TEACHING SOCIAL WORK WITH DIGITAL TECHNOLOGY

Copyright © 2019, Council on Social Work Education, Inc.

Published in the United States by the Council on Social Work Education, Inc. All rights reserved. No part of this book may be reproduced or transmitted in any manner whatsoever without the prior written permission of the publisher.

ISBN 978-0-87293-195-4

Printed in the United States of America on acid-free paper that meets the American National Standards Institute Z39-48 standard.

CSWE Press
1701 Duke Street, Suite 200
Alexandria, VA 22314-3457
www.cswe.org

TEACHING SOCIAL WORK WITH DIGITAL TECHNOLOGY

Laurel Iverson Hitchcock,
Melanie Sage,
and Nancy J. Smyth

Alexandria, Virginia

CONTENTS

VII		*Preface*
IX		*Acknowledgments*
1	CHAPTER 1.	Why Do We Need a Book About Technology in Social Work Education?
31	CHAPTER 2.	Digital Literacy
73	CHAPTER 3.	Pedagogical Approaches to Technology in Social Work Education
107	CHAPTER 4.	Technology in the Social Work Classroom
157	CHAPTER 5.	Online Classrooms
209	CHAPTER 6.	Online Programs
259	CHAPTER 7.	Field Education Online: High-Touch Pedagogy
309	CHAPTER 8.	Ethical Considerations for Faculty Members Who Teach With Technology
347	CHAPTER 9.	Technology for Professional Development
393	APPENDIX 1.	Assignment Compendium for Integrating Technology Into Social Work Assignments and Learning Activities
551	APPENDIX 2.	Technology-Based Learning Task List for Social Work Education
571	APPENDIX 3.	Technology in Social Work Education: Educators' Perspectives on the NASW Technology Standards for Social Work Education and Supervision
597	APPENDIX 4.	Reflection Questions for Digital Literacy in Social Work
607	APPENDIX 5.	Social Work Distance Education Assessment of Readiness

613	APPENDIX 6.	Technology Tips for Social Work Practitioners and Academics
631		*Glossary*
673		*Index*

PREFACE

We have no idea how many book collaborations begin on Twitter, but ours is probably not the only one.

But let's back up. Before there was a book, there were a few social workers hanging out on Twitter and figuring out how to get connected to each other. Most were on Twitter, at least in part, because of a cross-interest in technology and its potential utilities for social work. Most of us did not have colleagues in our own schools who were interested in the intersection of technology and social work. Some of us had been playing with technology in social work for many years, such as Linda Grobman, editor of the *New Social Worker* magazine. Some of us were innovating with new technology, such as Jonathan Singer, who hosts the *Social Work Podcast*. Few were deans of schools of social work, such as Nancy Smyth. Many of us were junior faculty members. Most of us were trying to figure out the potential of this medium, and we found each other.

Over time, organizational structures emerged in our Twitter community. We started using the hashtag #swtech (social work tech) to find each other, talk, and still stay within Twitter's then 140-character limits. Twitter chats were organized, and they brought groups of social workers together for live meetings during specific hours. We sent each other emojis and memes. Then, we started meeting up at conferences and attending each other's technology-related sessions. Before long, we were proposing collaborative conference sessions, working together on scholarly papers, and having interesting conversations about the future of social work in an increasingly tech-mediated world. Through discovering colleagues who could see the potential benefits of technology, and who brought thoughtful concerns (but were not overreactive) regarding potential risks, we had found our people.

When Jonathan Singer, chair of the Council on Social Work Education (CSWE) Council on Publications, put out a call for someone to write a new text about teaching social work with technology, Melanie Sage asked Nancy if she would consider collaborating on the book. Nancy, a well-respected school dean, and Melanie, a new faculty member at a rural school, were not a natural match for scholarly work, but technology has a democratizing impact on relationships. Nancy agreed, and Jonathan suggested we include Laurel Hitchcock as a coauthor. None of us had ever collaborated on a project of any kind at that point, but through a leap of faith that drew on our online connection, we partnered to form a three-woman team in an area of social work practice that had historically been dominated by older men.

Laurel took on the role of the organizer, scheduling meetings, making to-do lists, and keeping us on task. Melanie continually said, "How about we also do this?" which led to some detours along the way, and a few more appendices than planned. And Nancy pointed us in directions we did not know existed and continually helped us think bigger and deeper. We got together via GotoMeeting live video calls every 2 weeks for 3 years while writing this book; we sometimes stayed on task but eventually became more than writing partners.

Sometimes we had giggling fits, and sometimes inspired conversations. We turned to each other for advice. We became trusted colleagues and friends. We planned at least one or two more books, which we may or may not write. We laughed a lot. And we wrote a book!

We hope that this book inspires you, and maybe our story will too; your coauthors may be out there waiting for you, and we are a testament that writing with friends is better than going alone. We hope you like our book.

ACKNOWLEDGMENTS

Numerous people have contributed their knowledge and expertise to this book.

First, we would like to acknowledge our helpful colleagues who stepped in to cowrite Chapter 5, Denise Krause, and Chapter 7, Laura Lewis and Carol Schneweis. Our work is better for their contributions.

We drew on our peer networks with abandon. In 2015, when we started working on the book, we put out a call for assignment contributions. This became Appendix 1, the "Assignment Compendium." Then we reached out again, this time for general technology tips, and more educators came to the rescue—they helped us build Appendix 6, "Technology Tips for Social Work Practitioners and Academics." Contributors have been patient and supportive while waiting for their work to appear in print. We thank them for generously sharing their work with colleagues.

Similarly, we interviewed several educators, program directors, and deans about the workings of their programs. They not only gave us the behind-the-scenes details but also read drafts, edited copy, and answered a long list of questions for us. From small programs to large, and regional state schools to big private schools, we talked to busy people who care about the quality of their work and were kind to share it with all who pick up this book. You will find specific acknowledgments at the ends of chapters in which we used interviews and consultations to help illustrate concepts.

We field-tested much of the content for these chapters at various social work conferences, where we got support and feedback—so we want to thank all the people who have come to our sessions and asked good questions. Sometimes we grabbed a friend in the hall or across the country and asked them to read a thing or two and give feedback—often these were people who had already pitched in with an interview. The collaborative spirit of our colleagues has made this work enjoyable.

Allyson Varley, a doctoral student in public health who worked with Laurel as a graduate assistant not only cowrote the glossary but also provided countless hours of proofreading for our Word documents, managed our citations in Zotero, and screen-captured all the hyperlinks listed in the book. We thank her for all her efforts.

Finally, we leaned on family members, friends, and colleagues along the way. To devote time to this book, we put other projects on hold and stayed up too late or got up too early. Therefore, we must extend thanks to our social work departments at the University of Alabama at Birmingham, the University of North Dakota, and the University at Buffalo, who provided support and took this scholarship seriously, as well as our partners and colleagues whom we promised we'd spend time with again once the book was done.

Perhaps the only ones as excited as us to see this book in print is our fabulous professional learning network on Twitter. We're sending them a virtual hug for every time they asked if the book was done yet (they didn't mean it in a "are you even doing anything over there" kind of way but were genuinely anticipating its release)—it kept us going. Thank you!

CHAPTER 1

WHY DO WE NEED A BOOK ABOUT TECHNOLOGY IN SOCIAL WORK EDUCATION?

Imagine yourself in the following situation, one familiar to many social work educators: in an ambitious attempt to enliven a lecture or help demonstrate a concept about the role of hospice and end-of-life care during late adulthood for your Human Behavior in the Social Environment class, you do a quick search in your favorite Web browser and it brings you to a video from a national hospice advocacy agency. The video highlights how hospice works and provides the latest data on national trends. You play the 10-minute video for your class and then get back to your lecture, or maybe a classroom discussion about what the students watched. This is a common example described by social work educators about how they make good use of technology to supplement student learning.

But reimagine this same scenario: students still watch the video, this time before coming to class. During class, you connect via videoconference with the executive director of the hospice advocacy agency using Skype (a popular Web-based videoconferencing tool). The video call is projected from a computer to a screen in front of the class, and your students interact with your guest speaker, a nationally recognized expert in the field, through microphones and speakers. To supplement the lecture, your students follow the agency and the guest speaker on Twitter (a microblogging social media platform), and tweet questions during or after class, which the guest speaker answers following her presentation. Several students continue an ongoing conversation with the guest speaker via Twitter for several days after the class, asking questions related to a group project about hospice care that they are working on for another social work course.

If you had your choice, which experience would you want for your students? How do the learning outcomes differ in each scenario? How would you prefer to learn? This is one illustration of countless situations that emerge when you start to explore the broader universe of technology options in social work education. Social work educators are using digital avatars to role-play diverse characters, having students write their own textbooks via *wikis*, and asking students to create podcasts or videos instead of the traditional classroom presentations.

Technology has the power to help students access content in new ways, create open networks that link students to the practice world outside the classroom, and help educators share and collaborate on projects related to social work pedagogy in thoughtful and effective ways. And as an added benefit, students who work with these technologies in their courses then develop competencies in the use of technologies that will serve them later in their social work practice and professional development.

Our goal in writing this book is to help you as a social work educator, regardless of your skill with technology or the resources of your program, to move from that 10-minute video in the classroom to incorporating digital technologies in ways that are engaging, practical, and meaningful to teaching and learning about social work. This book is about teaching social work with technology and addresses many topics about how social work educators and administrators can design and implement successful technology-mediated learning environments. It does not offer advice about how to prepare students to conduct social work practice in an increasingly technology-saturated world, although they will learn much from your good modeling, and we do talk about how to improve their digital literacies through the ways in which you use technology in the classroom. This book does not address the many things that students need to learn regarding how to use technology in practice or what they need to know about digital and social justice issues. We cite other books that have been written on those topics and hope more will come. We do address the debate of whether technology-mediated education is acceptable in social work, but not ad nauseam. If you have picked up this book, we hope you are looking not for an answer to the debate about whether educators should deliver social work education using technology but instead are searching for tools for effective teaching and a deep understanding of what learning in technology-mediated environments looks like in social work.

Technology in social work education and practice is a hot topic at professional conferences, in journal articles, and among professional associations and regulation forums. The buzz is not surprising given trends in higher education. The National Center for Education Statistics (2015) reports that 2.9 million (29%) of undergraduate students took at least one online course in 2014, while half of those were enrolled in a completely online program. Similarly, Seaman, J.E., Allen, and Seaman, J. (2018) found that almost 1/3 of all college students have taken at least one distance course during the Fall 2016 semester. Further, 69% of chief academic leaders said that online education was critical to their long-term strategy. Online enrollment has grown each year for the last decade, with no sign of a plateau. The trends are not that different for social work education. According to 2016 data available from the Council on Social Work Education about online education (2015b), more than 300 accredited social work programs currently offer some or all their online courses, and 100 more programs plan to offer online courses in the future, including doctoral programs. CSWE's most recent data from 2017 reported that there are 73 fully online, accredited social work programs in the United States; 21 BSW, 44 MSW, six DSW, and two PhD programs (CSWE, 2018). Social work programs are under increasing demand to expand online offerings by universities, administrators, and students alike, for reasons that include revenue, competition, convenience, and access. These trends may be the reason you picked up this book, perhaps out of your personal interest to improve your teaching with technology, or from the agonizing external pressure to "get online."

TECHNOLOGY AND COMPETENCY-BASED EDUCATION

Beyond the mounting use of technology in higher education, most educators and administrators recognize that technology plays a role in competency-based social work education. The CSWE, the National Association of Social Workers (NASW), and the Association of Social Work Boards (ASWB) have recently revised their educational, practice, and regulatory standards to include the effective and ethical use of technology in practice as a valued competency for social workers (ASWB, 2015: CSWE, 2015a; NASW, 2017a, 2017b). Some of these standards are worth discussion, and we have attempted to weave them throughout this book. First is the NASW's Standards for Technology in Social Work Practice, which were developed in collaboration with CSWE, ASWB, and the Clinical Social Work Association (NASW, 2017b). These standards are lengthy (55 unique standards) and include guidance for micro- and macro-level practice as well as social work education and supervision (see Section 4 of the standards). We believe this is the first time NASW has ever produced practice standards for the educational setting.

CSWE is clear that education programs do not need to meet the NASW Technology Practice Standards under Section 4 of the technology standards document for accreditation purposes (CSWE, personal communication, June 30, 2017; NASW, 2017b), so we discuss these standards in relevant sections of the book only to offer guidance and best practices. Also, Appendix 3, "Technology in Social Work Education: Educators' Perspectives on the NASW Technology Standards for Social Work Education and Supervision," offers additional interpretations of the technology practice standards for education and supervision, based on a collaborative process with more than 25 social work educators and practitioners.

The second set of standards is the 2015 CSWE Educational Policy and Accreditation Standards (EPAS). As most of us in social work education know, these standards must be met for accreditation. The only specific mention of technology related to content that should be taught in the classroom is under the first entry in the section on Social Work Competencies: Demonstrate Ethical and Professional Behavior. Technology is included as one of the demonstrable behaviors for this competency. It states that "social workers also understand emerging forms of technology and the ethical use of technology in social work practice" (CSWE, 2015a, p. 7), and "use technology ethically and appropriately to facilitate practice outcomes" (CSWE, 2015a, p. 7). Concerning how social work educational programs should use technology to achieve the EPAS, CSWE does not prescribe the how to use technology but encourages educational programs to meet the standards based on their unique settings. Because this is a book for social work educators, we place most of our attention on the EPAS and how social work educators can look broadly at the accreditation standards to incorporate teaching with digital technology in their own programs.

Finally, the third set of standards we attempt to integrate throughout the book is the NASW Code of Ethics, which went through an extensive revision in 2017 to reflect how technology is being used in social work practice (NASW, 2017a). However, we want to make a clear distinction that our goal for incorporating the NASW Code of Ethics into this book is to advance the use of digital and social technologies in only social work education, not social work practice. Simply put, this book is for social work educators, not social work practitioners. We focus on how to teach with technology, and not what needs to be taught. It is about the role technology plays in the design and delivery of social work education, as a method for content delivery, as a tool for shaping learning activities, and in supporting beginning levels of competencies (digital literacy, etc.) needed for social work practice. As a result, the book does not cover the broad use of technology in social work practice, or even the wide variety of content that educators should teach students about the intersections of technology and social work. A great need exists for a book about the knowledge, skills, and values needed by social workers to use technology competently, professionally, and ethically in practice with clients and communities, about digital divides, the numerous ethical risks related to use of technology in social work practice, and using technology for assessments, interventions, and evaluation. We envision that book addressing issues such as how to practice telehealth with individuals and families; how to maintain privacy and confidentially when running an online support group on Facebook; how social media can be used to promote the mission of a nonprofit agency; how social workers can advocate for policy changes using e-activism and online petitions; and how social workers can use digital technologies to promote social justice and digital equity. Someone should write this book!

Along with the updates to standards that affect social work curricula, throughout this book we highlight stories from early adopters of technology in social work education who have willingly shared successes, challenges, and promising practices for using technology as a tool in teaching and learning social work competencies. Scholarship about online education is emerging, such as the effectiveness of online versus seated classrooms or the role of online labs to supplement a seated classroom (Cummings, Chaffin, & Cockerham, 2015; Elliott, Choi, & Friedline, 2013; Wilke & Vinton, 2006). Examples of technology-infused seated classrooms can also be found in the literature, from the use of mobile devices such as smartphones and tablets to adopting social media, such as

Twitter or Facebook (Baldridge, McAdams, Reed, & Moran, 2013; Buquoi, McClure, Kotrlik, Machtmes, & Bunch, 2013; Young, 2014). Additionally, an annual social work conference on distance education in the United States launched in 2015, with more than 400 attendees and more than 100 presentations on topics related to teaching and learning social work in distance-delivered environments (Indiana University School of Social Work & Council on Social Work Education, 2015). These are just a few illustrations of how social work educators are finding ways to share about teaching with technology to prepare students for the skills that they will need to practice in a technology-immersed societal and agency context.

CONCERNS FROM THE PROFESSION

Despite these efforts, as a profession, social work has been slow to adopt online education and other types of technology in the classroom. Concerns about student engagement and learning, the ability to assess students' acquisition of competency, gatekeeping, and ethical dilemmas such as dual relationships and privacy are chief concerns among some educators, who also worry that online education may disrupt the discipline's long-held value of the importance of human relationships (Kimball & Kim, 2013; Reamer, 2013; Voshel & Wesala, 2015). Some of these concerns are shared by employers; a 2015 study of North Carolina County Directors of Social Services (Marson, Pittman-Munke, & Stanton, 2016) found that most of the directors believed that distance and campus social work programs are not equivalent, and about a third reported they would not hire a social worker with an online degree. Qualitative comments in this study revealed specific concern about the possibility of virtual field placements and the importance of hands-on practice-skills courses. Concerns such as these are likely influenced by lack of understanding of distance teaching methodologies or exposure to poorly executed online courses.

Educators bring strong feelings about technology to the teaching environment, centered on their firsthand experiences, generational differences, comfort levels, and perceived impacts on professional social work education and practice. Educators also have many practical questions about the best ways to incorporate technology to their classrooms, driven by concerns about their own technology competence, their assumptions about student competence, the risk of relationship loss, worries about student privacy, and related laws, policy, or regulations, not to mention the effect of consumer and administrative-driven demands related to technology. We do not minimize these concerns (we have them too), but these problems also occur in seated classrooms, and we want to encourage thoughtful discussion about the effectiveness and rationale of our educational methods across all modes of delivery.

Although educators should take care to structure technology integration in such a way that the core values of social work are upheld, it is naïve to suggest that technology-facilitated education cannot be effective or relational. A third of America's marriages now start online (Cacioppo, Cacioppo, Gonzaga, Ogburn, & VanderWeele, 2013), and 69% of Internet users use social media with up to 74% of those users checking in daily (Pew Research Center, 2018); clearly, technological tools can be used to create and maintain relationships. Substantial research supports that no difference exists in learning outcomes in seated versus online class offerings across a number of disciplinary fields, a factor known as the No Significant Difference Phenomenon (Russell, 2001; U.S. Department of Education, 2010). A website dedicated to this phenomenon houses thousands of citations that support similar outcomes in online and traditional classrooms (see http://nosignificantdifference.org/). Ten years of research in the social work literature suggests that quality teaching and learning of social work content and skills can be done via online delivery (Cummings, Foels, & Chaffin, 2013; Forgey & Ortega-Williams, 2016; Siebert, Siebert, & Spaulding-Givens, 2006; Vernon, Vakalahi, Pierce, Pittman-Munke, & Adkins, 2009; Wilke,

King, Ashmore, & Stanley, 2016). With careful planning, educators can indeed design curriculum and classes that keep the relational parts of teaching in our work in online learning environments.

TECHNOLOGY CAN MAKE US BETTER EDUCATORS ACROSS LEARNING ENVIRONMENTS

The emergence of online social work courses attracts more critique than seated classrooms at many of our institutions, which is common when new educational models appear on the scene. Some institutions now require checklists and peer reviews for online courses such as those available from online educational organizations such as Quality Matters, Online Learning Consortium, and Educause, and some schools even hire professional staff or curriculum partners to assist with the development and presentation of online content.

Although evidence-based teaching as a practice is not well established in the social work literature, the critique of technology in social work education offers an opportunity for educators to assess quality, efficiency, and efficacy of our teaching methods, both in seated and online classrooms (Yaffe, 2013). Although technology is often incorporated into seated classes, they are usually not evaluated with the same critique as online classes as it relates to technology use or other pedagogical choices. Social work educators need to raise questions about pedagogical best practices across all types of classrooms, with consideration for the best methods for teaching practice competencies and assessment of learning. Research into the effectiveness of all instructional delivery methods in social work education can support improved educational outcomes for students and can increase the evidence about the most effective teaching and learning techniques to improve training for social work educators. A thoughtful social work educator will not only ask if online education is as good as the traditional seated classroom but also want to identify the hallmarks of quality social work skill development in any setting. In this sense, the critique of online education forces us to evaluate better all the ways that we deliver social work education.

Alongside the opportunity to critically assess the quality of social work education, technology-based pedagogy supports, encourages, and maybe even demands interdisciplinary collaboration in higher education. Other professions such as medicine, nursing, and education all have substantial bodies of research about how to incorporate technology into their courses, curricula, and internships settings, and have produced their own literature that can be relevant to social work education (George et al., 2013; Golonka, Bowles, Frank, Richardson, & Freynik, 2014; Raman, 2015; Sanford, 2010). Specifically, these disciplines are beginning to use meta-analyses or systematic reviews to understand broad trends of technology as educational tools in their disciplines as well as overall effectiveness related to student learning outcomes (Cheston, Flickinger, & Chisolm, 2013; Chipps, Brysiewicz, & Mars, 2012; Tondeur et al., 2012). Further, professionals and specialists from support systems, such as instructional design, information technology library services, and digital media centers, at our institutions have a variety of expertise and tools available to help social work educators create, implement, and assess technology-based assignments, courses, and even an entire curriculum. By looking outside our profession, we have an opportunity to improve social work education by drawing on the successful ways other practice professions are incorporating technology in their classrooms. If we fail to look outside our discipline for promising practices that can inform our work, social work educators risk having our own institutions do it for us through mandates, incentives, or top-down policies. In this text, we begin the process of drawing on best practices from across disciplines, as well as what is known in our discipline, to help inform and shape the future of technology-mediated social work education.

In summary, social work educators must make pedagogically

sound, rational, practical, and ethical decisions about technology integration in their social work programs. Further, they must learn how to effectively navigate the many options that will best prepare students for competent social work practice in a technology-driven world, bridging the relational opportunities offered via technology together with the best practices in technology-facilitated learning. The goal of this book is to help beginning and experienced social work educators navigate the vast and continually changing landscape of technology in social work education, specifically as it relates to teaching and learning social work knowledge, values, and skills.

A REMINDER: STUDENTS ARE AS CONFUSED AS YOU ARE—REALLY!

Although it is easy to assume that students are ahead of us in their ability and readiness to adapt to technological changes, this is often not the case. Familiarity and comfort with technology are not the same as digital literacy. Although students are exposed to technology at an ever-increasing rate, and those who enter our classrooms may have spent their whole lives with high-speed Internet and instantaneous access to information, they are not necessarily competent in understanding and using digital devices and social media (also sometimes called digital literacy). Noted author, journalist, and thought leader on digital culture Howard Rheingold (2012) observed that many young people today are not, in fact, entirely digitally literate. Moreover, even students who are continuously connected to devices require education, mentoring, and support about how to contextualize the values of social work in their technology-mediated education and practice.

Students are also affected by whether their learning takes place in a seated, hybrid, online synchronous, or online asynchronous classroom, and those with technology skills may not know the best ways to interact with or without technology in various settings. Although learning outcomes for a specific class offering may hold steady across delivery methods, best practices for engaging students vary significantly based on the method of classroom delivery, and it is up to the educator to know how to adjust the curriculum for the learning environment in order to best meet the learning goals and the needs of the student. Students will look to their teachers for the appropriate structure and advice. In this text, we hope to help prepare you to guide them in meaningful directions that support their best learning and your best teaching.

TECHNOLOGY INTEGRATION OCCURS ALONG A CONTINUUM

Throughout this book, we refer to the continuum of technology integration, with the understanding that social work educators and programs are at distinct stages and have diverse needs related to technology integration. The plethora of terms and jargon related to technology in higher education can be confusing and intimidating. When terms are introduced in this text, we flag the less common term in italic, so you can reference the glossary at the end of the book for more in-depth clarification. If you run across a technology term that is not in italic but still confusing, please also check out the glossary because we have defined many of the more common terms, too.

Many articles and books about teaching with technology attempt to categorize classes as online or traditional, but most of the time all classes use technology in some way. Because technology now allows for online courses to be taught face-to-face, we avoid using this term to refer to traditional campus-based in-person classrooms. Instead, the term seated classroom (also sometimes referred to as an on-the-ground class) is used to refer to the traditional classroom that meets at a predesignated time where students and instructor

WHY DO WE NEED THIS BOOK?

gather in their seats in-person on campus. Similarly, many programs use some online storage of content, often housed on a learning management system (LMS) such as Blackboard, Moodle, and Canvas. However, the storage of class-related information or documents online does not, by itself, make a class "online." The term online class is used by some to mean a class that is occasionally delivered via distance using the Internet, that the class is a hybrid, which indicates that at least half of the content is delivered over the Internet, or that a class is fully online, which indicates that all the material for a course are delivered over the Internet. Any class that uses online delivery may include any combination of content that is delivered synchronously, in "real time" in which class members meet over a distance at a designated time, or asynchronously, in which content is available for students to access at the day or time of their choosing. To further complicate matters, some seated classes are coordinated so that students can join the class synchronously via an online connection (streaming), or classes can be recorded (audio or video capture) so that students can later access the material asynchronously. When we refer to online classes in this book, we are referring to any class in which any part of the curriculum is moved to the Internet or another virtual environment for delivery, beyond simple access to supplementary class materials. Online programs, on the other hand, refer to entire degree programs that can be accessed through online classes, either synchronously or asynchronously, that require no regular, ongoing in-person contact for courses, although they may require an occasional campus visit.

All instructors and social work programs must find their ideal place in the range of possibilities on the technology-integration continuum. There is no best place on the continuum. Instead, the mission and goals of a program or class should match the best-suited delivery methods.

To further illustrate the idea of a technology continuum, we offer two examples of how a class might be face-to-face and online at the same time: (1) a traditionally seated classroom could use video recording so that students can watch the class either live or in recorded version on their own time, or (2) an online classroom could meet at a designated time each week for synchronous instruction and use an LMS such as Blackboard for online discussion boards and blogs, continuing their interaction throughout the week. Additionally, any given classroom may use a variety of technology integration methods for just a single class. Therefore, when we discuss the use of technology in social work education throughout this text, we address the use of technology across this continuum and recommend that technology infusion should occur in all social work programs.

FEELING LOST? HELP IS HERE!

Throughout this book, we demonstrate that technology in the social work classroom is practical and possible for all social work educators, students, and programs. Further, it is compatible (and necessary) to meet the standards of social work education and ethical practice. To achieve this end, we encourage three shifts in thinking about how the profession understands and uses technology in practice and education. The first shift is to appreciate the range of technology-mediated possibilities available to social work educators and administrators, starting with a single seated classroom, all the way up to an entire curriculum delivered through an online platform. This continuum of technology integration opportunities calls for thoughtful consideration about when, how, and why technology is incorporated into social work education. The second shift in thinking is the recognition that the use of technology for teaching and learning in social work is wholly compatible with the profession's mission, values, and educational and practice standards as outlined by the CSWE, the NASW, and the ASWB. In fact, educators have a growing awareness that understanding and using technology is an essential skill for twenty-first-century social workers. Finally, we encourage you to shift your thinking to consider technology only as a facilitative tool that can support your pedagogical practices, and not as a stand-alone method for teaching.

Common questions about the use of technology in social work education include the following:

- Don't students already know this stuff?
- How do I teach platform-specific skills that I don't even know? (What the heck is a tweet?)
- How can clinical and relational skills be taught online?
- How do we ensure gatekeeping in an online degree program?
- How do I engage students I can't even see?
- How do I motivate students to learn in an online environment?
- How will I find the time and supports to learn how to do this well?

The answers to these questions (and some you haven't even thought of yet) will unfold as you read this book. It is possible to engage, teach, gatekeep, and build strong relationships with your students online, and even us old dogs can learn new tricks.

A GUIDE TO THIS BOOK

We begin this book by offering some of the fundamental contexts about what it means to use technology in education, with an emphasis on social work's commitment to educate students who are prepared to serve vulnerable populations in complex and ever-changing environments, and who have learned the relevant social work competencies and practice behaviors that will equip them for this task. We recognize that today's social work educators have a range of knowledge and expertise related to technology in teaching and practice, and to address this wide range of readers, we offer the following tools to help the reader navigate not only the content but also the layout of this book.

A CONTINUUM OF TECHNOLOGY INTEGRATION FOR THE SOCIAL WORK EDUCATOR

The chapters of this book are ordered based on a learning continuum. The continuum begins with digital literacy, that is, what students most need to know for effective use of technology (Chapter 2), moving to pedagogical issues in using technology (Chapter 3), and then to infusing technology in seated classrooms (Chapter 4). From there, the continuum moves to online classrooms (Chapter 5) and online programs (Chapter 6). Two chapters offer a narrower focus on technology and social work and education: field education (Chapter 7) and ethics (Chapter 8). The continuum ends with the role and practice of technology in the lifelong learning of today's social work educators (Chapter 9).

OTHER RESOURCES

Each chapter offers a list of questions answered within the chapter, case scenarios or teaching tips, resources for further reading, and references. Four additional appendices offer the reader tools for assessing their own digital literacies, evaluating their program's readiness for an online program, navigating the new NASW, ASWB, CSWE, and Clinical Social Work Association (CSWA) Standards for Technology in Social Work Practice for educator, and using technology for academic productivity.

A COMPENDIUM OF COURSE ASSIGNMENTS AND LIST OF TECH-BASED LEARNING TASKS

Grounded in the firsthand experience of social work educators, this compendium offers an assignment guide for the practical integration of technology across the curriculum. The assignments are categorized by curricular areas (practice, human behavior in the social environment [HBSE], policy, research, and field education) and presented in a standardized format for ease of selection. They are submitted by social work educators who have designed and used them successfully in the classroom.

Additionally, we have developed a list of technology-based learning tasks based on the Council on Social Work Education's Social Work Competencies from the 2015 Educational Policy and Accreditation Standards (EPAS). This list provides example assignments and learning tasks that can be incorporated into social work courses, especially field education, and is in the appendices. In each of these example assignments, students should be directed to share their work with their class, seminar, or practicum field instructor. For assessment purposes, each assignment and learning task is grouped by competency and component behaviors and then labeled with the relevant competency dimensions. We introduce some of the assignments and learning tasks within the chapters, providing tips for implementing the assignment and connections to social work competencies and ethical considerations. Both resources include assignments and learning tasks that will help students learning about digital equity and digital inclusion.

A GLOSSARY OF DEFINITIONS AND LANGUAGE

A complex language is associated with our rapidly changing, technology-infused environments. As previously noted, this text includes a glossary (built with Allyson Varley's significant assistance) of terms to simplify the jargon. Terms such as seated classrooms, online courses, asynchronous versus synchronous content, hybrid courses, MOOCs (massive open online courses), and social and digital media are routinely part of the daily conversations in administrators' offices, faculty conversations, and curriculum committee meetings, as social work educators grapple to understand the available technology options and keep up with this new dictionary of terms and concepts. We also offer a second glossary of specific program names that are often used in teaching with technology, including proprietary software, hardware, classroom management systems, and social media platforms. In case you forget the difference between a Doodle, Moodle, and Noodle, you will find the distinctions there. When you see an unfamiliar term or software program, simply flip to the glossary to find the definition.

Across the text, these tools give educators the opportunity to quickly identify their level of expertise and comfort with technology in social work education, while also offering next steps for growth and understanding.

Although this book offers a linear roadmap to build the reader's knowledge of the confluence of technology and social work education, it can also be used as a practical reference text to answer your most pressing questions about technology. For instance, a reader with very rudimentary technology experience may first want to brush up on terms by flipping to the glossary, which covers the major jargon associated with technology used in this text. Field educators may want to turn directly to the section on field (Chapter 7) and then flip back to Chapters 3 and 4 to read more about the theory and practice of engaging students in technology-mediated environments. Those educators from programs newly considering online offerings may be interested in absorbing information across the text on models for launching online courses and moving from a campus-based to online program (Chapters 5 and 6). Those interested in theory, pedagogy, digital literacy, and foundations for understanding approaches to technology integration will find answers to their questions in Chapters 2 and 3, which review some of the effects of technology on learning and the differences in learning on the continuum from seated to fully online environments. Instructors who are either novice or experienced in technology will be excited to sift through the variety of practical examples offered in the assignment compendium of this book. Skeptics of technology in social work education may be very interested in the firsthand accounts, both positive and negative, of other educators, accounts that are offered throughout the chapters in the breakout boxes. Those who are ready to move beyond this text will find resources for further reading offered at the end of each chapter.

CHAPTER SUMMARIES: *A BRIEF OVERVIEW OF THIS BOOK*

When you are done here, you may want to move right on to Chapter 2, which explores ways in which digital media literacy can be integrated into social work education and professional practice. Given the complexities of digital and social technology and its effects on individuals, families, groups, communities, and organizations, we suggest that social work educators teach a holistic literacy of technology because it is mission critical to evaluating and using so many other tools in their future practice settings, as well as supporting clients and engaging in macro practice. We discuss the types of technology skills students need for successful use of technology and the ethical imperatives that necessitate that social workers have basic digital literacy skills, drawing from Howard Rheingold's (2012) concepts of digital literacy as a tool for personal empowerment and creating a more just society and Belshaw's (2014) elements of digital literacy. We offer some examples to show how educators can develop their own digital literacy, how they integrate digital literacy into course-level assignments, and how professional standards and guidelines inform digital literacy.

Chapter 2 will answer questions such as:

- Why must social workers be digitally literate?
- Don't students already know how to use technology?
- How does digital literacy apply to social work education?

In Chapter 3 we focus on pedagogy and the reasons that it takes a lot of planning and forethought to bring technology to the classroom in meaningful ways. We describe theoretical constructs relevant to teaching with technology, such as motivational principles, multimedia learning principles, and theories of self-regulation, as well as benefits of learning with technology, such as opportunities for repeated practice, reinforcement, and the use of technology-facilitated learning communities. To illustrate some of these concepts and help readers consider what these theoretical principles look like in practice, we share a case study from Portland State University's (PSU) School of Social Work, which is woven through the chapter, developed through interviews with PSU's inaugural master's of social work (MSW) distance director Sarah Bradley. We also identify the ways that educators can address some of the difficulties that come with distance education.

Chapter 3 addresses questions such as:

- How do adults learn online?
- How can I motivate learners?
- What does active learning look like in a distance environment?

We start Chapter 4 with a discussion of the digital technology continuum in social work education and how educators can begin integrating technology into the seated classroom. This chapter covers the range of activities and types of technology that can be infused into a single class session or across an entire course by drawing on pedagogical approaches discussed in Chapter 3. Examples include technology topics for in-class discussions, case studies, advice on how to update an established assignment to incorporate digital media such as podcast or videos, and guidelines for flipping the classroom with technology and developing a hybrid class (less than 50% online content). We will also explore the needs of social work educators new to using digital technology in the classroom, emphasizing the importance of collaboration (both within social work and interdisciplinary) and administrative support.

In Chapter 4, we answer questions such as:

- What is Bloom's Digital Taxonomy?
- How can I integrate technology into assignments or learning activities?
- How can I assess my new technology-based assignment?

In Chapter 5 we are accompanied by guest coauthor Denise Krause, clinical professor at the University at Buffalo (UB). In this chapter we talk about some of the unique issues involved with teaching an entirely online class, including how to convert a seated course into an online course and how one might modify the same activity across synchronous, asynchronous, and seated settings. In this chapter we cover such topics as managing student expectations, synchronous versus asynchronous activities, creating a class "culture," promoting opportunities for informal interaction, strategies for incorporating interactivity, and experiential learning strategies. Particular attention is given to best practices in student engagement, feedback, and quality instructor-student interactions in online environments. We also review different approaches that educators and social work programs take when transitioning from the on-ground to online classroom, ranging from an instructor-led conversion (organically driven within the curriculum) to an online educational specialist conversion (external to the curriculum).

Chapter 5 tackles questions such as:

- What do online courses look like in higher education?
- What do I need to know about teaching an online course in social work?
- How can I begin designing an online social work course?

Chapter 6 represents the other end of the digital technology continuum in social work education: the fully online social work curriculum. Instead of answering questions, we offer questions for your reflection as you consider taking your program online. We present our typology of approaches to deliver education in online environments. This typology includes curricula delivered fully online, hybrid programming, and blended online/seated classes. We cover the challenges of each and offer brief case studies related to each type of program with firsthand accounts from administrators. We offer some strategies for thinking about implicit curriculum issues. Finally, we discuss the methods through which degree programs can move to develop fully online programs: (a) organic (faculty and adjuncts converting over time) or (b) insourcing/outsourcing, which involves hiring an outside firm to put your program online, including varying approaches to the degree of faculty autonomy in developing and teaching an online course under this model. The pros and cons of each method will be explored.

Chapter 6 helps you consider questions such as:

- What is our capacity for distance delivery?
- What are special considerations for offering an undergraduate social work degree online?
- How will we get our program online?

Because none of us is a field educator, for Chapter 7 we invited some pros to help us navigate the ins and outs of distance field education: field director Laura Lewis from UB School of Social Work and distance director Carol Schneweis from the University of North Dakota helped write this chapter. Distance field education offers a unique set of challenges, especially for fully online programs operating outside of their geographical region. This chapter will address those challenges through discussion of the philosophical debates as well as the practical needs of field programs and the extra demands that technology places on field units. We discuss practices related to placement, including contacting the local social work program, face-to-face versus technology-assisted field site visits, online training with field instructors, and distance supervision. This chapter also covers the use of technology for managing field data and other software that is frequently used in field program management. We include examples from field offices across the nation to highlight promising organizational practices.

Chapter 7 will help you think through your school's practices by offering reflective and practical considerations for questions such as the following:

- What does the Council on Social Work Education, and other regulatory bodies, have to say about distance education and technology in field education?
- What are the differences between campus and distance field education?
- What technology skills do field coordinators, liaisons, and field instructors need?

Chapter 8 explores ethical debates in technology-mediated social work education, including issues of teaching human-services skills in a distance environment, issues related to student privacy, boundaries across digital environments, and the protection of student information. Although other emerging macro issues affect online social work education, such as net neutrality and the affordability and selectivity of online degrees, we give primary focus in this chapter to teaching educators how to navigate the ethics landscape online. This includes how to manage online identities, the benefits and risks of engaging with students/clients via social media, and how to handle these potential landmines ethically. Attention is paid to the variety of policies and standards developed and used by social work professionals for regulation (ASWB), practice (NASW), and education (CSWE), including the NASW Code of Ethics and the NASW technology practice standards (NASW, 2008; NASW, 2017b).

In Chapter 8, we address questions such as:

- What are the standards for technology use in social work education?
- What ethical concerns arise in teaching with technology?
- How can FERPA concerns be addressed?

Finally, Chapter 9 concludes our discussion by focusing on the developmental supports necessary for educators to operate successfully in a technology-mediated environment. It includes the basic skills necessary for any instructor who plans to teach in an online environment. We discuss best practices for preparing instructors and the importance of continuing professional development in the fast-changing world of distance education. We cover the use of professional learning networks (PLN) and how to create one, emerging trends related to technology in higher education (including data-driven decision-making), and training for adjuncts.

Chapter 9 we help the reader explore questions such as:

- What do I, as a 21st-century social work educator, need to know about technology?

- How can I use technology for professional development?
- How can I practice self-care when using technology professionally?

DISCLAIMER: *MOVING TARGETS AHEAD*

Although we offer a practical guide that helps address contemporary theoretical and practical challenges related to the use of technology in social work, it is difficult to write a timeless text on a rapidly changing topic. We are amid not only quickly changing technology but also an emerging body of literature about best practices with technology in educational settings. Where possible, we offer resources that will help you keep up to date on changes as they occur. Along with these resources, we encourage all social work educators reading this book to develop a PLN and use it as a tool to stay current on the developing literature on best practices for technology in higher education (Richardson & Mancabelli, 2011). Described in more detail in Chapter 9, a PLN is a process of networking with other professionals virtually and face-to-face about topics and issues of interest for lifelong learning. Social work educators are encouraged to use digital literacy skills to search, assess, and share the best available resources on technology in social work education. A PLN will be an excellent companion to this book on your journey to becoming a tech-savvy social work educator.

Finally, here is another a disclaimer: We offer several practice models and policy examples throughout this text. Please remember that administrative practices of a specific school change quickly, and the specific scenarios and roles of interviewees discussed in this book may have changed by the time you read them. Likewise, federal, state, and program policies we address in this book are also subject to change; before using this information to make decisions about your programming or practice, make sure you have the latest relevant policies and their interpretations.

REFERENCES

Association of Social Work Boards (ASWB). (2015). *Model regulatory standards for technology and social work practice: ASWB international technology task force, 2013–2014.* Culpeper, VA: Author. Retrieved from https://www.aswb.org/wp-content/uploads/2015/03/ASWB-Model-Regulatory-Standards-for-Technology-and-Social-Work-Practice.pdf

Baldridge, S., McAdams, A., Reed, A., & Moran, A. (2013). Mobile classrooms: Using mobile devices to enhance BSW education. *Journal of Baccalaureate Social Work, 18*(0), 17–32.

Belshaw, D. (2014). *The essential elements of digital literacies.* Retrieved from http://digitalliteraci.es/

Buquoi, B., McClure, C., Kotrlik, J. W., Machtmes, K., & Bunch, J. C. (2013). A national research survey of technology use in the BSW teaching and learning process. *Journal of Teaching in Social Work, 33*(4–5), 481–495. http://doi.org/10.1080/08841233.2013.833577

Cacioppo, J. T., Cacioppo, S., Gonzaga, G. C., Ogburn, E. L., & VanderWeele, T. J. (2013). Marital satisfaction and break-ups differ across on-line and off-line meeting venues. *Proceedings of the National Academy of Sciences, 110*(25), 10135–10140. http://doi.org/10.1073/pnas.1222447110

Cheston, C. C., Flickinger, T. E., & Chisolm, M. S. (2013). Social media use in medical education: A systematic review. *Academic Medicine, 88*(6), 893–901. http://doi.org/10.1097/ACM.0b013e31828ffc23

Chipps, J., Brysiewicz, P., & Mars, M. (2012). A systematic review of the effectiveness of videoconference-based tele-education for medical and nursing education. *Worldviews on Evidence-Based Nursing, 9*(2), 78–87. http://doi.org/10.1111/j.1741-6787.2012.00241.x

Council on Social Work Education (CSWE). (2015a). *Educational policy and accreditation standards for baccalaureate and master's social work programs.* Alexandria, VA: Author. Retrieved from https://www.cswe.org/Accreditation/Standards-and-Policies/2015-EPAS

Council on Social Work Education (CSWE). (2015b). *2015 statistics on social work education in the United States.* Alexandria, VA: Author.

Council on Social Work Education (CSWE). (2018). *2017 statistics on social work education in the United States*. Alexandria, VA: Author.

Cummings, S. M., Chaffin, K. M., & Cockerham, C. (2015). Comparative analysis of an online and a traditional MSW program: Educational outcomes. *Journal of Social Work Education, 51*, 109–120. http://doi.org/10.1080/10437797.2015.977170

Cummings, S. M., Foels, L., & Chaffin, K. M. (2013). Comparative analysis of distance education and classroom-based formats for a clinical social work practice course. *Social Work Education, 32*(1), 68–80. doi:10.1080/02615479.2011.648179

Educause. (2015). Home page. Retrieved from https://www.educause.edu/

Elliott, W., Choi, E., & Friedline, T. (2013). Online statistics labs in MSW research methods courses: Reducing reluctance toward statistics. *Journal of Social Work Education, 49*, 81–95. http://doi.org/10.1080/10437797.2013.755095

Forgey, M. A., & Ortega-Williams, A. (2016). Effectively teaching social work practice online: Moving beyond can to how. *Advances in Social Work, 17*(1), 59–77.

George, P., Dumenco, L., Dollase, R., Taylor, J. S., Wald, H. S., & Reis, S. P. (2013). Introducing technology into medical education: Two pilot studies. *Patient Education and Counseling, 93*(3), 522–524. http://doi.org/10.1016/j.pec.2013.04.018

Golonka, E. M., Bowles, A. R., Frank, V. M., Richardson, D. L., & Freynik, S. (2014). Technologies for foreign language learning: A review of technology types and their effectiveness. *Computer Assisted Language Learning, 27*(1), 70–105. http://doi.org/10.1080/09588221.2012.700315

Indiana University School of Social Work & Council on Social Work Education (CSWE). (2015). *Social work distance education conference* [Home page]. Retrieved from http://swde.iu.edu/index.html

Kimball, E., & Kim, J. (2013). Virtual boundaries: Ethical considerations for use of social media in social work. *Social Work, 58*(2), 185–188. http://doi.org/10.1093/sw/swt005

Marson, S. M., Pittman-Munke, P. & Stanton, R. (2016). Attitudes of employers toward online education of social workers. *Global Education Journal, 2016*(2), 183-202.

National Association of Social Workers (NASW). (2017a). *Code of ethics of the National Association of Social Workers*. Washington, DC: NASW Press. Retrieved from https://www.socialworkers.org/About/Ethics/Code-of-Ethics/Code-of-Ethics-English

National Association of Social Workers (NASW). (2017b). *NASW, ASWB, CSWE, & CSWA standards for technology in social work practice*. Washington, DC: NASW Press. Retrieved from https://www.socialworkers.org/includes/newIncludes/homepage/PRA-BRO-33617.TechStandards_FINAL_POSTING.pdf

National Association of Social Workers & Association of Social Work Boards. (2005). *Technology for social work practice*. Retrieved from https://www.socialworkers.org/practice/standards/NASWTechnologyStandards.pdf

National Center for Education Statistics. (2015). *Integrated Postsecondary Education Data System*. Retrieved from http://nces.ed.gov/ipeds/datacenter/

Online Learning Consortium. (2015). Home page. Retrieved from http://onlinelearningconsortium.org/

Pew Research Center. (2018). *Social networking fact sheet*. Retrieved from http://www.pewInternet.org/fact-sheets/social-networking-fact-sheet/

Quality Matters. (2014). Home page. Retrieved from https://www.quality-matters.org

Raman, J. (2015). Mobile technology in nursing education: Where do we go from here? A review of the literature. *Nurse Education Today, 35*(5), 663–672. http://doi.org/10.1016/j.nedt.2015.01.018

Reamer, F. G. (2013). Distance and online social work education: Novel ethical challenges. *Journal of Teaching in Social Work, 33*(4–5), 369–384. http://doi.org/10.1080/08841233.2013.828669

Rheingold, H. (2012). *Net smart: How to thrive online*. Cambridge MA: MIT Press.

Richardson, W., & Mancabelli, R. (2011). *Personal learning networks: Using the power of connections to transform education*. Bloomington, IN: Solution Tree Press.

Russell, T. L. (2001). *The no significant difference phenomenon* (5th ed.). Chicago, IL: International Distance Education Certification Center. Retrieved from http://www.nosignificantdifference.org/

Sanford, P. (2010). Simulation in nursing education: A review of the research. *Qualitative Report, 15*(4), 1006–1011.

Seaman, J. E., Allen, I. E., & Seaman, J. (2018). Grade increase: Tracking distance education in the United States. *Babson Survey Research Group.* Retrieved from https://files.eric.ed.gov/fulltext/ED580852.pdf

Siebert, D. C., Siebert, C. F., & Spaulding-Givens, J. (2006). Teaching clinical social work skills primarily online: An evaluation. *Journal of Social Work Education, 42,* 325–336.

Tondeur, J., van Braak, J., Sang, G., Voogt, J., Fisser, P., & Ottenbreit-Leftwich, A. (2012). Preparing pre-service teachers to integrate technology in education: A synthesis of qualitative evidence. *Computers & Education, 59*(1), 134–144. http://doi.org/10.1016/j.compedu.2011.10.009

U.S. Department of Education, Office of Planning, Evaluation, and Policy Development. (2010). *Evaluation of evidence-based practices in online learning: A meta-analysis and review of online learning studies.* Washington, DC: Author.

Vernon, R., Vakalahi, H., Pierce, D., Pittman-Munke, P., & Adkins, L. F. (2009). Distance education programs in social work: Current and emerging trends. *Journal of Social Work Education, 45,* 263–276. doi:10.5175/JSWE.2009.200700081

Voshel, E., & Wesala, A. (2015). Social media & social work ethics: Determining best practices in an ambiguous reality. *Journal of Social Work Values and Ethics, 12*(1), 67–76.

Wilke, D., & Vinton, L. (2006). Evaluation of the first Web-based advanced standing MSW program. *Journal of Social Work Education, 42,* 607–620. doi:10.5175/JSWE.2006.200500501

Wilke, D. J., King, E., Ashmore, M., & Stanley, C. (2016). Can clinical skills be taught online? Comparing skill development between online and F2F students using a blinded review. *Journal of Social Work Education, 52,* 484–492.

Yaffe, J. (2013). Guest editorial: Where's the evidence for social work education? *Journal of Social Work Education, 49,* 525–527. doi:10.1080/10437797.2013.820582

Young, J. (2014). iPolicy: Exploring and evaluating the use of iPads in a social welfare policy course. *Journal of Technology in Human Services, 32*(1–2), 39–53. doi:10.1080/15228835.2013.860366

CHAPTER 2

DIGITAL LITERACY

This chapter answers the following questions:

- Why must social workers be digitally literate?
- Don't students already know how to use technology?
- What does digital literacy really mean?
- How does technology figure into digital literacy?
- How can digital literacy apply to social work education?
- What are the elements of digital literacy?
- How do digital literacies come together?
- What do we know from research about digital literacies in social work?

Given the complexities of digital and social technology and its effects on individuals, families, groups, communities, and organizations, we argue that social work educators should teach a holistic literacy of technology to promote digital literacy, that is, the skills and knowledge to use information and communication technologies (ICTs) to find, critique, create, and share content (Heitin, 2016).

In this chapter, we present this perspective to provide a larger framework for teaching with technology. We do not suggest that educators systematically integrate all elements of digital literacy into their teaching in every class. Rather, we hope that the framework provides meta-thinking about how and why to integrate technology into social work education. As an educator begins integrating more technology into the education process, it will become evident how minor changes in the integration of technology can deepen digital literacy for students and educators. Further, a holistic view of digital literacy parallels the Council on Social Work Education (2015) competencies of professional practice, recognizing the need for students to assimilate knowledge, skills, values, and reflection into their use of technology for social work practice. We provide examples throughout the chapter to illustrate how this might happen. Finally, we do not endeavor to provide a comprehensive review of digital literacy, a topic that has generated a great deal of scholarship. Instead, we provide a framework to facilitate social work educators' understanding of this topic, so they can begin to reflect on digital literacies, focus on enhancing their own digital literacies, and begin to incorporate this knowledge into how they teach with technology. For those interested in learning more, we will recommend additional readings at the end of the chapter.

WHY MUST SOCIAL WORKERS BE DIGITALLY LITERATE?

When the topic of technology comes up in conversations with social workers, we often hear someone state some version of the following thought: "But social workers are 'people people,'" with the implication that being conversant in digital technologies is incompatible with a focus on connecting with people. And yet, most technologies are developed to connect people over the barriers of distance and time (Powers, 2010). Books share ideas between people who are separated by distance and time; all forms of transportation provide people with a way to connect with others who are far away; and the telephone facilitates communication between people (Powers, 2010). And even technologies that we think of as entertainment, such as TV and film, connect people to the experience of other people (Powers, 2010). Digital technologies, such as the initial development of the Internet, allowed people to communicate over distance and time through e-mail, LISTSERVs, and digital bulletin boards where people could share ideas about common interests. As digital technologies evolved to allow for more interaction, Web 2.0 emerged, marking the shift from using websites to communicate in one direction (from the website to the reader) to using websites as vehicles to facilitate interaction and collaboration among people. The term social media makes the purpose explicit: these are technologies that connect people. As social workers, we know how to connect people to each other—we just need to learn how to do so in the context of whatever tools we are using with our values for human relationships in mind, whether the connections occur through face-to-face dialogue, telephone, writing, or social media platforms.

Social media has become so ubiquitous that the majority of Americans are now using it. The Pew Internet Research Center reports that 69% of American adults use social media, whereas 10 years prior, the percentage was only 7% (Perrin, 2015; Pew Research Center, 2018). The reality is that digital technologies are becoming more and more a part of our world. Indeed, social media has become so much a part of the culture that one cannot be considered culturally competent without understanding it (Smyth, 2010; Zgoda, 2013). Social workers must become digitally literate to stay culturally competent; it is vital that social workers understand digital technologies so that clients' environments can also be understood. And digital technologies need to be understood deeply enough that social workers can help clients navigate the challenges in their worlds. For example, social workers have always helped individuals, families, groups, and communities set healthy boundaries, so it simply follows that a natural extension of this work should include skills for coaching clients about their social media use, exploring their own desired boundaries related to the role of technology in their lives, and setting healthy boundaries between social worker and client in technology-mediated communications.

Beyond just understanding the culture of technology, social workers need to be digitally literate to fully participate as professionals with other disciplines that are also using these technologies, and within the society as a whole. Social workers manage organizations, organize social action, and advocate for social policy—technology now plays an important role in all of these domains (Hill & Shaw, 2011; Perron, Taylor, Glass, & Margerum-Leys, 2010; Rheingold, 2012; Shirky, 2009). Perron et al. (2010) argue that effective use of ICTs applies to many social work ethical standards:

> ICTs are of critical importance to advancing the field of social work. Specifically, they provide efficent [sic] and effective ways for organizing people and ideas, offers greater access to knowledge and education, and increases the efficiency and collaboration of our work. . .. Many aspects of the NASW Code of Ethics (1999) can be advanced through careful and thoughtful application of ICTs. Thus, competencies with ICTs and ICT literacy should be required learning outcomes in social work education and continuing education. This includes having the knowledge and skills to understand and use ICTs to achieve a specific purpose (i.e., competencies), in addition to knowing the major concepts and language associated with ICT (i.e., literacy). (p. 69)

Digital literacy also is one of the cornerstone elements for a policy of digital inclusion, that is, strategies to ensure that all people have access to the information and opportunities provided through ICTs, given the increasingly important role that ICTs are playing in access to resources and opportunities in society. A recent report (Institute of Museum and Library Services, 2012) highlighted the critical need for digital inclusion strategies:

> The diffusion of the Internet and other information and communication technologies has enabled communities around the United States to reap the rewards of greater connectivity (FCC, 2010). Individuals and organizations from all sectors—including the public—have been able to expand and enrich their services through these new technologies. Not all members of a community benefit equally, and some excluded individuals and communities risk being deprived of basic needs such as education, employment, commerce, and social interaction that increasingly occur through the Internet and other advanced communication technologies. Communities have been left out altogether. These excluded individuals and communities risk being deprived of basic needs such as education, employment, commerce, and social interaction that increasingly occur through the Internet and other advanced communication technologies. (pp. 1–2)

Taken together, the rationale for social workers to be digitally literate is compelling: to empower us as professionals and to provide us with the expertise to then empower our clients, organizations, and communities. Therefore, we hold that social workers have an ethical imperative to be digitally literate, which means that social work education must include digital literacy.

DON'T STUDENTS ALREADY KNOW HOW TO USE TECHNOLOGY?

No. We know this answer flies in the face of the cultural mythology about digital natives versus digital immigrants (Prensky,

2001), that is, those who grew up using technology versus those who had to learn it later in life (Palfrey & Gasser, 2016). The digital native myth holds that people born after 1984 are proficient in the use of digital technology because they have been immersed in it from the beginning of their lives (Kirschner & De Bruyckere, 2017). And yet research indicates that today's young people, by and large, do not have the in-depth knowledge of technology implied by the term digital native, nor are they particularly skilled in how to use it to learn (Kirschner & De Bruyckere, 2017). Knowing how to use a tool like a smartphone or an application (app), does not mean one knows how to use the tool professionally and ethically (Karpman & Drisko, 2016; Sage & Sage, 2016). For example, one of us (Nancy), who serves as dean of a school, received an e-mail with a question from a student she had never met. The e-mail was written in "text speak," that is, it was very informal, using incomplete sentences and many abbreviations in place of words, and conveyed a very unprofessional tone. The student apologized when this was brought to her attention, confessing she just had not thought about it, and sent the email the way she might e-mail friends. This example highlights the significant difference in knowing how to use a tool and knowing how to use it in a range of contexts to meet many different goals.

It also bears mentioning that students will vary widely in their experiences with, and access to, digital technology, an issue that has been identified as key to ensuring digital equity (Davis, Fuller, Jackson, Pittman, & Sweet, 2007) and digital inclusion (Institute of Museum and Library Services, 2012). Clearly, it is hard to be digitally literate if one has limited access and experience, and at the same time, having access and experience with technology is not enough to ensure digital literacy. For all these reasons, it is best (1) to not assume anything about students' experiences and knowledge, and instead to encourage students to share their experiences and learning; and (2) to articulate the understanding that there can be wide variations given access issues and cultural differences.

WHAT DOES DIGITAL LITERACY REALLY MEAN?

Digital literacy is now discussed by educators of all types (Davidson, 2014; Hague, 2010; Jenkins, Clinton, Purushotma, Robison, & Weigel, 2001; Jenkins, Purushotma, Weigel, Clinton, & Robison, 2009). It is an ambiguous, complex concept (Belshaw, 2014; Hague, 2010) that is most often attached the ability to comprehend, communicate, and create and share content through knowledge and competencies associated with practical understanding and use of the Internet and a range of technological tools. The concept is discussed by many different names: competency in the use of ICTs (Colvin & Bullock, 2014; Hill & Shaw, 2011); media literacy (Livingstone, 2004); new media literacy (Jenkins et al., 2001; Jenkins, Purushotma, Weigel, Clinton, & Robison, 2009); and digital literacy (Davidson, 2014).

Although noting that digital literacy is a "complex and contested term," Hague defines digital literacy as "the ability to participate in a range of critical and creative practices that involve understanding, sharing and creating meaning with different kinds of technology and media" (2010, p. 3). For social workers, this means digitally literate professionals: (1) would understand the range of ways that social and digital technologies could be used within professional practice while respecting appropriate boundaries with clients and promoting professional ethics; and (2) have the skills to create professional content with various media (writing, images, video, audio), and to share it appropriately.

Davidson (2011) conducted a survey of her students at Duke University and asked them to list digital literacies. Their answers were far ranging, from possessing technical skills to working with a range of digital applications (e.g., Web video, WordPress, Facebook groups, and Wikipedia editing); adapting writing styles for the diverse audiences across various social media platforms (e.g., Twitter as compared to Instagram); and incorporating technology "efficiently and wisely" into work or educational settings (Davidson, 2011). See Breakout Box 2.1 for a complete list of these digital literacies. The diversity of these answers provides insight into digital literacy while illustrating the challenge inherent in providing one definition of digital literacy.

However, digital literacy should be understood in context. Belshaw (2014) observed that digital literacy is best thought of along a continuum, from skills to competencies to literacies, and that really multiple digital literacies exist that have eight essential elements: cultural, cognitive, constructive, communicative, confident, creative, critical, and civic. We will discuss each element in the next section, but key to understanding his framework is thinking of digital literacies as involving all these elements and being aware that specific contexts will involve Belshaw (2014) specific elements in differing degrees. He likens this to viewing the eight elements as ingredients in a recipe. One can have different recipes for different practice or client contexts (such as a hospital compared to a school setting or an individual client compared to a community) by changing the proportion of specific elements.

BREAKOUT BOX 2.1. THEORY TALK:
WHAT ARE DIGITAL LITERACIES?
LET'S ASK THE STUDENTS

- Using online sources to network, knowledge-outreach, publicize content, collaborate, and innovate
- Collecting, managing, and interpreting multimedia and online data and content
- Appreciating the complex ethics surrounding online practices
- Engaging successfully in an "Innovation Challenge," an exercise in simultaneous, multiuser, real-time distance collaboration, on deadline
- Developing a diversity of writing styles and modes of communication to best reach, address, and accommodate multiple audiences across multiple online platforms
- Demonstrating technical and media skills: Web video, WordPress, blogging, Google Docs, Livechat, Twitter, Facebook groups, and Wikipedia editing

- Participating successfully in peer leadership (without an authority figure as the leader to police, guide, or protect the collaborators), peer assessment, peer self-evaluation; making contributions to a group on a coherent and innovative project
- Cultivating strategies for managing the line between personal and professional life in visible, online communities
- Understanding how to transform complicated ideas and gut reactions about technology into flexible technology policy
- Learning how to champion the importance of the open Web and net neutrality
- Collaborating across disciplines and working with people from different backgrounds and fields, including across liberal arts and engineering
- Understanding the complexity of copyright and intellectual property and the relationship between "open source" and "profitability" or "sustainability"
- Excelling in collaborative online publishing skills and expertise, from conception to execution, implementation, and dissemination
- Incorporating technology efficiently and wisely into a specific classroom or work environment
- Leading peers in discussing the implications and ethics of intellectual collaborative discourse and engagement online and beyond
- Using the superior expertise of a peer to extend my own knowledge

Source: Davidson, 2011.

We are foregoing an in-depth and comprehensive review of all the definitions of digital literacy in favor of a more pragmatic focus to guide social work educators. To accomplish this, we present Belshaw's (2014) framework for digital literacies, which identifies the key elements for digital literacy that show up across the literature. This framework has the advantage of being comprehensive—it captures how "digital literacy" is being used—and is still flexible enough to accommodate diverse contexts, including that of social work education.

HOW DOES TECHNOLOGY FIGURE INTO DIGITAL LITERACY?

Belshaw (2014) notes that literacy of any type involves two types of knowledge: tool and content. For hundreds of years, tool knowledge, that is, our familiarity with the methods that convey information, was unchanging; tool knowledge required knowledge of printed material and pens—therefore, people focused on content knowledge when they discussed literacy and never even considered the impact of tools. But as technological change has accelerated, the relevance of tool knowledge has emerged. Someone might be able to understand the content in printed books but be unfamiliar with how to use hyperlinks on a Web page. The latter situation would mean they would miss some of the content knowledge on that Web page because they would not know to right-click on the hyperlinks. Therefore, if everything else is equal, in a culture where a large amount of knowledge is conveyed through hyperlinks, a person with the tool knowledge and skill of using hyperlinks would be more literate than the person who lacked the tool knowledge to use hyperlinks. Hence, content knowledge can be limited by deficits in tool knowledge.

Another challenge to defining digital literacy is a rapidly changing environment where new technologies are introduced and then adopted quickly. It is not enough for new technology to be created for it to affect digital literacy meaningfully for a given population; it also needs to be adopted by the population in question. Understanding the innovation adoption/diffusion curve (Rogers, 2003) can shed light on this phenomenon. Figure 2.1 shows the adoption curve, which is essentially a bell curve, with innovators and early adopters on the left, followed by early majority adopters, then the late majority, and finally laggards on the far right.

Smartphones become an excellent case in point to illustrate technology infusion and adoption. Although they originated in the early 1990s (McCarty, 2011), the use of smartphones would

*Figure 2.1. Innovation Adoption Lifecycle:
Digital Literacy & New Technologies*

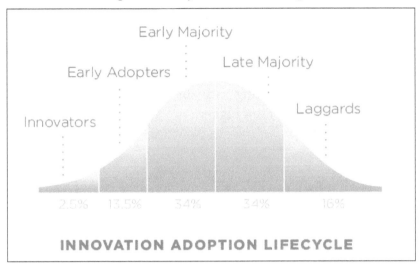

One of the challenges to defining digital literacy is a rapidly changing environment where new technologies are introduced and then adopted quickly. It is not enough for a new technology to be created to meaningfully affect digital literacy for a given population; it also needs to be adopted by the population in question. Understanding the innovation adoption/diffusion curve (Rogers, 2003) can shed light on this phenomenon. The adoption curve is essentially a bell curve, with innovators and early adopters on the left, followed by early majority, then late majority, and finally laggards on the far right.

Based on Rogers, 2003. Figure from "Diffusion of Innovation," Wikipedia, 2011, retrieved from https://en.m.wikipedia.org/wiki/File:DiffusionOfInnovation.png. CC Attribution License.

probably not have been included in someone's definition of an essential digital literacy skill at that time. However, when a new technology reaches the point where the majority of the population adopts the technology, one might make the case that the particular tool is a significant influencer in digital literacies. In 2011, 35% of American adults had smartphones (Perrin, 2015). By 2015 this percentage had almost doubled, with 64% reporting smartphone ownership and one in five Americans depending on smartphones for their Internet access (Perrin, 2015). As smartphones have now passed that mid-curve tipping point into the late majority category, the theory of technology diffusion suggests that use of smartphones becomes a vital component of tool knowledge (and, therefore, digital literacy) in American society, especially for those working with specific populations in which adoption rates may be even higher.

HOW CAN DIGITAL LITERACY APPLY TO SOCIAL WORK EDUCATION?

A social work faculty member, in a conversation with one of the authors, raised the following question about digital literacy: "Should we be teaching it in our courses, or should students have to complete a course covering this content?" This is a valid question that has been the subject of much debate (Hobbs, 1998) and harkens back to the dialogues that faculty members have about writing skills and critical thinking in the social work curriculum. However, at this time, we believe it is a straw man argument. Our assumption, as articulated in the previous section, is that social work practitioners at all levels of practice now need to be digitally literate. Currently, we know of no social work degree programs that require a course in digital literacy (although, hopefully, this will change soon) and yet the new National Association of Social Workers' (NASW) Standards for Technology in Social Work Practice (NASW, 2017b) and the recently revised NASW Code of Ethics (NASW, 2017a) require that all social workers develop the requisite knowledge and skills to ensure the professional use of technology. Within this context, it seems we need to begin teaching about technology in our courses immediately; work to develop required, stand-alone courses (such as the bachelor of social work [BSW] course described by Zgoda & Shane, 2018);

BREAKOUT BOX 2.2. CASE STUDY:
MAYA, TAKING THE PLUNGE INTO DIGITAL LITERACY

Maya, a faculty member who teaches in an MSW program, believes it is key for her students to deepen their knowledge and confidence using digital technologies in their roles as developing social workers. She understands this means she will need to find ways for them to have experience with several different social media applications. She also recognizes that her own experience with using social media professionally is limited. She uses Facebook (FB) a lot with friends and family but has never used it with colleagues. She also knows, from listening to colleagues at conferences, that some of them are using Twitter, Pinterest, and LinkedIn with their students. She feels overwhelmed at the thought of trying to learn all those apps, and she decides that she can start by broadening her knowledge of FB.

Maya starts by searching for "social workers" in the FB search box. It returns some results and gives her a choice of the types of listings to search. She chooses People from the tab and gets profiles where people list social worker as their job. However, from the nature of their public posts, she sees these social workers are not using FB professionally. The Pages tab results in a list of mostly organizations, which does not match her goal of learning how she can use FB professionally. The Groups tab yields many public groups that look promising. She clicks on several and is disappointed to find that they consist of some social work news postings with no comments, and a lot of spam.

At this point, Maya is pretty frustrated. She goes back to what she knows and posts a status update asking her friends and family (which includes some social workers) if any of them know of people who are using FB professionally. Within 24 hours she has some useful responses from her network that includes links to profiles of some people and groups that she can start to follow, observe, and interact with. A few days later, reflecting on her initial frustrations, Maya laughs as she realizes she did extend her knowledge with all that searching, just not the way she expected.

and also address the need for continuing education for faculties and alumni. Also, as previously mentioned, Belshaw (2014) argues that digital literacy is embedded in the context, and this matches our experience as social work educators. From this perspective, it becomes impossible to make digital literacy only a stand-alone course (although it would be wonderful to have such courses too)—it also needs to be embedded throughout the curriculum because the context of digital literacy changes across the curriculum. Our rationale for this embedded integration will become more evident as we discuss the elements of digital literacy as they apply to social work education.

Refer to Breakout Boxes 2.2, 2.3, 2.4, and 2.5, for a case study on how Maya, a faculty member in an MSW program, develops her digital literacy skills and shares these newfound skills with her students.

WHAT ARE THE ELEMENTS OF DIGITAL LITERACY?

Belshaw (2014) identified eight elements of digital literacies: cultural, cognitive, constructive, communicative, confident, creative, critical, and civic. We apply Belshaw's eight elements within the context of social work education and extend Belshaw's work to contexts that would be relevant for social work educators. Figure 2.2 lists all eight literacies that are discussed in this section.

Cultural Element of Digital Literacy

Belshaw (2014) placed Cultural context at the top of the list because of its importance, whereas he lists the other contextual elements in alphabetical order (p. 44). The context is a large part of what makes up the Cultural element related to digital and social technologies. He indicates that this context includes even specific tools, such as the type of device and the specific applications used. He writes,

DIGITAL LITERACY

Figure 2.2. Belshaw's 8 Elements of Digital Literacy

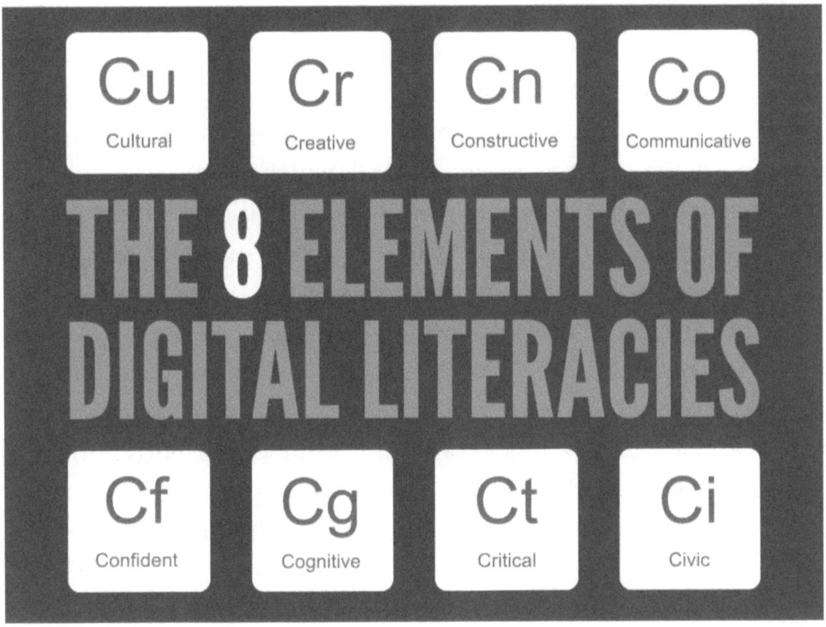

Cu	Cr	Cn	Co
Cultural	Creative	Constructive	Communicative

THE 8 ELEMENTS OF DIGITAL LITERACIES

Cf	Cg	Ct	Ci
Confident	Cognitive	Critical	Civic

Source: Belshaw, 2014.

> For example, I'm writing this particular paragraph whilst on a train using a non-linear word processing program called Scrivener. Every now and then I get a notification that I've got a reply or direct message on Twitter. This means several things, not least choosing whether to be distracted by those messages right now, but also (and more pertinently) how to navigate between the context of using a program such as Scrivener and TweetDeck, the app I use to interact with my Twitter network. (pp. 44–45)

Cultural also includes purpose, personal, social, and cultural aspects of the individual, along with environmental context. For example, mobile phones are used differently in Africa than in North America. Finally, Cultural includes the norms, habits, and expectations that are associated with all aspects of the technology

45

context, including the software application itself. For example, Twitter has different a different culture than Facebook. E-mail has different norms than texting. The best way to grasp the Cultural aspect of digital literacy is by immersion in the many diverse digital environments (i.e., social media platforms, video games, and learning management systems [LMS]), which requires learners to change their behavior to accommodate that digital environment (Belshaw, 2014). It is only by fully experiencing multiple digital environments that one fully understands the unique and shared elements of each platform's culture. For example, both Facebook and Blackboard, a brand of LMS, use text-based comments as the primary tool for communicating with others in the platform. However, Facebook is about communicating with friends and family, and Blackboard is about communicating with an instructor and classmates, so one would expect that different norms would apply to posting in each platform.

Some aspects of the Cultural element are unique to social workers, that is, the standards that guide the use of technology in social work. In the United States, organizations such as the National Association of Social Workers (NASW), the Association of Social Work Boards (ASWB), and the Council on Social Work Education (CSWE) are key to providing guidelines for practitioners and organizations (NASW), educators (CSWE and NASW), and state licensing boards (ASWB). The standards developed by these organizations are vital in shaping the context for the use of technology in social work. One example is the previously mentioned NASW Standards for Technology in Social Work Practice (NASW, 2017b), which include guidelines for the use of technology in social work education. Also, social workers need to understand the policy context in their individual agencies as well as state and local governments. For example, Erie County Department of Social Services added the use of social media to the tools that workers use to assess child safety (Erie County Child Protective Services, 2014), while other child protective service agencies might forbid the use of these tools. Ethical social work practice requires full disclosure and informed consent about whether and how social media will be used to gather information on clients, adding another Cultural contextual layer (NASW, 2017a, 2017b).

It is because context/culture is so important to digital literacy that digital natives (i.e., the younger generation of social work students and practitioners) need help understanding how to use technology effectively (Belshaw, 2014, p. 46). They may be facile with using text messages with friends, but those skills need to be adapted for different contexts, such as e-mailing a professor, sending texts to a client to change an appointment, or creating a professional profile on the Internet. In other words, knowledge about how to use particular apps, such as a text-messaging program that has been acquired for use in personal relationships, can only be successfully applied professionally after considering the various professional roles where it might be applied and reflecting how use of the app needs to change for each role and purpose.

Social work educators can highlight the Cultural element of literacy by asking students to reflect on what purpose they are pursuing (goal) while using digital media, including their target audience, consideration of their role, and the professional expectations relative to their audience. Following this, students need to consider norms and culture of the specific application in question. For instance, students can compare the user profiles and tweets for a Twitter account that is being used professionally, for networking and developing an online professional learning network (PLN), to a Twitter account that is being used more to connect with friends. After they do this, ask students to do the same for YouTube, the video-sharing application, and then to compare the similarities and differences between the observed cultures of YouTube and Twitter. Finally, ask students to find articles that describe the norms and cultures of each of the applications, and then have students compare those norms and cultures. Understanding these Cultural contextual elements helps students to develop skills that lead to competency in using technology professionally.

As Belshaw's (2014) earlier example of writing on a train highlighted, switching between applications and choosing whether to switch at a given moment is also a vital part of the context. In addition to the competence of switching between applications, competence in developing an awareness and the ability to work with attention is also important, something that Rheingold (2012) sees as the foundation for one's effectiveness in digital environments. He recommends practicing mindfulness to acquire the ability to manage one's attention online (Rheingold, 2012). Attention and awareness of one's goals are important in determining when to turn off technology to give full attention to a task or people who are present (Rheingold, 2012). Consider, for example, the question of when it is acceptable to use a smartphone in a meeting with a client or supervisor. An exploration of the answers to this question include understanding the larger purpose of the meeting and one's own goals in attending; how using a smartphone might affect those goals; and consideration of the unintended consequences of using the smartphone in the meeting (losing key content and conveying to others at the meeting that you are not interested in the content, that you are not behaving professionally, or that you don't think the meeting is important). In the same way, consider the impact of stopping at the beginning of a meeting and saying, "I want to turn this off, so we are not interrupted." This simple act conveys a powerful message about your attention and the importance that you place on the meeting, including the people in the meeting.

An important aspect of the Cultural context is the differences in how technology is used to create and express identity, and to build community, across a wide range of digital settings. Students will come from diverse backgrounds in their knowledge of, exposure to, and experiences in a wide range of digital Cultural contexts.

Norms can vary widely regarding creating *avatars*; referencing gender, sexual orientation, race, and other aspects of identity; and practices such as providing trigger warnings in an online post. Encouraging students to share, in class (or in small-group discussions), their observations about diverse and unique Cultural elements of various online environments can help to build shared understanding and to equalize differences in experience across all students. See Breakout Box 2.3 for a case study of how Maya, a full-time social work educator, created a group classroom activity that facilitated students sharing these experiences with each other. Maya's activities could easily be adapted to an online teaching environment through use of the SAMR Model discussed in Chapter 4, "Technology in the Social Work Classroom."

BREAKOUT BOX 2.3. CASE STUDY:
MAYA, CREATING CULTURAL LITERACY EXPERIENCES FOR STUDENTS

Motivated by her first exploration with digital literacy, Maya, who is teaching human behavior in the social environment (HBSE) for an MSW program, decides to incorporate some new content about technology into her learning module about culture, after learning about hashtags and how they are being used to shape conversations in social media such as #BlackLivesMatters and #MeToo. She is curious to help her students understand how diversity and difference can affect experiences with technology. Maya starts by asking her students to reflect on the following:

1. What digital technology do you have access to and use? Which ones don't you use, and what applications of technology do you feel most comfortable with?

2. Consider how your identity (e.g., race, gender, class, sexual orientation, age, and geographic location) affects experiences with technology and your confidence in using those technologies.

Maya then divides the class into groups to share their insights and has each group discuss what they learned about how their own identities intersect with their technology access, use, and experience.

Next, Maya asks students to identify their favorite social media app, such as Twitter, Snapchat, or Instagram, and then groups them with other students who also like that app. Each group is then asked to create a Cultural profile of that app using the following criteria:

- Type of content they or others typically post in the app
- People who are in the app community—and people who aren't
- How people use the app to help with developmental roles or tasks
- How the app might create challenges for human developmental roles or tasks
- Best practice guidelines and "norms" for how to use this app for someone who is new to it (dos and don'ts).

When Maya had some students who don't use social media at all, she asked them to discuss how nonuse can affect human development opportunities and challenges in today's society. After completing the profiles, the groups present their profiles to the entire class, which prompts several students to comment that they had not thought about how these different app platforms had their own cultural norms. Maya is pleased with her first attempt to explore culture and technology with her students.

Cognitive Element of Digital Literacy

The Cognitive element of digital literacy relates to expanding one's explicit knowledge relative to the structure and processes in digital environments (Belshaw, 2014). For example, cognitive literacy includes understanding the different components of a digital environment, such as that a website or application varies depending on the type of screen (i.e., computer monitor vs. smartphone), and branching logic within menus, hyperlinks, and digital download buttons. An understanding of the cognitive element can be developed by becoming acquainted with a range of digital settings, but Belshaw (2014) notes that reading about key aspects or practices in digital environments can help. For example, reading help guides or watching tutorials about how to use a social media app such as Instagram can directly enhance one's understanding of how to use the app. Such readings can accelerate learning from the specific to the general.

To help social work students develop the Cognitive element, educators can highlight common features, such as user profiles and privacy or notification settings, in platforms such as Blackboard as well as on social media platforms such as Twitter, WordPress, and LinkedIn.

Whenever students are being oriented to a new app, an opportunity exists to teach about the types of features that most apps have by simply moving the discussion from the specific (one app) to the general (noting how a feature is similar to or different from other apps). For example, while teaching students how to use an LMS discussion board, students can be told that most apps have options for adding comments but that the format, such as the view of the dialogue box, may vary from app to app. These similarities and differences can be highlighted across apps. For example, comment posting options such as undo, copy and paste, insert images, upload files, hashtags (or topic tags) are common digital tools for many apps. The concept of contextual menus, that is, menus that vary depending on where in the app you are currently working, can be introduced and highlighted as a common feature for apps. Common choices for setting up user profiles and choosing privacy settings can also be reviewed with students. This type of discussion offers the opportunity to bring in the Cultural element of digital literacy as well, since purpose, target audience, and app norms all have implications for privacy settings, profile photos, and bios. For example, students may want a more professional photo for their LinkedIn profile than for their Facebook profile.

Constructive Element of Digital Literacy

Belshaw (2014) defines the Constructive element of digital literacy as the ability to make (construct) something, typically content such as text, images, and video. Included here are skills such as copying and pasting content within and between apps, using an undo function, and writing and publishing a post or comment. Activities that promote the Constructive element include writing and publishing a blog post or discussion board posts, writing and publishing tweets, and recording, uploading, and editing a YouTube video. The Constructive element tends to emphasize the nuts and bolts of making content, whereas the Creative element (discussed later in the chapter) focuses on the act of making something new.

Higher-level knowledge related to the Constructive element includes understanding forms of licensing and how copyright law applies to digital content (e.g., using a Creative Commons license), how to build on others' work (remixing), how to cite others' work in digital environments (attribution), and knowing where to find public domain images. In our experience, students often have trouble in these areas, as they are unclear how copyright law applies to Web content and they cut and paste without appropriate citations in their papers and other constructed work. For example, when creating a podcast or video for a class assignment, students may incorporate music into the final product without understanding that use of certain music requires paying royalties and that they should use only royalty-free music. Educators have an opportunity to model social work ethics, such as using appropriate citations and remixing practices when presenting digital content to classes and when developing their own digital materials. Some of these practices include adding a Creative Commons license to work you've created, following fair use laws, and appropriately citing others. By modeling these practices, social work educators can begin educating students about these resources and processes. In a course where students might be creating materials to use with clients, such as a public service announcement or educational video, a discussion board could be devoted to answering questions of appropriate remixing and citation options to improve their skills in the constructive element of digital literacy. We have included, at the end of this chapter, some resources that provide an overview of copyright guidelines, fair use, and Creative Commons.

Communicative Element of Digital Literacy

Belshaw (2014) observes that the Communicative element of digital literacy is closely tied to the Constructive element in that it involves making content to share with others in digital formats. For this reason, the Communicative element is also intertwined closely with the Cultural element. That is, one must understand the norms, habits, and expectations within a specific digital setting (and for a particular purpose) to communicate effectively (Belshaw, 2014). For example, sending an e-mail to a friend requires an understanding of the different norms that would apply compared to sending an e-mail to a supervisor in a work setting. Belshaw also notes that the ability to understand and develop effective digital networks, what Howard Rheingold calls "network smarts" (Rheingold, 2012, p. 23), would be included in the Communicative element, such as knowing how to use digital networks to connect with people in real time and when to disengage with other users in a network because the connection is no longer meaningful or becomes hostile.

It is worth noting that someone might use many different applications, such as Facebook or LinkedIn, to acquire information but never have communicated in these environments, a behavior that sometimes is called lurking. Moving from lurking to communicating in environments with strangers can be scary, even for those who are comfortable sharing in other contexts, such as with friends and family. The faculty can help with this transition by scaffolding digital experiences when taking students through the process of learning and mastering a new digital environment for professional reasons. For example, ask students to start by brainstorming strategies to use for finding trustworthy people on Twitter who are sharing about a relevant topic (e.g., human rights), and then to use strategies to identify people and construct Twitter lists on specific topics. Next, instruct students to identify and share ways they can begin establishing relationships with one or more of these contacts. Relationships in digital spaces are built on mutuality—if you are asking people to share your content, but you have never shared theirs, you will likely be perceived as someone who is spamming or trying to sell something in absence of a relationship. It is worth the time to shift one's perspective when constructing a public post to ask reflective questions such as, how will this be viewed by other professionals? Other students? People receiving social work services? Prospective clients and employers? The public? (Kimball & Kim, 2013).

BREAKOUT BOX 2.4. CASE STUDY
MAYA, EXPLORING A NEW APP

Maya, the social work faculty member who began her quest to expand her digital literacy in Breakout Box 2.2, decides to attend a presentation on "Using Twitter in Your Classes" at an annual social work educators' conference. She doesn't have an account yet but has been interested to learn more about how to follow hashtags she hears about in the news such as #BlackLivesMatter and #MeToo. She is surprised to hear ways her colleagues are using Twitter with students, and what is most appealing to her is how her students can participate in live social work chats on the app, chats that include social workers, social work students, and educators from around the world. For this reason, she decides that she needs to learn how to use Twitter.

    Maya starts by finding the Twitter home page through a Google search using the key word "Twitter," but all she sees is an option to sign up or log in. She does not see any basic introduction about how to use the app. She checks through her notes from the presentation and sees that she made a note from the speakers that if you are looking for good basic introduction information you can search on "Twitter Tutorial" on Google or on YouTube. She decides to try the Google search and retrieves many links that look promising, including some YouTube videos. Twenty minutes later, after reading and viewing a few resources, she feels she has a better sense of how to start. She sets up a Twitter account, uploads a profile picture, and leaves the bio empty because she is not sure what to say. Then, she tries something that was suggested: she searches for the term "social work" in Twitter and is surprised at the types and quality of user profiles she gets back. She begins to "follow" some of these user profiles, and already she is noticing the ways in which Twitter is different than Facebook, the social media app she knows the best. She adds a few comments to her profile based on her review of the profiles of other social workers. She looks at the clock and realizes she has been working on this for an hour. "Time for a break!" she thinks. Her search for #BlackLivesMatter will have to wait until tomorrow.

Confident Element of Digital Literacy

The Confident element of digital literacy is a sense of mastery and competence related to one's ability to master digital environments. As social work educators, we think of it as digital self-efficacy (our term, not Belshaw's) because being a competent social worker requires skills as well as knowledge and adherence to social work values. Belshaw (2014) observes that the Confident element is not simply a function of acquiring confidence in the other elements of digital literacy but reflects a deep understanding of how to bring all the elements together and how to leverage the uniqueness of digital environments. Social work students acquire this element through practice in solving problems and directing their own learning through a wide range of digital settings (Belshaw, 2014). Faculty members can support students to acquire digital self-efficacy by presenting them with a range of different digital environments, especially those that will be available to them after they graduate. For this reason, we are hesitant to consider mastery of an LMS such a Blackboard and Canvas as true digital literacy. Although they provide good learning environments for hosting course assignments, readings, and the many components of an online course, most students will not be using an LMS after graduation. If students' digital experiences are only limited to an LMS environment, they will have much lower confidence than if they are using multiple digital environments, especially those available to them when they are no longer students. Therefore, helping students generalize from the LMS becomes important.

However, educators can draw on the previously described Cognitive element to facilitate generalization within an LMS by pointing out the similarities between tasks in the LMS and tasks that may arise in other contexts. For example, understanding notification and email settings in an LMS can be compared to an agency's internal email system, or writing discussion posts can be analogous to commenting on the agency's blog.

A key aspect of the Confident element is developing one's ability to master new digital environments. One way to foster this with students is to provide opportunities for exploration and risk-taking in an assignment, such as encouraging students to discover and explore new applications. For example, one might ask students to create a social work meme, that is, take a popular image and add social work–relevant text to it. This meme could then be shared on a social media platform such as Instagram.

Alternatively, the assignment could include finding and comparing two image-editing apps that are used to create memes, such as PhotoGrid or Canva. Students could write reviews that highlight the strengths and weakness of each app and describe what might be useful to other students. These types of exploration and risk-taking assignments are best implemented when they are included with class participation activities or graded in such a way as to support the effort and exploration behaviors, while placing less emphasis on the outcome.

BREAKOUT BOX 2.5. CASE STUDY
MAYA, REFLECTING ON PROCESS

Taking her break, Maya, sits with a cup of coffee at the student center and now reflects on some of the new things she had learned. She recalls how she started with exploring the ways that Facebook could be used professionally, next sought out some information at a conference, and then moved into exploring a new app, Twitter. She considers not just what she has learned but also how she learned it. Searching online, or within an app, yielded mixed results depending on where and how she searched. Her Facebook searches on "social work" were frustrating, whereas the same search on Twitter proved fruitful. Searching for tutorials on Google, as suggested at the presentation she attended, yielded helpful results. She then realized that a tutorial search on Google or YouTube would be a helpful starting point for learning any new app. Similarly, searching out colleagues who are using the apps was also a very helpful strategy.

Maya decides to share her learning journey with her students in her next HBSE class. She is more confident with her skills and thinks that having a discussion about technology and professional development will fit nicely after the recent group activity about the culture of social media platforms. While sipping her coffee, she jots a few notes in her notebook about what she wants to share and how she plans to follow this by inviting students to discuss strategies they may have employed to expand their knowledge of using digital technology professionally.

Creative Element of Digital Literacy

The creative element of digital literacy is quite simple. It involves constructing something that is new and that adds value (Belshaw, 2014). As with most of the other digital literacy elements, it is context dependent, that is, "what counts as 'valuable' and/or 'new' depends upon the context" (Belshaw, 2014, p. 52). When considering what is new and valuable, more emphasis is placed on the value added of the digital content, because very little content is completely original, especially within digital contexts (Belshaw, 2014, p. 53). To encourage development of the Creative element among social work learners, educators need to demonstrate this element themselves by creating digital content and designing learning activities to incorporate the unique capabilities provided by specific digital environments.

Additionally, learning activities need to empower students to take risks (Belshaw, 2014). Of these learning activities, Belshaw writes, "Aspects of randomness and discovery should flow through learning experiences, finishing with opportunities to synthesize these experiences. This sense-making is often where the 'creativity' occurs. The learner joins the dots in new, interesting and *contextually-relevant* ways" (p. 54–55).

Many potential learning activities in social work can support students taking risks to create new digital content. For example, learning challenging material, such as the neurobiology of addiction, can be facilitated by drawing students into the role of teaching others about the material through digital content. Although such a goal could be filled by asking students to find useful content on the Internet to help others learn, it is not likely to result in learning that is as deep as having students create their own content. And yet the same goal could be met by asking students to create their own content to teach other students (and perhaps, eventually, coworkers and clients) through video or animations, with the understanding that they can remix the work of others appropriately. For a plethora of social work learning activities that support this element, see Appendix 1, "Assignment Compendium for Integrating Technology Into Social Work Assignments and Learning Activities."

Critical Element of Digital Literacy

Belshaw (2014, p. 55) observes the Critical element of digital literacy comes closest to what is sometimes called media literacy and includes all of what is typically involved in developing the capacity for critical thinking, such as questioning the assumptions and perspective that is embedded in a piece of work or a text and evaluating the trustworthiness of a site and a source, what Rheingold (2012) calls "crap detection." However, within digital environments, the Critical element involves applying these skills to content such as hyperlinked pages, audio, video, and images. For example, a website that purports to rank the top MSW programs should be evaluated by examining the site sponsors, the top-level domain name, the authors' credentials and qualifications, disclosure of the ranking methodology, and citation of sources, to name just a few content-evaluating strategies. Similarly, a mental health app for anxiety reduction can also be evaluated in light of these strategies, for example, the credentials of the developers, the code sources used to construct the app, citations for any studies about the app's effectiveness, and reading reviews of the app. Breakout Box 2.6 summarizes some helpful content-evaluation strategies.

BREAKOUT BOX 2.6. PRACTICAL TIPS

STRATEGIES TO USE IN EVALUATING CONTENT

Ask Questions

- Who is the audience? Who is included? Who is excluded? (Belshaw, 2014, p. 56)
- What are the assumptions behind this text? (Belshaw, 2014, p. 56)
- Who is the author, and what are the author's sources? What are the author's credentials? (Rheingold, 2012, p. 79)

Other Strategies

- Check facts through hoax-checking websites like Snopes or Fact Check (Rheingold, 2012, p. 90).
- Look for an author; then search for the author's name to see what others are saying about this source (Rheingold, 2012, p. 78).
- Use the search protocol "Who is" to see who owns the URL; then search for the owner (Rheingold, 2012, p. 78).
- Triangulation: Search for confirming evidence from at least three other credible sources (Rheingold, 2012, p. 79).

- Evaluate the top-level domain name (e.g., .edu, .com, .gov, or .uk; Belshaw, 2014, p. 56; Rheingold, 2012, p. 79).
- Provide students with texts that come from different perspectives (Belshaw, 2014, p. 56).
- Do a search on Google's Reverse Image Search website to find similar images and see where the image originated (Brown, September 18, 2015).

To strengthen the Critical element of digital literacy among social work students, they could be asked to create a list of blogs to follow on a given topic, such as poverty. Then students could apply the strategies from Breakout Box 2.6 to each blog and discuss the credibility of the blogs, including the credentials of the authors and the credibility of a specific post, and also explain why they decided to follow or not follow specific blogs.

Civic Element of Digital Literacy

The Civic element of digital literacy focuses on the knowledge, attitudes, and behaviors that support participation in government and the larger society, including organizing for social action (Belshaw, 2014, p. 57). This includes applying the critical dimension to evaluate the digital media produced by governmental bodies and other key social organizations, as well as using a range of digital tools for advocacy and to organize people for digital and/or offline social change. Good examples of the Civic element are the role of hashtags such as #BlackLivesMatter and #MeToo in contemporary social action movements.

Activities that support the development of the Civic digital literacy in the classroom include asking students to provide online commentary or analysis on a proposed policy regulation at the website of a particular government agency; participating in online activities on websites hosted by local, state, or federal government agencies; writing and publishing a blog post advocating social action on a particular issue and then sharing it with others who might be interested in this issue via other social media; creating a petition on one of the social media petition sites (e.g., Change.org) and then organizing a dissemination campaign via other channels (online and offline) to gather supporters; following key political figures on social media and advocating for policy changes through interactions with them; raising awareness of a key issue through creating and sharing YouTube videos; or organizing an offline social action event through e-mail, social media, or other digital channels (Brady, Young, & McLeod, 2015; Goldkind, 2014; Young, 2014). The Civic element of digital literacy is clearly a critical digital literacy for social workers, given Ethical Principle 6 of the NASW Code of Ethics—the Social Workers' Ethical Responsibilities to the Broader Society (NASW, 2017b). In addition, the framework for professional action with the Civic element will be firmly grounded with the values and according to all the principles outlined in the NASW Code of Ethics (illustrating how the Code of Ethics, as a Cultural element, provides the key foundation for all professional Civic digital literacy).

HOW DO DIGITAL LITERACIES COME TOGETHER?

It bears mentioning one more time that most real-world situations involve the overlap and interplay of two or more digital literacy elements at the same time. It is helpful to think of digital literacies as taking place in the foreground and background of your digital assignments.

Figure 2.3 illustrates how this interplay occurs in the assignment example shared earlier in which students create and share social work memes. In this example, the Creative and Communicative elements are in the foreground of the assignment. This means students will draw on these literacies the most to complete the assignment, followed by the Cognitive and Constructive literacies. The Cultural element sits in the background, as student demonstration of this literacy, although essential to completing the assignment, is secondary to creating the social work meme.

Figure 2.3. Viewing Digital Literacies in Action: How Literacies Come Together

Source: Hitchcock, Sage, & Smyth, 2016.

Perhaps the most important point to consider in strengthening students' digital literacy is conveying that using ICTs in their assignments and their work is not really about learning specific skills, devices, or apps; it is about developing their digital literacies, which speaks much more to how they are evaluating, reflecting on, and understanding their use of ICTs through the lens of the many different literacies, including their professional roles, ethics, values, and context. The companion videos, embedded in the *Social Worker's Guide to Social Media* infographic created at the University at Buffalo School of Social Work (n.d.) can help students consider some key questions and issues in using social media and related ICTs, such as how they might build community online and how they represent the profession. These videos can help those students who are very confident about their use of social media in their personal lives understand that they need to develop more complex understandings of the use of ICTs now they are becoming social workers.

WHAT DO WE KNOW FROM RESEARCH ABOUT DIGITAL LITERACIES IN SOCIAL WORK?

The short answer to what is already known about digital literacy in social work is very little. Discussion occasionally surfaces about the need for digital literacy in social work and social work education, but little research on the topic exists (McAuliffe & Nipperess, 2017; Perron et al., 2010; Smyth, 2010; Zgoda, 2013). In the only study that we identified, Young (2015) adapted a new media literacy assessment scale (Literat, 2014) for social work education, sought to validate it, and then compared performance between social work educators and social work students. He found that social work educators scored lower on a 5-point Likert-type scale than social work students for four of the nine literacy subscales of his survey: networking (3.66 vs. 3.51), multitasking (3.69 vs. 3.59), simulation (3.60 vs. 3.47), and transmedia navigation (3.69 vs. 3.60). This suggests that social work educators need more training and practice with digital media than students. However, the scale itself assessed new media literacies, not digital literacy as we have defined in this book, within a relatively narrow Cultural context that may not reflect the social work educator's professional context in using new digital media. Although the differences observed by Young (2015) might be a bit difficult to interpret for social work educators, they do offer insight into the need for training about digital media for social workers in nonprofit agencies and macro-level practice settings.

A more recent study by Young (2018) is especially important in that he found that social work students' digital literacies were significantly improved, over time, after completing a course that infused digital literacy content, described by Young as "a course infused with social media, digital technologies, and content related to digital skill development" (p. 11). He also examined whether mode of course delivery (seated or online) made a difference in outcomes and found that there was no difference between the two course formats: both groups of students demonstrated significant improvement in their skills.

FINAL THOUGHTS

At a time when society is increasingly integrating digital technologies, social work practitioners and educators need to become digitally literate, especially considering the profession's new technology standards (NASW, 2017b) and a code of ethics that now addresses how technology applies across all ethical standards (NASW, 2017a). For many social work educators, this means beginning with deepening our own digital literacy, and then considering strategies for building and strengthening our students' digital literacy into all courses, especially providing them with opportunities to operate as new professionals in multiple digital environments. Additionally, digital literacy means having opportunities to reflect on the perspective and role changes that occur as students transition between specific digital environments and as they shift between personal and professional goals.

It is worth noting the speed of current technological change and the resulting changes in society that come with its adoption. As previously mentioned, social media use became ubiquitous in the past 10 years. The speed of change means that digital literacy is a moving target, and as new technologies develop, we are challenged to keep up our own learning as social work educators. As a result, we all need to develop strategies to stay abreast of the changes that are relevant to higher education and social work practice. This includes consideration of which digital literacies are covered within your courses and across your curriculum, and assessment of the ways that you are developing your own digital literacy skill set. It is helpful for all of us to ask reflective questions such as, how are we helping our students develop skills in digital literacy that prepare them for the types of practice experiences they are likely to encounter? For this reason, we have included Appendix 4, "Reflection Questions for Digital Literacy in Social Work," to help you assess your own digital literacy.

One strategy that has worked effectively to enhance digital literacy for many is developing a professional learning network (PLN). This is an online network of people to whom you stay connected to keep informed about new developments, explore ideas, and strategize about effective implementation. We have found PLNs so helpful in our own professional development that we have included how to create your own in Chapter 9, "Technology for Professional Development."

FURTHER READING AND RESOURCES

Belshaw, D. (2012, March 22). The essential elements of digital literacies: Doug Belshaw at TEDxWarwick [Video file]. Retrieved from https://youtu.be/A8yQPoTcZ78

Brown, P. (2015, September 18). Six easy ways to tell if that viral story is hoax. *Conversation*. Retrieved from https://theconversation.com/six-easy-ways-to-tell-if-that-viral-story-is-a-hoax-47673

Hitchings-Hales, J., & Calderwood, I. (2017, August 23). *8 massive moments hashtag activism really, really worked*. Retrieved from https://www.globalcitizen.org/en/content/hashtag-activism-hashtag10-twitter-trends-dresslik/

Institute of Museum and Library Services, University of Washington. (2012). *Building digital communities: A framework for action.* Technology & Social Change Group. Washington, DC: International City/County Management Association. Retrieved from https://tascha.uw.edu/publications/building-digital-communities/

Jenkins, H., Purushotma, R., Weigel, M., Clinton, K., & Robison, A. J. (2009). *Confronting the challenges of participatory culture: Media education for the 21st century.* Cambridge, MA: MIT Press.

Matthews, J. (2010, June 19). *Microsoft teacher guides: Developing critical thinking through web research skills.* Retrieved from http://learningonlineinfo.org/microsoft-teacher-guides-developing-critical-thinking-web-research-skills/

Rheingold, Howard. *Howard Rheingold.* http://rheingold.com/ (Includes links to his online articles and videos).

University at Buffalo School of Social Work. (n.d.). *Social worker's guide to social media.* Retrieved from http://socialwork.buffalo.edu/resources/social-media-guide.html (Includes an infographic and embedded videos).

Waters, S., & Burt, R. (2017, August 8). *The educator's guide to copyright, fair use, and Creative Commons.* Retrieved from https://www.theedublogger.com/copyright-fair-use-and-creative-commons/

REFERENCES

Belshaw, D. (2014). *The essential elements of digital literacies.* Retrieved from http://digitalliteraci.es/

Belshaw, D. A. J. (2011). What is 'digital literacy'? (Doctoral dissertation, Durham University, UK). Retrieved from https://clalliance.org/wp-content/uploads/files/doug-belshaw-edd-thesis-final.pdf

Brady, S. R., Young, J. A., & McLeod, D. A. (2015). Utilizing digital advocacy in community organizing: Lessons learned from organizing in virtual spaces to promote worker rights and economic justice. *Journal of Community Practice, 23*(2), 255–273. doi:10.1080/10705422.2015.1027803

Brown, P. (2015, September 18). Six easy ways to tell if that viral story is hoax. *Conversation*. Retrieved from https://theconversation.com/six-easy-ways-to-tell-if-that-viral-story-is-a-hoax-47673

Colvin, A. D., & Bullock, A. N. (2014). Technology acceptance in social work education: Implications for the field practicum. *Journal of Teaching in Social Work, 34*(5), 496—513. doi:10.1080/08841233.2014.952869

Council on Social Work Education (CSWE). (2015). *Educational policy and accreditation standards for baccalaureate and master's social work programs*. Retrieved from https://www.cswe.org/Accreditation/Standards-and-Policies/2015-EPAS

Davidson, C. (2011, April 21). What are digital literacies? Let's ask the students. DML Central. Retrieved from https://dmlcentral.net/what-are-digital-literacies-let-s-ask-the-students/

Davidson, C. N. (2014, February 17). *Practice digital literacies*. Retrieved from http://genius.com/Cathy-davidson-42-1-practice-digital-literacies-annotated

Davis, T., Fuller, M., Jackson, S., Pittman, J., & Sweet, J. (2007). *A national consideration of digital equity* (pp. 1–29). Washington, DC: International Society for Technology in Education. Retrieved from https://www.researchgate.net/publication/234680441_A_National_Consideration_of_Digital_Equity

Erie County Child Protective Services. (2014, March 18). *3/18/14: EC Child Protective Services adds social media to investigative arsenal* [Blog post]. Retrieved from http://www2.erie.gov/exec/index.php?q=31814-ec-child-protective-services-adds-social-media-investigative-arsenal

Goldkind, L. (2014). E-advocacy in human services: The impact of organizational conditions and characteristics on electronic advocacy activities among nonprofits. *Journal of Policy Practice, 13*(4), 300–315. doi:10.1080/15588742.2014.929073

Hague, C. (2010). *"It's not chalk and talk anymore": School approaches to developing students' digital literacy*. Bristol, UK: Futurelab.

Heitin, L. (2016, November 9). What is digital literacy? *Education Week*. Retrieved from https://www.edweek.org/ew/articles/2016/11/09/what-is-digital-literacy.html

Hill, A., & Shaw, I. (2011). *Social work & ICT*. London: Sage.

Hitchcock, L. I., Sage, M., & Smyth, N. J. (2016, April). *Incorporating digital and social technologies in social work education.* Presented at the 2nd Annual Social Work Distance Education Conference, Indiana University School of Social Work and the Council on Social Work Education, Indianapolis, IN.

Hobbs, R. (n.d.). The seven great debates in the media literacy movement. *Journal of Communication, 48*(1), 16–32. doi:10.1111/j.1460-2466.1998.tb02734.x

Information Policy and Access Center, University of Maryland College. (n.d.). *What is inclusion? Digital inclusion survey 2013.* Retrieved from https://digitalinclusion.umd.edu/content/what-digital-inclusion

Institute of Museum and Library Services, University of Washington. (2012). *Building digital communities: A framework for action.* Technology & Social Change Group. Washington, DC: International City/County Management Association. Retrieved from https://tascha.uw.edu/publications/building-digital-communities/

Ito, M., Gutiérrez, K., Livingstone, S., Penuel, B., Rhodes, J., Salen, K., ... & Watkins, S. C. (2013). *Connected learning: An agenda for research and design.* Digital Media and Learning Research Hub. Retrieved from http://eprints.lse.ac.uk/48114/

Jenkins, H., Clinton, K., Purushotma, R., Robison, A. J., & Weigel, M. (2001, October 19). *White paper: Confronting the challenges of participatory culture; Media education for the 21st century.* MacArthur Foundation. Retrieved from https://www.macfound.org/media/article_pdfs/JENKINS_WHITE_PAPER.PDF

Jenkins, H., Purushotma, R., Weigel, M., Clinton, K., & Robison, A. J. (2009). *Confronting the challenges of participatory culture: Media education for the 21st century.* Cambridge, MA: MIT Press.

Karpman, H. E., & Drisko, J. (2016). Social media policy in social work education: A review and recommendations. *Journal of Social Work Education, 52*, 1–11. doi:10.1080/10437797.2016.1202164

Kimball, E., & Kim, J. (2013). Virtual boundaries: Ethical considerations for use of social media in social work. *Social Work, 58*(2), 185–188. doi:10.1093/sw/swt005

Kirschner, P. A., & De Bruyckere, P. (2017). The myths of the digital native and the multitasker. *Teaching and Teacher Education, 67*, 135–142. doi:10.1016/j.tate.2017.06.001

Literat, I. (2014). Measuring new media literacies: Towards the development of a comprehensive assessment tool. *Journal of Media Literacy Education, 6*(1). Retrieved from http://digitalcommons.uri.edu/jmle/vol6/iss1/2

Livingstone, S. (2004). Media literacy and the challenge of new information and communication technologies. *Communication Review, 7*(1), 3–14. doi:10.1080/10714420490280152

McAuliffe, D., & Nipperess, S. (2017). E-professionalism and the ethical use of technology in social work. *Australian Social Work, 70*(2), 131–134. doi:10.1080/0312407X.2016.1221790

McCarty, B. (2011, December 6). The history of the smartphone. Retrieved from http://thenextweb.com/mobile/2011/12/06/the-history-of-the-smartphone/

National Association of Social Workers (NASW). (2017a). *Code of ethics of the National Association of Social Workers*. Washington, DC: NASW Press. Retrieved from https://www.socialworkers.org/About/Ethics/Code-of-Ethics/Code-of-Ethics-English

National Association of Social Workers. (NASW) (2017b). *NASW, ASWB, CSWE, & CSWA standards for technology in social work practice*. Washington, DC: NASW Press. Retrieved from https://www.socialworkers.org/includes/newIncludes/homepage/PRA-BRO-33617.TechStandards_FINAL_POSTING.pdf

Palfrey, J., & Gasser, U. (2016). *Born digital: How children grow up in a digital age* (Rev., exp. ed.). New York, NY: Basic Books.

Perrin, A. (2015, October 11). Social media usage: 2005–2015. Retrieved from http://www.pewinternet.org/2015/10/08/social-networking-usage-2005-2015/

Perron, B. E., Taylor, H. O., Glass, J., & Margerum-Leys, J. (2010). Information and communication technologies in social work. *Advances in Social Work, 11*(1), 67–81.

Pew Research Center. (2018, February 5). Social media fact sheet [Blog post]. Retrieved from http://www.pewinternet.org/fact-sheet/social-media/

Powers, W. (2010). *Hamlet's BlackBerry: Building a good life in the digital age* (1st ed.). New York, NY: Harper Perennial.

Prensky, M. (2001). Digital natives, digital immigrants, part 1. *On the Horizon, 9*(5), 1–6. doi:10.1108/10748120110424816

Rheingold, H. (2012). *Net smart: How to thrive online.* Cambridge MA: MIT Press.

Rogers, E. M. (2003). *Diffusion of innovations* (5th ed.). New York, NY: Free Press.

Sage, M., & Sage, T. (2016). Social media and e-professionalism in child welfare: Policy and practice. *Journal of Public Child Welfare, 10*(1), 79–95. htps://doi.org/10.1080/15548732.2015.1099589

Shirky, C. (2009). *Here comes everybody: The power of organizing without organizations.* London: Penguin.

Smyth, N. J. (2010, September 10). *When is cultural incompetence okay?* [Blog post]. Retrieved from https://njsmyth.wordpress.com/2010/09/10/when-is-cultural-incompetence-okay/

University at Buffalo School of Social Work. (n.d.). *Social worker's guide to social media.* Retrieved from http://socialwork.buffalo.edu/resources/social-media-guide.html

Young, J. (2014). iPolicy: Exploring and evaluating the use of iPads in a social welfare policy course. *Journal of Technology in Human Services, 32*(1–2), 39–53. http://doi.org/10.1080/15228835.2013.860366

Young, J. A. (2015). Assessing new media literacies in social work education: The development and validation of a comprehensive assessment instrument. *Journal of Technology in Human Services, 33*(1), 72–86. doi:10.1080/15228835.2014.998577

Young, J. A. (2018). Equipping future nonprofit professionals with digital literacies for the 21st century. *Journal of Nonprofit Education and Leadership, 8*(1), 4–15. doi:10.18666/JNEL-2018-V8-I1-8309

Zgoda, K. (2013, February 20). Luddite or love it: The ethical case for technology use in social work [Blog post]. Retrieved from http://swscmedia.com/2013/02/

luddite-or-love-it-the-ethical-case-for-technology-use-in-social-work/

Zgoda, K., & Shane, K. (2018). Digital literacy in social work education: A case study incorporating technology and social media within the social work curriculum. *Journal of Nonprofit Education and Leadership, 8*(1), 32–40. http://dx.doi.org/10.18666/JNEL-2018-V8-I1-8350

CHAPTER 3

PEDAGOGICAL APPROACHES TO TECHNOLOGY IN SOCIAL WORK EDUCATION

This chapter answers the following questions:

Teaching social work online: Where's the theory?
- How do adults learn online?
- How can I motivate learners?
    - What can I do to enhance student readiness to learn online?
    - Can I improve student motivation?
    - What is unique about teaching with multimedia?
- How do I capture student engagement?
    - Can I use collaborative learning in a distance environment?
    - How can I reinforce learning beyond the classroom?
    - What does active learning look like in a distance environment?
    - What does it mean to flip a classroom?

Social work educators are adapting to changes in teaching with technology in higher education and can benefit from the vast body of existing research borrowed from fields like education and psychology. In this chapter, we focus on andragogy (adult learning) and ways to meaningfully incorporate technology in the social work classroom, including adult learning strategies for effective classroom design. We describe theoretical constructs relevant to teaching with technology, such as motivational principles and *multimedia* learning, as well as benefits of learning with technology, such as opportunities for repeated practice, reinforcement, and the use of technology-facilitated learning communities. To illustrate some of these concepts and help readers consider what these theoretical principles look like in practice, we share a case study from Portland State University's (PSU) School of Social Work, woven through the chapter and developed through interviews with PSU's inaugural MSW distance director Sarah Bradley.

TEACHING SOCIAL WORK ONLINE: WHERE'S THE THEORY?

Although technology can enhance the social work classroom in many ways from a pedagogical lens, Web-based distance learning is a controversial mechanism for the delivery of professional social work education, especially for teaching clinical coursework (Vernon, Vakalahi, Pierce, Pittman-Munke, & Adkins, 2009). The Clinical Social Work Association's Distance Learning Committee offered a critical commentary on the inability of online education to meet standards related to using a "person in the environment" approach and suggested that online classrooms cannot address the complexity of learning about clinical assessment, professional ethics, and cultural awareness (CSWA, 2013). These critiques, if justified, would severely compromise the ability of any program to offer a full social work degree online.

Although critics of online social work education mostly cite concern about the ability of online learning to support transmission of skills such as engagement, judgment, and assessment, most research on distance education in social work to date has been atheoretical and does not describe how the change in the learning environment from campus-seated classes to online classes limits or facilitates learning. Assumptions that faculties cannot carry out social work education online adequately often come from individual experiences or biases related to technology-mediated instruction. Most social work educators have not critically examined the links between principles of online teaching and the theories that guide them to figure out how to move social work education to online settings and have instead mostly attempted to reconstruct their on-the-ground classrooms in the online environment. Only later do they realize this approach is inadequate for evaluating student learning; what works in the traditional class often does not work well online (Keengwe & Kidd, 2010).

On the other hand, extensive research on distance education suggests that online students perform as well, if not better, than face-to-face program students (Lim, Kim, Chen, & Ryder, 2008; U.S. Department of Education, 2010) in outcome-oriented assessments such as tests. Skills such as clinical judgment, transfer of learning, and ethical behavior can be assessed once instructors adequately operationalize outcomes. This chapter explores how learning theories and teaching strategies can inform the transmission of knowledge in the online environment, as well as the adjustments that must be made in the online classroom to capitalize on the unique opportunities and barriers offered by an online environment. We offer only a sampling of learning theories in this chapter to help social work educators begin to transition their teaching practices to online learning environments, and we encourage educators' exploration of learning theory beyond this chapter.

How Do Adults Learn Online?

Adult learners show up to the classroom in a way that is different from children and have different learning needs. *Andragogy* is a concept in adult education that refers to methods and practices of teaching adult learners, in contrast to the concept of *pedagogy*, which broadly refers to the art and science of instructing and typically refers to teaching children (Knowles, 1980). The assumptions of adult learning, according to the theory of andragogy, include the following: (a) adult learners are self-directed; (b) adult learners draw on their previous experiences to contextualize their learning; (c) adults are ready to learn what they need to know; (d) adults learn what they need to know now and what has utility in their lives; (e) adults are more internally than externally motivated; and (f) adults need to see the value of the instructional content and how it will be useful to them. Although some readers may argue that these qualities do not capture their learners, perhaps especially those who are emerging adults, we say that when presented with quality educational environments, these are intrinsic qualities of adults. Adults prefer to learn meaningful, engaging content, and part of their withdrawal that sometimes looks outwardly like poor attention or interest is, in part, a reaction to poor learning experiences, especially in online classrooms.

As you may conclude, androgogy has great relevance to educators in a technology-mediated classroom. Instead of a course design focus on the mechanism of teaching with technology (Can I teach clinical skills online? Should I use clickers? Should I show a video?), a theory-driven perspective allows educators to return to a focus on how to design a course that supports the ways that adults prefer to learn. A rapidly growing discipline of instructional design and technology gives more significant attention to developing and evaluation courses and assignments in consideration of adult learning theory (Knowles, Holton, & Swanson, 2015) and presents emerging best practices in using technology in university classrooms. Instructional designers (IDs) assist instructors with course development and improvement by helping them think through design issues, link assignments to objectives, chunk information, and incorporate adult learning theory in the classroom. See Breakout Boxes 3.1 and 3.2 for how the social work faculty at Portland State University began working with IDs.

BREAKOUT BOX 3.1. CASE STUDY
WORKING WITH INSTRUCTIONAL DESIGN, PART 1

Professor Sarah Bradley introduces the way that Portland State University School of Social Work worked with instructional designers (IDs) to support their mostly asynchronous online MSW program development, incorporating theories of adult learning. She also describes the learning curve related to the cross-disciplinary nature of working with instructional designers and understanding their role.

"Some of us had been talking about how to use technology to enhance classroom learning and we were exploring models of hybrid learning. The university offered a grant to departments who were willing to work with IDs to take new programs online, and we applied. After receiving the grant, we read the literature on what was unique about online learning and teaching and what was needed for success, such as building community, student, and faculty engagement. We thought we'd bring our grand vision about these things to the IDs and they would tell us what technology would support our work. When we asked them to help us figure out how to use technology to do online mind maps, they suggested we research it. I wanted to be able to talk about ecosystems and make animated videos to articulate the concepts, and at that point they didn't have a video person who could provide that kind of support, though that expertise was soon added.

"Over time, it became clearer what they saw as their expertise. Their expertise was in online instructional course design, not the technological tools to make the material engaging, and they would often tell us splashy technology was not necessary for successful online learning. Most of us in higher education had never had a course in curriculum design. We were usually given

> a syllabus and told to deliver the content over this many weeks, a more top-down approach. The IDs were asking us to design a course starting with the course outcomes and then distill that into weekly outcomes. How do you start with the end-point, learning outcomes, building from the back end? The IDs made us map our curriculum into weekly modules, each with very clear objectives for the week, identifying what students should be able to do or know. We had to justify how all the material and activities aligned with these weekly objectives. It was very painful. We thought, 'They have to read that article because it's a great article, everyone needs to read it!' But we had to cut it if it didn't align with our objectives."

Although instructional design principles are relevant to seated classes as much as to online classes, most social work educators are never formally trained in the scholarship of teaching and learning. The "sage on the stage" model of standing up and lecturing in front of the classroom has diminished in popularity in light of growing evidence that *active learning* models better promote learning (Krogh & Vedelsby, 1995), and we've caught on to this in social work education (Holmes, Tracy, Painter, Oestreich, & Park, 2015; Ní Raghallaigh & Cunniffe, 2013; Steiner, Stromwall, Brzuzy, & Gerdes, 1999). Active learning strategies offer a renewed focus on instructional design elements that place the learner at the center of the learning, with techniques such as group presentation and peer teaching, small-group work, and applied practice for skills such as interviewing. These techniques make sense considering our commitment to competency-based education, as they give students opportunities to demonstrate their learning. Challenges may come up for social work educators when trying to translate active learning practices online, which likely contribute to the critical lens by which many assess online education.

PEDAGOGICAL APPROACHES

BREAKOUT BOX 3.2. CASE STUDY
WORKING WITH INSTRUCTIONAL DESIGN, PART 2

Professor Bradley's team continued their course development with the instructional designers at their side, while also confronting cultural differences and negotiating understanding of each other's role.

"Every course was co-developed by two faculty members. I was co-developing a human development course. For each reading, I had to consider, 'How does this article tie to the objectives?' For every activity, 'How does it integrate knowledge, exploration, and demonstration?' I wrote my weekly overviews and objectives, and everything needed to align and have a rationale. Faculty members had to identify what they were going to do with everything that was required of the students. If there were discussions, would we read them all? Now this seems obvious to me but on the front end, it was a steep learning curve. I remember thinking the IDs were a pain in the neck. They wouldn't let us do anything until the whole course was mapped. We had 25-page course maps that outlined everything. We also realized the IDs were used to developing online content for undergrads and we had to push back on some of their ideas as we knew MSW students were adult learners committed to their education. So, some of what they expected was really about the pedagogy—I had never heard of andragogy."

By bringing theory to the forefront when deciding how to use technology in a course, we have an opportunity to build on cross-disciplinary research about how adults learn so we can structure our courses for student success. Emerging perspectives of adult learning in technology-enhanced environments draw on the classical conceptions of adult learning and further explain the way that adult learning occurs specifically in a technology-mediated environment. As seen in Figure 3.1, we group these perspectives into two groups—foundational theories and integrative theories—and offer some strategies about how the theories guide instructional design. This conceptualization is to help social work faculties find a starting point in the broad arena of educational philosophy. It is worth noting that we do not cover all theories of adult learning in this space; this is only a starting point for social work educators.

Figure 3.1. Strategies for Incorporating Theory in Technology-Mediated Teaching

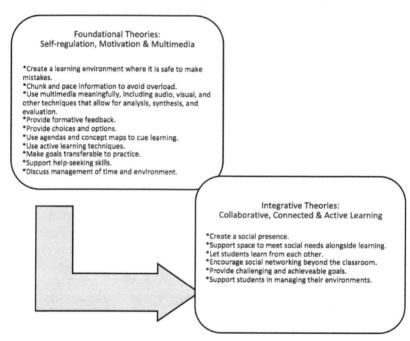

First, we offer some foundational theories: *self-regulation, motivation,* and *multimedia.* These three theories provide building blocks for any technology-mediated course or curriculum and focus on promoting the best practices and tools for adult learners in technology-enhanced classes.

Next are the integrated theories that encourage relational communication and collaboration, including *collaborative learning, connected learning,* and *active learning.* This group of theories focuses on creating and supporting a social environment in online education, which we noted previously is one motivation of adult learners.

Linkages between these theories and specific teaching methods exist for technology-mediated classrooms, and we illustrate some of them in this chapter, in breakout boxes throughout the book, and in other related teaching practice examples that you can find in the assignment appendix at the end of this text (Appendix 1).

How Can I Motivate Learners? Self-Regulation, Motivation, and Multimedia Theories

Technology-mediated learning and especially online learning requires a level of active participation beyond that practiced in a typical campus-based classroom. In the online class, students do not present as participants by merely showing up the way they can in physical spaces. Social cues deeply embedded into our culture, such as classroom seats, whiteboards, and physically raising a hand to ask a question, may be entirely absent in an online course, and replaced with log-ins, a laptop in the living room, and online discussion boards. Students may come to an online social work environment with prior experiences in online learning in which active engagement was not expected and assume their social work courses will be similar formats. Online social work instructors need to set clear expectations about online participation to help students integrate and understand the cues in online environments so they can effectively communicate in these spaces, which increases their motivation and ability for self-regulation.

Student motivation is not, of course, only in the hands of the educators. Specific characteristics of the learner and the learning environment facilitate success in online educational settings. However, educators have more control over the learning environment than of learner characteristics, and thus should capitalize on the opportunity to influence the learner through modifying the setting, as discussed in the following pages.

What can I do to enhance student readiness to learn online? Self-regulation and motivation are unique in the context of theories we discuss, in that they embody qualities of the learner more so than the learning environment, but a well-designed learning environment can bolster each of these. Self-regulation is the degree to which learners are metacognitively, motivationally, and behaviorally active in their learning (Zimmerman, 1994). Self-regulated learners monitor, evaluate, and adjust their learning strategies to achieve successful learning outcomes. Autonomy is essential for self-regulated learners, who must choose their own strategies for lifelong learning beyond the classroom. Skills that enhance self-regulation include motivation, self-efficacy, time management, management of the study environment, and help-seeking ability (Lynch & Dembo, 2004). Examples of self-regulation might involve ignoring distractions, prioritizing tasks, following directions, and focusing one's attention.

Although an instructor might assume learners' motivation and self-regulation is internal and not from the external factors, and therefore not worthy of attention in classroom design, good instructors can enhance the technology-mediated environment to respond to learner characteristics in several ways. For instance, student self-efficacy is increased when the learner knows where to find information, has transparency about assignment requirements, and receives regular formative feedback. Clarity and structure of timelines strengthen time management. Clarifying how and where students can access help increases help-seeking ability. Control of the environment can even be improved through things like mindfulness exercises to help students focus in the classroom, or worksheets that help students plan how they will create the time and space for the online learning environment. See Breakout Box 3.3 for an example of how PSU incorporated self-regulation tools into its online courses.

BREAKOUT BOX 3.3. CASE STUDY
INCORPORATING FOUNDATIONAL THEORIES, PART 1

Once roles were clear, Portland State University's team was able to embrace the value of IDs' perspectives related to issues such as supporting student self-regulation and self-efficacy through strategies such as consistency in course design and clarity of expectations.

Professor Bradley shares, "IDs reinforced the idea for us that there is a rhythm to courses; for instance, assignments are due Thursday, Saturday, and Sunday. Every week is the same. For every course in our online MSW program, the weeks of the course open sequentially. Each week opens Friday at 5:00 p.m., and the week goes through the following Sunday, so there's a two-day overlap between the finishing week and the next week. All the courses use the same template; they look identical so there's a look and feel that's the same, which helps students to know what to expect and where to find information.

"They urged us to develop appropriate structures that were also consistent across the course. Sometimes I had to figure out those structures by making mistakes. For instance, initially for discussion posts the students were required to make an initial post and then respond two more times, but there were no clear timelines. Some didn't post until late and then there was not time for people to respond. Now the structure is an initial post by Thursday and responses by Sunday. Instructional designers really encouraged us to do blind posts where students don't see other people's post until they make their own post. This way they bring their own perspective and experiences—it's even better than on campus where students can get away with not reading and riff off others who did read.

"Initially in the discussion posts I just gave some prompts, but it wasn't clear to me that they were actually integrating the material from the week. Now I say, 'The following are prompts to help you write a quality post; you do not have to address any or all of them. How have you seen these ideas in action? What experiences have you had that either confirm or conflict with information from this week? What did you learn this week? What was surprising, exciting, or confusing? What questions were raised? Please reference at least two of the readings/videos/podcasts that have influenced your thinking.'

> "I now offer some clarity about elements for responding to other students' posts: 'Your comments should add depth to the conversation by bringing in alternative perspectives, new ideas, or knowledge; integrating your experience; synthesizing themes, and so forth."

Can I improve student motivation? Instructors enjoy self-motivated students who come to class prepared to learn. In an online environment, motivation plays a significant role in student success. Online environments have fewer natural social motivators, and online students (who tend to be older and working) may encounter more distractions to learning in an online classroom.

Self-efficacy, beliefs of control, high levels of interest and value in material, and clear goals enhance student motivation in distance education (Abrami, Bernard, Bures, Borokhovski, & Tamim, 2011). Based on this conceptual model of motivation for adult learners, Pintrich (2003) offers several recommendations to enhance student motivation. Recommendations include providing formative feedback about the ways that learners show improved competence over time, acknowledging effort, offering tasks in which students are challenged but can be successful, providing opportunities for choice, and explaining learning outcomes and transferability to social work practice. Student motivation increases when learners understand the importance and future utility of an activity, and when a safe environment is created for making mistakes. Educators can outline learning objectives early to help cue students for what is to come and to explain the transferability of skills students are about to discover.

Collaborative learning also enhances motivation by allowing students to meet social and learning needs simultaneously. See Breakout Box 3.4 to see how Professor Sarah Bradley incorporated motivational theory into her online course.

BREAKOUT BOX 3.4. CASE STUDY
INCORPORATING FOUNDATIONAL THEORIES, PART 2

Professor Bradley shares how she incorporated foundational theories in her online classroom:

"We tell faculty who teach online that a normal seated class is six hours of preparation time for students and three hours in class a week, and it should be expected that online takes the same amount of time. We have debated things like quizzes for instant feedback—I don't use those for the most part. I do use a syllabus quiz to make sure they have read the syllabus. They don't get points for it, but the first week won't open until they pass the syllabus quiz. It is just a way to make sure they read the syllabus. There are other ways to make sure students are aware of the course requirements; for instance, in the first week there's a one-question extra-credit quiz, and the answer is in the course introductory video, so they only get the answer if they watch the video. The tools offer students motivation and clear expectations even though they are not linked to a grade."

She goes on to share more about the way that clarity and offering choices in the classroom support adult learning, but some experimentation is also required. "At one point, the IDs suggested that in terms of supporting online discussion, faculty should be more active at first, and then back off over time, and then at end of the term have students review their discussions and pull out evidence of the highest-quality discussion posts that demonstrate their critical thinking. We decided graduate students did not need that if you invite them with prompts and choice; most students have fabulous things to say if you give them some structure. Now I don't even give specific prompts—I have revised discussion board formats to give them much more choice. In the beginning, my prompts were very closely tied to the weekly activities, but they narrowed the discussion from my perspective. Now we are much more focused on their practice and lived experience as it relates to the course material."

How do I best deliver multimedia content? Multimedia learning theory, developed by Mayer, Heiser, and Lonn (2001), informs all technology-enhanced teaching. This research-supported concept of "dual processing" suggests that learners process verbal and written information differently and have limited capacity to handle a lot of information in either category but can absorb more information when it is delivered using multimedia approaches that are both verbal and written. Reliance on one type of information, such as written, decreases the amount of content students remember; however, at the other extreme, receiving all data in both audio and video format simultaneously may also be too much information to process. For instance, if students watch a closed-captioned video in which they must read all the text and process the visual story of the video simultaneously, they may experience cognitive overload. On the other hand, if instructors present students with visible bullet-point keywords alongside a lecture, they will have a better capacity to remember each.

Cognitive overload may also occur if too much material is presented, or the material moves too fast; the learners' brains have not had enough time to process and contextualize the information. When adult learners cannot connect their prior life experiences or other learning to the topic, new learning will take more capacity and chunking it into smaller pieces will help with retention. For instance, if students are learning about research methodologies and have no recent context for the material, they may need to learn the information in smaller chunks. They may be able to retain the material more effectively by linking it to contexts with which they are familiar, like popular media polling, and they will probably benefit from different forms of exposure such as demonstration of problems and an outline of key points.

> **BREAKOUT BOX 3.5. PRACTICAL TIPS**
> SUPPORTING STUDENTS TO MANAGE THEIR ENVIRONMENTS
>
> You can support student's mastery of their environment by introducing a short meditation at the beginning of each class—whether on the ground, asynchronous, or synchronous. Dialectical behavioral therapy manuals and videos (see examples on the Web and on YouTube) offer many brief mindfulness meditations that could help students focus on the present moment. This practice offers good training for managing distractions and chaotic environments that may be especially present for students who attend courses from home, and this skill is easily transferable to the field, where students can use mindfulness for themselves or teach the skill to clients.

To help students avoid cognitive overload, instructors can offer both auditory and visual materials that highlight fundamental concepts in writing or illustrate models graphically. Instructors can chunk the new or challenging ideas into small learning modules, offer previews of upcoming content to help prime students for further information, and offer signaling for critical concepts through outlines or concept maps. They can help prevent environmental distractions (Mayer et al., 2001) by encouraging students to prepare their learning space or by asking students to limit the availability of distracting information. For instance, a class might begin with a bulletin board reflective question about how students prepare for class time and ask students to post a picture of their study environment and share any kinds of tools (e.g., calendars, notebooks, and to-do lists) that help keep them organized and on task. See Breakout Box 3.5 for practical tips on helping students manage distractions in an online learning environment. Instructors, too, can remove unused tools from the learning management system (LMS) to direct students' focus. See Breakout Box 3.6 for examples of how PSU incorporated multimedia theory into its online courses.

> ## BREAKOUT BOX 3.6. CASE STUDY
> ### INCORPORATING FOUNDATIONAL THEORIES, PART 3
>
> Professor Bradley got help from instructional designers to chunk information and avoid student experiences of cognitive overload even though it meant professors had to make significant adjustments to their own traditional ways of teaching. "After we created the course map that included everything for the week, including the faculty content videos that needed to be developed, the IDs helped us chunk the information into 15–20 minutes. There are no 90-minute lectures or videos of lectures to watch. Some faculty were initially resistant to this, as we wanted to just record our long lectures. Instead, major lectures were broken down into shorter content videos, and there is always an associated visual (PowerPoint or outline) to accompany the lecture.
>
> "The IDs helped us with the pedagogy about how to deliver online curriculum, and then we had course builders who moved everything into the LMS using our standard template. This was a major time saver for faculty." (She notes that major class revision after changing a textbook and revising the course in the LMS system takes so much time!)

How Do I Capture Student Engagement? Collaborative, Connected, and Active Learning

Core concepts in social work include collaboration, understanding of the environment, relation-focused work, and hands-on practice, with field education as the signature pedagogy. Thus, it follows that collaborative, connected, and active learning also inform our theoretical framework for teaching social work with technology.

Collaborative learning requires the creation of social presence, which refers to the feeling of being together in the classroom. Feelings of connection come naturally in seated classrooms where the instructor and students can see each other, read body language, and communicate in real time. Social presence is equally central for an online class, but students achieve social interactions in different ways, such as through the active use of discussion boards, short video posts for introductions, and real-time office hours offered via videoconferencing software. The concept of social presence in the classroom provides essential parallels for social workers who will eventually interact with clients and others, and social work educators can help students understand the benefit to their future practice of active social engagement in the classroom by explaining how their effective communication skills in the online classroom transfer to the work environment.

Research suggests that collaborative and connected social learning promotes active learning and enhances student outcomes (Abrami et al., 2011). The online environment often introduces a new role for learners when it comes to social learning. In a traditional classroom, students can often participate somewhat passively, but in an online class, students must demonstrate that they are socially engaged.

One framework for thinking about social presence and engagement of both the teacher and the student is through the Community of Inquiry (COI) model (Garrison & Arbaugh, 2007). The researchers who developed this model defined themes related to student satisfaction and outcomes in online learning and broke the ideas up into three categories: social presence, cognitive presence, and teacher presence. As defined by Garrison, Anderson, and Archer (1999), social presence indicates social cohesion, open communication, and emotional expression. To assess for social presence, social work instructors can consider the extent to which they know who their students are, and to which students know their colleagues, outside of their identities as students. Cognitive presence indicates that exploration, interrogation, and resolution follow new learning (which they refer to as a "triggering event"); and teaching presence refers to instructional management and direction of learning. Although we generally associate cognitive presence (which includes thinking critically about information and integrating it into new knowledge) as the most valuable goal in education, the COI model argues that the students' ability to connect themselves to the learning community indirectly affects cognitive learning and increases critical thinking. The educator's instruction and facilitation, or teaching presence, are essential to students' ability to perform the other two functions. Multiple studies have tested the COI model and link these groupings of presence with positive outcomes (Kineshanko, 2016; Pollard, Minor, & Swanson, 2014; Rockinson-Szapkiw, Wendt, Whighting, & Nisbet, 2016). Therefore, to achieve ideal cognitive learning conditions, students must be socially connected to peers and the instructor, and the instructor should build these opportunities into the course design. Social work professors have drawn from the Community of Inquiry model to increase their social presence through activities such as having online students create video introductions, asking students to share personal and professional experiences with each other, encouraging co-creation of content through wiki tools, and setting the appropriate tone for discussion board posts (Bentley, Secret, & Cummings, 2015). Educators in our field acknowledge that creating an engaged and connected online classroom is extra work, given the planning, technology, and intentionality required, and that holding synchronous meetings alongside asynchronous class expectations assists in accomplishing community-building goals (Jones, 2015; Zydney, 2014).

Can I use collaborative learning in a distance environment? Collaborative learning, also known as social learning or cooperative learning, suggests that we learn best by interacting with others in a social setting. Behavioral theory contributes to this with concepts of imitation and reinforcement that peers provide in a classroom, and cognitive theory adds ideas about how students think when they observe their peers: peer observation offers opportunities to learn new ideas, learn about consequences, and think of problems as seen from another's perspective. For instance, when students review an ethical dilemma together in which the Code of Ethics provides contrary directions, students benefit from hearing how others in the classroom process and understand the ethical concern, and through this process, students talk through possible outcomes.

Although established as a principal element of learning, collaborative learning can be more challenging to translate from the campus-based class to the online course. Collaborative learning occurs through processes of socialization, working together, mentoring, peer learning, and developing identity.

Lev Vygotsky (Levykh, 2008) theorized that social and individual learning are very connected. He called this "sociocultural learning theory" and suggested that higher-order learning is embedded in cultural environmental symbols, which requires a shared social learning environment, as well as active involvement in a social learning process. He also proposed the concept of the *zone of proximal development,* which suggests that gaps in learning are supported by scaffolding or teaching in a way that moves students progressively toward greater independence by increasing task difficulty over time while offering challenging expectations and structured support. When an instructor integrates scaffolding and social learning together, students can support each other to solve problems in increasingly complex tasks, ask and answer each other's questions in pairs or groups, and seek feedback and clarity with each other.

Activities such as role-playing and problem-based learning offer more ways to scaffold learning and prepare students for actual practice. Instructors support scaffolding and sociocultural learning when they have students work together, build assignments that draw on previous learning, provide models that students can critically analyze before they make their own attempts at replication, and give valuable feedback. See Breakout Box 3.7 for an example on how PSU incorporated scaffolding into its online courses.

BREAKOUT BOX 3.7. CASE STUDY
INCORPORATING INTEGRATIVE THEORY, PART 1

Sarah Bradley shares about VideoANT, and how she used it to scaffold learning about technology and supervision. VideoANT is an annotation program that allows text to be added to an uploaded video. "For the first assignment I annotate each student's video to give them feedback on their skills. For the next assignment, I found a video about supervision and had them upload the video to VideoANT and annotate what they thought would improve the interactions. Then, for their last assignment, students are required to upload a video they recorded of themselves and annotate it. This way, before the final assignment is due they had done all the steps. I have had no glitches yet; they actually have been doing it beautifully."

Social presence enhances collaborative learning and is created instantly by the instructor in a traditional seated classroom; it begins with first-day icebreakers, explaining how the class works, and introductions. It is more work in an online classroom. It follows naturally that synchronous online education provides the closest proxy to the social presence created in a campus seated class (Moallem, 2015). In an asynchronous online class, it may be tempting to rely on written documents or simple introduction posts to a bulletin board, or to even skim over introductions all together and get right to work. However, an instructor's social presence predicts satisfaction in the online class for both students and instructors (Richardson & Swan, 2003), and should be a meaningful component of course development. Strategies for creating social presence to encourage student collaboration include creating introductory videos, using social media networks like Facebook that infuse personal with educational content, creating avatars or personal profiles, requiring all students to upload pictures for discussion boards, and providing frequent social check-in opportunities.

Students should have a sense of social presence for their instructors and their peers. See Breakout Box 3.8 for an example of how PSU incorporated social presence into its online courses.

> **BREAKOUT BOX 3.8. CASE STUDY**
> **INCORPORATING INTEGRATIVE THEORY, PART 2**
>
> Social presence may be one of the defining factors that sets a connected and coherent class apart from the awful stereotypes people imagine when they hear about online learning. Bradley shares PSU's plan for social presence.
>
> "We decided that there needed to be a synchronous component to all the required classes. IDs suggested this was helpful for addressing plagiarism, but we wanted faculty and students to actually be in face-to-face relationships with each other. Initially we required two synchronous sessions with the whole class, but there's been a slight morphing of that. In some cases, students meet with faculty in small groups, as opposed to meeting as a whole class. Other times the students meet together in small groups and videotape the meeting so I can watch them later for feedback if I can't attend. We really wanted it for face-to-face engagement between students, as well as for faculty. There are also office hours every week, on videoconferencing platform, in the evenings when students are available. Again, this was our decision about faculty presence."

Collaborative learning brings students together to solve complex problems or complete tasks synergistically and builds on collaboration skills that prepare for social work practice. In seated classrooms, collaborative learning often occurs via "group work." Examples of collaborative learning include group case-study review and problem-based learning in which students work together to discuss issues presented in a realistic scenario. Whereas group-based learning is sometimes a source of frustration in the traditional seated class due to asymmetrical contributions, online group work offers more opportunities for assessing individual contributions.

For instance, students can communicate primarily through a bulletin board system, which is accessible to the instructor, who is therefore able to assess the contributions of each group member. See Breakout Box 3.9 for an example of how collaborative learning theory was applied at PSU.

> ## BREAKOUT BOX 3.9. CASE STUDY
> ### INCORPORATING INTEGRATIVE THEORY, PART 3
>
> Professor Bradley shared that the IDs always asked, "what are you going to do with this?" for each activity, stressing the need for formative evaluation, and she offers the way they used collaborative learning by simplifying initial ideas to address some of this need. She says, "I think OMG, I have to give feedback on everything. What is the faculty time requirement if we have to give them feedback on all of these weekly activities? So in some cases we had to cut down the number of activities, as well as the type of feedback. In some cases, we designed peer feedback as a substitute, which also offered an opportunity to enhance social presence. For example, in teaching a supervision course, students had to do a synchronous supervision role-play with another student using canned cases they brought to supervision. They met the first week, which is the beginning of a supervision relationship—then for 2 weeks of actual supervision, and then they completed an ending role-play. I watch all the initial supervision videos and give them feedback using a VideoAnt to annotate the video. The following weeks I rotate who gets feedback, giving it to a third of the class each week. For their final assignment, the students had to take one of the videos and annotate it, noting what they did well and what they could have said instead. In hindsight, I would ask them to choose a video I did not annotate; we are always learning. In another practice class, I have the students annotate each other's role play videos."

How can I reinforce learning beyond the classroom? Connected learning embraces concepts from active and collaborative learning and adds an additional element to the process of learning in digital environments: the importance of using connections and networking to learn and teach. Developed by educators and researchers at the Connected Learning Research Network, the theory is grounded in the idea that learning is informed and empowered by the digital/information age of the 21st century (Ito et al., 2013). Connected learning does not focus on specific types of technology; rather, technology provides learners with new options to connect and network with peers and mentors both in and outside of the classroom. This is especially true for new media, such as blogs, wikis, and social media platforms that include interaction and sharing between users.

With connected learning, the student is the central focus of the educational experience. By developing and nurturing connections with peers, mentors, and the broader professional community through the extended networking opportunities that technology provides, learners can explore their interests while meeting the academic requirements of a course or program. For example, students can use social media platforms such as LinkedIn or Twitter to create a professional exchange with an expert from a national advocacy agency and then incorporate their learning into a social policy paper. In this way, they are engaged in the participatory culture, a form of civic and community engagement with low barriers to participation (Jenkins, Purushotma, Weigel, Clinton, & Robison, 2009). It is this environment of connectedness and participation that supports openness, sharing, and feedback with peers and others, and prepares students for professional networking in their social work careers.

What does active learning look like in a distance environment? Active learning is a pedagogical model that suggests learners should have active accountability for their education instead of receiving it passively, which creates a more engaging classroom and improves learner outcomes (Hake, 1998; Prince, 2004). Active learning is goal oriented and problem based (Johnson & Aragon, 2003). Because physical presence is evident in a seated classroom, it is much easier to be a passive recipient of knowledge of this environment. Still, many instructors incorporate active learning strategies in their seated classrooms already, such as discussion, presentation, problem solving, mock interviews, and group work. Active learning tools such as group presentations have replaced the old model of "sage on the stage" and have better outcomes through engaging students in the multiple roles of teacher, collaborator, and learner. In the technology-mediated classroom, the entire class structure is likely to be built on a foundation of active learning because little opportunity exists for passivity; the only way for students to demonstrate their presence is through active participation.

Many favorite active learning activities are translatable directly from the traditional on-the-ground class to an online environment. Examples include think-pair-share, short written exercises or reaction papers, and a class game. However, instructors often find that technology enhances active learning naturally and offers an expanded set of options by which students can participate in active learning. For instance, students can find online resources to share back in a discussion forum more efficiently in an online environment than in a traditional classroom.

Online collaboration tools make it easier to create documents with multiple authors and to demonstrate the input contributions of each student. Built-in modules in LMS often provide systematic ways for students to blog, journal, or use gamified learning such as a word search or crossword puzzle. It is easier to use technology such as video in online classes. See Breakout Box 3.10 to see how PSU's Professor Bradley views the online environment when it comes to active learning in online courses.

PEDAGOGICAL APPROACHES

> ### BREAKOUT BOX 3.10. CASE STUDY
> #### INCORPORATING INTEGRATIVE THEORY, PART 4
>
> Professor Bradley admits that she was once amongst the critics of online learning, especially as it relates to teaching practice skills, but her firsthand experience with effective active learning activities and exercises has changed her mind.
>
> "I actually think I can see much better what student practice skills are in the online environment—I can watch all students in videos online, whereas I just bounce from person to person on campus. Online I can see how students treat each other, see every video, observe every discussion. These are the same behaviors that we see on campus, but maybe not in as much depth; they are all observable in the online classroom. I see them flame each other, and we can have a discussion about it. In terms of monitoring ethical behaviors, I hear and see agency issues come up that I think I wouldn't see in the same way in the campus classroom."
>
> Sarah goes on to share, "there's something so interesting about the online world, a little less censoring, when they get in dialogues, if there is a lot of affect around an issue they are less hesitant to say x-y-z is happening. I feel like I see more deeply how they think/feel online. And you can't be silent online, so students who may sit in a 30-person class and not talk all term, they are present online."

Active learning is also enhanced when all users have the right equipment and digital skill sets. For instance, synchronous classes held using video platforms work best when students use headphones with a microphone and connect via wired high-speed Internet (Fitch, Cary, & Freese, 2016). Some active learning platforms, such as the program Flipgrid that allows users to upload short videos in a discussion board style, are easily accessed using smartphones. In either case, students with more previous technology exposure and skills will more easily integrate and participate actively in the online classroom. Research suggests that socioeconomic status plays a role in experience with digital content creation and digital literacy and that technology access correlates with academic achievement (Hargittai & Walejko, 2008; Jackson et al., 2008). Additionally, digital literacy affects online class participation, including peer engagement, and research has linked these factors to race and socioeconomic status (Prior, Mazanov, Meacheam, Heaslip, & Hanson, 2016). Online social work students say that the opportunity to hear diverse voices and experiences is essential to their online learning (Secret, Bentley, & Kadolph, 2016). Social work educators should consider technology access issues as part of the class design, and ways that their class expectations may be inclusive or exclusive to learners from a variety of backgrounds. For instance, a fully online degree program should make technology expectations clear at the time of application, and students with limited technology experience or exposure may need additional mentoring or support for learning new technologies. If students seem less engaged in the active learning components of the online classroom, instructors should check out whether it may be related to access to or comfort with technology and consider ways to encourage and support participation for the benefit of the whole class.

What does it mean to flip a classroom? Although not a theory of adult learning, the flipped classroom is an emerging model for technology-mediated teaching. Flipped classrooms separate the rote and technical learning activities from active learning activities and move the rote procedural learning to a pre-session before class discussion of the topic. The pre-session is commonly a video lecture but may also be a reading and quiz, a reading reflection journal, or another way to capture, before class activities, that the students have reviewed the learning materials and had time to think about them. The word *flipped* refers to the fact that teachers have historically taught the basic concepts of a topic in class and then give students an assignment outside of class to think critically about and apply the material. In a flipped classroom, students learn the basics of the material on their own and then demonstrate the critical thinking and application in class so that they can learn from each other's understanding of the material, be supervised and corrected by the instructor, or be prepared with questions for clarity at the critical time they most need it—when they are actually trying to use the material.

Additionally, the pre-session feedback, whether quiz or another tool, can be used by the instructor to assess which topics to review during the active learning component. In an online setting, it is exceptionally straightforward to use a flipped classroom model. For instance, a social work practice class that is teaching how to interview clients may have a partly asynchronous section where the students access multimedia materials on the topic of client engagement, including core concepts and indicators of engagement with clients. They may watch video examples and take a quiz about the signs of engagement to assess their understanding of the topic. Then the synchronous section of the class begins with a brief discussion of questions and clarifications, followed by direct practice in breakout groups where students practice engagement skills and can get feedback from colleagues and the instructor, followed by a debrief about how to use the concepts in the upcoming assignment. This type of active learning makes good use of scaffolding and may be more effective than the traditional model where students are taught engagement skills during the face-to-face class time and are then expected to demonstrate them in a homework assignment such as a video-recorded interview without the benefit of time to think, practice, and polish as a group in class.

A flipped classroom can be used in a fully asynchronous class by front-loading the technical material before students use discussion boards. It can be used in a fully seated classroom by having the students demonstrate they have completed all the course reading, completed an online module, or understood the technical part of the material followed by some type of assessment like a journal entry or brief quiz. This flipping leads to discussions in which student are better prepared, saves the faculty from covering basic material, and increases the time for applied and active learning.

BREAKOUT BOX 3.11. CASE STUDY

FINAL THOUGHTS

The Portland State University School of Social Work examples offered in this chapter touch on many of the concepts of adult learning theory and point out that quality online teaching that draws upon learning theory takes time, patience, investment, support, and a faculty-as-learner mindset. Bradley says that students report in evaluations that their courses make sense, are clear, and are unified, and are often vastly different than their previous experiences with online learning. A few students who have moved from the campus program to the online program noted there is higher student engagement with the material and with each other online versus on campus.

Finally, she offers this important reflection: "I know when I go back to teaching on campus it will be hugely different. I will flip stuff; I will use what I have them do online. One student said, 'I can't imagine how this class would be anything but online; we're doing all this videotape and review—how would we do this all on campus? I can't imagine how this would be a campus class." Professor Bradley and her students are converts thanks to well-designed coursework.

FINAL THOUGHTS

This chapter offered an overview of learning theories that inform the development of successful technology-mediated social work classrooms. Learning theory can also benefit the way you think about your seated classes. See Breakout Box 3.11 for Professor Sarah Bradley's final reflection on her experiences with online courses and how they influence her campus teaching. Although many social work educators have gut feelings about whether social work can be taught effectively online and may have concerns about technology-mediated education, a well-designed online course is likely to offer just as compelling a learning experience as a traditional seated classroom and may even provide unexpected opportunities.

A well-designed course extends attention far beyond the social work curriculum and carefully considers how to create a learning environment that supports adult learning as a lifelong process. A social work department that wants to support successful online programming will examine ways to equip the faculty with the tools and resources necessary to devote time to curricular development, which takes more than just uploading a seated-classroom syllabus to a learning management system. However, with the right support and time investments, faculty members may find that thinking about what it means to teach with technology enhances their traditional teaching too. In the next chapter, read more about specific ways of incorporating technology in the social work classroom.

FURTHER READING AND RESOURCES

Connected Learning Research Network. http://clrn.dmlhub.net/ (an interdisciplinary group of research associates with Digital Media and Learning Research Hub).

Flipped Learning Global Initiative. http://flglobal.org/ (a worldwide collaborative of educators and researchers committed to the flipped classroom).

Instructional Design Resources. http://www.instructionaldesign.org (a website by Richard Culatta, CEO of the International Society for Technology in Education).

International Society for Technology in Education. https://www.iste.org/ (an international membership group working to solve problems in education).

Milosch, T. (2018, January 17). Building a collaborative instructor-instructional designer relationship. *Inside Higher Ed*. Retrieved from https://www.insidehighered.com/digital-learning/views/2018/01/17/building-collaborative-instructor-instructional-designer

North American Council for Online Learning. https://www.inacol.org/ (a U.S.-based national organization for teachers, administrators, and policy makers interested in online education).

REFERENCES

Abrami, P. C., Bernard, R. M., Bures, E. M., Borokhovski, E., & Tamim, R. M. (2011). Interaction in distance education and online learning: Using evidence and theory to improve practice. *Journal of Computing in Higher Education, 23*(2–3), 82–103. doi:10.1007/s12528-011-9043-x

Bentley, K. J., Secret, M. C., & Cummings, C. R. (2015). The centrality of social presence in online teaching and learning in social work. *Journal of Social Work Education, 51*, 494–504. doi:10.1080/10437797.2015.1043199

Clinical Social Work Association (CSWA). (2013, September). *Report on online MSW programs.* Retrieved from http://www.clinicalsocialworkassociation.org/Resources/Documents/CSWA%20-%20Position%20Paper%20-%20Online%20MSW%20Programs%20-%20September2013.pdf

Fitch, D., Cary, S., & Freese, R. (2016). Facilitating social work role plays in online courses: The use of video conferencing. *Advances in Social Work, 17*(1), 78–92.

Garrison, D. R., Anderson, T., & Archer, W. (1999). Critical inquiry in a text-based environment: Computer conferencing in higher education. *Internet and Higher Education, 2*(2), 87–105. doi:10.1016/S1096-7516(00)00016-6

Garrison, D. R., & Arbaugh, J. B. (2007). Researching the community of inquiry framework: Review, issues, and future directions. *Internet and Higher Education, 10*(3), 157–172. doi:10.1016/j.iheduc.2007.04.001

Hake, R. R. (1998). Interactive-engagement versus traditional methods: A six-thousand-student survey of mechanics test data for introductory physics courses. *American Journal of Physics, 66*(1), 64–74.

Hargittai, E., & Walejko, G. (2008). The participation divide: Content creation and sharing in the digital age. *Information, Communication & Society, 11*(2), 239–256. doi:10.1080/13691180801946150

Holmes, M. R., Tracy, E. M., Painter, L. L., Oestreich, T., & Park, H. (2015). Moving from flipcharts to the flipped classroom: Using technology driven teaching methods to promote active learning in foundation and advanced masters social work courses. *Clinical Social Work Journal, 43*(2), 215–224. doi:10.1007/s10615-015-0521-x

Jackson, L. A., Zhao, Y., Kolenic III, A., Fitzgerald, H. E., Harold, R., & Von Eye, A. (2008). Race, gender, and information technology use: The new digital divide. *CyberPsychology & Behavior, 11*(4), 437–442.

Jenkins, H., Purushotma, R., Weigel, M., Clinton, K., & Robison, A. J. (2009). *Confronting the challenges of participatory culture: Media education for the 21st century.* Cambridge, MA: MIT Press.

Johnson, S. D., & Aragon, S. R. (2003). An instructional strategy framework for online learning environments. *New Directions for Adult and Continuing Education, 2003*(100), 31–43.

Jones, S. H. (2015). Benefits and challenges of online education for clinical social work: Three examples. *Clinical Social Work Journal, 43*(2), 225–235. doi:10.1007/s10615-014-0508-z

Keengwe, J., & Kidd, T. T. (2010). Towards best practices in online learning and teaching in higher education. *Journal of Online Learning and Teaching, 6*(2), 533–541.

Kineshanko, M. (2016). *A thematic synthesis of community of inquiry research 2000 to 2014.* Athabasca, AB: Athabasca University.

Knowles, M. (1980). What is andragogy. In *The modern practice of adult education: From pedagogy to andragogy*, 40–62. Chicago, IL: Follett.

Knowles, M., Holton, E., III, & Swanson, R. (2015). *The adult learner: The definitive classic in adult education and human resource development* (8th ed.). New York, NY: Routledge.

Krogh, A., & Vedelsby, J. (1995). Neural network ensembles, cross validation, and active learning. In G. Tesauro, D. S. Touretsky, & T. K. Leen (Eds.), *Advances in neural information processing systems, 7* (pp. 231–238). Cambridge, MA: MIT Press.

Levykh, M. G. (2008). The affective establishment and maintenance of Vygotsky's zone of proximal development. *Educational Theory, 58*(1), 83–101. doi:10.1111/j.1741-5446.2007.00277.x

Lim, J., Kim, M., Chen, S. S., & Ryder, C. E. (2008). An empirical investigation of student achievement and satisfaction in different learning environments. *Journal of Instructional Psychology, 35*(2), 113–119.

Lynch, R., & Dembo, M. (2004). The relationship between self-regulation and online learning in a blended learning context. *International Review of Research in Open and Distributed Learning, 5*(2). doi:10.19173/irrodl.v5i2.189

Mayer, R. E., Heiser, J., & Lonn, S. (2001). Cognitive constraints on multimedia learning: When presenting more material results in less understanding. *Journal of Educational Psychology, 93*(1), 187.

Moallem, M. (2015). The impact of synchronous and asynchronous communication tools on learner self-regulation, social presence, immediacy, intimacy and satisfaction in collaborative online learning. *Online Journal of Distance Education and E-Learning, 3*(3), 55.

Ní Raghallaigh, M., & Cunniffe, R. (2013). Creating a safe climate for active learning and student engagement: An example from an introductory social work module. *Teaching in Higher Education, 18*(1), 93–105. doi:10.1080/13562517.2012.694103

Pintrich, P. R. (2003). A motivational science perspective on the role of student motivation in learning and teaching contexts. *Journal of Educational Psychology, 95*(4), 667.

Pollard, H., Minor, M., & Swanson, A. (2014). Instructor social presence within the community of inquiry framework and its impact on classroom community and the learning environment. *Online Journal of Distance Learning Administration, 17*(2). Retrieved from https://www.westga.edu/~distance/ojdla/summer172/Pollard_Minor_Swanson172.html

Prince, M. (2004). Does active learning work? A review of the research. *Journal of Engineering Education, 93*(3), 223–231.

Prior, D. D., Mazanov, J., Meacheam, D., Heaslip, G., & Hanson, J. (2016). Attitude, digital literacy and self-efficacy: Flow-on effects for online learning behavior. *Internet and Higher Education, 29*, 91–97.

Richardson, J., & Swan, K. (2003). Examining social presence in online courses in relation to students' perceived learning and satisfaction. *Illinois Digital Environment for Access to Learning and Scholarship (IDEALS)*. Retrieved from http://hdl.handle.net/2142/18713

Rockinson-Szapkiw, A., Wendt, J., Whighting, M., & Nisbet, D. (2016). The predictive relationship among the community of inquiry framework, perceived learning and online, and graduate students' course grades in online synchronous and asynchronous courses. *International Review of Research in Open and Distributed Learning, 17*(3). doi:10.19173/irrodl.v17i3.2203

Secret, M., Bentley, K. J., & Kadolph, J. C. (2016). Student voices speak quality assurance: Continual improvement in online social work education. *Journal of Social Work Education, 52*, 30–42. doi:10.1080/10437797.2016.1112630

Steiner, S., Stromwall, L. K., Brzuzy, S., & Gerdes, K. (1999). Using cooperative learning strategies in social work education. *Journal of Social Work Education, 35*, 253–264.

U.S. Department of Education, Office of Planning, Evaluation, and Policy Development. (2010). *Evaluation of evidence-based practices in online learning: A meta-analysis and review of online learning studies.* Washington, DC: Author.

Vernon, R., Vakalahi, H., Pierce, D., Pittman-Munke, P., & Adkins, L. F. (2009). Distance education programs in social work: Current and emerging trends. *Journal of Social Work Education, 45*, 263–276. doi:10.5175/JSWE.2009.200700081

Zimmerman, B. J. (1994). Dimensions of academic self-regulation: A conceptual framework for education. *Self-Regulation of Learning and Performance: Issues and Educational Applications, 1*, 33–21.

Zydney, J. (2014). Strategies for creating a community of inquiry through online asynchronous discussions. *Journal of Online Learning and Teaching, 10*(1), 153.

CHAPTER 4

TECHNOLOGY IN THE SOCIAL WORK CLASSROOM

This chapter answers the following questions:

- What does technology look like in the social work classroom?
- What are learning management systems and e-learning tools?
- How can I bring technology to my social work course for active learning?
    - What is Puentedura's Model for Technology Integration?
    - So how can the SAMR Model help a social work educator?
    - What is Bloom's Digital Taxonomy?
    - How can Bloom's Digital Taxonomy help a social work educator?
    - What types of digital knowledge are needed for technology-fused assignments?
- How can I integrate technology into assignments or learning activities?
- How can I assess my new technology-based assignment?

TEACHING SOCIAL WORK WITH DIGITAL TECHNOLOGY

This chapter will focus on how social work educators can infuse technology into the social work classroom, from learning management systems (LMS) to assignments that require students to use social and digital technologies. We will cover diverse types of knowledge and skills needed for digitally based assignments, and how an educator can thoughtfully create or update a technology-based assignment from start to finish, from learning objectives to assessment. Although the focus will be on the seated classroom, we acknowledge that these assignments and practices can also be used in hybrid or fully online courses. Thus, this chapter represents all courses across our continuum of technology integration described in Chapter 1, "Why Do We Need a Book About Technology in Social Work Education?" We use examples from our assignment compendium (see Appendix 1) to help illustrate technology infusion in this chapter.

As we begin this discussion on technology in the social work classroom, it is helpful to distinguish between classroom technologies that are used for passive learning compared to active learning. As noted in Chapter 3, "Pedagogical Approaches to Technology in Social Work Education," active learning content requires students to engage and do something with the course content to promote knowledge, values, and skills. Technology assignments that include active learning could include using statistical software to analyze data or audio or video recording an informational interview with a practicing social worker. In contrast, passive learning requires very little of a learner. If technology is used in the classroom for passive learning, the sole purpose of the technology is typically for information consumption. Examples include watching a video recording of a lecture or reading Microsoft PowerPoint slides posted in an online course. Although technology tools can be valuable to help manage or deliver content for a class, from a single class session to an entire course, we consider the passive use of technology to be instructor focused versus student focused. Passive technology is sometimes appropriate when used in considering the theoretical perspectives discussed in Chapter 3. Throughout this chapter, we encourage incorporating digital and social technologies into assignments primarily for active learning, where social work students learn technology skills alongside course content.

WHAT DOES TECHNOLOGY LOOK LIKE IN THE SOCIAL WORK CLASSROOM?

Technology in the social work classroom dates to the mid-1950s: audiovisual equipment allowed educators and practitioners to show training videos to students and audiotape student interviews during practicum placements (Shorkey & Uebel, 2014). Thirty years later, personal computers and courses on how to use computers started to show up in social work classrooms, and by the mid-1990s, social work educators commonly used Internet-based tools such as e-mail and LISTSERVs (Shorkey & Uebel, 2014). Today, most social work educators use some sort of technology either in the classroom or as part of the educational process. A survey of BSW educators in the United States found that participants most commonly used e-mail technology (96.7%) followed by the Internet (93%) and then their institution's LMS (87%), such as Blackboard, Moodle, or Canvas (Buquoi et al., 2013). This matches national data that reports only 85% of all faculty members in higher education use their institutions' LMS, even though 99% of all universities and colleges in the United States have an active LMS in place (Dahlstrom, Brooks, & Bichsel, 2014).

A more in-depth look at the survey of BSW educators suggests that social work educators may not be early adopters of technology for active learning in the classroom. Buquoi et al. (2013) found that the use of DVD/CD players was prevalent (73.8%), but other electronic devices such as tablets, computers, and digital recording devices were employed by less than 50% of responding BSW educators. Software and applications such as social media, texting services, and online chat programs had lower rates of use; less than a third of all respondents (31%) reported using these technologies as part of their teaching activities. However, even though these data were published only 5 years ago, other studies suggest that technology use in social work education may be growing. A study found that social work faculty members and field educators in Canada overwhelming incorporated videos from YouTube into their teaching and assignments (Fang, Al-Raes, & Zhang, 2018). In another survey of field educators, this time in the South, Beal (2015) found that most used e-mail (100%), accessed the Internet (99%), and completed student documentation via learning management systems or other cloud-based services (79%), while less than half were using videoconferencing software as a tool for communications. Finally, a study by Quinn and Fitch (2014) found a gap between agency-level technology expectations for MSW-level students and what was being taught in the classroom. Responses from agency-based field instructors suggested a mismatch between the types of software students use in the classroom and those that are used in real-world practice settings (i.e., SPSS vs. Microsoft Excel for statistical analysis). This suggests that social work educators may be unfamiliar with the technology needs of today's social work practitioners or may not be thinking about transferability of skills to future practice settings. Additionally, social work educators may be more comfortable including technology in the seated classroom that is easy to use, ubiquitous, and readily available, and social work settings are not yet demanding that social work graduates possess technology skills. Educators may also have more comfort with passive methods for delivering digital content, rather than requiring students to engage with newer digital technology. For example, an instructor may feel more comfortable showing a video about motivational interviewing in class via a streaming service such as YouTube than asking students to digitally record role-plays of motivational interviewing and review the videos in class. Similarly, instructors might be comfortable using

Web-based platforms for e-mail and course management to help administer a course, or for activities such as sending out class-wide announcements or posting PowerPoint presentations.

Several reasons may account for the limited use of technology as a tool for engagement and active learning in social work education, especially in the seated classroom. First, social work educators may be unfamiliar with different types of technology, and thus unsure how to incorporate into assignments or the classroom environment (Buquoi et al., 2013). This may be partly related to an aging instructional workforce and generational comfort with technology (Wolf & Goldkind, 2016), but age and previous comfort do not have to limit exploration. Although an instructor may have experience using social media platforms such as Twitter or Instagram for personal reasons, understanding how these tools might support educational outcomes requires thinking about the technology in new ways (Ballantyne, 2008; Puentedura, 2013a). Second, some educators are wary of the resources and time commitments needed to learn and include different types of educational technology in classroom and learning activities (Jones, 2010; Perron et al., 2010). For example, an educator wanting to use video recorders in the classroom needs to have access to enough digital recording devices for all students, be familiar with how the software works, ensure that students know how to use the tools, and redirect class time to give attention to these matters, all before the learning activity begins.

This chapter offers suggestions to help social work educators address some of these possible needs and incorporate newer digital technologies into assignments or other active learning activities, irrespective of how the class is being taught (i.e., seated, hybrid, or online). We start with a short discussion on technology as a passive learning tool by describing learning management systems. The rest of the chapter focuses on how social work educators can begin to incorporate technology into their classroom activities for active learning and builds on the foundations of previous two chapters.

WHAT ARE LEARNING MANAGEMENT SYSTEMS AND E-LEARNING TOOLS?

Dozens of LMSs are used in higher education today, and their use ranges from supporting a seated classroom all the way to delivering a fully online course. Some are open sourced, others proprietary, and still others are developed by institutions to meet the unique needs of their organization. We want to focus on the functionality of software applications (apps) used in online education rather than on the specific names of platforms such as Blackboard, Moodle, and Canvas for two reasons. First, specific brands of LMS change as education, technology, and publishing companies buy, sell, and develop new or old systems. Second, universities that contract with companies for their LMS may change systems entirely when contracts end, moving from one system to another, or may contract for different services within one system, adding or deleting features. Similarly, some LMSs work with other apps for specific functions within their system. For example, systems such as Moodle and Canvas allow for users (i.e., institutions or instructors) to use a variety of different apps for recording lectures (e.g., Zoom, VoiceThread, or Kaltura), and these systems interface directly with the LMS. This means that educators need to understand the types of digital tools associated with their LMS and the functionality of the tools that are at their disposal for creating online content and courses. In Table 4.1, we briefly cover some essential definitions and offer a review of additional tools.

Table 4.1. Types of e-Learning Tools in Learning Management Systems

Type of e-Learning Tools	Purpose
Content capturing	Instructors can create content for courses such as video-recorded lectures, audio directions, or written formulas from a whiteboard. Examples include VoiceThread, Kaltura, and lightboards. Sometimes referred to as video or screen capturing.
Collaboration tools	These are often third-party apps that allow learners and instructors to work on projects in online environments at the same time in one location; examples include wikis, Google Documents, and cloud-sharing services.
e-Portfolios	This is a digital collection of student-completed work that is organized to demonstrate learning over time and can be created in a variety of platforms, from a blog to proprietary apps such as Taskstream and TK20 by Watermark.
Content repositories	These are digital databases that allow instructors to store, search, and retrieve digital content for inclusion in a course.
Academic integrity	These tools allow instructors and institutions to determine the identity of students and help to prevent cheating and plagiarism through proctoring, assessing writing, and locking down web browsers on computers. Examples include ProctorU, SafeAssign, Turnitin, and Respondus Lock Down Browser.
Video or audio conferencing	These services allow for two-way communication between persons in different locations via video or audio and are typically for synchronous classes or office hour meetings. Examples include Adobe Connect, Zoom, and GotoMeeting.
Streaming services	These services offer digital media content for use in the classroom. Content can come from textbook publishers, news outlets, and governmental agencies. Some institutions purchase subscriptions for direct upload into an LMS.

Defined, LMSs are platforms that store and deliver course content while also tracking who completes a course and tasks within it. Within these systems, instructors can use multiple tools to design how the content will be delivered, such as discussion boards, text boxes, hyperlinks, and video streaming. Although multiple users can interface with the platform, depending on their assigned role (such as administrators, instructors, and students), the goal of these systems is to provide a comprehensive learning environment for the student, while providing instructors with the ability to plan, administer, and track student participation in various learning activities. Built-in features for assessment and completion allow administrators and instructors to certify completion and levels of content mastery. Examples of LMS platforms include Blackboard, Canvas, and Moodle.

Other variations of learning systems include Learning Content Management Systems (LCMSs) and content management systems (CMSs). LCMS also deliver educational content, but the platform serves more as a repository for the learning content, and the goal of the platform is to provide tools for instructors to create and deliver content.

Examples might include an internal network at a community agency to train employees on required annual training. Similarly, CMSs are platforms that allow for managing course content for display on any website. The goal of these systems is to create a framework for storing and displaying content only. For example, although less common in higher education, some online content might be delivered through a professor's own website. More common is delivering continuing education opportunities via websites, open either to the public or as part of membership in an organization. In general, these options offer less functionality for the learner. One example in social work is the continuing education webinars offered by the National Association of Social Workers for their members (NASW, n.d.).

Learning to effectively deliver course content and engage with students with an LMS is an essential skill set for today's social work educators. As previously noted, Chapter 3 provides an overview of pedagogy that can help inform your curriculum design strategies. Chapter 5, "Online Classrooms," is devoted to using LMS to design and deliver an entirely online course.

Additionally, you will want to be familiar with how to apply universal design for learning (UDL) principles, which help to increase accessibility of digital content for people with disabilities, within an LMS and when designing technology-based assignments. See Chapter 6, "Online Programs," for an overview of UDL principles and Chapter 8, "Ethical Considerations for Faculty Members Who Teach With Technology," for the technology needs of students with disabilities. We encourage you to further develop your knowledge and understanding of LMSs by participating in training and professional development opportunities at your institution, attending presentations at social work education conferences, and connecting with other social work educators who are also using an LMS.

HOW CAN I BRING TECHNOLOGY TO MY SOCIAL WORK COURSE FOR ACTIVE LEARNING?

The rest of this chapter will focus on the nitty-gritty of planning or redesigning assignments that support the development of digital literacy among students and are informed by theories of adult learning. To achieve this outcome, we will introduce two technology-based frameworks, Ruben Puentedura's SAMR Model for Technology Integration and Bloom's Digital Taxonomy (Churches, 2009; Puentedura, 2013a; Puentedura, 2013b), which were designed to help educators create and adapt assignments and classroom activities to include technology either as part of the learning process or as the result of the assignment. We will first describe each framework, offering context for social work education, and then walk you through how to apply the frameworks.

What Is Puentedura's SAMR Model for Technology Integration?

Puentedura's (2013a; 2013b) SAMR (substitution, augmentation, modification, redefinition) Model for Technology Integration provides a guide to adapting assignments and learning activities for technology-mediated use, regardless of the curricular content. The model identifies hierarchical levels of technology adaptation that range from using technology to enhance an assignment at the lowest end of the spectrum to incorporating technology in such a way that the learning activity is transformed into something new at the highest end. Although an assignment can be adapted at any level of the model, some technology-enhanced modifications serve only to replace one traditional tool, such as a class role-play, for another tool, such as a YouTube video of a role-play. Other modifications change the assignment entirely and push students toward higher levels of thinking needed for digital literacy. The SAMR model can help social work educators reflect and evaluate how they are incorporating technology into a seated or hybrid classroom, across a range of assignments and activities. Figure 4.1 provides a visual of the SAMR model and defines four different approaches for incorporating technology into a sample class assignment. The dotted line in the middle of the figure represents an assignment that has gone from being enhanced by technology to being transformed by the inclusion of technology.

Figure 4.1. SAMR Model for Technology Integration

	Level of Technology Integration	Video Example
Transforming	**Redefinition** Technology allows for creating new, previously inconceivable tasks.	Creates how-to videos about interviewing technique, incorporating editing, and annotation software, to be posted on public video-sharing website
	Modification Technology allows for a significant redesign of the learning activity.	Video records role-plays, edits, and then annotates to label techniques used.
Enhancing	**Augmentation** Technology acts as a direct tool substitution with functional change in the learning activity.	Video records role-plays and then edits down to five minutes with video-editing software.
	Substitution Technology acts as a direct tool substitution with no functional change in the learning activity.	Video records role-plays rather than role-plays being performed in class.

The first level in the SAMR model is *substitution*. This is when technology works as a direct tool substitute, with no functional change to the learning task. For example, a social work educator might modify a role-play assignment for students by asking them to video-record the assignment rather than presenting the role-play during class. Students submit an unedited video file for grading at the end of the semester rather than doing an in-class role-play. After watching hours of unedited videos of role-plays at the end of one semester, our social work professor might decide to change the assignment slightly, which is *augmentation*. Students will continue to video-record their role-plays, but the professor now asks them to edit the videos to 5 minutes using video-editing software and identify and include only the most essential parts of the role-play. Although the video recording is still a substitution for the classroom, students are now using technology to streamline their videos and highlight the critical parts of the role-play, improving the quality and quantity of their final product, what Puentedura (2013a; 2013b) would call "improved functionality."

To transform this assignment, our social work professor might want to include a video-annotation tool that requires students to add words and symbols to their video. This tool could allow students to document what is happening in the video, label the techniques they used, and insert comments about what went well and what did not go well during the role-play. This is an example of *modification*, where the assignment is significantly restructured. Now in the process of editing, students review and critique their role-play. Finally, to apply *redefinition* to this video role-play assignment, the professor might incorporate a video-sharing website such as YouTube, so students can share their videos. By sharing videos publicly, the assignment can be transformed into one where students produce how-to videos demonstrating skills, or examples of good and bad interviewing techniques using all the technology tools of the previous levels, including video recorders, editing software, and annotation software. With this assignment, students are not only learning about and using different technology tools but also demonstrating some of Doug Belshaw's (2014) complex digital literacies skills, such as Communicative (i.e., professionally conveying how to conduct a specific interviewing technique) and Creative (i.e., combining the content of social work practice with multimedia).

So How Can the SAMR Model Help a Social Work Educator?

First, the model promotes the development of digital literacy through the transformation of assignments and learning activities. As noted in Chapter 2, Belshaw (2014) suggests that true digital literacy comes when an individual can effectively use digital tools, while also understanding the content and context associated with those tools. For example, if a small group of social work students is working on our video role-play assignment, they need to understand that creating a video for the public (context of the tool) requires awareness of social work professionalism and the subject matter of their role-plays. They also need to understand how to use a video-recording device, how to frame a shot, and how to record audio that is pleasing.

Second, the SAMR model supports the gradual inclusion of technology into a class assignment over time, giving the educator the opportunity to pilot test new technology tools and to experiment with an assignment from semester to semester. By taking measured steps in transforming an assignment, you can improve your own technology skills without overwhelming students with complex assignments beyond their skill levels. See Breakout Box 4.1 for some examples of how social work educators have started applying the SAMR model by enhancing their learning activities to include digital and social technology.

BREAKOUT BOX 4.1. PRACTICAL TIP
BEGINNING TO APPLY THE SAMR MODEL IN SOCIAL WORK EDUCATION FOR ENHANCEMENT

Presubstitution: Dr. Jonathan Singer of Loyola University's School of Social Work highlights the role of technology-mediated social work practice by assigning or teaching case studies or scenarios that were developed before today's technologies were commonplace. After reading the case study, students are asked to identify how the case study and related interventions/ethical dilemmas would be similar or different given today's technology. Although not the direct substitution of a digital tool as seen in the SAMR Model, learning comes from applying questions about current technology to case studies in contrast to the older technologies. (J. Singer, personal communication, October 25, 2017)

> *Preaugmentation:* Dr. Liz Fisher of Shippensburg University's Department of Social Work and Gerontology uses the social media platform Twitter to post events students can attend for extra credit. For example, she takes a photo of an event's flyer with her smartphone and then tweets it with the class hashtag. This activity replaces the instructor passing out a paper flyer in class and can be done almost any time by the instructor. The preaugmentation is that students need to have the digital literacy skills to use Twitter to find the extra credit opportunities. Additionally, the instructor could ask students to write a tweet about what they learned from the extra credit experience. Other ways to do this include using a discussion forum in an LMS or via email. (L. Fisher, personal communication, September 3, 2017)

You can also use the SAMR model to incorporate the educational practice of scaffolding, as discussed in detail in Chapter 3, into your technology-mediated assignments. Briefly, scaffolding is an instructional process whereby the instructor includes guidance, support, and advice early on during an assignment or activity and then slowly removes the supports so that students can practice and learn on their own. In our "Assignment Compendium for Integrating Technology into Social Work Assignments and Learning Activities" in Appendix 1, we have applied the SAMR model by labeling each assignment with its appropriate level of integration (i.e., substitution, augmentation, modification, or redefinition). This will help you quickly identify assignments across the different levels of integrations that you can use in your classes or as examples when developing your own assignments.

What Is Bloom's Digital Taxonomy?

Most social work educators will be familiar with Bloom's Taxonomy, which is a useful framework for developing student learning objectives and, ultimately, assessments in social work education (Anderson & Krathwohl, 2001; Bloom, 1956). The taxonomy includes multiple ways to articulate learning objectives that include the knowledge, skills, and cognitive and affective processes that are needed by students to complete learning activities successfully. Employing Bloom's Taxonomy when designing assignments and other learning tasks is consistent with the Council on Social Work Education (CSWE, 2015) approach to competency-based education in social work. Andrew Churches (2009) adapted Bloom's Taxonomy for 21st-century digital learning by identifying and linking knowledge and skills related to technology to the original taxonomy. We offer a synthesized version of the taxonomy for social work education, so you can quickly identify and write the learning objectives and identify the digital tools that students need to know to complete a technology-infused assignment successfully.

Bloom's Digital Taxonomy conceptualizes learning objectives and digital tools in two helpful ways. First is with the knowledge dimension, which includes four different types of knowledge (factual, conceptual, procedural, and metacognitive), that can be incorporated into a technology-infused learning activity. Figure 4.2 shows each kind of knowledge across the dimension with a brief definition and examples for digital and nondigital assignments. Using these four different categories of knowledge, you can decide what content needs to be included in a learning activity. For example, factual knowledge is the most essential information required to understand a concept or solve a problem. If educators plan to incorporate the use of a social media platform like Facebook into their classrooms, they need to start by making sure their students understand social media platforms and Facebook, and then discuss essential terms for Facebook, such as what it means to "like" something or "friend" someone. Next, they may focus on the procedural knowledge needed to use Facebook, such as understanding how to post content on Facebook or how operate the privacy settings in the platform. Finally, they may decide that students need to recognize and appreciate the broader cultural contexts of sharing personal information about themselves on Facebook, particularly as a future social work practitioner (metacognitive knowledge).

Figure 4.2. Bloom's Taxonomy for the Digital Age: Digital Knowledge Dimension

	Factual Knowledge of discrete, isolated content elements in the discipline	**Conceptual** Knowledge of the interrelationships among content elements in the discipline	**Procedural** Knowledge of how to do something in the discipline	**Metacognitive** Knowledge about how to think and self-awareness of one's own cognition as relates to the discipline
	⇩	⇩	⇩	⇩
General Examples	Create lists of vocabulary, symbols, and/or images. Recognize reliable sources of knowledge.	Understand systems of categories & classifications. Comprehend generalizations & principles for a discipline. Identify theories, models & structures in a field of study.	Demonstrate subject-specific skills, subject-specific techniques, and methods. Know the criteria for when to apply procedure.	Apply strategic knowledge, contextual and conditional knowledge, and self-knowledge.
Digital Examples	Search for content from a reliable website. Create an online list of resources with a bookmarking tool. Complete an online quiz.	Label or tag images using a social bookmarking tool. Comment on a blog post from a professional organization's website.	Use video-conferencing software to run a team meeting. Review the quality of content from online sources. Apply privacy and other types of settings with social networking sites.	Teach others how and why to use a social networking site. Conduct a social media audit. Develop criteria for whom to connect with on LinkedIn.
Sample Assignment: Developing a Professional Online Identity	Use different Web browsers. Conduct a search of your name (including an image search), and observe what you read and see.	Create an online list of various social media platforms. Describe how you could use each professionally.	Develop a professional profile on at least two social media platforms from your list.	Write a professional social media policy, and apply it to your professional online identity.

The second dimension of Bloom's Digital Taxonomy looks at cognitive process and includes six broad thinking skills that increase in complexity from lower-order to higher-order processes, which provide a range of possibilities for designing and assessing student learning activities. Simply put, this dimension focuses on the different ways students can learn how to retain and apply their knowledge of social work content, skills, and values. Figure 4.3 describes each of these thinking skills in order from low to high levels of thinking and provides examples from traditional and digital applications. For example, the thinking process of *remembering* focuses on how one can learn information for later recall or retrieval, such as memorizing definitions or dates from history, or stages of psychosocial development. On the other end of the scale is creating, the highest form of cognitive processing, which involves assembling an artifact or product from different sources of knowledge, such as a class presentation on how to do motivational interviewing or development of a resource directory for a local social service agency. Next to the traditional thinking skills in Figure 4.3, you'll see Churches' (2009) examples of digital thinking skills that connect to each of Bloom's traditional cognitive processes. Educators wanting their students to demonstrate an *understanding* of a critical social work concept for a technology-based assignment might require the students to annotate a video recording of a mock client interview or write comments on a class blog about important social work theories. Similarly, to demonstrate *analyzing*, students might be asked to create a wiki, instead of a group paper on a class topic, or examine a discussion on Twitter related to a current event or controversial social policy. Although the cognitive process remains the same, how the students demonstrate or implement the process looks different in a digital environment and requires the educator and students to learn new terminology, platforms, and skills. As the use of technology becomes more common in higher education, the distinction between these two skills sets will become unnecessary.

Figure 4. 3. Bloom's Taxonomy for the Digital Age:
Cognitive Process Dimension

Cognitive Processes	Traditional Thinking Skills	Digital Thinking Skills	
Creating	designing, constructing, planning, producing, inventing, devising, making	programming, filming, animating, blogging, video blogging, mixing, remixing, wiki-ing, publishing, videocasting, podcasting, directing, broadcasting	higher-order thinking skills
Evaluating	checking, hypothesizing, critiquing, experimenting, judging, testing, detecting, monitoring	commenting, reviewing, posting, moderating, collaborating, networking, refactoring, testing	
Analyzing	comparing, organizing, deconstructing, attributing, outlining, finding, structuring, integrating	masking, linking, validating, reverse engineering, cracking, media clipping	
Applying	implementing, carrying out, using, executing	running, loading, playing, operating, hacking, uploading, sharing, editing	
Understanding	interpreting, summarizing, inferring, paraphrasing, classifying, comparing, explaining, exemplifying	advanced searching, Boolean searching, blogging, tweeting, categorizing, tagging, commenting, annotating, subscribing	
Remembering	recognizing, recalling, listing, describing, identifying, retrieving, naming, locating, finding	bullet pointing, highlighting, bookmarking, social networking, favoriting, searching, Googling	lower-order thinking skills

Source: Churches, 2009; Anderson & Krathwohl, 2001.

So How Can Bloom's Digital Taxonomy Help a Social Work Educator?

Bloom's Digital Taxonomy is helpful to the social work educator in two ways. First, it offers language for writing learning objectives for technology-based assignments. Second, it provides concrete examples of what social work students can do with technology as learning tools in the classroom and in their future practice environment. For example, a project that involves students working in a group to write a paper traditionally has produced only a final product to be reviewed and graded by an instructor. Although students will use analyzing and evaluating skills to create this paper, the project becomes very different when the document is written using a wiki tool. Now, the social work educator can assess the quantity and quality of each student's contributions and participation within the wiki tool, along with content and writing skills. By combining Bloom's Digital Taxonomy skills along the continuum, you can quickly identify the specific learning tasks and the digital tools needed to complete a technology-based assignment, which helps support the assessment of the assignment and course-level student learning outcomes. Depending on the content of the assignment, these learning tasks can be mapped to the social work competencies and behaviors outlined by CSWE's Educational Policies and Accreditation Standards (2015).

Though Churches (2009) suggests that Bloom's Digital Taxonomy is not linear (you can start anywhere within the framework), he acknowledges that students need to have the lower-order thinking skills mastered before moving onto the higher-order skills. This means that educators need to provide necessary background information and skills development opportunities for students when integrating technology into an assignment. For our students who are now working on a wiki to write a group paper, we need to make sure they know how to use the different tools in the wiki platform to make edits, comment, and even highlight content. Examples of how to build this assignment based on lower-order thinking skills could include providing hyperlinks to videos or how-to guides in the course LMS, an in-class tutorial session about the wiki program, and a short practice assignment where each student must demonstrate how to use the tools before completing the assignment. Figure 4.4 provides an example of learning tasks for incorporating presentation software (i.e., Microsoft PowerPoint, Google Slides, or Prezi) as part of a classroom presentation, using a matrix from Bloom's Taxonomy. Additionally, we provide a copy of our "Technology-Based Learning Task List for Social Work Education" in Appendix 2 of this book, which maps technology-based learning tasks to CSWE's (2015) social work competencies.

Figure 4.4. Sample of Bloom's Taxonomy Matrix for Incorporating Presentation Software Into an Assignment

Cognitive Processes	Factual	Conceptual	Procedural	Metacognitive
Creating	List all the steps needed to create an effective digital presentation with a group.	Plan or outline a digital presentation with a group.	Create a digital presentation with a group.	Reflect on your own skills to create a digital presentation with a group.
Evaluating	Create a list of criteria for evaluating a digital presentation.	Develop a coherent checklist or rubric for evaluating a digital presentation.	Critique a classmate's digital presentation using the predefined checklist.	Critique your own digital presentation.
Analyzing	Identify parts of an effective professional presentation using software.	Write a list of best practices for effective digital presentations.	Create a slide that demonstrates a best practice for a digital presentation.	Discuss how your own digital presentation incorporates best practices or does not.

TECHNOLOGY IN THE CLASSROOM

Cognitive Processes	Factual	Conceptual	Procedural	Metacognitive
Applying	Collect articles & other resources for a digital presentation.	Create a reference list slide for a digital presentation.	Illustrate an idea on one slide using shapes, photos, or diagrams.	Describe the process used to identify sources for a digital presentation.
Understanding	Summarize text with limited amount of bullet points on a slide.	Give examples of course content with images & text on a slide.	Defend an argument with one slide.	Assess your own argument with one slide.
Remembering	Define vocabulary definitions on each slide.	Label diagram using shapes and text boxes. Describe objects & key events with images and text.	Create a list of effective digital presentations found from a search on the Internet.	Describe a previously viewed presentation, and discuss what made a digital presentation memorable.

So What Are the Digital Tools Described in Bloom's Digital Taxonomy?

The next step in using Bloom's Digital Taxonomy is to understand the different types of digital technology that can be used to support learning, such as mobile devices, software applications, and social media platforms. As we have previously discussed in this book, digital technology tools are ever changing due to updates, modifications, or products becoming obsolete when new ones are developed. New technologies are growing exponentially, and innovation will continue to improve the way we educate future social workers. For example, Moore's law suggests that computers and the systems that use them double their capabilities every 18–24 months (Emerging Future, 2012). This also means that developers of a digital platform may improve its features to include new tools, allowing for new ways to use the platform for learning activities. For example, YouTube has new video-editing tools that allow for more collaboration and creation of video content. Combined with the increase in royalty-free content available online, these new features dramatically expand how YouTube can be incorporated into an assignment. Further, it is not uncommon for an instructor to identify a free Web-based service that allows students to create a video with simple tools and use that service for a semester or two, only to have the service start charging monthly fees, or even disappear because the software company goes out of business.

Because of these challenges, we organize our discussion on technology tools by their functionality as outlined by Churches' Digital Taxonomy (2009). Additionally, we include only those tools that we consider to be of most use to the social work students, educators, and practitioners.

Tools for remembering. Remembering, the lowest level of the thinking skills as outlined by the taxonomy, is a student's ability to recall or retrieve content and knowledge from long-term memory, for example, recalling specific definitions or recognizing dates from history (Anderson & Krathwohl, 2001; Churches, 2009). The explosion in online content and data makes it almost impossible for a social work student or educator to keep up with the latest research findings, current news, or policy changes. A recent study by the company IDC suggests that the digital universe is doubling in size every 2 years, creating a vast amount of digital data that includes online written content, digital images, and videos (Turner, Reinsel, Gantz, & Minton, 2014). Given the large volume of information available online, it becomes essential for students to know how to use digital tools to locate, organize, and retrieve online content. Here are four crucial digital skills for remembering:

1. Searching or *Googling* is a widespread practice in social work, and it requires the use of search engines and keywords to locate content from the World Wide Web, online databases, and other types of websites. Students need to be able to pull up a Web browser or website on a device and enter keywords into the basic dialogue box to complete a simple search. The process of remembering is demonstrated when students can identify or recall the appropriate keywords needed for a successful search. Examples include using search terms with a Web browser such as Google or Bing or searching on database or wiki such as PubMed or Wikipedia.

2. Bookmarking or *favoriting* is when a student saves content from websites, files, and other electronic resources in an organized way. This can be done using a simple word processing document or through add-on tools in a Web browser. Online versions of bookmarking programs allow a user to save content with a Web-based application rather than to a device. Called social bookmarking, these programs offer additional features that allow for tagging and sharing information. Examples include Del.icio.us, Listly, and Diigo and reference citation managers such as EndNote or Zotero. Other examples include "read later" apps such as Pocket and Instapaper.

3. Social networking is the use of Web-based applications designed to help people connect and network with each other. These apps can be used to organize online content and locate other individuals and invite them to one's network. Examples include Facebook, Twitter, and LinkedIn.

4. Subscribing is the digital equivalent of putting one's name on a mailing list to receive notifications about an event, new information, or other types of content. Notifications or alerts can come in the form of an e-mail or a text, or through an RSS feed reader that automatically collects content from online sources and delivers to a user's account. Users can typically subscribe in one of two ways; first, through a website's own alert or notification system such as a social service agency's e-newsletter or a journal's table of content alert e-mail; or second, by using a third-party application that specializes in aggregating content such as RSS feed readers like Feedly, Digg, and The Old Reader, or even the RSS reader tool within an e-mail program such as Outlook.

Tools for understanding. A more advanced skill on the taxonomy, *understanding* is about building connections between bits of knowledge and content learned from textbooks, lectures, or other class activities, and assignments. Students should be able to explain or describe the relationships between concepts and processes and summarize these connections in their own words (Churches, 2009). For example, in social work, we would expect students to connect concepts such as research design and effect size, learned in research and statistics classes, with their understanding of evidence-based practice, often acquired in practice courses. Students can use digital tools to document and demonstrate their knowledge using the following digital skills:

1. Advanced and *Boolean searching* are more complicated search strategies that require knowledge about the topic of interest that is being researched, and how to successfully use the modifiers to obtain the best search results. Advanced searching typically involves using a series of predetermined settings in a database to narrow a research query, such as specifying dates or languages. Boolean searching requires students to use keywords in combination with modifiers such as *and, or, not*, and parentheses or quote marks. Examples of databases that accept advanced and Boolean searches include Google Scholar, WorldCat, and other databases available through campus or public libraries.

2. *Blogging* is the act of writing and publishing content through a blog or Web log, which can be shared publicly or privately through a website or other hosting platform. The content of the blog can vary depending on the goal of the website or class assignment. Students can demonstrate a basic understanding of content by writing a descriptive post about a social work intervention or can show higher levels of thinking when using a blog for discussion questions or working in groups to write a blog post. Examples of free blog sites include WordPress, Blogger, Tumblr, or Twitter, a microblogging platform.

3. *Tagging* or *labeling* is the process of attaching keywords to digital content such as blog posts, photos, and tweets to classify and organize the content. After using these features, content can be easily located by searching for the tag. A tag can be added through content on social media platform such as a hashtag in a Twitter post, or it can be added as a meta-tag, which is descriptive information that is attached to a data file such as the name of a song and artist that are frequently attached to MP3 files of songs. Most helpful to social workers is the ability to tag content in social media platforms such Del.icio.us or Flickr and to be able to read and locate meta-tags on all types of digital content, including audio and video files, spreadsheets, and Web pages.

> *4. Commenting* and *annotating* require students to review digital connect and then add their own thoughts or notes to that content. For example, students can work with Microsoft Word, Apple Pages, or Google Docs to write a report, and use the commenting tool in either program to write notes to each other about edits or suggestions. Other software programs allow students to add their own notes to a PDF document, a website, or a video file. Students can demonstrate their understanding of content by commenting on digital documents similar to handwriting notes on a paper handout or by using commenting tools to add or respond to content such as adding a written comment to a blog post or the discussion feature of a learning management system. Examples include PDF annotation tools, VoiceThread, and VideoAnt.

Tools for applying. Closely related to procedural knowledge, *applying* includes a student's ability to complete an exercise or solve a problem such as a role-play, a presentation, or a simulation by drawing on previous learning (Anderson & Krathwohl, 2001; Churches, 2009). Some of the required learning may come from other classes or experiences, and we expect students to apply this knowledge to social work settings, either in the classroom or during field education. Here are four skills that support the skill of application:

> *1. Running* and *operating* include the ability to work with software and hardware to complete an assignment or other learning activity. Common types of software programs that are used by social workers include word processing, spreadsheets, presentation, and e-mail software. Computers, laptops, tablets, and smartphones are common hardware devices used by students and social workers.

2. Editing is the process of correcting or revising some form of content such as a report, a presentation, or a multimedia project. Although editing has always been a common practice in social work education, it takes on unique aspects when it occurs in a digital environment. For example, students need to be able to use the editing features, such as cutting and pasting or track changes, of word processing programs.

3. Uploading involves transferring a digital file from a device to a server, typically operated by a Web-based service, to share the content. For example, a student might create a PowerPoint presentation about working with older adults and then upload the file to SlideShare, a service that allows users to share digital presentation. Other types of Web 2.0 tools that promote sharing include Flickr and YouTube.

4. Playing involves the ability to successfully operate and play a game for the purposes of learning. Game-based learning, the use of games for learning, or the application of gaming principles (called gamification) to meet defined learning outcomes is now often used in higher education and has even found use in the social work practice community, primarily when working with adolescents (Langlois, 2011; Sorbring, Bolin, & Ryding, 2015). Although game-based learning has been used in professional education since the first half of the 20th century, it has garnered renewed interest with the introduction of digital games (Lewis & Maylor, 2007). Potential ways that gaming could be incorporated in social work education include learning statistics or preparing for the social work licensure exam (Arena & Schwartz, 2014; Nevin et al., 2014). Gaming is often paired with badging, which is the award of a digital badge once a digital module or assignment is successfully completed.

Tools for analyzing. When students demonstrate the cognitive process of *analyzing*, they are breaking content into small parts or chunks and then deciding how all the parts relate to each other or to a larger structure or outline (Anderson & Krathwohl, 2001; Churches, 2009). Specifically, students need to be able to differentiate between the different parts of the content, know how to organize or rank those parts, and be able to provide context to the different parts. For example, a social work student might design and conduct a survey with online tools as part of a research class and then write up the results in a blog post. Following are some digital skills for analyzing:

> 1. *Linking* involves creating and building links within and outside of documents and Web pages, typically using a hyperlink. For example, students might create links between a digital presentation and YouTube videos or a website.
>
> 2. *Mashing*, or the process of creating a mash-up, is a digital project that integrates data, images, and other content from several different sources to create a single project, document, or visual representation. Because the process of incorporating different types of data can be sophisticated, online digital tools such as Wakelet or Google Maps that help integrate data in a visual form are extremely helpful to students. For example, social work students can create interactive and informative maps on social problems by collecting data from the U.S. Census Bureau and then using Google Maps tools to superimpose the data over a map, showing how data changes based on geography. Also, mind mapping tools such as MindMeister or Popplet can be used to create simple mash-ups between ideas and visual representations.

3. Students can also use digital tools for *surveying*, which may involve conducting surveys or collecting other types of data that are assessed and incorporated into a project. Tools such as Google Forms, Google Spreadsheets, and SurveyMonkey can be used to design digital survey forms, share the forms digitally with others to collect data, and then analyze data using spreadsheets.

4. Designing an *infographic* allows for visual displays of information and data on a theme in a single page/poster. Students can be asked to identify an important issue or question and then decide what content to highlight and how best to communicate that content visually. Although it is possible to create an infographic in a single slide in a program like PowerPoint or Apple Keynote, many apps, such as Canva, Piktochart, and Venngage, are designed for creating infographics.

Tools for evaluating. To successfully demonstrate the skills of *evaluating*, students must make judgments by reviewing or critiquing content, using learned criteria as a standard for the judgment (Anderson & Krathwohl, 2001; Churches, 2009). If presented with a newspaper article about the current status of children living in foster care in their country, students should be able to identify whether the content is valid and appropriate to share with a client and whether the article represents a credible source of information. Additionally, students should be able to offer productive feedback on digital content. Digital skills for evaluating include the following:

1. *Posting* and *commenting* are often used interchangeably to refer to the ability to use software and/or Web 2.0 platforms to write and share ideas, thoughts, opinions, and other forms of feedback about written or visual content

such as a blog post about social work practice, a question on a discussion board, or an electronic news article from the local newspaper. Good posts or comments require students to gauge the content within its context and then reply with thoughtful, structured comments that evaluate the content. Typical environments for posts or comments include blogs, discussion forums on learning management systems, and social networks such as Facebook, Instagram, and Pinterest.

2. Moderating involves reviewing other individuals' posts or comments and then assessing the post for quality, appropriateness, and contribution to the original content or discussion forum. For example, students who are moderating comments on their class blog will review the comments to determine if they are relevant to their blog, decide to make the comments public or not, and then decide whether they want to reply to the comments. Common blog tools include Blogger, WordPress, and Tumblr.

3. Collaborating requires learners to cooperate with each other to complete a task or project, using digital tools such as e-mail, video, or audio-conferencing tools, word processing software, and cloud-based storage servers that allow users to share documents. Skills include understanding and using a variety of digital tools as well being able to contribute to a team. Common digital tools for collaborating include Skype, Adobe Connect, or Google Docs, and GotoMeeting.

4. Networking is the ability to use technology to contact and communicate with other users. For learning purposes, students could use networking skills to engage with their peers, faculty members, staff members (such as librarians or student services on campuses), community-based agencies, and other professionals. Key to this skill is understanding and using social networking platforms such as Facebook, LinkedIn, or Twitter to make professional rather than personal connections.

Tools for creating. Lastly, *creating* is the highest level of the thinking skills as outlined by the taxonomy, and includes all the skills and knowledge needed to plan and produce an original product or artifact that demonstrates their learning (Anderson & Krathwohl, 2001; Churches, 2009). As creativity and originality are critical elements of creation, the digital tools that support this level of student learning often require advanced skills and practice along with specialty hardware. Social work educators should carefully plan when incorporating these skills and tools. Here are three essential digital skills for creating:

> *1. Videocasting* and *podcasting* include capturing original content through video or audio recorders that can be incorporated into a finished product such as a podcast interview with a social work researcher or video, demonstrating best practices for interview clients. Directing and producing a digital product such as a video or a podcast requires students to plan, organize, and combine content into a logical and comprehensible product. Hardware such as smartphones, video recorders, audio recorders, and tablets can be used to record content. Software such as Apple iMovie, Audacity, and Apple GarageBand provides tools for editing and converting files for viewing and listening.
>
> *2. Mixing* and *remixing* are about identifying available digital content, creating new digital content, and then combining the content using multimedia editing tools to create a new product. This technique is commonly used with music,

but social work students could capture photos and news clips to create a short video about a pressing social problem such as poverty or immigrant rights. This requires higher-order thinking as students must understand copyright laws and Creative Commons licenses.

3. *Publishing* includes all the activities necessary to share digital content, including written text, photos, videos, or audio files, with the public. Students need to understand and demonstrate skills to create content for an audience (outside the classroom), and then actually publish the content with Web 2.0 tools such as blogs, video blogs, and wikis.

Some of the skills and tools described in this section can be easily incorporated into social work classrooms, while others require more planning, equipment, and specialized training. As previously noted, the assignment compendium in Appendix 1 of this book includes more than 50 different technology-based assignments that represent the skills and tools from Bloom's Digital Taxonomy. As you review the compendium, you will notice that most assignments focus on one or two of the abovementioned tools. We recommend this approach rather than throwing the kitchen sink of technology at an assignment. Focusing on one or two technology-related skills is more than enough for one assignment or even one class, and take time to learn the tools yourself before adding them to an assignment. Integration of digital literacy skills as discussed in Chapter 2 develops over time by incorporating technology across a course or curriculum, or when practitioners include technology as part of their commitment to lifelong learning. Now that we've provided theories and offered examples, the remaining pages will help you think pragmatically about where to start and offer considerations regarding design and assessment of your new technology assignments.

HOW DO I GET STARTED WITH INTEGRATING TECHNOLOGY INTO ASSIGNMENTS OR LEARNING ACTIVITIES?

As described, the SAMR Model for Technology Integration and Bloom's Digital Taxonomy offer pragmatic tools for converting an existing assignment or designing a new learning activity that includes some form of technology (Churches, 2009; Puentedura, 2014). The ease of integration can range from little time and effort to complex tasks that require time for students and the educator to learn and apply the technology. We suggest using the SAMR Model and Bloom's Digital Taxonomy and their tools in one of two ways: (1) to infuse technology into an assignment that you already use in a course; or (2) to introduce a new technology-enhanced assignment into one of your classes, preferably one modeled from an existing assignment.

To infuse technology into an already existing assignment, the SAMR Model offers a clear and practical guide to identify where to start. When substituting or augmenting an assignment, use the skills and tools from Bloom's Digital Taxonomy to select technology that will enhance an assignment either without any real changes to the assignment or with some modification.

Examples include using e-books or YouTube videos rather than paper books or DVDs or asking students to search for resources online to supplement class content. When modifying or redefining an assignment, the technology tools and skills as outlined by Bloom's Digital Taxonomy can transform the learning activity significantly or into a whole assignment.

Examples include asking students to use Web-based productivity tools such as Google Docs to complete a group writing assignment, or to create a video or podcast instead of an in-class presentation. See Breakout Box 4.2 for a case study on how one social work educator works to apply the SAMR Model, and

Breakout Box 4.3 for a list of questions based on the model that can help you determine the best ways to integrate technology into a learning activity.

> ## BREAKOUT BOX 4.2. CASE STUDY
> ### MALIK—INTEGRATING TECHNOLOGY INTO AN EXISTING ASSIGNMENT
>
> Malik has been teaching a social welfare policy class for BSW students for the past year and wants to refresh the end-of-semester policy presentations that students do in small groups. He recently attended a faculty development workshop from his institution's Center for Teaching and Learning (CTL) about using different types of digital technology in the classroom. He was interested in the idea of video recording and having students create videos about different social welfare policies instead of a class presentation using PowerPoint slides but was unsure where or how to start. He meets with an instructional designer (ID) from the CTL, and she talks him through some of the details of video-based assignments, including the equipment and software requirements, storyboarding, and potential challenges for students. When discussing the type of technology needed for the assignment, Malik remembers that one his colleagues had problems last semester when some students did not have access to video-recording devices and asks about availability of equipment for students to borrow. The designer gives him a list of free and low-cost equipment resources for students. Finally, she encourages Malik to spend some time thinking through his goals for adapting his assignment from a presentation to a video and gives him a list of questions based on the SAMR Model (see the Breakout Box 4.3). Feeling the time pressure with less than 2 weeks before the next semester starts, Malik just wants to get the logistics of the assignment worked out. After 45 minutes of trying to pull the assignment together, he realizes incorporating technology into an assignment is not quick or easy and requires more than just knowledge about the technology. He pulls out the SAMR questions. First, he realizes that substituting the video recording for an in-class presentation with PowerPoint slides

means students will simply video-record their presentations. He can post the videos on the class management system, requiring students to watch outside of class, and then he would have more in-class time for other activities. He knows that students have free access to PowerPoint through the university and should be familiar with using it as presentation software is frequently incorporated into assignments in the School of Social Work. Next, he considers the augmentation question. By creating a video, he realizes that students could bring in multimedia components (i.e., news clips, music, and photos) and incorporate digital storytelling, enlivening the process of discussing social welfare policy. He looks at the list of free technology resources he got from the designer and sees that the library on campus loans out video-recording devices to students. He looks at the criteria for modification and notes that students could share their policy research with a larger audience than just the class if they developed a public video about their social policies and considered different target audiences. This would require posting the videos on a public video-sharing site and working with the students to develop skills for presenting to a larger audience than the class. As Malik reads through the redefinition questions, he pauses. He is unsure about how to answer these questions and feels a little overwhelmed. He decides to integrate the video-recording technology into the policy assignment at the augmentation level for this coming semester, asking students to create a short video about a social policy rather than simply record their presentations. As he maps out the assignment, he also develops some informal feedback questions to ask students at the end of the semester to help him assess the logistics of the assignment and makes notes for himself to see about the feasibility of having students publicly sharing their videos in future courses. He will also keep a notebook of his reflections about how this assignment goes so he can revise it, if necessary, before using it again.

> **BREAKOUT BOX 4.3. PRACTICAL TIP**
> QUESTIONS FOR TRANSITIONING ASSIGNMENTS WITH THE SAMR MODEL FOR TECHNOLOGY INTEGRATION
>
> - Substitution: What will I gain by replacing the older technology with the new technology?
> - Substitution to Augmentation: Have I added an improvement to the task process that could not be accomplished with the older technology at a fundamental level? How does this feature contribute to my design?
> - Augmentation to Modification: How is the original task being modified? Does this modification fundamentally depend upon the new technology? How does this modification contribute to my design?
> - Modification to Redefinition: What is the new task? Will a portion of the original task be retained? How is the new task uniquely made possible by the new technology? How does it contribute to my design?
>
> Source: Puentedura, 2013b.

As with any new assignment, introducing a brand-new technology-based assignment into a social work course or learning activity requires more time and effort on the part of the instructor. Start by reviewing different types of technology-based assignments, especially those that are already being used successfully in social work education, such as the ones in our assignment compendium, which is divided by subject areas—practice, human behavior in the social environment (HBSE), policy, research, field, and those assignments that apply to all subject areas, so it will be easy to find something that might work in your class. Another way to read through the compendium is by locating the type of technology or digital skill and knowledge that successful assignment completion requires. Although not a complete list, Figure 4.5 shows various kinds of learning activities organized by the type of technology with examples from the compendium. These activities range from case studies that incorporate technology to student-created media projects. Social work educators can also review technology-enhanced assignments and learning tasks from other disciplines in higher education. For suggestions, see the list of further reading at the end of this chapter.

Figure 4.5. Types of Technology-Enhanced Learning Activities

Name	Definition	Bloom's Digital Skills	Compendium Assignments (p. 393)
Discussions, reflections, and case studies	Topics focus on the role of technology in society and social work practice.	moderating, collaborating, social networking	Working Through an Ethical Dilemma; Learning Through Literature
Web-based projects	Using the internet to explore, search, and research content	searching, Googling, bookmarking, favoriting, subscribing, advanced and Boolean searching, tagging, labeling, commenting, annotating, posting, commenting	Screencasts of Literature Search; Lifelong Learning With Pinterest
Collaboration-based projects	Web 2.0 tools for creating content with two or more students	running, operating, editing, uploading, playing, linking, mashing, surveying, moderating, collaborating	Using Wikis for Human Rights and Social Justice; Skype Textbook Author
Social media–based projects	Web 2.0 tools to engage and network with others	social networking, tagging, labeling, commenting, uploading, linking, surveying, posting, moderating, collaborating, networking, publishing	Connecting with Peers and Professionals Using Twitter; Learning to Use LinkedIn for Professional Practice
Learning with mobile and handheld devices	Devices such as smartphones, tablets, and student response systems used to engage or create content in the classroom	running, operating, uploading, playing, moderating, collaborating, networking, videocasting, podcasting, mixing, remixing, publishing	Student Response System ("Clickers"); Using Smartphones to Access and Explore Secondary/Available Census Data

Name	Definition	Bloom's Digital Skills	Compendium Assignments (p. 393)
Game-based learning	Using gamification software or digital games	running, operating, playing, posting, commenting, networking, collaborating	World of Warcraft
Learning in virtual environments	Interactive computer programs that create a simulated experience for the user	social networking, running, operating, playing, networking, collaborating	Navigating the Virtual World of Second Life; Using Second Life as a Practice Lab
Student-created media projects	Hardware and software used by students to create or mix content	videocasting, podcasting, mixing, remixing, publishing	Community Assessment: Walking Video Tour; Field Placement Soundscape

HOW CAN I ASSESS MY NEW TECHNOLOGY-BASED ASSIGNMENT?

A final step to integrating technology into classroom activities is to determine how you will assess the quality of the completed assignment, specifically within the context of preparing student learners for social work practice. Bloom's Digital Taxonomy links to learning outcomes, and you can incorporate the multiple dimensions of competence (knowledge, values, skills, and cognitive and affective processes) outlined by CSWE (2015) in the most recent Educational Policy and Accreditation Standards. Next, it is important to connect these assignments to the real world of social work practice. To this end, educational and practice standards developed by accrediting bodies, professional social work organizations, and academic institutions from around the world are useful tools that can be incorporated into rubrics and other assessment tools at the assignment and course level. For example, the National Association of Social Workers (NASW) in the United States published Standards for Technology in Social Work Practice in 2017, which guide social workers on how best to incorporate technology into their own practice settings. By connecting or mapping these practice standards to the learning objectives developed through using Bloom's Digital Taxonomy, an educator can develop a rubric or grading checklist for assessment purposes and help students understand the value of the assignment for real-world practice. The educational and practice standards used by social work educators will depend on their location, as different countries and regions have adopted different standards. In this book, we demonstrate how the Social Work Competencies from CSWE (2015) can be mapped with Bloom's Digital Taxonomy to connect the student learning objectives and activities with program or curriculum assessments.

Consider Figure 4.6, which shows a completed Bloom's Digital Taxonomy matrix for an assignment that requires students to use presentation software to design and deliver a digital presentation. The learning activities or tasks are mapped to the learning objectives (which are also considered behaviors for social work practice) and one of CSWE's nine Social Work Competencies (Anderson & Krathwohl, 2001, Churches, 2009; CSWE, 2015). The actual content and focus of the assignment will vary depending on course content and course objectives. For example, refer to Malik, our social work educator in Breakout Box 4.2, who wants to revitalize a policy analysis assignment and have students create and publish a digital presentation on a social welfare policy instead of writing a paper. For his assignment matrix, he identifies two essential learning objectives (creating a digital presentation and analyzing one's own presentation) and several learning activities that students need to complete as part of the assignment. Because this is a social welfare policy class, we presuppose that the course will address the course objectives relevant to CSWE's Social Work Competency #5: Engage in Policy Practice. Additionally, the instructor's choice to include a self-critique on the presentation suggests the course will

*Figure 4.6. Assignment Matrix for
Digital Presentation on a Social Welfare Policy*

Assignment Task & Learning Activities	Learning Objective (Behavior of Social Work Practice)	Social Work Competency
1. Plan or outline the digital presentation. 2. Illustrate an idea in the presentation using shapes, photos, or diagrams. 3. Create a reference list slide for the presentation. 4. Summarize text with a limited amount of bullet points.	Create a digital presentation about a current social welfare policy. (Competency Dimensions = Knowledge & Skills)	#5: Engage in Policy Practice

also address the course objective relevant to CSWE's Social Work Competency #1: Demonstrate Ethical and Professional Behavior. Once all the critical parts of the assignment are identified (the competencies, the behaviors of social work, and assignment tasks), the educator can quickly create an assignment matrix similar to the one in Figure 4.6, which can be the basis for an assignment rubric or checklist, depending on how the instructor prefers to assess student assignments. To help social work educators identify learning tasks and activities linked with CSWE's Social Work Competencies,

Appendix 2 of this book offers a list of more than 100 technology-related learning tasks and activities that are mapped to each of CSWE's social work competencies.

A FEW PRACTICAL CONSIDERATIONS FOR ACTUALLY GRADING TECHNOLOGY-BASED ASSIGNMENTS

Although the focus of this book is not about how to develop rubrics or grading checklists, we recommend using some form of rubric with a technology-based assignment. Using rubrics is a good practice in all assignments for the theoretical reasons outlined in Chapter 3, including supporting self-regulation. Again, by working with Bloom's Digital Taxonomy to map your learning activities to learning objectives and educational standards, you will be able to create the skeleton of a rubric for your assignment. This will help with the grading process, and sharing the rubric with students provides them with a detailed understanding of how you will grade their assignment. This can help reduce anxiety about using unfamiliar technology as part of an assignment and increase understanding of how to successfully complete the assignment. Additionally, we recommend the practice of evaluating your assignment's rubric the first time you use it for grading with a meta-rubric (Stevens, Levi, & Walvoord, 2012).

Two other practical considerations for grading and assessing a technology-based assignment are deciding how to track and archive assignments, and how you ask students to submit assignments. Often, assignments that include social and digital media require the submitting a video or audio file rather than a printed paper or Word document, which may challenge students and instructors. For example, if an assignment is to post on a social media platform such as Twitter or Facebook, the entry may be hard to locate and grade on those platforms. Consider the situation of Malik from Breakout Box 4.2. He is planning on incorporating technology into his social welfare policy presentation assignments by having students create a video about a social policy instead of a class presentation. As he works through the assignment, he begins to think about the logistics of the assignment, such as what the students will turn in to him and how. The assignment logistics will not only inform what the students will do but also influence how the professor assesses the assignment. When thinking about tracking, storing, or archiving an assignment that uses digital or social media, you should consider where the assignment will be located (i.e., on a social media platform or as a file on a student's laptop). In Malik's case, he must decide whether he wants students to post their videos individually on a video-sharing website such as YouTube or to post all videos on a YouTube channel created for the class. Or maybe the videos will be stored on a private data storage system at his institution. The next step is to consider how students will submit their assignments to him. Most types of digital and text files can be uploaded through an institution's LMS, but some assignments, such as a blog post or review of a Twitter feed, may require students to submit a hyperlink. For example, if Malik asks his students to upload their own videos to a public video-sharing site, then students could send him a hyperlink to the video. In turn, he could create a list of hyperlinks of the videos and share with the class. Although the exact details of tracking and submitting assignments will vary depending on the technology and assignment, thoughtful consideration of these logistics will make assessment and grading easier.

FINAL THOUGHTS

On a final note, we recognize that both educators and students have different levels of comfort with, and understanding of, digital technology, especially as tools for learning. Before incorporating any form of technology into an assignment or learning activity, an educator should (a) understand and be able to use the technology with the proficiency that will be expected of students; and (b) consider students' access and readiness to technology. First, to help you assess your own comfort level with incorporating technology into a learning activity, Breakout Box 4.4 provides some self-assessment questions adapted from the Learning House Instructor Readiness Questionnaire (Learning House, 2013). If you answer yes to most of the questions, you are probably ready to integrate technology into your course learning activities. If you answered no to any question, then you have identified new knowledge that you can explore, think about in relation to the assignment, or include as a learning objective for your annual faculty review/meeting. Do not let any answers hold you back—practice makes perfect and is good modeling for students too. See Chapter 9, "Technology for Professional Development," for more information on professional development as related to the use of technology in social work education.

For student readiness to use technology, in Chapter 3, we discuss the role of pedagogy to help the answer the question, what can I do to enhance student readiness to learn online? In Chapter 5, Breakout Box 5.1 offers a list of common computer hardware, software, and skills needed by learners prior to taking an online course, which apply to all levels of technology use in the social work classroom. Other practical ideas include checking with your institution's e-learning office to see if they have online resources for student readiness such as a self-assessment tool for online learning and list of basic technology skills, including a statement in your syllabus about the technology requirements for the course, and partnering with your institution's library or digital learning lab to offer workshops on basic technology skills that students can take outside of class. There are also several scales that have been developed to assess student readiness for online learning such as the Student Online Learning Readiness (SOLR) instrument

(Wladis, Conway, & Hachey, 2016; Yu & Richardson, 2015). For student access to technology, as we have previously noted in this chapter, you should be mindful of the costs associated with requiring additional devices, Web-based software, or online accounts that work outside of one's LMS, and work to offer no-cost or low-cost options for students. Other ways to support student access to technology include being aware of and sharing information about campus-based resources such as disability services, computer labs, and the library or digital media center and advocating for student technology support within your program and at your institution. See Appendix 5 for the "Social Work Distance Education Assessment of Readiness" (SW-DEAR), which is a checklist related to best practices and resources for online social work education. Again, Chapter 8 includes a discussion about the technology needs of students with disabilities, and Chapter 6 provides an overview of UDL principles.

BREAKOUT BOX 4.4. PRACTICAL TIP
ARE YOU READY TO INFUSE TECHNOLOGY INTO YOUR COURSE?

1. Can you help troubleshoot student questions about file formatting, word processing, spreadsheet, or presentation software problems?
2. Can you explain to your students how to evaluate a website (e.g., define a URL construction or differentiate between a search engine and a search directory)?
3. Can you troubleshoot basic Internet connectivity, modem, and Web browser issues with your students?
4. Can you direct your students to the appropriate technology support services (either campus or noncampus)?
5. Do you already ask students to complete assignments using word processing, presentation software, and e-mail programs?

6. Are you comfortable using your institution's learning management system (LMS) tools? Specifically, consider the following tools: messaging, discussion forum, chat room, blogs, wikis, and questionnaire/survey/polls.
7. Are you comfortable communicating with your students via text messaging, Web pages, or social networking websites (e.g., Twitter, Facebook, etc.)?
8. Do you read about emerging technologies or utilities for social work education through RSS news feeders or other Internet news outlets?
9. Do you attend training sessions or workshops about emerging technologies or utilities for social work education?

Source: Learning House, 2013.

FURTHER READING AND RESOURCES

Campus Technology. https://campustechnology.com/home.aspx (a magazine that covers technology on college campuses for educators and administrators).

Journal of Medical Internet Research: Medical Education. https://mededu.jmir.org/ (a peer-reviewed journal focusing on how to train health professionals in the use of digital tools).

Journal of Teaching and Learning With Technology. http://jotlt.indiana.edu/ (an open-source journal focused on enhancing student learning in higher education with technology).

Multimedia Educational Resource for Learning and Online Teaching (MERLOT). https://www.merlot.org/merlot/index.htm (a repository of free and open online content and tools).

Open Educational Resources (OER) Commons. https://www.oercommons.org/ (a digital library of open educational resources from around the world).

Westwood, J. (Ed.). (2014). *Social media in social work education.* Northwich, UK: Critical (a practical book about using social media in social work education).

REFERENCES

Anderson, L. W., & Krathwohl, D. R. (2001). *A taxonomy for learning, teaching, and assessing: A revision of Bloom's taxonomy of educational objectives.* New York, NY: Longman.

Arena, D. A., & Schwartz, D. L. (2014). Experience and explanation: Using videogames to prepare students for formal instruction in statistics. *Journal of Science Education and Technology, 23*(4), 538–548.

Ballantyne, N. (2008). Multimedia learning and social work education. *Social Work Education, 27*(6), 613–622.

Beal, B. (2015). *The internet, technology, and social work education* (Unpublished Doctoral dissertation). University of Georgia, Athens, GA.

Belshaw, D. (2014). *The essential elements of digital literacies.* Retrieved from http://digitalliteraci.es/

Bloom, B. S. (1956). *Taxonomy of educational objectives: The classification of educational goals.* New York, NY: Longman.

Buquoi, B., McClure, C., Kotrlik, J. W., Machtmes, K., & Bunch, J. C. (2013). A national research survey of technology use in the BSW teaching and learning process. *Journal of Teaching in Social Work, 33*(4–5), 481–495. http://doi.org/10.1080/08841233.2013.833577

Churches, A. (2009). *Bloom's digital taxonomy.* Retrieved from http://edorigami.wikispaces.com/file/view/bloom%27s%20Digital%20taxonomy%20v3.01.pdf/65720266/bloom%27s%20Digital%20taxonomy%20v3.01.pdf

Council on Social Work Education (CSWE). (2015). *Educational policy and accreditation standards for baccalaureate and master's social work programs.* Alexandria, VA: Author. Retrieved from https://www.cswe.org/getattachment/Accreditation/Accreditation-Process/2015-EPAS/2015EPAS_Web_FINAL.pdf.aspx

Dahlstrom, E., Brooks, D. C., & Bichsel, J. (2014). *The current ecosystem of learning management systems in higher education: Student, faculty, and IT perspectives.* Louisville, CO: ECAR. Retrieved from https://www.researchgate.net/deref/http%3A%2F%2Fwww.educause.edu%2Fecar

Emerging Future. (2012). *Estimating the speed of exponential technological advancement*. Retrieved from http://theemergingfuture.com/docs/Speed-Technological-Advancement.pdf

Fang, L., Al-Raes, M., & Zhang, V. (2018). The use of social media by faculty and field instructors in social work education. Presented at the *22nd Annual Conference Achieving Equal Opportunity, Equity, and Justice*. Society for Social Work Research, Washington, DC. Retrieved from http://sswr.confex.com/sswr/2018/webprogram/Paper32990.html

Jones, P. (2010). Collaboration at a distance: Using a wiki to create a collaborative learning environment for distance education and on-campus students in a social work course. *Journal of Teaching in Social Work, 30*(2), 225–236. doi:10.1080/08841231003705396

Langlois, M. (2011). *Reset: Psychotherapy & video games*. Cambridge, MA: Chateau Escargot.

Learning House. (2013). *The Learning House new tool assesses instructor readiness, then offers training*. Retrieved from https://web.archive.org/web/20150826111431/http:/www.learninghouse.com/new-tool-assesses-instructor-readiness-then-offers-training/

Lewis, M., & Maylor, H. (2007). On the use of games in OM education and research. *International Journal of Production Economics, 105*(1), 134–149.

National Association of Social Workers (NASW). (n.d.). *Workshops and webinars*. Retrieved from https://www.socialworkers.org/About/Ethics/Ethics-Education-and-Resources/Workshops-and-Webinars

National Association of Social Workers (NASW). (2017b). *NASW, ASWB, CSWE, & CSWA standards for technology in social work practice*. Washington, DC: NASW Press. Retrieved from https://www.socialworkers.org/includes/newIncludes/homepage/PRA-BRO-33617.TechStandards_FINAL_POSTING.pdf

Nevin, C. R., Westfall, A. O., Rodriguez, J. M., Dempsey, D. M., Cherrington, A., Roy, B., & Willig, J. H. (2014). Gamification as a tool for enhancing graduate medical education. *Postgraduate Medical Journal, 90*(1070), 685–693. http://doi.org/10.1136/postgradmedj-2013-132486

Perron, B. E., Taylor, H. O., Glass, J., & Margerum-Leys, J. (2010). Information and communication technologies in social work. *Advances in Social Work, 11*(1), 67–81.

Puentedura, R. (2013a). *SAMR: A contextualized introduction*. Retrieved from http://hippasus.com/rrpweblog/archives/2014/01/15/SAMRABriefContextualizedIntroduction.pdf

Puentedura, R. (2013b). *The SAMR ladder: Questions and transitions*. Retrieved from http://www.hippasus.com/rrpweblog/archives/2013/10/26/SAMRLadder_Questions.pdf

Puentedura, R. (2014). *SAMR and Bloom's taxonomy: Assembling the puzzle*. Retrieved from https://www.graphite.org/blog/samr-and-blooms-taxonomy-assembling-the-puzzle

Quinn, A., & Fitch, D. (2014). A conceptual framework for contextualizing information technology competencies. *Journal of Technology in Human Services, 32*(1–2), 133–148. doi:10.1080/15228835.2013.860367

Shorkey, C. T., & Uebel, M. (2014). History and development of instructional technology and media in social work education. *Journal of Social Work Education, 50*, 247–261. http://doi.org/10.1080/10437797.2014.885248

Sorbring, E., Bolin, A., & Ryding, J. (2015). A game-based intervention: A technical tool for social workers to combat adolescent dating violence. *Advances in Social Work, 16*(1), 125–139.

Stevens, D. D., Levi, A. J., & Walvoord, B. E. (2012). *Introduction to rubrics: An assessment tool to save grading time, convey effective feedback, and promote student learning* (2nd ed.). Sterling, VA: Stylus.

Turner, V., Reinsel, D., Gantz, J. F., & Minton, S. (2014). *The digital universe of opportunities: Rich data and the increasing value of the Internet of things*. IDC. Retrieved from http://idcdocserv.com/1678

Wladis, C., Conway, K. M., & Hachey, A. C. (2016). Assessing readiness for online education: Research models for identifying students at risk. *Online Learning, 20*(3). Retrieved from https://olj.onlinelearningconsortium.org/index.php/olj/article/view/980

Wolf, L., & Goldkind, L. (2016). Digital native meet friendly visitor: A Flexner-inspired call to digital action. *Journal of Social Work Education, 52*(sup1), S99–S109.

Yu, T., & Richardson, J. C. (2015). An exploratory factor analysis and reliability analysis of the student online learning readiness (SOLR) instrument. *Online Learning, 19*(5), 120–141.

CHAPTER 5

ONLINE CLASSROOMS
Co-authored with Denise Krause

This chapter answers the following questions:

- What do online courses look like in higher education?
- Where can I go for help in finding online education resources?
- What do I need to know about teaching an online course in social work?
- How can I begin designing an online social work course?
- What do I need to know about delivering (teaching) on online social work course?

In this chapter we move along the continuum for technology integration and teaching introduced in Chapter 1, specifically reviewing some of the unique issues involved with teaching a completely online class. Both *asynchronous* and *synchronous* classes are discussed, including topics such as managing student expectations, designing synchronous versus asynchronous activities, creating a class "culture," and using experiential pedagogy to design and deliver an online course. Promising practices in student engagement, feedback, and quality instructor-student interactions in online environments get special attention in this chapter. We also review different strategies that social work educators can take when transitioning from a seated course to an online classroom, ranging from an instructor-led conversion (organically driven within the curriculum) to an online educational specialist conversion (external to the curriculum).

WHAT DO ONLINE COURSES LOOK LIKE IN HIGHER EDUCATION?

As we have previously mentioned, many scholars have addressed the question of whether online courses can be as effective as a seated course—researchers have found no significant differences between online and seated classrooms regarding learning outcomes for students (Russell, 2001; U.S. Department of Education, 2010). After 10 years of research in the social work literature, the debate is not whether we will do online education but how (Cummings, Foels, & Chaffin, 2013; Forgey & Ortega-Williams, 2016; Siebert, Siebert, & Spaulding-Givens, 2006; Vernon, Vakalahi, Pierce, Pittman-Munke, & Adkins, 2009; Wilke, King, Ashmore, & Stanley, 2016). Social work educators now have many choices for delivering content with digital technology to students. Several factors influence these choices, such as the structure of the course, the type of class content, and how students are expected to engage with the online content. Institutional factors also drive the look and feel of online courses, including the institution's learning management system (LMS) and the role of instructional designers across campus. Although we will reference institutional factors in this chapter, a more detailed discussion appears in Chapters 6, "Online Programs," and 7, "Field Education Online: High-Touch Pedagogy." For an overview of learning management systems, see Chapter 4, "Technology in the Social Work Classroom."

Types of Online Courses in Higher Education

The Online Learning Consortium (OLC), formerly known as the Sloan Consortium, offers seven categories that distinguish the range of e-learning that occurs in higher education (Mayadas, Miller, & Sener, 2015). We briefly review each category, highlighting the advantages, disadvantages, and variations for social work education. Due to the federal requirements for assigning credit hours, some institutions of higher education in the United States are concerned with ways to calculate seat times or time on task for online courses, equivalences of time for in-class and out-of-class time in online courses (New York State Education Department, 2016; Powell, Ice, Helm, & Layne, 2013). See Chapter 6 for a discussion about how this affects the design of an online program. Additionally, institutions or university systems sometimes set their own guidelines under which they label a course as "online"; the definition typically includes the percentage of course content that is carried out via distance. The most widely accepted standards are those developed by the Babson Survey Research Group in 2002, as part of their longitudinal research about online education in the United States (Mayadas, Miller, & Sener, 2015; Allen & Seaman, 2013). As shown in Table 5.1, the definition of a fully online course has historically included a percentage of online content (80%–100%), but today most institutions consider a course to be fully online when 100% of the content is delivered online (Mayadas, Miller, & Sener, 2015).

Table 5.1. Babson Survey Research Group's Definitions of Online Courses

Proportion of Content Delivered Online (%)	Type of Course	Typical Description
0	Traditional course	Course where no online technology is used
1–29	Web facilitated	Course that uses Web-based technology to facilitate what is essentially a face-to-face course; may use a course management system or Web pages to post the syllabus and assignments
30–79	Blended/hybrid	Course that blends online and face-to-face delivery; substantial proportion of the content is delivered online, typically uses online discussions, and typically has fewer face-to-face meetings
80–100	Online	Course in which most or all content is delivered online; typically without face-to-face meetings

Source: Allen & Seaman, 2013.

Traditional seated classroom course (0% online content). This course is the traditional college classroom that meets in a specific location at a set time and is quantified by the number of contact hours of in-person activities. Course activities may include the use of technology, but this is secondary to in-person activities. Examples of technology in a traditional classroom course include using a computer and projector to show a Microsoft PowerPoint presentation, meeting in a computer lab to learn about statistical software, or bringing in a guest lecturer from another location via videoconferencing. Students may bring their digital devices into the classroom for note-taking, but technology is not a critical component of the classroom. For social work education, this type of course represented the standard of instructional delivery until the introduction of online education about 10 years ago, when programs at Florida State University and the University of North Dakota launched online MSW programs (Florida State University, n.d.; University of North Dakota, n.d.). Advantages of the traditional classroom approach include the potential of high levels of contact between the instructor and students, social interaction within the context of the classroom, and instructor and student familiarity with the delivery modality. Disadvantages include the lack of flexibility and accessibility for students.

Web-enhanced course. The difference between a Web-enhanced course and a traditional classroom is that students need access to the Internet and hardware devices to complete Web-based course requirements, although their uses usually consist of less than 29% of the overall class activity (Allen & Seaman, 2013). Additionally, students may need devices and technical support from the institution to complete course requirements. Examples include the use of tablets or video and audio recording devices in the classroom, and the use of an LMS to retrieve course documents such as the syllabus or to submit course assignments. In social work education, faculty members have incorporated a wide range of technology including the use of tablets, social media, video-recording devices, and learning management systems to create Web-enhanced courses (Tandy, Vernon, & Lynch, 2016; Tetloff, Hitchcock, Battista, & Lowry, 2014; Young, 2014).

Advantages of these courses include increased access to Web-based course content and the opportunity to increase digital literacy and self-regulation among students (Cennamo, Ross, & Rogers, 2002). Disadvantages include the expense, maintenance, and support needed for instructors to bring digital devices into the classroom, and the cost for students to have their own devices and stable Internet access while off-campus (Wingard, 2004).

Synchronous distributed course. In social work, we often refer to this type of course as a synchronous online course or distance education course, because students are still required to attend class at a specific time to meet with an instructor and their classmates (i.e., in real time). Instructors and students still have face-to-face time, but this face-to-face time involves some use of technology such as a Web-based videoconferencing service, allowing students to access the course from a remote location. Variations can include classroom-based meetings where students gather at an off-campus location while the instructor is on-campus, a mix of students and instructors in on-campus and off-campus locations, or students and instructors meeting simultaneously via videoconferencing. One advantage is increased access to social work education, especially for those in rural communities (Reamer, 2013; Vernon et al., 2009). Additionally, the technology allows for the video or audio recording of class sessions for later review, and students get to interact with each other in a live setting. Challenges include decreased flexibility regarding time, issues with communicating via technology, and problems with students and instructors' comfort and ability to use the technology (Reamer, 2013; Vernon et al., 2009).

Blended or hybrid traditional classroom course. Like the Web-enhanced course, students complete some portion of coursework in an online or digital learning environment, which replaces time spent in a seated classroom, but students still spend most of the course in a seated classroom. The amount of online content in these courses ranges from 30% to 79% (Allen & Seaman, 2013). Examples include replacing one out of two class sessions per week with online content or meeting only for laboratory activities or tutoring sessions. One common method of achieving a blended course is called the flipped classroom, previously discussed in Chapter 3, "Pedagogical Approaches to Technology in Social Work Education." Advantages of the approach include the ability for students to review prerecorded lectures as often as needed, more time for instructors to assess students' understanding of the course material, and more social interaction between students and instructors during collaborative projects (Educause, 2012; Sage & Sele, 2015). Disadvantages include increased planning and preparation time for the instructor and the management of students' expectations about flipping content and activities. This pedagogical approach has been popular and successful with STEM (science, technology, engineering, and mathematics) courses in higher education, but little research exists about its effectiveness in social work education. One of us (Melanie) conducted a study about the use of reflective journals as a flipped classroom technique to encourage reading by students and found that the technique did increase students' preparation and completion of reading assignments (Sage & Sele, 2015).

Blended or hybrid online course. This type of course requires students to participate in online learning and activities with some in-person requirements such as participating in live simulations, attending guest lectures, or working with a small group on-campus or other onsite locations. Like the traditional hybrid course, the amount of online content in this type of course ranges from 30% to 79% (Allen & Seaman, 2013). The difference is that the students and instructor know upfront that the course is online.

Some social work educators and practitioners have concerns about how to teach skills to students without meeting those students in-person (CSWA, 2013; Duncan-Daston, Hunter-Sloan, & Fullmer, 2013). In social work education where educators grapple with the challenges of teaching social work skills courses in online environments, this method offers a way to supplement skills-based work (Ferrera, Ostrander, & Crabtree-Nelson, 2013; Phelan, 2015). The second half of this chapter discusses other teaching strategies to address this concern. Both types of blended courses (traditional and online) have similar advantages and disadvantages. Although students experience increased flexibility in how and when they can access course content, they still may encounter challenges related to geography.

Another consideration for hybrid courses is when to "load" the content for the learner. Front-loading means that students review online content such as readings, watch a video, and complete a quiz or other online assessment before participating in a face-to-face class. Learners are expected to review the content before seated class time, so the class time is reserved to discuss and apply the content at a higher level. This practice is considered effective for higher-level courses or advanced students (Chatfield, 2012). Back-loading content occurs after the seated class time, where students are introduced to a topic in class and then review online content that reinforces learning in the class meeting. An online assessment such as a quiz or discussion post is an example of a way to assess participation in back-loaded content. This practice is considered more effective with lower-level courses or introductory content for a major (Chatfield, 2012).

Online course. This type of course allows students to complete all course activities and requirements entirely online without any in-person meetings or on-campus activities. Students can access the course content at any time, which is referred to as an asynchronous online course. These courses offer a great deal of flexibility to students as they can participate in the course from any location and complete learning activities at their own pace, although the course syllabus may include frequent deadlines for segments of work. Most institutions use an LMS to deliver these types of courses and require 100% of the course interaction to be online (Mayadas, Miller, & Sener, 2015).

Additionally, social work educators should be familiar with massive open online courses (MOOCs), a unique type of online course that is characterized by being open and free to anyone and allows for large numbers of students to enroll and participate in the course (Gates & Walters, 2015). Although MOOCs remain largely untested in social work education, other disciplines have found mixed results with this type of online course. Advantages include increased access to educational opportunities, low-cost course credit for students, and the opportunity for institutions to reach large numbers of students with one course (Gates & Walters, 2015). However, many challenges exist such as impersonal learning environments, low completion rates, and concerns about cheating and plagiarism. Media hype over the past few years has resulted in research that has found that MOOCs may not provide the same benefits of smaller and limited-enrollment online courses (Straumsheim, 2014). Gates and Walters (2015) offer several recommendations for social work educators interested in developing MOOCs, which include securing funding, developing collaborative partners across institutions, and conducting educational research studies to assess effectiveness.

Flexible-mode course. With this type of course, content and instruction are offered to students through multiple delivery modalities, allowing students to select the delivery modality that best fits their schedules, learning preferences, and other educational needs. For example, lectures may be simultaneously cast live online, recorded as a video, and held in-person on-campus, giving students the option of which lecture to attend. Although no best way exists to design a flexible-mode course, two models have gained traction in higher education: the emporium model and the hyflex model (Miller, 2014). The emporium model replaces seated classrooms with on-campus learning resource centers where students can access online content and assistance from on-site instructors and tutors. Students attend at their preferred times and complete the course materials at their own pace. Several universities have used this model to redesign foundational undergraduate courses in math, English, and philosophy with improved learning outcomes and pass rates (Miller, 2014). A hyflex model course includes content in both online and in-person modalities, and students can choose their preference throughout the course. The course is not self-paced, but students can choose to attend an on-campus lecture one week, and then the next week view the lecture online (Educause, 2012). Although flexible-mode courses increase options and access for students, their implementation and success are dependent on the institutional context as these models require rethinking the use of space on campus, improved use of learning management systems, and buy-in from faculty and administration. For social work education, a flexible-mode class may prove a good alternative for courses such as statistics and research where students have varying levels of skill and report high levels of anxiety, which may be better relieved by an in-person presence (Elliott, Choi, & Friedline, 2013; Noble & Russell, 2013).

WHERE CAN I GO FOR HELP IN FINDING ONLINE EDUCATION RESOURCES?

Along with understanding the different types of online courses and delivery platforms, social work educators may find it helpful to consult with specialists in online education or access national clearinghouses that specialize in resources for online education. One place to start is your institution's office of online education or the equivalent. Because LMS platform management is handled by an administrator with an information technology (IT) background, most institutions of higher education employ professionals trained in instructional design and multimedia who can assist individual instructors with one-on-one consultation and training. See Chapter 3 for tips and guidelines on how to work with your institution's instructional designers. Additionally, several national organizations specialize in online education, such as the Online Learning Consortium and Quality Matters. Although these organizations are not necessarily content-specific to social work or any other discipline, they provide a wealth of information and resources related to faculty development, quality assurance programs, best practices in online teaching, and open-source digital teaching materials; they also host journals and conferences. Please see the further reading section at the end of the chapter for a list of these organizations.

WHAT DO I NEED TO KNOW ABOUT TEACHING AN ONLINE COURSE IN SOCIAL WORK?

Regardless of the type of course delivery and LMS, social work educators have some additional considerations when planning and delivering an online course. Because social work is a professional and accredited field of education, professors must help students achieve professional and ethical competency in a variety of knowledge, skills, and values (CSWE, 2015). Considerations include the education, assessment, and evaluation of professional and ethical behavior on the part of students, as well as how to present content related to being a professional and ethical social worker. Additionally, educators need to consider what professional comportment looks in online learning environments. For example, active listening is an essential skill for all social workers in establishing rapport and working through the change process with clients. Seated classrooms provide opportunities for educators to directly observe and assess a student's skill, give immediate feedback, and model as needed. Providing a similar educational experience is possible in an online environment and requires educators to shift their customary approach to planning and teaching a social work course.

To help with this shift in thinking about working within an online learning environment, we offer a simple, two-phase framework—design/delivery—to orient and guide instructors through the practical process of converting a course from seated to online. The *design* phase focuses on converting or developing content for online learning and platforms using instructional design principles, professional expectations, and multimedia. For example, the social work educator should offer students guidelines on how to engage respectfully in online discussion forums, which might include information about the Netiquette guidelines and the NASW Code of Ethics (Albion, n.d.; NASW, 2017). In contrast, the *delivery* phase focuses on how the educator actually teaches in the online courses, creating a collaborative learning environment that is relational and promotes learning. Ideally, social work instructors will model and manage online exchanges that occur between students, provide feedback, and intervene in disruptive or unprofessional behavior as needed.

The design/delivery framework builds on the content of previous chapters. By understanding the importance of digital literacy (Chapter 2), the foundational theories of pedagogy (Chapter 3), and digital tools (Chapter 4), an educator will be able to include design elements into their course that help promote learning in an online environment. By modeling digital literacy skills, applying the integrative theories of pedagogy, and being able to use and demonstrate the digital tools, the social work educator can effectively contribute to the overall delivery of an online course. The rest of this chapter focuses on practical steps that an instructor can use to both design and deliver an online social work course.

WHERE DO I START WHEN DESIGNING AN ONLINE SOCIAL WORK COURSE?

Effective course design is a predictor of student and instructor satisfaction with an online course (Kuo, Walker, Belland, & Schroder, 2013). Planning for the online environment is the secret to designing an effective online course. Instructors who are new to teaching online often start by converting an existing course (one they have been teaching in a traditional classroom format) to an online course. It is natural to want to replicate existing course content into the online format of their institution's LMS. Replication such as this draws on the substitution strategy of the SAMR model that we presented in Chapter 4 (Puentedura, 2013a; 2013b).

Educators taking this approach might convert one class session at a time to an online format, perhaps so that students can access content during a class session when an instructor is sick or traveling or to ensure equivalency between the campus-based and online course. Over time, this strategy will certainly result in a course that gets converted to a fully online format. However, in our experience, this strategy often results in a course that is disjointed in its online presentation and is confusing to students. In this section, we highlight the differences between designing a traditional seated class and designing an online course. The topics focus on incorporating pedagogy into the design of an online course, developing an online teaching persona, planning learning activities, course mapping and aligning, and specific types of design suggestions for online courses.

Start With Pedagogy

Creating the best online learning environment for social work content and practice skills begins with pedagogy, and the Community of Inquiry (COI) model offers a compelling approach to help guide the design of an online course (Garrison & Arbaugh, 2007). Introduced in Chapter 3, the COI model identifies teaching presence as a contributing factor for success in an online course. All instructors have a teaching persona, even online. When instructors make deliberate decisions about teaching presence, students can better manage their own expectations of feedback, e-mail responses, and etiquette for discussion boards (Garrison & Arbaugh, 2007). Further, social work instructors should be realistic about their own time demands, decide on a feasible amount of time for students to spend in an online course, and match the expectations of the social work program. Once an online course has begun, it is difficult to change a teaching persona without ramifications, especially related to when and how the instructor engages with students in the online course. As with all courses, students expect instructors to be consistent, approachable, present, and timely in their responses. They look to instructors to be clear with directions and requirements and to set high expectations for the quality of work (Kuh, 2009; Sheridan & Kelly, 2010; Zhang, Lin, Zhan, & Ren, 2016).

Generally, in social work practice courses, the instructor is expected to model good practice behaviors by giving frequent and detailed feedback to students and by promoting student-to-student engagement. For example, in a seated course, the instructor might create a teaching persona that balances engagement (i.e., checking in and remembering significant student events) with an expectation for coursework that includes excellence and adherence to the course syllabus (i.e., applying late penalties to everyone). In an online course, the instructor must also balance engagement with individual students and the class as a whole, and how students engage with the educational content such as audio recordings or photos. Practice with digital and social technologies, such as recording an introduction video for the course and developing a profile within an LMS that includes a photo, becomes important to the online teaching persona. One example of creating social presence is to create a closed Facebook group for a class where students post items that show their individuality, and the instructor can also share comments to demonstrate social presence. At the same time, the instructor can discuss contemporary social work-related issues and respond promptly to students concerns (whether observed directly or indirectly), both of which supports learning and cognitive presence in the course. Overall, you want your online teaching persona to remain consistent during an online course and model good use of technology.

Additionally, pedagogy informs the selection and application of specific social and digital technology tools that an educator will use in an online course. Multimedia learning theory, as well as the integrative learning theories described in Chapter 3 (active, collaborative, and connected learning), anchor learning for synchronous and asynchronous learning activities (Mayer, Heiser, & Lonn, 2001). If the objective is for the student to demonstrate assessment skills, the learning activities might begin with prerecorded video lectures and role-play demonstrations that present the concepts of how to assess a client (multimedia learning). The next learning task might require students to video-record their own demonstrations of assessment using a software program called VideoAnt (see Professor Bradley's example in Chapter 3), and then upload the file to a video-sharing website such as YouTube. The demonstration videos could also be linked from blog posts or discussion board posts in the LMS, directing students to give feedback through video annotation, discussion threads, and blog comments. This application of pedagogy enhances and reinforces learning across the entire assignment or learning task. In turn, this approach offers consistency, predictability, and a link between the technology and pedagogy. See Chapter 4 for more information on the types of digital technology tools that faculties can incorporate into an online course.

Several pedagogical theories offer ways to promote student success in online courses, such as self-regulation and motivation. Social work educators can apply these theories by using learning techniques such as scaffolding, incorporating progressive learning components, and employing adaptive release tools. Some instructors use progressive learning components and adaptive release tools for course materials that require students to have mastery over one concept before proceeding to the next concept. For example, dividing a learning module about ethics into two segments could require students to first watch a video lecture about the standards in the NASW Code of Ethics, and then take a knowledge-based quiz to demonstrate understanding of the Code of Ethics, before replying to a discussion post about a common ethical dilemma in social work practice. To successfully deliver this learning model, the instructor needs to use the LMS's release tools so that once students successfully pass the quiz in the learning module, the discussion board becomes available to them. Another benefit of using these design elements is that students who master basic concepts of a learning module ahead of other students can easily be directed to the next component or a more advanced version of the concept to individualize student learning. For example, students who bring previous experience with professional networking might want a more challenging assignment to complete rather than an informational interview over the phone. Some advanced learning activities involve professional networking via social media platforms such as Twitter or LinkedIn. Both activities can be incorporated into the online course, allowing students to select which level of the assignment they want to complete. Adaptive personalized learning, in which pretests and formative feedback from learners lead to changes in the curriculum to match their needs and learning styles, is not yet popular in social work education. Some posit that that this will be the next big innovation in online learning (Rani, Nayak, & Vyas, 2015).

Planning Learning Activities

The specific social work content of a course will also inform its design. For example, online practice courses, with their emphasis on skills acquisition and execution, require the inclusion of skills-based asynchronous or synchronous practice opportunities. Generally, designs that incorporate asynchronous learning require more time from the instructor to create the multimedia components of the learning activity, monitor student engagement with the activity, and give feedback to students as compared to synchronous activities. For example, a seated class or an online synchronous course covering content on social work ethical decision-making might include equal parts of lecture, class discussion on how to apply ethical decision-making in context, and an activity that gives students practice with an ethical dilemma. In this example scenario for an asynchronous course, the instructor needs to record and upload a video or audio lecture to the LMS. Then, class discussion needs to take place using some form of technology, such as a discussion forum in the LMS or on a social media platform like Twitter. Students need directions on how to use the discussion tools, expectations for how to participate in the discussion, an exemplar discussion post, and a deadline for when to complete their discussion posts. Finally, the instructor needs to monitor the discussion forum to reinforce the appropriate application of course content and correct misinformation.

Although online delivery does not need to mirror seated delivery, instructors should build a course with an understanding of how and when they, as instructors, will participate in and offer feedback for discussions and other learning activities, as well as how they expect students to participate. Thinking through the design planning in detail will help reduce common student complaints related to online courses including lack of clarity about how to progress through the course, inaccessibility of help (instructor and information technology services), and problems with using unfamiliar technology.

Instructors should also consider the workload of assignments for students. When assignments require that students use apps and social media platforms outside of the LMS, more time may be needed to complete the task. Making the value of these assignments explicit to the students, such as the transferability of the digital literacy skill development to their future practice as social workers, generally contributes to students' own appreciation of a learning activity. Further, it may seem like a great idea to require weekly live chats or discussion posts; however, they must be monitored and graded. Without graded feedback, students may devalue the learning activity or choose not to participate, and thus will not have the understanding necessary to improve their work for the next assignment. Thus, instructors should plan for the type of feedback needed for each learning activity in an online course. What seems realistic at the design stage may be too time consuming at the delivery stage.

One way to the assess workload requirement is to calculate the approximate time on task by estimating the time it will take a student to be in direct contact with the multimedia materials (i.e., how long to view slides and watch a video), complete an assignment, contribute to a discussion forum, and interact with other students and the instructor. These activities all count as seat time. The out-of-class time for students includes activities such as unsupervised research, reading, and preparing and completing assignments and activities. Often, instructors underestimate the amount of time that asynchronous online coursework takes, and because online courses require more demonstration than seated classes, participation in online coursework may require more time. It is easy for an instructor to overassign readings and add extra hyperlinks and Web-based content. Therefore, taking the time to review the time on task for assigned coursework is a helpful checkup for instructors and the program review processes when designing online learning activities.

Another important consideration when designing online learning activities is student perception, specifically the common perception that online courses are easier than seated courses. For example, students may believe that an online class consists of only watching a video lecture and completing a quiz. Instructors can address this perception by providing realistic expectations about student engagement and time expectations at the beginning of the course, offering an orientation before students enroll or begin online courses, and raising awareness about IT support and other help centers, including student self-assessment of technology skills in the course. All these activities enhance student self-efficacy and self-regulation, which can lead to higher satisfaction and motivation for learning. In some instances, students benefit from a "Learning How to Learn Online" course prepared by the social work program or the institution. In fully online programs, a distance program coordinator often has the role of preparing students with realistic expectations and online learning competencies.

An instructor must also purposefully plan opportunities to model social work practice and demonstrate the knowledge, skills, and values required to complete the course while integrating peer and instructor feedback. In practice courses, the design must include elements for practice and modeling (teaching presence); guidance and feedback (social presence); and exploration and execution (cognitive presence; Garrison & Arbaugh, 2007). In online courses, educators need to balance the synchronous and asynchronous course components to maximize opportunities for student practice and reflection in considering the best fit for the course content. To illustrate, during a lesson on teaching students how to help clients develop coping skills, the instructor might begin with a synchronous chat using videoconferencing software, asking students how they are managing all the demands in their life and inviting them to share their own strategies for coping. The instructor could then move the discussion to concepts about coping and how to use these concepts with clients or colleagues. After the live discussion, the instructor could require that students develop a one-page handout about coping. Table 5.2 provides examples of how learning activities might differ across different types of course delivery, from both the student and instructor perspective.

Table 5.2. Examples of Student and Instructor Learning Activities Across Different Types of Course Delivery (Design)

Sample Student Activities	Synchronous	Asynchronous	Seated
Syllabus Treasure Hunt: to locate certain elements of a course (assignments, due dates, etc.)	Instructor discusses this via online chat, in a video, or during live class.	Students are directed via written directions or recorded video to locate elements on their own.	Instructor discusses this in-person during class time.
Small-group role-plays with instructor prompts	Instructor uses real-time private message technology to prompt student in social worker role during a live role-play.	Instructor uses checklists or other feedback mechanisms for student self-evaluation and plan for improvement.	Instructor uses real-time feedback in classroom to prompt student in social worker role.
Small-group consultations without instructor (copy of feedback form is given to the instructor after)	Students are asked to give live feedback to each other using checklist or form during group meetings.	Students are asked to give public feedback to each other using checklist or form in a discussion board.	Students are asked to give public feedback to each other using checklist or form during an in-person class session.

Sample Student Activities	Synchronous	Asynchronous	Seated
Reaching Inside of Silence	Instructor asks students what their silence is about during a synchronous video class session.	On a post with no discussion, the instructor can e-mail the class or post a comment that asks what the reasons for a lack of response.	Instructor asks students what their silence is about during an in-person session.
Professional comportment	Either via e-mail or phone, when students' communication is unprofessional, couch feedback around the expectations of the program, after validating their primary concern.	Either via e-mail or phone, when students' communication is unprofessional, couch feedback around the expectations of the program, after validating their primary concern.	In-person after class time or during office hours, when students' communication is unprofessional, couch feedback around the expectations of the program, after validating their primary concern.
Demonstrating practice skills through role-play	Students are moved in to separate break-out groups, and instructor moves between groups to observe, prompt, or support students.	Students post video to a site (VideoAnt or Flip-Grid) where peers and instructor can provide recorded or annotated feedback.	Students are moved into separate break-out groups, and instructor moves between groups to observe, prompt, or support students.

Course Mapping and Aligning

Effective course design also includes beginning with the end in mind, for both the course objectives and the role of the course in the larger degree program. Known as *backward mapping* in instructional design, this type of course mapping starts with the course objectives and connects all course assignments and learning tasks such as readings, discussions, and role-plays to one or more of the objectives. If an assignment or reading cannot be connected to a course objective or learning module objective, then it does not go into the course. This elimination exercise challenges a social work educator to provide a rationale for including all materials in a course, from a reading to assignments to Web links. Saying that students need to read an article for a course because it is important does not meet the threshold for inclusion. Rather, based on thoughtfully developed course and module objectives, instructors should identify a learning task that gives students the opportunities to develop knowledge about a concept, theory, or principle (factual and conceptual knowledge); to demonstrate skills or application (procedural knowledge); and to self-reflect or critically think about how the knowledge fits for the learner (metacognitive knowledge; Anderson & Krathwohl, 2001; CSWE, 2015; Knowles, Holton, & Swanson, 2015). See the Further Reading and Resource list at the end of this chapter for information on how course mapping can be done using a spreadsheet or a table in a Microsoft Word document.

Once you map the course assignments and learning tasks, the next step is to make decisions about how to present the course content in the LMS, using the tools within the system as well as digital and social technologies outside the LMS. Other considerations are the digital literacies needed by students to complete learning tasks in online platforms, as well as the ways you will present the content. E-learning tools can work well for some social work classes and not others. For example, asynchronous content delivery via video-recorded lectures might work well for a Human Behavior in the Social Environment (HBSE) course, but some practice course exercises may benefit from a synchronous class meeting via a videoconferencing tool so students can practice skills and demonstrate them for the instructor. Although Web-based software might be a terrific choice for some course material, such as learning how to construct a genogram or create an infographic, instructors should also consider students' access to that software and their ability to operate it. A key question to ask is how the course plan will account for the time and resources needed to learn this technology. Digital knowledge requirements are also a critical question for instructors who teach seated classes. For example, an instructor teaching a statistics course should consider whether students need to know how to use Statistical Package for the Social Sciences (SPSS) or if another data management software would be better for students, such as Microsoft Excel or Google Spreadsheets. In an online course, the question might be how many hours students should spend learning video-annotation software to record their own practice demonstration videos. Strategic approaches can help answer the question of how to balance time learning technology and time on course content. One strategic approach is scaffolding, as discussed in Chapter 3, in which the instructor divides an assignment into steps or even smaller assignments. In our example of helping students learn how to use video-recording software, the instructor may first require students to complete a 3-minute practice video to make sure they have the knowledge to use the technology appropriately. This scaffolding can occur across the curriculum by using the same video-recording software for assignments in different courses. Other strategies include providing students with a list of basic computer hardware, software, and skills needed prior to taking an online course (see Breakout Box 5.1 for an example list); incorporating how-to videos or guides, so students can quickly learn the technology outside of the classroom; and working with their institution's library or digital media lab to offer tutorial sessions for students.

> **BREAKOUT BOX 5.1. PRACTICAL TIPS**
> **COMMON COMPUTER HARDWARE, SOFTWARE, AND SKILLS NEEDED PRIOR TO TAKING AN ONLINE COURSE**
>
> Basic Hardware & Software
>
> - Computer
> - Speakers
> - Internet connection
> - Word-processing software
>
> Basic Computing Skills
>
> - Use a keyboard and mouse
> - Save, open, and edit various file types
> - Open, send, reply, and attach and open attachments to e-mail messages
> - Upload and download files from and to your computer and the Internet
> - Navigate the Internet
> - Navigate the course environment in the LMS
> - Create online accounts
> - Download and use software and/or add-ons as specified by your instructor

Design Suggestions

As with any new course prep, creating a new online course requires planning well in advance of course delivery. Although we offer no hard and fast rule for how long it takes to create an online course, we encourage educators to start building online content for a course about a semester before they teach it. A useful place to start with any course is creating an instructor planning grid such as a table in a Word document or a spreadsheet that includes columns for the names of the course learning units, readings, ancillary materials, assignments, manner of content delivery including technology used, manner of feedback, and anything else significant to the design and delivery of a specific learning component. You can convert a grid later to a student roadmap or lesson outline. By placing the roadmap in the LMS's course shell, students can follow along as they complete learning modules, which will help them to see where the course is going and allow them to plan for when and how they will complete course content. See the Further Reading list at the end of this chapter for directions on how to create student roadmaps and sample planning grids for an online social work course.

In traditional seated courses, a component of learning is usually called a class session. In an online environment, a key component might be called a learning module, a pod, or a learning unit. Once an instructor has made decisions about course content based on such factors as the course syllabus, learning objectives, and number of weeks in the course, the next step is to match the content to the e-learning tools in the LMS. We recommend working with an instructional designer (ID) on this step, as the ID can help review existing tools and identify what resources are available within a given institution. For example, an instructor might want to include synchronous course activities on weekends, but this might present challenges if the institution does not provide online support for technological problems on weekends. Other constraints might include an instructor's skill set with technology, the availability of certain e-learning tools, and a program or institution's policies related to the online course. For example, to promote academic integrity, an instructor may want to use an online proctoring service. But if the Department of Social Work or institution does not cover the costs, then the only option is to require students to pay for the service. An ID can also help with issues such as universal design, which includes creating transcripts for video lectures and alt-text for visual images so that students with visual or hearing impairments can still access the course content. See Chapter 8 and Appendix 3 for more information about ethics related to technology in social work education.

Another important design element for online courses is consistency, specifically in presentation, format, and structure of content within the LMS. Consistency allows students to navigate through the course with ease, improving self-efficacy and self-regulation. Breakout Box 5.2 offers some key elements for consistency that can help students successfully navigate an LMS environment. Ideally, all the online courses within a degree program have a consistent LMS design so that students can navigate the course environment quickly and effectively across all their courses. Asking a colleague or instructional designer to preview the course before it goes live is a helpful way to determine the consistency and intuitiveness of a course structure and presentation.

BREAKOUT BOX 5.2. PRACTICAL TIPS
CREATING CONSISTENT COURSE DESIGN

- Keep the same color scheme, font type, and font size throughout the course.
- Develop a scheme for organizing the content of the course, such as similar headings across all modules, placing all learning modules in one place, or having the same place for each type of learning activity (e.g., all class discussions on the discussion forum page).
- Include hyperlinks to connect resources, readings, and other material to the appropriate learning module.
- Include due dates for key assignments in headings of modules or learning activities so students do not have to toggle between the activity and course calendar.
- Provide completion time estimates so students can decide when best to do each activity.

Source: Meyer, 2014

WHAT DO I NEED TO KNOW ABOUT DELIVERING (TEACHING) AN ONLINE SOCIAL WORK COURSE?

For any social work educator, managing the online course environment begins with clear expectations for the course interactions. With a solid design that considers the topics from the previous section of this chapter, delivery of an online course relies on the execution of the design components and on the elements of instructor and student engagement. As with any course, it is helpful to consider the beginning, middle, and ending phases of an online course, as well as the number of weeks available to teach the course (i.e., a 15-week semester, a 10-week quarter, or another timeframe). In this section, we focus on creating a class culture; supporting student engagement with the content; facilitating instructor-student and student-student engagement; and finally, giving feedback in an online course.

Creating a Class Culture

Creating a class culture begins with the overall design of the course. A student-centered learning environment is defined as a course designed in a way that is most useful to the learner. To start the course, the instructor should include a "Where to Begin" or "Getting Started" audio or video recording that only requires students to click on a hyperlink. This introduction can be recorded using a variety of video or audio recording apps such as Jing, Audacity, or Zoom. It is also useful to ask students to introduce themselves to each other via recorded videos or in a written format using discussion boards.

Choose a medium that all students will be successful with to start. During this introduction time, instructors benefit from an active presence in the course by posting their own comments and welcoming statements, and modeling engaged interaction in the same medium as the students. Good introductions set the stage for approachability. To the degree that students judge an instructor to be approachable, the instructor can head off potential problems, engage in a learning discourse, and challenge students to be their best learner selves.

Instructors can benefit from planned time for monitoring the course and communicating with students via tools such as e-mail, text, Twitter, or instant messaging. These tools offer contact that is analogous to office hours. It is important to monitor the course regularly, especially at the beginning of the semester. Students need information about what to expect from the instructor regarding communication, such as when the instructor will respond to e-mail and how long a response should take. The perception of instructor availability is correlated to student satisfaction (Richardson & Swan, 2003). Additionally, instructors can and should model professional decorum in their online communication. Deliberate decisions must be made by the instructor related to the type of language to use in e-mail and texts, options for contacting the instructor such as cell/home phone number, and the number of posts they will publish in shared spaces. Unless instructors establish and share their expectations, students will not know when and how to best communicate with their instructor and boundaries may become blurred. See Breakout Box 5.3 for an example of how one instructor creates a class culture around feedback.

BREAKOUT BOX 5.3. CASE STUDY

ESTABLISHING A CULTURE OF COMMUNICATION IN AN ONLINE COURSE, BY CAROLYN SHERLET GENTLE-GENITTY

It is the middle of the day, and during the daily hustle, e-mails keep coming in from students for tonight's assignment. A hard grin appears on your face as you bite down on your teeth in frustration, stating, "Why can't they ask these questions long before?" As you type, you realize you are typing the same answers in response to varying versions of the same questions and you decide just to cut and paste. You think a better way must exist to handle this heavy volume of e-mails. This segment shares three quick tips: (1) establishing a mandatory presession of Q&A before assignments; (2) sending e-mail feedback after assignments; and (3) establishing a course policy to guide feedback and queries on assignments.

1. Establishing a mandatory pre-session before assignments. Establish a pattern of mandatory presession Q&A with instructor on established days and times (e.g., every Wednesday at 8:00 p.m. in the chat room or forum). This accomplishes two objectives: (1) students will know long before when you are hosting the session and can plan to attend; and (2) hosting it in a chat room or forum means the information will be stagnant and students who miss or e-mail asking the same questions can be rerouted to review the notes in the chat room. This reduces the number of emergency, clarifying, and assignment e-mails. Because it is mandatory, also set requirements for them to log in at least once before, during, or after the session on the assigned day.

2. Sending e-mail feedback after an assignment. After grading each assignment, consider sending a general e-mail reminding about any feedback e-mail policies, how students performed in meeting required aspects of the assignment (use rubric as a guide to present feedback in bulleted form), and what areas of growth are still expected for the next assignment with due dates, and so forth.

3. Establishing a course policy to guide feedback and queries on assignments. The policy must allow students to spend time reviewing feedback and generating constructive evaluation rather than knee-jerk reactions to a grade. It also values the time that you, the instructor, have taken to give assignment feedback and allows the instructor time to plan for student responses and have scheduled time to respond.

Instructors also need to be flexible as the course progresses. They may need to adjust activities and assignment based on technological difficulties. For example, a due date for a discussion post may need modification due to institution-wide power outages. Also, unanticipated challenges can arise throughout the delivery of a new online course related to LMS issues such as program software updates and changes to third-party digital tools that support the LMS. By being on top of the course, the instructor facilitates a culture of importance, sends a message of respect ("I respect your time and effort"), and creates positive and professional expectations for student behavior. Breakout Box 5.4 offers a case study about Kadim and an example of how creating a class culture might look over time, emphasizing the importance of flexibility.

BREAKOUT BOX 5.4. CASE STUDY
KADIM CREATES HIS FIRST ONLINE COURSE

Kadim is creating an online section of a practice class he has been teaching for several years. In his seated class, he divided each class into a lecture, an exercise (discussion, video, etc.), and then a role-play to demonstrate the concept. He decides to replicate this online. He records 14 lectures for 14 weeks and then creates a discussion board space for each lecture with the expectation that students will engage around the material he presented. Every other week he holds a voluntary synchronous video chat where students can role-play the skills of the previous two weeks. Kadim is very excited about this model and helping students learn the skills. For the first 2 weeks, students post one or two comments in the discussion board and most students attend the first chat. After that, attendance and interaction fall off.

Instead of becoming disenchanted with online teaching, Kadim asks his students what he could do differently to increase discussion and involvement. They tell him they want to be engaged but feel there are disparities in the course (the same students comment/show up) and they receive no credit for it. Also, the assignments are not tied to the discussions, so they prioritize their time on the assignments. Finally, they want to hear from him more.

Kadim is appreciative of their input and makes some minor changes to the current course so he takes a more active role in the discussion board by outlining specific content that is associated

> with assignments. Also, he assigns each student a section of the reading to pull in their comments. Kadim posts an audio file in the course announcements each week to alert students to upcoming work, what he has been noticing about the class progress, and any tips for success. The biweekly video chats become a space for students to talk with each other about assignment ideas and a place to share resources. Kadim uses these first-time experiences to adjust the course going forward. He elicits feedback from some students about redesign and integrates best practices to increase engagement and skill development.

Instructor and Student Engagement With the Course

Although participation matters in all courses, participation will look different in online learning compared to the seated classroom, and online courses with elements of interaction enhance students' learning experiences (Meyer, 2014; Randolph & Krause, 2002; Zepke, 2014). Engaged students spend more time on learning, and experiential learning may promote higher levels of engagement for all students (Richardson & Newby, 2006; Umbach & Wawrzynski, 2005). Remember that the concept of scaffolding applies with engagement as well as learning content. Starting small and building the activities of engagement will help students' efficacy in an online course. For instance, if students are asked to share and defend personal opinions, scaffolded assignments might start with concrete and low-risk opinion sharing, such as a favorite book, and progress toward high-risk sharing, such as one's opinion about a controversial public policy, as students become more comfortable with the technology, instructor, and class members.

As with all learning components, the balance between enough and too much engagement requires attention. Also, it is crucial for social work educators to attend to students who appear disengaged with the material, classmates, and instructor, or are inappropriately engaged (Gilbert, Morton, & Rowley, 2007). Mirroring a seated classroom, the instructor can reach out with concern and guidance to assess and help the students make the best choices for themselves related to the online course. A check-in can occur via e-mail, a videoconference call, or direct messaging tools in the LMS. Noticing individual students allows an instructor to pave the way for professional relationship building and modeling of engagement skills. Throughout the semester, a social work educator has many opportunities to communicate with students, such as commenting on discussion board posts, engaging in individual conversations via e-mail, and mandating office hours. Breakout Box 5.5 offers best practices for increasing student engagement in an online course.

BREAKOUT BOX 5.5. PRACTICAL TIPS
BEST PRACTICES FOR ENGAGEMENT

1. Model engagement by being regularly and consistently present and by monitoring activities.
2. State expectations for student engagement clearly, in the beginning of the course (Hu & McCormick, 2012).
3. Create spaces for engagement through LMS tools or use of social media.
4. Reinforce engagement activities through graded and ungraded activities (Laird & Kuh, 2005).
5. Provide experiential learning activities, especially those that are student run, such as
   a. Immersion exercises
   b. Case studies
   c. Simulations
   d. Role plays
   e. Creating multimedia products
6. Offer learning activities that allow for choice and autonomy (Stefanou, Perencevich, DiCintio, & Turner, 2004).

Establishing policies and boundaries regarding instructor-student engagement complements the teaching persona. Additionally, these teaching practices reinforce expectations for an online course, which helps promote cognitive presence, or a student's ability to learn through reflection and discussion (Garrison & Arbaugh, 2007). Breakout Box 5.6 provides some guidelines for responding to students in online courses. Instructors should always share their guidelines as part of the course syllabus. The transparency of these guidelines is more important than the policy itself. Successful online instruction can include a 24/7 availability or weekly responses (with urgent responding when necessary). The key is that the instructors share their availability and the nature of preferred contact (i.e., e-mail, text messaging, or phone calls), and then adhere to their own policy throughout the course. A common practice is to create some sort of discussion forum either in the course or on a social media platform where students can publicly post general questions and instructors can post public answers, when appropriate. Often an additional discussion forum is created for technology-specific questions as well. Instructors should have a habit of daily monitoring of this virtual space. Many messaging platforms have automatic notification settings that can alert an instructor when a posting occurs. Social work educators may be tempted to make themselves available to student questions at all times of the day. This is a difficult pattern to sustain over time, and when the instructor cannot respond in the established time frame, students may interpret this as disinterest. To help build professional relationships with students in an online course, educators can personalize their interactions with students just as they might in a seated course. Breakout Box 5.7 offers tips on ways that instructors can engage students. Key to this practice is to ask students informal questions professionally and then remember (or record) their responses so you can integrate the knowledge into later student-instructor interactions.

BREAKOUT BOX 5.6. PRACTICAL TIPS
GUIDELINES FOR RESPONDING TO STUDENTS

- Fast acknowledgment of receipt of messages and of when a return will be expected
- One-day turnaround on questions
- Feedback on assignments within 1–2 weeks and before next assignment is due
- Alerts to technology or content problems in the course
- Willingness to adapt the course based on student feedback

BREAKOUT BOX 5.7. PRACTICAL TIPS
WAYS TO "NOTICE ME"

- Learn about student by asking some personal information during one-on-one times, such as e-mails or video calls. Keep track of their lived experiences, such as where they live, placements, children, other careers, and major events.
- Integrate above knowledge when appropriate into e-mails or other communications. When students are struggling, ask them to volunteer or provide recommendations.
- Make a personal connection by asking about silly things, such as a favorite snack, places they travel, and so forth. This can be done via photos or memes.
- Share hyperlinks to resources based on student's interest.
- During weekly course announcements, give a shout out when someone is recognized in the news, school award, and so forth.

Promoting formal and informal interactions can be challenging in an online course. The nature of online interaction and the time between the interactions can enhance or hinder the connection between the instructor and student. In social work education, we are particularly attuned to communication and often strive to model appropriate professional interactions with our students that mirror real-life practice. Instructor-student interaction establishes a beginning benchmark for appropriate exchanges that will occur in future practice with clients. The instructor's teaching presence can be both formally and informally professional. Through formal interaction, such as synchronous communication or learning activities, the instructor can model skills, techniques, and strategies of professional social work practice. Through less formal interaction, such as a closed Facebook group or a professional Web page, the instructor can share personal interests and aspects. In addition, components of the course can offer and require student-instructor interaction. Examples include virtual office hours where the instructor is available via a videoconferencing platform, phone, or text-messaging tool. Learning elements within an online course can also be added to increase this level of engagement. One example is the coaching format adopted from Fiske and Burns (2010), where students are required to meet with the instructor at least once per semester, either virtually or by phone, to discuss their progress in the course and to outline next steps. See Breakout Box 5.8 for a practice tips on coaching instructor-student engagement. An example of how this coaching session might look is provided in Breakout Box 5.9, as Kadim continues working on his online course.

BREAKOUT BOX 5.8 PRACTICAL TIPS
COACHING INSTRUCTOR-STUDENT ENGAGEMENT

1. What is your best hope for our conversation?
2. Suppose that your best hope is realized in this course. What will be different for you? What will the instructor notice is different?
3. On a scale of 1 to 10, where 10 is that your best hope is realized and 1 is the opposite, where are you now? What tells you that you are at, say, a 4? What else? How do you know you are not a 3? What is the first thing you will notice as you move up the scale?
4. What are you doing that is on track? What else?
5. What is your next step?
6. Compliment the student.

Source: Fiske & Burns, 2010

BREAKOUT BOX 5.9. CASE STUDY
KADIM APPLIES THE COACHING GUIDE

Instructor: What is your best hope for our conversation?

Student: My best hope is for you to tell me how to get an A on this assignment.

Instructor: Well, I want to be helpful to you. Suppose I could tell you; what would be different for you?

Student: I wouldn't feel so lost about this paper.

Instructor: What would you feel instead?

Student: I would feel like I knew what I was doing.

Instructor: So, you want to feel like you know where to go with this.

Student: Yes.

Instructor: When you feel like you know where you are going, what will I notice different about your work?

Student: You'll notice all the work I put into this.

Instructor: What else will I notice?

Student: Well, you have told me to be more clear and concise, so I suppose you would notice this.

Instructor: So, being more clear and concise is something you are aiming for?

Student: Yes, I have the ideas in my head, but I can't get them out the way I want. Then I try and add literature and it doesn't flow well.

Instructor: Is there anything else I would notice?

Student: Yeah, I would spell out contractions, use APA format, and proof.

Instructor: Wow, you have a lot of thoughts about this ... On a scale of 1 to 10, where 10 is that you feel pretty sure you can do these things (list them) and 1 is the opposite of this, where are you?

Student: I am a 4.

Instructor: Really? You are almost halfway. What tells you are at a 4?

Student: I know what I have to do.

Instructor: What else?

Student: I am pretty sure I can do it. I wish I had more time.

Instructor: I am curious, what tells you are not a 3?

Student: Good question ... I have started thinking about it and I have talked to others.

Instructor: What else?

Student: My field educator gave me some ideas and I know I can use the tutor.

Instructor: You really are on top of things. What do you think you can do to move up just a little on the scale, maybe a 4.5?

Student: You could tell me what to do ...

Instructor: Smiles/laughs ... (waits)

Student: Really, talking about this is helpful. I think I should go back and reread the comments on my other papers.

> Instructor: How will that be helpful?
>
> Student: It will get my brain on track.
>
> Instructor: And when your brain is on track, what will you be doing that you are not doing now?
>
> Student: I will make an outline that has my ideas, the literature that goes along with it, and draw lines that connect ideas.
>
> Instructor: You seem sure that this will help.
>
> Student: Yes, it has helped me in the past.
>
> Instructor: You mentioned that you are doing . . . (lists things). What else are you doing to be on track with getting an A?
>
> Student: I thought about asking my roommate to read my paper out loud to me.
>
> Instructor: You have a number of ideas and next steps. Where will you start?
>
> Student: Knowing me, I will start with writing down my ideas and then I will check them out with you.
>
> Instructor: I am impressed with how important this is to you and how you seriously you take feedback on assignments.

Student-student interaction is another critical element of online learning. Like the seated classroom, these interactions can be built into assignments, such as dividing students into groups for activities, using collaborative tools such as wikis or Google Docs for completing assignments and creating a private social media group outside of the LMS. More informal opportunities include self-introductions on discussion board or posting video selfies throughout the course. To promote student-student engagement activities, we recommend balancing the type of design of the activities with delivery factors. Figure 5.1 shows how the design and delivery go together to promote student-to-student engagement in a course.

ONLINE CLASSROOMS

Figure 5.1. The Balance of Enhancing Student-Student Connection in Online Learning

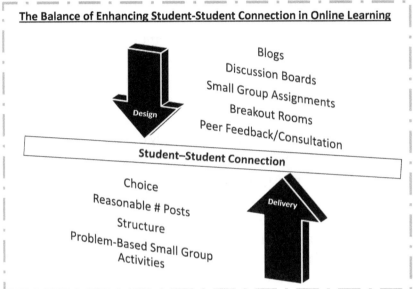

(Note. This work is licensed under the Creative Commons Attribution 3.0 Unported License. To view a copy of this license, visit http://creativecommons.org/licenses/by/3.0/ - Denise Krause 2016.)

The first key delivery factor for student-student interaction is choice. When students are required to engage with their classmates via asynchronous assignments (e.g., blogs, discussion boards, and wikis), they want to choose how and who they reply to, and what they comment on to make the class relevant to their own interests. For example, students who are asked to create blog posts based on their skill development can also be asked to comment on their classmates' entries based on criteria such as responding to at least two other classmates of their choice or responding to a classmate's post that looks very similar or very different from their own post.

The second element that encourages student-student interaction is requiring a reasonable number of posts (i.e., comments, replies, or entries) in the online environment. "Reasonable" is somewhat contingent on the assignment, but guidelines could include establishing a timeframe for posts and comments that allow replies to last-minute entries. Thus, it might make sense to require a student who is starting a threaded discussion to begin the discussion by a certain date, and then require that the same student post comments by a later date. Other examples include assigning only a small number of discussion entries (i.e., only one entry) when depth or detail is required in a reply/comment; encouraging students to respectfully engage with the person whose post they are replying to, even when they disagree; and using language that specifies expectations of the post, such as "you must respond to at least two classmates before the due date." Along with the number of posts, an instructor should provide information on the quality of students' posts. Examples might include noting that their comments will be graded based on appropriateness, timing, professionalism, and depth.

Structure is another element that can promote student-to-student connection. Providing structure to any assigned activity moves students from anxiety to focus. Although a lack of structure may be part of the task (i.e., demonstrating small-group process principles), most often this is not the case for online environments and detracts from the learning. In synchronous and asynchronous interactions, written instructions are helpful even when you have given verbal directions. Time frames for the various components of a learning activity are also helpful, and if students are assigned to take on roles as part of a case study, an explanation of those roles is useful. To illustrate, the instructor may want a small group to work together to practice a specific skill—one student is the social worker, another student is the client, and another student is an observer. Each student receives separate instructions for his or her specific role. For example, if the observer is expected to take notes and report on the interaction, that person receives written instructions about how to perform the role. Several online tools can be used to facilitate this type of activity, such as a synchronous videoconferencing software, which allows for smaller breakout rooms, a live chat tool, or asking students to schedule themselves to interact with each other synchronously outside of class time.

An additional delivery practice that instructors can use to promote student-to-student interaction is problem-based, small-group activities. Requiring this type of student-to-student interaction must have a purpose that is evident to the students, especially at the beginning of a course. For example, this can be done by adding a reflection component to the small-group discussion or by asking students to report back to the entire class. Another way to do this is to provide an explicit goal for the small-group activity. An instructor might want students to experiment with different ways to begin a discussion on race. By explaining to students that this is the goal, not only will students be more prepared for the activity, they also are more likely to investigate the best ways to do this. After their small-group discussions, the instructor may process not only the ways they began the discussion along with the content but also the group processes that occurred in the small-group discussion.

Case presentations or consultations are other types of problem-based activities frequently used in social work practice courses. In addition to the feedback process at the core of these learning activities, students can connect on the use of practice skills, a vulnerable area of practice. After years of experimenting with several case presentation models, one of us (Denise) has landed on a model that includes a structure for the process, a way for students to develop useful practice skills, and space for the emotional safety for the presenter and group. Students appreciate the guidelines as well as the reinforcement of techniques they are learning about, and an opportunity to connect with their peers that is both safe and productive. See Breakout Box 5.10 for these guidelines, which are appropriate for both online and seated classes.

> **BREAKOUT BOX 5.10. PRACTICAL TIPS**
> 30-MINUTE CASE PRESENTATION
> GUIDELINES FOR STUDENTS
> - Presenter sends group members brief target system description that includes (a) desired outcome for the presentation, (b) brief description of the target system with only generic identifying information, (c) description of ecological systems and "fit," (d) target system strengths, (e) the nature of your contact(s) with the target system, (f) your role(s) with the target system, and (g) your thoughts about the struggle.
> - Facilitator and presenter touch base prior to group meeting.
> - Facilitator leads the group using the Solution Focused Case Consultation Guide (Fiske & Burns, 2010).
> - Group compliments the presenter.
> - Facilitator debriefs the group.

Feedback

Providing feedback in any learning environment can facilitate task engagement and encourage metacognitive monitoring processes (Ferrara & Butcher, 2012). Feedback in online courses is an essential component of successful experience for the students as well as the instructor. As in seated classrooms, online feedback can be individualized for one student or target the entire class. General principles about feedback to keep in mind are timeliness, clarity, and depth (Cicco, 2011; Stein, Wanstreet, Slagle, Trinko, & Lutz, 2013). Offer feedback on one assignment before the next assignment is due so that students can improve their work and seek help if necessary. Scaffolding in this way also supports learning that is gradual and builds on previous course content. It is also helpful to capture themes of student work from online discussion forums or assignments and share those back to the whole class. For asynchronous feedback, an instructor can also record a brief audio or video file or write a discussion post with examples that help give specificity and reinforce the instructor's presence. Synchronous mechanisms for feedback in an online course include direct messaging chats, videoconferencing calls, and phone meetings. Private messaging features in an LMS allow instructors to give in vivo feedback and support. Other examples of feedback include nongraded quizzes used for formative assessments, sample answers, and draft reviews. Instituting multiple ways to deliver feedback will ensure students can self-assess and make decisions related to their own learning course. Breakout Box 5.11 provides a list of different ways that educators can provide feedback in an online course.

BREAKOUT BOX 5.11. PRACTICAL TIPS
GIVING FEEDBACK USING MULTIPLE METHODS
- Use different methods for feedback:
  - Written comments using track changes in a Word document
  - Audio recordings of grading comments
  - Direct annotations of a student video using VideoAnt
- Track themes for individuals and the class as a whole and give feedback.
- Always balance positive with critical.
- Send out tips for the entire class.
- Track comments and refer to previous comments.

Giving and receiving feedback appropriately marks a crucial professional social work competency. For this reason, instructors must build opportunities into the course for students to give peer feedback, give examples of what useful feedback looks like, and monitor and give feedback on the students' use of feedback. Although it is not best practice for instructors to delete posts due to unpopular opinions or poor writing, sometimes this kind of intervention is warranted. For instance, a student may post a practice video about working with someone of a different culture and might have "played" the client in a very stereotypic way that is insulting and offensive. The instructor has a "teachable moment" for the individual student and the whole class. The instructor could ask the student to delete the video and request that the student record another video. Other options include asking that students submit all videos to the instructor before posting, or the instructor could have a conversation with the student privately.

Finally, an instructor may want to incorporate offline tools to help track feedback and other online facilitation. You can create a spreadsheet or table in a Word document to track feedback provided to individual students and reflect on progress over time. Another option is to use a checklist for online facilitation to help you track your own participation in a course, such as your teaching and social presence in the course (Bart, 2010).

FINAL THOUGHTS

Just like teaching in the seated classroom, all social work educators must develop and apply their teaching philosophy, practical applications of pedagogy, and teaching persona. Development of these approaches takes time, practice, and patience. When using the design/delivery framework to create an online course, we recommend instructors allot enough time to plan their design. As previously noted, to convert a seated course to online, the ideal is to begin at least one full semester before the online class launches. Allow for three times the number of hours to prepare for a seated delivery for all learning components (at least until you have a lot of experience as an online educator). Similarly, when developing a new course in an online format, begin at least 1 year before delivery when possible. Finally, develop a support or resource network for yourself by attending training about online education, create a professional learning network of online educational experts (see Chapter 9), and use on-campus resources.

FURTHER READING AND RESOURCES

Educause. http://www.educause.edu/ (a nonprofit association with the mission to advance higher education through information technology).

European Distance and E-learning Network (EDEN). http://www.eden-online.org/ (a not-for-profit international organization focused on open and distance education).

Krause, D., Hitchcock, L. I., Sage, M., & Smyth, N. J. (2018, March 8). Course mapping for online social work courses [Blog Post]. Retrieved from https://www.laureliversonhitchcock.org/2018/03/08/course-mapping-for-online-social-work-courses/

Online Learning Consortium. http://onlinelearningconsortium.org/ (a nonprofit professional online learning society).

Open SUNY Course Quality Review (OSCQR). http://oscqr.org/ (a free and open-sourced quality-review rubric for online courses).

Quality Matters. https://www.qualitymatters.org/ (an international organization that promotes quality assurance in online education).

Social Work Distance Education Conference. http://swde.iu.edu/ (established in 2015 by the University of Indiana and CSWE, the conference is now sponsored by Our Lady of the Lake University: http://www.ollusa.edu/s/1190/hybrid/18/wide-hybrid-ollu.aspx?sid=1190&gid=1&pgid=8191)

Zgoda, K. (2018, February 20). *Social work educator tips: Guidelines for online discussion*. http://www.laureliversonhitchcock.org/2018/02/20/social-work-educator-tips-guidelines-for-online-discussion-forums/

REFERENCES

Albion. (n.d.). Netiquette [Home page]. Retrieved from http://www.albion.com/netiquette/

Allen, I. E., & Seaman, J. (2013). *Grade change: Tracking online education in the United States*. Oakland, CA: Babson Survey Research Group. Retrieved from http://www.onlinelearningsurvey.com/reports/gradechange.pdf

Anderson, L. W., & Krathwohl, D. R. (2001). *A taxonomy for learning, teaching, and assessing: A revision of Bloom's taxonomy of educational objectives*. New York, NY: Longman.

Bart, M. (2010, February 8). *A checklist for facilitating online courses* [Blog post]. Retrieved from https://www.facultyfocus.com/articles/distance-learning/a-checklist-for-facilitating-online-courses/

Cennamo, K. S., Ross, J., & Rogers, C. (2002). *Evolution of a Web-enhanced course incorporating strategies for self-regulation*. Retrieved from http://er.educause.edu/articles/2002/1/evolution-of-a-webenhanced-course-incorporating-strategies-for-selfregulation

Chatfield, K. (2012, January 25). Content "loading" in hybrid/blended learning. Retrieved from https://secure.onlinelearningconsortium.org/node/1787

Cicco, G. (2011). Assessment in online courses: How are counselling skills evaluated? *Journal of Educational Technology, 8*(2), 9–15.

Clinical Social Work Association (CSWA). (2013, September). *Report on online MSW programs*. Retrieved from http://www.clinicalsocialworkassociation.org/Resources/Documents/CSWA%20-%20Position%20Paper%20-%20Online%20MSW%20Programs%20-%20September2013.pdf

Council on Social Work Education (CSWE). (2015). *Educational policy and accreditation standards for baccalaureate and master's social work programs*. Alexandria, VA: Author. Retrieved from https://www.cswe.org/Accreditation/Standards-and-Policies/2015-EPAS

Cummings, S. M., Foels, L., & Chaffin, K. M. (2013). Comparative analysis of distance education and classroom-based formats for a clinical social work practice course. *Social Work Education, 32*(1), 68–80. doi:10.1080/02615479.2011.648179

Duncan-Daston, R., Hunter-Sloan, M., & Fullmer, E. (2013). Considering the ethical implications of social media in social work education. *Ethics and Information Technology, 15*(1), 35–43. doi:10.1007/s10676-013-9312-7

Educause. (2012). *7 things you should know about flipped classrooms*. Retrieved from https://library.educause.edu/resources/2012/2/7-things-you-should-know-about-flipped-classrooms

Elliott, W., Choi, E., & Friedline, T. (2013). Online statistics labs in MSW research methods courses: Reducing reluctance toward statistics. *Journal of Social Work Education, 49*, 81–95. http://doi.org/10.1080/10437797.2013.755095

Ferrara, L. A., & Butcher, K. R. (2012). Exploring students' perceived needs and ideas about feedback in online learning environments: Implications for digital design. *International Journal of Cyber Behavior, Psychology, and Learning, 2*(2), 48–70.

Ferrera, M., Ostrander, N., & Crabtree-Nelson, S. (2013). Establishing a community of inquiry through hybrid courses in clinical social work education. *Journal of Teaching in Social Work, 33*(4–5), 438–448. doi:10.1080/08841233.2013.835765

Fiske, H., & Burns, K. (2010). The 10-minute solution focused interview. In T. Nelson (Ed.), *Doing something different: Solution-focused brief therapy practices* (pp. 145–147). London, UK: Routledge.

Florida State University. (n.d.). *Overview of the College of Social Work*. Retrieved from http://csw.fsu.edu/about-csw/overview/

Forgey, M. A., & Ortega-Williams, A. (2016). Effectively teaching social work practice online: Moving beyond can to how. *Advances in Social Work, 17*(1), 59–77.

Garrison, D. R., & Arbaugh, J. B. (2007). Researching the community of inquiry framework: Review, issues, and future directions. *Internet and Higher Education, 10*(3), 157–172.

Gates, T., & Walters, A. (2015). Are MOOCs the next trend in social work? Implications for practice education. *Advances in Social Work, 16*(1), 184–201.

Gilbert, J., Morton, S., & Rowley, J. (2007). E-learning: The student experience. *British Journal of Educational Technology, 38*, 560–573.

Hu, S., & McCormick, A. C. (2012). An engagement-based student typology and its relationship to college outcomes. *Research in Higher Education, 53*, 738–754.

Knowles, M., Holton, E., III, & Swanson, R. (2015). *The adult learner: The definitive classic in adult education and human resource development* (8th ed.). New York, NY: Routledge.

Kuh, G. D. (2009). The national survey of student engagement: Conceptual and empirical foundations. In R. M. Gonyea & G. D. Kuh (Eds.), *New directions for institutional research: No. 141, Using NSSE in institutional research* (pp. 5–10). San Francisco: Jossey-Bass.

Kuo, Y. C., Walker, A. E., Belland, B. R., & Schroder, K. E. (2013). A predictive study of student satisfaction in online education programs. *The International Review of Research in Open and Distributed Learning, 14*(1), 16-39.

Laird, T. F., & Kuh, G. D. (2005). Student experiences with information technology and their relationship to other aspects of student engagement. *Research in Higher Education, 46*(2), 211–233.

Mayadas, F., Miller, G., & Sener, J. (2015, July 7). *E-learning definitions*. Retrieved from http://onlinelearningconsortium.org/updated-e-learning-definitions-2/

Mayer, R. E., Heiser, J., & Lonn, S. (2001). Cognitive constraints on multimedia learning: When presenting more material results in less understanding. *Journal of Educational Psychology, 93*(1), 187–198.

Meyer, K. A. (2014). Student engagement in online learning: What works and why. *ASHE Higher Education Report, 40*(6), 1–114.

Miller, M. D. (2014). *Minds online: Teaching effectively with technology*. Cambridge, MA: Harvard University Press.

National Association of Social Workers (NASW). (2017). *Code of ethics of the National Association of Social Workers*. Washington, DC: NASW Press. Retrieved from https://www.socialworkers.org/About/Ethics/Code-of-Ethics/Code-of-Ethics-English

New York State Education Department. (2016). Determining time on task in online education. Retrieved from http://www.highered.nysed.gov/ocue/ded/policies.html

Noble, D., & Russell, A. C. (2013). Research on webbed connectivity in a Web-based learning environment: Online social work education. *Journal of Teaching in Social Work, 33*(4–5), 496–513. doi:10.1080/08841233.2013.829167

Phelan, J. E. (2015). The use of e-learning in social work education. *Social Work, 60*(3), 257–264. doi:10.1093/sw/swv010

Powell, K., Ice, P., Helm, J. S., & Layne, M. (2013). *APUS online learning contact hour calculator: An adaptive model for calculating contact hours.* Retrieved from https://secure.onlinelearningconsortium.org/effective_practices/apus-online-learning-contact-hour-calculator-adaptive-model-calculating-contact-

Puentedura, R. (2013a). *SAMR: A contextualized introduction.* Retrieved from http://hippasus.com/rrpweblog/archives/2014/01/15/SAMRABriefContextualizedIntroduction.pdf

Puentedura, R. (2013b). *The SAMR ladder: Questions and transitions.* Retrieved from http://www.hippasus.com/rrpweblog/archives/2013/10/26/SAMRLadder_Questions.pdf

Randolph, K. A., & Krause, D. J. (2002). Mutual aid in the classroom: An instructional technology application. *Journal of Social Work Education, 38*, 259–271.

Rani, M., Nayak, R., & Vyas, O. P. (2015). An ontology-based adaptive personalized e-learning system, assisted by software agents on cloud storage. *Knowledge-Based Systems, 90*(Supplement C), 33–48. doi:10.1016/j.knosys.2015.10.002

Reamer, F. G. (2013). Distance and online social work education: Novel ethical challenges. *Journal of Teaching in Social Work, 33*(4–5), 369–384. http://doi.org/10.1080/08841233.2013.828669

Richardson, J. C., & Newby, T. (2006). The role of students' cognitive engagement in online learning. *American Journal of Distance Education, 20*(1), 23–37.

Richardson, J. C., & Swan, K. (2003). Examining social presence in online courses in relation to students' perceived learning and satisfaction. *Journal of Asynchronous Learning Network, 7*(1), 68–88.

Russell, T. L. (2001). *The no significant difference phenomenon* (5th ed.). Chicago, IL: International Distance Education Certification Center. Retrieved from http://www.nosignificantdifference.org/

Sage, M., & Sele, P. (2015). Reflective journaling as a flipped classroom technique to increase reading and participation with social work students. *Journal of Social Work Education, 51*, 668–681.

Sheridan, J., & Kelly, M. A. (2010). The indicators of instructor presence that are important to students in online courses. *MERLOT Journal of Online Learning and Teaching, 6*(4), 767–779.

Siebert, D. C., Siebert, C. F., & Spaulding-Givens, J. (2006). Teaching clinical social work skills primarily online: An evaluation. *Journal of Social Work Education, 42*, 325–336.

Stefanou, C. R., Perencevich, K. C., DiCintio, M., & Turner, J. C. (2004). Supporting autonomy in the classroom: Ways teachers encourage student decision making and ownership. *Educational Psychologist, 39*(2), 97–110.

Stein, D. S., Wanstreet, C. E., Slagle, P., Trinko, L. A., & Lutz, M. (2013). From "hello" to higher-order thinking: The effects of coaching and feedback on online chats. *Internet and Higher Education, 16*, 78–84.

Straumsheim, C. (2014). *Data, data everywhere*. Retrieved from https://www.insidehighered.com/news/2014/06/10/after-grappling-data-mooc-research-initiative-participants-release-results

Tandy, C., Vernon, R., & Lynch, D. (2016). Teaching student interviewing competencies through second life. *Journal of Social Work Education, 52*, 1–6. doi:10.1080/10437797.2016.1198292

Tetloff, M., Hitchcock, L., Battista, A., & Lowry, D. (2014). Multimodal composition and social justice: Videos as a tool of advocacy in social work pedagogy. *Journal of Technology in Human Services, 32*(1–2), 22–38. doi:10.1080/15228835.2013.857284

Umbach, P. D., & Wawrzynski, M. R. (2005). Faculty do matter: The role of college faculty in student learning and engagement. *Research in Higher Education, 46*(2), 153–184.

University of North Dakota. (n.d.). *Fact about the UND Social Work Department*. Retrieved from http://www.nursing.und.edu/departments/social-work/facts.cfm

U.S. Department of Education, Office of Planning, Evaluation, and Policy Development. (2010). *Evaluation of evidence-based practices in online learning: A meta-analysis and review of online learning studies*. Washington, DC: Author.

Vernon, R., Vakalahi, H., Pierce, D., Pittman-Munke, P., & Adkins, L. F. (2009). Distance education programs in social work: Current and emerging trends. *Journal of Social Work Education, 45*, 263–276. doi:10.5175/JSWE.2009.200700081

Wilke, D. J., King, E., Ashmore, M., & Stanley, C. (2016). Can clinical skills be taught online? Comparing skill development between online and F2F students using a blinded review. *Journal of Social Work Education, 52*, 484–492.

Wingard, R. G. (2004). Classroom teaching changes in Web-enhanced courses: A multi-institutional study. Retrieved from http://er.educause.edu/articles/2004/1/classroom-teaching-changes-in-webenhanced-courses-a-multiinstitutional-study

Young, J. (2014). iPolicy: Exploring and evaluating the use of iPads in a social welfare policy course. *Journal of Technology in Human Services, 32*(1–2), 39–53. http://doi.org/10.1080/15228835.2013.860366

Zepke, N. (2014). Student engagement research in higher education: Questioning an academic orthodoxy. *Teaching in Higher Education, 19*(6), 697–708.

Zhang, H., Lin, L., Zhan, Y., & Ren, Y. (2016). The impact of teaching presence on online engagement behaviors. *Journal of Educational Computing Research, 54*, 887–900.

CHAPTER 6

ONLINE PROGRAMS

This chapter addresses the following questions:

- Why do we want to go online?
- What is our capacity for online or distance delivery?
- Who are our students?
- How will we get online?
- Who are our teachers?
- On who's turf?
- What program funding model will we use?
- How do we support the implicit curriculum in distance education?
- Do we need campus visits?

In this chapter we turn the focus from how to incorporate technology in the curriculum to the possible approaches for taking a social work degree entirely *online*. We start at the beginning, by helping the reader consider the reasons for starting online programming and offering a list of early considerations to help assess readiness. First, we discuss the methods through which degree programs can develop fully online programs: (a) organic (faculty members converting over time, adjuncts converting over time); (b) launching designated online cohorts; or (c) insourcing (hiring faculty members to teach online) and outsourcing (hiring an outside firm to put your program online), and give examples of varying degrees of faculty autonomy in developing and teaching online courses. We present typologies that range from fully asynchronous courses with no campus meetings to fully synchronous programs with campus meetings, all of which can be offered at the bachelor's, master's, or doctoral degree levels. The chapter includes the benefits and challenges of each method of online programming, enhanced by case studies that explore the firsthand accounts and experiences of social work program administrators, from deans and directors to educators, whom we interviewed about their programming. They share stories ranging from software considerations to instructor preparation. Please remember that administrative practices of a specific school change quickly, and the specific scenarios and roles of interviewees discussed in these chapters may have changed by the time you read them. Those who provided information are acknowledged at the end of this chapter.

Beyond the leap into an online programming format, programs should consider campus-wide issues before launching any type of fully online programming. These considerations include the ways in which online programming makes education more, or less, accessible to different populations of students, gatekeeping concerns, and implicit curriculum issues. Throughout this chapter, we will ask questions to help prompt your thinking about these questions and about the development of online social work programs.

This chapter offers a beginning conversation about implicit curriculum in online programs. Some gatekeeping concerns are touched on in this chapter but explored more in more depth in Chapter 7. We also include an assessment checklist in Appendix 5 called Social Work Distance Education Assessment of Readiness (SW-DEAR), which programs can use to assess readiness to launch an online program or identify where they may have opportunities to strengthen current online programming. Other issues, such as the Americans With Disabilities Act (ADA) and Family Educational Rights and Privacy Act (FERPA) also affect program design. We save these issues for Chapter 8.

WHY DO WE WANT TO GO ONLINE?

This first reflective question is perhaps the most important one and the hardest to answer: what drives your program administrators to take their full curriculum online? Social work educational programs move to online education for many reasons. Sometimes the pressure is internal: students or faculty believe online programming will meet a need. Perhaps your program is in a very rural community where students travel a great distance for education, and online learning is more practical and fits your school's mission to serve a broad geographic region. On the other hand, maybe you are a large urban school that serves many kinds of students and working students would appreciate the flexibility of online programming, and your faculty is willing to help make the leap to meet market demands.

Conversely, the pressure may be external: your university administration may see online education as an opportunity to increase revenue and enrollment, or your whole university could be moving to expand online offerings. Maybe you are dubious. Maybe your institution does not clearly understand the accreditation issues related to teacher-to-student ratio and assumes you can launch larger classes online, failing to account for the fact that online programs often take more infrastructure and labor than campus-based classes. If this is the case, this chapter may help you educate administrators about the challenges and risks associated with online social work degrees. We attempt to clarify the many decisions and resources that it takes to mount a high-quality online program. Regardless of your goals, we hope you come away from this chapter equipped with knowledge about the choices involved in going online and are inspired to guide your social work program toward decisions that are the best fit for your context.

WHAT IS OUR CAPACITY FOR ONLINE OR DISTANCE DELIVERY?

With this question, we ask you to consider infrastructure and institutional supports available for an online program at your university and within your academic unit. Some social work programs have a strong tradition of online or hybrid education going back many years, and for this reason, they can move to fully online programs more efficiently than a program that is newer to online education. Examples from our interviews include the University at Buffalo (UB), Indiana University (IU), and the University of North Dakota (UND), three different public universities that moved to online master's of social work (MSW) programs using their own resources based on their history of teaching some technology-mediated classes. On the other hand, Arizona State University (ASU) had a robust university infrastructure supporting online education, ASU Online, and was able to use those resources, in addition to the resources in the school, to design, implement, and scale up their new MSW program rapidly.

Programs with less infrastructure and experience can develop their own online programs by using university resources, or by identifying financial resources to build their own infrastructure at the school or department level. When there are fewer supports available at the start, this process will take longer as the program needs time to locate resources, to develop its online curriculum, and to educate the faculty and the staff. Institutional supports needed for online educational programs include

- university services (enrollment, library, tutoring, testing, etc.) available via distance,
- Institutional support for the program's move to online education,
- a distance education committee to develop and carry out institutional policies and practices,
- tech support and training for the faculty and students,
- clear online/distance tuition model, and
- fees to support infrastructure or travel.

Departmental supports needed for online educational programs include

- a clear mission that helps define online student target audience;
- a distance coordinator to provide faculty and student support;
- access to equipment, software, and faculty training;
- an advising structure that supports distance students;
- opportunities for students to participate in social work clubs and culture;
- broad support among faculty members for offering online courses, learning best practices, and engaging in online teaching;
- support for staff members who are knowledgeable about the program and can answer questions;
- a deployment model that acknowledges the extra work to launch and maintain online courses;
- field placement policies, practices, and supervision for distance students; and
- gatekeeping policies that allow identification of students who are struggling online.

It is essential to know which resources are available institutionally, including tuition model expectations. Some institutions have well-developed models for distance tuition, which are often different from the on-campus tuition models. Tuition for distance education may include out-of-state fees, technology access fees, or clinical and field fees. Some institutions may limit the types of fees a department can charge, which will affect the design of the program, including the number of students and where those students are located. If tuition for distance students remains very low, for instance, it may be impossible to support the faculty to travel out of state to see students in a distance field placement, or to hire separate online field coordinators or liaisons. If tuition is too high, issues of access and social justice should be considered. See more about this topic in Chapter 8.

Schools launching a new fully online program must often create a proposal and route it through the university, outlining budgetary effects, competition with other state or local universities, and market analysis. A plan should include all the possible costs of educating social work students, including what it will cost to meet Council on Social Work Education's (CSWE) requirements related to field contracting and visits, costs of new technology and technology supports for faculty and students, course release for faculty to prepare for online teaching, travel costs, additional field staff to manage distance placements (including developing new agreements and relationships), and other specialized costs related to the program you envision. You should not assume that distance programs are less costly to administer than campus-based programs, a mistake that administrators often make. To help establish fiscally related needs, it is helpful to conduct a comparison of tuition with other similarly situated distance social work programs, and to bring in stakeholders from your region, such as potential students, community agency leaders, and those who have experience in distance program development, to help you consider the actual expenses and needs of a quality online program.

WHO ARE OUR STUDENTS?

In the broad market of distance social work education, it is essential to know what differentiates you from other programs; a useful place to start is to consider which students you hope to serve. In many areas of the country, regional students make up the target population. Some students appreciate earning their degrees from a local university because if they plan to work in the local community, future employers are likely to know the name and reputation of their alma mater. If that is the case, where will the regional geographic boundaries for the online program be drawn, and will any exceptions be made (i.e., will you admit students from outside your state if you live close to the state border)? This critical choice may direct whether or how often you expect students to come to campus, and where and how often you will need to form new relationships with field agencies. For instance, in a regional program, after a few years, you may develop good relationships with field sites statewide and recontract with them regularly for student placements. But if you are placing students nationally, the field office is much more likely to have to periodically negotiate with new placement sites, which is more time consuming. This is discussed further in Chapter 7. If you decide on a national audience, there are more considerations. For instance,

- Who is your target market? Is there an institutional mandate to serve specific student populations?
- Does your institution have permission to operate in a potential student's state? (See information on National Council for State Authorization Reciprocity Agreements [NC-SARA] information later in this chapter.)
- How will you differentiate yourself from other national distance programs?

- Will your online program have a different concentration and approach (and thereby necessitate a separate CSWE accreditation review) than your campus program?
- For undergraduate students, will they have access to other prerequisites of your institution's degree program? Who will negotiate transfer issues?
- How will you handle gatekeeping issues or other concerns over a long distance?
- How will students access support services (library, disability services, etc.)?

In a local market that is likely to attract regional students, social work programs may be able to give less attention to marketing. This is a different story when students are choosing between national online programs. Schools should make sure their listings are up to date in CSWE's list of accredited online programs and work with their institution's extended education office, or other university offices that help with marketing online degree programs. Often these offices send personnel to recruiting events across the country. By establishing a relationship with these recruiters, you can equip them with the information they need to understand and promote your program to a national audience. They will likely encourage you to think about what sets your program apart. For instance, UND calls itself a small high-touch program. UND operationalizes this approach in the following ways: (a) all students are taught by a core campus-based faculty via synchronous education; (b) students get to choose their own advisors; (c) students stay in the same cohort of about 30 students over 2 to 3 years; and (d) all students have a face-to-face visit (either in-person or technology mediated) with a faculty member whenever they enter field placement, no matter where they live. This is a good match for the student who wants an online program that is as much like an on-the-ground program as possible. In contrast, the University of Southern California (USC) differentiates itself as a much larger program and can offer students a high degree of choice by scheduling many classes across the day and evenings, allowing students to customize their schedules, which is perfect for students who need flexible scheduling. Their broad alumni network helps connect graduates who have attended USC.

Some programs incorporate a topical focus for their online programs. For instance, UB offers a trauma-informed and human rights focus, and Humboldt State University provides an indigenous-focused curriculum based on concepts of decolonization. Both schools offer some blend of asynchronous and synchronous online learning. In contrast, IU designed their degree to meet the needs of working adults who were juggling work and parenting (or other caregiving responsibilities) and created an advanced generalist curriculum with a primarily asynchronous structure. The topical focus at UND (also an advanced generalist program) integrates rural and tribal issues into their curriculum. To do this, they collaborate closely with rural county offices and tribal colleges for recruitment and needs assessment. These examples illustrate the degree to which the students you decide to serve may influence your methods of delivery, curriculum development, and other important decisions.

Consider how your program might stand out to students and what claims you will be able to make about what you do online, for whom, and how you do it. Following are some ways you can help inform students about how your online program works:

- clear orientation about how to access university resources via distance, including disability services, counseling, and tutoring;
- provide a self-assessment students can use to see whether they are a good match for online learning;
- clear assessment about whether the student is a good match for online learning;
- clear expectations before enrollment about the distance model used, including technology and presence requirements;

- opportunities to participate in departmental and extracurricular activities; and

- opportunities to engage in relationship building with peers and professors.

HOW WILL WE ACCOMMODATE STUDENTS WITH ACCESSIBILITY NEEDS?

Although accessibility and flexibility provided by distance education is a major strength that draws students to online learning, accessibility must also be considered as it relates to the online environment and the types of disabilities affecting students. For instance, students who have vision impairments often use screen readers or magnifiers to help translate written content, and screen readers may not be able to recognize text from certain types of digital documents. The ADA mandates that educational programs are accessible to students with disabilities, so social work educators should consider the accessibility of online materials, their relationships with their institution's disability services programs, and how to refer and connect students to help when it is needed from a distance. Disability service offices are gaining understanding of ways to assist both students and faculty members with online classes, but some of the traditional accommodations that have been used over the years in university settings may be more difficult to implement in online settings that rely on auxiliary department services, such as the use of sign language interpreters or one-to-one tutoring.

One of the easiest ways to accomplish the goal of accessible online education is by using *universal design for learning (UDL)* principles in all your curriculum development. Rather than taking the approach of trying to convert a curriculum for a specific student's needs, this approach improves accessibility for students with a range of needs, including students who do not have identified disabilities. However,

UDL training is a resource investment. Most faculty members do not have training in UDL, and they may need formal professional development or peer support to learn effective UDL strategies, such as using multimedia, assessing for understanding, formative feedback, and supporting student learning communities (Seok, DaCosta, & Hodges, 2018). See Breakout Box 6.1 for more information on UDL, and our further reading suggestions at the end of this chapter. Chapter 8 provides additional answers about accessibility mandates.

BREAKOUT BOX 6.1. PRACTICAL TIPS
UNIVERSAL DESIGN FOR LEARNING

Universal design for learning (UDL) is a framework for how to design material so it is accessible by people with different learning styles or needs. It originates from concepts of federally mandated universal design in architecture, which were created to support accessibility in buildings. When applied to online learning, UDL informs the ways in which materials are made available to learners. CAST (n.d.) offers some applied guidance that uses concepts from UDL:

- Include a welcoming access statement in all syllabi.
- Provide simple, consistent navigation.
- Choose tools carefully—make sure they accommodate.
- Model and teach good discussion board etiquette, including how to organize new topics.
- Use color with care—provide good contrast, and do not rely on color alone for meaning.
- Make sure text is readable: Ariel and Helvetica fonts are best.
- Provide accessible document formats. Word files and most PDF files are accessible.
- Describe graphics and visual elements—including charts and graphs.
- Caption videos and transcribe audio clips.
- Rethink and redesign PowerPoint presentations. Check the "outline" view to see that all text appears.

WHAT ARE SPECIAL CONSIDERATIONS FOR OFFERING AN UNDERGRADUATE SOCIAL WORK DEGREE ONLINE?

Although social work MSW and doctoral programs are typically self-contained and governed within schools or departments of social work, undergraduate programs offer additional complexities as students must be able to access the cross-campus curriculum, often known as general education courses or the core curriculum, including liberal arts courses such as English, math, and psychology. This is probably one reason there are still few completely online bachelor of social work (BSW) degrees. However, as more institutions begin bringing their core undergraduate coursework online, it becomes easier for students to access a completely online undergraduate degree. Schools that currently offer online BSW degrees typically provide their curriculum as a degree-completion online course of study, requiring students to transfer in a certain amount of credits related to the liberal arts curriculum, or to have already completed all the coursework that falls outside the social work curriculum. If students transfer in with significant coursework completed in other institutions, extra work is necessary to demonstrate course equivalency of transfer credits, and degree completion programs require extra advising time, articulation agreements, and identification of other potential barriers. University systems might limit the ability of students to bring in all their non-social-work transfer units, for instance, by mandating that students earn a certain number of credits at the host university or by not transferring courses in as general education equivalencies. It is valuable to know who makes these decisions in your university and engage in discussions before establishing an online degree. Programs that do have significant university offerings outside their discipline that can accommodate a full degree completion should determine which institutional units they will need to work with, and which administrative staff members will help with the extra work of answering questions, steering students toward the online offerings that best supplement social work courses, supporting students to understand transfer credits, developing articulation agreements with feeder schools, and the other efforts that it will take to launch this kind of program.

WHO ARE OUR TEACHERS?

This question focuses on the role of instructors in developing and implementing a fully online program. In small programs, the campus faculty is often expected to teach across distance and campus classes, and some may eagerly volunteer to teach online, but faculty members may also face the task with uncertainty or trepidation. As a program moves online, the faculty should have time for training to learn about online teaching resources and understand the reasons for moving the program coursework online. In some programs, it may be possible for some of the faculty to opt out of online teaching. It is increasingly evident from faculty recruitment ads that schools have learned to clarify their expectations about online teaching from the onset and are actively seeking faculty members who are willing to engage in online teaching, and who also understand the best practices related to teaching online. Online programs can set themselves apart by having faculty members who are skillful in online teaching and online student engagement. This will aid the reputation of your program. See Breakout Box 6.2 on dealing with reluctant faculties and Breakout Box 6.3 for tips on supporting faculties to teach online.

BREAKOUT BOX 6.2. THEORY TALK
ENGAGING RELUCTANT EDUCATORS TO TEACH ONLINE

Administrators who understand the reasons educators resist or adopt technology can then address those issues by providing information, resources, support, and recognition. The following reasons for resisting or adopting teaching online were summarized in a literature review of 67 empirical studies.

Reasons educators resist online teaching:
- Technical problems with hardware/software
- Not as optimistic about online education as administrators
- Not enough clarity about institutional goals related to technology
- Not enough institutional support for technology adoption
- Worry about assessment of their teaching skills (for promotion or evaluation)
- Technology seeming inappropriate for the task
- Concerns about issues of academic honesty
- Concerns about student access and knowledge related to technology
- Technology use increasing workload

Reasons that educators adopt technology:
- Confidence about technology skills
- Value of continuing education
- More satisfaction with using online tools after appropriate training
- More positive about online teaching after direct experience
- Previous success with technology use leading to more openness
- Seeing how students benefit from its use
- Knowing that learning objectives are clearly enhanced by using technology
- Receiving incentives (money or time) for teaching with technology
- Teaching with technology increasing flexibility
- Valuing professional development that comes with teaching with technology
- Availability of training, mentoring, and support
- Online teaching being recognized by the institution

Source: Adapted from Wingo, Ivankova, & Moss, 2017.

BREAKOUT BOX 6.3. PRACTICAL TIPS
STRATEGIES TO SUPPORT YOUR FACULTY IN THE MOVE TO ONLINE TEACHING

- Contact your university technology center to see what training they already provide, and see whether they might customize some training for your faculty.
- Have your faculty sit with other faculty members at your university already engaged in online teaching to hear about their successes and strategies.
- Hire a consultant: Often, faculty members at schools with established distance programs are willing to contract to support new programs.
- Form a book group, and use this text to share ideas and guide the development of your program and teaching strategies.
- Acknowledge the extra time, stress, and learning required to take on this extra work, and address related workload concerns
- Send the faculty to training at conferences, online training, or through your school's instructional design courses, often offered in education departments. This can increase confidence and skill.
- Provide adequate time for planning and transition.
- Identify champions in and outside your program.

Program administrators who are taking their full curriculum online often must carefully scale their new online offerings so they grow at a pace that allows for the growth of faculty positions. Although it is often assumed that online teaching takes less time or energy than a seated classroom, the opposite is the case. This is especially true initially because it takes a lot of time to design an online classroom, build in a learning management system, and convert from a traditional on-the-ground class (Freeman, 2015), as illustrated in Chapter 5. Extra time may be required to deliver the content online, including typing out responses on message boards, learning new technologies, and monitoring what is happening in the online classroom

(Allen & Seaman, 2013; Bezuidenhout, 2015). In consideration of these extra time requirements, some programs offer faculty members extra time toward their workload for new preparations, weight the time of online classes more heavily than on-the-ground classes when calculating workload, or provide other kinds of extra supports. For instance, at Columbia University, faculty members are trained to teach online and are also paired with live support specialists and associates, who provide a variety of assistance to both the instructor and the students. The live support specialists, who are typically MSW alumni who have taken at least one online class, are trained to set up the *Adobe Connect* online room each week, participate in every live class to manage the technology, and help if students or instructors experience any technical problems. The course teaching associate, another paid support personnel for the instructor, helps monitor the chat boxes and provides grading assistance. See Table 6.1 for the ways Columbia uses the associate and specialist in the online synchronous classroom.

Table 6.1. Differences Between the Live Support Specialist and Associate Positions in Columbia University School of Social Work's Online Campus

Live Support Specialists	Associates
Work 5 hours/week/course, plus 10 hours prior to the start of the semester to prep with the instructor & associate	Work 7–10 hours/week/course, depending on the needs of the week & the instructor
Role focuses on the quality and implementation of technical aspects of live class sessions for online courses	Role focuses on supporting the instructor in academic aspects of the online courses, for example course site prep, class lesson & material prep, grading, etc.
Qualified candidates pass the Institute on Technical Skills for Online Events and pass the application process are assigned to courses by the online campus administration	Qualified candidates pass the Institute on Pedagogy and Technology for Online Courses are invited to virtual interviews and then are potentially selected by instructors

Live Support Specialists	Associates
Position is a variable hours officer position, with a maximum of 20 hours/week	Position is an academic appointment, with a maximum of 3 academic appointments/year at Columbia University, including all Schools & academic roles
Paid the hourly rate biweekly after submission of timesheets	Paid a stipend biweekly, starting after the semester has begun
Potential opportunities for additional projects, such as working on quality assurance of online course sites in Canvas	No opportunity for additional projects
Candidates must be CSSW alum who took an online course as a student. If a CSSW alum did not take an online course as a student, they can meet this requirement by passing the Institute on Pedagogy and Technology for Online Courses.	Candidates must have a MSW, DSW, or PhD

Increasingly, universities are using adjuncts and distance faculty to fill online teaching roles (Amirault, 2012; Bedford, 2009). This raises concerns for full-time academics and adjuncts alike, as often substantial disparities exist regarding pay, benefits, job security, academic freedom, and workload. The disparities can create a hierarchical structure that negatively affects relationships between campus-based and online faculty members (Shulman, 2016). Faculty members who teach from a distance are also more likely to feel isolated and underappreciated by the institution (Dolan, 2011). We recommend that administrators and faculties of social work educational programs discuss these issues ahead of establishing their program and choose administrative and hiring practices that are consistent with the field's values for social justice, including efforts toward equity and appreciation. In the following paragraphs, we review some ways to address these concerns; other considerations are beyond the scope of this book, such as how to hire, evaluate, and promote distance faculty.

Although hiring distance faculty can widen the pool of talent and offers benefit to the curriculum and students, considerations are warranted related to who will support the distance faculty, how values and expectations will be translated to the distant hires to create a cohesive student experience, and how faculty monitoring, supervision, and instructional feedback will be provided from a distance. Support for adjunct and distance faculty is critical (Barbera, Ward, Mama, & Averbach, 2017; Rogers, McIntyre, & Jazzar, 2010; West et al., 2009), including how they will be oriented to the implicit curriculum, integrated at faculty meetings, and gain knowledge of accreditation processes. Faculty members who work at a distance may also need additional support in developing a sense of community. For instance, Schwartz, Wiley, & Kaplan (2016) researched relational experiences among online social work faculty members and found that they appreciate working with diverse students across the country but had limited opportunities for informal networking with each other and with students. Several found it easier to develop relationships with students than colleagues because of access and exposure. Some research participants wished for additional opportunities for peer networking such as online or regional faculty meetings and structured occasions to visit and connect.

Although few schools have opted to hire full-time distance faculty, it is not unheard of. For instance, USC employs full-time clinical faculty members in its distance program who work away from campus, and schools without regular brick-and-mortar settings such as Walden University and the University of Phoenix employ most or all their full-time faculty via distance. USC uses several strategies to bring the virtual faculty together, including semiannual Virtual Academic Center faculty retreats, monthly hybrid faculty meetings, and virtual spaces and activities such as a virtual water cooler for informal networking, online wellness activities, and a virtual book club (Schwartz, Weiss, & Wiley, 2016). The biannual, expenses-paid, face-to-face, retreats are mandatory for full-time distance faculty, and one of the meetings occurs in conjunction with CSWE's annual program meeting.

In large online programs, it may take significant energy to recruit, train, retain, and support distance and adjunct faculty. Simmons College (SC) incorporates a mini-lesson into their adjunct interview process to identify which faculty members have the skills for online teaching. Specifically, potential faculty members work through an online module in which they receive training on the technology, and then they teach in front of the camera for 15 minutes on any topic of their choice in a recorded lecture. This screening tool offers would-be adjunct faculty members an opportunity to demonstrate their instructional style and decide whether they are comfortable teaching with technology. ASU, University of Central Florida (UCF), SC, and USC all use lead instructor models, where a campus-based faculty member creates a core curriculum and offers instructional support to adjuncts who teach the same course. In some instances, the lead instructor designs the curriculum, from which the online instructor cannot diverge. Although this approach helps standardize curriculum and outcomes, it can disempower adjunct instructors, affecting their experience of self-efficacy and agency.

Smaller social work programs also use distance faculty and see the benefits and challenges. Dr. Becky Anthony, the MSW online coordinator at Salisbury University (SU), directs an online program where about 60 new students are admitted each year in both traditional and advanced standing cohorts. She notes that using adjunct faculty members who live far away from campus increases their faculty diversity, and they can draw from a larger pool of instructors to fill specific curricular needs. To meet the needs of adjuncts, social work faculty members and their instructional designers created an online, self-paced professional development training program using *Canvas*, their LMS, where adjunct and full-time faculty members learn about best practices for teaching online.

Though this in-house support for adjuncts is helpful, some universities rely on the institution to provide adjunct support. For instance, at UCF, the university offers centralized support that includes a course on how to teach online, policies on online teaching, and instructional designers that support all faculty members, including adjuncts. Further along the spectrum of insourced versus outsourced training, some schools pay for faculties to participate in trainings from national organizations such as Quality Matters or the Online Learning Consortium or provide learning materials such as the book you are reading now. See Chapter 5 for a review of national organizations that provide faculty support.

DECISIONS, DECISIONS: HOW WILL WE GET ONLINE?

Programs embarking on online curriculum must make decisions about the speed and scope of an online launch. Closely related to this is a program's starting position and reason for going online. A significant design choice must be made about whether to use a decentralized approach through a commercial *online program manager* such as *2U*, *Cengage*, or *Pearson*, or to choose a centralized approach to administer the online program through the institution (Alkaff, Qomarudin, Alkaff, & Bilfaqih, 2018; Dhanatya, 2017; Newton, 2016). An in-between approach is also possible, where some tasks are decentralized, such as admissions, while other tasks are centralized, such as advisement (Bergeron & Fornero, 2018). Each of these options has very different consequences related to workload, program size, and tuition remission.

The choice of a commercial partner nearly ensures rapid program growth, as well as the outsourcing of some of the time-consuming aspects of online student management, such as recruitment, application management, and getting coursework online. Reasons for choosing a commercial partner might be that your institution lacks some of the services or supports necessary for online learning or does not want to take on those administrative burdens. Several schools have chosen the partnership path. Commercial partners typically work on a commission basis and take a percentage of tuition that can total 40%–80% or more of tuition (Newton, 2016), depending on the vendor and types of services they manage. Because of the commission, these partners have the incentive to support program growth and may expect a minimum annual enrollment of hundreds of students. Beyond this, they may suggest other strategies to increase enrollment, such as encouraging programs to offer many enrollment dates for new students throughout the school year so students can begin classes within months of choosing a school, or they may ask schools to lower other barriers to entry such as pretesting, admissions essays, or grade-point average requirements. These partners will often work with a master curriculum your school has created and will help with the design of modules that fit into your LMS. They may locate field placements and field instructors for you. They can also help with program assessment by using LMS data to help identify students who are not logging in or completing work, and their services may include student coaching or tutoring to help keep students enrolled. In large programs such as these, efforts to maintain enrollment are essential, and management of a student body of several hundred students would require the addition of several noninstructional staff members in a centralized model. The decentralized model outsources this labor. The partner benefits from continued student success linked to tutoring and other support because of the commission-based model, and their supports improve retention and help get students to graduation. Their funding structure often requires a higher tuition differential, and this model is commonly seen at large private institutions.

The MSW programs at USC and SC use the commercial partner *2U*. This partner agency actively recruits students and advertises online. A person searching online for a distance MSW program is likely to encounter a targeted ad from one of these schools or another school that contracts with a corporate partner for advertising, as these partners give significant attention to *search engine optimization (SEO)* and paid advertising. These private schools each have large enrollments of more than 1,000 online social work students. Although these large student bodies may make campus visits and cohort models impractical, classrooms are typically broken up into very manageable class sizes of 15 students or less and include synchronous and asynchronous instruction. As the large student body size also makes it difficult to draw enough instructors locally, a program of this size benefits from recruiting faculty members from across the nation. This means that administrative resources are also needed to manage many instructors who may never visit the campus, and programs must decide on methods for screening, hiring, orienting, integrating, and supporting their large distance faculty as noted earlier. Although we have heard critiques and concerns related to quality in programs of this size (mostly from colleagues with little or no experience teaching online and who do not know the practices of large programs), our experience of talking to instructors and students who work and learn within these models is that the large program size has several advantages. These include flexible course offerings for students; the opportunity for the faculty to develop expertise and experience in delivery of the online model; a large enough student body that students can form their own governance structures, and not rely on integrating with the student association for on-the-ground students; and access to technology that supports best practices such as the use of small synchronous video-facilitated classes and other collaborative programs.

Cheryl Parks, the dean of social work at SC, shared the story of her program's online partnership. SC decided to take the leap to grow their reputation nationally through *2U* before her arrival as dean. The program has attracted a national audience, with about four out of five online students enrolling from outside the school's normal catchment area. Students are admitted five times during the year and can complete their MSW in four, six, or eight terms. Currently educating 1,000 online students using blended synchronous and asynchronous learning in each course, students earn the same degree and pay the same tuition whether taking classes on-campus or online. The private school status offers more flexibility and a higher tuition rate, which helps support the School of Social Work's resources. Dean Parks has appreciated *2U*'s efforts to work with their faculty to get their curriculum online, and the technology supports offered through *2U* benefits the program significantly in managing the large enrollment. She concedes that there were some initial culture clashes related to *2U*'s business model that focused on recruitment and growth, and her own school's nonprofit model and faculty inclination to grow slowly. They had to find ways to collaborate that honored the values and goals of each, and she reports they were successful in doing so. Some other challenges include that online students cannot be funded through traditional school scholarships due to the tuition split between the university and *2U*. They also had to figure out how to scale up university services, such as library and disability support access for the online students. The frequent start dates that accommodate students who want to begin classes soon after program application, as well as the 14-week terms, have workload implications for the faculty and the staff. It can be difficult to provide the faculty with predictable breaks between terms, and the academic calendars do not match between the online and on-ground programs.

Online program managers can offer schools flexibility for their students in other ways. Marilyn Flynn, the former dean of social work at USC, noted that their social work program has an online enrollment of about 2,500 MSW students. She sees the online program is an extension of the campus-based programs. Online students at USC's social work program enroll from almost every state and several countries. Although most students complete traditional field placements in their own communities, the size of the program also allows for some unique options. For instance, very rural and out-of-country students may complete their field placements in a telehealth setting, helping consumers virtually from their computers. The scope and financial resources of the school also allow for creativity. Dean Flynn has used funding generated by the distance program to study the effectiveness of their field approaches, such as the use of virtual encounters as a precursor to fieldwork. They are also able to employ data collection through *Salesforce*, a commercial software application that they use to manage and track communications between the school and their students, and which provides additional insights about student needs. Students can choose from coursework throughout the day and evening, as multiple sections are offered for each course.

Programs of this size are the exception, yet because of the sheer volume of students educated in these large-scale programs, thousands of social workers will graduate from just a handful of these schools each year. This large scale-up seems to occur almost exclusively in private institutions, where tuition for an MSW degree can be as high as $100,000 for a full MSW program of study. If you are thinking about going this route, it is vital to negotiate contracts carefully. Partnering agreements often involve multiyear contracts, and the partner may hold rights to the course and other materials they develop as part of the partnership. Usually the partners front money for staff and faculty expansion and schools pay it back over many years. It may be hard to dissolve agreements and change paths after an investment in this approach. It is also good to know a range of business partnerships exist. For example, a collaboration with a publisher such as Cengage can provide curriculum support and student monitoring and help with some of the responsibility of program management at a lower cost but leave more freedom—and more work—in the hands of the school.

IF YOU WANT TO DO IT YOURSELF...

Some schools decide they want to launch online and maintain the control of the programming and all the work that comes with it—the do-it-yourself (DIY) or the centralized organic model. In this case, enrollment in the hundreds right from the start is much less likely. ASU is an exception to this situation. Former director Michelle Carney describes how they increased from 60 to 400 MSW students in just 1 year. However, having a robust university infrastructure in ASU Online was one key factor facilitating this quick scale-up. ASU Online provides some instructional design services, and contracts with Pearson for student recruitment, marketing, and student success services.

A school using the DIY model is more likely to choose to convert its curriculum slowly, giving existing campus-based students the opportunity to take some classes online until the school can move all its courses to an online option. The UB School of Social Work where one of us (Nancy) is dean began moving into online education in 2001 in this way, providing online courses to expand options for students enrolled in their existing geographically dispersed distance program. However, over time, after closing the cohort-based extension programs and increasing online offerings for all students, the faculty realized that it might be possible for individual students to graduate from the program with 50% of their classes online. As a result, they needed to register their degree as a distance education program with the New York State Education Department, because New York State has set 50% as the criteria for defining a degree as offered in a distance education format (New York State Education Department, n.d.). Initially, UB offered its practice course in foundation interventions as only a hybrid course, with skills "workshop sessions" provided in-person on a few Saturdays each semester. Over time, the faculty gave students a choice to participate in these interventions skills sessions through live video streaming (students can also choose to come to campus), thereby transitioning the UB program to an entirely online MSW program. The UB School of Social Work continues to mix its online student and on-the-ground student populations in many of its online classes, although online students receive registration preference in required courses. Online degree students must apply specifically for the online program, and the MSW Program Admissions Committee (which makes recommendations for all MSW applicants) assesses their appropriateness for online education, as well as for the MSW program, during the application process. UB currently admits about 45 students a year online: 30 to the foundation year and 15 as advanced-standing students. The school does plan to double admissions soon because of high demand for their trauma-informed and human rights online MSW curriculum. The example of their move to online education highlights the necessity of understanding the individual state regulatory context for higher education distance programs and demonstrates what it might look like to scale up slowly.

A more common path to online degrees is to admit online students only to an institution's online social work program, without mixing them with on-the-ground students. Most schools use this strategy, maintaining a separate enrollment and application process for their online students and using an online program coordinator who works with the program director to help guide the admissions, onboarding, and student support processes. Students often move through programs of this type as a cohort, but not always. Some programs have established guidelines and practices that allow students to move back and forth from an online program to on-ground or vice versa depending on student needs, such as changes in life circumstances or poor fit with online learning environments.

Carol Schneweis, the distance MSW coordinator at UND, described the launch of their fully synchronous online degree. As early adopters of distance education, beginning with a state-wide interactive video network in the 1980s that dispersed interactive television to satellite sites around the state (before online programming was widely available), the distance MSW program formally launched online in 2006 with a cohort of 15 students. Initially, they used *Adobe Connect,* a *videoconferencing software,* for synchronous online delivery. In 2018 the university moved to *Zoom* for videoconferencing. Both these software programs have improved over the years and allow students to log in to the classroom with their video cameras and microphone headsets. See Breakout Box 6.4 for a list of other types of videoconferencing products. Students are required to attend and participate in the weekly synchronous classes and are required to use their microphones and cameras to increase the sense of community. Now, after 10 years, the program still admits only 60 students per year, 30 to the foundation cohort and 30 to the concentration cohort. Schneweis explains that the small cohorts allow for close relationships between the core faculty and students. As the program coordinator, she knows each student, helps orient them to the program, and is a key contact if concerns arise. Nearly all faculty members who teach in the online program also teach on-the-ground courses, and she believes that experience with online teaching also enhances on-the-ground teaching, as faculty members must be creative and think about their assignments and engagement in new ways. The program is competitive, with only 15%–25% of applicants admitted each year. She notes that in the past they have resisted program growth because of the high-touch model, which keeps the program unique and fills a different niche than other online schools. However, they are considering ways that they might grow and maintain their value for high-touch experiences.

> ## BREAKOUT BOX 6.4. PRACTICAL TIPS
> ### SOFTWARE FOR SYNCHRONOUS MEETINGS
> If you are exploring software to help you conduct face-to-face meetings with your students or the faculty online, the best place to start is within your institution. Does your school already support a product? Here are some popular products and packages that allow Web conferencing or live streaming:
>
> - Adobe Connect
> - BigBlueButton
> - Blackboard Collaborate
> - Canvas
> - Google Hangouts (Google for Education offers additional features)
> - GotoMeeting
> - Skype (business and personal versions have different features)
> - Tegrity
> - Zoom

Schneweis also shares her belief and experience that online education can be more rigorous than on-the-ground classes in a program like UND's. For example, the initial acceptance is more competitive, and the faculty must work harder to meet the intellect and experience of the students who often come with years of community practice. It is easier to notice who participates and who doesn't, as an electronic trail exists for all student encounters. When considering the drawbacks of a model like this, she says it is easy to stagnate because investments in software are high for universities and faculties, often prohibiting change. She encourages those who are launching programs to consider technology choices carefully by assessing university technical support and recommends that schools periodically reevaluate whether the current tools still are the best matches to accomplish program goals. She also notes that it is important to consider the isolation of distance rural students and the ways the school can support students who fall into this category. The implicit curriculum outcomes are harder to meet in the distance cohort in her experience: her program attempts to meet these challenges by working with campus support units to educate them about the distance student body and make resources available, and by giving students informal places to chat and connect. Examples include their private *Facebook* groups, a message forum in the LMS, regional gatherings, and access to student activities via Web streaming. Students also come to campus for four days per year for intensive workshops and social time, which supports engagement and connection to the faculty, the university, and each other.

IU was also an early adopter of online education. Led by Professor Bob Vernon, the online MSW launched at IU in 2012 as a mostly asynchronous program. The online program was branded as *MSW Direct*, with a single concentration (advanced generalist) instead of the five concentrations offered in their on-the-ground campus program. Students enroll from across the United States, Europe, and Canada. Instead of a cohort model, students can move at their own pace and adjust their workload and participation to meet their own needs, with most working adults completing the program within 3 years. Although IU began with an on-campus orientation requirement lasting three days, this proved burdensome to students, so the orientation was moved online. A core group of on-campus faculty members teach most of the online courses and are given a class curriculum that they can customize. Rolling admission is offered so that students can join in spring or fall to provide as much flexibility as possible. Continuous enrollment is not required to stay in the program. For example, if students have a family problem and need to leave for a few semesters, they can return to MSW Direct and immediately start where they left off. About 300 students are enrolled in the program at any given time, with about 15% of those on a break from the program.

When asked about lessons learned, Vernon shared the need to screen for students who are a good programmatic fit. They have found a student's previous grade point average (GPA) to be a valuable indicator of who might have problems with online learning; students with higher GPAs also have better grades in the graduate program. He also shares that rumor control is more important in the online environment. Students talk amongst each other through social media when they hear something about program happenings, so it is important to communicate well about programmatic issues. Also, Vernon notes the importance of having a clear process for assessing whether the program has all the needed student support resources. His program was in a planning stage for 2 years before opening enrollment, and his dean gave them a million dollars to ensure a successful program launch. This money was used to build infrastructure, hire faculty, and prepare for the program kickoff. They made sure support personnel were immediately available. The program admitted a student with significant disability challenges early on, which helped define and address access and participation problems. The student subsequently completed the degree. They hired a coordinator to serve as a point of contact for any distance student concerns, whether the concerns originated with student or faculty member. Now the program is investing in additional staffing resources such as a dedicated instructional designer, full-time lecturers, and two field coordinators.

Portland State University (PSU) developed its asynchronous MSW program online in yet a separate way. PSU had a competitive internal grant process for any faculty or program interested in developing new curricular offerings that used technology or increased access. The MSW program was awarded a grant to convert the MSW curriculum into a fully online option. The grant provided faculty support for project management and course development and supported the course development by providing instructional designers to ensure a pedagogically strong approach. This funding was provided in advance of program startup, which gave faculty members time to study best practices in online education and to convert their courses into the online format. PSU chose to begin by offering only their macro concentration online to increase access to advanced macro practice for students around the state, as previously only the clinical concentration was offered to students by distributed learning at off-site locations outside the Portland metro area. This also allowed faculty members who were cautious about whether quality clinical training could be provided in an online setting to understand the pedagogy and technology to support the development of micro practice skills. The program admits primarily students from the Pacific Northwest region and follows the standard campus program calendar.

THINKING OUTSIDE THE BOX: NONTRADITIONAL TIME CLOCKS

On campus, classes typically adhere to a traditional time clock set by the university, whether semester or quarter system. However, online courses provide the opportunity for programs to adjust their schedules and consider unique alternatives. ASU and UCF both offer rolling admissions, for instance, where students take either one or two courses per term in shortened time blocks. This may allow students additional focus on fewer classes, and numerous entry points allow students to begin graduate school closer to the date that they are most ready. Although IU began its program with this model in place, the administrators found that being off the traditional calendar made it more difficult for the faculty to teach simultaneously in on-the-ground and online courses, and this concern caused a return to a conventional term-based model. Program administrators note that nontraditional scheduling also makes it more difficult for the faculty to take time off between terms, as new courses start at the tail of the last ones, raising concerns of faculty burnout.

SEAT TIME

Credit hour time, also referred to as seat time, is the amount of time it takes for students to complete coursework per credit hour in class. One concern of online programs, especially those offered asynchronously, is the concept of whether students are achieving enough seat time and how the department should demonstrate this. College credit hours are set by the Department of Education and derived from a unit of time called the *Carnegie unit* (initially designed to measure time in high school hours), which equates to 120 total hours of class contact time (Shedd, 2003; Silva, White, & Toch, 2015; Silva et al., 2015) and translates to about 1 hour a day for classes in a high school year. A credit, on the other hand, is 12 hours of contact time, which typically equals about 50 minutes per week over the course of a semester; thus, a 3-credit class meets 50 minutes three times per week. Institutions that use quarter systems or other alternative clocks must adjust the hours-per-week requirement to meet the seat-time credit hour requirement. For every clock hour of seat time, 2 hours of out-of-class work is also expected. This definition of a credit hour is broadly adopted in federal law and by accrediting agencies, although some variations are possible based on competency-based evaluation approved by an accrediting body. CSWE does not permit competency-based evaluation in exchange for college credit currently. See the *Federal Register*, 34 CFR 600.2, for more information on the Carnegie unit and credit hours (Silva, White, & Toch, 2015).

Online courses should demonstrate equivalent seat time to campus-based offerings. However, there is no actual expectation of hours spent in a traditional seated course, only an expectation that the amount of work assigned is matched to the credit hours it takes to complete the assigned work. For instance, a 3-credit course on the semester system calendar should take 150 minutes in class and 300 minutes out of class per week to finish. In a fully synchronous course, this calculation is equal to on-the-ground requirements; students appear in the online classroom for the same amount of time they would in a campus classroom. However, in asynchronous or blended classes, programs are expected to document how they calculate the time it takes to complete course assignments so they align with campus-based or synchronous offerings. Institutions, and not individual programs, agree to abide by these rules related to seat time as part of their institutional accreditation processes.

COMPETENCY OUTCOME ASSESSMENT

CSWE also plays a role in ensuring that online programs offer the same rigor of study as campus-based programs, including equivalency in learning and coursework expectations.

CSWE's Educational Policy and Accreditation Standards (2015, p. 18) require that competency outcome assessments be completed for each degree program option. For this reason, social work programs should be able to distinguish social work competency data in their online versus campus-based cohorts separately so that each can be evaluated on its own merits. Student competency scores should differentiate between students who matriculate in a campus-based program versus a distance program when the programs consist of two distinct options. For instance, if a school offers an online MSW and a campus-based MSW, and data is collected from each group for program assessment required by CSWE, programs should be able to demonstrate that their assessment outcomes are generally consistent between the online and campus programs and that each program individually meets all CSWE expectations.

HOW DO WE SUPPORT IMPLICIT CURRICULUM IN ONLINE EDUCATION?

The explicit curriculum of a social work program is visible in the coursework, the list of faculty members, and the required assignments. The implicit curriculum is also evident but in separate ways. It includes all the things that make up what it feels like to be part of a program, such as student supports, relationships with faculty members and students, advising, opportunities to engage in extracurricular activities, and the types of messages students receive from all program stakeholders. In on-the-ground programs, the university often creates much of the context for implicit curriculum through student activities, and the social work program also offers messaging through bulletin boards, social work clubs, and student diversity events. In the online setting, a program must be more intentional to create an implicit curriculum that supports and invites students to join in the programming, and additionally supports the emotional and social development of students. CSWE defines a program's implicit curriculum as made up of "the program's commitment to diversity; admissions policies and procedures; advisement, retention, and termination policies; student participation in governance; faculty; administrative structure; and resources" (CSWE, 2015, p. 14) and asks schools to report on the ways they are assessing this component of their programming.

Michelle Carney, former director at ASU, took a thoughtful approach to implicit curriculum in their online MSW program development. Students are admitted each semester as a cohort, and each group has its own cohort page in the learning management system. Students are also mapped geographically and encouraged to connect with other students who live in their regions for peer support. Additional ways they support student connection to the campus is by sending students branded water bottles and T-shirts at program entry, and they prepare videos and podcasts about student services offered through the university that are available to distance students. A dedicated distance student services staff member and distance field director are the main contact people for distance students, which improves student access to supports. The distance team meets weekly to identify challenges and to adjust its processes accordingly, and Carney attributes this, in part, to its ability to adapt and grow quickly from 60 students in 2014 to more than 400 students by 2016.

One advantage of large online programs like SC and USC is that they have enough online student bodies to foster a diverse online student support system. Between them, these schools have several unique student-affiliated organizations that have formed online, such as groups for students of color, first-generation students, military students, and a newly created chapter of the National Association of Black Social Workers organized by online students. At USC, virtual students have their own student caucus in the student government. Distance students also communicate directly with the online program director, much as students for the on-the-ground program would do with the campus-based program director. Often, distance students represent more diverse populations than campus-based students (Quinn & Barth, 2014), and these cross-cultural exposures also influence the implicit curriculum. Online students at USC also get all the same e-mails and school-wide communications as the students in the on-the-ground program, even though they may not be able to take advantage of all those opportunities. But when there are events that can be done in local communities, such as an advocate with state government event, the online students participate in those events as they desire.

Smaller programs address implicit curriculum differently. UB works to stream and record student services workshops that are provided in their on-the-ground program. All student services staff members are trained and skilled in providing services through distance platforms, and one student services staff member is the primary contact person for online students. Ongoing, synchronous support sessions are also offered for the online students that cover issues such as study skills and stress management, and individual sessions are scheduled when a student is identified as in need of extra support. An online orientation and frequent e-mails ensure that students know about resources and how to access them.

TEACHING SOCIAL WORK WITH DIGITAL TECHNOLOGY

DO WE NEED CAMPUS VISITS?

Is it possible to graduate social work students without a member of your faculty ever seeing them in person? Possibly. Many programs have moved to entirely online offerings and rely on field placements for in-person assessment of students. However, many distance programs require students to attend a campus visit during the program. In a survey of 16 distance-delivered programs, Quinn and Barth (2014) found that 75% of the campuses mandated that either students visit the campus or faculty members visit students. The most common reasons for these visits included orienting students to program expectations, helping develop cohort connections, teaching clinical skills, and engaging in in-person gatekeeping. Schools that have opted out of campus visits report reasons that include the extra expenses of these visits as a justice issue, that technology now allows for similar goals to be met via distance, and that students may be on different time clocks and not in cohorts. Program administrators who are planning a distance program and contemplating the campus visit should consider the following: (a) their perceptions about the goals of a campus visit and whether the goals can be met just as well another way; (b) the types of students the program is serving and the burden the required visit might create, such as time away from caretaking or employment; (c) the time and activities that will be needed to facilitate the goals of such a visit; and (d) the consequences of not attending the required visit, including possible alternatives to the visit. The expectations about a required visit and expenses involved should be explicit before students enroll in the program. Most important, students should see the value in the campus visit and that it is an effective use of their time. Campus visits may be referred to as intensives, residencies, orientations, or just plain old campus visits.

Some distance programs adopt a regional program focus, which makes campus visits more practical. For example, when students are only admitted within the state, the financial hardship of an occasional campus visit may be mostly diminished. Regional programs can choose to have these students visit at regular intervals to support skill development and cohort building. The University of Minnesota Duluth applies this approach in their mostly online BSW model by having students come to campus every other week for classes. Although initially the program was designed to meet less often in person, the students in the early cohorts requested more campus time, and the program adjusted to meet the needs of the students.

Other programs may draw from a broad geographic region, yet still require time on-campus. At UND, where all classes are offered synchronously, students get to know each other and develop relationships by seeing each other regularly via videoconferencing software in the online classroom. Additionally, the students in the part-time 3-year degree program visit campus twice during their time in the program, and the advanced-standing students visit campus once. They stay on-campus for approximately 4 days, where they meet several times with each of their practice classes to strengthen their skills; participate in a faculty advisor fair, where they learn about faculty interests so they can choose an advisor for their special topics cumulative paper; and meet with the field team to prepare for their field internships. The visits occur later in the program, so students learned the theory needed to prepare for practice skills development during the campus visit, as the main goal for a visit is enhancing students' readiness for field and practice. The visits are a mix of practice, policy, and community building. Students usually report that the time on campus was important, even if inconvenient as they arrange for time away from home. These students pay for their own airfare and hotel rooms during their visit, although the university does offer low-cost stays in dormitories as an option. The department provides most meals and lots of structure for at least 8 hours of each day, which they see as valuable for demonstrating to students that their time is important. Shared meals and face-to-face activities contribute to a sense of community, and students often arrange after-hours activities together, such as dinners, attendance at sports activities, community runs, or other social time. Faculty members at the school report that the campus visit positively affects online classroom cohesion. They emphasize the importance of ensuring students understand the campus visit obligation even as they apply to the program, as well as the approximate costs and the visit timeline, as far in advance as possible. Because visits typically occur in the summer, students may have to plan vacations, weddings, and work coverage around the time away. It is also important that the program has a policy in place for what happens if a student misses the campus visit. At UND, a student cannot enter the field until they have participated in a campus visit.

Other schools opt for an early campus visit, with the primary goal of orienting students to the expectations of the program. At PSU, the faculty feels that students can demonstrate practice skills very well in the online environment, maybe even better than on-campus, because mock interviews are recorded by students and can be replayed with online feedback provided by the faculty. So, the 2-day campus visit is offered first at the beginning of the program as an opportunity to prepare students for the rigorous requirements of graduate school, to ensure they are familiar with the technology, and to begin the process of building community within the cohort. The students visit a second time in the fall for 2 days before beginning their generalist field placement and generalist practice classes. They are introduced to field requirements and become familiar with the technology used in the practice classes. Using a 3-year cohort model in the mostly asynchronous program, instructors also constantly reinforce social presence by requiring students to use pictures, videos, chat forums, and collaboration so they connect with each other and with the faculty despite not having a shared live classroom time. Social presence is also facilitated through periodic online live meetings, one-on-one between the faculty and students. See Chapters 3 and 5 for more ideas on how to promote social presence in online courses. Many schools have decided to forgo the campus visit entirely and rely on technology, citing convenience to students as the primary motivator. Students may still have opportunities to engage in-person though. For instance, Dean Marilyn Flynn at USC explains that all students are expected to attend graduation, and students are also invited to regional conferences such as for the Society for Social Work Research and CSWE annual program meetings, where they are welcome to share a scheduled dinner with other students and the faculty. The school holds a national fundraising bicycling event where they coordinate their students across the country to participate, an event she describes as "an effort to export our culture."

ON WHO'S TURF?

So far in this chapter we have discussed the numerous ways to get online but have not addressed the possible stressors related to bringing your university's program to someone else's backyard. With a growing demand for online education, all social work programs must be aware that students have a vast amount of choices when it comes to achieving their degrees, and it is essential for each program to differentiate itself in a highly competitive market. Putting a program online does not necessarily mean you are encroaching on someone else's backyard. You may be serving students who could not access their local programs for one reason or another.

Many schools consider issues of encroachment in their admissions process, prioritizing students who live in geographically close areas for admission. Regional admissions may be important institutionally for those schools with missions that include service to the region. Some schools, such as UND, also consider whether applicants are in rural or urban areas and whether they have regional schools nearby with distance programs that might also provide an educational option. This consideration is based on their value of distance education as a tool that promotes access to social work education. As a regional fully online program Salisbury University offers admission only to students in their state (Maryland) and four other adjoining states, and it does not fear encroachment from other institutions. Online program coordinator Dr. Becky Anthony at SU explains that students in her region want to earn their degrees from local, regional schools so they will be connected to institutions that their local employers recognize. We have also heard stories of schools that try to maintain friendly relationships with their colleagues from other institutions and call or send an e-mail when they're placing a student in another school's region, sometimes even getting advice about the reputation of an agency or seeking information about placement possibilities in the area. Outreach like this is helpful; we have heard stories of schools that attempted to place students in their local community and found that an out-of-state school had already placed several students at the agency and there was no more space. Local schools also have good information about the reputations and practice experiences of local agencies. Cooperation may enhance relationships and diminish some concerns about turf.

Admissions committees also need to be aware of state practice regulations for social workers that may also have implications for students. For instance, Minnesota and California are two states that require a specific number of hours be obtained in specific settings or courses during the MSW degree program for social work licensure; topics may include human behavior, domestic violence, or child abuse reporting. Some states require internships in school settings to earn certification as a school social worker, or in substance abuse settings for a chemical dependency credential. For licensure, graduates may have to demonstrate where and how they met these specialized requirements; therefore, the field office and students should be aware of any special rules mandated by states from which they accept students. When students hope to enroll in a distance social work program in another geographic area, whether state or country, the school and the students should both be aware of issues that can affect their ability to practice in their home region, and these issues should be disclosed during the admission process before it becomes a problem for the graduate.

Before admitting online students, schools should check the latest state members of the National Council for State Authorization Reciprocity Agreements (NC-SARA). A federal rule titled State Authorization Rule 34 CFR § 600.9 mandates that universities comply with state laws where the student resides when placing students in states where the school does not have a physical presence, and schools must obtain the permission of that state. Whereas this law has been interpreted to not apply to students engaged in online learning from home, it does apply once a student enters field placement and has an education-related physical presence in the community. Placement is easier if the home institution is an NC-SARA member and the student is the resident of an NC-SARA-member state. When students reside in nonmember states, the school must enter into an agreement with the state, which can cost thousands of dollars. To address this issue, some states programs will not admit students from nonmember states. State members of NC-SARA have provided agreements for a university outside the state to deliver education within the state if the individual institution is an NC-SARA member. Although most states are now members, exceptions exist. Applications to NC-SARA occur at the state and then the institution level, not at the program level. Additionally, your university must also be a member of NC-SARA to benefit from the reciprocity, which costs between $2,000 and $6,000 annually, depending on the number of students enrolled in out-of-state education. As of this writing, all states are NC-SARA members except California, with Massachusetts just joining this year. When a state is not a member, institutions within the state cannot join and therefore cannot send students to out-of-state agencies through the agreement.

Similarly, schools that have applicants who live in California must go through a separate approval agreement with the state if the student will perform their field placement work in California. One reason for resisting NC-SARA membership is fear that it will reduce consumer protection; for instance, for-profit career colleges could market to vulnerable students.

Although NC-SARA makes it easier to enroll students outside the state, it does not cover human resources issues related to employing people out of state. Labor laws are complex and vary by state. It is vital that departments work closely with their own institutions to ensure they are following legal procedures that will address issues such as liability, unemployment and workers compensation, income tax, and other laws that affect employing out-of-state instructors who are conducting business on behalf of the institution but reside outside of the state. Some of these complications are avoided by hiring out-of-state faculty members as independent contractors, but states have different guidelines about who qualifies as an independent contractor versus employee. Again, it is valuable to consult with your human resources office or legal counsel at your institution.

Why do we need to consult with lawyers and human resources when designing our distance social work education that spans state lines? When it comes to paying employees out of state, such as to hire liaisons, supervisors, or others in the home state of the student, multiple laws and practices may apply. Some states have reciprocity agreements related to tax and unemployment insurance collection for out-of-state employees. Your institution may have to apply for an employer's tax account to hire an out-of-state employee or contractor. The payroll office and university legal team can be helpful in navigating these issues and should be consulted during program planning in case the state of student residence has specific requirements that may pose problems down the line.

WHAT PROGRAM FUNDING MODEL WILL WE USE?

Adding an online degree in a brick-and-mortar university environment can carry a high price tag to support the additional and needed infrastructure. Types of required infrastructure expenses include adding instructional designers, offering ongoing support and training for the faculty and students, obtaining specialized software, having student success services, ensuring that other campus services (e.g., libraries, disability services, registrars, financial aid, and judicial services) are equipped to serve online students, and having the appropriate information technologies infrastructure and support. Also, in a social work program, additional field staff and supports are needed.

As noted earlier, contracting with external partners usually involves significant tuition sharing to cover the cost of all the infrastructure they support, and this elevated level of tuition sharing makes financial sense for a degree program only if the program admits a large number of students. When universities provide their own infrastructure, the additional costs of online degrees are generally met through either specific online fees or a differential tuition rate for online degrees, or sometimes both. For example, IU applies an online education fee, and ASU has a separate tuition rate for online degrees (and students pay for every credit, even if they are taking more than 12 credits, whereas their campus program tuition caps out at the cost of 12 credits) and an online fee. However, in the State University of New York (SUNY) system, UB is prohibited from charging on online fee, and online students pay the same rates as on-the-ground students. This means that the additional costs of providing online education will only be covered if some portion of degree-seeking students are outside the state and paying out-of-state tuition rates. Although UB has minimal centralized university support for online education, the School of Social Work has been able to leverage aspects of Open SUNY, the statewide online education arm of the SUNY system, as well as to take advantage of its proximity to Southern Ontario, Canada, to attract international students who also pay a higher tuition rate.

The UCF School of Social Work was the first Florida program within the university to scale up quickly in size and became a model of quality distance program for the university. The university supported its request to develop a significant online degree presence. The university, the social work director, and the social work faculty explored using an external partner to launch their program. However, in the end, the university decided to develop its own infrastructure for online education, including hiring instructional designers and student service staff. Also, they were able to set a higher, market-rate tuition for the online degree program at the time they began the program (which endures, even though the state of Florida had put this option on hold for new programs at the time of the interview with UCF program director Bonnie Yegidis). Having the university see social work as a trailblazer for university-wide change is a wonderful political asset for a department, school, or college. The downside of being the school leading the university on a new initiative is that the university infrastructure will take more time to develop and mature. In UCF's case the support to market the online programs was the last piece the university put into place. Although this was not much of a problem in recruiting students in their own region, it slowed down their move into a national market.

Although the funding model of an online program often matches that of the institution's campus-based programs, variations do exist. For instance, some social work programs align their programs with the continuing education unit of the institution rather than the academic unit. In some cases, this allows for more autonomy. The social work department may be able to recapture a more significant percentage of its tuition dollars with less redistribution across the university. On the other hand, these self-funded program models are typically reliant on generating their own profits and may not receive the same institutional support for initial program growth and work on more of a traditional market-driven model. In times of program enrollment decline, they may have to lay off faculty members or cut costs.

FINAL THOUGHTS

This chapter offers many technical and practical considerations for moving a degree program online and still does not dip a toe into the emotional work necessary to move processes through committee, support dubious faculty, develop an institutional argument for resources, or learn new technologies. A to-do list cannot capture the time and energy requirements of taking the leap to fully online programming. However, interviews with faculties and administrators who are doing the work demonstrate the many rewards that come with a job well done. These include the opportunity to serve students who would not otherwise have access to social work education, the creative joys that come with dreaming about new ways of connecting, and yes, even the new market of students that may be discovered and the revenue that follows them. According to the 2015 CSWE data report, 76% of MSW programs are at least partially online or have online coursework in development (CSWE, 2016). Student access to online social work coursework will soon be the expectation and not the exception, which demands that we all take inventory of our capacity for online education, so we can articulate the reasons for or against joining this club.

It should also be clear from the program examples throughout this chapter that going online with a degree program is very context dependent, influenced by state and regional policy, regional characteristics, and the university institutional and social work program context. We've presented a number of case scenarios, but not all of them, and have not led you in a single direction; we hope you've realized that one size does not fit all, and that the program design you choose must fit your resources and program values. Understanding one's own context is critical—for this reason, it can be helpful to see if there are other professional programs in your university or at a similar institution offering online degrees; if there are, reach out to them to explore how they have made the journey online. Additionally, entire books are written about the design and structure of online programming, and if you feel you have got more questions than answers, you can explore further. One book you might consider is *Leading and Managing E-Learning: What the E-Learning Leader Needs to Know* (Piña, Lowell, & Harris, 2018).

ACKNOWLEDGMENTS

We express our gratitude to the following social work educators who provided information and support via interviews and e-mails about their various program models: Bob Vernon, Indiana University; Bonnie Yegidis, University of Central Florida; Carol Schneweis, University of North Dakota; Cheryl Parks, Simmons College; Marilyn Flynn, University of Southern California; Matthea Marquart, Columbia University; Michelle Carney, University of Kansas; Rebecca Anthony, Salisbury University; Sandra van den Bosse, University of Minnesota Duluth; and Sarah Bradley, Portland State University.

FURTHER READING AND RESOURCES

Higher Education Compliance. http://www.higheredcompliance.org/resources/disabilities-accommodations.html (provides regulations and guidance about disability accommodations).

National Council for State Authorization Reciprocity Agreements (NC-SARA). http://nc-sara.org/ (provides state-to-state agreements for reciprocity for distance students).

Silva, E., White, T., & Toch, T. (2015). *The Carnegie unit: A century-old standard in a changing education landscape.* Stanford, CA: Carnegie Foundation for the Advancement of Teaching. https://www.carnegiefoundation.org/resources/publications/carnegie-unit/ (defines student seat time).

CAST. http://www.cast.org/about#.WGczlRsrJPY (provides resources to improve curriculum accessibility).

REFERENCES

Alkaff, A., Qomarudin, M. N., Alkaff, S. D., & Bilfaqih, Y. (2018). Modelling online course services and comparison of its major providers. *International Journal of Emerging Technologies in Learning (iJET), 13*(1), 65–81.

Allen, I. E., & Seaman, J. (2013). *Changing course: Ten years of tracking online education in the United States.* Retrieved from https://eric.ed.gov/?id=ED541571.

Amirault, R. J. (2012). Distance learning in the 21st century university: Key issues for leaders and faculty. *Quarterly Review of Distance Education, 13*(4), 253.

Barbera, R., Ward, K., Mama, R., & Averbach, J. (2017). Improving teaching: Training program for social work adjuncts. *Journal of Baccalaureate Social Work, 22*(1), 17–30.

Bedford, L. A. (2009). The professional adjunct: An emerging trend in online instruction. *Online Journal of Distance Learning Administration, 12*(3), 1–8.

Bergeron, M. Z., & Fornero, S. C. (2018). Centralized and decentralized approaches to managing online programs. In A. A. Piña, V. L. Lowell, & B. R. Harris (Eds.), *Leading and managing e-learning: What the e-learning leader needs to know* (pp. 29–43). Cham, Switzerland: Springer.

Bezuidenhout, A. (2015). Implications for academic workload of the changing role of distance educators. *Distance Education, 36*(2), 246–262. doi:10.1080/01587919.2015.1055055

Code of Federal Regulations. 34 CFR 600.2. Retrieved from https://www.law.cornell.edu/cfr/text/34/600.2

Council on Social Work Education (CSWE). (2015). *Educational policy and accreditation standards for baccalaureate and master's social work programs.* Alexandria, VA: Author. Retrieved from https://www.cswe.org/getattachment/Accreditation/Accreditation-Process/2015-EPAS/2015EPAS_Web_FINAL.pdf.aspx

Council on Social Work Education (CSWE). (2016). *Annual statistics on social work education in the United States.* Retrieved from https://www.cswe.org/getattachment/992f629c-57cf-4a74-8201-1db7a6fa4667/2015-Statistics-on-Social-Work-Education.aspx

Dhanatya, C. L. (2017). From strategic thinking to a plan of action: The process of mapping organizational quality; A case study of the USC Rossier School of Education. In D. E. Neubauer & C. Gomes (Eds.), *Quality assurance in Asia-Pacific universities* (pp. 37–53). New York, NY: Palgrave Macmillan, Cham Springer. doi:10.1007/978-3-319-46109-0_3

Dolan, V. L. (2011). The isolation of online adjunct faculty and its impact on their performance. *International Review of Research in Open and Distributed Learning, 12*(2), 62–77.

Freeman, L. A. (2015). Instructor time requirements to develop and teach online courses. *Online Journal of Distance Learning Administration, 18*(1), n1.

New York State Education Department (n.d.) *Approval and registration.* Retrieved from http://www.highered.nysed.gov/ocue/aipr/guidance/gpr17.html

Newton, D. (2016, June 7). How five companies are gaining millions in profit off education at nonprofit schools. *Atlantic.* Retrieved from https://www.theatlantic.com/education/archive/2016/06/for-profit-companies-nonprofit-colleges/485930/

Piña, A. A., Lowell, V. L., & Harris, B. R. (Eds.). (2018). *Leading and managing e-learning: What the e-learning leader needs to know.* Cham, Switzerland: Springer.

Quinn, A., & Barth, A. M. (2014). Operationalizing the implicit curriculum in MSW distance education programs. *Journal of Social Work Education, 50,* 34–47. doi:10.1080/10437797.2014.856229

Rogers, C. B., McIntyre, M., & Jazzar, M. (2010). Mentoring adjunct faculty using the cornerstones of effective communication and practice. *Mentoring & Tutoring: Partnership in Learning, 18*(1), 53–59.

Schwartz, S. L., Wiley, J. L., & Kaplan, C. D. (2016). Community building in a virtual teaching environment. *Advances in Social Work, 17*(1), 15–30. doi:10.18060/20875

Seok, S., DaCosta, B., & Hodges, R. (2018). A systematic review of empirically based universal design for learning: Implementation and effectiveness of universal design in education for students with and without disabilities at the postsecondary level. *Open Journal of Social Sciences, 6*(5), 171.

Shedd, J. M. (2003). The history of the student credit hour. *New Directions for Higher Education, 2003*(122), 5–12.

Shulman, S. (2016). The costs and benefits of adjunct justice: A critique of Brennan and Magness. *Journal of Business Ethics*, 1–9. doi:10.1007/s10551-017-3498-2

Silva, E., White, T., & Toch, T. (2015). *The Carnegie unit: A century-old standard in a changing education landscape.* Stanford, CA: Carnegie Foundation for the Advancement of Teaching. Retrieved from https://www.carnegiefoundation.org/resources/publications/carnegie-unit/

CAST. *Universal Design for Learning.* Retrieved from http://www.cast.org/our-work/about-udl.html#.W5k33kZKg2w

West, M. M., Borden, C., Bermudez, M., Hanson-Zalot, M., Amorim, F., & Marmion, R. (2009). Enhancing the clinical adjunct role to benefit students. *Journal of Continuing Education in Nursing, 40*(7), 305–310.

Wingo, N. P., Ivankova, N. V., & Moss, J. A. (2017). Faculty perceptions about teaching online: Exploring the literature using the technology acceptance model as an organizing framework. *Online Learning, 21*(1), 15–35.

CHAPTER 7

FIELD EDUCATION ONLINE: HIGH-TOUCH PEDAGOGY
Co-authored with Laura Lewis and Carol Schneweis

This chapter answers the following questions:

- What do the Council on Social Work Education and other regulatory bodies say about distance education and technology in field education?
- What are the differences between campus and distance field education?
- What technology skills do field coordinators, liaisons, and field instructors need?
- Why do field offices need specialized software or databases?
- How do we prepare distance students for field placement?
- How do we find placements in another state?
- Does a field coordinator or liaison need a face-to-face meeting with students?
- How do we use technology to maintain a sense of community and communication?

When we offer up the topic of technology in social work field education, we have found that social work educators often fall into two categories: the nonbelievers and the believers. Often the nonbelievers jump to concerns about technology-based field experiences and worry that in-person contact will be replaced with the use of avatar clients and virtual field experiences. These concerns come with emotional responses about the roles of social workers and how social work education may be negatively affected by technology-mediated practice; skeptics tend to believe that online social work education is a negative move for the field overall. On the other hand, the believers understand that distant students can practice in their home community while enjoying expanded access to social work education, and that the university helps increase social justice by promoting access to education of social work professionals in underserved communities. They may even see the benefit of the use of telehealth placements and avatar-based practice. The reality is that even in online distance-delivered degrees in social work education, it is quite rare that social work students complete field placements without any face-to-face client contact and supervision. Schools that provide liaison supervision via technology increasingly use video technologies that are similar to face-to-face in-person meetings. Compared to students who relocate for schooling, students who can stay in their own communities while continuing their education are more likely to remain in the community once the degree is earned (Moran et al., 2014; Reichert, Cromartie, & Arthun, 2014; Rérat, 2014). In this chapter, instead of introducing arguments about the pros and cons of technology-mediated field education (although you may guess our opinion), we attempt to break down the divide and focus on the continuum of technology applications in field education, from the campus-based field office that is trying to efficiently integrate new technology to the fully online program innovators who are dreaming about the future of technology in field education.

Field coordinators (also known as field directors, field staff, or other titles, depending on the program) are sometimes anxious about adopting technology. They are prized for their in-person clinical skills that allow them to simultaneously develop relationships with field site instructors (also known as field site supervisors or field educators) and with students, and do not want to lose sight of their relational work. We know that these relationships open doors to much of the experiences students are afforded in communities, and field coordinators often enjoy maintaining their valued collaborations with local agencies. They have a foot in both worlds, with an on-the-ground understanding of what is happening in the field alongside their home base in a social work educational program. Therefore, the field staff may also express reluctance to take the technology plunge for field activities such as meeting with potential agency contacts, supervisors, and students via a videoconferencing software platform such as *Zoom* instead of in-person and will need extra support in understanding the value of technology in field education.

The expectations about the use of and competence with technology among field coordinators are shifting. Many are familiar with field coordinator roles such as (a) matching students with a qualified field agency for placement, often drawing on their relationships in the local community to convince students as well as agencies of a mutually beneficial match; (b) teaching seminar courses; (c) navigating tough gatekeeping situations with students; and (d) serving in the role of liaison, or the practitioner who meets with the agency and student to discuss learning opportunities and progress (although sometimes this role is held by contractors, social work faculty, or others). Field coordinators must now manage all these roles while integrating digital technologies, often working with practitioners and agency staff members who sometimes do not have access to or training in how to use the technology. Also, as technology used in universities and social work programs has grown more complex, field coordinators must adapt to new requirements. All areas of social work education, including field, are expected to be more accountable, use data to improve their education programming, and to innovate (Asakura, Todd, Eagle, & Morris, 2018). Field coordinators now need to be tech-savvy not only because of new responsibilities related to distance education but also because of the development of technology needs in traditional seated social work programs. Now, field coordinators may have new tasks related to technology such as collecting data for program assessment via a Web-based assessment management programs such as Taskstream or via spreadsheet software; offering video recording lectures to be delivered via a learning management system (LMS); hosting meetings via videoconferencing software; and training students to use electronic forms in a variety of Web-based applications. Further, a field coordinator may need to make initial contacts with a new field site using only technology (i.e., host small meetings via live video services, and exchange important documents online). Savvy social work field programs as at the University at Buffalo (UB) and the University of Houston are going even further to find innovative ways to use technology tools such as geographic information system (GIS) software to match students to the closest field opportunities and to help geographically distant students connect to each other. See Breakout Box 7.1 for more information about how one field office is using GIS.

BREAKOUT BOX 7.1. PRACTICAL TIPS
APPLICATIONS FOR GIS IN FIELD EDUCATION

Jamie Parker, director of field education at University of Houston Graduate College of Social Work, along with Nivisha Shah, hybrid/online field coordinator, originally set out to use a Geospatial Information System (GIS) to provide a visual representation of the locations of their field placement sites. They chose to use the cloud-based software ARC GIS because other academic units at the university were already using it. As they began exploring, additional functionality was discovered, such as the ability to more quickly match students to placements based on their home locations. They also use the software to label agencies by categories, which enhances the ability to place students in preferred matches. The software does not interact directly with other field resource databases, so addresses of field sites must be manually uploaded to the GIS program, which means maps are static instead of interactive. Still, Jamie Parker and Nivisha Shah see additional ways the platform could enhance field program knowledge; for instance, in the future they might add a data layer that includes locations of all students or field liaisons to further improve efficiency, matching, and visual storytelling.

Online distance education also offers a whole new set of technology-based learning and role development for field coordinators. In short, it takes more than a team with good clinical skills to make the most of a field education experience in our increasingly digital environments—it also requires advanced technology-facilitated administrative practice skills. For instance, students may have limited technical skills when using specialized software for developing an online learning plan and tracking field hours. Field coordinators must often fill the gap by providing the additional software training. Further, because potential social work field agencies and the public have limited knowledge about how online social work programs teach students, field coordinators must often educate and engage potential field placement sites and community professionals to help them understand online programming. The field coordinator often provides information about the efficacy of online learning, because as potential distance field site instructors may lack experience working with a distance-educated student and may bring their own biases or assumptions about the effectiveness of online education. Distant field sites may also have loyalty to local schools or serve as a host site for students from other universities who have different calendars and policies or are in another state. An agency is unlikely to have the preexisting relationships with field coordinators or social work programs from other states in the way that occurs in communities local to the campus. Therefore, attending to field placement requirements in new communities takes more time for field coordinators. As with any new agency, there are many steps to developing a new field placement agreement (i.e., paperwork, addressing barriers, and building trust). Imagine doing all of this from a distance and then never having another student in that geographical region or agency setting again, which means frequent fresh starts.

Field placement is also a high-stakes experience for students. It is known to be the most anxiety-provoking part of the social work educational experience (Wilson, 2013). Some students have no previous experience in a work setting, and the classroom experiences of mock interviews or simulations only partially prepare students for the real-life work of sitting with clients. Traditional-aged students come from a background in which social technologies are infused in every part of their lives, including as a mediator to in-person conversations, and this has implications for new social workers who attend field practice in settings where communication is typically not technology mediated (Ahmedani, Harold, Fitton, & Shifflet Gibson, 2011). Field coordinators, as a result, must keep their clinical skills sharp enough to ease tensions between students and the field agency, and help students through these difficult types of transitions, even by distance using some of the same technologies. For example, the field coordinator might be e-mailing, video conferencing, or texting with a student to discuss the importance of in-person engagement with clients and colleagues.

To successful navigate these types of student technology-mediated encounters, we encourage the use of a high-touch pedagogy. What do we mean by high-touch pedagogy (MacFadden, Maiter, & Dumbrill, 2002)? In its simplest terms, we are talking about emotionally connected work, regardless of the role of technology in facilitating communication or learning. High-tech and high-touch teaching are often seen as dichotomous, but we believe they can exist mutually. Every communication with a field liaison, an agency staff member, and student is another opportunity to engage in a relationship, whether it is an in-person meeting, a videoconference, or an e-mail. In practical terms, field coordinators can set metrics or guidelines that help inform what high-touch connection looks like, such as three outreaches per week by a liaison for a student in a current field placement, at least one of which is unrelated to field (i.e., happy birthday/happy holidays note or a general supportive outreach), with the other outreaches serving as placement-related or reminders of upcoming activities. When paired with technology, some of these outreaches can be automated and personalized, but automation should not take the place of person-to-person communication. We encourage field coordinators to incorporate technologies that we know to be most relational from a high-touch lens into their own practice with students and field agencies. Examples include videoconference meetings with Zoom or Skype or texting students with apps such as Remind or GroupMe. Metrics and automation cannot replace relational experiences, but yes, we can use video calls and text messages with an ethical and caring approach! See Breakout Box 7.2 for practical tips on how to extend emotional support in the field via technology.

BREAKOUT 7.2. PRACTICAL TIPS
EXTENDING EMOTIONAL SUPPORT IN FIELD WITH TECHNOLOGY

Field coordinators can extend the emotional and instructional support with technology, whether students attended coursework in a local seated program or are involved in distance programming. Examples of communication tools include video-conferencing calls with Skype or Zoom, audio recordings uploaded to an e-mail or learning management system (LMS), and group text messages through a program such as Remind that allows for automated and personal messaging while maintaining privacy. Online calendar scheduling software such as agreeAdate and Doodle allow students to arrange timely meetings with field personnel separate from e-mails, eliminating frustrating back and forth communication.

Arizona State University keeps up with its students by delivering podcasts and videos that students can access during their field placements. Podcasts may be especially accessible for students who travel distances for fieldwork and can connect to the audio while commuting.

When field placement agencies do not have access to video-conferencing calls because of technology barriers, University of North Dakota's field office mails a video kit that contains a Wi-Fi device and tablet, so the agency can participate in a virtual field visit.

This chapter is framed from our perspectives that social work field education must be relational and that technology can be deployed for relational purposes. The discussion in this chapter is informed by interviews with social work field coordinators across universities who employ various technology-based strategies that fit well in their institutions. See the acknowledgments at the end of this chapter for more information about our interviews. Administrative roles and school practices can change quickly, so examples and descriptions used in this chapter were accurate at the time of this writing but may have since changed. We acknowledge the unique challenges related to the use of technology in field education programs by incorporating discussions of the philosophical choices as well as the practical needs of field offices throughout this chapter. We have also incorporated field education into our digital technology continuum for social work education, recognizing that field education is social work education (see Chapter 1 for an overview of this continuum). Topics in this chapter related to technology in field education include (a) preparing and screening students for field via distance; (b) placement, including contacting the local social work program; (c) face-to-face versus technology-assisted field site visits; (d) online screening and training with field instructors; and (e) distance supervision. This chapter also covers the use of technology and software choices for managing field data and outreach. We offer case studies related to organizational practices such as field visits (hiring regional people, distance visits via video calls, or flying to see students) and initial placement identification (student, field office, or partner driven). Finally, we use the terms "distance" and "online" programs interchangeably throughout this chapter as both are used across the nation. Although social work educational programs have been doing distance education for many years (i.e., via closed-circuit TV or sending faculty members to remote locations), most programs use a combination of online software and learning management systems now to deliver their content via distance (Shorkey & Uebel, 2014).

WHAT DO CSWE AND OTHER REGULATORY BODIES SAY ABOUT DISTANCE EDUCATION AND TECHNOLOGY IN FIELD EDUCATION?

Referred to as the *signature pedagogy* of our profession, field education is an opportunity for students to demonstrate their ability in the real world and to practice what they have learned in the classroom (CSWE, 2015). Field is also often a setting in which the Council on Social Work Education (CSWE)–required data are collected by the social work program about students' competency in practice settings, holistically defined as the application of social work knowledge, values, skills, and cognitive and affective processes, also known as domains of competency (CSWE, 2015). Although CSWE offers some guidance about the role of technology in field education, field coordinators should also look to other regulatory and professional bodies (i.e., the National Association of Social Workers [NASW] or their state's licensing board) as well as their own institution for further direction.

Although CSWE does not differentiate between standards for seated versus online social work education for field, they do require that students demonstrate competence through the in-person application of skills with clients or constituents during field education (CSWE, 2015). Live and virtual simulations in which students interact with actors or avatars are becoming more common in social work education, yet they cannot be the only way that programs assess student competency in field (Bogo, Rawlings, Katz, & Logie, 2014). For example, the University of Southern California (USC) School of Social Work has been using virtual clients to help train students in their MSW program before their field experience, but students still work directly with clients for their field hours. A group of USC MSW students does work remotely with live clients via a telehealth program when they have other significant barriers to direct practice access (such as living out of the country) and can benefit from video-assisted supervision from licensed practitioners when they work in those settings. If social work programs can demonstrate student competency across the required domains (knowledge, skills, values, and cognitive/affective processes) in the field settings, placements may occur at a call center, such as a crisis line, or a video-assisted coaching and counseling program like those often offered to military families (CSWE, 2015).

Field programs must articulate their field methods for their online programs for CSWE accreditation by describing their process for selecting agencies and field instructors, as well as checking in with students during their time in field education (CSWE, 2015). Social work field programs must also be able to explain the ways they provide orientation for students in online programs and ongoing training for field instructors in distant locations (CSWE, 2015). Accomplishing these tasks at a distance can be resource intensive, and this is an essential consideration for social work programs considering their methods of distance or online programming.

As we have noted in other parts of this book, NASW has recently updated their Standards for Technology in Social Work Practice, which include an entire section devoted to education and supervision (NASW, 2017). Although CSWE does not require educational programs to meet these standards (CSWE, personal communication, June 30, 2017), the standards do provide guidance and include one section related to field education (CSWE, personal communication, June 30, 2017). See Chapter 8 and Appendix 3 for a more detailed discussion of these standards.

Another essential regulatory consideration for distance programs is the state authorization for field internships through either membership with the National Council for State Authorization Reciprocity Agreements (NC-SARA) or separate agreements with unaffiliated NC-SARA states (NC-SARA, n.d.). For a detailed discussion of this process, see Chapter 6. It is essential to have access to legal representation when developing education affiliation agreements between social work educational programs and field placement agencies, especially across state lines or international borders. Although many agencies will readily accept your program's affiliation agreement, many others will have their own contracts, and state requirements for contract content may vary across jurisdictions. In this event, a legal consult can help navigate the differences between states relative to regulations and expectations.

WHAT ARE THE DIFFERENCES BETWEEN CAMPUS AND DISTANCE FIELD EDUCATION PROGRAMS?

In small social work programs, assessing student readiness for field education may be similar across campus and distance delivery models. Differences, or the need to implement different strategies, may only become apparent when a concern arises. Examples include when a gatekeeping meeting is needed; a student's potentially concerning online behavior is hard to decipher; or a field instructor reports a student concern. Whereas these difficulties would traditionally be assessed during an office-based check-in, the online environment requires a different approach. Thus, field coordinators should plan for managing difficulties in both the seated and online learning environments. See Breakout Box 7.3 for a list of common elements associated with online or distance field education programs.

BREAKOUT BOX 7.3. THEORY TALK
UNIQUE CHARACTERISTICS OF DISTANCE FIELD EDUCATION PROGRAMS

If you have a campus-based field program and are just moving to distance education, you may be wondering about the differences between the two delivery options for field education. Although we have highlighted several differences already in this chapter, this list covers common elements of distance field programs discovered from our interviews:

- Managing distance placements takes more time due to travel, continuous development of new field agency agreements, and other paperwork issues.
- Out-of-state field placements or use of out-of-state liaisons may involve human resources or legal staff in developing contracts and placement agreements.

- Student orientation to field and placement arrangements occur earlier in the social work curriculum, and should be assessed during student admission.
- Initial identification of agency placements often start with the student, not the field staff.
- Models and protocols for student/agency visits and managing concerns that come up during placements require more travel for field staff or hiring out-of-state staff.
- Training for field instructors needs to include technology-based options.

When implementing a distance field program, it is essential to identify the mechanisms currently being used to assess student readiness for field throughout the program and ensure there is a means to replicate them or use differential practices that meet the same goals in the online environment. For instance, if you typically rely on seated classroom experience with students to assess the critical-thinking skills that indicate readiness for field and are now considering a primarily asynchronous model of content delivery, course development will need to include assignments designed to demonstrate critical-thinking and practice skills in the online learning environment. One way to accomplish this is by requiring students to provide video demonstrations of their practice skills development. In some social work programs, specific assignments designed to prepare students for field are added to the curriculum before students enter their field placement. For instance, Sarah Bradley, inaugural MSW online option coordinator and associate professor of practice at Portland State University (PSU), shared their requirement for students to map the scope of practice in their home community as part of their coursework. In this assignment, students explore what level of professional licensure or degree is required and describe typical work in various practice settings (i.e., hospitals or prisons) in their individual communities. This has the advantage of helping provide field coordinators with some first notions about potential placements. For more information on how to design practice skill courses, see Chapter 5. For more examples of field assignments, see Appendix 1.

Additional insight can be gained about student readiness through student comments posted in online discussion boards, where educators can post questions about professional and ethical practice, and assess whether students are experiencing communication problems or other concerns related to professionalism. A video-based discussion tool such as Flipgrid or VoiceThread may be better for assessing communication difficulties related to nonverbal skills that might be warning signs for field readiness. Some programs use campus visits to supplement assessment of readiness, requiring students to come to campus to attend didactic sessions and meet with field education faculty members. This way, all faculty members have an in-person opportunity to assess for communication styles and offer correction if needed. In social work education, these types of visits are most frequently used in regionally based distance programs, but a few national programs also include a campus visit.

Early planning and coordination of field orientation and other placement activities are critical in distance programs. Students must be well informed of the time commitments and expectations for their physical presence in an internship. This is particularly important in asynchronous programs when students expect a great deal of flexibility related to when and how they can complete their coursework. Students new to online learning may assume that the whole degree provides more flexibility than is possible in field settings. Beginning preparations for field early in a social work program allows students time to explore whether work-based placements are an option, and also provides time to talk with their employers regarding scheduling and release time for an internship. Employment-based placements are a popular option for students already employed at a human service agency. If the student and employer can identify new tasks and supervision that meet the learning plan objectives, this simplifies the process of placing distance students who live in remote locations. Whether campus or distance, work-based field placements often require extra vetting to clarify expectations of new learning activities and develop clear boundaries separating the students' internship and their employment. In many programs, students are required to submit a proposal for an internship in their place of employment that demonstrates explicit support from the agency's administration and delineates the steps to be taken to ensure unimpeded learning during the internship. This proposal is reviewed by the field education office to determine whether students will have a placement opportunity that meets CSWE's criteria regarding new learning for work-based field placements (CSWE, 2015).

When a social work program's explicit curriculum does not have a specific class designed to prepare students for field, coordinators typically schedule a detailed interview with the student to develop a personalized learning plan. The meeting clarifies previous work and volunteer experiences as well as identifies career goals and helps guide the field placement search process. The information gleaned from this interview can be invaluable for field coordinators looking for learning environments that will provide the students with professional growth and development beyond social work skills already mastered in previous experiences. The interview is also a time for field faculty to coach students about how to network to identify possible contacts and internship sites in schools where that is a role of the student.

WHAT TECHNOLOGY SKILLS DO FIELD COORDINATORS, LIAISONS, AND FIELD INSTRUCTORS NEED?

Although the requisite technology skills of field coordination are increasing, for both campus and distance programs, field coordinators and liaisons who are assigned to oversee online student placements from a distance may require a technical skill level beyond the knowledge and skills traditionally needed for local placements. Knowing how to engage students, such as developing relationships, disseminating knowledge effectively, and problem solving via distance and with digital tools requires expertise like that of the online classroom instructor (see Chapter 5 for more information about online courses). Field programs may have to hire from outside of their standard pool of field liaisons or assist in the skill development by providing training. Comfort with modern technologies is a necessity, and many of the tools used in the online classroom can be adapted to perform critical functions in field education. See Breakout Box 7.4 for a description of the technology mindset that supports creating or working in a distance field program.

BREAKOUT BOX 7.4. PRACTICAL TIPS
TECHNOLOGY MINDSET FOR FIELD EDUCATION

Not all field coordinators, liaisons, or supervisors are a good fit for technology-mediated education or supervision. The right mindset, however, might be even more important than a specific set of technology skills. University at Buffalo's collective practice wisdom from the field office indicates that a good match as a field coordinator, liaison, or supervisor is someone who matches the following traits:

- Is not risk averse and is willing to try new instructional approaches
- Is curious about modern technology options that improve personal communication
- Weighs potential benefits of technology for their work alongside the risks, having a balanced perspective
- Views the deployment of technology as an opportunity to be creative and innovate with teaching and learning
- Sees the potential for technology as a tool to promote relationship building (versus a belief that technology harms relationships)

> - Understands that in-person approaches may not always translate well to distance communication, maintaining a focus on desired objectives (i.e., high-quality learning for students and well-prepared field educators)
> - Is willing to experiment with technology as a means of getting the same desired outcome (i.e., uses technology to achieve an outcome, not as a trade-off)
> - Is not intimidated by technology (i.e., tolerant of the minor challenges inherent to learning about technology)
> - Is often an innovator or early adopter of technology, per Rogers's (2003) Diffusion of Innovations Theory
>
> Heather Craig-Oldsen, former BSW director at Briar Cliff University, summarized this mindset best when she described her experience in taking a social work program online: "My colleague and I were in our 60s when we decided to develop an online program. You have to have an 'anything's possible' attitude to make it happen."

One way to support technology development among field coordinators in an online program is to have dedicated field education positions just for distance education. Midsize to larger schools may find they want to increase their staffing and assign some field coordinators to the distance students only, because the work does have some nuances that require additional skill sets. Most midsize to large programs hire a field coordinator who works under or parallel to the program's field director and whose role is to manage only the distance-educated students. Schools typically use field liaisons to act as a bridge between the university and community setting to ensure appropriate learning opportunities are available and to assist in gathering assessment data. Some schools use faculty or community-based liaisons who connect with students via travel or technology, while others hire liaisons in or near the regions where students reside, or some mix of both. The following discussion of roles for technology-based tasks in social work field programs may help schools develop job descriptions, orientations, training, or other program improvements.

Field Director, Coordinator, or Distance Coordinator for a Field Program

The general duties of this type of position are to coordinate the field program and establish policies and procedures. Technology tasks and technology applications for this role are as follow:

- *Coordinates technology use across the social work field program:* Establishes policies and procedures for distance and technology-mediated field education; ensures integration of field policies, practices, expectations, and timelines for distance/online programs in all school processes from program preadmission application to graduation. Shares data with the social work program and other constituents to inform curricular needs and program integrity.
- *Develops policies and procedures regarding technology use in field:* Policies and procedures address data management, FERPA/HIPPA compliance, technology-mediated placements, federal and state laws, institutional guidelines, accreditation issues, and expectations for training on technology hardware and software, and technology-mediated communications including policies or practices regarding the use of communication technologies such as social media when policies are not in place at the field agency.
- *Evaluates program needs and secures necessary resources:* Needs include hardware, software (for data management and technology-mediated communication), and training for all stakeholders from the faculty to students.
- *Orients and trains field staff on use of technology and best practices in the field program:* Training topics include technolo-

gy-related standards for field placement, communication, and data management; hardware and software use; and best practices for technology use.

- *Participates in learning networks:* Networks with field directors across social work and other professional programs to stay abreast of best practices and issues that affect field related to CSWE or other regulatory bodies.

- *Ensures programmatic data collection via technology for field program:* Data is systematically collected, integrated, analyzed, and used to inform change.

Field Staff

Field staff members place students, support agency contracting, and may serve as liaisons. Typical tasks and technology applications for the role are as follow:

- *Develops curriculum, trains others, and effectively uses field-related software:* Is knowledgeable about the software used for data collection and communication and can train stakeholders in these tools via distance or in person. Develops asynchronous or synchronous training and orientation modules to orient stakeholders to field policies, procedures, and technologies via distance.

- *Effectively uses technology to carry out job tasks:* Uses technology for recruitment, contracting, training, and communication with new placement sites in consideration of laws and policies; establishes and carries out procedures related to ongoing one-on-one communication with liaisons, supervisors, and students via technology, including frequency, and best practices.

- *Helps stakeholders understand effective uses of technology:* Educates community members regarding how distance education is equivalent to campus-based programming and provides systematic training to field liaisons, supervisors, and students regarding field technologies and best practices.

Field Liaisons

Field liaisons, whether staff members, faculty members or contractors, serve as a bridge between the university and placement, and they monitor student learning contracts. Typical tasks and applications are as follow:

- *Monitors student and agency needs and competencies in technology use:* Communicates clear expectations to supervisors and students regarding technology-mediated communication and field-based learning; supports students and supervisors in the use of electronic forms, data management systems, or technology-mediated field education plans; ensures supervisors understand technology-related competencies that students are expected to demonstrate; and helps supervisors and students identify any gaps in policies or practices related to technology-mediated communication in the field setting
- *Effectively uses technology to carry out job tasks:* Carries out procedures related to ongoing one-on-one communication with field office, supervisors, and students via technology, using best practices related to frequency and technology

Field Instructors/Supervisors or Task Supervisors

The general duties of field instructors/supervisors or task supervisors are oversight of student field work, supervision of learning plans, and providing regular supervision. A typical technology task for this position is monitoring student use of technology.

The instructor/supervisor ensures students have opportunities to build and demonstrate competence in technology-mediated social work practice in areas of ethical behavior, assessment, treatment, and evaluation, and provides feedback related to professional use and expectations in the field.

Field Students

Field students demonstrate competency in social work practice. Typical tasks and applications are as follow:

- *Effectively communicate via technology:* Demonstrate the ability to communicate effectively using a variety of technologies, including e-mail, text, and video as appropriate; choose the best technologies in various situations; seek help when appropriate; are timely and professional in using e-mail, field plans, time logs, case notes, and other technologies
- *Use technology for practice:* Demonstrate the ability to choose and use technology for assessment, intervention, and evaluation as appropriate
- *Understand ethical use of technology:* Manage boundaries related to technology, professional online identity, password protection, client privacy, and other standards; consult appropriately about technology questions or accidental misuse of technology

Social Work Faculty Members

Social work faculty members prepare students for social work practice. Typical technology tasks and applications associated with this role are as follow:

- *Prepare students for technology-mediated practice in the field:* Integrate technology-related case studies into class to help prepare students for issues that might arise in fieldwork, including best practices for technology-mediated communication, assessment, intervention, evaluation, and ethical concerns; teach students to access and apply technology-related standards from EPAS.

- *Build digital literacy and provides opportunities for technology-related skill building:* Assignments require students to use a variety of technologies, inside and outside the LMS. Students are given feedback about their use of technology.

- *Notify field faculty members of concerns related to student technology use:* If students demonstrate concerns related to ethical or expected use of technology, the faculty members communicate with the field office after giving feedback to students if remedial supports are necessary for student success in field placement.

Stakeholders Across the Curriculum

All stakeholders across the curriculum ensure program and student success. Typical technology tasks and applications for stakeholders are as follow:

- *Effectively use technology for communication*: Communicate the best ways for stakeholders to reach you via technology tools and respond within timelines established by the field office

- *Use technology ethically:* Know how to access appropriate supports related to technology disruptions or other problems related to distance learning; consult as appropriate in novel situations or when an ethical issue emerges related to technology or distance learning; engage in continuing education to keep up-to-date with best practices regarding the use of technology in social work; review and understand new standards relevant to technology-mediated social work education and from the Code of Ethics and technology standards;

maintain student and client privacy

- *Model lifelong learning in technology use:* Share emerging technologies that pose promise or concerns that can affect policies or practice in field education; model ethical and effective use of technology

Although CSWE does not require a specific student-to-field liaison ratio, field offices should consider that liaisons who manage distance students may need more time (and a reduced staff-to-student ratio) to travel or manage technology. *Pearson*, a for-profit educational company that supports online curriculum and provides other services, recommends that schools add one full-time field program staff member to help with placement development and orientations, and an additional liaison every time the social work program enrollment grows by 50 students. You may want to think about the student-to-coordinator or student-to-liaison ratio (depending on the structure of the job roles at your university) for your own online program, and how this is calculated depends on such variables as the location of the student, whether the placement is new or well established, and what kind of coordinator travel or contact may be required to manage the placement.

Another approach to supporting technology mindsets and development among all levels of field education personnel, including field instructors, is through continuing education. Field coordinators may assume it would be challenging to attract field instructors to online training, but this is likely not a correct assumption. A survey of more than 200 Michigan field instructors were asked about their willingness to engage in online learning, and the study found that 82% were willing to attend online training relevant to their roles as field coordinators (Dedman & Palmer, 2011). These field instructors also saw other opportunities for the use of technology, such as connecting with other field instructors and the university as a whole. Online engagement with field instructors via these trainings also offers an opportunity for field offices to model the ways that social workers can use technology for professional purposes. One of us (Carol) offers a monthly synchronous "Lunch in the Field" continuing education meeting for all field instructors at the University of North Dakota (UND). Through a videoconferencing platform, field instructors are encouraged to log in once a month to learn about a new topic, with different faculty members leading the discussions. They earn a continuing education hour for attending the meeting, get experience related to online education in a way similar to the distance students, and meet some of the program's full-time faculty members. Training can be focused on issues that students are bringing up in field seminar, such as the ethical use of technology with clients, or can be related to CSWE outcomes issues, such as how to give students a good research experience in the field setting. The "Lunch in the Field" makes training more accessible, and the free continuing education credit supports the field instructors and acknowledges their contributions to the program.

In speaking about the technology learning curve with field liaisons or students, Sarah Bradley, at PSU, mentioned that every time she incorporates technology into her training and instruction, she must figure out how to use it first. With this knowledge, she can then develop how-to videos for the students and troubleshoot in advance any potential issues. In this case, the faculty member is identifying a useful technology tool and learning alongside or just ahead of the liaisons or students. No one person can know every new digital tool, but approaching technology with the spirit of a curious innovator as described above goes a long way in supporting distance field education. For more information on how to assess one's own level of technology readiness, see Chapter 4. Additionally, Chapter 9 provides many suggestions on how social work educators can increase their own skills, such as developing a professional learning network.

Although we have shared some advice for helping with

technology-mediated communication, field offices should be mindful of the frequency of technology issues that arise in field placements and the importance of mentorship that students receive from their field instructors and liaisons related to these experiences. For example, students may be placed in a child welfare agency where workers have degrees in a variety of fields, and some workers are using social media to search for clients without clear agency policy guidance and without an obligation to follow a code of ethics, risking poor modeling for the social work intern. In contrast, students may be placed at a juvenile justice center where Internet is blocked, limiting access to technology-assisted field liaison visits and the ability to log placement hours from the work setting. In many cases, students may be savvier with technology than others in their workplace, including field instructors, especially about the latest trends.

Regardless, students (and the instructors!) may need help thinking about these issues with a social work lens, especially related to ethical dilemmas. For instance, what considerations guide whether a student should friend field instructors or other social workers at the agency, especially if the agency culture encourages its employees to make many social network connections. Field offices can help field agencies stay abreast of such issues through Web-based webinar trainings, e-mail blasts, and short "did you know" communications. Additionally, the field office should be aware of agency culture at its various field placement sites, as opinions and values about using and integrating technology may vary based on the type of agency, individual values, and past experiences. For example, social media is widely used among adoption agencies to promote foster care and adoption to the general public, whereas domestic violence shelters may be concerned about privacy and confidentiality when using technology with their clients. It also helps for social work educators to be digitally literate about the cultures of different types of social media platforms and how they may be used in different field agency (i.e., why might an agency have a Facebook account but not an Instagram account). For more information about digital literacy, see Chapter 2. For more guidance on how technology affects field education, see Appendix 3.

WHY DO FIELD EDUCATION OFFICES NEED SPECIALIZED SOFTWARE OR DATABASES?

Virtually all social work programs rely on a database to catalog or track essential student, placement, and field instructor and agency information. Many key program functions, such as tracking attendance of student and field instructor orientation as required by CSWE, and student selection of placement and placement assignment, depend on a well-maintained system of record keeping, and technology can aid in all these tasks. Field programs may begin the placement process by surveying agency partners and field instructors about their continued interest in hosting students, and a plethora of Web-based survey tools exist that can help accomplish this goal. Google Forms, part of Google Docs, is a free tool, for example, that can be used to create customized forms to collect information about new field opportunities. Survey platforms such as SurveyMonkey and Qualtrics, offer similar utility. These data can then be converted into a spreadsheet and imported into a database. From there, the database can be uploaded to a GIS program to provide a visual map of field locations and can be filtered in various ways. At the other end of the spectrum, some schools, such as USC, use a high-powered database system called Salesforce, where every contact with a field stakeholder can be logged in the system and analytics run to explore demographics and other factors based on types of contact or field site. See Breakout Box 7.5 for examples of software commonly used by social work field offices.

BREAKOUT BOX 7.5. PRACTICAL TIPS
UNDERSTANDING SOFTWARE FOR FIELD EDUCATION

Many types of software and applications (apps) can be used for field education. Some are free, and others are proprietary with financial costs. Some examples of how software can be used in field education are as follows:

- Manage field applications and learning plans (IPT and Sonia)
- Track learning outcomes (Taskstream by Watermark)
- Keep lists of student cohorts, placement sites, liaisons (Microsoft Excel or Google Sheets)
- Map students' distance to sites (GIS)
- Make video-conference calls (Zoom and Skype)
- Host classes (LMS, Zoom, and Adobe Connect)
- Collect survey information (SurveyMonkey or Qualtrics)
- Record meetings (GotoMeeting or Adobe Connect)
- Send e-mail and text messages (Microsoft Outlook and Remind)
- Network students to each other (Facebook, Flipgrid, and LinkedIn)
- Build practice communities (LISTSERVs and program websites, Facebook, or Flipgrid)

Does your analog field office want to make an easy first step to integrate some timesaving technology? Consider moving your field application to Google Forms, a free software where data can be exported to Excel or viewed online. For more information about all of these software programs and apps, see the section titled "Specific Brand Name Products and Organizations" in the Glossary.

Other needs in field education include recording student data related to placement preferences, which are generally collected and maintained as part of the student's application to field practicum. What student information is deemed relevant may vary by program but typically includes student geographic preference, practice area of interest or concentration, and perhaps more critically, any accessibility needs. Some programs still collect handwritten student forms and go through a process of matching that involves adhesive notes and handwritten lists, which may be acceptable and efficient in smaller programs. For field programs with larger student bodies, the act of matching individual students to available placements becomes more complicated. Some programs have designed their own custom-made digital systems for managing field data. Increasingly, Web-based placement management systems are available for purchase and are marketed across programs that use field placement experiences. Many of these can be customized and cost money; the programs may have institutional fees based on student body size, monthly maintenance fees, or creation and editing fees. Some of these programs have been designed for teacher field education programs and can be customized for managing social work placements; examples of the programs include Taskstream, TK20, and LiveText, all under the company Watermark. A smaller number of specialized programs are designed specifically for social work, such as Intern Placement Tracking (IPT) and Sonia. See Breakout Box 7.6 for tips on how to decide which digital tracking system is best for your program.

BREAKOUT BOX 7.6. PRACTICAL TIPS
QUESTION TO ASK WHEN PLANNING TO ADOPT A FIELD TRACKING SOFTWARE

Are you deciding which field tracking systems make the most sense for you? Consider the following:

1. Does your university already use and support a system that might work for you?
2. Do you need a system that can connect to key software and databases (e.g., university enrollment systems, an agency database, and a student database)?
3. Does your program retain ownership of the data? Who else has access?
4. Is the data stored locally on a university server, or is the data stored remotely?
5. Is storage on a secure server, or is storage Cloud based?
6. What are the costs of implementation, ongoing fees, and updates?
7. What level of support is provided?

Because this is a high-stakes decision in terms of money, time, and other resources, programs may want to create an ad hoc decision-making committee, talk with other social work program administrators who have already adopted specific brands of software, and invite company representatives to campus for a product demonstration.

Field programs have increasingly invested in data management systems since 2008 when CSWE updated its Educational Policies and Accreditation Standards (EPAS) to require collection and reporting of assessment data to the public (CSWE, 2008, 2015). Which software systems make the most sense for a program? The answer is that it depends on the program needs. Depending on available resources and program size, field education offices may want to choose a system that simultaneously helps to manage the process of field placements and data collection. Features of digital tracking systems can vary but may include basic data storage and retrieval; electronic survey forms; document tracking; bulk e-mailing and e-mail merges; automated matching of student and field placement attributes; and automated e-mail referral of students to placements. Ideally, but infrequently, the field software can "talk" to other software used by the field office or institutions through connected databases. For instance, when the same software is not used for both field plans and assessment reporting, it is ideal if the data from the field plans can import directly into the database used for program assessment. Accredited programs must be able to collect and report on evaluation data related to student learning outcomes and the implicit curriculum, so ideally, at a minimum, the field plan program should offer the option to create reports from a database.

In-house designed options can work where there is technical support on-campus (i.e., an information technology [IT] department at your institution) that will handle system development, implementation, and most importantly, ongoing updates. Many schools find it easier to use a vendor or packaged software solution. One type of simple and less expensive field tracking software used by schools such as University of Central Florida and UND is Intern Placement Tracking (IPT), also known as ALCEA. This system, like many in the field database category, is a Web-based program. Created by the spouse of a social work educator to meet the need of social work programs, this software provides field education offices with predeveloped time log forms and the ability to create new custom forms. Other features include customized *user* roles within the system for the liaison, student, and field coordinator.

Depending on the individual's position (and assigned user role) within the system, the user can create, review, edit and approve different digital forms related to student hours and evaluations. Prompts are provided by e-mail when forms are ready for review. ALCEA allows for some reporting features, as well as sorting and label printing. As of this writing, many of the add-on features to

IPT such as customized digital forms are available at an additional cost. Some schools, such as Arizona State University (ASU), have paired the use of IPT with DocuSign, a Web-based program for collecting authenticated signatures, for their field agreements with community-based agencies. Most field offices eventually settle on some combination of off-the-shelf products like this.

At the other end of this spectrum, highly customizable and robust programs, such as Sonia, are available. This Web-based program includes e-portfolio tools, accreditation data tracking tools, mobile apps, social media integration, and field placement databases. It can also support linkages to your university's enrollment databases and can be used across multiple school sites. With user-friendly dashboards, data about field student and placement demographics are easy to share with other staff members. Schools interested in such a system can expect fees, such as set-up costs, student access fees, and monthly maintenance dues. This may be practical for social work programs at institutions with substantial enrollments or state schools connected across multiple sites where it is easier to bring down the per-pupil roll-out expense.

UB uses Taskstream by Watermark to collect student competency data during field placement. The ability to have multiple people view a student's learning contract and evaluation was an essential feature for the UB field office, as was the functionality of reporting field education data. As of this writing, no set-up fee is required, but there is a cost for student accounts. A variety of payment options are available with this software; one possibility is a direct charge to students, and the other is for a social work program to purchase a site license and absorb the student costs. Students can buy their own multiyear license for less than the price of a typical textbook. Taskstream also offers other digital tools such as an accreditation management database, which carries with it additional cost. Although it is proprietary Web-based software, the program's databases are built within the institution's IT systems, and the university maintains ownership of the database. It allows for many of the same features as does Sonia, with more build-your-own customization versus custom-build dashboards. Following is a sample of tools and features to consider when selecting a field tracking software for your program.

- Data storage and retrieval
- Document tracking
- Filtering and matching student and agency attributes
- Assessment of learning outcomes
- Off-site (nonuniversity) log-in
- Interoperability with other software or databases
- Electronic forms
- Bulk e-mailing; e-mail merging
- Automatically generated e-mails for placement interviews
- Data and outcome reporting
- Dashboards
- Import and export features

Although it takes some time to set up and convert paper-based reporting processes to a digital system, including time to learn how to use the features, the time savings appears to pay off in the long run. One risk with any proprietary system is that if the system goes offline or the company goes out of business, a university may not control the database and may lose information. Additionally, some universities express concern about external noncontracted platforms holding student data. The state system that oversees higher education may even have a policy prohibiting this practice. Finally, university technical support will often not provide troubleshooting help for programs that are not licensed through the university system. Because of these challenges, we recommend consulting with your institution's IT department when deciding about adopting a system. The University of Alabama at Birmingham and Indiana University (IU) both created an ad hoc committee to help with the decision process that included representatives from the faculty, the field office, agency settings, and their campus IT departments.

HOW DO WE PREPARE DISTANCE STUDENTS FOR FIELD PLACEMENT?

Regardless of the type of social work program (seated or online), preparing students for field education starts far ahead of the placement process. Distance education students, because they often engage in online study due to their work schedules, often need early (preadmission) clarity about the requirements for field placement including the number of hours and the expectations about employment during this period. Technology can help with this in many ways. For instance, students can sign an online document where they express their understanding of field requirements during their application process, or they can watch a short online preapplication video that outlines expectations of the field experience as part of a preenrollment orientation, followed by a short assessment to ensure understanding.

When students do not live in the region, field planning may need to start sooner than in traditional campus-based programs. This allows extra time to locate, screen, and contract with a field placement site in geographic locations where the field office may not have any current contacts. Some online social work programs start as soon as students apply for admission to the program by asking students to identify potential placements for the field upfront. This is especially valuable in rural or out-of-country contexts. An early field identification process allows the field office to start mapping plans for outreach and determine whether a student's preidentified site can meet student learning outcomes. Information about possible placement options can be captured by students via online forms, and e-mail can be set up to auto-send links to these forms to automate some of the work processes. Along with this practice, students should be informed about the purpose of the task, and specifically that identifying a potential agency upfront does not guarantee a field placement.

Student participation in identifying a field site varies among online social work programs. Some programs strictly instruct students not to approach potential placement sites in their community, whereas others may encourage initial outreach. Alternatively, the students can suggest places that they would like the field office to contact. If social work students lead the outreach, schools should provide clarity about when and how to approach the agencies professionally and to inform them of next steps. Some schools give the student a letter or documentation they can use to initiate contact with a possible field placement agency to aid in a student-outreach process. This student-initiated method should only be used with significant student guidance about how to approach an agency, and with clear guidance about how the field office will facilitate next steps. After the student contacts a potential agency to ask very basic questions (e.g., Do you take social work student interns?), the field office should follow up with the agency to help finalize the potential match, clarify expectations and site requirements, and support the process of the formal student interview.

Along with the field site planning process, the program's explicit curriculum can include elements that help students plan for their field experience through assignments focused on professionalization for the field, classroom discussions about what to expect during field, and continuously linking assignments to practice in their future field placement. Often, field programs hold an early orientation for students several terms before their field placements that is designed to help explain the field placement process. This can ease student anxiety and remind them of important due dates and the field timeline. The social work faculty can further help students build their technological readiness by incorporating technology-mediated assignments, case studies, and ethical dilemmas in the curriculum. See Breakout Box 7.7 for examples of how different social work programs help prepare their students for field placement.

> ## BREAKOUT BOX 7.7. CASE STUDY
> ### PREPARING STUDENTS FOR FIELD PLACEMENT IN DISTANCE PROGRAM
>
> Arizona State University (ASU) developed a creative approach for professionalizing students to the field of social work. During a formal "socialization to the profession" course, students are assigned a field ambassador. The field ambassadors are program graduates who are matched by geography to students, and their role is to talk to students about their own experiences and help them prepare for field. During a 15-week course period, they orient students to the field plans. At the end of the term the field ambassadors hand the students off to field staff. The ambassadors become additional social work mentors in the students' community. ASU also has a "field brigade" model, in which they activate field liaisons in the community to go out and help on-site if a student issue requires additional attention.
>
> University of Southern California offers a Virtual Field Practicum class proctored by a professor in which a paid actor plays the role of a client in crisis so students experience realistic practice scenarios prior to entering field. Distance students practice their intervention skills via live video.

HOW DO WE FIND FIELD PLACEMENTS IN ANOTHER STATE?

Sometimes an out-of-state agency is hesitant to take students because of their commitment to other social work programs with which they are already contracted and have developed relationships, especially those programs in their own geographic region. Additionally, some agencies may be reluctant to provide internships for online distance social work program because of their own lack of familiarity or bias about online education. In each case, the field staff should seek the opportunity to describe the way in which social work competencies are met within the online program (CSWE, 2015) to at least open the door for a conversation about possible placement and student interviews. Field coordinators will have to develop rapport quickly, establish the credibility of the program, and explain their processes and policies for giving proper attention to students and field instructors from a distance. See Breakout Box 7.8 for creative ways USC meets the placement needs of distance students.

BREAKOUT BOX 7.8. CASE STUDY
FIELD PLACEMENTS OUTSIDE THE BOX

University of Southern California (USC) has developed two unique field placement options to help meet student needs in their distance MSW program. First, they have developed successful partnerships with field agency sites in which they are able to provide agency funding and supervision for a whole unit of student interns. Second, they also run a campus-based telehealth program, and all international students conduct their field placements via distance in the telehealth program, which is supervised by licensed clinical faculty. Third, they are able to pay out-of-state field supervisors. While these USC programs offer unique learning opportunities for their students, these models are uncommon for social work education because they are expensive, are resource intensive, and operate on large scales.

Schools with fewer resources can use their creativity to develop low-cost ways to recognize field instructors. For instance, we have heard of programs that offer their field instructors tuition remission for a class or free continuing education units, $10 coffee shop gift cards, university-branded swag, and certificates of appreciation. These gestures alongside other practices (i.e., organized and transparent procedures, proper supports, early planning, and reputable programming) improve the likelihood of successful placement matches.

Another option to ease field placement identification is to contract with a corporate partner, also known as an online program management (OPM), that assists with this task. For instance, 2U hires staff that provides the field office with placement finding and matching services. The OPM may provide other technical supports such as identifying instructors or intervening when students are experiencing difficulties. This often comes with heavy administrative fees, upward of 50% or more of student tuition. This topic is discussed more thoroughly in Chapter 6.

When a student is successful during his or her interview with a potential field agency, the contracting process is a next step. Because the legal language in placement agreements varies from state to state and site to site, you may have to negotiate the affiliation agreement. Even after years of distance education, distance field coordinators will be continuously developing agreements with new sites. For instance, even after 10 years of distance education, the UND reports that approximately 60% of their distance internship placements each year are in new locales and require generating a new field education contract. Agreements with hospitals and other medical facilities, due to extra state-by-state protections regarding health workers, may be especially challenging to manage and require consultation with legal representation to ensure the contract is acceptable to the social work program's institution. Some field agencies may require extra student health screenings and immunizations. This can be a lengthy process, and on occasion an agreement cannot be reached, requiring an alternative site for the student.

DOES A FIELD COORDINATOR OR LIAISON NEED A FACE-TO-FACE MEETING WITH FIELD SUPERVISORS AND STUDENTS?

We have heard a variety of approaches and perspectives regarding quality field placements in our interviews with field coordinators. Some feel strongly about an in-person orientation for students in online programs, usually administered during a mandatory campus visit in which the field director outlines expectations and answers questions. Other social work programs started with this model and later moved to online orientations, and some always had fully online models. Other social work programs send campus-based field coordinators or liaisons out to approve field sites, especially for initial agreements, whereas others conduct this work remotely or hire a regional liaison to visit the potential field site. All the social work programs we spoke with have, minimally, a plan for getting someone (from the field office or a local liaison) to a field site in the case of a potential placement disruption, whether related to student or site concerns. For example, if a student cannot perform developmentally appropriate competencies or reports inadequate learning opportunities, an in-person visit may be required to resolve the situation. Many schools use technology-mediated liaison visits in their distance programs when the field work is going as expected but opt for in-person response in times of trouble. Technology-mediated visits include *audio*-only conference calls but are often enhanced by videoconferencing software so that the parties can see each other during the field liaison visit.

Most field and task supervision of the student occurs in-person. Some programs, but only a few, use video-mediated field supervision with students. We heard that recruiting and maintaining a pool of high-quality field sites and instructors is a universal challenge for all field education programs and locating placements with qualified instructors in remote regions can be particularly challenging. Nonetheless, social work field programs still mainly rely on the placement sites to provide the needed social work supervision. If social work supervision is not available at the agency (typically due to the lack of a social work supervisor on site), field offices generally prefer to contract with supervisors in the region to provide the supervision in-person. Remote video or telephone supervision from the field office is often used as the last option. When technology is employed for social work supervision, it is typically used only in special situations. For instance, Elizabeth Hayward, field coordinator at ASU, noted one instance where distance supervision was used for a student in Ecuador. This was considered an exception in that the field instructor supervising the student was also in Ecuador but working at another nongovernmental organization, so she understood the local culture. Silvana Castaneda, field director at Simmons College (SC) School of Social Work, similarly states that they occasionally allow non-routine, social work supervision by field instructors via Skype or other technology. She shares that this can work when a task supervisor is on-site who can coordinate with the field supervisor who works at a distance from the agency and is also available to join the technology-mediated supervision meetings. If a social work program uses technology-supported field instruction, it is essential to consider state laws regarding supervision. Field supervision often falls under state social work licensure laws, and if a student is in a different state than the field liaison or instructor, this could place the field supervisor in a position of practicing without a license in the student's resident state.

Many programs use field seminar as a supplement to on-site field supervision. For instance, Carrie Dorminey, field director at Valdosta State University, reports that in their regional hybrid distance program, they use a combination of in-person and technology-supported meetings. They offer an off-site supervision group individual supervision via phone or Skype video calls, asynchronous reflection assignments, and an on-campus supervision group that meets on weekends. UND, on the other hand, offers a field seminar course in a synchronous online setting where students share about their field experiences once a month.

The efficacy of models of distance supervision remains mostly untested in the social work literature. This may speak to a collective reluctance to replace the in-person elements of field supervision with online communication tools. Also, there may be a presumption that CSWE or other accreditation guidelines dissuade distance field supervision. Actually, no rules (that we are aware of) prohibit technology-mediated field supervision or liaison contact.

Understanding whether a distance approach to field supervision is effective, and under what conditions, will be a crucial area for further research by social work educators. As online programs grow and technology improves, it is likely that technology-mediated approaches to field supervision will become increasingly used and accepted. How do we use technology to maintain a sense of community and communication during field?

The social needs of adult learners are well documented and presented in previous chapters. Specifically, see Chapter 3 for the theory behind social presence in online learning environments and Chapter 5 for practical tips on developing and supporting social presence in online courses. Do not forget that field coordinators, liaisons, and agency-based supervisors are also adult learners who have needs for connection and support, and that we are all modeling and learning from each other during professional interactions. We have discussed the importance of relationship building as part of social work education, but professional relationships take maintenance, especially if they are with social workers who live a thousand miles away. Further, we often compartmentalize training needs for field education. For instance, when training new field staff in a software program, we may forget that students, liaisons, and field instructors also need the training. Or we talk to students about professional and ethical social media use but forget to include the faculty or field instructors in those conversations; or we only offer local field instructors a training opportunity and forget to make training accessible to distance instructors.

On the other hand, the field experience itself can feel compartmentalized and disconnected from the rest of the explicit curriculum, whether students are in campus-based or distance programs. When students enter field placement, it is essential that connection to the broader community within the social work program continues so that students maintain a sense that their educational community (i.e., instructors from previous courses and their peer cohort) is still accessible them, and they still identify as learners while in field placement. Similarly, field instructors need to know that even though a social work program is at a distance, support from the institution and the field office is always available to them.

Our interviews found that field offices attempt to meet challenges related to creating a sense of community and connection via distance in many ways. Programs can bolster student satisfaction, community connection, and alumni relations by giving students a sense of pride in their university, beyond just the quality of the social work program by also identifying with a place. Several social work programs describe efforts to encourage the esprit de corps in their students no matter where they reside. For instance, USC encourages students to attend away games of the USC sports teams when they come to the students' community; UND encourages students to attend a hockey game when they are on-campus for their mandatory campus visit; and ASU sends newly admitted distance students branded swag such as water bottles and T-shirts. Because online learning sometimes feels isolating or carries the stigma of not being as high quality as campus-based programs, students may be comforted by these gestures and a connection to a real-life place.

Another option for creating a sense of community for online students is by connecting students to each other geographically.

For instance, with their permission, UND's distance program director invites current students to meet for dinner with recent graduates when she travels to see students for field placements. Many of their students live in rural areas where issues of isolation may be especially prevalent during their education, and even after graduation. Community connections built during their field education may help protect students against loneliness and provide professional community networks. As UND's distance director also joins the students for dinner, she is engaged in ongoing relationship work with students and alumni, which she also sees as development work for the program, as the students often become future site instructors and a source of program referrals for future students. See Breakout Box 7.9 for considerations on creating a university-affiliated social media group for field students, which is another way to build community.

BREAKOUT BOX 7.9. PRACTICAL TIPS
SUPPORTING STUDENT-LED VIRTUAL COMMUNITIES FOR FIELD EDUCATION

It is very common for students to rally together to create their own communities using social media tools, such as a private Facebook group, if the department has not formalized this process. This is a way for students to gather around a virtual water cooler. Pros and cons should be weighed in deciding whether to create a university-hosted group or encourage students to develop their own group. On one hand, students are likely to bring up concerns or complaints in these groups that can quickly become rumors that worry or stress students unnecessarily, and program administrators may want some oversight. Conversely, it is another group to monitor if it is university administered and deprives students of the opportunity to self-police. A better approach may be to support student leadership and offer training related to how to manage problems and address concerns that emerge in the group.

Live or technology-assisted group communication is another way to establish a sense of support in distance programs and is possible to achieve through many digital tools and for a number of processes pertinent to field education. Field programs in early stages of technology adoption might begin by incorporating Web-based tools in routine field processes. For instance, they may post resource materials and a list of placement agencies on their public websites or behind a log-in website if they do not want the information publicly available. Other options to adopt technology include live streaming field-related training or uploading prerecorded videos to YouTube or an LMS so students can watch later. For example, like our discussion about the hyflex online course model in Chapter 5, field orientations and other training sessions can be made more accessible by offering both in-person and online sessions for participants and offering participants the choice of which to attend. Archiving the material for later watching allows access for those who cannot attend a live session or for later reference by all participants. A range of videoconferencing applications are available, such as GotoMeeting, Blackboard Collaborate, and Zoom. Some applications are free (usually with limited time or features), and others have costs. Zoom, a robust, moderately priced software that allows live streaming, locally saved recording or cloud storage, text chat, and breakout rooms, starts at about $100 a year per host as of this writing. Videoconferencing tools generally have functions that facilitate remote participation, which include settings that allow either full audio privileges or the use of chat boxes where questions can be posted. Skype can be used for smaller classes and include live streaming features. With live streaming, communication is often only available one way from instructor to the participant. When selecting a virtual option for a meeting or training session, the best first option is to identify your need and then see if your university licenses a specific software that meets the need. After that, you can reach out to your professional networks—other field coordinators across social work programs—and find out what works for their programs.

For a very high-touch approach, field education programs use technology to overcome the emotional and physical distance between themselves and their students. As we described earlier in this chapter, high-touch communication with students is more frequent and intentional, designed to foster a sense of community and support and engage students as learning occurs instead of only to deliver a task-related message. This might include regularly scheduled videoconference call check-ins between students and field instructors to strengthen their engagement and to facilitate more timely discussion of concerns, as well as frequent e-mail check-ins, timely process-journal feedback, and the other strategies described in Chapter 5 that demonstrate a caring approach.

LEVERAGING THE UNIQUE ROLE OF THE FIELD OFFICE WITH TECHNOLOGY FOR COMMUNITY BUILDING

Field education programs are uniquely situated between the social work program and its community constituents and are therefore well positioned to diminish the divide between the two with the assistance of technology. Online social networking sites such as Facebook and LinkedIn can be used, for example, to create virtual communities of practice gathering spaces, which provide an alternative to in-person meetings and conferences. These virtual affinity groups may be more accessible to social work practitioners and adjunct faculty members than expensive conferences. Various options can be employed to bring the community to the university. For instance, UND's "Lunch in the Field" model reengages distance field instructors with the university learning community and with the expertise of various faculty presenters.

Another option is an online group hosted by your institution for field instructors, which supports communication about shared interests and concerns. For example, a closed Facebook group allows for text-based discussion about common challenges and a forum to answer questions. Field instructors might share the realities of their work and find support from other field instructors across the country regarding common challenges. Virtual communities of practice have the potential to bridge the gap between research and practice (Adedoyin, 2016). Field instructors, for example, can connect with each other and with the social work faculty to explore ideas related to best practices in student supervision or other evidence-based practices relevant to their settings. Having the field office establish and support these virtual spaces will help ensure positive outcomes for these conversations.

There is also a larger online community for field online education. To facilitate a community of practice among field coordinators, in 2015 the Social Work Distance Education Field Consortium formed as a peer network. The consortium meets at CSWE's Annual Program Meeting, the Social Work Distance Education Conference in the United States, and virtually throughout the year. They are addressing problems, resource sharing, mentoring, and promoting best practices relevant to field education administered in distance education programs. Along with in-person and Web-facilitated meetings, they also host a website and a LISTSERV. More information can be found in our further reading list at the end of this chapter.

FINAL THOUGHTS

Field education can be enhanced by technology, but at the end of the day, we desire to minimize any quality differences between distance and campus-based social work field education and maximize the use of technology in ways that improve our educational programs and teaching practice. Technology has not wholly rewritten the role of field programs as some feared. For instance, field education is still predominantly located in community-based agencies rather than virtual practice settings, and field supervision is still primarily done on-site at a field agency. Some field coordinators are still reluctant to innovate with technology in their education and supervision practices but are trying to figure it out as the quality of digital communication tools improve. As a profession, social work educators are still exploring the indicators of quality field placements and evaluating evidence about what works in field education across several technology and nontechnology related issues. Examples include the ways to assess competencies in field settings and the ideal number of field hours. Advents in technology offer opportunities to critically analyze the way we do business in field education, to incorporate new models, and test the bounds of what is possible.

When asked to look to the future of field education in social work, several field directors we spoke with said greater collaboration between social work programs, given their shared territory, would enhance their own work. The most commonly mentioned innovation by these field coordinators was a universal training or orientation, which spanned geography and institutions, for field instructors. This would allow site-based field instructors to go through a single training and then accept students from multiple universities within a country. This kind of resource sharing may still be beyond our current level of collaboration, but conversations about innovations such as this are likely given that communication technology enables field coordinators to better network across schools to discuss these kinds of possibilities.

Research about technology and the role it plays in social work practice and education is moving the entire profession forward, and field offices need to keep pace and allow innovation and research evidence to inform our work. For example, supervision for remote placements is becoming more common and is sanctioned by licensing bodies in most states with approval, even at the clinical licensure level. If licensure supervision can occur via distance with technology tools, we should keep abreast of best practices regarding these experiences to inform our virtual work with social work students in field. Although some in the profession have resisted telehealth or online counseling, technology-assisted placements may offer additional learning opportunities, such as the benefit of video recordings so students can rewatch their interactions with clients, or receive other in vivo supervisor or guided assessment with peer or field instructor review (Rousmaniere & Renfro-Michel, 2016). These innovations offer promising potential for teaching and learning in social work education and should not be dismissed summarily. Imagine the ways in which virtual field fairs could provide exciting agency previews and timely meetings between students and community agencies. The landscape of field education is likely to look very different in 10 years, and we need to embrace our roles as lifelong learners, leading the way to understand what contributes to success and how to bridge gaps between education and practice.

ACKNOWLEDGMENTS

We express our gratitude to the following social work educators who provided information and support via interviews and e-mail about their program models: Bonnie Yegidis, University of Central Florida; Carrie Dorminey, Valdosta State University; Elizabeth Hayward, Arizona State University; Jamie Parker, University of Houston; Marilyn Flynn, University of Southern California; Michelle Brandt, Social Work Distance Education Field Consortium; Michelle Carney, University of Kansas; Sarah Bradley, Portland State University; and Silvana Castaneda, Simmons College.

FURTHER READING AND RESOURCES

Cole, S. (2015, March 10). 5 big ways education will change by 2020. *Fast Company*. Retrieved from https://www.fastcompany.com/3043387/5-big-ways-education-will-change-by-2020

Council on Social Work Education (CSWE). (2018, April). *Envisioning the future of social work: Report of the CSWE Futures Taskforce*. Retrieved from https://bit.ly/2tMHEIx

Curington, A., & Hitchcock, L. I. (2017, July 28). *Social media toolkit for social work field educators*. Retrieved from http://www.laureliversonhitchcock.org/?s=social+media+toolkit

North American Network of Field Educators and Directors. https://nanfed.com/cswe/ (a group for field educators).

Social Work Distance Education Field Consortium. https://sites.google.com/site/swdefieldconsortium/ (a network of field directors and coordinators who operate in distance education programs).

REFERENCES

Ahmedani, B. K., Harold, R. D., Fitton, V. A., & Shifflet Gibson, E. D. (2011). What adolescents can tell us: Technology and the future of social work education. *Social Work Education, 30*(7), 830–846. doi:10.1080/02615479.2010.504767

Asakura, K., Todd, S., Eagle, B., & Morris, B. (2018). Strengthening the signature pedagogy of social work: Conceptualizing field coordination as a negotiated social work pedagogy. *Journal of Teaching in Social Work*, 1–15.

Bogo, M., Rawlings, M., Katz, E., & Logie, C. (2014). *Using simulation in assessment and teaching: OSCE adapted for social work*. Alexandria, VA: Council on Social Work Education.

Council on Social Work Education (CSWE) (2008). *Educational policy and accreditation standards*. Alexandria, VA: Author. Retrieved from https://cswe.org/Accreditation/Standards-and-Policies/2008-EPAS

Council on Social Work Education (CSWE) (2015). *Educational policy and accreditation standards for baccalaureate and master's social work programs*. Alexandria,

VA: Author. Retrieved from https://www.cswe.org/getattachment/Accreditation/Accreditation-Process/2015-EPAS/2015EPAS_Web_FINAL.pdf.aspx

Dedman, D. E., & Palmer, L. B. (2011). Field instructors and online training: An exploratory survey. *Journal of Social Work Education, 47,* 151–161.

MacFadden, R. J., Maiter, S., & Dumbrill, G. C. (2002). High tech and high touch: The human face of online education. *Journal of Technology in Human Services, 20*(3–4), 283–300.

Moran, A. M., Coyle, J., Pope, R., Boxall, D., Nancarrow, S. A., & Young, J. (2014). Supervision, support and mentoring interventions for health practitioners in rural and remote contexts: An integrative review and thematic synthesis of the literature to identify mechanisms for successful outcomes. *Human Resources for Health, 12*(10). doi:10.1186/1478-4491-12-10

National Association of Social Workers (NASW). (2017). *NASW, ASWB, CSWE, & CSWA standards for technology in social work practice.* Washington, DC: NASW Press. Retrieved from https://www.socialworkers.org/includes/newIncludes/homepage/PRA-BRO-33617.TechStandards_FINAL_POSTING.pdf

NC-SARA. (n.d.). Retrieved from http://nc-sara.org/

Reichert, C. von, Cromartie, J. B., & Arthun, R. O. (2014). Reasons for returning and not returning to rural U.S. communities. *Professional Geographer, 66*(1), 58–72. doi:10.1080/00330124.2012.725373

Rérat, P. (2014). The selective migration of young graduates: Which of them return to their rural home region and which do not? *Journal of Rural Studies, 35,* 123–132. doi:10.1016/j.jrurstud.2014.04.009

Rogers, E. M. (2003). *Diffusion of innovations* (5th ed.). New York, NY: Free Press.

Rousmaniere, T., & Renfro-Michel, E. (2016). *Using technology to enhance clinical supervision.* Alexandria, VA: American Counseling Association.

Shorkey, C. T., & Uebel, M. (2014). History and development of instructional technology and media in social work education. *Journal of Social Work Education, 50,* 247–261. doi:10.1080/10437797.2014.885248

Wilson, G. (2013). Evidencing reflective practice in social work education: Theoretical uncertainties and practical challenges. *British Journal of Social Work, 43*(1), 154–172. doi:10.1093/bjsw/bcr170

CHAPTER 8

ETHICAL CONSIDERATIONS FOR FACULTY MEMBERS WHO TEACH WITH TECHNOLOGY

This chapter answers the following questions:

- Can social work practice skills really be taught online?
- What are the standards for technology use in social work education?
- What ethical concerns arise in teaching with technology?
- How can HIPAA concerns be addressed?
- How can FERPA concerns be addressed?
- How can we ensure our courses are accessible?
- How can we address boundary issues?
- Should degree programs establish social media policies?
- How can we ensure academic integrity in technology-mediated courses?

To start this chapter, we want to acknowledge that the ethical concerns related to social work practice and technology are far ranging, touching on an assortment of issues: how technology is employed in practice (Reamer, 2013); the implications of failing to be knowledgeable and competent in using technology, especially technology being used by the populations that one serves (Smyth, 2010; Zgoda, 2013); digital justice concerns such as clients not having access to technology and being controlled by technology (Eubanks, 2011; Eubanks, 2014); Internet access as a human right (Jackson, 2011); being an ethical compass to monitor and guide the use of big data and artificial intelligence so that current inequalities are not perpetuated by algorithms (Edes & Bowman, 2018); net neutrality (Erreger, 2017; Escoto, 2017); and the social work grand challenge to use technology for social good (Berzin, Singer, & Chan, 2015). Though fascinating and clearly relevant to social work, they are all topics that are worthy of their own books—topics that are important to social work policy and practice. We mention them here to provide some sampling of the broader societal and professional context, and yet for this book, we focus primarily on the ethical issues involved in teaching with digital technology, or technology-mediated education.

There is also one more ethical issue that deserves mention before we shift to more specific discussions of the considerations that arise in teaching social work with digital technology: that of the impact in the growth of online education. Specifically, the rise of for-profit businesses that are benefiting from tuition-sharing profits with nonprofit degree programs has raised questions about the excessive cost of online degrees and reduced selectivity of admissions (Newton, 2016). As we mentioned in Chapter 6, quality online courses incur higher costs, including the need for good instructional design and student support, combined with the challenges of developing and supporting students in far-ranging field education sites. Students, especially at private nonprofit schools that use corporate academic partners, often incur significant debt in student loans, raising more issues related to justice (Newton, 2016). The Council on Social Work Education's (CSWE) 2017 annual survey report on social work education does not include admissions selectivity data, nor does it include comparative data for online and on-the-ground programs (CSWE, 2018). However, based on our own experiences and discussions with social work administrators in online degree programs, we suspect there is wide variation in selectivity rates correlated with the size and cost of degree programs. If true, students who are potentially less qualified may be at risk for the highest debt burdens. We would certainly support having data on selectivity and cost publicly available on all types of social work degrees as well as further discussion and debate on the impacts of these issues.

These issues aside (the ethics of technology in social work practice and the high tuition costs associated with online social work education), there are still many specific ethical issues related to teaching social work with digital technology that we will cover in this chapter. These debates include challenges of teaching human-services skills (i.e., active listening and therapeutic interventions) in a distance learning environment, student privacy concerns, boundaries across digital environments, access issues, and the protection of client information. We offer an overview of the broader ethical considerations but give primary focus in this chapter to guiding social work educators in navigating the ethics landscape online. As part of this discussion, we discuss the benefits and risks of engaging with students/clients via social media, and how to ethically manage potential landmines.

WHAT ETHICAL CONCERNS ARISE WHEN TEACHING WITH TECHNOLOGY?

We identify four categories of ethical concerns for social work educators and higher education administrators: privacy and confidentiality; digital access for faculty members, students, and agency-based instructors, including accessibility for people with disabilities; boundaries in digital environments, which encompasses the boundaries between educators and students, as well as boundaries for students and educators between personal and professional uses of technology; and finally, academic integrity (including copyright). All these ethical concerns require familiarity with the legal and ethical context to ensure compliance, and all these concerns can be managed by following best practices. As you read through the chapter, we offer a brief review of each ethical category followed by discussions on some best practices. As we have mentioned before in this book, technology is ever changing and improving, especially in educational settings. These changes may bring new ethical concerns, and we encourage all social work educators to stay current and aware of the ways that technology changes affect ethical practices in the social work field.

Academic integrity—most commonly plagiarism—concerns are not unique to online learning environments. However, they can come up more often when using technology-mediated assignments, especially because students are often not familiar with how and when content (text, images, audio, and video) must be attributed, or because an exam is being administered in an online course without a proctor. Online education skeptics raise concerns about whether work, or perhaps even a whole degree, could be completed by someone other than the enrolled student. Clearly, many of these ethical concerns, along with the laws and regulations, relate to education in general, not just technology-mediated education. However, it is useful to explore the situations that are more likely to arise in teaching social work with technology.

CAN SOCIAL WORK PRACTICE SKILLS REALLY BE TAUGHT ONLINE?

When talking with social workers and social work educators about online education, people still typically express skepticism about the value of online social work degree programs and, in particular, the ability for students to learn social work practice skills in an online learning environment. The position paper of the Clinical Social Work Association (CSWA) mentioned in Chapter 3 exemplifies this perspective (CSWA, 2013). When we probe this perspective with colleagues, what usually emerges is that the skeptic is only familiar with a model of online education in which the student sits in front of a computer watching videos of a faculty member lecturing, makes posts to an online discussion board, and then completes an online exam (behaviors most closely associated with outdated methods of asynchronous delivery). In these discussions, the social work seated classroom is held up as the gold standard. And yet seated social work classes can easily drift into lengthy discussions about practice, providing very little opportunity for actual practice skill development.

As we have discussed in the earlier chapters of this book, quality online education begins by designing a course with focus and objectives in mind. For this reason, online courses on social work practice, such as foundation intervention courses, need to be designed to ensure that students receive sufficient opportunities to develop, rehearse, and receive feedback on their practice skills. This can be achieved in multiple ways, such as live modeling of practice skills via videoconferencing software (which can be recorded and replayed, if desired), modeling practice skills through video recordings, and providing multiple opportunities for students to practice their skills. Student skill practice can occur through real-time (i.e., synchronous) role-playing by using webcams with Web-based software from a laptop or tablet, responding to simulations with recorded video responses, or recording role-plays with a video recorder and uploading them to an online classroom (hosted by a learning management system, or LMS) where the instructor (and peers) can view the recordings and provide feedback. In our experience, after describing these options to skeptics and showing them examples of recorded classrooms, many express surprise that online education includes these types of opportunities for learning and thus are less concerned. As we have previously mentioned in this book, more than a decade of research on this very questions exists in the social work literature, and most studies report that clinical skills can be taught in online learning environments (Cummings, Chaffin, & Cockerham, 2015; Forgey & Ortega-Williams, 2016; Siebert, Siebert, & Spaulding-Givens, 2006; Washburn, Bordnick, & Rizzo, 2016). See Chapter 5 for more in-depth focus on this question.

WHAT ARE THE STANDARDS FOR TECHNOLOGY USE IN SOCIAL WORK EDUCATION?

It is important to note that our profession has standards on technology use in social work (and that these standards, and their interpretation, also include technology use in social work education, continuing education, and supervision; NASW, 2017b). Known as the Standards for Technology in Social Work Practice, the standards were updated in 2017 as a collaborative effort of the National Association of Social Workers (NASW), the Association of Social Work Boards (ASWB), CSWE, and CSWA. Also, the most recent update to the NASW Code of Ethics addresses technology use throughout the ethical code (NASW, 2017a). Finally, ASWB has issued model technology standards for state licensing boards (ASWB, 2015). These documents define the U.S. professional social work policy framework related to technology when taken together. We have also found that policies from our international colleagues are excellent resources for faculties and students and provide us with a more global perspective. For example, both the British Association of Social Workers (BASW) and the Canadian Association of Social Workers (CASW) have their own social work and social media guidelines (BASW, 2012; CASW, 2014).

The NASW Standards for Technology in Social Work Practice are broken up into four sections, with the first three sections covering social work practice with technology. We do not

ETHICS FOR TEACHING WITH TECHNOLOGY

cover issues related to practicing social work with technology in this book. Section 4, "Social Work Education and Supervision," is most directly relevant to educators; most—but not all—of the ethical issues we discuss in this chapter are mentioned in this section of the standards (NASW, 2017b). The 2017 update of the social work technology standards was a much-needed, far-ranging project that involved a great deal of work for the committee members. The committee sought feedback at several points throughout the life of the project. Because of the broad scope of the technology standards updates (which focus primarily on social work practice), there were actually very few full-time social work educators on the committee and subcommittee. For this reason, we sought perspectives on the standards for education, and especially on the interpretations, from a larger group of social work educators. These are published online (Hitchcock, Sage, & Smyth, 2017), in a booklet format, by the University at Buffalo School of Social Work (Hitchcock, Sage, & Smyth, 2018), and we have included these interpretations for you in this text in Appendix 3. Breakout Box 8.1 includes a list of all 12 education- and training-focused standards from Section 4 of the Standards for Technology in Social Work Practice, and we encourage you to review them so you can think more deeply about the issues that we highlight in this chapter. As we discuss the ethical issues in this chapter, when they connect to one of the NASW technology standards, we identify that standard by number in our text to assist readers in linking what we discuss to the NASW technology standards for education; the exceptions are Standards 4.02 (Training Social Workers About the Use of Technology) and 4.03 (Continuing Education), because those standards focuses on teaching about technology use for social work practice (a topic that is outside the focus this book, which focuses on teaching with technology but not teaching about technology for practice). For those who are interested, these two standards are discussed in Appendix 3.

BREAKOUT BOX 8.1. THEORY TALK

A FRAMEWORK FOR UNDERSTANDING ETHICAL ISSUES IN TECHNOLOGY-MEDIATED LEARNING; SECTION 4: EXCERPTS FROM SOCIAL WORK EDUCATION AND SUPERVISION OF THE NASW STANDARDS FOR TECHNOLOGY IN SOCIAL WORK PRACTICE (NASW, 2017B)

- *4.01. Use of Technology in Social Work Education:* Social workers who use technology to design and deliver education and training shall develop competence in the ethical use of the technology in a manner appropriate for the specific context.

- *4.02. Training Social Workers about the Use of Technology in Practice:* Social workers who provide education to students and practitioners concerning the use of technology in social work practice shall provide them with knowledge about the ethical use of technology, including potential benefits and risks.

- *4.03. Continuing Education:* Social work educators who use technology in their teaching and instruct students on the use of technology in social work practice shall examine and keep current with relevant emerging knowledge.

- *4.04. Social Media Policies:* When using online social media for educational purposes, social work educators shall provide students with social media policies to provide them with guidance about ethical considerations.

- *4.05. Evaluation:* When evaluating students on their use of technology in social work practice, social work educators shall provide clear guidance on professional expectations and how online tests discussions, or other assignments, will be graded.

- *4.06. Technological Disruptions:* Social work educators shall provide students with information about how to manage technological problems that may be caused by loss of power, viruses, hardware failures, lost or stolen devices, or other issues that may disrupt the educational process.

- *4.07. Distance Education:* When teaching social work practitioners or students in remote locations, social work educators shall ensure that they have sufficient understanding of the cultural, social, and legal contexts of the other locations where the practitioners or students are located.

- *4.08. Support:* Social work educators who use technology shall ensure that students have sufficient access to technological support to assist with technological questions or problems that may arise during the educational process.

- *4.09. Maintenance of Academic Standards:* When social work educators use technology to facilitate assignments or tests, they shall take appropriate measures to promote academic standards related to honesty, integrity, freedom of expression, and respect for the dignity and worth of all people.

- *4.10. Educator-Student Boundaries:* Social work educators who use technology shall take precautions to ensure maintenance of appropriate educator-student boundaries.

- *4.11. Field Instruction:* Social workers who provide field instruction to students shall address the use of technology in organizational settings.

- *4.12. Social Work Supervision:* Social workers who use technology to provide supervision shall ensure that they are able to assess students' and supervisees' learning and professional competence.

The final key context regarding these revised standards on using technology for social work education is at the level of organizations, that is, the standards and policies of your university or college, and for our students, the standards and policies of their field agencies or workplace. Educators need to stay up to date with the standards of their institutions and need to remind students of the need to be knowledgeable about the contexts of the expectations in which they practice (see NASW Technology Standard 4.11 in Breakout Box 8.1). Additionally, we would encourage social work educators to consider becoming members of key decision-making bodies at your institutions (i.e., a campus-wide technology committee or online advisory council) or local and statewide professional committees on technology that influence social work education and practice in your geographic area (i.e., the technology council of your state-level NASW chapter). These decision-making groups often influence social work education, policy, and practice, and offer an opportunity for social work educators to help shape the development of ethical use of technology within their own communities.

PRIVACY AND CONFIDENTIALITY WHEN TEACHING WITH TECHNOLOGY

Regarding privacy and confidentiality, two primary federal laws in the United States influence the use of technology in social work education: the Health Insurance Portability and Accountability Act (HIPAA; HIPAA, 1996) and Family Educational Rights and Privacy Act (FERPA; U.S. Department of Education, 2015), each pertaining respectively to the privacy of health-care information and of student information. Social work educators should know when and how student information can be shared with third parties, including how student information is shared digitally during class-related activities or is stored on digital devices. Similarly, as students often bring their casework experience to the classroom, educators must prepare themselves and their students to hold client privacy to the highest standards of the HIPAA law.

How Can HIPAA Concerns Be Addressed?

In the United States, client privacy concerns are addressed at a federal level primarily through HIPAA (HIPAA, 1996), which includes many regulations related to health-care coverage and health-care information. In social work education, HIPAA applies to the privacy and confidentiality of all health-care medical records that instructors and students may encounter during field education, and to client information that an instructor (or a student who presents a case) might discuss in a class. This means that all client information, including names, diagnoses, and any other information that could potentially identify a client or constituency, must be kept private and confidential at all times. HIPAA issues are most easily addressed in the classroom by making it clear to students from the beginning of a class how client information is to be managed in the course before any content is presented. See Breakout Box 8.2 for practical tips on how to manage HIPAA issues.

> ## BREAKOUT BOX 8.2. PRACTICAL TIPS
> ### MANAGING HIPAA ISSUES IN THE SOCIAL WORK CLASSROOM
>
> 1. Include a statement about the need for HIPAA compliance in your syllabus. Ideally, this statement should have language vetted by program administrators and be included by all instructors in their syllabi. This statement can also be included in program handbooks and easily converted into an acknowledgment form for students to sign as part of the course.
>
> 2. Highlight and review the syllabus statement with students and the faculty at multiple times across the curriculum. Examples include a unique digital course announcement that draws attention to the HIPAA statement and then summarizes it during orientations and as part of field educators' trainings.
>
> 3. If your course will involve students using case examples from work or field, provide an example of managing HIPAA issues:
>
> - Present a fictitious case, with identifying information included.
>
> - Present a HIPAA-compliant reworking of the case, disguising all information that could be used to identify a client.
>
> - Discuss the decisions that you made in adapting the case, so students gain insight into your thinking—this could be done easily with a video or audio recording for an online course.

If students are going to post information about real patient cases on the Internet, or in some other public space, the issues become much more complicated. A blog post on the Internet is considered a type of publishing. Whereas a de-identified case is technically HIPAA compliant, if the case represents a particular individual, that person should grant written consent for the example to be shared in any capacity. A client might stumble on a public blog post, so everything about the posting should be vetted with the individual client. This might apply to a scenario such as student-recorded interviews posted for review and feedback. The reality is that the HIPAA issues are more easily resolved than are the ethical issues. A related ethical issue is whether a client is genuinely free of coercion in providing consent, given the power imbalance in the relationship with a staff member, a student intern, and the agency. Additionally, publishing about a case may require Institutional Review Board (IRB) review to ensure that human subjects' rights are protected—check with your institution's IRB to be sure you comply.

An easy solution to the dilemma of publishing cases in digital environments is to (1) keep specific cases de-identified and shared within the private classroom environments such as a learning management system (LMS) that requires user authentication and a secure log-on or (2) design any public case posts to be about fictitious cases (with the cases clearly labeled as fictional so that anyone who reads it understands that the case is not real).

How Can FERPA Issues Be Addressed?

FERPA is the federal law in the United States that protects the privacy of student educational records. The purpose of FERPA is to give students access to their educational records, the ability to have the records amended, and control over the disclosure of some of the information from the records (U.S. Department of Education, 2015). We reviewed mixed professional opinions about the settings in which FERPA applies. Lindsay (2005) argues that FERPA does not apply to settings in which students have direct control of documents, as is the case of social media and blogs. However, Drake (2014), in an Educause paper, cautions that when educators ask students to share content in public venues such as social media platforms, they must still be careful about replies that may publicly identify the student's personal academic information. Specifically, when using a social media platform or another public venue with students, educators should not share information that would be considered part of the educational record (e.g., grades, course enrollment, class schedule, disciplinary action, financial aid). Some institutions and educators are overly cautious about the application of FERPA and assume it means that students should not be asked to engage in work for a public audience or on social media. This is not accurate. Some educators also express concern about the third-party ownership of data and information that is inherent in the use of public, for-profit programs such as Twitter and in for-profit partnerships with commercial providers. We agree that terms of service, information sharing, and data use is worthy of discussions with students to improve their digital literacy about the ubiquitous use of data exchange in our society, from online shopping to social media and search engines. For-profit data exchange in public education is not a new concern; many college students have their financial aid disbursed to for-profit bank cards that collect student information, universities distribute national surveys that collect student data, educators use survey response software or digital textbook supplements in class where students register with private companies, and universities work closely with other for-profit vendors who are also data brokers. We believe best practice includes giving students options related to their public identities in assignments where they are asked to post information publicly or create a user profile with a for-profit website. We also advocate for further conversations about data in society and the ways in which participation in university systems mandates or facilitates private data sharing. Many of the assignments in Appendix 1 include using social media platforms as an integral part of the learning activity, and we recommend that educators apply the FERPA strategies discussed later in this section when using those activities with social work students.

Given the student privacy issues involved in FERPA, some educators prefer to teach entirely within the protected environment of an LMS. And yet there are excellent reasons for asking students to share their work in public spaces such as Twitter, YouTube, Instagram, or public blogs. As was noted in Chapter 2, assignments that ask students to share their work in public places (as opposed to only within an LMS) offer pedagogical advantages. First, students develop the knowledge and skills to use those specific apps professionally, and these are the same environments they have access to in their professional lives. This exposure to the ethical and professional use of publicly available tools increases their digital literacy and increases the likelihood they will use these tools ethically and professionally when they graduate. Second, research suggests that students produce higher-quality work when they know it is intended for an authentic audience (Lieberman, 2018; Trammell & Ferdig, 2004). Third, students have the option to highlight specific digital products in professional public spaces, such as LinkedIn or on a blog, in essence, creating a digital portfolio of their work.

Some students may be cautious about identifying themselves in public online settings for a variety of reasons, including past or current experiences with online or in-person harassment. Fortunately, it is relatively easy to modify assignments so that student privacy is respected. The easiest option is to allow students to decide how they present themselves in the profiles that they set up for classes. Nevertheless, prior to students making that decision, it is best to discuss with all students the pros and cons of setting up a professional presence on the Internet (see NASW Technology Standard 4.04 in Breakout Box 8.1). Breakout Box 8.3 offers a list of these pros and cons that could be used to start a class discussion. Other best practices include ensuring that content in all syllabi makes it clear that the students are not required to use their real names in any public profile. Administrators can develop, with faculty input, recommended language for all faculty members to use, emphasizing that students can choose to use pseudonyms in place of their names, and images (of objects, or game image avatars) in place of their names and personal photos. All students should be instructed to use the chosen names of classmates in any public post/comment if people decide not to use their real names. Instructors should also never post grades, or grading-related feedback, publicly.

BREAKOUT BOX 8.3. PRACTICAL TIPS
PROS AND CONS OF PROFESSIONAL ONLINE PRESENCES (FOR STUDENTS)

Pros

- You can provide content for prospective and current clients, colleagues, and employers that highlights your knowledge and skills.

- You can develop online resources to which you can refer clients, colleagues, or the public.

- Content published under your name will come in searches, which can make older, less desirable content harder to find.

- Other professionals will be able to find you, which could help you develop strong online professional networks.

Cons

- Comments, if permitted, can raise concerns about your clients identifying themselves without having an in-depth understanding of the risks. Discussing those risks with clients in the beginning of the relationship is key, as well as how you will manage the risks.

- As a student, you are learning, and your content might include mistakes.

- Establishing a public presence allows anyone to find you, which can be a personal concern for people who do not want to be identified (e.g., had problems with a stalker).

- Social media users have limited control about how for-profit companies use their personal data. Privacy and marketing options change frequently.

Finally, FERPA speaks to the need for overall privacy of student records, which includes digital communications with students, such as *e-mail* and texting. This requires that educators protect student privacy by ensuring appropriate privacy protections for their devices, and to specific applications that include student data.

One final note about privacy is in order: The European Union (EU) 2016 legislation, General Data Protection Regulation (GDPR, EU 2016/679), went into effect in May 2018. Although the law itself technically applies only to those countries in the EU, because major companies, universities, and publishers serve a wide international audience, the effects of GDPR are projected to be much wider ranging (Tiku, 2018). GDPR requires that companies provide information about data that they collect, provide consumers with the option to delete data, and require that individuals opt in to data collection. It also applies stricter privacy controls to the collection of sensitive data, such as race, religion, and sexual orientation (Tiku, 2018). Major changes in policies related to user data have already been made, and it is predicted that users all over the world will continue to see major improvements in privacy controls (Tiku, 2018). Although it is too soon to identify the specific impact on privacy in terms of teaching in North America, improvements in privacy protections for all users will be helpful to educators and students as well.

ACCESS AND ACCESSIBILITY WHEN TEACHING WITH TECHNOLOGY

Regarding access and accessibility, the legal context is set by the Americans With Disabilities Act of 1990 (ADA), and legal regulations are outlined in the 2010 ADA Standards for Accessible Design (U.S. Department of Justice, 2010). The most common concern of access related to online education is ensuring that the needs of visually impaired and hearing-impaired students are accommodated, and yet students with learning disabilities may also have unique needs. For this reason, it is essential to have support services and resources for both the faculty and students.

Further, access is an ethical concern that is larger than the ADA focus. It also encompasses issues of availability of the technology and of appropriate technical support for programs, the faculty (including adjuncts), and students. As was noted in Chapter 2, "Digital Literacy," there are vast differences in the access that various groups and communities have to digital technologies, and this can seriously limit people's access to information and opportunities (Institute of Museum and Library Services, 2012). This problem requires an emphasis on digital inclusion strategies to ensure that all people have access to the information and opportunities provided through information and communication technologies, given the increasingly important role that they are playing in access to resources and opportunities in society (Institute of Museum and Library Services, 2012).

The last access issue relates to NASW Technology Standard 4.06, preparing students and oneself for the inevitable technology disruptions that will arise, whether because of a power outage or simply because something stops working as planned, a not uncommon problem that follows in the wake of software updates (NASW, 2017b).

How Can We Ensure Our Courses Are Accessible?

Whether we are teaching a traditional seated course that incorporates technology into assignments or teaching a fully online course, it is critical to make sure all courses are accessible for students with disabilities. Because technology evolves rapidly, it can be hard to stay abreast of the full range of assistive devices that students can use to access a course, as well as to keep pace with the current legal standards for ensuring access. For this reason, it is essential to work closely with campus-based experts in disability access and instructional design to ensure we are following the current standards and best practices for access under the ADA and other guidelines for each course and for the curriculum as a whole. We should be prepared for any student who might need reasonable accommodations. See Breakout Box 8.4 for examples of how to apply accessibility practices across a curriculum.

BREAKOUT BOX 8.4. PRACTICAL TIPS
APPLYING ACCESSIBILITY PRACTICES ACROSS A CURRICULUM

Ms. Matthea Marquat of Columbia University and Dr. Beth Counselman-Carpenter of Southern Connecticut State University share tips they have learned from colleagues:

- Caption all media that will be used during the first week, in every course, and then selectively caption the rest of the semester as needed on a course-by-course basis. This ensures that students who are deaf can enroll in any course and participate starting the first week and saves the cost of fully captioning all courses.
- Live-caption sporting events as a matter of course, so that anyone in the community can follow the announcers. Use a variety of captioning approaches, including using third-party vendors Cielo24 and 3PlayMedia, requiring students to caption media they create for assignments (in VoiceThread), requiring instructors to caption media they use in class, and using auto-captioning via Kaltura to start and then manually correcting the mistakes to bring the captioning up to standards. (Marquart & Counselman-Carpenter, 2017)

Though the requirements for ADA compliance continue to evolve, it is helpful to become facile in core practices for creating course content that will ensure content is accessible from the beginning. Some key practices include using the heading structure of your word processing software or learning management system, ensuring that students can navigate content using only a keyboard (and do not have to use a mouse); adding brief descriptions of what an image shows with captions or using alt-text; using descriptive names for hyperlinked content rather than the URL (uniform resource locator); and avoiding PDF files as the sole way to present content (Burgstahler, 2017). See Breakout Box 8.5 for examples of how Ms. Matthea Marquat of Columbia University and Dr. Beth Counselman-Carpenter of Southern Connecticut State University have used captioning in an online course with students who are hard of hearing.

BREAKOUT BOX 8.5. CASE STUDY
TEACHING ONLINE WITH STUDENTS WHO ARE DEAF

Ms. Matthea Marquart and Dr. Beth Counselman-Carpenter of Columbia University School of Social Work share their experiences of making online courses accessible to students with disabilities, including how they managed unexpected changes in course delivery.

From our perspective, there are three critical components to success:

1. Never assume. When choosing media for your course, never assume that the captions provided are of the level and caliber in terms of accuracy. YouTube videos are not equal access compliant, as they are often inaccurate, or their timing is off. All media selected by the instructor must be captioned by the institution's captioning services or be reviewed for accuracy by the Office of Disability Services prior to being assigned, shown, or posted. This also includes transcribed videos shown from the library, when transcription has been completed by outside sources, and for podcasts.

2. Attention to the timeline. Captioning often requires a 3- to 4-week turnaround for all captioning, which requires having your media organized and well placed in the semester's calendar prior to the start of the semester (if possible). It is not equal access to show a video in class and ask for it to be captioned later. Planning ahead and being confident in your choices is critical. Should something unexpected, such as a snow day or a server being down (which happened this past year and led to an unexpected asynchronistic class recorded lecture being posted), communicate actively with your student about their needs and be flexible about deadlines when asking for an "emergency" captioning of media. Also, be mindful of the amount of student-generated audio and video that is posted asynchronistically and the turnaround time frame for all of those assignments to be captioned (usually it is 48–72 hours).

3. The all-important backup plan. Live captioners, who work in multiple shifts during a synchronistic class, can occasionally have technical difficulties and need to reenter the classroom during live lectures. To manage this, our backup plan was for the course teaching associate to step in and provide captioning (as well as possible) while the professor and student e-mailed both the Office of Disability Services and the captioning service emergency support while class continued. The teaching associate was aware of their responsibilities when this happened, and although the captioning was not perfect, it allowed for students to continue to participate until the situation was remedied. There are many departments and people involved in supporting students who need accommodations, including the university's Office of Disability Services, the school's disabilities liaison, the Advising Office, the Field Office, the Student Services team, and the instructors, teaching associates, and technical support specialists. The students who need accommodations need to be looped in as well (Marquart & Counselman-Carpenter, 2017).

As noted earlier, a digital inclusion perspective on access requires us to cast a wider lens on all the factors that can influence students' access to, and use of, technology. Within a given classroom, this means educators need to be aware that students can vary widely in their access, use of, and experience with a range of digital technologies. In addition, students' cultural context, in general, influences all aspects of their education, and educator's need to understand the context for all their students (see NASW Technology Standard 4.07 in Breakout Box 8.1). It is key to assess students access and use of digital devices, applications (apps), and information technology (IT) support and to recognize that diverse factors, such as socioeconomic status, geography, gender, race, age, religion, ability, and culture, can affect students' access and experience with these technologies. For the same reason, it is essential to be specific about grading criteria involved in grading specific elements of digital assignments, so that no prior knowledge of the digital context is assumed (see NASW Technology Standard 4.05 in Breakout Box 8.1).

When ensuring a digital inclusion approach, it is important to note that all the same factors that relate to students also affect the faculty, the staff, and adjunct instructors in higher education, so we need to consider these differences in providing education and support in the academic workplace. Moreover, in social work we also need to consider and respond to the access needs and cultural context of field instructors and agency-based personnel who work with our students in the community.

Ensuring that everyone can access and successfully navigate digital technologies is vital, and this may mean providing a range of different types of IT support (see NASW Technology Standard 4.06 and 4.08 in Breakout Box 8.1). In addition, within a given classroom, it is important to ensure that students of all experience backgrounds have the opportunity to participate fully. One of the best ways to do this is to facilitate students learning from each other (which will help to equalize differences among students). Chapter 2 includes an example in Breakout Box 2.3, "Case Study: Maya, Creating Cultural Literacy Experiences for Students," which illustrates one way this can be accomplished.

As noted earlier, access also encompasses the need to ensure that the technology is available to students, and that appropriate technical support is provided too. The latter issue is discussed in more depth in Chapter 6. The issue of availability of technology requires that we consider that students will access courses through different types of operating systems and devices. For example, a student may be using a smartphone to access course content via an app rather than a desktop computer. These are key factors to consider in designing courses, and instructional designers can be helpful resources on such issues. Also, it is good to plan ahead for access problems in course delivery, such as videoconferencing software that stops working in the middle of a synchronous session (always have backup option), and to be flexible with deadlines for students if they encounter access problems that interfere with assignment deadlines (such as the LMS shuts down for an extended period of time or the student loses Internet access at home). Reviewing these options at the beginning of a course can go a long way toward alleviating student anxiety and managing problems when they occur. For a discussion of more on this topic, see Appendix 3.

BOUNDARY ISSUES WHEN TEACHING WITH TECHNOLOGY

Dual relationships between social work students and their professors have always been a concern for social work education, long before the development of social and digital communication tools (Congress, 1996; 2001). The NASW Code of Ethics addresses educator-student dual relationships in Section 3.02, "Education and Training," and clearly states that "educators or field instructors for students should not engage in any dual or multiple relationships with students in which there is a risk of exploitation or potential harm to the student (NASW, 2017a, para. 29). When revising the code in 2017 to include digital and social technologies, NASW specifically states that not engaging in dual relationships also extends to "social networking sites or other electronic media" (NASW, 2017a, para. 29). NASW Technology Standard 4.10, "Educator-Student

Boundaries" (see Breakout Box 8.1), also encourages social work educators to avoid dual relationships when engaging students with technology-mediated platforms. Key to avoiding dual relationships with students is for social work educators to set explicit, fair, and culturally appropriate boundaries.

How Can We Address Boundary Issues?

Boundary issues always have the potential to present ethical concerns regardless of the classroom setting. Generally, two sets of boundary issues come into play in digital environments: (1) dual relationships and (2) personal and professional boundary management. These issues relate directly to NASW Technology Standard 4.10 (see Breakout Box 8.1).

The phrase "dual relationships" pertains to the boundaries between students and educators (and administrators) that encompass all aspects of their relationships, from seated venues to digital contexts, including via e-mail, social media, and LMS. Key to understanding those boundary issues is first to acknowledge the power imbalance that exists between students and educators, and then to consider how to manage this power imbalance as an educator. For example, if an educator sends a Facebook "friend request" to a student, the power imbalance makes it difficult for that student to decline the request. The second issue is that when students and educators connect on social media, they both have access to the others' personal and professional content. This can blur the boundaries between personal and professional roles. It also raises questions that need consideration, such as how an educator would manage learning something about the student on social media that raises concerns (i.e., illegal drug use). Similarly, what will students learn about their educators' personal life, and how will this play out in the classroom?

A general principle in sorting out dual relationship issues online is to consider how we manage these issues *on-the-ground*.

Closely connected to this is the use of self-disclosure with students. There is a considerable amount of variation among educators regarding self-disclosure in teaching, with some sharing many examples from their lives with students, and others sharing very little (Wyrick, 2017). It is likely that educators who disclose more in the classroom will feel more comfortable doing so on social media. When posting online, ask yourself if the information is something you would feel comfortable sharing in your seated classroom (Kimball & Kim, 2013). The same applies to posting visual images, that is, consider if the images shared are ones that would be appropriate in one's office or in a classroom.

As with the use of self-disclosure in therapy, it is essential to consider the purpose of self-disclosure in teaching. Are we sharing to fill our needs for feeling close and to develop personal relationships with students? Or are we attempting to model a process for students (Dean, 2012)? For example, it might be helpful for students to hear that a faculty expert in technology in social work feels a need to disconnect sometimes and has struggled to find the right balance in seeking digital boundaries. When using self-disclosure, faculty members need to be cognizant of the power differences in their relationships with students (Dean, 2012; Wyrick, 2017) and consider how they are representing themselves as professionals (Wyrick, 2017). In addition, it is important to remember that self-disclosure can blur boundaries in relationships. At the same time, some research indicates that teacher self-disclosure may play a more critical role in online education, compared to on-the-ground education, in contributing to student satisfaction and the educator's social presence in the class (Song, Kim, & Luo, 2016).

Educators can take many different approaches to social media use with students. Some people set clear rules, such as never "friending" students, and others establish personal and professional accounts, and encourage students to do the same, and then it becomes acceptable to accept friend requests from students. Still others choose to keep all postings in their social media accounts at a level that would be congruent with the boundaries of their professional roles, that is, only posting personal content that they would be comfortable with the general public knowing. Think through these issues ahead of time, and explore your personal boundaries with students, much in the same way that we would with clients in a clinical setting. Effective management of these boundaries will consider the impact of power imbalances in the educator-student relationship; the purpose of one's specific social media accounts; and the ethical guidelines on dual relationships, such as in the NASW Standards for Technology in Social Work Practice (NASW, 2017b).

Of course, all these boundary issues apply to relationships beyond that of educator-student, such as supervisor-employee, client-therapist, and colleague-colleague. Because social work educators are preparing students for these professional roles, it is essential to educate them on technology-mediated boundary issues (see NASW Technology Standard 4.04 in Breakout Box 8.1). We see this connecting back directly to the Cultural digital literacy, which includes our profession's ethical code as a key element of setting the context for digital engagement. When we discussed digital literacy in Chapter 2, we noted that when we move between different online roles and platforms, we especially need to ask, which content and use of technology applies to this new role and situation? The *Social Worker's Guide to Social Media* from the University at Buffalo is an online, interactive digital infographic that includes short embedded videos, and it is a free tool that can be used with students for reflective practice (University at Buffalo School of Social Work, n.d.) and help them begin to consider the ethical issues involved with how to be online as a professional. The videos are short and provide good prompts for launching a discussion.

Should Degree Programs Establish Social Media Policies?

Many social work programs have established social media policies for their students. Some policies get very detailed and prescriptive (Karpman & Drisko, 2016). Others, like the policies at University at Buffalo's School of Social Work (2017), are very general, placing their policy with the other general statements on abiding by professional ethics:

> Students are expected to follow the NASW Code of Ethics and University standards of behavior at all times, including, but not limited to: classes, field placements, volunteer work, and digital contexts. Digital contexts include, but are not limited to, online social networks (e.g., Facebook, Twitter, YouTube, Google Plus, Instagram, LinkedIn, MySpace, etc.), text messaging, blogging, virtual worlds, and e-mail. (p. 15)

The problem with very specific policies is that they often leave out situations. For example, many policies assume that students are using social media for personal reasons only and do not provide much guidance in the event social media is being used to establish a professional presence online or to create a professional learning network (PLN). As we have previously noted, the purposes of specific social media platforms can vary widely and can change over time, so it becomes cumbersome to be very specific about behavior in online platforms while ensuring that the policy will encompass all goals and roles of students.

It certainly makes sense for every program to have some statement on social media and professional roles and ethics, simply because society is still struggling with the "realness" of digital environments and behavior in those settings (Humphrey, 2014; Karpman & Drisko, 2016). A statement like the one used at University at Buffalo is straightforward, and yet it alerts students that professional ethics apply within digital environments.

However, it does not educate students on all the ways that professional roles and ethics can play out in digital settings. Karpman and Drisko (2016) recommend that social work programs develop policies that outline six different domains, including understanding social media, legal obligations, the implications of personal and professional online presence, institutional obligations to the social work program, productivity implications, and possible consequences for violations of the policy (p. 1). Some social work programs have used this approach and are clearly using these policies as tools to educate their students on the specific kinds of situations that should be avoided. The best social media policies will capture the full scope of digital environments and roles, especially given how rapidly technology evolves; administrators will expect the policy not to do all the teaching but to provide a context for teaching. Policies in practice should be discussed and reinforced in the social work classroom to prepare students to think critically about ethics related to digital practice.

Additionally, faculty members may want to develop their own individualized social media and technology policies or guidelines for use in the classroom (Brady, McLeod, & Young, 2015; Curington, Hitchcock, & Carroll, 2018; NASW, 2017b; see NASW Technology Standard 4.04 in Breakout Box 8.1). Brady et al. (2015) pose a useful framework encompassing instructor, student, institutional, and professional dimensions that considers questions for instructors to consider in developing their course policies. Instructor guidelines can be shared on the course syllabus and could address when and how devices, recorders, or tablets might be used in the seated classroom, discuss expectations for professional e-mail communications, and outline when and how the instructor will engage with students via social media. These types of guidelines may vary by educator and can be used to support class discussions, assignments, and other learning tasks. For example, these instructor guidelines could serve as a model, and students can prepare for their future role as a social worker by writing their own individualized social media policy to share with the class for feedback. See examples of other assignments related to social media policies in Appendix 2.

ACADEMIC INTEGRITY WHEN TEACHING WITH TECHNOLOGY

Academic integrity—or plagiarism—concerns are not unique to online learning environments. However, they can come up more often when using technology-mediated assignments, especially because students are often not familiar with how and when content (text, images, audio, and video) must be attributed, or because an exam is being administered in an online course without a proctor. Online education skeptics raise concerns about whether work, or perhaps even a whole degree, could be completed by someone other than the enrolled student.

Clearly, many of these ethical concerns, along with the laws and regulations, relate to education in general, not just technology-mediated education. However, it is useful to explore the situations that may be more likely to arise in teaching social work with technology.

How Can We Ensure Academic Integrity in Technology-Mediated Courses?

Academic integrity, that is, maintaining high standards in scholarship, research, and education, is core to quality higher education. More specifically, the International Center on Academic Integrity (ICAI) defines academic integrity as "a commitment, even in the face of adversity, to six fundamental values: honesty, trust, fairness, respect, responsibility, and courage" (ICAI, n.d., para. 1). Academic integrity needs to be a focus in all types of education, and yet the advent of recent technologies has made it easier for students to cheat (Fishman, 2014, p. 11). Beyond copying and pasting content from websites and documents on the Internet, practices that students use to cheat include purchasing prewritten papers or hiring someone to write a paper (Thomas, 2015a; 2015b). Other concerns include having someone other than the enrolled student take an exam and sharing questions from online exams or quizzes (Lee-Post & Hapke, 2017). These issues relate directly to NASW Technology Standard 4.09 (see Breakout Box 8.1).

Approaches to managing online academic integrity violations fall into two categories: prevention and enforcement (Lee-Post & Hapke, 2017). Prevention focuses on creating an environment where academic integrity is clearly defined and highly valued. Specific practices include honor codes, educating student and faculty, enlisting faculty members' commitment to make academic integrity a priority, and developing institutional processes to address and monitor violations (Lee-Post & Hapke, 2017). Enforcement centers on detecting violations, through user authentication, that is, verifying user identity, and defensive strategies, such as software that blocks screenshots or printing of test questions, or apps like SafeAssign or Turnitin that are available to assist educators in screening for plagiarized text (MIT Comparative Media Studies, n.d.). Common user authentication strategies include limiting course access to registered students with a photo ID, using biometric methods (i.e., fingerprints), and using video monitoring by proctoring services such as requiring a webcam to be on while the student is logged into an online course or taking an exam (Lee-Post & Hapke, 2017). Though we have heard few examples related to use of authentication strategies in online social work programs, plagiarism checkers such as SafeAssign are often used by individual teachers or embraced by departments.

> **BREAKOUT BOX 8.6. PRACTICAL TIPS**
> EXAMPLES OF FREE AND OPEN-SOURCED CONTENT FOR ASSIGNMENTS
>
> **Multiple Types of Content**
> - Wikimedia Commons
> - Flickr: The Commons
> - The Internet Archive
> - Search engine on Creative Commons' website
>
> **Photos & Images**
> - Unsplash
> - Public Domain Pictures
>
> **Music & Audio**
> - Free Music Archive
> - Jamendo
> - Freesound
>
> **Videos**
> - Videvo
> - Pexel Videos
>
> **Books & Texts**
> - Project Gutenburg
> - U.S. Library of Congress

Finally, academic integrity begins with educators. As social work educators, we have a crucial role in educating students about academic integrity and in modeling it in all aspects of our work (Thomas, 2015b). We can model appropriate use of text, images, audio, and video when we create our own content, and provide students with sources for content that is in the public domain or can be used under a Creative Commons license when completing

ETHICS FOR TEACHING WITH TECHNOLOGY

multimedia assignments (see "Further Reading and Resources" at the end of this chapter). See Breakout Box 8.6 for some examples. Educators and students who are competent in digital literacies will be better positioned to demonstrate strong academic integrity, because as noted earlier, academic integrity includes responsibility, which means we need to share from credible sources. Similarly, when we model lifelong learning through professional learning networks (PLN), we demonstrate the academic integrity value of responsibility and the social work ethical value of competence (see NASW Technology Standard 4.01 in Breakout Box 8.1). See Chapter 9 for a discussion on PLNs. Finally, we demonstrate our own competence and integrity as social work educators when we take steps to ensure that we are effectively assessing students' knowledge and skills related to technology use. This means using best practices for educational assessment and supervision (i.e., grading or supervision feedback (see NASW Technology Standard 4.12 in Breakout Box 8.1). Chapter 3 provides an overview of adult learning theory that can be used to help design educational assessments, and Chapter 4 offers practical tips on grading technology-based assignments.

FINAL THOUGHTS

This chapter provides an overview of some ethical considerations and best practices for using technology in social work education. Although not a complete list of all ethical possibilities that one might encounter in an online program or course, the issues outlined here offer a starting point for learning and using technology in ethical ways with your students. Appendix 3 offers more examples of best practices for preventing ethical dilemmas related to technology in the classroom. Most important, given how quickly technology changes, all educators should focus on continuing professional development to stay abreast of ethical issues and strategies to manage them. Chapter 9 discusses how to use technology to address this challenge.

FURTHER READING AND RESOURCES

Brady, S. R., McLeod, D. A., & Young, J. A. (2015). Developing ethical guidelines for creating social media technology policy in social work classrooms. *Advances in Social Work, 16*(1), 43–54.

Burgstahler, S. (2017, January 30). ADA compliance for online course design. *Educause Review*. Retrieved from https://er.educause.edu/articles/2017/1/ada-compliance-for-online-course-design

Creative Commons. https://creativecommons.org/ (provides guidance for protecting work published online or through other means of distribution).

Future of Privacy Forum. http://fpf.org (a think tank for the responsible use of data and related implications; offers a focus on student data privacy).

Institute of Museum and Library Services, University of Washington. (2012). *Building digital communities: A framework for action*. Technology & Social Change Group. Washington, DC: International City/County Management Association. Retrieved from https://tascha.uw.edu/publications/building-digital-communities/

Toner, H. (2016, September 27). *Copyright for educators*. Retrieved from http://www.pbssocal.org/education/copyright-for-educators/

University at Buffalo School of Social Work. (n.d.). *Social worker's guide to social media*. Retrieved from http://socialwork.buffalo.edu/resources/social-media-guide.html (including embedded videos; additional resources: http://socialwork.buffalo.edu/resources/social-media-guide/resources.html).

Use and Remix. https://creativecommons.org/use-remix/ (sources with a Creative Commons license).

REFERENCES

Adedoyin, A. C. A. (2016). Deploying virtual communities of practice as a digital tool in social work: A rapid review and critique of the literature. *Social Work Education, 35*(3), 357-370.

Association of Social Work Boards (ASWB). (2015). *Model regulatory standards for technology and social work practice: ASWB international technology task force, 2013–2014*. Culpeper, VA: Author. Retrieved from https://www.aswb.org/wp-content/uploads/2015/03/ASWB-Model-Regulatory-Standards-for-Technology-and-Social-Work-Practice.pdf

Berzin, S. C., Singer, J. B., & Chan, C. (2015). *Practice innovation through technology in the digital age: A grand challenge* (Grand Challenges for Social Work Initiative Working Paper No. 12). Cleveland, OH: American Academy of Social Work & Social Welfare. Retrieved from http://aaswsw.org/wp-content/uploads/2013/10/Practice-Innovation-through-Technology-in-the-Digital-Age-A-Grand-Challenge-for-Social-Work-GC-Working-Paper-No-12.pdf

Brady, S. R., McLeod, D. A., & Young, J. A. (2015). Developing ethical guidelines for creating social media technology policy in social work classrooms. *Advances in Social Work, 16*(1), 43–54.

British Association of Social Workers (BASW). (2012). *BASW's social media policy*. Retrieved from https://www.basw.co.uk/resource/?id=1515

Burgstahler, S. (2017, January 30). ADA compliance for online course design. *Educause Review*. Retrieved from https://er.educause.edu/articles/2017/1/ada-compliance-for-online-course-design

Canadian Association of Social Workers (CASW). (2014). *Social media use and social work practice*. Retrieved from https://www.casw-acts.ca/en/social-media-use-and-social-work-practice

Clinical Social Work Association (CSWA). (2013, September). *Report on online MSW programs*. Retrieved from http://www.clinicalsocialworkassociation.org/Resources/Documents/CSWA%20-%20Position%20Paper%20-%20Online%20MSW%20Programs%20-%20September2013.pdf

Congress, E. P. (1996). Dual relationships in academia: Dilemmas for social work educators. *Journal of Social Work Education, 32*, 329–338. doi:10.1080/10437797.1996.10778464

Congress, E. P. (2001). Dual relationships in social work education. *Journal of Social Work Education, 37*, 255–266. doi:10.1080/10437797.2001.10779052

Council on Social Work Education (CSWE). (2018). *2017 statistics on social work education in the United States* (p. 32). Retrieved from https://www.cswe.org/Research-Statistics/Research-Briefs-and-Publications/CSWE_2017_annual_survey_report-FINAL.aspx

Creative Commons. (n.d.). Creative Commons [Home page]. Retrieved from https://creativecommons.org/

Cummings, S. M., Chaffin, K. M., & Cockerham, C. (2015). Comparative analysis of an online and a traditional MSW program: Educational outcomes. *Journal of Social Work Education, 51*, 109–120. http://doi.org/10.1080/10437797.2015.977170

Curington, A. M., Hitchcock, L. I. & Carroll, M. J. (2018). *Social media toolkit for social work field educators*, 2nd ed. Retrieved from https://www.laureliversonhitchcock.org/2018/11/05/revised-social-media-toolkit

Dean, A. K. L. (2012, December 3). Teaching vs. preaching: Conversational ethics in the classroom. Retrieved from https://ethicist.aom.org/2012/12/teaching-vs-preaching-conversational-ethics-in-the-classroom/

Drake, P. (2014, February 24). *Is your use of social media FERPA compliant?* Retrieved from http://er.educause.edu/articles/2014/2/is-your-use-of-social-media-ferpa-compliant

Edes, A., & Bowman, E. (2018, February 19). *"Automating inequality": Algorithms in public services often fail the most vulnerable.* Retrieved from https://www.npr.org/sections/alltechconsidered/2018/02/19/586387119/automating-inequality-algorithms-in-public-services-often-fail-the-most-vulnerab

Erreger, S. (2017, February 26). *Net neutrality and the under-served?* [Blog post]. Retrieved from http://stuckonsocialwork.com/2017/02/26/net-neutrality-and-the-under-served/

Escoto, W. (2017, July 19). *Net neutrality: The social justice issue of our time.* Retrieved from https://www.publicknowledge.org/news-blog/blogs/net-neutrality-the-social-justice-issue-of-our-time

Fishman, T. (2014). *The fundamental values of academic integrity* (2nd ed.). Greenville, SC: Clemson University. Retrieved from http://www.academicintegrity.org/icai/assets/Revised_FV_2014.pdf

Forgey, M. A., & Ortega-Williams, A. (2016). Effectively teaching social work practice online: Moving beyond can to how. *Advances in Social Work, 17*(1), 59–77.

General Data Protection Regulation (GDPR), Pub. L. No. 679, EU (April 27, 2016). Retrieved from https://eur-lex.europa.eu/eli/reg/2016/679/oj

Health Insurance Portability and Accountability Act (HIPAA), Pub. L. No. 104–191, 110 Stat 1938 (1996). Retrieved from https://aspe.hhs.gov/report/health-insurance-portability-and-accountability-act-1996

Hitchcock, L. I., Sage, M., & Smyth, N. J. (2017, November 30). *Technology in social work education: Educators' perspectives on the NASW technology standards for social work education and supervision*. Retrieved from http://www.laureliversonhitchcock.org/2017/11/30/technology-in-social-work-education-educators-perspectives-on-the-nasw-technology-standards-for-social-work-education-and-supervision/

Hitchcock, L. I., Sage, M., & Smyth, N. J. (Eds.). (2018). *Technology in social work education: Educators' perspectives on the NASW technology standards for social work education and supervision*. Buffalo, NY: University at Buffalo School of Social Work, State University of New York.

Humphrey, M. (2014, February 6). Is online community real, "virtual" or something else? Retrieved from https://www.forbes.com/sites/michaelhumphrey/2015/04/06/is-online-community-real-virtual-or-something-else/

Institute of Museum and Library Services, University of Washington. (2012). *Building digital communities: A framework for action*. Technology & Social Change Group. Washington, DC: International City/County Management Association. Retrieved from https://tascha.uw.edu/publications/building-digital-communities/

International Center on Academic Integrity (ICAI). (n.d.). *Fundamental values of academic integrity*. Retrieved from https://academicintegrity.org/fundamental-values/

Jackson, N. (2011, June 3). United Nations declares Internet access a basic human right. *The Atlantic*. Retrieved from http://www.theatlantic.com/technology/archive/2011/06/united-nations-declares-internet-access-a-basic-human-right/239911/

Karpman, H. E., & Drisko, J. (2016). Social media policy in social work education: A review and recommendations. *Journal of Social Work Education, 52*, 1–11. doi:10.1080/10437797.2016.1202164

Kimball, E., & Kim, J. (2013). Virtual boundaries: Ethical considerations for use of social media in social work. *Social Work, 58*, 185–188.

Lee-Post, A., & Hapke, H. (2017). Online learning integrity approaches: Current practices and future solutions. *Online Learning, 21*(1), 135–145.

Lieberman, M. (2018, January 31). High-impact practices enliven staid online course format. *Inside Higher Ed*. Retrieved from https://www.insidehighered.com/digital-learning/article/2018/01/31/high-impact-practices-enliven-staid-online-course-format

Lindsay, C. (2005). *The college student's guide to the law: Get a grade changed, keep your stuff private, throw a police-free party, and more!* Lanham, MD: Taylor Trade.

Marquart, M., & Counselman-Carpenter, B. (2017, June 23). *Supporting the success of online students who are deaf: Lessons presented at #SWDE2017* [Blog post]. Retrieved from http://www.laureliversonhitchcock.org/2017/06/23/supporting-the-success-of-online-students-who-are-deaf-lessons-presented-at-swde2017/

MIT Comparative Media Studies. (n.d.). *Resources for teachers: How to detect plagiarism* [Blog post]. Retrieved from https://cmsw.mit.edu/writing-and-communication-center/resources/teachers/detect-plagiarism/

National Association of Social Workers (NASW). (2017a). *Code of ethics of the National Association of Social Workers*. Washington, DC: NASW Press. Retrieved from https://www.socialworkers.org/About/Ethics/Code-of-Ethics/Code-of-Ethics-English

National Association of Social Workers (NASW). (2017b). *NASW, ASWB, CSWE, & CSWA standards for technology in social work practice*. Washington, DC: NASW Press. Retrieved from https://www.socialworkers.org/includes/newIncludes/homepage/PRA-BRO-33617.TechStandards_FINAL_POSTING.pdf

Newton, D. (2016, June 7). How five companies are gaining millions in profit off education at nonprofit schools. *Atlantic*. Retrieved from https://www.theatlantic.com/education/archive/2016/06/for-profit-companies-nonprofit-colleges/485930/

Reamer, F. G. (2013). Social work in a digital age: Ethical and risk management challenges. *Social Work, 58*(2), 163–172. doi:10.1093/sw/swt003

Siebert, D. C., Siebert, C. F., & Spaulding-Givens, J. (2006). Teaching clinical social work skills primarily online: An evaluation. *Journal of Social Work Education, 42*, 325–336.

Smyth, N. J. (2010, September 10). *When is cultural incompetence okay?* [Blog post]. Retrieved from https://njsmyth.wordpress.com/2010/09/10/when-is-cultural-incompetence-okay/

Song, H., Kim, J., & Luo, W. (2016). Teacher-student relationship in online classes: A role of teacher self-disclosure. *Computers in Human Behavior, 54*, 436–443. doi:10.1016/j.chb.2015.07.037

Thomas, A. (2015a, August 7). *Dishonest academics may make students think plagiarism is acceptable*. Retrieved from http://theconversation.com/dishonest-academics-may-make-students-think-plagiarism-is-acceptable-45187

Thomas, A. (2015b, August 19). *Forget plagiarism: There's a new and bigger threat to academic integrity*. Retrieved from http://theconversation.com/forget-plagiarism-theres-a-new-and-bigger-threat-to-academic-integrity-46210

Tiku, N. (2018, March 19). How Europe's new privacy law will change the web, and more. *Wired*. Retrieved from https://www.wired.com/story/europes-new-privacy-law-will-change-the-web-and-more/

Timm, D. M., & Duven, C. J. (2008). Privacy and social networking sites. *New Directions for Student Services, 2008*(124), 89–101. doi:10.1002/ss.297

Toner, H. (2016, September 27). *Copyright for educators*. Retrieved from http://www.pbssocal.org/education/copyright-for-educators/

Trammell, K. D., & Ferdig, R. E. (2004). Pedagogical implications of classroom blogging. *Academic Exchange Quarterly, 8*(4), 60–64.

University at Buffalo School of Social Work. (n.d.). *Social worker's guide to social media*. Retrieved from http://socialwork.buffalo.edu/resources/social-media-guide.html

University at Buffalo. (2017, September). *Masters of social work student handbook 2017–2018*. Retrieved from http://socialwork.buffalo.edu/content/social-work/home/current-students/msw-student-info/student-handbooks/_jcr_content/par/download_123743111/file.res/2017-2018%20handbook-Final.pdf

U.S. Department of Education. (2015, June 26). *Family educational rights and privacy act (FERPA)*. Retrieved from http://www2.ed.gov/policy/gen/guid/fpco/ferpa/index.html

U.S. Department of Justice. (2010). *2010 ADA standards for accessible design*. Retrieved from https://www.ada.gov/2010ADAstandards_index.htm

Washburn, M., Bordnick, P., & Rizzo, A. (2016). A pilot feasibility study of virtual patient simulation to enhance social work students' brief mental health assessment skills. *Social Work in Health Care, 55*(9), 675–693. doi:10.1080/00981389.2016.1210715

Wyrick, A. J. (2017, June 19). Professor Goldilocks and the three boundaries. Retrieved from https://www.facultyfocus.com/articles/teaching-and-learning/professor-goldilocks-three-boundaries/

Zgoda, K. (2013, February 20). Luddite or love it: The ethical case for technology use in social work [Blog post]. Retrieved from http://swscmedia.com/2013/02/luddite-or-love-it-the-ethical-case-for-technology-use-in-social-work/

CHAPTER 9

TECHNOLOGY FOR PROFESSIONAL DEVELOPMENT

In this chapter, we help you explore the following questions:

- Who are today's tech-savvy social work educators?
- What is my own comfort level with using technology in my professional life?
- What do I, as a 21st-century social work educator, need to know about technology?
- How can I use technology for professional development?
- How can I practice self-care when using technology professionally?

Chapter 9 concludes our discussion on technology in social work education by focusing on strategies that support successful navigation by social work educators in a technology-mediated educational environment. We briefly return to topics from previous chapters to help synthesize knowledge and skills needed by today's tech-savvy social work educators across the technology spectrum, such as the basic skills necessary for managing one's workload and professional development. We discuss technology-mediated tools for work productivity and the importance of continuing education in the fast-changing world of distance education. We explain the use of professional learning networks (PLN) and where to find them, discuss emerging trends related to technology in higher education (including data-driven decision-making), and offer ideas about how to use technology to create and disseminate scholarship. We wrap up with a brief discussion on ways to practice self-care in the digital age.

WHO ARE TODAY'S TECH-SAVVY SOCIAL WORK EDUCATORS?

Generally, faculty members in higher education, at least in the United States, use technology professionally and as part of their teaching. Most professors use learning management systems (LMSs) to communicate and share course content with students and e-mail to communicate with students and colleagues (Allen & Seaman, 2016). About 32% of faculty members have taught an online course, and 40% have taught some form of hybrid course (Straumsheim, Jaschik, & Lederman, 2015). Social and digital media, on the other hand, have slightly different user engagement profiles. A majority of faculty members in U.S. higher education (70%) use social media for personal reasons, a similar rate of use to the 70% of all Americans and others worldwide who are reportedly social media users (Pew Research Center, 2017; Straumsheim, Jaschik, & Lederman, 2015). Professionally, about 50% of faculty members use social media for work-related tasks such as networking, with the majority coming from the disciplines of professional or applied sciences (Seaman & Tinti-Kane, 2013). Despite evidence that Twitter and other social media platforms increase dissemination of scholarship to other academics, policy makers, and the public (Darling, Shiffman, Côté, & Drew, 2013; Parsons, Shiffman, Darling, Spillman, & Wright, 2014), a survey by *Inside Higher Ed* reported that only 6% of faculty members in the United States use social media to discuss or share their scholarship (Straumsheim, Jaschik, & Lederman, 2015). We offer a detailed discussion of the available research about technology use by social work educators in Chapter 4, which generally finds that social work educators use common technology tools such as their institution's LMS and e-mail programs but are slow to adopt new and innovative technologies into their teaching and learning such as social networking platforms or text messaging. In a more recent survey, Goldkind, Wolf, and Jones (2016) found strong patterns of technology use among social work field supervisors, with high numbers using e-mail (99%) and text messaging (83%) for work, as well as electronic records (68.4%), cloud computing (56.8%) and online survey tools (70.4%). They argue that practicing social workers in the community may not be as technophobic as conventional wisdom leads us to believe.

It is not enough that new technologies are emerging in higher education, nonprofit management, or individual social workers' productivity; the actual adoption and embrace of technology by social work educators and practitioners is also important. One theory that helps us understand the reasons social work educators may be less inclined to adopt technology into their professional lives is Everett Rogers' (2003) diffusion of innovations (2003). We introduced this theory in Chapter 2 as part of our discussion on digital literacies. Rogers notes that adoption of new technologies is often a social process influenced by five factors:

1. The innovation itself (i.e., how well the technology translates to the educational process, for instance, presentation software compared to handwriting on a whiteboard);

2. Who the adopters are (e.g., university administrators compared to faculty members);

3. The communication patterns between the adopters (e.g., how a new assistant professor convinces a tenured faculty member to use a professional social network such as LinkedIn);

4. How long the technology has been around (i.e., whether it is in beta or a well-established platform); and

5. The makeup of the larger social system of the adopters (e.g, internal influences such as comfort level with technology and external influences such as popularity, cost, policies).

Based on these five factors, Rogers suggests an individual fit into one of five types of technology adopters. See Figure 9.1 for a description and list of characteristics of the five types. Generally, innovators adopt because the technology is new, and they are willing to risk failure to see how the technology applies in the classroom or their work environment. Innovators are relatively a small group of people within an organization, community, or working group. They do not typically exert a lot of social influence with the other adopters; rather, they are individuals viewed as those who will try the latest educational fad. In contrast, early adopters are also quick to adopt new technology but are more risk averse, preferring to protect their reputations by not adopting a new technology too quickly. Innovators influence early adopters when it comes to new technology. However, because early adopters are more careful in their assessments and applications of new technology, they tend to have more social influence with other types of adopters.

Majority adopters are the critical mass of social work educators needed to ensure that technology is adopted in the educational arena, and Rogers identifies two types of majority adopters. Early majority adopters value the practical benefits of using the technology and embrace a new form of technology when it has a proven track record, or the benefits outweigh the costs. Late majority adopters typically adapt to technology use out of necessity rather than personal interest. Everyone else is doing it (for instance, using the LMS), so they need to jump on the bandwagon too. Late majority adopters often need and expect assistance in learning and applying the technology to the classroom and their teaching. These are the faculty members who don't use the LMS until they are told they must, and then they get someone to help them. Finally, laggards are the last to adopt technology for the classroom and are often resistant to the technology and its use as an educational tool. Though it may be tempting to value one type of adopter over another, understanding where you fall on this continuum of adoption will help you understand your preferences for using technology in your own professional work life and how that preference affects others in your environment. Can you identify where you fall along the spectrum of innovation adopters?

Figure 9.1. Spectrum of Innovation Adopters

Innovators (2.5%)
- Characteristics include risk tolerance, willingness to fail, and adventerousness.
- Adopts technology to drive change and try out new ideas
- Respected by early adopters whereas majority of adopters doubt efforts

Early Adopters (13.5%)
- Chacteristics include intentionality, willingness to embrace change, and being opinion leaders.
- Adopts technology because likes trying new things and ideas
- Highly influential among majority adopters and enjoys sharing with others

Early Majority Adopters (34%)
- Chacteristics include pragmatism and preference for slow, paced change.
- Adopts technology when benefits outweight costs
- Feels comfortable with technology when it is shown to be benefical

Late Majority Adopters (34%)
- Chacteristics include being skeptical, cautious; likes to know the rules.
- Adopts technology when it is nessecary but not by choice
- Feels comfortable with new technology only when it is proven and established

Laggards (16%)
- Characteristics include being risk averse; values tradition and is wary of change.
- Adopts new technology only when no other option is available
- Feels threatened or uncomfortable with change or uncertainty

WHAT IS MY OWN COMFORT LEVEL WITH USING TECHNOLOGY IN MY PROFESSIONAL LIFE?

Instruments and measurement tools can help you empirically assess what type of innovation adopter you are or pinpoint your own comfort level with using technology. But because technology is an ever-changing presence in the professional lives of social workers, we also suggest a reflective approach to help gain insight about your own willingness and comfort level when it comes to adopting new technical knowledge and skills. Adapting Schon's (1984) reflection frameworks, start with reflecting on your current use of technology in your professional and personal life (reflection on action). See Breakout Box 9.1 for an overview of questions you can ask yourself as you reflect on your technology use. The first step is to understand the values that drive your use of technology at work or at home, including the types of technology you use and how you use them, to best understand how you view technology and its role in social work education and practice. Consider where you fall on the Diffusion of Innovations spectrum previously described in this chapter. Are you an early adopter of technology or do you prefer not to use it all? Though one is not better than the other, it is important to understand your own views about technology in social work education and practice so you can be intentional in understanding your own worldview. You could also consider the professional values and policies that influence your use of technology in teaching and learning. Possible examples include those that appear in the National Association of Social Workers' Code of Ethics and Standards for Technology in Social Work Practice, the Council on Social Work Education's Educational Policy and Accreditation Standards, the Association of Social Work Boards' Model Regulatory Standards for Technology and Social Work Practice, state-level licensure laws, institutional guidelines, and your personal teaching philosophy (ASWB, 2015; CSWE, 2015; NASW, 2017a, 2017b). Chapter 8 offers a detailed review of the

TECHNOLOGY FOR PROFESSIONAL DEVELOPMENT

social work ethical considerations for the educational environment. Because social justice and human rights are core values that are uniquely woven into the social work profession, we encourage all social work educators to use the lens of social justice (i.e., digital justice) in their worldview of technology (Eubanks, 2012). This means thinking about Internet access as human right; understanding how net neutrality benefits individuals and communities; understanding racism, sexism, homophobia, and all the other isms and what the response to these -isms look like on social media (e.g., the use of hashtags such as #BlackLivesMatter and #MeToo); and understanding how digital platforms can be used to promote e-advocacy, digital equity, and digital inclusion. Because a detailed discussion of digital justice is beyond the scope of this book, see the further reading list at the end of the chapter.

BREAKOUT BOX 9.1. PRACTICE TIPS
REFLECTING-ON-ACTION WITH TECHNOLOGY IN SOCIAL WORK EDUCATION: SCHON'S FRAMEWORK

To help you reflect on your own use of technology in your personal and professional life, consider the following questions:

1. What is your own worldview related to technology? Consider where you stand on the Diffusion of Innovations spectrum, and the professional values and guidelines that help shape your worldview.

2. What is your current level of knowledge and skill related to technology? For personal use? For professional use?

3. What does your technology-learning environment look like? How do you stay abreast of what you next need to know in terms of technology? What are your environmental supports?

Key to this part of the reflection process is to gain insight into the competing values that often create dilemmas when incorporating technology into the classroom. What are the conflicting values or ethical principles that apply when using social media in the classroom? The value of teaching e-professionalism in a networked culture versus privacy of students and faculties may be a relevant example. Further, Brady, McLeod & Young (2015) suggest that competing values of innovation versus resistance to change influence a social work educator's decision to incorporate social media into the learning environment. They offer an ethical framework of guiding questions that social work educators can ask themselves and others to guide decision-making about whether to use social media in class.

Once you understand your own worldview, the next step is to assess your technology skills. The "Reflection Questions for Digital Literacy in Social Work" in Appendix 4 offer opportunities to think about your current technology practices and understanding, and reading Chapter 2 helps explain Belshaw's (2014) digital literacy skills on which these questions are based. Your responses to the digital literacy questions will help you identify your current level of skill and provide insight into areas of growth for your technical knowledge and skills. For the final step in this reflection process, assess your larger educational environment and its role in supporting when, how, and why you use technology in your professional life. For example, how does your own social work program incorporate technology into its curriculum? The "Social Work Distance Education Assessment of Readiness" checklist available in Appendix 5 and discussed in Chapter 6 provides one tool for evaluating the status of technology supports in your own academic home.

As a final practice of reflection for teaching with technology, you can practice Schon's (1984) reflection-in-action model when using technology either personally or professionally; that is, reflect on the good, the bad, and the ugly while you are using technology to teach, conduct research, or complete other work tasks. Borton (1970) offers three reflections questions that you can use in the moment to help you assess your immediate situation with technology and contemplate your next steps to resolve a problem or appreciate a success. For example, you can reflect-in-action when Skype is or is not working for a classroom guest lecture. We have adapted these questions to focus on using technology as a social work educator:

1. *What?* Identify what is/was going on in the experience (i.e., what is going on with the technology, the user, or both?). This is when you are self-aware about the situation and can describe it. What is/was the problem or the success with the technology? What is/was your role as the user of technology? What happened as the result of using the technology? What am I doing/did I do with the technology?

2. *So what?* Ascertain what is important about this experience of using technology to achieve an outcome. This is when you analyze how your role or actions influenced the outcome of the situation. What is/was so important about using technology in this situation? What is/was different to what I knew or did previously with this technology? What am I learning/did I learn about this type of technology, or using technology in this situation?

3. *Now what?* Reflect on your options with technology in this type of situation. This is when you synthesize your answers to the previous questions and choose what you are going to do next. Now, what do I need to do with the technology? What might be the consequences of my actions with this technology? What do I do to resolve the situation or make it better with this technology?

Key to this process is the ability to reflect about yourself as a *user* of the technology and about how the specific type of technology is used in the learning environment. As a user, consider your knowledge and skills related to the specific learning technology. For example, when you have a guest speaker in the classroom via videoconferencing software, if a problem comes up during the class, you will want to think about your understanding of, and your ability to, operate and troubleshoot the software. Further, you need to reflect on the guest speaker's ability to use Skype, the physical hardware that is available to you in the classroom, and the students' understanding about how to interact with someone via videoconferencing. To see how this process might work, Breakout Box 9.2 offers a case study about how one educator reflects-in-action while using Skype with a guest speaker.

BREAKOUT BOX 9.2.
JESSICA'S REFLECTING-IN-ACTION WITH VIDEO-CONFERENCING SOFTWARE

Jessica is a social worker for a child welfare agency and an adjunct instructor at the local university's School of Social Work. She teaches a child welfare elective as a seated course once a week. As part of a module on the Indian Child Welfare Act, Jessica reaches out to a national child welfare expert, who lives in another state, about guest speaking to her class via Skype. She wants to include the perspective of this expert because he is Native American and works in a tribal community. Jessica knows technology will help her incorporate this expert and his ideas into her course. The expert agrees, and Jessica plans for the following week. The evening of the guest lecture, Jessica arrives early and begins her reflection as she moves to turn on the classroom desktop computer:

> Okay, I got to class early and am able to pull up and log onto Skype without any problems [*What?*]. Good thing I tested the software on this computer last week [*So what?*]. I need to do that every time I Skype someone into the class [*Now what?*].

Jessica quickly cycles through the reflections questions as she opens Skype. Then, she begins checking the hardware:

TECHNOLOGY FOR PROFESSIONAL DEVELOPMENT

> Okay, testing whether the speakers and microphone are working. OMG, the speakers are not working! Without the speakers, the students won't be able to hear. Okay, deep breath; what did I do the last time this happened to me? I can check the volume on the computer and the receiver. As a backup, I can call the IT help desk or get a student up here to help me with the volume.

Jessica checks the volume controls on the desktop computer, which are at an appropriate level, and then checks the receiver and sees the volume-level knob was turned all the way down. She turns the volume up, and now the speakers are working. Jessica mentally pats herself on the back for solving the problem. She continues setting up the hardware by making sure the projector is on and is showing what is on the desktop monitor. She then contacts the guest expert who answers the video call. After chatting for a few minutes, she starts class and introduces the guest expert, who then begins to lecture. Jessica sits down near the computer in case she needs to do something with the computer or Skype and begins to monitor the students:

> Whew, let's see what is going on with the class ... some are paying attention, taking notes—wait, I see Alyssa's hand; she is miming that she can't hear, and she is in the back row. The rest of the back row is miming the same thing. They need to hear what the guest expert is saying. I'll turn up the volume. Okay, done. Alyssa is giving me the thumbs up sign. Next time, I'll ask if everyone can hear before we start, like a sound check.

Throughout the lecture Jessica monitors the students and the Skype video call. When the guest expert is done, she asks if the class has any questions. Several hands go up, and Jessica calls on one student in the back row, who asks his question but the guest speaker says she can't hear. Jessica begins her reflection again:

> Drat! The microphone is up here with me and the student is in the back. She can't answer the question if she can't hear it. I'll repeat the question, so she can answer it. I can continue to repeat the questions. I can ask the students to come up to the computer to ask their questions, or they can write them down. I could type them into the chat box—What to do? Here is what I will do ...

> Jessica tells the class that she will repeat the questions for the guest expert, and to help save time she asks the students to write down their questions on a piece of paper and pass them forward. After the class, she spends a few minutes reflecting on how the Skype session went:
>
>> Whew, I am glad that is over, my first time using Skype with a guest speaker. I was so nervous. The students were able to hear from a national expert and I had problems with the volume and questions. I am so glad I played around with Skype on the classroom computer and talked with guest speaker on Skype earlier in the week. I wonder how much the students learned from the guest speaker, especially over Skype. I was able to use Skype with the guest expert, solve the volume problem, and get the students' questions answered. How could I do this better next time? I can ask the students for feedback about using Skype. I can make a checklist for the next time. And I can ask students to write their questions down during the lecture. I can also ask IT about the microphone. I am definitely going to try this again!
>
> She writes these ideas down on an index card right away and staples them to her master syllabus so she remembers that she needs to address these issues when planning out her class next term.

WHAT DO I, AS A 21ST-CENTURY SOCIAL WORK EDUCATOR, NEED TO KNOW ABOUT TECHNOLOGY?

We offer three areas of knowledge all social work educators can reflect on related to the role of technology in their teaching and learning in the 21st century. These include (1) keeping up to date about the intersections of technology and social work practice; (2) using technology in higher education for teaching and program assessment; and (3) deciding how technology can aid in academic work productivity. We briefly touch on each of these trends and provide some concrete tips and strategies for how you can stay informed and develop your own technology-based skills. Appendix 6 provides real-world advice from many diverse social work educators.

Technology in Social Work Practice

What do you need to know to teach the next generation of social workers about technology? This question focuses on the knowledge, values, and skills that social workers need to be effective practitioners with clients and groups who use technology daily, and within organizations that operate with the help of technology. Increasingly, new practices such as telehealth and videoconferencing mediate the client-practitioner relationship. Agencies and practice settings use technology to manage and administer programs for clients and communities. As discussed in Chapter 2, knowing when, how, and the best ways to use social and digital technologies is now an essential skill for all social workers. In a recent editorial in the *Journal of Social Work Education*, one of us (Nancy) wrote about the need to incorporate content about technology into all types of social work courses, not just those delivered online (Robbins, Regan, Williams, Smyth, & Bogo, 2016). Social work students need to understand, for example, how to ethically use text message *apps* with clients, what it means to be part of a gaming culture, and how to help clients search for reliable information on the Internet. One of the American Academy of Social Work and Social Welfare's (AASWSW) Grand Challenges is *harnessing technology for social good*, through the incorporation of technology such as on-demand, self-paced, and individualized and flexible services through technology-enabled devices (AASWSW, n.d.; Berzin, Singer, & Chan, 2015). Another growing body of literature suggests that social work graduates need to be aware of ethical decisions related to information and communication technologies (ICT); the role of big data and integrated medical records in program administration and research; how to use and interpret apps and wearable technology, and working with geographic information system (GIS) data (Coulton, George, Putnam-Hornstein, & de Haan, 2015; Felke, 2014; Goldkind & Wolf, 2015; Mishna, Bogo, & Sawyer, 2015). The innovation of social work practice through technology relies on well-trained social workers who know how to use it effectively. Further, social work educators must present relevant discussions in the classroom that reinforce the profession's ethical commitment to social justice, including the spread and growth of technology to all persons, regardless of background and resources (NASW, 2017a; Goldkind & Wolf, 2015). As previously noted, Chapter 8 provides a more detailed discussion of ethical concerns related to technology; however, a risk focus as it relates to technology may create technology-phobic social workers who are inclined to avoid technology. A well-rounded curriculum should include the potential benefits of technology and the value of social workers who can engage in critical decision-making about technology. Although the focus of this book is not technology in social work practice, we have some suggestions about how you can stay informed about how technology is affecting the social work profession.

Using Technology Effectively in Social Work Education

We have committed most of this book to helping social work educators understand and develop the skills needed to effectively use technology in their classrooms and across their programs' curriculum. Chapter 2 and Appendix 4 provide an overview of digital literacies, whereas Chapter 3 reviews theoretical constructs related to incorporating technology into one's pedagogy. Chapter 4; Appendix 1, and Appendix 2 offer numerous tools, assignments, and learning activities that can be used to build technology competency among social work students. Finally, Chapters 5, 6, and 7 discuss how to teach in a technology-mediated environment. It is clear from research that online education can be just as effective as the seated classroom option and that online education is here to stay (Cummings, Chaffin, & Cockerham, 2015; Elliott, Choi, & Friedline, 2013; Wilke & Vinton, 2006). What is less clear are answers to the following questions: Which social work students benefit the most from online courses as compared to hybrid or seated courses? How do we best develop implicit curriculum in an online education environment? And what training will equip the next generation of social work educators to use technology in the classroom? We need more research and support in the scholarship of teaching and learning as it relates to efficacy and best practices of technology in social work education, and the specific skills needed of educators. Additionally, as the profession shifts to competency-based education with more emphasis on student learning outcomes, social work educators should be knowledgeable and skillful in collecting assessment data through computer or cloud-based software programs and should be able to consider how the development of big data in social work education could affect key education practices such as admission policies, gatekeeping, summative evaluation, and program accreditation (Coulton et al., 2015; Robbins et al., 2016).

Managing Work Productivity With Technology

Managing one's own work productivity is essential for today's social work educator. Along with the growth in technology tools such as tablets, smartphones, and cloud-based computing comes the ability for academics to manage their work productivity in new and more efficient ways. E-mail and text messaging have increased communication between professors and their students and colleagues. Online searchable databases allow for quick and easy access to research, and reference management software and bookmarking tools can organize research. Statistical analyses software, online survey tools, and Web-based collaboration tools such as Google Docs or videoconferencing programs have expanded opportunities for scholars to conduct research. Further, dissemination of social work scholarship has been enriched by podcasting, social media apps such as Twitter and Facebook, and academic social networking sites such as ResearchGate and Academia.*edu*. Social media tools are used to track the impact of scholarship by counting the number of shares, likes, and mentions of an article to calculate an altmetric impact score (Altmetric, n.d.). Despite the plethora of these technology tools, learning and using them can be expensive and involve significant time commitments. It is easy to sign up for the latest e-mail management app only to discover that you are spending more time trying to figure out how to run the app than actually dealing with your e-mail. Further, colleagues or institutions will suggest, impose, or restrict the types of technology that one uses to accomplish work tasks in higher education, including learning management systems, file-sharing services such as Dropbox, or e-mail software. Social work academics need to be aware of their own work style and must also develop their own digital literacy skills to assess, use, and manage the available technology tools.

As already noted, other chapters of this book cover topics such as how to incorporate technology into an assignment or how to become more digitally literate, and other topics are beyond the scope of this book (i.e., how to use technology in social work practice). In the rest of this chapter, we focus on how to use technology for one's own professional development. Specifically, we review how to use technology to manage workload, develop a professional learning network, collaborate digitally with others, and disseminate scholarship. We answer questions such as how to stay current with technology and how to stay connected to what you need to know about technology. See Breakout Box 9.3 for an example of how a professional learning network can be used to stay current and connected with technology.

BREAKOUT BOX 9.3. CASE STUDY
THE POWER OF A PROFESSIONAL LEARNING NETWORK (PLN)

This excerpt is taken from Dr. Nancy J. Smyth's blog post on October 14, 2016, from Social Work Synergy, the blog of the University at Buffalo (UB) School of Social Work:

> A true story from a UB colleague, Dr. Phillip Glick, illustrates the power of PLNs. One of his medical residents contacted him in the middle of the night, concerned about a child's non-response to emergency treatment. Seeking to advise the resident on what might help, Dr. Glick immediately searched Medline, an online database of biomedical articles, but he was unable to find anything useful. Next, Dr. Glick reached out to his Twitter network (using general statements, so as to not disclose protected health information). A few hours later, he had a suggestion from a doctor in Sweden who was writing up a series of similar cases—that suggestion saved the child's life. What's important to highlight is that Dr. Glick had already done the work, prior to the crisis, to build a trusted, professional learning network on that social media platform. How lucky for that child and family that they had a physician who was globally connected. (Smyth, 2016)

HOW CAN I USE TECHNOLOGY FOR PROFESSIONAL DEVELOPMENT?

Given the fast-paced and expansive world of technology, it is challenging to stay current on everything, use every work productivity app, and be constantly connected. The reality is that you will never know everything, but you can use technology to help you stay current on trends, improve your work habits, collaborate with others, and share your scholarship with broad audiences. In this section, we cover how you can develop your own professional learning network (PLN) to promote your own lifelong learning, share practical tips from other social work academics about how to best manage one's workload with technology, describe how collaboration tools such as videoconferencing software and Web-based Word documents can be used to improve interactions and productivity with colleagues, and how technology can be used to disseminate scholarship beyond traditional venues.

Using Technology for Lifelong Learning: PLNs

Competent and ethical social work practice requires educators to stay up to date and share information about current news, practice knowledge, and the latest research findings (CSWE, 2015; NASW, 2017a). Although there are many strategies, one robust strategy is the PLN; (also referred to as personal learning networks). Simply stated, PLNs employ, within an online environment, the same strategy that social work professionals have used for centuries: the practice of connecting to people who share interests and can learn from each other. PLNs are a well-established practice in the field of education (Richardson & Mancabelli, 2011). The term comes from the educational technology learning communities and has its origins in connectivism, a learning theory developed by George Siemens (2005) to explain how network-based learning occurs in the digital age. Specifically, connectivism suggests that learning is the process of connecting sources of information together across networks, shifting learning from an individual process to a community effort. Thus, learning includes the skills of managing the flow of information, determining what is and is not useful information, and maintaining connections with others to facilitate ongoing learning (Siemens, 2005). All of these skills are developed and applied with a PLN.

In social work, the word *personal* in personal learning networks can raise some concerns for clinical social workers who are especially sensitive to the need to keep boundaries between their personal and professional personas. For this reason, we use the word *professional*, not *personal*. A PLN exists when a social worker uses social media to collect information related to professional interests, shares this information with others, and collaborates with others in their professional networks on projects (Richardson & Mancabelli, 2011). For example, social workers might use their PLNs to collect e-mail alerts from online newspapers, blogs, and scholarly journals about child welfare research, which they then share with employees, colleagues, or students via Twitter or a curated list on Diigo. A PLN includes the tools and processes used by a social worker to stay up to date and share information about current news, practice knowledge, and the latest research findings.

Prior to the explosion in online content and tools, a PLN might have included an article from a trusted daily newspaper or a print version of a child welfare journal, which a social worker might copy to share with employees or colleagues (or, if a social work educator, with students as part of a class discussion). Along with using digital tools, reciprocity is a distinguishing characteristic of PLNs. Professional relationships in social media are developed and maintained through social exchange. For example, you will only build a network of followers on Twitter if you start following others and commenting on their posts along with posting your own content. PLNs also often move to in-person networks. We (Laurel, Melanie, and Nancy) initially "met" by following each other on Twitter because of our interests in technology in social work education and practice. This online communication led to in-person meetings at conferences and ultimately collaborative work projects.

You will discover many benefits from developing a digital PLN. First, you can develop a network of trusted resources (individuals, organizations, and publishers) that you can access at almost any time. Although learning from other professionals is nothing new, social media expands the number and variety of content, people, and groups that you can access, such as professionals from other countries, open-access peer-reviewed scholarship, and firsthand accounts of other people's experiences. Second, you can easily stay up to date on any professional interest and quickly add or expand an interest in your network. For example, if you are interested in homelessness, you might start by following local and national housing advocacy agencies on Twitter, and in the process, you might discover individuals who are tweeting about their personal experiences with homelessness. Also, given the diverse sources and opportunities with an online PLN, social workers can use their networks to access information and resources when working with complex situations, with clients with rare conditions, or in isolated practice settings (Chen, Rittner, Manning, & Crofford, 2015; Robbins et al., 2016). Third, a digital PLN allows you to create and share content with others in real time, offering tools that allow you to contribute meaningfully to professional conversations and public discourse. Maybe you do not want to write a blog, but you can share interesting articles with your colleagues about self-care practices or other professional interests via a Facebook group, or answer a request for specialized knowledge. Today's social work educators need to create and maintain their PLN while helping students to develop their own PLNs. See Breakout Box 9.4 for tips on how to get started with your own PLN.

BREAKOUT BOX 9.4. PRACTICAL TIPS
HOW TO SET UP A PLN

1. Identify and set up two to three free social media accounts for professional use with networks such as Twitter, LinkedIn, and Facebook. Spend time setting up your profiles with your professional interests.

2. Start following other social workers and organizations on your social media accounts, based on your interests.

3. If you aren't familiar with the norms, etiquette, and culture of the social media application you are using, search on "best

practices for [app name]" and choose entries that are more recent (because apps change over time).

4. Join an online group or community based on your interests.

5. Actively participate by commenting on what other social workers are posting on social media or through their blogs. Consider joining a live video conference call to talk with others or participate in a live Twitter chat such as the #MacroSW chats or the NASW live chat series.

6. Review your PLN frequently by reading information shared by others, listening to podcasts, or watching videos. Nurture your network each day for about 20 minutes.

Along with using one's PLN to network and share content, educators can use digital tools to manage the content (i.e., newspaper articles, blog post, and academic publications) obtained from their PLN. Numerous content management tools exist to help with favoriting or filing information within a social media platform, social bookmarking or curating tools, reference management software, and note-taking or word documenting programs. Chapter 4 includes a discussion of some of these tools. Tool selection is a personal choice and will depend on factors such as your personal preferences for devices and software (e.g., design, ease of use, etc.) and the features of the devices and apps (e.g., cost, sharing, syncing, etc.). No one right way exists for designing and managing a PLN, and everyone has a unique process for organizing a network. Breakout Box 9.5 provides a case study about Carlos, an assistant professor, who uses the "Professional Learning Network Worksheet" that we designed to help plan out his PLN (Hitchcock, Sage, & Smyth, 2017). You may also want to spend time reflecting on how you plan to use your PLN (for networking, sharing information, curating information, or all three), given your own digital literacy skills. For ideas on how to incorporate PLNs into assignments for students, see Appendix 1 and Appendix 2. Both provide example assignments and learning tasks that can be used with students to help them develop their own PLN.

> ## BREAKOUT BOX 9.5. CASE STUDY
> ### CARLOS SETS UP HIS PROFESSIONAL LEARNING NETWORK
>
> Carlos, a brand-new assistant professor, attended a session about professional learning networks at a national social work conference and decides this would be a great tool to help him connect with others and stay current on his primary area of research, HIV prevention and treatment. Using a worksheet provided at the conference session, he spends the time on his return flight planning out his PLN.
>
> The first question on the worksheet asks, What do you want to learn? "That's easy," thinks Carlos, "I want to stay up to date on the latest research findings on HIV prevention and treatment, both in the medical and the social work literature. Also, I know several of the top HIV researchers from the medical community and at my institution, but I am less familiar with who in social work is doing HIV prevention work. I'd like to meet more social work academics working on HIV. And I think it would be a good idea to keep better track of the local practitioners and agencies working on HIV in my state. I really hate that I missed the HIV awareness event sponsored by the city's AIDS Outreach program."
>
> As he sits for a minute, Carlos remembers one of the workshop presenters talking about social justice and digital equity. "There is so much stigma related to HIV work, even today," he thinks and sighs. "I wonder what this stigma looks like on social media and what social workers are doing about it." He adds a goal on his worksheet to learn more about digital equity as it relates to HIV.
>
> Feeling confident in his learning goals for his PLN, Carlos reads the next question on the worksheet: How do you want to participate? He remembers from the session that the presenters discussed different types of quality interactions using social media platforms. "I don't really use Facebook for work, but I did accept Maria's friend request, and she posts a lot of information about the work at her HIV treatment clinic. Thinking about it,

TECHNOLOGY FOR PROFESSIONAL DEVELOPMENT

I did post a comment to her question about evidence-based prevention programs, and we had a good exchange." Based on this experience, Carlos decides he would like to share his own knowledge with others while also connecting with people across the nation and locally.

The next question on the worksheet intimidates Carlos: What digital tools do you want to use? He sighs again, thinking, "I don't have time to keep up with a bunch of social media accounts. I like Facebook, so maybe I can start there by creating some professional connections. I wonder if there is a local HIV prevention group on Facebook that I could join. But is that enough?" He recalls that the speakers at the session used Twitter as part of their PLN and that one speaker mentioned that medical researchers commonly use Twitter to share their findings. He decides to set up a Twitter account next week.

Carlos sees the next question: How will you manage it? "If I spend an hour a day on Facebook like I did after the conference reception last night, I'll never manage a PLN! Wait, didn't one of the speakers say she only spend 15 minutes a day on her PLN? What if I just start with 15 minutes a day and see what happens?"

The final question on the worksheet is, How will you connect it with your face-to-face network? Carlos instantly feels better. He likes talking with people, especially in person. "I can start by following people I know on Twitter. I wonder if Maria is on Twitter. I'll also be local for the researcher from California that I meet yesterday after my session." Within a few minutes, Carlos has a list of people he plans to follow on Twitter, including the speakers from the PLN session so he can see how much they tweet, and a few national advocacy organizations. He also wonders about HIV patients who share their personal experiences with treatment in their own words, something that's not easy to find at conferences or in journal articles!

Carlos scans the worksheet and jots down three actions items in the last section of the worksheet:

1. Find an HIV research group on Facebook and join it.
2. Set up a Twitter account.
3. Follow Maria, Dr. Kendall, and the PLN speakers on Twitter.

He adds next Friday's date for when he wants to complete these actions and smiles as he puts the worksheet into his backpack.

Using Technology for Productivity: Managing the Academic Workload

Technology has shaped the 21st-century work environment in many ways, presenting new benefits and challenges. Benefits include the ability to communicate quickly and easily with clients and colleagues via e-mail, text messaging, and videoconference calls, and challenges include managing higher volumes of digital information and the need to learn how to stay abreast of new tools and technologies. In this section, we discuss how you can use technology tools to help manage the academic workload of teaching, research, and service. Further, in Appendix 6 we offer several technology tips from social workers about how they use technology to manage their workload.

E-mail is one of the most common forms of technology-based communication in social work practice settings, including higher education (Goldkind et al., 2016; Pignata, Lushington, Sloan, & Buchanan, 2015). In 2014, John Ziker and his colleagues completed a time study with 30 faculty members at Boise State University to better understand how academics spent their time. Though they spent most of their work time on teaching and research, participants reported spending 13% of their weekday work time on e-mail, both related to research and teaching. Research studies over the past decade have found that e-mail communication improves organizational productivity but can decrease an individual's productivity and increase personal stress (Jerejian, Reid, & Rees, 2013; Kushlev & Dunn, 2015; Mark et al., 2016). Key to understanding the dilemma of e-mail is that the ease of sending an e-mail allows for more communication between individuals or groups of people, and that the sender is always favored in the communication process, as the receiver spends more time decoding the meaning of an e-mail than does the sender (Pignata et al., 2015). To successfully manage the volume of e-mails received during the workday, academics should incorporate digital tools, such as creating a schedule for checking e-mail and using automatic reply add-on tools or scheduling software to reduce the back-and-forth communication that is common with e-mails, and use e-mail guidelines with students (Pignata et al., 2015; Weiss & Hanson-Baldauf, 2008).

Two other important digital tools that can help manage one's workflow include electronic calendar software and workflow or to-do list applications. Calendaring software minimally includes a digital calendar and frequently includes other features such as an appointment book for scheduling events and a contact or address list. Although data does not exist on the number of social workers or educators who use calendaring software, it is commonly used in governmental agencies, academic institutions, and nonprofit agencies across the globe to keep track of appointments and assist in shared scheduling. Brands of electronic calendars include Google Calendar, iCloud Calendar, and calendar features that come with e-mail software such as Microsoft's Outlook or Apple's Mac Mail. Advantages of using an e-calendar include the ability to sync appointments across a calendar on multiple devices, allowing others to access and manage one's calendar for consensus scheduling, alerts and reminders for upcoming events, and integration with e-mail software. Additionally, learning management systems often include a calendar tool for course management that professors can then sync to their e-calendars.

Disadvantages to calendaring software include the learning curve required to understand and fully use the software, and devices that are unable to access a calendar due to interoperability errors, a drained battery, or a technology glitch. Similar to digital calendar software, online workflow apps or software (such as a digital to-do list) can be useful to manage one's workflow, replacing the paper to-do list. Examples include Trello, Todoist, or Wunderlist. Common features that make digital to-do lists particularly useful include syncing across devices (such as laptop, tablet, and smartphone), list sharing, and integration with calendar and e-mail software.

Though this section offers examples of different tools, apps, and ways that social work academics can use digital technology for managing their workload, we do not recommend any one app or tool. Rather, we encourage you to consider the broader needs you desire in a tool (e.g., scheduling, maintaining a task list, etc.). Thinking about the purpose rather than tool will help you understand why you might want to select one tool over another and what types of features you prefer in an app. Further, some apps and Web-based programs have a free version with basic features and a paid version with more features. You will want to compare the differences between the two versions before investing money and time into learning the program. Finally, we recommend you consult with your institution's information technology office to see if the software or app you are planning to use is compatible with or supported by the institution's other systems. You can also inquire about whether they provide access to a similar program at no cost and with training.

Using Technology for Collaboration: Virtual Communities of Practice

Jean Lave and Etienne Wenger's 1991 theory of communities of practice (CoP) has been adapted for online communities and is known as virtual communities of practice (VCoP; Adedoyin, 2016; Hara, Shachaf, & Stoerger, 2009). The idea of CoP describes a group of people who are passionate about something that they do and form a community to learn more about it. The typology is often used to describe the continuing professional education undertaken by practitioners, such as physicians who want to learn more about how to use social media in their practice or lawyers who are interested in family law. In this model, members interact and learn from each other concerning a similar activity or practice. Lave and Wenger stress the depth of these connections and the enduring commitment of constituent members. In the virtual iteration, VCoPs describe professional online communities that exist to improve work and education for disciplines and professions. No longer tied to geography, these online communities can provide professionals with opportunities to connect and engage with other similarly engaged professionals around the world. Examples of VCoPs appear in medicine, nursing, and social work (Adedoyin, 2016; Rolls, Hansen, Jackson, & Elliot, 2016; Schwartz, Wiley, & Kaplan, 2016). Common reasons professionals engage with VCoPs include networking and collaborating with peers, reducing professional isolation, and improving clinical practice (Adedoyin, 2016; Rolls et al., 2016; Schwartz et al., 2016). Additionally, a VCoP (which involves group work to get a task or process done) may be part of your PLN, which is individualized to your learning only, to support lifelong learning and professional development.

Several examples of VCoPs exist in social work education. For example, the online community called Social Work and Technology, which was started by a social worker, Dr. Jonathan Singer, is a VCoP. It is a virtual space for practitioners who "believe that technology can and should be used by social workers to make the world a better place" (Singer, n.d.). This community has more than 1,200 members, both practitioners and educators, who share news stories, research articles, event happenings, photos, apps, and other ideas about technology and social work practice. Another VCoP in social work is the #MacroSW community (#MacroSW, n.d.). #MacroSW uses Twitter (@OfficialMacroSW) to host weekly conversations among social work practitioners, educators, and students about macro-level social work practice. Topics range from policy and advocacy issues to skills needed to work with communities and organizations. Additionally, members can engage in asynchronous conversations by responding to each other's tweets over hours or days. Some VCoPs in social work education use e-mail LISTSERVs to create an online community. The e-mail LISTSERV from the Association of Baccalaureate Social Work Program Directors (abbreviated BPD) offers a good example of this type of online community. The purpose of the BPD LISTSERV is to create connections between members and the organization by providing a venue where members can share ideas and consult about issues related to baccalaureate social work education (BPD, n.d.). Adedoyin (2016) reports on different VCoPs based in academic institutions in other countries besides the United States, ranging from student-focused communities connected with a course to an online community that connects social work educators and practitioners.

Using Technology for Scholarship: Creating and Sharing Your Work

In this section, we discuss how you can use technology to create meaningful scholarship and then how to disseminate scholarship via social and digital venues to increase impact and access. For social work academics, publishing research is a meaningful and ethical way to contribute to the profession and improve well-being outcomes for clients and communities.

Publishing is also often necessary to obtain an academic position, earn tenure or promotion, and obtain extramural funding. Although publishing requirements for social work professors vary by position and institution, current trends in social work scholarship suggest that academics are becoming more collaborative with their research projects, are writing longer articles, and are increasingly focused on publishing in high-impact journals (Hodge, Lacasse, & Benson, 2012; Kahn, 2014). It is less clear how social and digital technologies can influence and support the creation and dissemination of social work–based research findings.

Social scholarship is an alternative to traditional publishing mechanisms. Greenhow and Gleason (2014) define *social scholarship*, based on Boyer's (1990) classic framework in *Scholarship Reconsidered*, as the integration of social and digital tools throughout the scholarship process, from conceptualization and implementation of a research study to publication. Publishing of ideas, draft work, and other information via social media is faster and more collaborative than traditional publications such as journals and books, making it an ideal starting point for projects (Daniels, 2013). We can share ideas via blog posts or social networking platforms quickly and receive feedback through comments or responses just as quickly. For instance, if social workers were developing a new conceptual idea to describe technology-mediated romantic relationships, they might post a working draft on a wiki or Google Doc so that others could post comments, and then alert their social media network that they are seeking feedback about their draft work. Then they might ask some of the commenters to cowrite an article on the subject, collect themes related to the topic by using hashtag searches on Twitter, and share the final work, or infographic summaries of it, on social media.

The use of social media to share and discuss research is a great equalizer. Social work practitioners and students (even some of us in academics) may not have access to high-priced journals and databases or expensive conferences. By tweeting, blogging, podcasting, and posting about our own research and the research of others, we can share with other professionals and even the public, which may have limited access to the scholarship due to cost or time. If we take it a step further by providing context and explanation, we can help translate the process of scientific inquiry into practical and usable knowledge, especially the social work literature. This approach to information sharing fits with our profession's commitment to social justice and promoting competent practice (NASW, 2017a).

Social work educators can employ social media to create original content for scholarship in multiple forms, but blogging is perhaps the most obvious and popular. With more than one billion websites on the Internet, it is hard to determine the number of blogs that exist worldwide, including the number of academic bloggers (Real Time Statistics Project, n.d.). Several reasons exist for blogging as part of scholarship, including as a practice to improve writing, a way to share ideas early in the creative process, and a venue for feedback and mentoring (Mewburn & Thomson, 2013; Perry, 2015). Research about academic blogs found that posts written by academics fall into categories ranging from career advice to discussing their research for a lay audience.

Blogging can involve creating one's own blog or writing posts for another blog, such as your institution's blog or a professional organization. All three of us have experience blogging, and we each maintain our own blogs as part of our academic work. Nancy's blog is called *Virtual Connections* (Smyth, n.d.), and she uses the free version of WordPress to host the blog. Her blog explores the human connections that we make in virtual spaces as well as the interface between social work and technology, especially Web 2.0. She sometimes features topics related to education, higher education, social work, and technology. Nancy also uses a Creative Commons license to copyright her work and cross-posts some of her blog posts with her school's blog, *Social Work Synergy* (Creative Commons, n.d.; University at Buffalo School of Social Work, n.d.).

Melanie's blog is *Melanie Sage, Social Work Geek* (Sage, n.d.), and she hosts her blog via Blogger, a free platform from Google. The purpose of Melanie's blog is twofold; the first is to showcase her work as a social work scholar, including research dissemination and summaries of her latest interests, and the second is to provide resources for her students or other readers. As a scholar, Melanie blogs about her research and includes a list of her publications and presentations, serving as a de facto CV. Additionally, she curates blog sites of other social work educators, useful software programs, and other types of information. For students, Melanie has detailed blog posts about how to prepare for the licensure exam and how to find research articles and regional resources.

Finally, Laurel's blog, *Teaching and Learning in Social Work* (Hitchcock, n.d.), focuses on practical information for today's social work educator such as sample assignments, tips for incorporating technology into the classroom, and narratives about the learning experiences of students and other social work educators. Using the paid version of WordPress, the blog is a way for Laurel to share work quickly and get feedback before incorporating into an article. For example, she wrote a series of blog posts about using Twitter in social work education.

Based on feedback and comments from peers, she was able to write and publish a peer-reviewed article from those blog posts with a colleague. Another blog post about how to participate in live Twitter chats had more than 400 unique views and was republished by the New Jersey chapter of NASW in their newsletter. Laurel also uses her blog to share materials from conference presentations and workshops, and any peer-reviewed publications. To copyright her work, she includes a Creative Commons license on her blog, which also guides her readers about how they can incorporate ideas and tools from the blog into their own educational practice (Creative Commons, n.d.).

Depending on the target audience, it may be more useful to translate your research to practice via a short video or infographic. You can use free tools to create these kinds of products, and a well-delivered message can easily go viral, racking up hundreds or thousands of views. Although white papers are the more traditional method for translating research to practice, these documents may not gain as widespread dissemination and often lack the attention-getting graphics of contemporary media. Some journals even encourage their authors to pair their published work with a short descriptive video. A scholar could also decide to turn each publication into an easily shareable infographic in a program like Piktochart. Scholars should make these decisions with an audience in mind but also know that the information might reach anyone. It is important to consider these issues carefully when it relates to high-interest or controversial social issues that could be taken out of context when the reader only sees a snapshot of data or findings.

Other ways to create content and conduct research via social media include participant outreach and recruitment. First, social media platforms can reach high-stigma participants such as people with HIV or people undergoing gender reassignment therapies. Second, social work scholars can create interventions, such as health interventions, and carry them out in Facebook groups or on Skype video calls. Third, social media can be a data source, through tools that allow you to download hashtag data from Twitter, or photo information from Facebook public profiles. NVIVO qualitative software helps manage social media data. Some research projects analyze social media data, such as the Our Data Helps Project or Patients Like Me, which collects social media data to further research about suicide and other health conditions (Hitchcock & Sage, 2017; Our Data Helps, n.d.; Patients Like Me, n.d.).

Recognition is growing regarding the value of digital or social scholarship as a part of tenure and promotion decisions (Cabrera et al., 2017; Langdorf & Lin, 2016; Sherbino et al., 2015). Advantages of social media–based scholarship include free and open access, wide reach, timely dissemination, and the promotion of innovation and collaboration (Sherbino et al., 2015). Whereas specific criteria are lacking for social work education, models exist in other professions. Sherbino et al. (2015) developed criteria for social media-based scholarship for educators in health professions education such as medicine and nursing. Using a consensus process, the authors developed a definition of social media–based scholarship for case-based health education. Specifically, they use the following criteria:

- Be original.
- Advance the field of health professions education by building on theory, research, or best practice.
- Be archived and disseminated.
- Provide the health professions education community with the ability to comment and transparently provide feedback that informs wider discussion. (p. 552)

Additionally, they note the importance of assessing the impact of social media–based scholarship on educators as a whole and for authors. For example, alternative metrics, such as the number of page views or the number of shares or likes, can be used as a stand-in for influential factors to demonstrate the impact of a blog post (Bornmann, 2015).

Although creating digital or social scholarship may not fit with every academic's research, time, and comfort level, disseminating or sharing scholarship via technology should be standard practice. Technology can be used to disseminate scholarship beyond traditional venues through methods such as turning articles into infographics to increase research-to-practice dissemination, using tools such as Piktochart or Canva, and then sharing those images via social networks such as Facebook or Twitter. Similarly, researchers can record and post podcasts or videos of themselves discussing a recently published article or summarizing a conference presentation in order to reach a wider audience and support research impact.

FINAL THOUGHTS

To close out this chapter, we want to briefly discuss the importance of practicing self-care when engaging with technology in your professional and personal lives. One of us (Nancy) wrote a blog post about self-care with technology titled "Self-Care in the Digital Age" (Smyth, 2014). Though we offer no single right way to practice self-care with technology, in this discussion we draw from Nancy's blog post to highlight a key self-care practice with technology: being intentional about when and how you use social and digital technologies in your professional and personal lives. Most of our devices allow us to engage with our work environments 24 hours a day, seven days a week. E-mail programs and social networking apps send us notifications around the clock to let us know that someone is trying to reach us or likes what we had to say. Setting our own guidelines about when and how to engage with our technology, and then practicing those guidelines, is one way to incorporate digital self-care into your teaching, research, and service obligations as a social work educator (Carter, 2015; Kanter & Sherman, 2016).

Technology-related self-care is not only about limiting technology. More and more, technology-based tools offer gateways to self-care. For instance, tools like Fitbit watches remind us to get up and take a walk after sitting too long at the computer, and several apps offer coaching for deep breathing or meditation. Other apps remind users to drink enough water or track other kinds of healthy activities. Because technologists (and not social workers or medical professionals) create many apps, it is important to screen the practical utility of these kinds of tools instead of assuming they are useful or evidence based.

Another way to develop your own digital self-care guidelines is the reflection-on-action practice we discuss earlier in this chapter. By thinking deeply on your own knowledge, skills, and preferences, as well as your larger social environment, you will understand your own needs and desires for technology in your work life. Then you can make decisions about when you want to check your e-mail (e.g., only twice a day), how you want to default your notification settings (e.g., sound, icon, or no notification at all), and where you will store your devices during your downtime (e.g., not keeping your tablet in the same place as where you sleep). Technology can have a rewarding quality, with alerts and buzzes that are designed to make people engage frequently, but some people find that technology infringes on their productive time. The Center for Humane Technology (n.d.) is working on design standards to inspire tech companies to provide more options that support well-rounded technology use to encourage reflection about these issues.

Many very active social media users who are also social work scholars set very firm boundaries regarding their technology use

TECHNOLOGY FOR PROFESSIONAL DEVELOPMENT

because they know the possibilities of it creeping into all parts of their lives. Boundaries can include restricting time of technology tool use to certain hours of the day, setting a total time limit, not using social media on the mobile phone, or prescheduling Twitter posts for once a week using software like Hootsuite or Social Pilot instead of engaging daily. The technology tips from other social work educators introduced this chapter and explained in Appendix 6 include many ideas that you can incorporate into your daily or weekly routine. Implicit to the discussion on these tips is the need to be intentional with your technology engagement for self-care purposes. See Breakout Box 9.6 for a practical tip on how to set up digital boundaries.

BREAKOUT BOX 9.6. PRACTICAL TIP
SETTING UP DIGITAL BOUNDARIES ON YOUR PERSONAL DEVICE

Beth Kanter, author of *The Happy Healthy Nonprofit*, describes why and how she sets up digital boundaries on her smartphone:

> Like many professionals in today's connected age, I carry my mobile phone with me all the time. It contains everything I need to run my personal and business life. I can do everything—from checking my bank balance, booking a restaurant reservation, getting driving directions, or reading work documents or e-mail. And that can be a problem—a lack of boundaries between work and personal technology.
>
> I used to marvel at the fact that I could do work anywhere, anytime, because of my mobile phone. I could be waiting for my plane in an airport and check in with e-mail and knock a few tasks before boarding. I didn't have to wait until I was "back at the office." But these days, without boundaries, I could be sitting on the beach in Hawaii enjoying the sun and ocean and all of sudden hear that all too familiar beep for an incoming e-mail or text and the next minute be transported (mentally, of course) back to work.
>
> I have now learned that it is very necessary to learn

> boundary management and enforcement, especially when it comes to use of technology for work outside of work hours and the workplace. One of the things I do now is that on weekends and vacations, I move all my work-related apps and social media and put them many screens back in a folder. The reason is that your thumbs have "thumb memory," and without even knowing it, you are tapping your e-mail and reading. So, by moving the apps and breaking that pattern, I'm able to set a boundary when I need to. (B. Kanter, personal communication, January 19, 2018)

Along with establishing some digital self-care practices, you may want to practice mindfulness techniques when you do engage with technology. Instead of habitually dreading e-mail or mindlessly responding to the beeps from your digital device, try spending a moment to remind yourself why you are checking e-mail (e.g., to be responsive to students and colleagues) or take ten deep breaths before looking at your Facebook account (Willard, 2016). See Breakout Box 9.7 for examples on how Nancy incorporates mindfulness into her digital life.

BREAKOUT BOX 9.7. PRACTICAL TIPS
WHAT DOES SELF-CARE LOOK LIKE IN THE DIGITAL AGE?

Here Dr. Nancy J. Smyth (one of this book's authors) describes what she has learned about taking care of herself in the digital age her blog post *Self-care in the digital age* from her blog Virtual Connections (https://njsmyth.wordpress.com).

Instead of mindlessly doing something on a device, I start by asking myself, *What do I need right now?* And when I say this, I actively check in with all of me—my body, my soul, and my mind. I try to notice what I'm doing and turn my attention inward and notice my physical sensations, my energy level, and my feelings and then use this information to ask what's needed. Here are some of the practices I use depending on what I need:

- Set boundaries for myself regarding technologies—times to be off e-mail and other work-related contacts, and time to eat and enjoy food and the people I'm eating with, especially toward the end of a day.
- Keep my body moving, taking frequent breaks from sitting still working on a device.
- Have experiences that are doing and being and interacting with the world (and the people) around me, especially being outside. This means putting the technology down at these times.
- Disconnect—even from fun things like games and Second Life—at least an hour before bedtime. I don't sleep as restfully when I don't, and the research on the impact of backlit screens on sleep confirms this. And I turn off notifications on my phone then, too.
- Plan some "open" mind time for mind wandering. Sometimes I just need to stand in line or sit in the doctor's waiting room and just let my brain wander, because my mind just feels too full. Sometimes I need to drive in silence, not listening to a recorded book or having my phone read articles to me. Research suggests the need to allow for some mind wandering, since it seems to enhance creativity.
- And sometimes I need to listen to that recorded book or that article while I'm driving, or work on e-mail in that doctor's waiting room.

Yes, I do realize that my last two points suggest opposite actions. That's because it's not about formulas for living. It's about stopping for a few seconds, asking what's needed, and making choices. And it's about observing how things affect me, so I can make choices and find the right mix and come up with some general principles to guide my life to create my own personal "owner's manual" of sorts. You will probably never find me doing e-mail at 5:30 a.m. But I have a colleague who does that regularly and identifies it as something that works well for her. We have to allow room for differences among us, while working together to share what works and dialogue with each other about the process.

Throughout Chapter 9, our focus has been to provide insight and practical advice on how to use technology to enhance one's own work productivity. Understanding how your peers use technology, and other digital trends in social work education, allows you to begin exploring the options for increasing your own use of technology. Further, reflecting on your current knowledge and skill set will help you determine how to best enhance your own learning with digital and social technologies. Given financial costs of technology, the speed of change, and time to learn new technology tools, this self-reflection may be the most important step. Self-knowledge about your goals, obligations, and boundaries will help you to make the best decisions for incorporating technology into your work life.

FURTHER READING AND RESOURCES

American Academy of Social Work and Social Welfare. (n.d.). *Harness technology for social good*. Grand Challenges for Social Work. Retrieved from http://aaswsw.org/grand-challenges-initiative/12-challenges/harness-technology-for-social-good/

Center for Humane Technology. http://humanetech.com/

National Digital Inclusion Alliance. https://www.digitalinclusion.org/

Shieber, J. (2017, May 15). *Using tech to uproot systemic racism*. Retrieved from https://techcrunch.com/2017/05/15/using-tech-to-uproot-systemic-racism/

Social Media at the Mayo Clinic. https://socialmedia.mayoclinic.org/

University at Buffalo School of Social Work. (n.d.). *Our self-care starter kit*. Retrieved from https://socialwork.buffalo.edu/resources/self-care-starter-kit.html

REFERENCES

Adedoyin, A. C. A. (2016). Deploying virtual communities of practice as a digital tool in social work: A rapid review and critique of the literature. *Social Work Education, 35*(3), 357–370. doi:10.1080/02615479.2016.1154660

Allen, I. E., & Seaman, J. (2016). Online report card tracking online education in the United States. Babson Survey Research Group and Quahog Research Group. Retrieved from https://onlinelearningconsortium.org/read/online-report-card-tracking-online-education-united-states-2015/

Altmetric. (n.d.). Home page. Retrieved from https://www.altmetric.com/

American Academy of Social Work and Social Welfare (AASWSW). (n.d.). *Grand challenges initiatives.* Retrieved from http://aaswsw.org/grand-challenges-initiative/

Association of Baccalaureate Social Work Program Directors (BDP). (n.d.). Home page. Retrieved from http://www.bpdonline.org/

Association of Social Work Boards (ASWB). (2015). *Model regulatory standards for technology and social work practice: ASWB international technology task force, 2013–2014.* Culpeper, VA: Author. Retrieved from https://www.aswb.org/wp-content/uploads/2015/03/ASWB-Model-Regulatory-Standards-for-Technology-and-Social-Work-Practice.pdf

Belshaw, D. (2014). *The essential elements of digital literacies.* Retrieved from http://digitalliteraci.es/

Berzin, S. C., Singer, J. B., & Chan, C. (2015). *Practice innovation through technology in the digital age: A grand challenge* (Grand Challenges for Social Work Initiative Working Paper No. 12). Cleveland, OH: American Academy of Social Work & Social Welfare. Retrieved from http://aaswsw.org/wp-content/uploads/2013/10/Practice-Innovation-through-Technology-in-the-Digital-Age-A-Grand-Challenge-for-Social-Work-GC-Working-Paper-No-12.pdf

Bornmann, L. (2015). Usefulness of altmetrics for measuring the broader impact of research: A case study using data from PLOS and F1000Prime. *Aslib Journal of Information Management, 67*(3), 305–319. doi:10.1108/AJIM-09-2014-0115

Borton, T. (1970). *Reach touch and teach: Student concerns and process education*. New York: McGraw-Hill.

Boyer, E. L. (1990). *Scholarship reconsidered: Priorities of the professoriate*. Princeton, NJ: Carnegie Foundation for the Advancement of Teaching.

Brady, S. R., McLeod, D. A., & Young, J. A. (2015). Developing ethical guidelines for creating social media technology policy in social work classrooms. *Advances in Social Work, 16*(1), 43–54.

Cabrera, D., Vartabedian, B. S., Spinner, R. J., Jordan, B. L., Aase, L. A., & Timimi, F. K. (2017). More than likes and tweets: Creating social media portfolios for academic promotion and tenure. *Journal of Graduate Medical Education, 9*(4), 421–425. doi:10.4300/JGME-D-17-00171.1

Carter, C. (2015, February 2). Don't fool yourself: Use technology intentionally. *Greater Good*. Retrieved from https://greatergood.berkeley.edu/article/item/dont_fool_yourself_use_technology_intentionally

Center for Humane Technology. (n.d.). Calling all technology makers. Retrieved from http://humanetech.com/designers/

Chen, Y. L., Rittner, B., Manning, A., & Crofford, R. (2015). Early onset schizophrenia and school social work. *Journal of Social Work Practice, 29*(3), 271–286. doi:10.1080/02650533.2015.1014328

Coulton, C. J., George, R., Putnam-Hornstein, E., & de Haan, B. (2015). Harnessing big data for social good: A grand challenge for social work (Grand Challenges for Social Work Initiative Working Paper No. 11). Cleveland, OH: American Academy of Social Work and Social Welfare. Retrieved from http://aaswsw.org/wp-content/uploads/2015/12/WP11-with-cover.pdf

Council on Social Work Education (CSWE). (2015). *Educational policy and accreditation standards for baccalaureate and master's social work programs*. Alexandria, VA: Author. Retrieved from https://www.cswe.org/Accreditation/Standards-and-Policies/2015-EPAS

Creative Commons. (n.d.). Creative Commons [Home page]. Retrieved from https://creativecommons.org/

Cummings, S. M., Chaffin, K. M., & Cockerham, C. (2015). Comparative analysis of an online and a traditional MSW program: Educational outcomes. *Journal of Social Work Education, 51*, 109–120. http://doi.org/10.1080/10437797.2015.977170

Daniels, J. (2013, September 25). *From tweet to blog post to peer-reviewed article: How to be a scholar now*. Retrieved from http://blogs.lse.ac.uk/impactofsocialsciences/2013/09/25/how-to-be-a-scholar-daniels/

Darling, E. S., Shiffman, D., Côté, I. M., & Drew, J. A. (2013). The role of Twitter in the life cycle of a scientific publication (No. e16v1). *PeerJ*. Retrieved from https://peerj.com/preprints/16v1

Eubanks, V. (2012). *Digital dead end: Fighting for social justice in the information age*. MIT Press, Cambridge, MA.

Eubanks, V. (2014). Want to predict the future of surveillance? Ask poor communities. *The American Prospect, 15*.

Elliott, W., Choi, E., & Friedline, T. (2013). Online statistics labs in MSW research methods courses: Reducing reluctance toward statistics. *Journal of Social Work Education, 49*, 81–95. http://doi.org/10.1080/10437797.2013.755095

Felke, T. P. (2014). Building capacity for the use of geographic information systems (GIS) in social work planning, practice, and research. *Journal of Technology in Human Services, 32*(1–2), 81–92. doi:10.1080/15228835.2013.860365

Goldkind, L., & Wolf, L. (2015). A digital environment approach: Four technologies that will disrupt social work practice. *Social Work, 60*, 85–87. doi:10.1093/sw/swu045

Goldkind, L., Wolf, L., & Jones, J. (2016). Late adapters? How social workers acquire knowledge and skills about technology tools. *Journal of Technology in Human Services, 34*(4), 338–358. doi:10.1080/15228835.2016.1250027

Greenhow, C., & Gleason, B. (2014). Social scholarship: Reconsidering scholarly practices in the age of social media. *British Journal of Educational Technology, 45*(3), 392–402. doi:10.1111/bjet.12150

Hara, N., Shachaf, P., & Stoerger, S. (2009). Online communities of practice typology revisited. *Journal of Information Science, 35*(6), 740–757. doi:10.1177/0165551509342361

Hitchcock, L. (2015, July 1). *Personal learning networks for social workers* [Blog post]. Retrieved from http://www.laureliversonhitchcock.org/2015/07/01/personal-learning-networks-for-social-workers/

Hitchcock, L. I. (n.d.). *Teaching and learning in social work* [Blog]. Retrieved from http://www.laureliversonhitchcock.org/

Hitchcock, L. I., & Sage, M. (2017, May 4). *Harnessing social media for social good at #CG4SW* [Blog post]. Retrieved from http://www.laureliversonhitchcock.org/2017/05/05/harnessing-social-media-for-social-good-at-cg4sw/

Hitchcock, L. I., Sage, M., & Smyth, N. J. (2017, April 15). *Day two of #SWDE2017: Professional learning networks for social work* [Blog post]. Retrieved from http://www.laureliversonhitchcock.org/2017/04/15/day-two-of-swde2017-professional-learning-networks-for-social-work/

Hodge, D. R., Lacasse, J. R., & Benson, O. (2012). Influential publications in social work discourse: The 100 most highly cited articles in disciplinary journals, 2000–09. *British Journal of Social Work, 42*(4), 765–782. doi:10.1093/bjsw/bcr093

Jerejian, A. C. M., Reid, C., & Rees, C. S. (2013). The contribution of e-mail volume, e-mail management strategies and propensity to worry in predicting e-mail stress among academics. *Computers in Human Behavior, 29*(3), 991–996. doi:10.1016/j.chb.2012.12.037

Kahn, J. M. (2014). Social work scholarship: Authorship over time. *Journal of Social Work Education, 50*, 262–273. doi:10.1080/10437797.2014.885253

Kanter, B., & Sherman, A. (2016). *The happy, healthy nonprofit: Strategies for impact without burnout.* Hoboken, NJ: Wiley.

Kushlev, K., & Dunn, E. W. (2015). Checking e-mail less frequently reduces stress. *Computers in Human Behavior, 43*, 220–228. doi:10.1016/j.chb.2014.11.005

Langdorf, M. I., & Lin, M. (2016). Emergency medicine scholarship in the digital age. *Western Journal of Emergency Medicine, 17*(5), 511–512.

#MacroSW. (n.d.). Home page. Retrieved from https://macrosw.com/

Mark, G., Iqbal, S. T., Czerwinski, M., Johns, P., Sano, A., & Lutchyn, Y. (2016). E-mail duration, batching and self-interruption: Patterns of e-mail use on productivity and stress. In *Proceedings of the 2016 CHI conference on human factors in computing systems* (pp. 1717–1728). New York, NY: ACM. doi:10.1145/2858036.2858262

Mewburn, I., & Thomson, P. (2013). Why do academics blog? An analysis of audiences, purposes and challenges. *Studies in Higher Education, 38*(8), 1105–1119. doi:10.1080/03075079.2013.835624

Mishna, F., Bogo, M., & Sawyer, J.-L. (2015). Cyber counseling: Illuminating benefits and challenges. *Clinical Social Work Journal, 43*(2), 169–178. doi:10.1007/s10615-013-0470-1

National Association of Social Workers (NASW). (2017a). *Code of ethics of the National Association of Social Workers*. Washington, DC: NASW Press. Retrieved from https://www.socialworkers.org/About/Ethics/Code-of-Ethics/Code-of-Ethics-English

National Association of Social Workers. (2017b). *NASW, ASWB, CSWE, & CSWA standards for technology in social work practice*. Washington, DC: NASW Press. Retrieved from https://www.socialworkers.org/includes/newIncludes/homepage/PRA-BRO-33617.TechStandards_FINAL_POSTING.pdf

Our Data Helps. (n.d.). *Home page*. Retrieved from https://ourdatahelps.org/

Parsons, E. C. M., Shiffman, D. S., Darling, E. S., Spillman, N., & Wright, A. J. (2014). How Twitter literacy can benefit conservation scientists. *Conservation Biology, 28*(2), 299–301. doi:10.1111/cobi.12226

Patients Like Me. (n.d.). *Home page*. Retrieved from https://www.patientslikeme.com

Perry, D. (2015, November 11). 3 rules of academic blogging. *Chronicle of Higher Education*. Retrieved from http://www.chronicle.com/article/3-Rules-of-Academic-Blogging/234139

Pew Research Center. (2017, January 12). *Social media fact sheet*. Retrieved from http://www.pewinternet.org/fact-sheet/social-media/

Pignata, S., Lushington, K., Sloan, J., & Buchanan, F. (2015). Employees' perceptions of e-mail communication, volume and management strategies in an Australian university. *Journal of Higher Education Policy and Management, 37*(2), 159–171. doi:10.1080/1360080X.2015.1019121

Real Time Statistics Project. (n.d.). *Internet live stats: Internet usage and social media statistics.* Retrieved from http://www.internetlivestats.com/

Richardson, W., & Mancabelli, R. (2011). *Personal learning networks: Using the power of connections to transform education.* Bloomington, IN: Solution Tree Press.

Robbins, S. P., Regan, J. A. R. C., Williams, J. H., Smyth, N. J., & Bogo, M. (2016). From the editor: The future of social work education. *Journal of Social Work Education, 52,* 387–397. doi:10.1080/10437797.2016.1218222

Rogers, E. M. (2003). *Diffusion of innovations* (5th ed.). New York, NY: Free Press.

Rolls, K., Hansen, M., Jackson, D., & Elliott, D. (2016). How health care professionals use social media to create virtual communities: An integrative review. *Journal of Medical Internet Research, 18*(6). doi:10.2196/jmir.5312

Sage, M. (n.d.). *Melanie Sage, social work geek* [Blog]. Retrieved from https://melaniesagephd.blogspot.com/

Schon, D. A. (1984). *The reflective practitioner: How professionals think in action.* New York, NY: Basic Books.

Schwartz, S. L., Wiley, J. L., & Kaplan, C. D. (2016). Community building in a virtual teaching environment. *Advances in Social Work, 17*(1), 15–30. doi:10.18060/20875

Seaman, J., & Tinti-Kane, H. (2013). *Social media for teaching and learning.* Babson Park, MA: Babson Survey Research Group. Retrieved from http://www.meducationalliance.org/sites/default/files/social_media_for_teaching_and_learning.pdf

Sherbino, J., Arora, V. M., Melle, E. V., Rogers, R., Frank, J. R., & Holmboe, E. S. (2015). Criteria for social media-based scholarship in health professions education. *Postgraduate Medical Journal, 91*(1080), 551–555. doi:10.1136/postgradmedj-2015-133300

Siemens, G. (2005). Connectivism: A learning theory for the digital age. *International Journal of Instructional Technology and Distance Learning, 2*(1). Retrieved from http://www.itdl.org/Journal/Jan_05/article01.htm

Singer, J. B. (n.d.). *Social work and technology: Google+.* Retrieved from https://plus.google.com/communities/115588985317830085141

Smyth, N. J. (n.d.). *Virtual connections* [blog]. Retrieved from https://njsmyth.wordpress.com/

Smyth, N. J. (2016, October 14). *Online connections for professional learning* [Blog post]. Retrieved from http://njsmyth.wordpress.com

Straumsheim, C., Jaschik, S., & Lederman, D. (2015). 2015 Inside Higher Ed survey of faculty attitudes on technology. *Inside Higher Ed*. Retrieved from https://www.insidehighered.com/booklet/2015-survey-faculty-attitudes-technology

University at Buffalo School of Social Work (n.d.). *Social Work Synergy*. Retrieved from https://socialworksynergy.org/

Weiss, M., & Hanson-Baldauf, D. (2008, February 13). E-mail in academia: Expectations, use, and instructional impact. Retrieved from https://er.educause.edu/articles/2008/2/email-in-academia-expectations-use-and-instructional-impact

Wilke, D., & Vinton, L. (2006). Evaluation of the first Web-based advanced standing MSW program. *Journal of Social Work Education, 42*, 607–620. http://doi.org/10.5175/JSWE.2006.200500501

Willard, C. (2016, March 22). Before you scroll, try this mindful social media practice. *Greater Good*. Retrieved from https://greatergood.berkeley.edu/article/item/before_you_scroll_try_this_mindful_social_media_ practice

APPENDIX 1

ASSIGNMENT COMPENDIUM FOR INTEGRATING TECHNOLOGY INTO SOCIAL WORK ASSIGNMENTS AND LEARNING ACTIVITIES

Why Did We Select These Assignments?
When we started this book, we issued a call to our fellow social work educators, asking them to share their technology-based assignments and learning activities. This appendix represents the best of those submissions along with our own assignments. We selected assignments based on how the technology was integrated into the assignment, to represent a variety of topics and technologies, and how the assignment contributed to skills development. Some assignments were combined because of similarities, and credit is given to each contributor throughout the compendium.

How Do I Navigate This Assignment Compendium?
Each assignment includes a variety of information ranging from learning objectives to editors' comments. Here is a breakdown of information for each assignment:

Title and Subject Area
The assignments are organized by subject area for courses, with the following areas in parentheses after the titles: any (course),

field, human behavior in the social environment (HBSE), practice, and research.

Editors' Introduction
This section offers a brief description of the assignment written by the book authors.

Author's Name and Contact
The author's name and contact information are listed here. Please note that author's affiliations may change over time; please conduct a web search for the latest email address when necessary. If you have questions about a specific assignment or come across a non-working link, you are encouraged to contact the author directly. The author will be able to answer comments or questions better than the book's authors. Besides contacting the assignment's contributor, you can also access additional resources for these assignments on the book's YouTube channel: https://goo.gl/aoCkuV.

Approximate Prep Time for Faculty
The approximate amount of preparation time in hours for the instructor.

Average Assignment Time for Students
The average amount of time students will need to complete the assignment, as estimated by the contributor.

Council on Social Work Education (CSWE) Competencies Addressed
For each assignment, the contributors have linked CSWE's 2015 Social Work Competencies to each entry. To conserve space, we included only the competency numbers rather than the titles. Please use the following list to fully identify each competency:

> Competency 1. Demonstrate Ethical and Professional Behavior
>
> Competency 2. Engage Diversity and Difference in Practice

Competency 3. Advance Human Rights and Social, Economic, and Environmental Justice

Competency 4. Engage in Practice-Informed Research and Research-Informed Practice

Competency 5. Engage in Policy Practice

Competency 6. Engage With Individuals, Families, Groups, Organizations, and Communities

Competency 7. Assess Individuals, Families, Groups, Organizations, and Communities

Competency 8. Intervene With Individuals, Families, Groups, Organizations, and Communities

Competency 9. Evaluate Practice With Individuals, Families, Groups, Organizations, and Communities

Learning Objectives
Each assignment contains at least three learning objectives developed by the assignment's author.

Assignment Description
This section includes a short description of the assignment.

Notes for Instructor
Here the authors provide practical suggestions, including tips for the instructor and advice for helping students with the technology. Many of the assignments in this compendium require the instructor to possess technological knowledge and skills in order to promote successful learning. We always recommend that social work instructors complete an assignment on their own or have a solid understanding of the technology before asking students to use the same technology. Besides contacting the assignment's contributor, you can also access additional resources for these assignments on the book's YouTube channel: https://goo.gl/aoCkuV.

Technology Required

This section will include a list of devices and specific applications/software that are incorporated into the assignment. Almost all of these assignments require that the instructor and student have high-speed and reliable Internet access and know how to use a Web browser and search engine software to access information, a learning management system, a social media platform, or software for word processing. The type of device (computer, tablet, or smartphone) and the type of Web browser (Safari, Chrome, Firefox, etc.) will affect the look and functionality of applications and software for students. For example, the mobile version of Twitter shows different features compared to the Web-based version that is available on a desktop computer. Additionally, older hardware or devices may limit the functionality of software or may be incompatible and not allow the software to operate.

Some authors recommend that you consult with institutional resources on your campus. This will vary by institution, and you will need to identify the specific offices and individuals on your campus. Examples of institutional resources include information technology departments, instructional designers, digital media labs, and digital librarians. We strongly encourage all social work educators to consult with someone at their institution to help best integrate technology into an assignment, to learn how to use technology, and as support for students completing an assignment. Additionally, a quick search of the Internet can provide more information about the devices, social media applications, and software referenced in these assignments.

Here is a list of the different types of common technology found in these assignments:

- Audio recorder
- Computer
- E-reader
- Microphone
- Smartphone

- Social media (specific types listed)
- Software (specific types listed)
- Tablet
- Video recorder
- Webcam
- Website (specific sites listed)

Finally, software can range from free and open access to expensive and proprietary. Educators should consider this when making decisions about using software for an assignment or learning activity. Requiring students to purchase software may not be necessary when free or low-cost options are available. For example, though teaching students to use Statistical Package for the Social Sciences (SPSS) is a common practice in social work education in the United States, most social service agencies do not use the software, preferring to use the statistical analytic tools in a spreadsheet software program such as Google Spreadsheets (free) or Microsoft Excel (low cost). When a software recommendation appears in the assignment, it can often be swapped with another option.

Editors' Variations
The editors offer adaptations for each assignment.

SAMR Level of Technology Integration
The SAMR model was developed by Dr. Ruben Puentedura to help educators integrate technology into course assignments and learning activities. A detailed discussion of this model can be found in Chapter 4 of this book. We have applied this model to our assignment compendium by identifying the level of technology integration for each assignment. This will help you in selecting assignments that best fit your level of comfort with technology and available resources at your institution. The levels of technology integration are as follows:
- *Substitution.* Technology acts as a direct tool substitution with no functional change in the learning activity.

- *Augmentation.* Technology acts as a direct tool substitution with functional change in the learning activity.

- *Modification.* Technology allows for a significant redesign of the learning activity.

- *Redefinition.* Technology allows for the creation of new task, previously inconceivable.

Terms may require more explanation than can be provided in the assignment. A more detailed explanation of these terms is provided in the book's glossary. Additionally, a quick search of the Internet can provide more information about the technology terms used in this book.

Ethical and Legal Considerations for Assignments
In Chapter 8, we cover several different ethical and legal guidelines that affect the use of technology in social work education, which may have implications related to these assignments. Some of these guidelines include the National Association of Social Workers' (NASW) Code of Ethics; the NASW Standards for Technology in Social Work Practice; and in the United States, the Health Insurance Portability and Accountability Act (HIPAA) and Family Educational Rights and Privacy Act (FERPA). When using technology with assignments and learning activities, we encourage social work educators to follow national, state, and local laws; the profession's ethical and practice standards; practicum agency's policies; and the policies of their institution of higher education. Please see Chapter 8 for a full discussion of how these laws and standards affect the use of technology with the assignments in this compendium. Additionally, we encourage educators to incorporate Netiquette guidelines into all assignments with social media (http://www.albion.com/netiquette/).

ASSIGNMENT COMPENDIUM
TABLE OF CONTENTS

Navigating the Virtual World of Second Life (Any)	402
Exploration of a New Culture via the Virtual World of Second Life (Any)	406
Connecting With Peers and Professionals Using Twitter (Any)	410
Educational Website as a Small Group Project (Any)	412
Spiritual Journey Digital Story (Any)	414
Infographics to Promote Advocacy and Brokering Skills (Any)	416
Learning Through Literature: Social Work Book Group (Any)	419
Using Wikis for Human Rights and Social Justice (Any)	422
"Fill in the Blanks" Slides Activity (Any)	424
Live Tweeting for Social Work Education (Any)	426
Field Journal Website (Field)	429
Data Collection: Using Informatics in Social Work Practice (Field)	431
LinkedIn for Professional Practice (Field)	435
Electronic Media Project: Field Placement Overview (Field)	438
Field Placement Soundscape (Field)	440
Preparing for Lifelong Learning With Pinterest (HBSE)	443
Skyping Human Behavior Theory (HBSE)	445
Blog and Digital Poster Assignment (HBSE)	448
Reviewing the Use of Health-Promoting	

Smartphone Apps (HBSE)	451
Agency Infographic Assignment (Practice)	456
DSM5 Practice and Trauma Assessment: Using Interactive Video (Practice)	457
Engaging in YouTube E-advocacy for LGBTQ Issues (Practice)	460
Social Issue: A Persuasive Speech (Practice)	463
Engaging in Social Work Advocacy: Policy Critique Exercise (Practice)	465
Agency Tutorials (Practice)	468
Advocate Policy Change: Fact Sheet and Online Mock Testimony (Practice)	470
Twitter Chats (Practice)	473
Electronic Human Rights Advocacy Service-Learning Project (Practice)	475
Social Work Practice With Non-Western Client Populations (Practice)	478
Video Case Presentation (Practice)	480
Professional Social Media Profile (Practice)	482
Social Media and Technology Use Policy Assignment (Practice)	484
Social Justice Video Presentation (Practice)	487
Exploring Communities Using the American FactFinder (Practice)	489
Interdisciplinary Ethics Exercise (Practice)	492
Skills Practice With Role-Play Videos (Practice)	495
Agency Informational Interview Podcast (Practice)	497
Using Twitter in Professional Development (Practice)	499

World of Warcraft (*WoW*) Assignment (Practice)	502
Media-Savvy Social Work: Radio Interviewing (Practice)	504
Community Assessment: Walking Video Tour (Practice)	508
Macro Podcast Assignment (Practice)	510
Second Life as a Practice Lab for Assessment and Reflection (Practice)	513
Design an Online Support Group (Part 1) and Implement a Simulated Online Support Group (Part 2) (Practice)	516
The Virtual Self: Professional Use of Social Media (Practice)	520
Video Vignettes of Practice Interventions (Practice)	523
Working Through an Ethical Dilemma (Practice)	525
Experiential Service Learning Group Video (Practice)	527
Student Response System ("Clickers") (Research)	530
Theoretical Constructs and Measures (Research)	533
Screencasts of Using Library Databases for Literature Reviews (Research)	535
Skewed? Analyzing Statistics in the Popular News Media (Research)	538
GIS Exploration for Community Assessment (Research)	541
Designing, Developing, and Delivering an Online Survey (Research)	544
Using Smartphones to Access and Explore Census Data (Research)	547

NAVIGATING THE VIRTUAL WORLD OF SECOND LIFE (ANY)

Editors' introduction: Virtual environments offer students opportunities to engage with diverse groups of people from around the world. This is the first of two assignments that provide students with opportunities to engage with diverse cultural communities in the virtual world of Second Life. This first assignment orients students to virtual worlds and introduces them to some of the diverse cultural resources that can be engaged there.

Author's name and contact: Scott P. Anstadt, Florida Gulf Coast University, sanstadt@fgcu.edu

Approximate prep time for faculty: 10 hours

Average assignment time for students: 5–7 hours

CSWE competencies addressed: 1, 2, 6, and 7

Learning objectives: After completing this assignment, students will be able to
- demonstrate ability to follow basic directions to navigate a virtual platform;
- demonstrate and articulate reflection on learning skills in the virtual environment; and
- apply basic netiquette skills when interacting in the virtual environment, such as when asking for assistance.

Assignment description: The purpose of this assignment is to learn and become comfortable in using the virtual world Second Life (SL). You may do this in a number of ways. You will be paired with another team member as you may find it easier to learn SL

ASSIGNMENT COMPENDIUM FOR INTEGRATING TECHNOLOGY

navigation as mutual supports. Complete the following steps in the order outlined:

1. View the video the Professor made that outlines the steps for registering and logging on, and explains how to use the Community Cultural Hub (CCHub): https://drive.google.com/file/d/0B9zp1GwuNuzTXzRWcWtPQWNwN00/edit?usp=sharing.
2. Download Firestorm Viewer software: http://www.firestorm-viewer.org/downloads/.
3. Register a free account at Second Life: http://secondlife.com/.
4. When logging on, type "Inspiration Island" in the box for Start Location and then Landmark this location and other important locations as described in the video.
5. Complete the following Self-Guided Tours of Basic SL Skills:

- Walk across the yellow bridge where you have landed toward the building with the green sculpture with the Earth on top; this is the CCHub.

    - Left-click on the poster to the left of the entrance to the CCHub that says, New Resident Self-Guided Training Courses.
    - Click Accept to the notecard, which will go into your Notecard Folder in your Inventory.
    - You will see a screen with five Landmarks. You can click on any of them. This will open a screen asking if you want a teleport. Click Yes and teleport to the location.
    - Then, take the self-guided tour of basic SL skills offered at any of the above locations (approximately 1/2 hour). You may use these as often as you like until you feel comfortable navigating around SL. During the tour, you will learn how to navigate your avatar, change clothes, take a picture, create and obtain your Landmarks, and visit sites (sims).

6. Select an outfit that best expresses you from the outfits in your Inventory Library. When you find an outfit in the clothes folder in the Library, just drag it onto yourself to make the change. To illustrate this process, there is a video created by the Professor for "Changing Clothes": https://drive.google.com/file/d/0B9zp1GwuNuzTemVxMUhDd2M0Y0E/view?usp=sharing

7. Go the Buddhist community of Hikari. Click on the Hikari poster in the Spirituality Section of the CCHub. See video as to how to do this step: https://drive.google.com/file/d/0B-9zp1GwuNuzTZUt4UTJXd1d1LWs/view?usp=sharing. You may make an appointment with the Professor during his SL Office Hours at the CCHub.

8. Write a short paper that recalls your orientation experiences. This paper should cover the following: (a) Overview of what you did (Why did you choose the avatar that you did? What did you like/not like about the avatar you chose?); (b) Overview of who assisted you (or not); (c) Overview of what you learned about yourself, in terms of your learning style, asking for help, and messages you give yourself about how you can overcome challenges confronting you; and (d) Self-reflective summary of above. Submit the paper with a picture you took of your avatar in SL (with new outfit on) at the community of Hikari.

Notes for instructor: This is a jumping-off assignment that gives students a basic introduction and orientation to Second Life (SL). Any further assignments in SL would rest on both the navigation skills and student awareness of what they might expect as they travel to various SL Communities.

Without these basic skills, students may remain confused and frustrated with the many particulars of this unique platform. The links provided relate to Professor Anstadt's course. The videos show students how to get the viewer and get started with SL. He has students using Firestorm Viewer, which is an alternative to the SL viewer (also, it's free and can be downloaded from https://secondlife.com/ so all of his instructions assume the use of the Firestorm Viewer. There also are many "how-to" videos to orient people to SL in YouTube, or instructors can make their own using a screen-capture program. The CCHub is a structure in SL developed by Dr. Scott Anstadt that is free to anyone. It is a central teleportation hub, meaning avatars can easily transport themselves to a selected SL community listed in the CCHub. The CCHub is organized by categories of communities in SL that include Spiritual, Arts, Role Plays, Families, Social Services, Educational, and Others. Once entering into the CCHub building, the avatar will see these categories displayed on the walls with posters underneath each one. Each poster has a picture of the community featured. By clicking on the poster, the avatars receive a notecard on their screen. The notecard has information about the community and a URL, known as a landmark. Clicking on the landmark link transports the avatar to the community location. This process makes it easy and convenient for students to navigate to these communities.

Technology required: computer; software: Second Life and virtual world viewer

Editors' variations: Virtual worlds like Second Life offer the opportunity for immersive experiences that are not available to students in other ways, for example, providing simulation of what it's like to experience hallucinations or develop posttraumatic stress disorder (Smyth, 2011).

Level of technology integration (SAMR Model): Redefinition

TEACHING SOCIAL WORK WITH DIGITAL TECHNOLOGY

EXPLORATION OF A NEW CULTURE VIA THE VIRTUAL WORLD OF SECOND LIFE (ANY)

Editors' introduction: Virtual environments offer students opportunities to engage with diverse groups of people from around the world. In this assignment, students participate in three activities of a specific cultural group within Second Life and write a reflection paper on their experience. This assignment is meant to follow the "Navigating the Virtual World of Second Life" assignment (pp. 00–00).

Author's name and contact: Scott P. Anstadt, Florida Gulf Coast University, sanstadt@fgcu.edu

Approximate prep time for faculty: 10 hours

Average assignment time for students: 5–7 hours

CSWE competencies addressed: 1, 2, 6, and 7

Learning objectives: After completing this assignment, students will be able to

- demonstrate the use of a virtual platform (Second Life) to immerse themselves into represented cultural community traditions;
- use the immersive experience to augment more traditional research methods about cultures; and
- identify valued elements of the immersive activity that can be translated into useful client interventions.

Assignment description: This assignment provides an immersive experience in new cultures through the virtual world of Second Life (SL), so that you can expand your appreciation and respect for cultural communities. You will attend three different community activities in the Community Cultural Hub (CCHub) in a community that you have studied in your literature review. This is your opportunity to experience the simulated culture in an immersive way. Your task will be to compare and comment on your experience in the activity with the information you have researched about that culture. Please complete the following steps.

1. Use the CCHub to teleport and visit your selected community. Take note of how to join their group for activity notices, take down their schedule from their calendar board, and seek out a principle representative with whom you can dialogue about the upcoming events.

2. Attend the events and make notes that describe the activities and, most importantly, how you are learning by taking an immersive part in them. Make special note of your previous biases or assumptions that are reformulated after experiencing these events.

Then, write a paper and include the following areas, giving examples to illustrate for each point:

A. Experience of Community and Culture: Apply a cited definition of culture and community to what you experienced and then discuss the following: (1) Did you sense a community and its cultural expression? Be specific about what you saw and what you experienced that gave you your impression. (2) What values, traditions, belief systems are conveyed and spread within the community and were used during the activity? Which activities helped reinforce what made the community unique, special, and purposeful? (3) What architecture, objects, or artifacts associate with real-life places? Which have been embellished or changed to make them "unique" to the SL community cultural activity experience? (4) What opportunities for social interaction are afforded by this community in being able to do this activity that may not be as readily available in real life? (5) Describe the member interactions that you witnessed. What does this say about the community cohesiveness? And (6) is there more or less a feeling of "we" over "me" or vice versa, or is it on a continuum? How did the activities support this process?

B. The Activities: Give your impressions regarding how the activity helped strengthen community around the activity: (1) Were there particular prescribed traditions, ways of interacting, or rituals you witnessed that participants did to fully benefit from the community practices you experienced? (2) Did you feel interested or compelled to take part, or could you simply observe? and (3) How did that feel to you as someone new to the community?

C. Social Network Analysis: Who seemed to talk the most? Who seemed to get the greatest responses from others when they spoke? How did they speak? Text? Voice? Who was ignored? Why do you think? Did you attempt to communicate? What happened?

D. Your Personal Experience: (1) Were there behaviors persons can do in Second Life that make the overall experience more intense, intimate, creative, and so forth? Did you use any? (2) Were you able to understand all that you observed and participated in? Did you need the assistance of asking some of the participants or doing literature research to achieve better understanding? (3) Did you find the anonymity of your character helped you to say or do things that you would not have normally done in real life? Give examples. (4) Did the size of the community event you observed/participated in affect your comfort level in that participation? (5) Did you meet folks from other diverse cultures? And (6) conjecture on what your involvement may have become should you have been able to spend additional time exploring the sim culture.

E. Summary: Describe what information you collected in both your Second Life community interactions and your outside research.

Give a few examples of how these coincided and differ.

Notes for instructor: The instructor should make sure students are comfortable with the basic use of Second Life and be available for regular consults when questions arise (see assignment "Navigating the Virtual World of Second Life" [pp. 00–00]). Students should also consult with instructor about their progress in doing the necessary background research on the culture they are studying. This prepares them to attend the activities. Incorporating several focus groups in this assignment provides a rich opportunity to share experiences between the students and to give further coaching in using Second Life and the CCHub. The focus groups consist of the instructor and the students. If the class is large enough, it might be divided into groups of no more than eight students. The questions asked concern the following:

- Mastery of SL navigation
- Dressing the avatars in a way unique to the student
- Using the Community Cultural Hub for transport to SL communities
- Availability and information gleaned from key informants in the communities explored
- The ways that the information and experiences in SL enhance student appreciation of various cultures around the world

Technology required: computer; software: virtual world viewer

Editors' variations: Virtual worlds like Second Life offer the opportunity for immersive experiences that are not available to students in other ways, for example, providing simulation of what it's like to experience hallucinations or develop posttraumatic stress disorder (Smyth, 2011).

Level of technology integration (SAMR model): Redefinition

CONNECTING WITH PEERS AND PROFESSIONALS USING TWITTER (ANY)

Editors' introduction: This assignment shows students how to create a digital network of professionals and resources on Twitter to be used throughout a course and for their lifelong learning.

Author's name and contact: Becky Anthony, Salisbury University, rsanthony@salisbury.edu

Approximate prep time for faculty: 10–30 hours

Average assignment time for students: 15–25

CSWE competencies addressed: 1, 2, 3, 5, and 6

Learning objectives: After completing this assignment, students will be able to

- demonstrate ethical and professional behavior on Twitter;
- increase their knowledge of current events as they relate to class material; and
- engage with peers, social work professionals, and organizations about events that directly relate to social work practice at the micro, mezzo, and macro levels.

Assignment description: The purpose of this assignment is to help students gain insight about the ethical use of social media and to think critically about how course material connects to current events, social injustices, and advocacy opportunities. This assignment also allows students the opportunity to connect with peers and other social work professionals and broaden their social work network. For this assignment, students are expected to create a free Twitter account for professional purposes and initiate one tweet (writing a post) each week. You may include a hyperlink to an article, video, and/or picture on a topic related to the weekly class material. Include our course hashtag on all of your posts. Please note that Twitter only allows 140 characters per tweet; therefore, you must be critical, concise, and brief in your comments. Additionally, you will be expected to reply to at least two tweets submitted by your classmates.

Notes for instructor: Professors should be comfortable with using Twitter, have their own account, and be prepared to actively use it throughout the semester. A course hashtag will need to be created and the professor will need to remind students to use the hashtag in all class-related tweets (including replies). Twitter tutorial videos (which can be found online via YouTube) about how to create a Twitter account and how to use Twitter were included in the beginning of this course. This assignment can be incorporated into a variety of social work courses and/or assignments, such as policy, research, and practice sequences. Additionally, professors have found this to be a successful way to connect with students outside of class and enhance their learning experience, particularly in distance and online learning courses.

Technology required: computer, tablet, and/or smartphone; social media: Twitter

Editors' variations: Another networking task with Twitter is to have students create a public list, which is a feature on Twitter that allows for the grouping of other users into one list. Students can title and describe the list, and others can subscribe to the list. Further, an instructor could use Twitter to create networking opportunities between different social work courses with their program or with students at other institutions.

Level of technology integration (SAMR Model): Modification

EDUCATIONAL WEBSITE AS A SMALL GROUP PROJECT (ANY)

Editors' introduction: This assignment invites students to use their creativity while producing an evidenced-informed educational resource for classmates and social work professionals. Working in small groups for this assignment can help ensure a variety of skill sets contribute to the project and also imitate real-world collaborative teams.

Author's name and contact: Tobi DeLong-Hamilton, University of Utah, Tobi.hamilton@socwk.utah.edu

Approximate prep time for faculty: 1–2 hours

Average assignment time for students: 10–12 hours

CSWE competencies addressed: 1, 2, 3, 4, and 5

Learning objectives: After completing this assignment, students will be able to

- describe multilevel practice roles and skills for working with marginalized populations;
- create a website to educate about a specific client population of interest; and
- explain social work intervention strategies for working with the population of interest.

Assignment description: The goal of this project is to demonstrate multilevel practice roles and skills in promoting work with populations that have been systematically marginalized in society due to racism, classism, sexism, heterosexism, ethnocentrism, ageism, disability discrimination, and/or inequitable distribution of resources. Over the course of the term, students will work in groups to construct an educational website that targets professionals working with the oppressed or underserved population chosen. This assignment is designed to increase understanding and appreciation for diversity and to become familiar with intervention strategies to combat the dynamics and impact of oppression. Please note that each group will present the website to the class at the end of the semester. Each group has complete creative freedom to develop the website. Websites can be developed in any free website builder, for example, Google Sites or WordPress. Each group should complete the following steps: (1) Construct your group website; (2) develop the outline for the website; (3) research the issue and interventions; (4) construct the content; (5) move forward with the content; (6) review and revise the website; and (7) unveil the final product to your peers by presenting the website to the class. Your assignment will be evaluated using the assignment grading rubric. All content for this project should be submitted in APA format.

Notes for instructor: Students enjoy this assignment because it does not feel as if they are writing a paper, although they are putting together information that would equal a traditional paper. As an instructor, I enjoy this assignment because it is not a typical paper or presentation and allows students to show their creativity. Possible website topics include racism, classism, sexism, heterosexism, ethnocentrism, ageism, disability discrimination, and inequitable distribution of resources.

Technology required: computer, tablet, and/or smartphone; software: blogging

Editors' variations: Students could be asked to make the website publicly available, which frequently improves the quality of work produced by students and requires students to present content in different ways (e.g., targeting nonprofessionals or using direct and jargon-free language). Additionally, student groups could work with local community agencies to create and design content for the organization's websites, incorporating a service learning component to the assignment.

Level of technology integration (SAMR Model): Augmentation

SPIRITUAL JOURNEY DIGITAL STORY (ANY)

Editors' introduction: Digital storytelling is telling a story (or delivering a message) through words, images, and sound. This assignment encourages students to explore their own spirituality through technology.

Author's name and contact: Stephanie Hamm, Abilene Christian University, stephanie.hamm@acu.edu

Approximate prep time for faculty: 1 hour

Average assignment time for students: 4 hours

CSWE competencies addressed: 1 and 2

Learning objectives: After completing this assignment, students will be able to

- use reflection and self-regulation to manage personal values and maintain professionalism in practice situations;
- demonstrate professional demeanor in behavior; appearance; and oral, written, and electronic communication; and
- apply self-awareness and self-regulation to manage the

influence of personal biases and values in working with diverse clients and constituencies.

Assignment description: Students will develop a digital story by writing a script, reading the script, and putting images and music (or ambient noise) to that script. Students will be graded on the quality of their narrative, the use of resources, and their critical appraisal of their own spiritual journey (or other, depending on the use of this exercise). This is a wonderful opportunity to gain self-awareness to further one's practice and grow spiritually. Students will start with writing a script/story of about 300 words. Try to answer the following questions: Why this story? Why now? What is it about the story that matters to your life right now? The "story" is read aloud into a microphone on a computer. Then, apply images and music to create a three- to 4-minute digital story. Choose a computer program that works well for you such as GarageBand or iMovie or possibly even Microsoft PowerPoint. The digital story can also be used to illustrate injustice or a policy, and to explore other areas of self-awareness.

Remember the following elements to good digital storytelling:

(1) Own your own story—this is a story that only you can tell.
(2) Show, instead of telling the watchers, what they are supposed to hear/know.
(3) Find the moment of some kind of change/transition.
(4) Hear your story: use music and other ambient sounds (water, dog barking, car driving, etc.).
(5) Assemble/share your story (3 to 4 minutes).
(6) Identify where in the story you would use explicit story/images and where you would put images that are implicit, and put ambient effects; let images sometimes tell the story.
(7) Know that your script is the foundation.
(8) Maybe start with an arresting moment, instead of chronologically, and then go to the backstory.

(9) take the watcher on the journey. The destination is not always the key. You can get by with as few images as ten. Music is the last element to add. Keep in mind your audience. Choose audio to help you tell the story—silent time is okay. Speak at the pace in which you converse. Don't rush it. Pause appropriately and naturally.

Notes for instructor: I use this assignment for a spirituality course; however, it can be used in many ways and in several courses. Students have enjoyed this process and report that the assignment is formative as well as summative. Students can use intellect and creativity in this critical thinking exercise.

Technology required: computer, tablet, and/or smartphone; video and/or audio recorders; software: digital presentation, video editing, and/or audio editing

Editors' variations: Students could also be encouraged to explore the difference between personal and professional values, comparing their own personal values to the six core social work values.

Possible alternatives to a personal story could be a digital story about a diverse client population, the development of a social policy, or the career of a social work pioneer.

Level of technology integration (SAMR model): Augmentation

INFOGRAPHICS TO PROMOTE ADVOCACY AND BROKERING SKILLS (ANY)

Editors' introduction: In this assignment, students create and publicly share an infographic about a social problem. Through a step-by-step process, students develop, review, and revise their infographic that they will disseminate via social media.

ASSIGNMENT COMPENDIUM FOR INTEGRATING TECHNOLOGY

Author's name and contact: Nathalie P. Jones, Tarleton State University, NJONES@tarleton.edu

Approximate prep time for faculty: 5 hours

Average assignment time for students: 10–15 hours

CSWE competencies addressed: 1, 3, and 4

Learning objectives: By the end of this assignment, students will be able to

- create an infographic that provides awareness and/or describes preventative measures related to a social problem;
- conduct research to identify statistics, resources, and other data relevant to a social problem; and
- demonstrate communication and advocacy skills by sharing and promoting one's infographic via social media.

Assignment description: The purpose of this infographic assignment is to help students practice advocacy and brokering skills as it relates to a social problem, a human service issue, or another relevant topic. Students are expected to create an infographic that provides statistics and/or facts on a chosen topic. The assignment has six steps. First, students should create a Twitter account and provide their Twitter *username* within the class learning community. Second, students will locate and share two infographics, one found from the Web search and one from search on Twitter, related to human rights, advocacy, or awareness for their chosen topic. Then, they will provide a one- to two-page comparison on how the infographic was distributed, what was learned, and how this resource pertains to their topic. Third, students will create a free account with an infographic software platform. After reviewing the tools in the platform, students will complete a draft storyboard of an infographic, including text and images. Students should consider what the message might be and how they will use images to create the infographic. Fourth, students will critique a classmate's infographic, providing a one- or two-page summary on what was learned by viewing the peer's infographic. Students will assess its quality as a resource and explain its relevance to social work. Fifth, students will revise their infographic and submit a final version for grading. Additionally, students will send a tweet of their infographic, tagging organizations or individuals that would be interested in their infographic. Sixth, students will write a reflection assignment on how the infographic was created, what was learned, what were the strengths and limitations of this assignment, and how using infographics could impact future work as a social work practitioner.

Notes for instructor: Infographics can be a creative and critical thinking tool that enhances student knowledge and allow students the opportunity to create a resource to share publicly online. Students will need assistance with data sources and with using the infographic tools. Assistance from one's institution, such as a digital media lab or library, can be helpful. The students are initially apprehensive about the assignment, but during the semester they typically become interested in the process and their creations, and ready to present to the class. Students must remember to add a section for references on the infographic. Instructors should provide information about copyright rules, plagiarism, and crafting a professional online identity via Twitter.

Technology required: computer, tablet, and/or smartphone; social media: Twitter; software: infographic designing

Editors' variations: Almost any social work topic could be used for infographic. For example, students could create an infographic for one research article or social work theory. It could be an alternative to a traditional research paper. Students can also report on how well their infographics were shared on Twitter to support a discussion about dissemination.

Level of technology integration (SAMR model): Modification

LEARNING THROUGH LITERATURE: SOCIAL WORK BOOK GROUP (ANY)

Editors' introduction: For this learning activity, students read a work of fiction and participate in a book group discussion, either in a seated experience or virtually through digital and social media platforms. Any book could be used to apply and develop knowledge, values, and skills found across a social work curriculum. Using technology to enhance this assignment could create a larger and more diverse learning community.

Author's name and contact: Amanda L. Taylor, University of Central Lancashire, United Kingdom, amltaylor@uclan.ac.uk

Approximate prep time for faculty: 30 minutes

Average assignment time for students: 10 hours

CSWE competencies addressed: 1, 2, and 3

Learning objectives: After completing this assignment, students will be to

- critically examine and evaluate the lived experiences of others in context;

- apply social work knowledge, theories, values, and skills to the fictional characters and their circumstances; and
- reflect on learning using dialectical journaling and a book group discussion.

Assignment description: The purpose of book groups in social work education is to assist students at any stage of their professional training to meet as a community of learning after reading a piece of fiction as if it were a case file. Choose a piece of fiction relevant to the learning objectives and content of the course and group. While reading the book, students are encouraged to annotate the text, using headings such as knowledge, values, and skills. To maximize the learning potential of the group, readers should make notes as they read through the text, identifying points that will eventually assist them to contribute fully to the book group discussion. The nature of the group will dictate how, where, and when the book is read and the overarching format of the group. Group leaders should have prepared questions for the discussion. To create a virtual component to the group, use of a live video stream and a Twitter account (ours is @SWBookGroup) along with a hashtag (#swbk). Others can watch the live stream and post comments or follow the discussion on Twitter. Additionally, e-reading devices have been integrated into this group. Prior to the event, student can use and share the highlighting and comments functions on e-readers to share initial learning points for discussion. In postgroup discussions, students can be encouraged to identify and record areas for future development and methods of addressing any knowledge gaps.

Notes for instructor: For more detail about this learning activity, see "Using a Book Group to Facilitate Student Learning About Social Work," by J. Scourfield and A. Taylor, 2014, *Social Work Education*, *33*, pp. 533–538, retrieved from http://www.tandfonline.com/doi/abs/10.1080/02615479.2013.832190. Respective professional standards, reflecting the layers of capability and competency, should be evidenced throughout the dialectical journaling and discussion elements of this learning activity. For a more detailed template of prompts for annotating a fictional text in this manner, see "When Actual Meets Virtual: Social Work Book Groups as a Teaching and Learning Medium in Social Work Education," by A. Taylor, 2014, in J. Westwood (Ed.), *Social Media in Social Work Education* (pp. 40–52) (Northwich, UK: Critical Publishing). See also "Fiction, Book Groups and Social Work Education," by A. M. L. Taylor, 2015, in G. Brewer and R. Hogarth (Eds.), *Creative Education, Teaching, and Learning* (pp. 167–177) (Houndmills, UK: Palgrave MacMillan).

Technology required: computer, tablets, and/or smartphones; e-readers; social media: Twitter; software: video streaming; video recorders

Editors' variations: Professional social workers could be included in the book groups, or a group could be developed between multiple classes. Using blogs or other social networking platforms such as Facebook or Goodreads could increase communication between book groups. Live video streaming is ideal to increase size of the group or collapse geographical boundaries.

Level of technology integration (SAMR model): Augmentation

USING WIKIS FOR HUMAN RIGHTS AND SOCIAL JUSTICE (ANY)

Editors' introduction: This assignment incorporates the use of wikis to promote learning about human rights and help students develop teamwork skills using technology tools.

Author's name and contact: Cecilia L. Thomas, University of North Texas, Cecilia.Thomas@unt.edu

Approximate prep time for faculty: 2 hours

Average assignment time for students: 4–6 weeks

CSWE competencies addressed: 2, 3, and 5

Learning objectives: After completing this assignment, students will be able to

- collaborate effectively with others to improve learning in the classroom;
- understand and analyze complex aspects of human rights and social justice and
- explore ways to advocate for human rights and social justice, becoming an agent of change.

Assignment description: Students are expected to examine intersectionality, how different systems of oppression can impact a human rights issue, and gain knowledge on advancing social justice to alleviate oppression. Students will use wiki technology to develop an online document that critically examines a human rights issue from a global perspective. A wiki is an interactive tool that allows users to share content digitally, while supporting teamwork so multiple students can contribute to the content. Therefore, the document is constantly changing, enabling the entire team to be creative together. Students will select a topic and form a collaborative team. The draft of the project will be developed in a private, designated wiki space available online. This project requires extensive research using scholarly resources (journal articles, books, etc.) and all of the required, key content must be included. The project must apply knowledge of race, class, gender, and other issues of diversity.

Further, the human rights issue must be analyzed in consideration of its economic, political, and social dimensions. Each team will decide how to best present the information (use various methods such as bullet points, graphics, videos, pictures, and written text). The final project will essentially be a Web page, so a report with extensive narrative and text is not expected. The final project will be uploaded and published, allowing it to be viewed for the entire class to review and provide feedback. The final project must include (1) historical analysis, (2) description of population(s) affected, (3) aspects of power and privilege evident for an issue, (4) description of intersectionality and levels of oppression, (5) key documents and policies, and (6) change strategies.

Notes for instructor: This assignment requires that students receive concrete guidelines on conducting research and other expectations. It is also beneficial to provide students with examples of previous projects that have been successfully completed. Using the wiki is not complicated, operating much as any word processing tool. It is important to understand that students are often frustrated with teamwork. I have been more successful in allowing students to self-select this assignment and voluntarily choose to conduct it individually or with a team. This assignment reinforces learning and promotes collaboration, a sense of community, and relevance in dealing with real-world issues. Grading criteria for this assignment include (1) knowledge of subject manner; (2) adequate use of scholarly resources; (3) inclusion of all required content adequately addressed; (4) evidence of research; (5) a clear, concise message; (6) a well-organized presentation; (7) use of creativity to enhance project; and (8) a compelling charge for advocacy.

Technology required: computer, tablet, and/or smartphone; software: wiki

Editors' variations: Using a real-world application, students could create content or make changes to content to appropriate pages in Wikipedia (e.g., content about special populations and their needs). Also, consider incorporating teamwork or collaboration skills as part of the grading criteria for wiki-based assignments.

Level of technology integration (SAMR model): Augmentation

"FILL IN THE BLANKS" SLIDES ACTIVITY (ANY)

Editors' introduction: This learning activity applies the "fill-in-the-blank" approach to lecture material using slide presentation software. During the lecture, students must answer the questions or items to move on to the next topic.

Author's name and contact: Ruth T. Weinzettle, Northwestern State University of Louisiana, weinzettler@nsula.edu

Approximate prep time for faculty: 5–8 hours

Average assignment time for students: Length of lecture

CSWE competencies addressed: 1, 2, 3, 4, 5, 6, 7, 8, and 9

Learning objectives: After completing this assignment, students will be able to

- recall course content;
- identify sources of information related to course content; and
- practice with answering questions during lectures.

Assignment description: The purpose of this learning activity is to help students integrate course materials. This activity does not have any points value attached to it and will not be graded. It is strictly for the students' own learning, but it will greatly assist them in learning the material and being prepared for the tests. Microsoft PowerPoint slides related to all units of course content are posted in the learning management system. Students will note that the slides have "blanks" scattered throughout. The students' task is to obtain the material to correctly fill in those blanks. Students may find materials to complete those blanks through a combination of the following avenues: (1) During classroom lectures the professor may lecture on that slide and advise students of the correct information; (2) slides presented in class that accompany the lecture have information; (3) recorded lectures are posted on the course site in the learning management system for each set of slides; (4) textbook readings and other reading materials are required as part of the course. The students do not submit anything for the activity. They retain the completed slides and can use them for study/learning purposes.

Notes for instructor: This activity was designed to assist students to be more engaged in the learning process, particularly when listening to lectures accompanied by PowerPoint slides. It was originally designed for the in-class section of a practice class. However, when that class had to be taught online, it was also very useful in requiring the online student to be more engaged in the learning process. To obtain the best results from this activity, it is best for instructors to create their own PowerPoint slides rather than using those that are provided with the text. After creating the slides, instructors should select words to eliminate from the set of slides. The instructors will also need to record lectures (especially for the online classes) to accompany the slides. Although I like to think I am a very engaging lecturer, using lots of great examples and asking students strategic questions, I found using fill-in-the-blank slides kept students more alert during periods of lecture. It also helps the students engage one additional learning method for those who do not learn as well through listening only.

Technology required: computer; software: lecture recording, media playing, and digital presentation software such as PowerPoint

Editors' variations: Students could use this technology to create their own study guide of course materials, a study guide for peers, or as part of a class presentation.

Level of technology integration (SAMR model): Augmentation

LIVE TWEETING FOR SOCIAL WORK EDUCATION (ANY)

Editors' introduction: Young's assignment incorporates the use of hashtags and tweeting about documentary films to promote critical thinking and engaged conversations. We have added an additional assignment from Samantha Teixeira and Kristina Hash under the editor's variation because of its similarities in combining live tweeting with documentaries.

Author's name and contact: Jimmy A. Young, California State University San Marcos, jyoung@csusm.edu.

Approximate prep time for faculty: 2 hours

Average assignment time for students: 1 hour

CSWE competencies addressed: 1, 2, 3, 4, 5, and 6

Learning objectives: After completing this assignment, students will be able to

- think critically about content related to the course;
- engage and communicate with others while processing content related to their specific course; and
- develop knowledge, skills, and values that contribute to their professional development.

Assignment description: This assignment involves using Twitter to live-tweet while viewing a documentary or similar content in the social work classroom. Students will obtain a free Twitter account and use their mobile devices to share their learning, perspectives, or other interesting takeaways while viewing a documentary in the classroom. Students are effectively live-tweeting their reactions/responses to the film as if they were live-tweeting their reactions to a TV program such as *American Idol*. Students will use a hashtag for each of their tweets during the film and should share 10 tweets at a minimum.

Notes for instructor: Sharing a film in class or assigning it to students to view on their own and having them live-tweet their reactions/responses while using a specific hashtag provides the opportunity for interaction and connection without the constraint of time. Students who are also too intimidated to share their thoughts live in the classroom can share their thoughts via Twitter with the class. Using a hashtag can also provide an archive of the tweets, which I have used to revisit during an actual in-class discussion. This has really enriched the in-class discussions and provided a means for deeper engagement in my online courses. I have also done this activity during presidential debates. If students do not have access to technology that allows them to live-tweet while watching the films, they can tweet their responses later. An in-class tutorial on Twitter use and social media ethics is held at the beginning of the course. If used as a stand-alone assignment, ethical and professional use of Twitter should be discussed prior to engaging students in Twitter use. The benefit of using Twitter is that students can comment in real time and connect with students from other sections of the course. The films could also be streamed online so students could view from their own homes. Additionally, students could be encouraged to live-tweet during a guest lecture, symposium, or conference.

Technology required: computer, tablet, and/or smartphone; social media: Twitter

Editors' variations: Contributions from Samantha Teixeira of Boston College (samantha.teixeira@bc.edu) and Kristina Hash of West Virginia University (kmhash@mail.wvu.edu) offer variations to this assignment. They suggest tweeting during an HBSE Film Festival. The purpose of the assignment is to give students a chance to practice writing professional tweets over time and provide students with the opportunity to engage in public conversations with each other inside and outside of the classroom. This exercise allows students to apply critical thinking and creativity in discussions and effectively use technology tools and resources available to communicate and interact with their colleagues. Students watch two or more films, either in or outsides of class. During the film, students send at least three tweets that reflect their reactions to the film. Students should indicate which film they are viewing in each tweet and use the course hashtag. They should also respond to tweets of other classmates or instructors viewing the same film.

Level of technology integration (SAMR model): Modification

FIELD JOURNAL WEBSITE (FIELD)

Editors' introduction: For this assignment, students learn how to create a private website and then use it to keep an ongoing reflective field journal throughout their field experience. Ongoing feedback is then provided to students in the field Web journal by field liaisons or field educators. This assignment requires an institutional subscription to Microsoft Outlook e-mail but could be adapted for other platforms.

Author's name and contact: Amy Bullas, California State University, Monterey Bay, abullas@csumb.edu

Approximate prep time for faculty: 1 hour

Average assignment time for students: 20 minutes/week

CSWE competencies addressed: 1 and 2

Learning objectives: After completing this assignment, students will be able to

- use reflection and self-regulation to manage personal values and maintain professionalism in practice situations;
- integrate, apply, and reflect on social work values as implemented in field practice settings; and
- apply self-awareness and self-regulation to manage the influence of personal biases and values in working with diverse clients and constituencies.

Assignment description: You will be creating a private website to record weekly field journal entries. This website will be shared with your faculty field liaison (and field instructor) who will provide feedback within your website throughout the semester. This journal is a tool for digesting and integrating what is happening with you and your internship. Your journal should be updated weekly, and you will receive periodic feedback from your field liaison throughout the semester. To create your website, follow these steps:

1. Log into your e-mail account and click on the nine small boxes in the upper right corner. Select sites from the nine boxes.

2. Choose the site template Social Work Field Journal from the list of templates.

3. Select from a variety of backgrounds—taking the time to personalize it can be helpful.

4. After choosing a background, click Create; then share the site with your faculty field liaison by clicking Share and typing in your liaison's e-mail address. Be sure to click on Can Edit so your liaison can provide comments and feedback on your journal.

5. You will see four prompts each week, and you should respond to each prompt. Sample responses are shown in Week 1 to give you an idea of the type and depth of content.

Notes for instructor: Our university uses a Moodle interface, which gives us access to Google tools and their blogging features. You will need to create a template for your students on your website. The template I created has four prompts for students: (1) activities and tasks, (2) reactions and reflections, (3) learning, and (4) self-care and supports. You may choose these or something else depending on which competencies you would like to address. I find the website journal easy to access, and both the student and faculty field liaison can access it at the same time. With one click, information is saved, without having to upload or open anything. I like to provide a video and written tutorial for students to set up their sites, and encourage students to pull out their laptops and set up their sites as I demonstrate and walk them through the steps with a student volunteer. Student have shared that this journaling tool has helped them process their internship experiences each week and integrate what they have seen and learned.

Technology required: computer or tablet; software: blogging or website development

Editors' variations: This online journal could be used in any course to encourage a reflective process on how course material applies to key content, such as current events (social policy or social action courses) or group dynamics in a class (group work).

Level of technology integration (SAMR model): Augmentation

DATA COLLECTION: USING INFORMATICS IN SOCIAL WORK PRACTICE (FIELD)

Editors' introduction: This assignment starts with students viewing a video and measuring behavior two different ways (without using technology and then using technology) and then comparing these two methods. Next, students design and implement a semester-long client behavior change project (single system design) using technology as a tool for ongoing measurement of client behavior. A final written report on the project is completed, as is a class presentation.

Author's name and contact: Susan E. Elswick, University of Memphis, selswick@memphis.edu

Approximate prep time for faculty: 3–5 hours

Average assignment time for students: 10–12 hours

CSWE competencies addressed: 1, 6, 7, 8, and 9

Learning objectives: After completing this assignment, students will be able to

- demonstrate data-collection skills and importance in evaluating clinical outcomes using technology;
- analyze social science/behavioral science data-collection systems;
- identify through critical reflection the benefits and challenges of using technology in social work practice for data-collection purposes; and
- identify a way in which the data-collection process/technology could be advanced for future practitioners.

Assignment description: The purpose of this assignment is to help students practice assessment and evaluation skills related to applied social work/behavioral science practice while learning about the importance of technology in the applied setting. This assignment has two parts:

1. Review and practice using assessment, data-collection practices, and evaluation in a single-subject format for clinical cases. You will learn best practices in assessment, data collection, evaluation, and intervention for single-subject work. We will also investigate the differences in accuracy of data collection (hand-collected data versus technology-assisted data collection). We will cover single-subject design, multiple assessments, data-collection methods, evaluation procedures, and evidence-based interventions. To better prepare you for collecting data in the field, we will practice data-collection methods (frequency/event recording, momentary time sampling, duration, latency, etc.). You will use the handout

provided by the instructor ("Behavior Change Project and Data-Collection Assignment"). On this handout, you will click on the YouTube links to watch the identified video. You will be provided explicit instructions on the target client, target behavior, and the type of data-collection method you will be expected to use. These prompts will indicate when to start and stop the video for viewing, which data-collection method to use for each video, and how to capture the data for each video. *You will do this assignment twice.* The first time you complete the assignment, you will collect data by hand directly on the sheet. During the second trial, you will use an app-based data-collection system (of your choice or from samples provided) while watching the videos. Once completed, we will discuss and analyze both data-collection attempts in class. This will assist you in understanding and interpreting the processes of data collection (barriers and challenges), and understanding and evaluating inter-observer agreement.

2. Semester-long behavior-change project. You will complete a behavior-change project during this semester within this course. You will be required to identify a need in the client population served at your field agency. Through research, you will identify an appropriate evidence-based intervention to implement with the clientele (group or individual). You will collect data (including baseline and intervention data) through supportive technology (app-based data system or data-collection download/software), implement the identified evidence-based intervention, monitor client progress during the intervention, collect data throughout the intervention that best captures the target being observed, and make changes during the intervention if success is not noted. You will need to identify a data-collection app/software download that can be used in direct practice to collect live data of the identified client's target behavior. Make

sure that you choose an application that is collecting data in the format you need for this project (duration, frequency, latency, momentary time sampling, etc.). Take into account whether or not the data you are collecting is compatible with the application chosen. Also take into consideration the usefulness of the technology you are choosing, making sure it is not intrusive and distracting to the client while you are collecting the data. You may also choose to have the client collect self-report data. If you are choosing this method, make sure the app/technology chosen is accessible to the client, that the client understands the system, and that on conclusion of the assignment, you get feedback from the client on the client's thoughts/perceptions of using technology for self-monitoring purposes. After concluding the intervention assignment, you will create a graphic display of the data collected during the intervention and complete a written report and class presentation.

Notes for instructor: The handout referenced ("Behavior Change Project and Data-Collection Assignment") includes a link to the YouTube video that illustrates some behavior that will be measured. Provide video examples of frequency/event recording, duration, momentary time sampling, and group-based data systems. YouTube video searches can yield some great examples (e.g., "temper tantrum"). The handout includes links to multiple videos and a place to record the behavior count for different types of behavior measurement. Each link and video represents a different data-collection method being practiced. Downloading an app is easy, and oftentimes low-cost technology is ideal for undergraduate/graduate students. Most students can afford to use their phone technology to download an app for this assignment. There are many free data-collection apps, especially if the student researches them in advance. Provide sample data systems/apps that can be used, and model using these systems within the classroom. Students need to be reminded that many free/low-cost data systems are not HIPAA approved, secure, or confidential. Partner with your institution's technology support department to help students use app-based programs and computer software.

Technology required: computer, tablet, and/or smartphone; social media: YouTube; software: apps

Editors' variations: This assignment could be easily used in a research methods class, a practice evaluation class, or even an advanced intervention methods classes where students are assessing the changes in a behavior after implementing an intervention. The written report and class presentation could be easily adapted to a fully online classroom by using a blog post, an e-poster, or a multimedia presentation.

Level of technology integration (SAMR model): Augmentation

LINKEDIN FOR PROFESSIONAL PRACTICE (FIELD)

Editors' introduction: For this assignment, students use the social media platform LinkedIn to create an electronic resume.

Author's name and contact: Laurel Iverson Hitchcock, University of Alabama at Birmingham, lihitch@uab.edu

Approximate prep time for faculty: 3 hours

Average assignment time for students: 6–7 hours

CSWE competencies addressed: 1

Learning objectives: After completing this assignment, students will be able to

- develop a professional LinkedIn account for social work practice;
- demonstrate how to network with students, instructors, and professional social workers via social media; and
- reflect on one's use of social media as an ethical social work professional.

Assignment description: LinkedIn is a business-oriented social networking site, used for professional networking. To complete this part of assignment, each student will need to do the following tasks:

(1) Create a free LinkedIn account at https://www.linkedin.com. If students already have an account, they can use that account but need to make sure they complete all parts of the assignment.

(2) Develop a public profile to include the following: a professional-looking photo, a summary, experience to date, education to date, skills and endorsements, interests, and contact information.

(3) Connect with the instructor, all the other students in the class, and at least 10 other people in field of social work.

(4) Join the class group and at least three other groups. Participate and observe in the class group conversation with at least five posts.

(5) Research an organization on LinkedIn that you might like to work for in the future.

(6) complete four journal entries over the semester about using LinkedIn. The four journal entries should include

written self-reflections about creating a LinkedIn account, participating in a LinkedIn group, researching an organization, and the overall use of LinkedIn over the semester.

Notes for instructor: Detailed instructions should be provided on how to establish a LinkedIn account, connect with other users, and join groups. Your own LinkedIn profile can be used as a model for the students. It is recommended that you create a closed group for students to join so students' posts can be private, and you can share-class specific content as needed. Additionally, students can remain in the group after the class, creating a network of alumni to who might be willing to interact with students. Instructors can also facilitate class discussions about how to use social media professionally, such as how to develop a professional online presence, what content is appropriate for social workers to post on social media, and how to use privacy settings with social media. Also, consider partnering with your institution's career services office that might be able to offer a class presentation about how to use LinkedIn. For grading, have students submit a copy of the URL address of their LinkedIn account.

Technology required: computer, tablet, and/or smartphone; social media: LinkedIn

Editors' variations: LinkedIn can also be used as a platform for an electronic student portfolio.

Level of technology integration (SAMR model): Modification

ELECTRONIC MEDIA PROJECT: FIELD PLACEMENT OVERVIEW (FIELD)

Editors' introduction: Students create and share short media projects that present an overview of their field agencies and the role of social workers and social work intern within those agencies. They also review and comment on others' projects.

Author's name and contact: Alyssa Lotmore, University at Albany, State University of New York, alotmore@albany.edu

Approximate prep time for faculty: 2 hours

Average assignment time for students: 10 hours

CSWE competencies addressed: 1, 2, and 3

Learning objectives: After completing this assignment, students will be able to

- describe the field placement agency to demonstrate an understanding of the organization as a whole and the role of the social worker within the agency;
- assess the impact of discrimination, oppression, and injustice on a specific population and demonstrate knowledge, skills, and values of cultural competence and cultural sensitivity through the project; and
- learn about other agencies and the services offered by reviewing peer projects.

Assignment description: This 5-minute Electronic Media Project is an opportunity for you to display what you are learning at your agency and what the agency has to offers. This can be displayed through a narrative PowerPoint, a video recording, or a complete movie. When you are working on this project, please consult with your field supervisor to ensure there are no confidentiality issues.

1. Create your project. The project focus should be on social work within the agency setting and should incorporate the following information: purpose of agency, services provided by the agency, procedures obtaining services, the practice model (approach, philosophy, etc.) used by the agency, and the role of the student intern. Projects must be submitted electronically. Many students upload the project to YouTube (as an unlisted video) and submit the link to the instructor. Do not wait until the last minute to decide how you will submit it.

2. Participate in media project peer review. Links to the media projects will be posted on the course media project blog. You will review the media projects of four peers and write a two-paragraph (at least five sentences in each paragraph) response to each project. This can be posted in the Comments section under each project post. The response could include what you learned from watching the project. how the resources of that agency may be helpful to clients you work with, and so forth. As social workers, we share resources to learn about other agencies and services that may benefit our clients, and viewing the projects are a way to learn about services offered in the local community.

Notes for instructor: Partner with your institution's media and learning center staff to obtain equipment or technical assistance for instructors and students. Remind students about copyright laws and protecting client confidentiality. This project evolved from a paper into a media project that can be shared and viewed easily by classmates. It is a way for students to creatively demonstrate an understanding of their agency and the role of social workers within the agency. If needed, you can help students focus further by asking them to answer specific questions about the agency, for example, What's the mission of the agency? What's the agency's history? How is it funded? How does funding influence agency activities? Who are the populations served? Are other disciplines present, and how do they interrelate with social worker roles? How do clients enter (i.e., eligibility, intake policies, and procedures), progress, and leave/terminate the agency? What examples show the agency's commitment to the community and the areas it serves?

Technology required: computer or tablet; social media: YouTube or other video-sharing platform; software: video editing; video recorder

Editors' variations: Media projects could be used in place of papers or presentations for any course. If appropriate, media projects could be posted on a public site and made available as a Web resource.

Level of technology integration (SAMR model): Redefinition

FIELD PLACEMENT SOUNDSCAPE (FIELD)

Editors' introduction: Students record and edit an audio file to tell a story about their field agency.

Author's name and contact: Jonathan B. Singer, Loyola University Chicago and *Social Work Podcast*, jonathan.b.singer@gmail.com

Approximate prep time for faculty: 2 hours

Average assignment time for students: 10–20 hours

CSWE competencies addressed: 2, 3, 6, and 7

Learning objectives: After completing this assignment, students will be able to

- understand how to use audio recording and editing technology;
- think critically about how sounds reflect environmental justice; and
- analyze the audio environment in which their clients receive services and how that might influence what clients need or want from services.

Assignment description: Students are asked to record the sounds from the environments associated with social services, such as their client's neighborhood, their field site, and their own neighborhood. Students will create a soundscape (audio montage) that is intended not to tell a narrative story but rather to capture the sounds associated with going to, being at, and leaving social service delivery.

Students will record no less than 10 minutes of raw audio, edit it down to a 60–90 second audio file, and a submit a 500–700-word description of what they learned from the experience. There are three separate time periods that students should record: before, during, and after. First, students should record the sounds of arriving at the field site. For example, if clients take public transportation to the field placement, they should record the sounds on that public transportation. Next, students should record approaching, entering, and being in the field site. To maintain client privacy, any identifiable sounds need to be removed or masked during audio editing. For example, if the recording in the waiting room captures the sounds of a staff members calling a client ("Lucinda, are you ready to come back?"), the student will need to edit out the client's name. Last, students should record leaving the field site. Questions that students can ask while recording include the following: What does it sound like approaching your field site? What do clients hear as they walk through the halls or sit in the waiting room? What sounds do you hear leaving? How does the quality of sound change as the client leaves the agency? What are the sounds from nature, from the human-made environment, and from people themselves? This project is intended not to tell a linear story but rather to capture the essence of the sounds associated with service use. For example, if a student's placement is in a correctional facility, he or she might record the sounds of different doors opening and closing and edit them together sequentially. Then the student might record the sounds of walking in various locations around the prison. Alternately, the student could sequence the sounds leading up to, being in, and leaving the correctional facility.

Notes for instructor: Every smartphone can record high-quality audio. The closer the phone is to a specific sound, the better the quality of the audio. Students can watch videos on YouTube to learn how to use equipment. The soundscape can be an audio file with sounds placed next to each other sequentially. Students can present their soundscapes in class for group feedback. During student presentations, have all the students close their eyes and listen to the audio without introduction. You can partner with your institution's digital media staff to do a brief presentation in class about audio recording. You can record you own version by recording the School of Social Work.

Technology required: audio recorder; computer, tablet, or smartphone; software: audio editing

Editors' variations: Although the purpose of this assignment is to allow the sound to speak for itself, an alternative assignment could include a voice-over that includes the name of the field site and the purpose of the agency. If their soundscape follows the "narrative" of traveling to, being at, and leaving the field placement, then students can narrate that, for example, "I'm on the 59 bus. I'm about to walk in the front door. I'm sitting in the waiting room. I'm in the office. I just left the building, and I'm now in the parking lot." Students can take photos of the places where the sounds were recorded and create a video (using PowerPoint, iMovie, etc.) where the images are timed with the video.

Level of technology integration (SAMR model): Redefinition

PREPARING FOR LIFELONG LEARNING WITH PINTEREST (HBSE)

Editors' introduction: Students use the social media platform Pinterest to curate list of resources related to HBSE content.

Authors' name and contact: Lisa R. Baker, Samford University, lrbaker2@samford.edu; and Laurel Iverson Hitchcock, University of Alabama at Birmingham, lihitch@uab.edu

Approximate prep time for faculty: 3 hours

Average assignment time for students: 10–12 hours

CSWE competencies addressed: 1, 2, 3, 6, 7, 8, and 9

Learning objectives: After completing this assignment, students will be able to
- research, critically assess, and link external sources of information with required course material;
- integrate and develop a professional use of self in a public environment; and
- develop a professional repository of resources and information that could bridge content across the curriculum and into field education.

Assignment description: Students are required to create a HBSE Pinterest page that will be used to pin items that relate to content throughout the semester. Students are encouraged to create a professional account separate from a personal account. Students should view the Pinterest boards as a collection of resources that may be added to over time to develop their professional knowledge base. Students are encouraged to follow the course instructor's account in Pinterest along with all the other students in the class. Students should create a board for each of the course learning modules. Students should pin content to each of the boards that illustrates at least two concepts from the learning modules. Each board must contain at least five pins total with one pin from each of the following categories: (1) information/education, (2) advocacy or support, and (3) practice resource. Each pin must include a photo and hyperlink to the original content and have a comment that explains the linkage to the learning module. Pins may include podcasts, websites, pictures, Web pages, and so forth. Please view the instructor's board for examples. Students should also review their classmates' board. From other students' boards, students can identify a concept from each learning module that they did not illustrate on their own board. Re-pin as least three pins related to this concept. These pins can be from one or multiple students, but the concept must be the same. Students should provide a comment on each one of these pins about why they are re-pinning and a brief assessment of the concept and content of the pin. Pinterest boards should be completed by the end of the corresponding learning module. After completing all the required boards and pins, students should write a self-reflection about the experience of using Pinterest as a tool to assess and collect resources related to the content of this course. Write between 300 and 500 words that address the following questions: What process did you use to identify pins for your Pinterest boards? How was your experience of using Pinterest different from what you expected? What did you like/dislike about using Pinterest for this assignment? What did you learn about human behavior in the social environment as a result of this assignment? Did you learn a new skill or clarify an interest as a result of this assignment? How can you use your Pinterest boards in your future practice as a social worker? What else would you like to learn about using Pinterest?

Notes for instructor: Detailed instructions should be provided on how to establish a Pinterest account, create pins and boards, and *follow* other users. Because some students will already have an established account for personal use, the instructors should provide additional instruction on differentiating between personal and professional accounts and distinguishing what content is appropriate for the different boards. Instructors can also facilitate class discussions about how to use social media professionally, such as how to develop a professional online presence, what content is appropriate for social workers to post on social media, and how to use *privacy settings* with social media. This assignment can easily be incorporated across multiple courses in a sequence. For grading, have students submit a copy of the URL address to their board.

Technology required: computer, tablet, and/or smartphone; social media: Pinterest

Editors' variations: Students could create a Pinterest board about almost any topic or could use a board to create a study guide for licensure exams.

Level of technology integration (SAMR model): Modification

SKYPING HUMAN BEHAVIOR THEORY (HBSE)

Editors' introduction: By using Skype, or some other type of videoconferencing software, students are able to dialogue with the author of their human behavior textbook in this classroom activity.

Authors' name and contact: Patricia Chase, West Virginia University, patricia.chase@mail.wvu.edu; Elizabeth Hutchison, University of Nevada–Reno, ehutch@vcu.edu; and Kristina Hash, West Virginia University, kmhash@mail.wvu.edu

Approximate prep time for faculty: 1 hour

Average assignment time for students: 0.5 hour

CSWE competencies addressed: 6

Learning objectives: After completing this assignment, students will be able to

- describe different views on the nature of human behavior;
- articulate their views on the nature of human behavior; and
- discuss theories regarding human behavior with an expert in the field.

Assignment description: This week in class, we will be engaging with the author of your textbook, Dr. Elizabeth Hutchison, via the videoconferencing software Skype. We will engage with her and discuss the questions included in the exercise "Getting in Touch With Your Theoretical Framework." There will also be time to ask other questions of our guest. We will Skype for approximately 30 minutes.

Agenda:

A. Introductions (The guest speaker is introduced, and students go around the room and introduce themselves to the guest speaker and share their specific interests in the field of social work and related to human behavior.)

B. Exercise: Getting in Touch With Your Theoretical Framework (handout).

　　i. What are your core beliefs about human beings and human behavior?

　　ii. Why do people do the things they do—what motivates behavior?

　　iii. Can people change? If so, what is the process? How does that change occur; can change be facilitated?

What does that facilitation need to look like? What are barriers, or obstacles, to change?

C. Final questions and comments

Notes for instructor: This is a very simple assignment to implement, and no supporting materials are needed. It is helpful to give the guest speaker and the students the exercise questions ahead of time. A handout with the questions should be passed out in class. Students should also read the introductory chapter of the human behavior textbook. The students in this course used the following textbook: *Dimensions of Human Behavior: Person and Environment* (4th ed.), by E. D. Hutchison, 2010 (Thousand Oaks, CA: SAGE). This exercise is well suited for graduate-level students in the foundation of human behavior course. Student feedback regarding this exercise was overwhelming positive. They were thrilled to be able to discuss theories and issues of human behavior with an expert in the field and the person who wrote their textbook. They also mentioned that it helped them feel more connected to the content as they continued to do the course readings. The Skype address and phone number of the guest should be retrieved and tested prior to the class session. If possible, a technology specialist should be on hand to problem-solve any difficulties that may arise.

Technology required: computer; social media: Skype

Editors' variations: Although this is described as an assignment in an on-the-ground class, it could be modified for a virtual classroom environment, with the guest author on screen and students taking turns on video to ask questions and discuss. In addition, the activity could be modified to bring in any guest speaker that would be appropriate to the topic. However, this kind of assignment has the most impact on students when they can hear from someone they would not have heard from without the technology, that is, someone who is geographically distant from the class.

Level of technology integration (SAMR model): Substitution

BLOG AND DIGITAL POSTER ASSIGNMENT (HBSE)

Editors' introduction: Students create a digital or multimedia poster and a blog post focused on description and analysis of a social problem or issue. These products are posted in a learning management system, and students participate in group discussion of each other's content. We have added an additional assignment from Denise Orpustan-Love under the editor's variation because of similarities in using digital poster presentations.

Author's name and contact: Laura A. Lewis, University at Buffalo SUNY, lalewis@buffalo.edu

Approximate prep time for faculty: 5 hours

Average assignment time for students: 20 hours

CSWE competencies addressed: 1,4, and 9

Learning objectives: After completing this assignment, students will be able to

- present information on the scope/prevalence of a pressing issue or concern for social work, and prevailing theories of causation;
- analyze the extent to which the prevailing theories consider human behavior and development at diverse social locations including the impact of poverty, inequality, oppression, exposure and vulnerability to trauma, and violations of human rights; and
- analyze the extent to which prevailing theories consider environmental factors in understanding human development and change over the life span.

ASSIGNMENT COMPENDIUM FOR INTEGRATING TECHNOLOGY

Assignment description: Identify a social problem. Examples include depression and suicide, refugee status, and school failure. You will create a digital poster summarizing your work and a blog post that presents your analysis with more detail. Complete the following parts of the assignment:

1. Create a digital poster (Prezi or Microsoft PowerPoint), using primarily images with brief, explanatory text and focusing on the following: (a) overview of why this problem/issue merits the attention of social work (3–5 slides); (b) scope of the problem (e.g., How widespread is this problem? Who is affected? What is the incidence and prevalence) (3–5 slides); (c) circumstances or conditions in the United States that may also contribute to the problem identified above (e.g., poverty, grief/loss, violence, lack of access to education, etc.); include citations (1–2 slides); (d) personal aspects: multimedia element (online interview, video, quote from newspaper, etc.); you might interview a social work practitioner or researcher/faculty member that works in the identified area (2–3 slides); and (e) context (If attention is shifted to the larger context, what could social workers do to alleviate conditions that lead to the issue or problem? What would the implications be for policy and practice?) (2–3 slides).

2. Create a blog post with a more detailed discussion of all the major points in the poster that are related to the problem: (a) Present and discuss all the points in the poster. In addition, consider, how is the problem identified? What are the perceived causes? Can it be prevented? Completely resolved? (b) Discuss theories of causation commonly associated with the problem and then analyze them. (c) Analyze the extent to which the prevailing theoretical approach considers human behavior and development at diverse social locations including the impact of poverty, inequality, oppression, exposure and vulnerability to trauma, and violations of human rights. When analyzing theories, be sure to address the following

questions: Whose interests does the theory serve? In what ways is it related to power and oppression? What are the limitations of the theory for the given issue/community? And in what ways is the theory relevant or not to social work? (d) Analyze the extent to which the theoretical approach considers environmental factors in understanding human development and change over the life span. Reference relevant literature if available. (e) Name two alternate theories of human behavior that might help to widen the lens. Explain. (f) References: Complete reference citations must be included following American Psychological Association guidelines.

3. Discussion. Students are required to view classmate digital posters and blogs and participate in discussion, including posting 5–6 times in the classroom discussion board for each of the scheduled presentation weeks. Discussion grades are based on frequency (up to 4 points) and quality (up to 4 points). To earn full points for frequency in a given week, students must post 5–6 times for each schedule presentation week. To earn full points for quality in a given week, student posts must demonstrate knowledge and interest in topic.

Notes for instructor: The blog format allows students to add their own voice to the topic and to think creatively about how theory can be applied in practice. It also requires students to write more concisely about their topic than they would in a paper. It is helpful to provide one or two sample blogs and digital posters made by students from a previous semester or by the instructor as exemplars. Remind students that they cannot use any content that is copyrighted, including music. They also generally need information on how to cite images. Provide information on best practices for PowerPoint and Prezi, and on designing a digital poster.

Technology required: computer, tablet and/or smartphone; social media: Prezi or software: digital presentation

Editors' variations: This assignment could be modified to any topic where one would typically ask students to write a paper or do a presentation. A contribution from Denise Orpustan-Love of California State University Monterey Bay (dorpustan-love@csumb.edu) offers such a variation on this assignment, in which she has students identify, research, and describe the theoretical perspectives they feel will be most influential in guiding their current/future social work practice. Students complete a five- to seven-page paper describing their professional theoretical orientation. Then students create a technology/multimedia poster demonstrating their knowledge of the main points of the paper (history, key elements/assumptions, interventions, strengths/cons, human experience, and research findings). The poster is a computer-generated, one-page poster, using a multimedia poster program, such as Glogster, PowerPoint, or Camtasia, which is then uploaded to the LMS.

Level of technology integration (SAMR model): Augmentation

REVIEWING THE USE OF HEALTH-PROMOTING SMARTPHONE APPS (HBSE)

Editors' introduction: Using health-promoting apps is increasingly common among smartphone users. In this assignment, students review apps to increase their understanding of the software and make recommendations on how apps might be incorporated into social work practice.

Author's name and contact: Elise Johnson, California State University Dominguez Hills, eljohnson@csudh.edu

Approximate prep time for faculty: 8 hours

Average assignment time for students: 15–20 hours

CSWE competencies addressed: 1, 2, 3, 6, 7, and 8

Learning objectives: After completing this assignment, students will be able to

- demonstrate ability to incorporate technology into practice;
- identify through critical reflection the challenges and benefits of using technology in direct practice with clients; and
- evaluate and critically assess the personal and clinical value of health-promoting smartphone applications.

Assignment description: Students will critically assess information learned by using three mobile phone applications (apps) over the course of a semester. Students will participate in a shared communication tool, write a concluding paper, and include the information learned in their final class presentation. Directions are as follows:

1. On a smartphone or tablet, download, compare, and contrast three health-promoting apps and use them on a regular basis. Students are encouraged to choose one more app that might benefit them as the consumer and one or more apps that might benefit your field placement client population. Students will search either iTunes or Google Play and choose at least one app from the following list (note that some of the following apps are free of cost but others require a onetime fee of $4.99): Anxiety Coach, DBT Diary Card and Skills Coach, Happify, Moodkit, Pacifica, Pocket CBT, SAM, Smiling Mind, SuperBetter, or What's Up. Up to two apps may be chosen by the student as long as they are health-promoting in nature. For example, students can compare three similar topics that interest them as the consumer (e.g., three mental health promoting apps) or a combination of any topic (e.g., two fitness apps and a mindfulness app).

The topic must promote physical or mental health. Ideally, the students should find an app or two that might apply to your field placement client population.

2. Over the course of the semester, students will contribute to an online working document (a wiki or Padlet). Using the same guidelines as those for the paper (listed below), this communication tool among students will provide up-to-date feedback on apps and technical support as well as discussion on any clinical issues that may arise (within the confines of confidentiality). The instructor will curate and moderate the site.

3. Students may incorporate app use with field placement clients only with field placement supervisor's approval and supervision.

4. Students will submit a two- to three-page essay that will critically assess the information learned by using three mobile phone applications over the course of a semester. Students will also include this information as part of their presentation to their peers at the conclusion of the semester.

Directions for the essay: Introduce the app. How would you categorize the topic? (e.g., mental health, mindfulness, stress reduction, diet, exercise, general health, spirituality, substance abuse, etc.). Describe the elements of confidentiality or security. Describe any clear community or population to whom it may appeal. What is the affiliation? (Who or what company is the developer?) How did you find it? Why did you choose it over others? Note the date you began using the app to the date you ended using it. Include how many times per week you used it. If you found that you wanted to abandon the app, note at what point you lost interest and why. Using the article by Stoyanov et al. (2015) as a general guide, evaluate each app through the lens of two points of view: The first shall be from your point of view as the customer. The second shall be as a potential client's perspective. Rate the app on a five-star criterion, with a one-star maximum for each category:

(1) Critique the aesthetics, the graphics, layout, and the visual appeal.

(2) Critique the level of engagement and gaming, entertainment, customization, interactivity, fit to target group, and motivating elements. Is there cross-cultural or linguistic relevance? Are there options in multiple languages? If so, which ones?

(3) Critique the functionality. Describe the performance, navigation, gestural design, and ease of use for potential clients?

(4) Critique the information provided. Describe the quality, quantity, visual information, credibility, and evidence base. How is education incorporated? Does the app include the recommendations from the article discussed in class (Bakker, Kazantzis, Rickwood, & Rickard, 2016)? If so, which ones and to what degree?

(5) The last section is more subjective in nature. What is the price? (If it's free, does it remain free or does it seek payment after a certain time? If it charges a fee, how would clients pay if they don't have a credit card?) From your point of view, is it worth recommending? Does it stimulate repeat use?

(6) Finally, go back to iTunes or Google Play and write a review of each app. What is your overall rating? What feedback would be helpful to the developers?

Notes for instructor: The instructor was open with students about the novelty of the assignment and asked students for their participation, flexibility, and feedback. Consequently, this created an open dialogue between the class and the lecturer that was mutually informative. Moreover, the students expressed excitement that they could be at the forefront of an emerging intervention for clients of all ages and socioeconomic levels. At the conclusion of the semester, the students' feedback was extremely positive in nature.

Although most students could be described as "digital natives," many had not used apps for personal benefit and described being excited to use the apps for personal use. They expressed further excitement that they had, in some cases, become their field placement's resident "expert" in an emerging technology use with clients, particularly with the use of apps that promote self-awareness, meditation, and mindfulness. Recommended readings for this assignment including the following:

> Bakker, D., Kazantzis, N., Rickwood, D., & Rickard, N. (2016). Mental health smartphone apps: Review and evidence-based recommendations for future developments. *JMIR Mental Health, 3*(1). doi:10.2196/mental.4984
>
> Stoyanov, S. R., Hides, L., Kavanagh, D. J., Zelenko, O., Tjondronegoro, D., & Mani, M. (2015). Mobile app rating scale: A new tool for assessing the quality of health mobile apps. *JMIR mHealth and uHealth, 3*(1), e27. doi:10.2196/mhealth.3422

Technology required: tablet and/or smartphone; software: apps

Editors' variations: This assignment could be adapted for a research assignment where students use the app to collect data for a single-system design study. Additionally, parts of the assignment could be incorporated into an intervention-based assignment where students need to search for an app to meet a client's need after completing a psychosocial assessment. Other types of apps could be reviewed depending on the topic of a course, such as homework assistance apps, medical information apps, and productivity apps for agencies.

Level of technology integration (SAMR model): Redefinition

AGENCY INFOGRAPHIC ASSIGNMENT (PRACTICE)

Editors' introduction: In this assignment, students develop an infographic to help promote a social service organization in their community.

Author's name and contact: Suzanne Potts, University of Texas at Austin, Spotts@utexas.edu

Approximate prep time for faculty: 30 minutes

Average assignment time for students: 4–6 hours

CSWE competencies addressed: 1, 4, and 5

Learning objectives: After completing this assignment, students will be able to

- develop an engaging infographic depicting a data source in graphic form for key stakeholders;
- increase the ability to interpret and communicate program data; and
- expand knowledge and practice with macro social work policy focus and infographic Web resources.

Assignment description: Create one infographic or marketing graphic project about a social service organization of your choice. Students must also develop the topic, outline, content, and references on a separate sheet along with the infographic. Students may use any online or visual reference to create this marketing and information resource. Pick a section of a program, an organizational goal, or some aspect of the agency that you think would lend itself well to an infographic, and help "tell the story" for that organization. Please include the organizational mission or core standards. What information stands out to you? What information is intriguing? What can you pull from the information system or reports that helps shape the infographic?

Notes for instructor: Students should be encouraged to search for information, data, and graphics on the Internet. Tutorials can be developed, but there are many articles and videos that students can access via a quick Web search. Infographic software that students can use for free is Piktochart. Students should be reminded of copyright laws and encouraged to use only free or royalty-free graphics or designs in their assignments.

Technology required: computer or tablet; software: infographic or digital presentation (PowerPoint)

Editors' variations: This assignment lends itself well to service-learning and community-engaged scholarship as students could work directly with an agency to create an infographic for real-world use or distribution by the organization. Students could work in groups or with students from other disciplines such as marketing or design to create the infographic.

Level of technology integration (SAMR model): Modification; Redefinition if shared with an agency

DSM5 PRACTICE AND TRAUMA ASSESSMENT: USING INTERACTIVE VIDEO (PRACTICE)

Editors' introduction: This learning activity uses a video to create an interactive learning experience for students. The instructor uses a combination video-editing and digital presentation software. Students are expected to watch the video with embedded questions before coming to class. This specific lesson is on diagnoses and assessment with trauma survivors in a Trauma and Resilience class, but an interactive video could be done for almost any type of lecture. To create this video, the instructor can use a software program such as PlayPosit or VoiceThread that will embed questions and track student progress.

Authors' name and contact: Johanna Creswell Báez, University of Texas at Austin, jbaez@smith.edu; and Ginger Lucas, University of Houston, vlucas@central.uh.edu

Approximate prep time for faculty: 3 hours

Average assignment time for students: 8 hours

CSWE competencies addressed: 6, 7, and 8

Learning objectives: After completing this assignment, students will be able to

- understand diagnosis in the assessment process with survivors;
- understand examples of providing a *Diagnostic and Statistical Manual of Mental Disorders*, 5th edition (DSM5) diagnosis for a trauma survivor; and
- practice providing a DSM5 diagnosis for a case example that will be further discussed in class.

Assignment description: The overall objective of this assignment is to watch an online video lecture on the DSM5 and trauma assessments and complete the embedded formative assessments. This assignment should be completed before they get to class and is posted on the online learning management system.

Step 1. Read the chapter on "Diagnosis in the Assessment Process," by K. A. Heimsch and G. B. Polychronopoulos, 2014, in E. Neukrug and R. Fawcett (Eds.), *Essentials of Testing and Assessment: A Practical Guide for Counselors, Social Workers, and Psychologists* (pp. 43–58) (Stamford, CT: Cengage Learning). Available at https://view.officeapps.live.com/op/view.aspx?src=http://ww2.odu.

edu/~eneukrug/DSM5/DSM5.doc

Step 2. Read a clinical case example of a domestic violence survivor (or another case example; case examples are included in the above website), and think about what DSM5 diagnosis should be provided.

Step 3. View a posted example of a short case (could use Tracey from the above website, p. 18) and diagnosis (to show students how a diagnosis is written).

. Post a link to a video via an unlisted (private or your institutions) *YouTube* channel or in the online learning management system. This video will cover content in both the reading and case example with embedded questions to test for mastery of content.

Step 5. The instructor can monitor students' progress and answers to modify lecture content in PlayPosit. Further, the instructor can plan the lecture around application and practice diagnosing other case examples.

Notes for instructor: When using interactive videos, you are transforming what is usually passive video content into an active experience for students. This lesson uses a video to create an interactive learning experience using the online program PlayPosit. A Microsoft PowerPoint slide deck with the instructor's video embedded is posted to the class online learning management system. During the video, formative assessments (questions with answers and open-ended questions) are embedded to support accountability and mastery of content using PlayPosit. Instructors begin by creating a YouTube video using screencasts (using software such as Screencast-O-Matic or Jing) of their lecture. This lecture is then uploaded to PlayPosit and embedded questions are added. Students are expected to watch the video with embedded questions before coming to class.

Technology required: Audio and/or video recorders; computer; social media: YouTube; software: digital presentation, screencasting, and specialized educational software called PlayPosit.

Editors' variations: This lesson is ideally used in a flipped classroom where content is delivered before class, to allow class time for further exploration and application.

Level of technology integration (SAMR model): Modification

ENGAGING IN YOUTUBE E-ADVOCACY FOR LGBTQ ISSUES (PRACTICE)

Editors' introduction: By creating their own advocacy-based video, students develop critical-thinking skills while demonstrating policy advocacy skills concerning lesbian, gay, bisexual, transgender, and queer (LGBTQ) issues. With this assignment, students practice all the steps of using video to promote social justice and will create a multimedia project.

Author's name and contact: Trevor G. Gates, University of the Sunshine Coast, tgates@.usc.edu.au

Approximate prep time for faculty: 2 hours

Average assignment time for students: 3 hours

CSWE competencies addressed: 2, 3, and 5

Learning objectives: After completing this assignment, students will be able to

- identify social justice advocacy issues affecting lesbian, gay, bisexual, transgender, and queer (LGBTQ) communities using Web-based newspapers, magazines, radio, and/or television sources;

ASSIGNMENT COMPENDIUM FOR INTEGRATING TECHNOLOGY

- engage in e-advocacy, influencing citizen, legislative, community, and media outlets about an important LGBTQ social justice issue; and
- critically reflect on the strengths and challenges of e-advocacy using YouTube.

Assignment description: The purpose of this assignment is to familiarize students with current issues affecting LGBTQ communities and to use YouTube for e-advocacy to influence stakeholders about the issue. The assignment is to be completed in the following order: (1) identify a social justice issue; (2) create a YouTube video; and (3) reflect on the experience. First, identify a current LGBTQ social justice issue in the news, including but not limited to LGBTQ relationship equality, violence and hate crimes, poverty, racism, and discrimination. The news piece identified should have been written or recorded within the last 90 days and can be found using a variety of search tools, such as Google News. You may also search the websites of traditional media outlets, such as CNN, ABC, NBC, BBC, *USA Today*, the *Washington Post*, and other news outlets. Next, film a YouTube video advocating for the LGBTQ social justice issue. You may use any digital video camera, including your iPhone or Android phone. Before filming the video, decide on a target audience for your e-advocacy, which might include direct citizens, legislators, community leaders, or media outlets. Then, upload the video to YouTube. Post a link to social media such as Twitter and Facebook using hashtags appropriate for the issue, for example #senatorbrown, #transviolence, or #hatecrime. Consider posting a transcript or creating a closed-captioned video so that people with differing abilities can access the video. Last, write a 100-word reflection on your experience creating an e-advocacy video regarding an important LGBTQ social justice issue. What worked well for you? What were you challenged by? Are there other considerations that might limit the use of e-advocacy? For example, e-advocacy efforts may only reach a limited audience, such as people who are not deaf and have regular access to the Internet.

Notes for instructor: Identify several e-advocacy videos that are currently available on YouTube and provide several examples prior to assigning the project. Find several videos that are not effective, for example, poor lighting, inadequate sound, speaker presenting a message that is either too long or too short, or unclear message. Provide tips for creating a successful YouTube video, including the "best" videos from the previous term. Be sure to get permission from your previous students to share past class assignments. Consider whether heavy editing is helpful. Especially for very current news events, it is often more helpful to get out the e-advocacy message rather than spending hours editing the video. Timeliness and relevance may be more important than form.

Technology required: computer, tablet, or smartphone; social media: YouTube; software: video editing; video recorder

Editors' variations: Almost any policy-based topic or social justice issue could be used to complete this assignment, including a review of a specific policy or telling the story of a person affected by discrimination or oppression. This assignment also works well for group work as creating videos are complex and involve storyboarding ideas, filming, editing, and postproduction audio.

Level of technology integration (SAMR model): Redefinition

SOCIAL ISSUE: A PERSUASIVE SPEECH (PRACTICE)

Editors' introduction: For this assignment, students use podcasting technology to present and review a speech.

Author's name and contact: Retchenda George-Bettisworth, University of Alaska, rbgeorgebettisworth@alaska.edu

Approximate prep time for faculty: 4 hours

Average assignment time for students: 3 weeks

CSWE competencies addressed: 1, 3, and 5

Learning objectives: After completing this assignment, students will be able to

- demonstrate effective oral communication when working with individuals and colleagues;
- distinguish, appraise, and integrate multiple sources of knowledge, including research-based knowledge and practice wisdom; and
- engage in practices that advance social and economic justice.

Assignment description: This assignment has two parts. This first presentation is a persuasive speech. A persuasive speech is used many times by politicians, specifically during electoral debates. The speakers are trying within their speech to sway the audience to their position. Students can choose from a list of current social issues provided, or if a specific social issue is not on the list, students should discuss with the professor to determine if an issue is appropriate. Students will be trying to sway the audience to their position. To complete the speech, students will complete a 2–3 minute SoundCloud that is an introduction to their topic. This should include the position statement and up to three main points supporting the students' position. Then, all students will complete peer reviews on the SoundCloud intros and are expected to comment using the SoundCloud comment tools or on the course blog. The peer review could include an opposing argument to the position stated, questions about the topic, supporting comments to their main points, and opposing arguments to their main points. Types of comments not allowed are as follows: "Good job," "I agree," "I disagree," "Wow," "That's interesting," and such within this same theme. Students will then listen to all responses and reply to at least two, either directly back to the statement or on the cloud or blog. This process is meant to help develop the students' final speech. For the second presentation, students will submit a final 8-minute SoundCloud presentation on their identified social issue. Students will listen to their SoundCloud and do a critique on their final speech, using the following criteria: clear organization; definitive statement/position; main points clearly defined and supported; time requirement/vocal presentation; and areas needing improvement. The self-critique will be submitted on the course blog with their final SoundCloud link.

Notes for instructor: I teach an oral intensive class both face-to-face and by distance. I use the format outlined for both sections. The use of SoundCloud allows students to interact and helps them develop their argument. Just listening to the audio focuses on the vocal presentation itself—but you could use YouTube as a visual option as well. I have taught the campus section, where the final speech is done in the classroom, and used a free software, Poll Everywhere, to poll the class at the beginning to gage the audience position, and then after to see if the speech actually persuaded students positions. The polling outcomes were not added into the final grade. Students really enjoy the SoundCloud tool and find it beneficial. This is an evolution from the traditional debate format.

Technology required: audio recorder; computer, tablet, or smartphone; microphone; social media: SoundCloud; software: Poll Everywhere

Editors' variations: Creating a podcast is a great alternative to almost any assignment requiring an interview or presentation. Examples include an informational interview with a social worker about their agency or presentation about latest research on a current social work topic. Asking students to listen to and review a podcast prior to completing the assignment will help students become familiar with podcasts in general.

Level of technology integration (SAMR model): Augmentation

ENGAGING IN SOCIAL WORK ADVOCACY: POLICY CRITIQUE EXERCISE (PRACTICE)

Editors' introduction: Using local, state, or national Web-based media platforms, this assignment encourages students to write about policy for a public audience, contributing to the public discourse about social welfare policy.

Author's name and contact: Lauren B. McInroy, University of Toronto, lauren.mcinroy@mail.utoronto.ca

Approximate prep time for faculty: 2 Hours

Average assignment time for students: 8–10 Hours

CSWE competencies addressed: 1, 3, and 5

Learning objectives: After completing this assignment, students will be able to

- analyze and articulate a critique of a federal, state, or local policy of relevance to the social work profession and the student's personal social work practice;
- identify an online platform/website appropriate for engaging in social work advocacy; and
- demonstrate professionalism and professional self-reflection in written electronic communication, and potentially contribute positively to a professional online presence.

Assignment description: The purpose of this assignment is to engage in social work advocacy by analyzing and critiquing a policy relevant to practice. This assignment is intended to encourage students to participate in a professional capacity in public discourses relevant to social work practice. The assignment is to be completed individually in four steps. First, students select a federal, state, or local policy relevant to a population or community they desire to practice with in the future (or are currently practicing in their practicum). Second, students compose a brief analysis and critique, for or against the selected policy (approximately 500 words). The analysis should include a brief description of the policy and its most salient points; strengths and/or weaknesses of the policy as it affects the selected population (e.g., well-being and access to services); and a discussion of what changes (if any) the student perceives the policy to require. Third, students select a relevant and appropriate online platform or website to submit their policy critique to (e.g., a website, a blog, an online magazine, or a newspaper). Students should format their assignments following the instructions of the selected platform and submit a copy of those guidelines with the assignment to the instructor. When the policy critique is complete, they submit it to the chosen platform and blind carbon copy (BCC) the instructor if sent by e-mail. If the submission is completed via an online form, they e-mail the instructor and attach a copy of the submission. The acceptance or rejection of the policy critique by the platform will have no bearing on the final grade. Finally, students should write a self-reflection on the assignment (approximately 150 words). In this self-reflection, students should include a justification of why they chose the selected platform to submit their policy critique and their experience of the process.

Notes for instructor: It may be helpful to have a few preselected platforms as examples for students (e.g., local or regional websites, newspapers/e-magazines, or blogs that accept outside submissions). You should allow ample class time to demonstrate and discuss the important elements of a policy critique, as well as your expectations. Depending on the size of your class, you may wish to set up a separate e-mail address for students to BCC when submitting their policy critiques to their platform to avoid overwhelming your mailbox. If all students are in practicum, you may choose to mandate that students complete the assignment on their current practice population. This assignment and its expectations can be adapted to be appropriate for both undergraduate and graduate students.

Technology required: computer, tablet, or smartphone

Editors' variations: To scaffold the assignment, students could search for an example policy critique from a Web-based media platform and review the critique or write a response to the critique and post using the platform's commenting tools prior to completing their own critique. Students could also develop and run their own policy-based blog for the course, developing criteria for submission and posting peer-reviewed comments.

Level of technology integration (SAMR model): Augmentation

AGENCY TUTORIALS (PRACTICE)

Editors' introduction: Using a free educational platform called Tes Teach, students create a lesson for their classmates about a local social service agency. This assignment incorporates elements of storytelling to describe and assess at the organizational client system.

Author's name and contact: Amy Hayes McLean, University of Tennessee at Martin, amclean1@utm.edu

Approximate prep time for faculty: 1–2 hours

Average assignment time for students: 5–7 hours

CSWE competencies addressed: 5 and 7

Learning objectives: After completing this assignment, students will be able to

- analyze agency websites for sufficient content and efficiency of use;
- demonstrate ability to create tutorials that are effective learning tools; and
- identify Web-based material that has potential benefits to client populations or social work professionals.

Assignment description: The purpose of this assignment is to learn more about agencies and resources available to serve a variety of client populations, along with assessing the agency's website. By using the online tool Tes Teach, students will have access to each student's lesson and be able to access the information in the future. There are three parts to this assignment: (1) create a lesson on an assigned agency; (2) present a brief overview of the lesson to the class; and (3) complete a reflection of the assignment and the agency website. To start, students will create a lesson on an agency assigned by the instructor. The lesson should be educational and help other students understand the agency's services, referral procedures, and eligibility requirements. Students may include agency websites, YouTube videos, and other Internet resources. Students should use information that is relevant, valid, and reliable. Once the student completes the assignment (and classmates review it), classmates should know who is eligible for services and how to make a referral. The last tile of the lesson should be a quiz covering the information provided in the lesson. The quiz questions should focus on services available, referral procedures, and eligibility. The lesson should contain the following: (1) six to nine elements; (2) one or two YouTube clips; (3) one quiz with a minimum of 10 questions; (4) no more than one picture element; and (5) useful information related to the topic. Students will need to share the lesson with the class on Tes Teach before the in-class presentation. Second, students should be prepared to present a brief overview of the agency to the class (5–10 minutes). In the overview, discuss the following: (1) the agency and its purpose/mission; (2) why specific information was included in the lesson; (3) what the student learned; and (4) any particular tiles in the lesson that the students think are important. For the final part of the assignment, students should assess their experience according to the following: (1) describe the experience of using the agency website; (2) describe the experience of using the website from the perspective of a potential client or professional; (3) describe what should be changed on the website or the method of accessing the information; (4) describe the experience learning about the agency; (5) describe what new information was learned as a result of this assignment; and (6) describe individual assessment of the assignment as a learning method.

Notes for instructor: Tes Teach is a Web-based software for creating digital lessons and offers free accounts. A sample lesson may be found at this link: https://www.tes.com/lessons/aQM5Djmh5_aySQ/

modern-racism. Tutorial videos exist on YouTube and the Tes Teach website. The instructor should set up a class space in Tes Teach prior to the students beginning the project, which will allow students to upload their lessons directly to the class.

Technology required: computer, tablet, or smartphone; software: Tes Teach

Editors' variations: Another addition to this assignment is to have the students visit the agency or conduct a phone interview. Students could also interview a client for their experiences. Students could also work directly with the agency to create a how-to tutorial for clients or conduct a focus group about the agency's website as a quality improvement practice.

Level of technology integration (SAMR model): Augmentation

ADVOCATE POLICY CHANGE: FACT SHEET AND ONLINE MOCK TESTIMONY (PRACTICE)

Editors' introduction: This assignment offers a supplemental activity to a written policy analysis. By video recording a short position or testimonial statement, students can learn technology skills while developing policy practice skills.

Authors' name and contact: Jeanette McQueen, University of Denver, jeanette.mcqueen@du.edu; and Stephanie Begun, University of Denver, stephanie.begun@du.edu

Approximate prep time for faculty: 3 hours

Average assignment time for students: 5–7 hours

CSWE competencies addressed: 1, 3, 5, and 8

Learning objectives: After completing this assignment, students will be able to

- demonstrate professional demeanor in behavior, appearance, and oral, written, and electronic communication;
- apply their understanding of social, economic, and environmental justice to advocate for human rights at the individual and system levels;
- apply critical thinking to analyze, formulate, and advocate for policies that advance human rights and social, economic, and environmental justice; and
- negotiate, mediate, and advocate with and on behalf of diverse clients and constituencies.

Assignment description: The primary purpose of creating a policy fact sheet and providing testimony is to help students develop the skills of critical thinking and advocacy on behalf of diverse constituencies. Another purpose is to engage the learning community in the discussion of current policy issues and advocacy strategies to advance human rights and social, economic, and environmental justice. Students will use the written policy analysis of a state legislative proposal assignment, completed earlier in the term, to develop a fact sheet and deliver testimony. The intended audience is policy makers and legislative staff. This is a three-part assignment. First, students prepare a one-page, visually appealing fact sheet that clearly states their position on the legislative proposal, with concise reference to supporting evidence that prompted their policy position. Students may use both sides of the paper, including citations and references and contact information. Next, students should video-record the delivery of 3 minutes of succinct, persuasive testimony in favor of, or opposed to, the legislative proposal. The testimony should include compelling evidence for their position with oral references to sources used, and be of the caliber of a presentation to a legislative committee. The dress and professional communication style should reflect this expectation. Finally, students should review their colleagues' facts sheets and testimonies and provide constructive and respectful feedback to all colleagues concerning their professional communications, evaluation of their critical analyses of their respective bills, and clarity of their advocacy strategies. Students should post written feedback to their colleagues by selecting Reply To their respective fact sheet and testimony posts so all responses may be easily read and organized by specific fact sheet and testimony.

Notes for instructor: This assignment builds on a traditional seven- to ten-page academic written policy analysis of a state legislative bill proposal. This assignment is appropriate for both BSW and foundation MSW introductory policy courses. Students have expressed appreciation for the applied nature of this assignment, noting that their knowledge of the breadth of policy issues and the development of advocacy skills contributed to increased desire to participate in the policy-making process. This is traditionally the final assignment in the course.

Technology required: computer, tablet, and/or smartphone; software: video editing; video recorder.

Editors' variations: Students could also create a podcast of their testimony. To deepen self-analysis of their testimony, students could annotate their own video recording. Students should provide a written copy of their testimonial or create captions in their videos to improve accessibility. Posting these statements in a public video-sharing website would allow students to contribute to the public discourse on social policy debates. Additionally, students could work with a local advocacy-based agency to help develop testimonial videos from staff or clients or individuals affected by the policy.

Level of technology integration (SAMR model): Augmentation

TWITTER CHATS (PRACTICE)

Editors' introduction: This assignment by Jimmy Young shows how Twitter can be used to engage and connect students in real time about social problems or politics. We have added an additional assignment from Retchenda George-Bettisworth under the editor's variation because of its similarities in tweeting about politics.

Author's name and contact: Jimmy A. Young, California State University San Marcos, jyoung@csusm.edu

Approximate prep time for faculty: 10 hours

Average assignment time for students: 4 hours

CSWE competencies addressed: 1, 3, 5, and 6

Learning objectives: After completing this assignment, students will be able to

- engage with others from around the country or world through a live chat conducted via Twitter to enhance their professional communication and development of a professional identity;
- think critically and attend to multiple perspectives that emerge from and through the live chat; and
- reflect on their learning through two different written assignments.

Assignment description: Students will watch the documentary *Inequality for All* on their own or in class (or a film of your choosing), and then write a brief reaction to the movie, including if they agreed with the filmmaker's position (why or why not?) and how the movie informed their understanding of poverty in the United States (500–700 words). Students then participate in a 1-hour live Twitter chat on a specific date/time with other students, educators, or professionals. This does require some preparation beforehand to ensure participation. Questions will be based around the film as well as the overarching topic of inequality (or the topic of the chosen film). Students will need a free Twitter account and will demonstrate participation during the chat by (a) posting responses to at least three of the discussion questions; and (b) responding to at least three other chat participants. If you or your students are new to *Twitter*, you can find several guides on the Internet to help you get started. After the live chat, students will write a self-reflection about the experience of participating in the chat that includes a summary of the chat, lessons learned from the chat, and how the experience could inform future social work practice (300–500 words).

Notes for instructor: Students will need a free Twitter account and familiarity with the platform. Dedicating a portion of class time can be useful to better understand the mechanics of Twitter and demonstrate how Twitter chats function with hashtags. Class discussions about how to become consumers of current events, news, and politics within a technological age are helpful. For the documentary chat, partnering with an established group hashtag for the chat can also help promote the chat to a broader audience, such as #MacroSW or #NASW. Coordinating a multiclass chat does require some preparation beforehand to ensure participation. Students have indicated this assignment changed their perceptions of social media and enhanced their learning. They enjoyed connecting with others from around the country and realized that they can use their voice to advocate for a cause.

Technology required: computer, smartphone, or tablet; social media: Twitter

Editors' variations: From the University of Alaska (rbgeorgebettisworth@alaska.edu), Retchenda George-Bettisworth's version is "Twitter State-of-the-State": Students will watch the state-of-state address by the governor and live-tweet with the instructor and classmates, posting about thoughts, quotes, and reactions from the address. Students should use the hashtags #AKStateofstate and #GovernorWalker. After the address, locate at least two media resources (newspaper articles, opinion pieces, or videos) reacting to the governor's address that provide opposing viewpoints. Then, write a two-page reaction paper that includes an overview of the address, reactions to the address, the two media sources, and reactions to the live tweeting. Alternative content can include the president's State of the Union address, political debates, almost any documentary film, or the local or national news. Students could also create a transcript of their tweet or all the tweets from the chat, and annotate the transcript.

Level of technology integration (SAMR model): Modification

ELECTRONIC HUMAN RIGHTS ADVOCACY SERVICE-LEARNING PROJECT (PRACTICE)

Editors' introduction: This assignment requires students to search the Internet for human rights websites, identify a nonprofit's calls to action, and prepare responses to the calls. Students must use skills related to navigating the Web and learn about how agencies involve individuals in community action.

Author's name and contact: Martha Addison Armstrong, Ohio Dominican University, armstrom@ohiodominican.edu

Approximate prep time for faculty: 1 hour

Average assignment time for students: 4 hours

CSWE competencies addressed: 3 and 5

Learning objectives: After completing this assignment, students will be able to

- advocate for human rights and social justice;
- engage in practices that advance social and economic justice; and
- collaborate with colleagues and clients for effective policy action.

Assignment description: Employ Internet *searches* to identify three current human rights campaigns sponsored by three separate human rights organizations. These campaigns must focus on international, that is, not primarily domestic, human rights and social justice issues/violations. Select and prepare a campaign action response as requested by each of the three organizations for each of the three campaigns selected. In the interest of academic freedom, you may choose to stop short of completing the requested action, for example, you might draft a requested letter but choose not to forward it to the intended recipient. (Note: making a monetary donation to a human rights campaign does not fulfill this part of the assignment.) On each of three due dates, submit in class the following: a paper copy of one human rights organization's website that includes a description of the organization's current human rights campaigns and the actions requested by the organization specific to one of the campaigns underway; and documentation that you prepared one of the requested campaign actions. Be ready to discuss your selected human rights campaign, including whether and in what specific ways the campaign is compatible with the International Federation of Social Workers Statement of Principles as well as the Universal Declaration of Human Rights and, as applicable, the Convention on the Rights of the Child.

Notes for instructor: This assignment is used in a macro practice course. By sharing information in class regarding their selected campaigns, the students expand their awareness of current global human rights issues. Students frequently become avid supporters of campaigns for which they have prepared an action response. Starting the Internet searches in a laptop classroom is invaluable in helping to get everyone on the same page regarding assignment requirements. Viewing the UNICEF photo essay "The Rights of the Child," parts 1 and 2, which is available on the Internet, helps the students to focus on human rights. The full text of the International Federation of Social Workers Statement of Principles, the Universal Declaration of Human Rights, and the Convention on the Rights of the Child are easily accessible on the Internet.

Technology required: computer, tablet, and/or smartphone

Editors' variations: This assignment could help students learn about social work ethics by also asking students to explore the website's compatibility with the National Association of Social Workers' Code of Ethics. Additionally, students could be asked to use social bookmarking software such Pocket or Diigo to curate or keep up with the information from their searches.

Level of technology integration (SAMR model): Substitution

SOCIAL WORK PRACTICE WITH NON-WESTERN CLIENT POPULATIONS (PRACTICE)

Editors' introduction: This assignment consists of three separate article reviews, by which students gain a greater understanding of culturally informed practice by locating scholarly articles related to working with specific populations. The instructions ask students to use scholarly databases, locate recent articles, and to focus on articles authored by social workers—with each step giving students opportunities to hone their skills related to literature search. Finally, by sharing the information with their peers, students practice public speaking and presentation.

Author's name and contact: Martha Addison Armstrong, Ohio Dominican University, armstrom@ohiodominican.edu

Approximate prep time for faculty: 30 minutes

Average assignment time for students: 3 hours

CSWE competencies addressed: 2 and 6

Learning objectives: After completing this assignment, students will be able to

- recognize and communicate their understanding of the importance of difference in shaping life experiences;
- discover, appraise, and attend to changing locales, populations, and emerging societal trends to provide relevant service; and
- analyze the quality and variety of scholarly information available on the Internet.

Assignment description: You will conduct three *electronic database* or Internet searches to locate three current (last 5 years) scholarly journal articles than can inform direct social work practice with non-Western client populations (those that are not part of the Western tradition primarily influenced historically by countries of western Europe and North America). Give preference to articles authored by social workers. Consider beginning your search using key words regarding a region/country of interest to you, a specific non-Western client population, or a life challenge directly affecting non-Western client populations. On each of three scheduled due dates, submit in class the following: (a) one copy of the first three pages of the journal article; and (b) a one-paragraph summary of the information obtained from the article that you consider most significant for informing direct social work practice with the non-Western client population under discussion in the article. On each of the due dates, be prepared to share with the other class members the information found in the journal article submitted that day that you consider most significant for informing direct social work practice with one or more non-Western client populations.

Notes for instructor: This assignment works well during the second half of the semester in an upper-level, undergraduate direct practice course. Having access to a laptop classroom has proven helpful in getting the students started with the assignment. Requiring that the focus be on non-Western client populations ensures that the students consider a global perspective.

Technology required: computer, tablet, and/or smartphone

Editors' variations: Although this assignment suggests a series of three assignments, this number could be scaled up or down. This could be a helpful assignment leading up to a final paper about using a specific intervention with a specific population, and offers an opportunity to give students feedback on the quality of the literature they are using to inform their work. Additionally, students could be asked to use social bookmarking software such Pocket or Diigo to curate or keep up with the information from their Web searches.

Level of technology integration (SAMR model): Substitution

VIDEO CASE PRESENTATION (PRACTICE)

Editors' introduction: Students post a case presentation via video to the learning management system and comment on each other's work. Case staffing is an important component of many practice settings, and this exercise offers students an opportunity to consider confidentiality issues, key case elements, and positionality, and to use peer feedback. This assignment lends itself to all types of classes, including on the ground, synchronous, or asynchronous settings.

Author's name and contact: Kia J. Bentley, Virginia Commonwealth University, kbentley@vcu.edu

Approximate prep time for faculty: 20 minutes

Average assignment time for students: 1 hour

CSWE competencies addressed: 1, 2, 4, 6, and 8

Learning objectives: After completing this assignment, students will be able to

- articulate specific practice roles and activities related to psychiatric medication in a real-case scenario and connect them to course content;

- reflect on the challenges of using a partnership approach to practice; and
- demonstrate (and observe in others) self-awareness and the ability to critically evaluate their own practice and their own levels of client empathy.

Assignment description: Be prepared to post a brief video case presentation (no more than 7 minutes) about one of your real clients in the field/at work (past or present) and the relevance of the course content to your work. Begin by very briefly describing a case (camouflaged) and then, in more depth, discuss your use of the specific content, knowledge, and skills in fulfilling new roles for assisting the client with her/his medication-related concerns. Your video should focus on your roles and activities, *not* on a long description of the case or "what happened next." We need to see that the case presentation is clearly for a class in social work and psychopharmacology that stresses partnership practice. Your ability to demonstrate self-awareness and an appreciation of the consumers' experience is essential to this assignment. In addition, you should demonstrate a progression of learning, as well as the ability to stimulate creative thinking and expanded applications of content in the rest of us. You are expected to review at least a dozen of your peers' videos.

Notes for instructor: Students will need a computer or other device that allows them to record a video and then be able to upload to class through the learning management system. This assignment is ideal for an online course.

Technology required: computer, tablet, and/or smartphone; software: video recording; webcam

Editors' variations: If students do not yet have access to real clients, they could instead create case presentations based on a book, a movie, or an assigned scenario, or even use in lieu of/as a supplement to the common psychosocial assessment assignment.

Level of technology integration (SAMR model): Substitution

PROFESSIONAL SOCIAL MEDIA PROFILE (PRACTICE)

Editors' introduction: For this assignment, students create a professional social media profile and consider their public presentation. Professional online presence is valuable. Although it is easy to assume that "digital natives" come naturally by these skills, they do not; instructor guidance can support students in using a professional voice. By exploring social media settings and privacy, this assignment also offers an opportunity for a classroom discussion about how social workers interact with clients in the online environment. Students are also asked to sharpen their advocacy skills as well as consider their audience and prepare messages that speak to this group. Public social media assignments offer engagement with an audience outside the classroom.

Author's name and contact: Erica D. Shifflet-Chila, Michigan State University, shiffle6@msu.edu

Approximate prep time for faculty: 4–5 hours

Average assignment time for students: 4–5 hours

CSWE competencies addressed: 1 and 6

Learning objectives: After completing this assignment, students will be able to

- create a professional social media profile;
- understand how to use privacy settings on social media profiles to target a specific audience; and
- use a social media platform for advocacy.

Assignment description: The purpose of this assignment is to create a professional social media profile that is effective at reaching a target audience and follows the ethical and legal considerations of the profession. The assignment has three parts:

1. Create a social media profile on a recognized social media platform (Facebook, Twitter, Instagram, LinkedIn, etc.). You will create a social media profile on a popular social media platform. You can use your real name, real organization's name, or an alias or make-believe identity. You need to choose the platform that you think will best reach your target audience (clients, community members, or other professionals). What your profile will include depends on the platform you choose, but it may include photos, links to other organizations/websites, a personal or organizational bio, informative content, and so forth.

2. Adjust security settings. Research the security/privacy settings of the platform you have chosen, and adjust your settings to allow access for your target audience. Include the settings for posting/sharing or linking to your profile. You also must make sure that your instructor can access your profile.

3. Use your profile for advocacy. How you accomplish this will depend on your chosen platform. You can provide information through blog posts/tweets, links to other advocacy organizations, and so forth. The purpose here is to choose an area of advocacy (can be advocating for clients, raising awareness of an issue, promoting yourself as a professional, etc.) and using your profile to share information or inform constituents.

Notes for instructor: Make sure you have a basic understanding and an active profile on the social media platforms you allow students to use for this assignment. For example, if you do not have a Twitter account, do not allow students to use that specific platform.

Technology required: computer, tablet, and/or smartphone; social media: various

Editors' variations: This can be a onetime assignment or carried throughout the semester. For instance, students may create a blog about local trauma resources that they update throughout the term. Instructors should consider ways for students to react or comment on each other's contributions. Do bring the conversation about professional social media engagement back to the classroom and reflect together on what is off limits for online posting, and how to handle a critical comment or client engagement via social media. Consider having students read an article on best practices for attention-grabbing social media posts.

Level of technology integration (SAMR model): Redefinition

SOCIAL MEDIA AND TECHNOLOGY USE POLICY ASSIGNMENT (PRACTICE)

Editors' introduction: This assignment not only allows students to practice agency policy making by creating a social media policy but also forces them to consider their own values regarding social media use alongside ethical guidelines. Although many agencies have general technology-use guidelines, few focus on issues related to client searches or client interaction. Given the ubiquity of social media and its use across personal and professional settings, this is valuable content for exploration.

ASSIGNMENT COMPENDIUM FOR INTEGRATING TECHNOLOGY

Author's name and contact: Erica D. Shifflet-Chila, Michigan State University, shiffle6@msu.edu

Approximate prep time for faculty: 2–3 hours

Average assignment time for students: 4–5 hours

CSWE competencies addressed: 1, 5, and 8

Learning objectives: After completing this assignment, students will be able to

- draft an agency policy to guide employee use of technology and social media;
- demonstrate understanding of the ethical and legal considerations of the use of social media and technology in the social work profession; and
- create supports/consequences that encourage appropriate use of social media and technology.

Assignment description: Imagine that you are a supervisor at a social service agency. You have had several reports recently of staff members using technology and social media while on the job, and some reports that staff members are posting information about the agency or clients to their personal social media profiles. You are concerned that this use may be illegal, unethical, or unfavorable to your organization and its clients. Your assignment is to create a social media policy to be used in your human service agency to address these concerns. You can use a real or fictitious agency. Make sure your policy includes the following: (a) purpose of the social media/technology use policy (Why has this policy been created? What is the overall goal? Do you want to encourage use? Discourage it?); (b) appropriate use of social media and technology in the workplace (What activities are allowed? Prohibited? What is allowed during the workday? In the workplace? At home?); (c) references to agency or clients in personal social media (What is allowed? What is prohibited? How will this be monitored?); and (d) consequences of inappropriate behavior on social media. Your policy should be no more than two pages, clear and concise, and in accordance with the materials you have read for class.

Notes for instructor: Provide some examples of employee/staff policies for students to critique/refer to prior to this assignment. Students will need to read/discuss legal and ethical considerations of social media use and confidentiality prior to completing this assignment, including Health Insurance Portability and Accountability Act (HIPAA) regulations, the National Association of Social Worker (NASW)'s Code of Ethics, and the NASW Standards for Technology in Social Work Practice.

Technology required: none

Editors' variations: This assignment would fit well in a policy class. It may be helpful to precede this class with reading and discussion related to the pros and cons of searching for and communicating with clients or other professionals via social media, including beneficial aspects such as locating missing clients, family finding in child welfare, or conducting emergency safety assessments. Encourage students to discuss value conflicts related to their personal use versus professional use, and client privacy versus practitioner convenience. Several scholarly articles report on frequency of work-related social media use by professional helpers and promising practices for policy making. Consider these articles as primers for a class discussion:

> Brady, S. R., McLeod, D. A., & Young, J. A. (2015). Developing ethical guidelines for creating social media technology policy in social work classrooms. *Advances in Social Work, 16*(1), 43–54.

Sage, M., & Sage, T. (2016). Social media and e-professionalism in child welfare: Policy and practice. *Journal of Public Child Welfare, 10*(1), 79–95.

Additionally, you can request a free copy of the "Social Media Toolkit for Social Work Field Educators," by A. Curington and L. I. Hitchcock, July 28, 2017, retrieved from http://www.laureliversonhitchcock.org/?s=social+media+toolkit

Level of technology integration (SAMR model): none

SOCIAL JUSTICE VIDEO PRESENTATION (PRACTICE)

Editors' introduction: This group assignment encourages students to explore community resources by developing a video about a local agency, institution, or organization.

Author's name and contact: Elizabeth P. Cramer, Virginia Commonwealth University, ecramer@vcu.edu

Approximate prep time for faculty: 15 hours

Average assignment time for students: 8 hours

CSWE competencies addressed: 2 and 3

Learning objectives: After completing this assignment, students will be able to

- gain knowledge about a specific social justice–related place (site), organization, and/or activity in your state;

- demonstrate knowledge and skills in the phases of video production, including capturing images and video, storyboarding and creating co-narratives, editing, and final production; and
- learn how to use Creative Commons/open-source resources.

Assignment description: You will work with a group to create a 5-minute audiovisual presentation on a social justice–related place (site), organization, and/or activity in your state. Your video can be captured using any equipment, and you can produce and edit the video using any program you desire.

Include in your video the aspects of this place, organization, and/or activity that have been most challenging to you and those aspects that have been the most powerful and thought provoking. You may use photographic images that you take or that you find on the Internet. You will be working in groups and you will co-create the story or narrative for the video. You are encouraged to be creative, honest, and engaging in your video presentation. You will show your video to the class. The instructor must be sent a copy of the video. All students will also complete a self-evaluation and assign their own grade. Possible video-editing software are Educreations and WeVideo. Sample student group videos are on the course learning management system site.

Notes for instructor: Administer a brief survey to students in the beginning of the semester to identify their familiarity with video editing and production. (Put those with little to no experience into a group with students who have plenty of experience.) Recommended maximum number of students per group is four. In an early class session, go over the assignment in detail and provide examples of storyboards. Show students some student-made videos as examples, not just ones that are technically high in quality that your students could never imagine making. Distribute a tip sheet. Give students four to 8 weeks to complete the project. Offer an orientation for software or hardware use for students who are not comfortable with technology. Point students to Creative Commons resources for videos and photographs; remind them to cite sources and respect copyright.

Technology required: computer, tablet, and/or smartphone; software: video recording and video editing; video recorder

Editors' variations: You can ask students to meet with agency representatives and visit the agency before creating the video. Consider creative ways to use these videos; for instance, they could be posted to a website or blog as a community resource directory or shared directly with the agency so they can use them promotionally. If they use them for promotional materials, students should work with the agency for guidance. If the videos focus on agencies that offer field placements, they could be used to help students select or prepare for field placements.

Level of technology integration (SAMR model): Redefinition

EXPLORING COMMUNITIES USING THE AMERICAN FACTFINDER (PRACTICE)

Editors' introduction: Using the American FactFinder tools from the U.S. Census Bureau, students completing this assignment collect data and create maps to complete a community-level assessment.

Author's name and contact: Thomas P. Felke, Florida Gulf Coast University, tfelke@fgcu.edu

Approximate prep time for faculty: 4 hours

Average assignment time for students: 6–8 hours

CSWE competencies addressed: 4, 5, and 9

Learning objectives: After completing this assignment, students will be able to

- locate data on a topic of their interest from the U.S. Census Bureau online datasets;
- create maps of an identified community using data on a topic of their interest; and
- recognize potential community needs and assets based on an analysis of the created maps.

Assignment description: The purpose of this assignment is to provide students with an opportunity to explore a selected geographic community using freely available data and tools found at the U.S. Census Bureau website. Students create a presentation on a selected topic for an identified geographic area. To accomplish this, students are asked to do the following:

Identify the problem. Consider a selected geographic area (neighborhoods, counties, regions, etc.) that is of interest to you, as well as a social issue or a gap in services that is affecting the selected area. Using academic, organizational, and public media sources, research the issue in the selected area and provide a two-page outline of your research on the selected topic for the selected geographic area.

Examine the datasets. Using the American FactFinder website, explore the different datasets and accompanying variables that may assist you in describing the problem or the need for services in the selected geographic area. You can use the search options navigation tools to locate variables related to your topic of interest. For example, you may consider variables such as "veteran status" and "service connected disability" from the American Community Survey datasets if looking at the need for programs to assist military veterans in a selected geographic area.

Create a dataset and maps. Use the American FactFinder website to compile a dataset of variables that assists in describing the social issue or need for services in your selected geographic area. First, select the geographic area that you wish to explore, such as "all counties in Florida." Use the search options to once again locate the variables that assist you in describing your selected topic. Once you have located a variable, use the Create Map tool found on the American FactFinder website to create a visual representation of your variable data. Save the maps as image files so you can include them in your final presentation. In addition to creating and saving your maps, use the Download tool to download your data into a Microsoft Excel file so you can manipulate the data for presentation purposes.

Analyze and present. Create a Microsoft PowerPoint or Prezi presentation that incorporates the research on your selected topic, the data you located, and the maps you created. Provide recommendations for addressing the social issue or gap in services based on your findings.

Notes for instructor: This assignment is as much about data location and management as it is about map creation. By making the geographic and demographic selections, students are learning about what types of data are or are not available via the U.S. Census Bureau website as well as gaining an understanding of the different types of datasets produced by the U.S. Census Bureau. Demonstrate the map-creation process in class prior to having the students attempt the assignment on their own. Provide detailed, step-by-step instructions for the assignment. Students need to know that not all topics are covered using data obtained through the U.S. Census Bureau, such as direct counts of homelessness.

Technology required: computer, tablet, and/or smartphone; website: U.S. Census Bureau's American FactFinder (http://factfinder.census.gov/faces/nav/jsf/pages/index.xhtml)

Editors' variations: Students could also focus solely on a community, such as the community where their practicum agency is located, and search for data on multiple indicators such as poverty rates, food insecurity, and demographics. The presentation then becomes a report care of a community.

Level of technology integration (SAMR model): Redefinition

INTERDISCIPLINARY ETHICS EXERCISE (PRACTICE)

Editors' introduction: This assignment conducted with social work and nursing students is designed to present health-care-system ethical dilemmas that could be experienced in real-world practice by having interdisciplinary students discuss case studies in a shared online forum.

Author's name and contact: Joan Groessl, University of Wisconsin–Green Bay, groesslj@uwgb.edu

Approximate prep time for faculty: 5–8 hours

Average assignment time for students: 3.5 hours

CSWE competencies addressed: 1 and 2

Learning objectives: After completing this assignment, students will be able to

- apply the code of ethics of the professional discipline to practice scenarios;
- compare and contrast perspectives between the two disciplines; and

- effectively communicate personal and professional perspectives to promote interprofessional understanding.

Assignment description: Using case study materials such as readings or videos, students have the opportunity to understand and interact with other professions. Students familiarize themselves with background and supporting information supplied by the instructor prior to entering the online discussion forum.

Assignment Process:

(1) Students review case study materials (readings and/or video).

(2) Students then post an analysis of the situation of the case study to the discussion forum responding to the following prompts: (a) Explain what action should be/should have been taken in the case study; (b) describe which moral principle (beneficence, malfeasance, autonomy, or justice) influenced your decision-making (Note: These are the biomedical ethical principles.); (c) identify aspects of your profession's code of ethics that provide assistance with decision-making; (d) identify which one of the following theories provided guidance in your decision-making and explain how the theory did so—utilitarianism, deontology, caring, intuitive (minimum 400 words).

(3) Peer reply: Reply to a student of the other discipline who has a different perspective on this situation. Respectfully compare your perspective to the other student's perspective; include parallels and contrasts within respective code of ethics and outline your rationale for the comparisons (250 words).

Notes for instructor: Content to be covered in the course prior to the implementation includes moral theories, ethical decision-making, and interprofessional practice. Codes of ethics of both disciplines should be included as support materials. The ethical situation is developed jointly with the faculty member of the other discipline to ensure that both disciplines would be challenged and have potentially differing interpretations. The case study can be developed from a video that presents a situation with ethical overtones, presents news stories of controversial situations, or is created using other known situations. Examples used with nursing students have included situations related to genetic engineering, medical procedures with ethical overtones, and scenarios with differing interpretations of potential outcomes based on differing philosophical perspectives of the two disciplines. Debriefing after the session can help students to gain perspective on the differences and ensure learning is consistent. Two courses from the two different disciplines join for the assignment. A joint forum (separate course shell) needs to be created to allow the groups to communicate with each other; consult with your university's technology support unit.

Technology required: computer, tablet, and/or smartphone

Editors' variations: Instructors can choose from a variety of professions that social workers might encounter for this assignment, including students who study education, physical therapy, medicine, and so forth. As a supplement to this assignment, students can compare and contrast professional ethical standards and the roles of each discipline in intervening in the offered scenario. They may discuss the differences in how each discipline is prepared through the curriculum or field experience for intervening in the case to develop knowledge about each other's discipline and respect for what each field brings to the collaboration.

Level of technology integration (SAMR model): Substitution

SKILLS PRACTICE WITH ROLE-PLAY VIDEOS (PRACTICE)

Editors' introduction: This semester-long assignment involves video recording four role-plays, focusing on interviewing and clinical skills. Students work in groups and conduct peer and self-assessments.

Author's name and contact: Linda Ayscue Gupta, Virginia Commonwealth University, lagupta@vcu.edu

Approximate prep time for faculty: 9–11 hours

Average assignment time for students: 6–8 hours

CSWE competencies addressed: 1, 2, 3, 6, 7, 8, and 9

Learning objectives: By the end of this assignment, students will be able to
- identify, synthesize, and assess multiple perspectives and sources of knowledge with individuals and families to arrive at professional judgments and practice decisions;
- apply knowledge of human behavior and the social environment to data gathered with individuals and families to produce assessments that recognize strengths and source of difficulties; and
- identify, select, and practice selected intervention techniques from practice theory and analyze the results of those interventions postinterview.

Assignment description: This assignment will use assigned case scenarios that you will role-play online, record, and then post for reflection, feedback, and assessment. First, with the assigned scenario, plan and video record a role-play with classmates. Please meet ahead of time to discuss how you will proceed—who will ask what, when the next person will take over, and so forth. You want to be sure that each of you has an opportunity to ask the "client" one or two questions before moving on to the next person. Have fun with this! You may dress the part if you wish. You will be graded not on your acting but on your analysis of the role-play in the discussion board later on. Limit your role-play to 20–30 minutes. Next, watch your recorded role-play, and using the "Outline for Skills Practice Reflection," write an original discussion post that answers each of the questions under the assigned sections for each scenario by the due date. Check the appropriate Skills Practice Rubric and Course Folder for the week to determine the assigned sections. Remember to answer all the questions under each assigned section. Now, write your reflection response, posting to another class member's original discussion post, by the due date.

Notes for instructor: You will need four case scenarios with teaching points embedded, for example, a social or economic justice issue, an ethical issue, and so forth. You will need a writing prompt, in this assignment called a Skills Practice Reflection, with one or more questions under each of several headings—countertransference, identity as a professional social worker, ethical issues, social and economic justice issues, engagement, assessment, and intervention. This actually involves the ability to Web-conference so that students can sign in from wherever they are, along with the ability to record audio and video of that Web conference. I use Blackboard's Collaborate, but it could be done with Zoom or similar tools.

Technology required: computer, tablet, and/or smartphone; microphone; software: video recording such as Zoom or Collaborate

Editors' variations: Students could role-play and video-record examples of good and not good interviewing techniques to be shared with the class for discussion. Also, students could use annotation tools with the videos to directly identify strengths and challenges of the role-plays.

Level of technology integration (SAMR model): Augmentation

AGENCY INFORMATIONAL INTERVIEW PODCAST (PRACTICE)

Editors' introduction: This assignment incorporates podcasting technology in place of a written paper. Students start by listening to a podcast and then create their own podcast based on an informational interview with a professional social worker.

Author's name and contact: Laurel Iverson Hitchcock, University of Alabama at Birmingham, lihitch@uab.edu

Approximate prep time for faculty: 2 hours

Average assignment time for students: 10–12 hours

CSWE competencies addressed: 1, 6, and 7

Learning objectives: After completing this assignment, students will be able to

- analyze a social work podcast for content and production value;
- demonstrate assessment and interview skills for engaging with and assessing a human service organization; and
- identify through critical reflection the benefits and challenges of using technology in social work practice.

Assignment description: The purpose of this assignment is to help students practice assessment skills related to a human service organization while learning about podcasting technology. The assignment has three parts. First, students review a podcast. They will select and listen to a social work podcast (at least 30 minutes long) and then write a review about the podcast, providing the following: (a) title and description of podcast including hyperlink; (b) introduction and conclusion; (c) content; (d) delivery; and (e) technical production. Second, students create a podcast based on an informational interview conducted with an employee of a local social service agency. The podcast should be no less than 5 minutes and no more than 10 minutes and should describe and assess the agency using the following framework, discussed in class. The audience for this podcast will be the general public, and students can be creative with this podcast. It should reflect professional behavior, such as appropriate language, and no obscene music or sounds. Along with the podcast, they will create a one-page handout describing their agency using the framework. The podcast will need to be submitted as an MP3 or MP4 format file. Third, students complete a self-reflection about the experience. After submitting the podcast, they can write at least 200 words that reflect on how they created the podcast, what they learned from creating the podcast, what were the benefits and challenges of the assignment, and how they will use podcasts in future practice as a social worker.

Notes for instructor: Partner with your institution's library or digital media lab that can provide equipment or technical assistance to you and your students, including tutorials. Podcasting is an easy and low-cost technology that makes it ideal for undergraduate students. Most students can record an interview on a smartphone and then download free software to edit.

Provide one or two sample podcasts made by students from

previous semesters as exemplars. Students need to be reminded that they cannot use any content that is copyrighted, including music.

Technology required: Audio recorder; computer, tablet, or smartphone; microphone; software: Audacity or GarageBand

Editors' variations: Students could create a podcast on almost any topic related to a social work course. Additionally, listening to and reviewing a podcast could be incorporated into a course as an independent assignment.

Level of technology integration (SAMR model): Augmentation

USING TWITTER IN PROFESSIONAL DEVELOPMENT (PRACTICE)

Editors' introduction: This Twitter-based assignment allows students to communicate about a focused topic: motivational interviewing. By using this public social network, students can observe which other professions and areas of the world are interested in this topic while they practice their professional networking and presentation skills.

Author's name and contact: Melinda Hohman, San Diego State University, mhohman@mail.sdsu.edu

Approximate prep time for faculty: 1 hour/week

Average assignment time for students: 10 minutes/week

CSWE competencies addressed: 1, 4, 6, 7, 8, and 9

Learning objectives: After completing this assignment, students will be able to

- demonstrate empathy through reflective listening and other interpersonal skills;
- define and apply key concepts of motivational interviewing;
- demonstrate professional demeanor in electronic communication with other professionals; and
- use social media to enhance professional development and learning.

Assignment description: With the growth of social media, it is important for students to learn how to use it professionally, particularly as they prepare for a social work career. The purpose of this assignment is for students to use social media (Twitter) in developing a professional identity through their interactions. Further, another purpose is to demonstrate knowledge and skills regarding an evidence-based practice, motivational interviewing. The assignment also helps students understand the potential for social media in social work practice. Students will complete the following steps:

(1) Establish a free Twitter account. If they are already using Twitter for personal use, they may wish to create a second account for professional use.

(2) Learn how to use Twitter. Students usually know someone who uses Twitter to ask for help or they may ask the professor if they are unfamiliar with Twitter. Students are instructed to use the course number with a hashtag (#SW381) in all posts to identify themselves as part of the course. Further, students are asked to use #motivationalinterviewing or #MI in all posts as well so that others in the professional community can find their posts and respond to them.

(3) Respond to Twitter posts. Students are informed that the faculty member will post at least one question per week on

Twitter that they are asked to respond to. The question can either be about course content or be a role-play response to a simulated client.

(4) Create one's own post or re-tweet. Students may also re-tweet other posts that they find that relate to course content or can ask questions themselves of their classmates and community professionals. Video links and other sources demonstrating motivational interviewing can also be posted. Again, the course hashtag must be included.

(5) Provide a self-reflection. Students who participated in the project are asked, in lieu of a quiz, to write a one-page paper regarding how they used Twitter, what their experiences with it were in the larger professional community, and what they learned.

(6) NASW Code of Ethics and social media visibility are important to remember in writing on Twitter as a social worker.

Students are reminded that content is public and to conduct themselves accordingly.

Notes for instructor: I am a member of the Motivational Interviewing Network of Trainers so I was able to write to our membership LISTSERV regarding the class and ask other members who use Twitter to respond to students. Only a handful of people tweeted, but students were thrilled with interactions. This could be done by any instructor who is a member of a professional group. Similarly, faculty members could collaborate with peers teaching a similar course in another university and ask students to respond to each other. I had to read Twitter daily and make notations of which students posted. Students who posted regularly throughout the semester were able to earn full points.

Technology required: computer, laptop, and/or smartphone; social media: Twitter

Editors' variations: This assignment can be applied to any topic. Have students read, search, and reply to content from other professionals. Have students review compelling posts and compare what types of posts/posters generate the most feedback. Additionally, other platforms could be used, such as FlipGrid.

Level of technology integration (SAMR model): Redefinition

WORLD OF WARCRAFT (WOW) ASSIGNMENT (PRACTICE)

Editors' introduction: In this assignment, students are asked to become familiar with culture and norms of gamers. To work with clients, practitioners must become knowledgeable about new environments. Here they get experience with gaming culture and use reflection. This is transferable to work with kids and adolescents and offers opportunity to practice metaphors. Leveling up in a game is a way to explain persistence through obstacles. In this game, student can witness/intervene in bullying, build social skill opportunities, and learn about culture.

Author's name and contact: Mike Langlois, University at Buffalo, malanglo@buffalo.edu

Approximate prep time for faculty: 6 hours

Average assignment time for students: 20 hours

CSWE competencies addressed: 1, 3, 4, 7, and 9

Learning objectives: After completing this assignment, students will be able to

- create a video game character and use it in a multiplayer environment;
- demonstrate skills for engaging with gaming technology individually and with others; and
- identify through critical reflection the benefits and challenges of using video games in social work practice.

Assignment description: The purpose of this assignment is to help students become familiar with key concepts in video games as they relate to human experience and reflect on the psychological experience of playing them. Participants will be expected to download, install, and play World of Warcraft (WoW) throughout the course. You can play this for free until you reach level 20, and you will receive the percentage equivalent of your level for this portion of the grade (i.e., if you hit level 5, you get 5%; if you hit level 20, you get the full 20%). Register, download, and check to make sure you have the capacity to save and play on your computer. Downloading this software takes time, so please do so as soon as possible before class. When you create your character, you will be asked to choose a server. Please be sure and choose the server for this class. If you do not, you will not be able to interact with the rest of the class or me. You will also be asked to choose between the factions Horde and Alliance. Make sure you choose the class race (Horde and Alliance), or you won't be able to speak the same language as the rest of us. Along with playing the game, a blog will be used for reflective learning. Two blog postings will be expected each week, one of which should be your reflections on your play. For the second one, post not just journal-like entries but also images, videos, podcasts, and other things related to WoW that catch your interest. Blog postings will be part of the class participation grade. When you set up your blog, be sure to set it to private so that only other students and I can read it. Posts do not have to be long; in fact, more frequent short posts are preferred to weekly posts of length.

Notes for instructor: Familiarize yourself with the technical specifications required to download the game, as well as what would be the best platform for your class to share blog posts. It may be more accessible to use free blogging platforms such as *WordPress*. Encourage students to scan all software downloads for viruses. Be sure to clearly identify which game server you want all students to use so they create characters on the same one and are able to play together. This assignment is a lengthy one and should be expected to provide a substantial portion of the coursework time and grade. Consider dropping the level requirement to a lower number if this is a concern. Encourage collaboration during *gameplay*.

Technology required: computer; server; social media: WordPress or Blogger; software: World of Warcraft

Editors' variations: Students could be asked to play almost any game such as Minecraft or Words With Friends. Alternatively, students could be asked to review a video game for therapeutic use or as a tool to create community or learning collaboratives.

Level of technology integration (SAMR model): Redefinition

MEDIA-SAVVY SOCIAL WORK: RADIO INTERVIEWING (PRACTICE)

Editors' introduction: For this assignment, students prepare short audio clips and provide each other with feedback before completing a final assignment: a 30-minute "radio show" related to social work. This exercise provides the opportunity to prepare students to speak on behalf of an issue, to prepare thoughtful questions, and to learn more about an area of interest while using new and familiar technology.

Author's name and contact: Alyssa Lotmore, University at Albany SUNY, alotmore@albany.edu

Approximate prep time for faculty: 5 hours

Average assignment time for students: 5 hours

CSWE competencies addressed: 1, 4, 6, and 7

Learning objectives: By the end of this assignment, students will be able to

- research a specific topic and create relevant questions to ask the chosen guests;
- demonstrate the ability to engage with the interviewee and the general audience while providing insight on the chosen topic; and
- identify through self-reflection and peer critiques the benefits and challenges of seeing the "public as the client" and using the medium of radio to reach individuals and constituents.

Assignment description: This assignment is part of a larger course on media-savvy social work, in which students use the medium of radio and other forms of technology for advocacy and social justice. To prepare for this assignment, students can first work in pairs to create 5–10-minute radio segments. Students gain experience of being both the host of a show and a guest. When in the interviewer role, the focus is on the student's ability to control the interview, keep the conversation on topic, form questions, and engage the listener. As guests, the students experience explaining the area they were being interviewed on, balance providing facts with engaging conversation, and learn to communicate in a clear, concise manner. Students not only provided peer critiques of the radio segments but also created self-critiques about how they felt during the experience. For the peer critiques, students answer the following questions:

- Were you engaged in the show?
- Did you find the host asked quality questions?
- Were there questions that you would have asked if you were the host?
- Did the guest get the point across?
- As a listener who may be unfamiliar to the topic, was the show easy to understand and follow without being knowledgeable in the field?
- What was your overall impression of the set-up, the production quality, and show content?
- What were aspects that you liked about the show?
- What aspects would you have changed?

Practice and peer review prepares students for the final assignment of a 30-minute radio segment and a reflection paper. Assignment: Choose a social work topic of your interest (a population such as veterans or an issue such as self-care or vicarious traumatization). You will conduct three 10-minute interviews with individuals who can give information about your topic. For example, if your topic was veteran posttraumatic stress disorder (PTSD), you could interview a social worker at the Department of Veterans Affairs (VA) to discuss PTSD, a veteran, and a worker at a nonprofit organization that provides resources to veterans. Through those three interviews, the listener can learn information about PTSD from the social worker, the personal story from the veteran, and what resources are available to veterans from the person at the nonprofit. Be sure to skillfully incorporate sources of your information and resources for the listeners. With your final audio segments, include the promotional summary. This should be creative and informative, as you want to use it as a tool for people to tune in and listen. It should include the show name and highlights of the content covered. As you complete your assignment, you will reflect on the project. Answer the following questions in a paper: What caused you to choose the topic you did? Why do you feel that the topic should be addressed? Remember to cite sources of information and statistics, if applicable. Who is your goal audience? What are the main points you wanted to get across to the listeners? Why did you choose the individuals you interviewed? What did you want them to bring to the segment? What made you choose the questions you did? Did the guest say anything that surprised you? Were you able to accomplish what you wanted with the segment? Who would you like to share your segment with and why?

Notes for instructor: Partner with your institution's interactive media center/library that can provide equipment or technical assistance to both instructors and students. Using audio software and podcasts is fairly simple and low cost. There are online audio platforms, such as BlogTalkRadio, but many students simply use their smartphones to record. Uploading audio clips to *YouTube* allows students to easily share their content with peers and the class. Students can edit audio on YouTube or in a freeware program like Audacity. Remind students about copyright laws and referencing sources when on air. Students can be introduced to radio and podcasts by listening to samples and critiquing them.

Technology required: audio recorder; computer, tablet, or smartphone; social media: YouTube; software: BlogTalkRadio

Editors' variations: Instead of a topical area, interviews could focus on life stories focused on developmental stages for a HBSE class, a research study where students interview researchers for a research class, or profiles of community leaders for a macro focus. Variations are endless, and these media skills have high transferability for community-based practice.

Level of technology integration (SAMR model): Redefinition

COMMUNITY ASSESSMENT: WALKING VIDEO TOUR (PRACTICE)

Editors' introduction: The traditional community assessment is usually formatted as a long report, which is rarely seen by anyone besides the instructor. This technology twist has students complete their community assessment via a video walking tour. All the same criteria can be applied; when presented via video, students must give even closer attention to highlighting key points, and the end product can easily be shared with the class and stakeholders.

Authors' name and contact: Ginger Lucas, University of Houston, vlucas@central.uh.edu; Aabha Brown, University of Houston, abrown28@uh.edu; and Donna K. Amtsberg, University of Houston, dkamtsbe@central.uh.edu

Approximate prep time for faculty: 1 hour

Average assignment time for students: 12 hours

CSWE competencies addressed: 1 and 7

Learning objectives: After completing this assignment, students will be able to

- delineate the tasks involved in the process of assessment;
- conduct a strengths-based assessment with clients at the community level; and
- discuss the collaborative nature of assessment and its relationship to social work values.

Assignment description: The overall objective of this assignment is to complete an assessment of a community of your choosing.

ASSIGNMENT COMPENDIUM FOR INTEGRATING TECHNOLOGY

Community is defined as a place with specific geographic boundaries. This assignment is best completed in steps:

Step 1. Complete a historical assessment of the community, identifying relevant history as well as current impacts of that history. Special attention should focus on assessing power structures both past and current in the community.

Step 2. Using video-recording technology (a smartphone or tablet can be used), conduct a walking assessment of the community, video recording your observations. Pay special attention to the sights, sounds, smells, and structures within the community.

Step 3. After obtaining written consent, identify at least three community members to interview in your video. Students should attempt to interview an adult resident of the community, a person who works to serve the community, and a youth resident in the community (if possible).

Step 4. Edit the video information collected into an 8–10 minute video that provides audio/visuals needed to complete an assessment of the community. Your video should explicitly identify strengths/assets as well as challenges.

Step 5. Upload your video to the class YouTube channel, saving your video as the name of the community you assessed (e.g., Houston Heights).

Step 6. Students will then be assigned a classmate's video to view and will be asked to conduct their own assessment based on the audio and visual information collected in the video.

Notes for instructor: In an online environment, this assignment offers several advantages. Students can learn about communities and neighborhoods in various regions throughout the country, thus providing an opportunity to discuss the vast diversity within a geographic region. Second, viewing the videos fosters a connection and understanding among the online students and builds a sense of community within the online class. Finally, on debriefing, many students left with a sense of pride in the community they chose to assess, an unintended consequence. Using a strengths-based perspective offers students an opportunity to identify assets that might go unnoticed in a traditional assessment. Faculty members need to set a class page to share the videos (YouTube or learning management system).

Technology required: computer, tablet, or smartphone; social media: YouTube or other video-sharing platform; software: video editing; video recorder

Editors' variations: This can be an individual or group project, where students take various roles (editing separate sections of research and interviews, etc.). Using a similar format, students could also assess their field agencies, a local social-work-related issue facing the city council, or a community or campus issue such as underage drinking.

Level of technology integration (SAMR model): Modification

MACRO PODCAST ASSIGNMENT (PRACTICE)

Editors' introduction: A podcast is an audio file that can be uploaded to the Internet for sharing and listening. In this assignment, students record a podcast for possible sharing on the nationally acclaimed *Social Work Podcast* website.

Authors' name and contact: Suzanne Potts, University of Texas at Austin, Spotts@utexas.edu; and Jonathan B. Singer, Loyola University, jonathan.b.singer@gmail.com

Approximate prep time for faculty: 1 hour

Average assignment time for students: 6–8 hours

CSWE competencies addressed: 1, 4, and 5

Learning objectives: After completing this assignment, students will be able to

- research and evaluate a relevant macro social work topic for a podcast;
- increase knowledge about podcast development from design to implementation; and
- demonstrate ability to use research to inform practice in macro social work.

Assignment description: This project includes planning, researching, and developing a macro-focused social work podcast. Listen to an episode of the *Social Work Podcast* (http://socialworkpodcast.blogspot.com/) to get an idea of how the episodes are constructed and delivered. There are lecture-style episodes and expert interview-style episodes. Once you have an idea of what the episodes sound like, think of a topic of interest for macro social workers. Include in your project the social significance to the field of social work and importance to the profession. A well-documented literature review is also required. Though it is not necessary to "cite" in the podcast itself, it is important in the transcript to cite relevant information. For example, in the recorded version of the podcast, one might say, "Logic models have been in use for the past 15 years." In the transcript, a citation would be included. If one were summarizing the work of a specific author, one might say, "Hasenfeld (2010) argues that effective policy requires…." Key terms must be identified and defined for the audience. Describe the core content of the podcast in two to four paragraphs. Include any take-home language from each section. A content outline is required for this assignment. Please include core content sections for the podcast.

Research and suggest speakers who are considered subject matter experts (SME) for this topic. Please include a short list of potential speakers who could cover the material proposed, including why they are considered SMEs for this topic. A demo version may be recorded and sent via e-mail to the instructor. This is not required but may help shape the final product if selected. Students may submit an audio recording, a video recording, or a text version of the podcast. One final podcast may be selected to be recorded and shared on the *Social Work Podcast* website. By participating in this assignment, you are giving Jonathan Singer permission to record your episodes if selected to be developed into a full podcast. All episodes that are selected will include a short introduction that the topic was researched and written by you and as part of this class at the University of Texas at Austin.

Notes for instructor: Faculty members are encouraged to be familiar with podcast content, style, and format before assigning. Clear expectations about the content outline will help focus research for podcast content. Identify as a class types of macro social work podcast episodes that may be relevant to meet project expectations. Review podcasts as previous assignment so students are familiar with content, style, and format. Include grading rubric in assignment and review expectations and outcomes on the project. Test out the microphone and recording system on your computer to better explain how to record content, if applicable. Clearly outline whether students are expected to submit a written content outline or also include a .wav file that has been recorded.

Technology required: audio recorder; computer, tablet, or smartphone; microphone; video recorder; software: audio and/or video editing; webcam

Editors' variations: Almost any topic can be the focus of a podcast, such as an interview with a practitioner, a review of a theory, or a presentation of a current social welfare policy. Podcasting technology is easy to learn and use, so students can also work independently on this assignment.

Level of technology integration (SAMR model): Redefinition

SECOND LIFE AS A PRACTICE LAB FOR ASSESSMENT AND REFLECTION (PRACTICE)

Editors' introduction: This assignment uses Second Life, a virtual online environment, as a tool to simulate a client-practitioner interaction.

Author's name and contact: Kelley Reinsmith-Jones, East Caroline University, reinsmithjonesk@ecu.edu

Approximate prep time for faculty: 2 hours

Average assignment time for students: 4 hours

CSWE competencies addressed: 1, 2, 6, 7, 8, and 9

Learning objectives: After completing this assignment, students will be able to

- demonstrate ethical and professional conduct in a virtual environment;
- increase knowledge of current events as they relate to class material; and

- engage with peers, social work professionals, and organizations about events that directly relate to social work practice at the micro, mezzo, and macro levels.

Assignment description: The goal for this activity is to have each student role-play both a social worker and a client. They work in pairs and use forms that the course instructor has provided, and explained, ahead of time. It is also important that the students use the "chat" method of communicating while in Second Life to create a written document of their sessions. To start, have each student choose (from examples the instructor provides) or create a client profile and then work in pairs. Students should then complete the following tasks:

(1) Complete each assessment form as assigned, and follow each session with case notes using the format provided by the course instructor. This is most often Subjective, Objective, Assessment, and Plan (SOAP) or SOAP or Data, Assessment, and Response (DAP).

(2) Each student social worker will meet with his or her client in Second Life to complete the following activities:

  (a) Meet, establish rapport, and begin assessment process with a provided biopsychosocial form.

  (b) Meet to continue working on the biopsychosocial and complete a spiritual assessment as well. I use the Faith, Importance, Community, and Address in Care (FICA) assessment. The social worker and client meet as many times as is necessary to complete these assessments.

  (c) Meet to review the biopsychosocial summary, with an instructor-provided form.

  (d) Cooperatively complete a care plan, using an instructor-provided form.

  (e) Meet, as many times as is desired, to review and amend the care plan as needed.

(f) Termination is possible when appropriate and if sufficient time is given for the activity.

(3) During this process, and after each session, the students copy and paste their session conversation into a separate document that the students role-playing as social workers then use to self-evaluate their skills (rapport building, interviewing, note-taking, assessing, etc.). The two students must complete the entire process, having role-played both the counselor and the client.

Notes for instructor: The East Carolina School of Social Work is fortunate to have its own Second Life Social Work Island, a part of the larger university presence. We have created various activities for our students to do, depending on assignment activity. However, it is always available for students to use as a safe space for practicing skill building in interviewing, becoming familiar with specific types of forms, treatment planning, case note formulation, and self-assessment. It would be ideal if students from two different classes could pair up for this activity. However, it is often difficult for students to work with others outside of their classrooms. If working with another class, it is imperative that both instructors require the activity as a mandatory assignment in their syllabus. Otherwise, if the activity is voluntary, it is too convenient for students to decide that they do not have the time for activity completion.

Technology required: computer; software: Second Life

Editors' variations: Although this institution has their own island, there are other ways for instructors to access space in Second Life— cooperative shared spaces by educators and nonprofits. The reality is that students could use any number of public spaces to role-play because the chat will be private, so they will just be talking somewhere.

Level of technology integration (SAMR model): Augmentation

DESIGN AN ONLINE SUPPORT GROUP (PART 1) AND IMPLEMENT A SIMULATED ONLINE SUPPORT GROUP (PART 2) (PRACTICE)

Editors' introduction: This two-part assignment has students develop and implement an online support group to be used in an online chat and offers a perfect opportunity to discuss issues related to online practice, including confidentiality, record-keeping, consent, and interstate practice.

Author's name and contact: Jill L. Russett, Christopher Newport University, jill.russett@cnu.edu

Approximate prep time for faculty: 4–6 hours

Average assignment time for students: 20–30 hours

CSWE competencies addressed: 1, 2, and 4

Learning objectives: After completing this assignment, students will be able to

Part 1
- apply the principles and techniques of generalist social work practice to group work;
- understand and apply basic concepts of group work, including recruiting and selecting members, leadership, and facilitation; and
- acquire generalist knowledge of evidence-based models, principles, and methods of social group work practice.

Part 2
- acquire foundational knowledge of types and use of groups in social work practice, group formation, and identify stages of group development;

- apply basic social work skills, techniques, and strategies in engaging, assessing, contracting, intervening, evaluating, and terminating with social work groups;
- identify self as it relates to social work roles in working in group practice;
- identify diverse populations to benefit from virtual group support; and
- explore ethical practice and social work values in a virtual group support setting.

Assignment description: Traditionally, support groups are held in-person. Advancements in technology allow opportunities for online support groups on a variety of topics in the privacy of the participant's home. They increase accessibility for numerous at-risk populations and reduce a sense of isolation potentially experienced in geographic localities (rural settings), with physical/medical conditions (housebound clients or clients with disability), or social constraints (nontraditional work hours, house arrest, transportation, or language). The purpose of this assignment set is to have students design, implement, and participate in a simulated online support group as a group facilitator and member.

Students will write a support group proposal and then gain skills in creating and facilitating a support group run exclusively online. In addition, students will gain insight and perspective on client experiences in online support groups.

Part 1 Instructions:
1. Identify an online support group platform. Multiple Web-based platforms and software exist to facilitate online group interaction. Research, identify, and describe a program you believe would be beneficial to implement a future online support group; include associated costs (Note: you do not have to purchase the software); benefits and limitations of

the program; and technology required by user (audio/visual, computer, Internet access, etc.). Some sites provide audio, visual, and typing capability. Examples of sites appropriate for this assignment include Tinychat, and Skype.

2. Select a format. Determine the type of interaction that will occur: live, written discussion, or a combination. Consider how the facilitator will engage with group members. Synchronous groups function with members participating in real time on a designated day and time. They may use screen names with pseudonyms or with live interaction. Asynchronous groups provide opportunities for posting messages 24 hours at their convenience. Support your rationale for your format, and include benefits and limitations of your choice.

3. Ethical concerns. Develop an informed consent form applicable to online support groups. This form should include confidentiality and group rules. How will you recruit and screen potential group members? Reference the NASW Code of Ethics.

Part 2 Instructions:

1. Form a mock support group. The instructor will establish groups of five to six students to participate in a simulated online group experience. Each student will be assigned 1 or 2 weeks to serve as the group facilitator. During the remaining weeks, students will participate as active group members and contribute to the conversation. Groups will be monitored by the instructor for content, skills, and experience.

2. Select a topic and population. An approved list of topics appropriate for online support groups will be provided by the instructor. Student groups will select a topic to simulate during their online group experience.

3. Group format. Students will be required to set up Google Hangouts, which will be used to facilitate live, synchronous groups. This format allows for both videoconferencing and text chats. An in-class demonstration will be provided. Students will meet in class to establish a consistent meeting time and format for the online support group. Student teams will identify a name for the group and discuss appropriate netiquette to guide online conversation. Student will select dates to serve as facilitator.

4. Facilitator role. Each week a different student will be assigned as the group facilitator. Your job as the facilitator will be to lead the weekly support group, including starting and ending the group and guiding the discussion. Group facilitation will last 1 hour. On completion of your role as facilitator, write a reflection on your experience. Note what skills you used, the stage of group development, and challenges and benefits.

5. Participant role. Students will participate weekly as members of the online support group. Members are responsible for establishing appropriate content for discussing and engaging in the group process. Participants need to sign into the group on time and remain engaged for the entire group process. After each weekly support group, write a reflection on your experience. Note what it is like to be a member: How are you supported? Do you feel included? What was helpful or not? How so?

6. Reflection paper. On completion of the group experience, students will turn in a final paper. Included in the paper will be your weekly reflection (with each date/time your group met) and a final written summary of the experience as a whole.

Notes for instructor: Have students read NASW Code of Ethics Standard 1.04 Competence and Standard 1.05 Cultural Competence and Social Diversity. Provide sample list of topics appropriate for an online support group. Provide information on Google Hangouts, which is currently the most accessible free software.

Technology required: computer, tablet, or smartphone; software: videoconferencing

Editors' variations: These instructions can easily be implemented in a LMS with tools such as Adobe Connect, which limits some student privacy risks but does not expose students to learning software that they can take with them to practice. Google Hangouts, and other software, allows for recording, which may allow peer and instructor reviews; thus, groups can occur outside of class time. Consider assigned roles and scenarios instead of real-life self-disclosure in the group to minimize FERPA concerns.

Level of technology integration (SAMR model): Modification

THE VIRTUAL SELF: PROFESSIONAL USE OF SOCIAL MEDIA (PRACTICE)

Editors' introduction: Social media is a powerful tool for personal and professional networking and relationship maintenance, and increasingly it is used as a tool by nonprofits. In this exercise students explore social media sites and profiles and learn how to develop a professional profile. Issues related to privacy and professional boundaries are explored.

Author's name and contact: Jill L. Russett, Christopher Newport University, jill.russett@cnu.edu

Approximate prep time for faculty: 2–4 hours

Average assignment time for students: 4–6 hours

CSWE competencies addressed: 1

Learning objectives: After completing this assignment, students will be able to

- identify private conduct and professional responsibilities related to social media forums;
- reduce potential for dual relationships in a virtual environment; and
- establish a professional social work identity.

Assignment description: Social media provides numerous opportunities for virtual connectivity. The increasing adoption of and ever-changing social networking sites presents students with challenges to manage social media for both personal and professional purposes. Engaging in social media also presents a source of concern about exposure to liability for social workers involved in online communication. The purpose of this assignment is to help students separate personal and professional use of social media, and establish a work-life balance while developing a professional identity.

Students will distinguish between social media networking sites and personal use and learn to protect their personal information. After reviewing personal social media profiles, students will write a two- or three-page paper about their experiences with their virtual identity. Complete the following steps:

1. Searching yourself. Using any Web-based search engine, search your name and see what you find. Are there any surprises? What information could a client find out about you? Also search images.

2. Social media protection. Identify each form of social media in which you have a personal account (if you do not engage in social media, select sources to review). You must review a minimum of three sources in depth. For each account, review the settings and ensure the strictest level of privacy is in effect. Review the policy: What types of personal data are collected, and how are they used? What other ways can you protect your privacy while engaging in social media use? Social media and online forums to consider as part of your search: Facebook, Twitter, Instagram, Snapchat, LinkedIn, Pinterest, online dating sites, blogs, and accounts by friends and family that may contain access to your personal information and others.

3. Professional identity. How does the NASW Code of Ethics inform your use of social media? How would you manage client interactions with your virtual identity (how would you respond if a client wants to "follow you" or if you accidently identified a client account)? What other ways can you maintain control over your professional reputation online? Identify an agency and search their policy on social media use as it relates to their employees.

Notes for instructor: Instructors should complete this task themselves and share examples with the class.

Technology required: computer, tablet, and/or smartphone; social media: various platforms

Editors' variations: Consider using this assignment in combination with the social media policy assignment, or having students conduct "background checks" on the Internet for each other to see what information can be discovered.

Level of technology integration (SAMR model): Redefinition

ASSIGNMENT COMPENDIUM FOR INTEGRATING TECHNOLOGY

VIDEO VIGNETTES OF PRACTICE INTERVENTIONS (PRACTICE)

Editors' introduction: In this assignment, students demonstrate practice skills on video as a way to develop skills in professional presentation, technology, and practice interventions.

Author's name and contact:

Approximate prep time for faculty: 3 hours

Average assignment time for students: 4 hours

CSWE competencies addressed: 1, 4, and 8

Learning objectives: After completing this assignment, students will be able to

- consider their professional public persona for the Internet;
- demonstrate, on video, their ability to apply research to practice;
- describe and model a practice intervention; and
- effectively use technology for social work practice.

Assignment description: The students will choose an evidence-based intervention and describe and demonstrate how the intervention is carried out during a video in less than 5 minutes. Videos are recorded and uploaded using YouTube. The intervention could be an existing intervention from a workbook, but students must be able to link it to evidence and theory. Alternatively, it could be a brief intervention of the students' own creation, as long as it is guided by evidence. For instance, the students could describe using an ecomap with a family and demonstrate its use or demonstrate a way to use calming breaths when working with children who are anxious. Students must submit or cite at least one peer-reviewed article that supports the theoretical constructs for using the intervention—this supports their ability to link practice to research.

Notes for instructor: If the students want to demonstrate their intervention with another person, a release of information should be signed so that the other video participants are clear about how the video will be used. Although this is only a brief video, students may need time to learn to use the technology and research their assignment. I used the assignment for a children's mental health course and uploaded the student work each semester to a public blog. This blog became a video library repository of brief interventions that can be a resource for others in the profession.

Technology required: computer, tablet, or smartphone; social media: YouTube; software: video editing; video recorder

Editors' variations: Several variations are possible. For instance, instead of brief practice interventions, at the end of the semester have students record brief tips related to any class, such as research, policy, or HBSE. These could be shared with the next class to help them prepare for the course. Instead of video blogs, have each student create a client worksheet with instructions. For a research class, have students record an explanation of a behavior or diagnostic measure.

Level of technology integration (SAMR model): Modification

WORKING THROUGH AN ETHICAL DILEMMA (PRACTICE)

Editors' introduction: This assignment has students consider possible outcomes at each stage of a case related to ethical decision-making. A story is programmed by the instructor using a free Web-based software, Twine, and then shared with students. The story pauses at decision points, and the viewer chooses a path. Different paths lead to different storylines. After demonstrating this, students can build their own stories in groups and share them with other class members. Storylines must follow ethical guidelines, giving students a creative way to exercise their ethics muscles.

Author's name and contact: Jane Sanders, University of Toronto, jane.sanders@mail.utoronto.ca

Approximate prep time for faculty: 6 hours

Average assignment time for students: 8–10 hours

CSWE competencies addressed: 1

Learning objectives: After completing this assignment, students will be able to

- understand the complexity of an ethical dilemma;
- be able to identify key points for social work consultation; and
- be able to identify guidelines for ethical behavior in the field of social work.

Assignment description: The purpose of this assignment is to build comfort and confidence in the area of social work ethics. Students will have an opportunity to work through an ethical dilemma using the open-source technology called *Twine*, which can be used to create a storyline similar to choose-your-own-adventure books. This technology will be used to help identify and work through case example and practice dilemmas, learning about ethic decisions using a tool for telling interactive, nonlinear stories. There are, identified below, three suggested instructional options, which can stand-alone or build on each other toward the completion of the assignment. *Option 1*: Instructors can use the technology in a lecture format, pulling ideas and discussion from the class. Using a digital projector, the instructor would walk through a scenario that introduces an ethical dilemma. A Twine story is built with a series of "passages," similar to digital cue cards, to create each page of the story. On each page of a completed Twine, the reader is given options. The instructor can prepare a complete storyline in advance or use class discussion to build a scenario with two "ethical decision points." The class will vote on one of two options. Based on the class discussion, the instructor will continue with the story until the next decision point. Instructors can choose how and when to foster additional discussion, at the end of the storyline or at each decision point. Instructors also have the option to go back to either (or both) decision point to work through the alternate options, discussing the ramifications of those choices.

Option 2: Instructors divide the class into groups of two to four students. Each group will be asked to create a Twine of ethical decisions. The groups must then map out the ethical situation and what happens on both sides of the decision points. The class will have an opportunity to review and discuss the Twines created by the other groups.

Option 3: Twine assignment. The class will be given an ethical Twine created by the instructor. Students are asked to document their ethical roadmap. In the assignment students will be asked to explain each decision point, supported by literature in social work ethics. Students are asked to identify when and how they would consult regarding the situation, identify the complexity of the ethical situation, and identify the social work ethics that are guiding their decisions.

Notes for instructor: Twine is an open-source tool and thus has no cost. The instructor must become familiar with the Twine tool. The Twine wiki has an online guide (http://twinery.org/wiki/twine2:guide), and there are multiple YouTube video tutorials (search for "Twine 2 tutorial"). View example Twines on the Twine home page (http://twinery.org).

Technology required: computer; software: Twine

Editors' variations: As presented, this assignment focuses on ethical dilemmas. However, the same software could be used for other kinds of decisions, such as diagnosis/clinical decision-making where the bridges lead to different therapeutic modalities. Students could select the best modality fit for the diagnostic presentation—their selections could lead to different outcomes dependent on whether complementary therapies are chosen for the diagnosis.

Level of technology integration (SAMR model): Modification

EXPERIENTIAL SERVICE LEARNING GROUP VIDEO (PRACTICE)

Editors' introduction: This assignment asks service-learning students (in Jamaica for this example) to make a short video about the culture of the place they visit. Any trip could be substituted. The assignment neatly lays out rules and foci for this group assignment, which includes identifying the role of social workers in a new environment. The product could be shared with and enjoyed by many.

Students develop video-editing, production, storyboard, interview, and presentation skills while they learn about using likes and sharing videos for the public and intercultural communication.

Author's name and contact: Leslie Yaffa, University of New England, Lyaffa@une.edu

Approximate prep time for faculty: 2 hours

Average assignment time for students: 10 hours

CSWE competencies addressed: 2 and 3

Learning objectives: After completing this assignment, students will be able to

- demonstrate knowledge of several perspectives in social work from a Caribbean context;
- demonstrate knowledge of the influence of Caribbean social, economic, and political policy on the lives of citizens in that region; and
- demonstrate knowledge of strategies/interventions related to developing trust and serving as "co-learners" in cross-cultural and international settings.

Assignment description: While in Jamaica, within your groups, you will be filming and taking pictures to be used for a video production that your group will work on over the course of the rest of the term. To do this, you will need to agree within your group who will be working on what. Some of you may be more comfortable doing most of the filming/photography/interviewing; others will be eager researchers; others will be better writers; and still others will jump at the chance to do some narration or the editing. Deciding those details is up to you and your group in Jamaica. If some students are unable to fulfill a specific role for one reason or another (a technological or a personal reason, for instance), then the rest of the group should accommodate those students by giving them a responsibility that they can fulfill.

Because you will be filming others, it is important that you respect laws regarding permission to use a person's likeness or portraying their property. Recordings done in public places rarely require model releases because persons or objects in public are, to some extent, fair game (which is certainly not a license to be rude). If a person asks not to be recorded, or asks that recordings made not be used, those are wishes that need to be honored. However, recordings done of private property, or arranged interviews with individuals, may require a model release. In case you think you need a model release, a template is available.

The objective of this assignment is to create a 10-minute video of your experiences as a social work student in Jamaica. Please use the organizations we visit and help viewers understand the individuals, community, and groups we encounter. This video can be set up in any way you see fit but must explain your experience and how social work is viewed in Jamaica. It is, in essence, a way to get at the first learning objective in this course: "Demonstrate knowledge of several perspectives in social work from a Caribbean context." Once you've returned from Jamaica, you should begin working with your online group to assemble the footage, pictures, and whatever else you accumulated from the week in Jamaica into a video. After you've submitted it, the video will be posted to a school of social work YouTube channel.

Notes for instructor: Whether they use Microsoft Windows or Apple MacOS operating system, students have a native video editor already installed: Mac uses iMovie, Windows uses Movie Maker. Students can use whatever tools they have to record the video, such as a cell phone. Students love this assignment; some technical difficulties were reported, but overall, they loved contributing to the course.

Here are some examples of videos: https://www.youtube.com/watch?v=d8fiOaXHts4 and https://www.youtube.com/watch?v=ISOXiX67arI.

Technology required: computer, tablet, and/or smartphone; social media: YouTube; software: video editing; video recorder

Editors' variations: Consider ways in which this format can be used for community assessment, foreign exchange or study abroad trips, or even local service-learning projects.

Level of technology integration (SAMR model): Redefinition

STUDENT RESPONSE SYSTEM ("CLICKERS") (RESEARCH)

Editors' introduction: This class activity using clickers (a student response system) provides a way to engage the entire class and check students' comprehension of key concepts.

Author's name and contact: Phyllis Black, Marywood University, Black@marywood.edu

Approximate prep time for faculty: 2 hours

Average assignment time for students: varies

CSWE competencies addressed: 1, 4, and 9

Learning objectives: After completing this assignment, students will be able to

- demonstrate enhanced engagement in research content;
- engage interactively in research class discussions; and
- attain competency in understanding research concepts.

Assignment description: Current emphasis on empirically informed social work practice, reflected in the 2015 Educational Policy and Accreditation Standards (EPAS), heightens the need for approaches to augment student engagement in research. There is longstanding recognition of student antipathy to research. A proposed in-class activity, iClickers is an interactive technological tool that promotes student involvement in attaining research competency.

Multiple-choice research questions are displayed on a screen as slides in a Microsoft PowerPoint format, with numbered options for response. Graphics and humor are incorporated to support student engagement. Examples of PowerPoint slides are as follows: (1) A hypothesis concerning social work practice poses the question of identifying the independent variable; (2) students are asked to identify the level of measurement (nominal, ordinal, interval, or ratio) of a specified variable; and (3) a study is presented that used a convenience sample; students are asked to indicate the external validity of the study.

Students are asked to identify the statistical test to assess the relationship between two nominal variables: professional attire (neck or bowtie) and client trust of practitioner (yes, no) as either ANOVA, Mann-Whitney, or chi square. Each student is provided with a clicker, a handheld electronic device on which the students anonymously select the number that corresponds to their response choice. Immediately following the "click voting" by the students, a bar chart presenting the aggregate response distribution of the class is electronically shown on the screen. Students then volunteer the rationale for their personal selection of responses, which generally prompts a lively interactive exchange. The correct answer to the question is then shown on the screen, frequently prompting additional discussion and requests for clarification of embedded research concepts in the slides. The key feature of this experience lies in the class discussion. The clickers serve as a technical conduit to stimulate the discussion and thereby enhance student participation in grappling with the concepts under consideration.

Notes for instructor: An advantage of clickers is that students can provide their responses anonymously and avoid embarrassment. Furthermore, students who might ordinarily be reluctant to participate in class discussions may be energized by the activity and become involved in the discussion. Students report enjoying this mode of learning, which in turn, prompts heightened interest in the subject matter. On the other side of the desk, instructors benefit from being able to gauge the collective level of student understanding of the material under study and can use this information to inform their future curricular plans. The clicker exercise promotes a nonthreatening learning environment in which otherwise dry, challenging research concepts can become more comprehensible. The element of novelty and fun inherent in the technique diminishes student resistance, engages interest, and enhances research competence.

Technology required: clickers; software: PowerPoint or other presentation software

Editors' variations: There are now smartphone apps that provide clickers for free, so these could be used in place of actual clickers (search for "clicker apps for classroom"). This assignment could be used in any class where core concepts could be displayed in a question/answer format through slides. Similarly, this could be used in a fully online classroom in a synchronous session if smartphone clicker apps were employed. Though smartphones do provide clicker technology free of charge, not all students have access to smartphones or smartphones with sufficient space to download the app.

Level of technology integration (SAMR model): Augmentation

THEORETICAL CONSTRUCTS AND MEASURES (RESEARCH)

Editors' introduction: This assignment allows students to apply knowledge about measurement constructs while connecting to an online, professional, collaborative community, as well as giving them access to a great resource for assessment measures.

Authors' name and contact: Nurit Fischer-Shemer, University at Buffalo, nf24@buffalo.edu; and Heather Orom, University at Buffalo, horom@buffalo.edu

Approximate prep time for faculty: 3 hours

Average assignment time for students: 10 hours

CSWE competencies addressed: 4, 7, and 9

Learning objectives: After completing this assignment, students will be able to

- understand theoretical constructs in behavioral science, their definitions, and their associated theoretical foundation, and how they are assessed, along with advantages and disadvantages of using these assessment approaches;
- become involved in building a cumulative base of knowledge about theory and measurement by contributing and updating existing information in the Grid-Enabled Measures (GEM) Database; and
- access and share useful information and evaluation of evidence-based assessment tools used in behavioral science with a virtual community of scholars.

Assignment description: This assignment will (a) familiarize you with Grid-Enabled Measures (GEM) Database, a collaborative website where behavioral, social science, and other scientific construct and measures are compiled and organized with contributions from experts in the field; and (b) increase your knowledge and understanding of theoretical constructs and associated measures used within your area of interest. The assignment has three parts.

Part 1. Visit the GEM website "About GEM: Grid-Enabled Measures Database," at https://www.gem-measures.org/public/About.aspx. Watch the Informational video by Richard P. Moser, PhD, and familiarize yourself with the site.

Part 2. Go to the database site (http://www.gem-measures.org/Public/Home.aspx) and register as a user (top right-hand corner of this page). GEM contains structures and associated measures. For this part of the assignment, please spend some time exploring the kinds of constructs that are included in the database. You may want to focus on constructs that are relevant to your practice or research area of interest. Choose four constructs (preferably constructs that are lacking a full description in the GEM database), and in a Word document, using APA table format, complete entries for the five categories (Definition, Related Content Areas, Theoretical Foundation, Similar Constructs, and Keywords). For the Theoretical Foundation heading, try to list only those theories that include the constructs as part of their framework. Add any references below each table. In addition to the four constructs, choose one more measure. In your own words, summarize (for up to two measures) the available information on that measure (including references, characteristics, and history). Suggest a title for a study you might conduct using one of the measures. Submit the document to your instructor. Your instructor will provide you with feedback that you can use to fine-tune your contribution for GEM. After your entries have been approved you will upload all your information to the GEM site.

Part 3. Go to the workspace in the site and familiarize yourself with it. In a Word document, suggest a topic in social work for a new workspace and describe it (at least 100 words). This document will be handed in to your instructor.

Notes for instructor: GEM is an interactive website containing behavioral, social science, and other scientific measures organized by theoretical constructs. GEM enables researchers to collaborate with others, encourages using common measures, and facilitates sharing harmonized data (National Cancer Institute, n.d.).

Technology required: computer, tablet, and/or smartphone; website: Grid-Enabled Measures (GEM) Database

Editors' variations: This assignment could be adapted to a practice class where students are asked to consider evaluating the use of identified measures in practice.

Level of technology integration (SAMR model): Redefinition

SCREENCASTS OF USING LIBRARY DATABASES FOR LITERATURE REVIEWS (RESEARCH)

Editors' introduction: This assignment asks students to create screencasts to introduce themselves and also to capture their search strategy for each type of research study on which the course focuses.

Author's name and contact: Christine McKenna Lok, @altSWtxtbks

Approximate prep time for faculty: 2 hours

Average assignment time for students: 2 hours

CSWE competencies addressed: 2, 4, and 9

Learning objectives: After completing this assignment, students will be able to

- describe their strategies for using the college library databases to find relevant journal articles;
- evaluate the strength of the research designs in journal articles; and
- identify which subsets of the population are represented (or not) in the study.

Assignment description: The goals of this assignment are to (a) help you become more efficient with your searches of the Internet, in general, and library databases in particular; and (b) find compelling examples in your desired area of practice for each of the research methods we will study this semester. What is a screencast? Even if you do not recognize the term, you most likely have watched a screencast. It is a video that allows you to watch what is happening on someone's computer screen while the video's creator explains and demonstrates the steps involved in a task, such as attaching a file to an e-mail or changing your privacy settings on Instagram.

Introduction. Create a 10-minute screencast in which you walk us through approximately 5 to 10 of your photos (perhaps in a PowerPoint presentation you have assembled) and tell us the stories behind the pictures. Your job is to help us get to know you while you practice the software. Upload your video in a message to the course discussion board. Before the following class, watch the screencasts of at least two classmates you do not know well.

Research Method of the Day. You will be completing several specific literature searches during the semester as you develop your final project, an Institutional Review Board application form for original research that could be completed in one semester. The form asks you to summarize research on your topic that has been done in the past and to describe how those studies have shaped your proposal. To prepare you to write that section of the form, you are to search for at least one peer-reviewed journal article on your topic for each research design covered in the course. You will be creating one 15-minute screencast for each research method that we are discussing. The 15-minute screencast will be your efforts to find peer-reviewed journal articles that demonstrate the research method we are discussing. You must search using the library database. Each screencast is due on the first day we will be discussing each method: (1) survey; (2) experiment; (3) program evaluation; (4) ethnography *or* "case study" *or* "life history"; (5) focus group; (6) participatory action research; and (7) content analysis of documents, images, case files, or other available records not created by the researchers' own effort (e.g., not transcripts of interviews done by the researcher) or secondary analysis of large-scale survey data or historical analysis.

Notes for instructor: Through the assignment, I saw how frustrating it was for students who had not mastered the search strategies taught at the start of the course. By the end of the semester, students were generally working more quickly and better able to pinpoint what made some articles more useful than others. End-of-semester surveys showed greater confidence in finding Internet and other information sources. Grading was time consuming but less so than when students were submitting written summaries of peer-reviewed journal articles they had found. I simply kept a Word document open alongside the video to write brief notes to each student, stopping the video while I jotted down suggestions, and then cut and pasted those notes into our learning management system grading feature.

Technology required: computer, tablet, or smartphone; software: screen capturing

Editors' variations: Screencasts can be valuable assignments for any assignment where how something is accomplished needs to be shown. Search strategies would be helpful to capture to illustrate finding community resources, or for illustrating fact checking or assessing the trustworthiness of digital sources (i.e., "crap detection"; see Chapter 2 about digital literacy).

Level of technology integration (SAMR model): Augmentation

SKEWED? ANALYZING STATISTICS IN THE POPULAR NEWS MEDIA (RESEARCH)

Editors' introduction: This class activity has students searching for a news article, evaluating the credibility of the article based on a framework, and sharing their findings in class.

Author's name and contact: Lauren B. McInroy, University of Toronto, lauren.mcinroy@mail.utoronto.ca

Approximate prep time for faculty: 30 minutes

Average assignment time for students: 1 hour

CSWE competencies addressed: 4

Learning objectives: After completing this assignment, students will be able to

- efficiently complete a general online search for information on a topic relevant to social work practice;

- effectively assess the use, quality, and accuracy of research statistics in popular news media; and
- articulately discuss researching a topic or population relevant to social work practice.

Assignment description: Once social work practitioners are in the field, much of their knowledge on contemporary social issues and current research come from online resources and news. It is important to learn how to evaluate this content critically to ensure research-informed practice. The purpose of this assignment is to effectively assess research statistics in popular news media, as well as the quality and accuracy, on a topic or population relevant to social work practice.

Additionally, this assignment is intended to encourage participation in a professional capacity in public discourses. This in-class activity is completed in pairs and comprised of three steps. Please read the instructions carefully. All three components are completed in class (including the search for the news article).

Component 1. Do an Internet search for a recent news article on a population or topic of your choice using research statistics. The topic or population should be relevant to social work. Hint 1: Use the News tab, rather than the Web tab, for your search to pull up recent articles. Hint 2: Include the word *statistics* in your search (e.g., "homelessness + statistics" or "older adults + statistics"). Ideally, the news article your pair selects should have been published in the last year. If you are having trouble finding an article that is appropriate, ask the instructor for assistance.

Component 2. Evaluate the article using the following framework:

  (a) What are the search terms used to find the article?

  (b) What is the title of the article?

  (c) When was the article published?

(d) What is the source of the article (e.g., name of newspaper, magazine, or blog)?

(e) Do you know anything about the source? Does the source seem neutral or partisan? How do you know?

(f) What is the article's main argument?

(g) How does the article use research to support its arguments?

(h) What study, studies, or research does the article reference? What information is provided about those studies and about those studies' methodologies (e.g., sample, location, population, and method)

(i) What is your assessment of the research in the article? (e.g., Are the statistics used relevant to the topic of the article? Do the statistics seem to be used in an accurate/ethical way? Are the statistics and their sources adequately explained?)

Component 3. As a class we will discuss your findings. Each pair gets 2 minutes to share their findings, and then the instructor will facilitate a larger class discussion. Be sure to hand in your framework at the end of class for completion marks.

Notes for instructor: The instructor may want to have links to a few suitable articles ready on a number of topics in case some groups are unable to find an appropriate article to evaluate. If you are concerned about time, you may ask students to search for the article between classes and bring it to class to complete Component 2 and 3 of the assignment. You may decide to format the framework as a handout that students can fill in as they work in pairs. This activity and its expectations can be adapted to be appropriate for both undergraduate and graduate students.

Technology required: computer, tablet, or smartphone; software: Web browser

Editors' variations: This exercise could be used in any social work class, assuming students have already had a research methods class. It could be modified to incorporate more "crap detection" strategies discussed in Chapter 2. It also could be adapted to a fully online classroom with either synchronous sharing or sharing through blog posts, discussion boards, or multimedia presentations.

Level of technology integration (SAMR model): Substitution

GIS EXPLORATION FOR COMMUNITY ASSESSMENT (RESEARCH)

Editors' introduction: Geographic information system (GIS) software allows students to create sophisticated maps highlighting community problems such as poverty rates and the location of social service agencies. This assignment shows how GIS can be used by students for organizational outcomes.

Author's name and contact: Kelly L. Patterson, University at Buffalo, klp27@buffalo.edu

Approximate prep time for faculty: 10 hours

Average assignment time for students: 16–20 hours

CSWE competencies addressed: 1, 4, 7, and 9

Learning objectives: By the end of this assignment, students will be able to

- construct maps using GIS technology for communicating information to diverse audiences;

- interpret and describe map results to a nontechnical audience; and
- develop an agency PowerPoint presentation displaying, describing, and interpreting created maps.

Assignment description: This assignment explores different uses of GIS and spatial analysis within social work. Specifically, students learn how GIS can be used by practitioners to visually map data such as the prevalence of lead contamination in the surrounding neighborhood, the location of subsidized housing in their service area, or the proximity of services to their clients. This information can enable practitioners to integrate neighborhood information in direct service provision. Additionally, it can help them plan interventions and evaluate services. There are four parts to this assignment:

1. Choose a database. There are three different agency folders that contain information about the agency and a specific issue they are working on, including the questions they believe could be answered through mapping. The agency data that you will need to create your maps is also located in the folders. Look through the folders, read over the information, and choose an agency you would like to use.

2. Geocode the data. Each folder contains an address database for you to create your maps. The data has already been formatted so that the GIS software can process it. You must geocode the data so that address locations can be placed as points on a map and analyzed with other spatial data. You also need a GIS data layer that you will use as the geographic reference layer, for example, a city's street center-lines layer. A street file is also included in each folder.

3. Join the data to current census data. You will join the address data with census tract data so you will be able to show and discuss the neighborhood characteristics of the agency data.

Make sure you use the most current American Community Survey 5-year estimates.

4. Create maps based on what the agency is looking for. Develop a Microsoft PowerPoint presentation with the maps to present to the agency. Write up a description of each map that includes an interpretation of what each map reveals about the agency's data. The presentation should include an explanation of how mapping the data was useful in answering the agency's questions and how seeing the data visually can potentially help practitioners identify troublesome patterns, make referrals, target services, and so forth.

Notes for instructor: Instructors need to create agency databases for student use. These can be invented or based on real examples from community partners. The following information will be needed from each agency: a concise description of the problem, an explanation of what information they are looking for, and the administrative data they want mapped. This assignment uses ArcGIS software (available on some campuses free for students, available in campus computer labs, and available as a 180-day free trial version with textbook). Instructors should practice with the software on their own and consider enlisting the help of campus partners such as the digital media lab staff.

Technology required: computer; software: geographic information system

Editors' variations: Students could create maps for almost any assignment that focuses on a community or organization. Examples might include mapping their practicum agency's community prior to field placement, mapping their own community and comparing to state-level or national-level data, or mapping changes over time in a community.

Level of technology integration (SAMR model): Redefinition

TEACHING SOCIAL WORK WITH DIGITAL TECHNOLOGY

DESIGNING, DEVELOPING, AND DELIVERING AN ONLINE SURVEY (RESEARCH)

Editors' introduction: Students use this assignment to evaluate and then create an online survey. After classmates take the survey, they write up the methods and results in a brief research paper. This offers exposure to several skills, including survey development, analysis, and reporting research.

Author's name and contact: Sarah Serbinski, University of Western Ontario, sarah@serbinski.com

Approximate prep time for faculty: 5 hours

Average assignment time for students: 15–20 hours

CSWE competencies addressed: 1, 2, 4, and 5

Learning objectives: By the end of this assignment, students will be able to

- evaluate the strengths and weaknesses of online research surveys within the human service sector;
- develop a user-friendly online survey that answers key research questions, builds on current social work knowledge, and adheres to current laws, policies, and practices; and
- discuss and disseminate research findings to individuals, groups, organizations, and communities.

Assignment description: The purpose of this assignment is to help students practice their skills related to survey design, development, delivery, data analysis, and dissemination of research while using online survey technology. The assignment has four parts:
Part 1. Review an online survey. You will select and review one

nonmarketing online survey. Please have your survey preapproved by the instructor. Then, you will write an analysis about the survey's objective, target sample, consent process, types of questions asked, and how participants can access the survey findings. Also include your thoughts/feelings on how this survey engages diverse and different participants, how it complies with current laws and policies, and how this online survey can build or hinder knowledge development.

Part 2. Design and develop an online survey. Create an online survey with 15 to 20 questions on a social issue important to you. The survey should include key elements discussed within class, including what the survey is about, what is involved for the participants, confidentiality, risks/benefits, compensation, and what happens with the results. For learning purposes, the last two questions you must include are, What was good about this survey? And what was not good about this survey? Your survey will need to be submitted as a PDF format file to the instructor.

Part 3. Complete three to five surveys from fellow classmates. Once approved by the instructor, you will e-mail your survey link to three to five classmates for them to complete online. You will also be asked to complete the surveys that have been e-mailed to you by your classmates.

Part 4. Conduct data analysis and report writing on survey findings. Once classmates have completed your online survey, you will analyze your findings. Due to the small sample size, you will not be required to use any online data management software for qualitative or quantitative data analysis. However, if you would like to experiment with it, you can. In a final research report, you will include title page, table of contents, background and literature review, methods, results of survey, discussion, concluding remarks, and references. As an appendix, write a three-page, double-spaced self-reflection on your experience in designing, developing, and delivering a survey to participants. Consider: What have you learned from the online survey process? How can you create a diverse and inclusive survey? Do the current laws and policies help or hinder your research process? What are the benefits and weaknesses of your online survey? How will you use online surveys within your social work practice? Your final report will need to be submitted in a PDF format file to the instructor.

Notes for instructor: Designing an online survey can be lots of fun! To learn how, you can use the free tutorials provided with your selected survey software, partner with your technology department, or consider inviting a computer science student to provide tutoring. Free survey software such as SurveyMonkey is available online, or your institution may subscribe to a survey product such as Qualtrics. Many surveys are available to view online.

Technology required: computer, tablet, and/or smartphone; software: online survey development

Editors' variations: The use of online surveys could be applied to a wide range of other classes if students are charged with gathering feedback about projects that they have created.

Level of technology integration (SAMR model): Augmentation

USING SMARTPHONES TO ACCESS AND EXPLORE CENSUS DATA (RESEARCH)

Editors' introduction: This class activity asks students to download the U.S. Census Bureau app, fill out their neighborhood preferences, and then discuss their reactions to the exercise.

Author's name and contact: Karen Zgoda, University of Massachusetts Boston, karen@karenzgoda.org

Approximate prep time for faculty: 5 minutes

Average assignment time for students: 1 hour

CSWE competencies addressed: 4

Learning objectives: After completing this assignment, students will be able to

- retrieve available census location data using a smartphone;
- compare and contrast findings with other students; and
- identify and critique the strengths and limitations of using available/secondary data for research.

Assignment description: For this classroom activity, students are encouraged to use their smartphones. We are going to explore the advantages and disadvantages of using secondary or available data. In addition, you will learn how to access location-based demographic data quickly for upcoming assignments in this and other courses. Download the Dwellr app from either Google Play or the iTunes to access and use neighborhood census data. Once the app is downloaded, you will be asked a series of questions about your personal lifestyle preferences to discover your ideal neighborhood. You can even tailor the results further by using the slider bars to express stronger preferences. This should take about five minutes to complete.

After you are finished, you will be given a list of top places you should live. Do you agree with the results? Were you surprised by the recommendations? Why/why not? Check in with a classmate sitting near you. What did your classmate learn from the app? To learn more about another specific location, tap the compass button on the bottom of the screen. You can now check neighborhood data for your current location, or type in a city/town name to learn about another location. For group discussion: What was your experience like using this app? Would you use it again? Would you recommend it to others? Why/why not? What did you learn about using secondary or available data?

Notes for instructor: This classroom activity takes advantage of the smartphone more and more students are bringing with them to class and provides students with a valuable opportunity to use it for educational and research purposes. It typically takes 30–45 minutes to complete the activity. Students may use the U.S. Census Bureau's website if a smartphone not available, and this often adds complexity and resource-sharing to the classroom discussion. I have used this activity with both BSW and MSW students with positive feedback. Students have commented that they enjoy the activity and learning how to use their technology devices in a new way, agreeing or disagreeing with the recommendations (which leads to great discussion about strengths and limits of available data), and like having a new, convenient resource for accessing data to use for their assignments in their courses.

Technology required: tablet or smartphone; software: Dwellr app

Editors' variations: This activity could be easily adapted to a fully online classroom with students posting results to discussion boards and responding to each other's posts. In addition, for a practice class, students could be asked to consider if this app might be useful to clients and, if so, to discuss how they would introduce it to clients, as well as how they would discuss the results with clients. These scenarios could then be role-played.

Level of technology integration (SAMR model): Redefinition

References

Smyth, N. J. (0000, March 00). *Virtual worlds as immersive treatment settings: The PTSD sim* [Blog post]. Retrieved from https://njsmyth.wordpress.com/0000/00/00/virtual-worlds-as-immersive-treatment-settings-the-ptsd-sim/

National Cancer Institute. (n.d.). *Gem: Grid-enabled measures database.* Retrieved from https://www.gem-beta.org/public/Home.aspx?cat=0

APPENDIX 2

TECHNOLOGY-BASED LEARNING TASK LIST FOR SOCIAL WORK EDUCATION

Learning Tasks from this list are Licensed under a Creative Commons Attribution-NonCommercial-ShareAlike 4.0 International License. Contact Laurel Hitchcock (lihitch@uab.edu), Melanie Sage, or Nancy Smyth for questions.

Using the Council on Social Work Education's (CSWE) social work competencies from the 2015 Educational Policy and Accreditation Standards, this list provides example assignments and learning tasks that can be incorporated into social work courses, especially field education. For each task students should be directed to share their work with their class, seminar, or practicum field instructor. For assessment purposes learning tasks are grouped by competency and component behaviors and labeled with the relevant competency dimensions using the following key: K=Knowledge, V=Values, S=Skills, and CA=Cognitive and Affective Processes.

Competency 1: Demonstrate Ethical and Professional Behavior
Behavior 1: Make ethical decisions by applying the standards of the NASW Code of Ethics, relevant laws and regulations, models for ethical decision-making, ethical conduct of research, and additional codes of ethics as appropriate to context.

Technology-Based Learning Tasks
1. Be familiar with ethical standards that address dilemmas related to the use of digital and social technology in social work (such as the Association of Social Work Boards Model Regulatory Standards for Technology, NASW Standards for Technology in Social Work Practice, and NASW Code of Ethics). Write up a case study of one possible ethical dilemma with technology in practice. (K, V)
2. Locate and review policies and regulations that oversee the use of digital technology at one's practicum agency or learning institution. Assess whether the policies provide guidance related to use of social media or Internet searches of clients. Create a list of these policies and policy gaps. (K, S, CA)
3. Recognize that federal, state, local, and agency regulations and policies that govern the use of digital technology and be familiar with how to locate and review such policies when needed. Create a list of these policies. (K)

Behavior 2: Use reflection and self-regulation to manage personal values and maintain professionalism in practice situations.
Technology-Based Learning Tasks
1. Search for information about yourself on the Internet, including websites, social media accounts, and other online resources Review the content, including words and images, for quantity, quality, and accuracy. Write down your findings in a brief 300-word reflection. (S, CA)[1]
2. Write a personal digital and social technology policy that reflects your professional use of social and digital technologies

---

1. This task was adapted from the Association of Social Work Boards' 2015 *Model Regulatory Standards for Technology and Social Work Practice*, available at https://www.aswb.org/wp-content/uploads/2015/03/ASWB-Model-Regulatory-Standards-for-Technology-and-Social-Work-Practice.pdf.

in social work practice that could be shared with a client to let them know how to contact you and detailing your policies about use of technology with clients. (K, S, V, CA)
3. Conduct an audit of your personal and professional social media accounts by creating a spreadsheet that lists all your accounts and describes your profile and your activity with each account. Include your assessment of what a client or prospective employer might conclude about you if they viewed accounts associated with your name. (K, S, CA)

Behavior 3: Demonstrate professional demeanor in behavior; appearance; and oral, written, and electronic communication.
Technology-Based Learning Tasks
1. Create a handout that describes the benefits and challenges related to electronic communication with client systems and colleagues such as e-mail, text messaging, video conferencing, mobile phone calls, and social media. Include resources that social workers can use for professional decision-making. (K, S, CA)[1]
2. Describe and/or record examples of appropriate electronic communication between a practitioner and a client or colleague using various technologies such as e-mail, text messaging, video conferencing, mobile phone calls, and social media. (K, V, CA)[1]
3. Create and compare multimedia examples of appropriate and inappropriate electronic communications between a practitioner and a client or colleague using various technologies. (K, S, CA)
4. Review the Netiquette website (http://www.albion.com/netiquette/) and create a list of professional electronic communication tips for yourself and your practicum agency. (K, S, CA)

Behavior 4: Use technology ethically and appropriately to facilitate practice outcomes.

Technology-Based Learning Tasks

1. Create a professional social media profile on a social media site such as Twitter, LinkedIn, or Facebook. Connect with other professionals and share resources. (K, S, CA)
2. Develop and implement an online support group to be used in an online chat format for clients at your practicum agency. Ensure that you have appropriate permissions, are following all applicable polices and laws, and that clients know risks and benefits. (K, S, V, CA)
3. Using data from the U.S. Census Bureau, create a digital map about the community where you live or where your practicum agency is located. (K, S, CA)
4. Develop a local agency resource list on a wiki site that can be edited by other students or practitioners. (K, S, CA)

Behavior 5: Use supervision and consultation to guide professional judgment and behavior.

Technology-Based Learning Tasks

1. Identify and establish rapport with instructors, colleagues, or supervisors in your learning environment who have relevant expertise with digital technology. (S, CA)
2. Write brief case studies for at least three situations in which you might need to seek consultation from an instructor, supervisor, or colleague about digital technology in social work practice. (K, V, CA)
3. Discuss a case scenario with your instructor about an ethical conflict related to social media, such as when a client sends a friend request. Discuss potential responses, the risks and benefits of each, and which ethical standards inform your decision. (K, V, CA)

Competency 2: Engage Diversity and Difference in Practice

Behavior 1: Apply and communicate understanding of the importance of diversity and difference in shaping life experiences in practice at the micro, mezzo, and macro levels.

Technology-Based Learning Tasks

1. Create a digital slideshow presentation that describes and compares how mobile phones are used in different parts of the world. Upload the presentation to a slide-sharing website. (K, S)
2. Develop a list of hashtags used by a specific population served by your practicum agency, such as LGTBQ youths or Black Americans, and explain the context of each hashtag in a blog post. (K, S, V)
3. Assemble a list of best practices for interprofessional teams working in virtual spaces, including collaborative writing spaces (wikis, Dropbox), video conferencing (Skype or Zoom), and digital to-do-lists (ToDoist or Wunderlist). (K, S, CA)

Behavior 2: Present themselves as learners and engage clients and constituencies as experts of their own experiences.

Technology-Based Learning Tasks

1. Develop a digital professional learning network and present it to a class or group of your colleagues. Identify the strategies you used to develop the network in a written self-reflection. (S, V, CA)
2. Curate a list of Web-based hyperlinks relevant to understanding cultures served by your practicum organization. Alternatively, curate similar resources with a Pinterest board. (K, S, CA)[2]

---

[2] This task was adapted from Ellen Belluomini's blog, *Bridging the Digital Divide in Social Work Practice*, available at http://socialworksdigitaldivide.blogspot.com/.

3. Ask a client to create a curated digital compilation on a site such as Tumblr or Pinterest of things that make them feel positive. Review the compilation together, and let the client explain the meanings. (K, S, CA)

Behavior 3: Apply self-awareness and self-regulation to manage the influence of personal biases and values in working with diverse clients and constituencies.

Technology-Based Learning Tasks
1. Locate and complete a survey that assesses your skill level with social and digital technology. Write a 300-word self-reflection about what you learned. (K, CA)
2. Interview an older adult about digital technology and their use of technology. Write a paper comparing their use of technology with your own. (K, V, CA)
3. Search for information about e-mail etiquette in professional settings and create a best-practices list for social workers at your practicum agency. Complete a short reflection paper on how your preassignment e-mail etiquette measures up to the best practices. Identify changes you think you need to make. (K, S, V, CA)

Competency 3: Advance Human Rights and Social, Economic, and Environmental Justice

Behavior 1: Apply their understanding of social, economic, and environmental justice to advocate for human rights at the individual and system levels.

Technology-Based Learning Tasks
1. Read about digital rights in sources such as Electronic Frontier Foundation's website (https://www.eff.org) or Ranking Digital Rights (https://rankingdigitalrights.org/) and write a

750-word blog post about digital rights for a client population served by your practicum agency. (K, CA)
2. Curate a reading list (at least 10 items) about digital rights that can be used by other social workers with the bookmarking program Diigo, providing a description and tag for each item. (K, S)
3. Search the Internet for information about human rights and access to the Internet in your community and in the United States. Create a digital story comparing the locations using Storify. (K, S, V)
4. Choose a specific client population and describe five ways that social media can be used as an advocacy tool for each one. Give an example of current efforts to use social media for advocacy for this population. (K, S, V)

Behavior 2: Engage in practices that advance social, economic, and environmental justice.
Technology-Based Learning Tasks
1. Find your local, state, and federal elected officials online and send them an e-mail in support of or against legislation affecting a population of interest to you.[2] (K, S)
2. Read about technology-enhanced advocacy tools such as online petition and fundraising websites, digital storying, and/or photovoice. Write a memo to your practicum supervisor describing and recommending one tool for your practicum agency. (K, CA)[3]
3. Plan, implement, and evaluate an educational group for clients or workers at your practicum agency, informing

---

[3]. This task was adapted from the American Academy of Social Work & Social Welfare's report titled "Practice Innovation Through Technology in the Digital Age," available at http://aaswsw.org/wp-content/uploads/2013/10/Practice-Innovation-through-Technology-in-the-Digital-Age-A-Grand-Challenge-for-Social-Work-GC-Working-Paper-No-12.pdf.

them about digital rights such as privacy with electronic data, open access, and transparency. (K, S, CA)

Competency 4: Engage in Practice-Informed Research and Research-Informed Practice

Behavior 1: Use practice experience and theory to inform scientific inquiry and research.
Technology-Based Learning Tasks
1. Use Google Forms to create a survey that answers a research question based on your practicum experience (e.g., What do social workers at my agency know about using technology in practice?). (K, S, V, CA)
2. Identify a technology-use problem experienced by a client at your practicum agency and develop a single-system research study to address the problem. (K, S, CA)
3. Identify a technology-use research question based on a problem experienced by the staff at your practicum agency and design a research study to answer the question. (K, S, CA)

Behavior 2: Apply critical thinking to engage in analysis of quantitative and qualitative research methods and research findings.
Technology-Based Learning Tasks
1. Use Google Spreadsheets to analyze the data from a survey that you created. Use descriptive and inferential statistical formulas. (K, S)
2. Conduct a focus group with clients about your agency's website and then analyze the results in a report for your supervisor. (K, S, CA)
3. Review and create a list of free survey tools to share with other social workers at your practicum agency. (K, S, CA)

4. Complete an online institutional review board training and reflect on how issues of privacy, informed consent, and confidentiality apply to online surveys. (K, V, CA)

Behavior 3: Use and translate research evidence to inform and improve practice, policy, and service delivery.
Technology-Based Learning Tasks
1. Conduct a literature search on a technology topic that affects social service agencies in your community (or at your practicum agency). Compile an annotated reading list using Pocket, Instapaper, or another save-for-later reading platform. (K, S)
2. Review the website Information for Practice (http://ifp.nyu.edu/). Write a 750-word blog post about how social workers at your agency could use the website as part of practice. (K, S)
3. Create an infographic about an evidence-based intervention targeting elected officials or key decision makers in your local community (e.g., best interventions to prevent electronic aggression in adolescents for the local school board). (K, S, CA)

Competency 5: Engage in Policy Practice

Behavior 1: Identify social policy at the local, state, and federal level that affects well-being, service delivery, and access to social services.
Technology-Based Learning Tasks
1. Read about Section 508 of the Rehabilitation Act of 1973 (https://www.access-board.gov/guidelines-and-standards/communications-and-it/about-the-section-508-standards/section-508-standards), which requires that all website content be accessible to people with disabilities. Review your agency's website for compliance with one of the checklists from the U.S. Department of Health & Human Services

(http://www.hhs.gov/web/section-508/making-files-accessible/checklist/index.html). (K, S)
2. Create a public service announcement video about a local or state policy that affects social service agencies in your community. Post it on a video-sharing website such as YouTube or Vimeo. (K, S, CA)
3. Attend a local advocacy conference or event in your community. Record audio interviews with attendees and sounds at the event for a podcast about the conference. (K, S, CA)
4. Develop a list of online policy resources from your local and state governments and the federal government (e.g., the US Government Printing Office website (https://www.gpo.gov/)). (K, S)

Behavior 2: Assess how social welfare and economic policies affect the delivery of and access to social services.
Technology-Based Learning Tasks
1. Search the Internet for current local, state, and national policies related to cyberbullying. Write a 750-word blog post that informs social workers in your community about those policies. (K, S, V)
2. Create a Twitter list of national and state advocacy and policy-based agencies focused on issues affecting clients at your practicum agency. (K, S, CA)
3. Select a social policy that affects clients at your agency. Write about that policy for a public audience in a Web-based media platform such as a local newspaper or the blog of a state-wide advocacy agency. (K, S, V)

Behavior 3: Apply critical thinking to analyze, formulate, and advocate for policies that advance human rights and social, economic, and environmental justice.
Technology-Based Learning Tasks

1. Read the blog post "Social Media: What Is the Policy Where You Work?" by Ellen Belluomini and then analyze your practicum agency's social media policy. (K, S, CA)
2. Review and analyze at least 10 social media policies from nonprofit or governmental agencies from the Social Media Policy Database (http://socialmediagovernance.com/policies/). Create a list of best practices for your practicum agency. Consider how these practices would affect clients, employees, and community constituents before sharing with your supervisor. (K, S, V)
3. Create a video about a human rights issue specific to your community that will inform social workers. Post it on YouTube. (K, S, V)
4. Create a podcast about a current social problem affecting your practicum agency or community that advocates for a system-wide change (i.e., take a stand on a social problem and try to persuade your audience). (K, S, V)

Competency 6: Engage With Individuals, Families, Groups, Organizations, and Communities

Behavior 1: Apply knowledge of human behavior and the social environment, person-in-environment, and other multidisciplinary theoretical frameworks to engage with clients and constituencies.
Technology-Based Learning Tasks
1. Listen to a podcast about technology and social work and write a review of it. (K, CA)
2. Using the Pew Research Center's website (http://www.pewresearch.org/), search for information about the use of technology in the United States based on age, race, gender, SES, etc. Create a one-page digital handout for the staff at your practicum agency focused on one of the populations served by the agency. (K, S, V)

3. Create a digital list of articles, videos, and/or blog posts about how social workers at your practicum agency can best use social media to engage with clients or communities served by the agency. (K, S)
4. Develop a list of questions for clients at your agency about their digital communication preferences, such as e-mail, texting, and video conferencing, that can be used on a referral questionnaire form or during the first session with a client. (K, S)
5. Interview three or four parents about their challenges in digital parenting, that is, parenting children on issues related to children's use of technology. Next, research the best practices for parents for digital parenting issues. Create some type of digital resource (e.g., slide show, video, infographic) to share digital parenting resources and tips for parents and share it on a public site as well as with the parents you interviewed. (K, S, CA)

Behavior 2: Use empathy, reflection, and interpersonal skills to effectively engage diverse clients and constituencies.
Technology-Based Learning Tasks
1. Participate in a live Twitter chat with other social workers or professionals about a topic of interest to you (e.g., #MacroSW). (K, S)
2. After writing your own professional social media policy, practice discussing it with clients at your agency as part of your informed consent process. (K, S, V, CA)
3. Create a video that informs social workers about best practices for verbal and nonverbal communication with a client via a face-to-face video conference call. (K, S)

Competency 7: Assess Individuals, Families, Groups, Organizations, and Communities

Behavior 1: Collect and organize data and apply critical thinking to interpret information from clients and constituencies.
Technology-Based Learning Tasks
1. Create a list of questions that could be used to assess whether a client's needs could be met with services provided electronically. (K, S)
2. Create a technology ecomap with a client or family by asking about how they use technology or experience technology, including positive and negative impacts of technology in their lives. (K, S, V)
3. Create an instrument to help families self-assess the use of digital devices and screen time. (K, S, V)
4. Read "Big Data's Impact on Social Services" (Getz, 2014) and then formulate two or three research questions that could be answered from mining data at your practicum agency. (K, CA)
5. Collect data about poverty from the U.S. Census Bureau website (https://www.census.gov/) and use it to create a digital map showing how poverty is distributed across your state. (K, S, CA)

Behavior 2: Apply knowledge of human behavior and the social environment, person-in-environment, and other multidisciplinary theoretical frameworks in the analysis of assessment data from clients and constituencies.
Technology-Based Learning Tasks
1. Locate, assess and curate a list of websites that will inform and empower a special population group (such as people with disabilities, New Americans, etc). (K, S)[2]
2. Read "A Digital Environment Approach: Four Technologies That Will Disrupt Social Work Practice" (Goldkind

& Wolf, 2015). Create an infographic on how these four trends could affect your practicum agency. (K, S, CA)
3. Using a wiki, draft a list of questions that assess cultural, environmental, and linguistic issues related to digital and social technologies that social workers could ask clients or constituents from your practicum agency. Share with other social workers at your agency, asking for comments and additional questions. (K, S, CA)[1]

Behavior 3: Develop mutually approved intervention goals and objectives based on the critical assessment of strengths, needs, and challenges in clients and constituencies.
Technology-Based Learning Tasks
1. Create a list of smartphone apps that can be used to monitor emotions and moods and then write goals and objectives that could be used in a treatment plan for clients at your agency. (K, S)
2. Develop a work plan for your practicum agency to establish and maintain a social media account such as Facebook, Twitter, or Instagram that will inform clients and the community about the agency. (K, S)
3. Research texting programs such as Text for Baby (https://www.text4baby.org/) and write a summary for your practicum supervisor about how the program could be worked into case plans at your agency. (K, S, CA)

Behavior 4: Select appropriate intervention strategies based on the assessment, research knowledge, and values and preferences of clients and constituencies.
Technology-Based Learning Tasks
1. Read about gamification/gaming as a practice intervention and identify client populations at your agency that might benefit from a gaming intervention. (K, V)

2. Create a 1-hour slideshow presentation for the staff at your practicum agency about Internet safety. Share these slides using a free Web-based slide-sharing program. (K, S, V)
3. Review two or three mental health apps for use with clients at your practicum agency. Present your findings to your field supervisor. (K, S, V)
4. Using the Social Media Policy Database (http://socialmediagovernance.com/policies/), create a draft social media policy for your agency and share it with your supervisor and three other employees at your practicum agency for feedback. Write a report for your supervisor that discusses how you used the tool, your policy, and the feedback from others about the policy. (K, S, V, CA)

Competency 8: Intervene With Individuals, Families, Groups, Organizations, and Communities

Behavior 1: Critically choose and implement interventions to achieve practice goals and enhance capacities of clients and constituencies.
Technology-Based Learning Tasks
1. Work with a client or family from your practicum agency to develop a family media use plan that outlines screen time, the use of the Internet, and media exposure. (K, S)
2. Review two or three collaborative work space applications such as Loomio or Slack, and write a report recommending one application for use at your practicum agency, along with the potential benefits and risks. (K, S)
3. Write a proposal that incorporates best practices for a private Facebook group for a client population at your agency. (K, S, CA)

Behavior 2: Apply knowledge of human behavior and the social environment, person-in-environment, and other multidisciplinary theoretical frameworks in interventions with clients and constituencies.
Technology-Based Learning Tasks
1. Develop and facilitate a live Twitter chat for social workers about a topic relevant to a client population at your agency. (K, S)
2. Search the Internet for human rights websites and identify a call to action that is relevant to clients or populations serviced by your agency. Prepare a response to the call. (K, S, V, CA)
3. Using systems theory, create a list of possible interventions that could be used to address the problem of sexting among adolescents in the United States. (K, S, V)[2]
4. Prepare a staff development presentation about how diversity can influence group interactions in virtual work environments such as a video conference call. (K, S)
5. Using an online database such as PubMed or Google Scholar, research the difference in efficacy of online and in-person mental health therapy for a client population (e.g., children, women, people of color, immigrants). (K, S)

Behavior 3: Use interprofessional collaboration as appropriate to achieve beneficial practice outcomes.
Technology-Based Learning Tasks
1. Use a video conferencing tool to facilitate an interprofessional team meeting at your practicum agency or with different agencies in your community. (K, S, CA)
2. Draft guidelines and instructions for how an interprofessional team can use digital collaboration tools such as Google Docs or a cloud-based document sharing service to complete a report or agency project. (K, S)
3. Practice using three professional collaboration tools such as Doodle, MindMeister, Evernote, or Wunderlist, and then

write a short report about the advantages and disadvantages of each tool. (K, S, CA)

Behavior 4: Negotiate, mediate, and advocate with and on behalf of diverse clients and constituencies.
Technology-Based Learning Tasks
1. Create a document in Google Docs that could be used with caregivers of elderly clients to communicate about the plan of care for the client. (K, S)
2. Develop a resource list for clients about free and low-cost Internet and cell phone access options in your community. (K, S, V)
3. Based on the client population served by your practicum agency, create a list of strengths and limitations for using video conferencing software as a tool for delivering services. (K, S, V)

Behavior 5: Facilitate effective transitions and endings that advance mutually approved goals.
Technology-Based Learning Tasks
1. Design an online after-care group for clients at your agency who will be transitioning out of care, such foster care children who are aging out or children with special health care needs who will be transitioning to adult health-care systems. (K, S)
2. Curate a digital list of resources for your agency's website that could be used by clients or constituencies after the completion of services. (K, S)
3. Create a video that shows examples of effective and ineffective techniques for the last session with a client or group. (K, S, CA)
4. Reflect on your time at your practicum agency and create a digital story that captures your learning and accomplishments that you can share with your practicum instructor and/or supervisor. (V, CA)

Competency 9: Evaluate Practice With Individuals, Families, Groups, Organizations, and Communities

Behavior 1: Select and use appropriate methods for evaluation of outcomes.
Technology-Based Learning Tasks
1. Use an online survey instrument to create a consumer satisfaction survey for your practicum agency. (K, S)
2. Identify and rate different online data resources such as the Kids Count Data Center (http://datacenter.kidscount.org/), County Health Rankings & Road Maps (http://www.countyhealthrankings.org/), or the Center for Enterprise Development's Local Data Locator (http://assetsandopportunity.org/localdata/) that could be used to obtain data about populations served by your agency. Describe the kinds of data available and how they might inform a specific agency. (K, S, CA)
3. Review your agency's client database and assess how it could be used to answer an evaluation question such as where client referrals come from or how many days there are between initial referral and first contact with a client. Present a list of research questions to your practicum supervisor. (K, S, CA)

Behavior 2: Apply knowledge of human behavior and the social environment, person-in-environment, and other multidisciplinary theoretical frameworks in the evaluation of outcomes.
Technology-Based Learning Tasks
1. Create a list of free online digital research tools that could be used by various groups or constituencies in your community, such as a youth, social action, or immigrant group, to conduct a needs assessment. (K, S)
2. Research the advantages and disadvantages of using of online surveys with various clients based on age, race, gender,

and so forth. Create a PowerPoint presentation with your findings. (K, S, V)
3. Develop a digital reading list of articles and research reports that considers the effectiveness of online therapies and other services relevant to the cultural and geographic needs of diverse clients and members of vulnerable populations in your community. (K, S, V)[1]

References

Belluomini, E. (2014, March 17). "Social media: What is the policy where you work?" Retrieved from http://socialworks-digitaldivide.blogspot.com/2014/03/social-media-what-is-policy-where-you.html

Getz, L. (2014). Big data's impact on social services. *Social Work Today*, *14*(2), 28–29. Retrieved from http://www.socialworktoday.com/archive/031714p28.shtml

Goldkind, L., & Wolf, L. (2015). A digital environment approach: Four technologies that will disrupt social work practice. *Social Work*, *60*, 85–87. Retrieved from http://doi.org/10.1093/sw/swu045

APPENDIX 3

TECHNOLOGY IN SOCIAL WORK EDUCATION: EDUCATORS' PERSPECTIVES ON THE NASW TECHNOLOGY STANDARDS FOR SOCIAL WORK EDUCATION AND SUPERVISION

Technology in Social Work Education:
Educators' Perspectives on the NASW Technology Standards for Social Work Education and Supervision

Editors
Laurel Iverson Hitchcock, University of Alabama at Birmingham (lihitch@uab.edu)
Melanie Sage, University at Buffalo (msage@buffalo.edu)
Nancy J. Smyth, University at Buffalo (sw-dean@buffalo.edu)

Copyright Information
Technology in Social Work Education: Educators' Perspectives on the NASW Technology Standards for Social Work Education and Supervision is licensed under a Creative Commons Attribution-NonCommercial-Share with Attribution, No Derivatives International License. The *NASW, ABSW, CSWE, & CSWA Standards for Technology in Social Work Practice* are copyrighted by NASW Press and content from the *Standards* appear in this document as materials under fair use. Contact Laurel Hitchcock (lihitch@uab.edu) with questions.

TABLE OF CONTENTS

Editors 1
Copyright Information 1
Table of Contents 2
Suggested Citation for Blog Post 3
Suggested Citation for Book 3
Contributors 4
Forward 5
Introduction 6
Standard 4.01: Use of Technology in Social Work Education 7
Standard 4.02: Training Social Workers about
    the Use of Technology in Practice 8
Standard 4.03: Continuing Education 9
Standard 4.04: Social Media Policies 10
Standard 4.05: Evaluation 11
Standard 4.06: Technological Disruptions 12
Standard 4.07: Distance Education 13
Standard 4.08: Support 13
Standard 4.09: Maintenance of Academic Standards 14
Standard 4.10: Educator-Student Boundaries 15
Standard 4.11: Field Instruction 16
Standard 4.12: Social Work Supervision 17
References 19
Resources 19

Suggested Citation for Blog Post
Hitchcock, L. I., Sage, M., & Smyth, N. J. (Eds.). (2017, November 30). Technology in social work education: Educators' perspectives on the NASW technology standards for social work education and supervision [blog post]. Retrieved from http://www.laureliverson-hitchcock.org/2017/11/30/technology-in-social-work-education-educators-perspectives-on-the-nasw-technology-standards-for-social-work-education-and-supervision

Suggested Citation for Book
Hitchcock, L. I., Sage, M., & Smyth, N. J. (Eds.). (2018). *Technology in social work education: Educators' perspectives on the NASW technology standards for social work education and supervision.* Buffalo, NY: University at Buffalo School of Social Work, State University of New York.

Contributors
  Becky Anthony, Salisbury University, School of Social Work
  Lisa Baker, University of Alabama at Birmingham, Department of Social Work
  Ellen Belluomini, Brandman University, Department of Social Work
  Shane R. Brady, University of Oklahoma, School of Social Work
  Beth Counselman Carpenter, Columbia University, School of Social Work
  Stephen Cummings, University of Iowa, School of Social Work
  Allison M. Curington, University of Alabama, School of Social Work
  Katherine D. Ferrari, Independent Practitioner
  Ellen Fink-Samnick, George Mason University, Department of Social Work
  Lauri Goldkind, Fordham University, Graduate School of Social Service
  Laurel Iverson Hitchcock, University of Alabama at Birmingham, Department of Social Work

Janet M. Joiner, University of Detroit Mercy, Department of Social Work

Nathalie P. Jones, Tarleton State University Department of Social Work

Dione M. King, University of Alabama at Birmingham, Department of Social Work

Matthea Marquart, Columbia University, School of Social Work

Jennifer Parga, University of Southern California, Suzanne Dworak-Peck School of Social Work

Carlene Quinn, Indiana University Bloomington, School of Social Work

Liz Rembold, Briar Cliff University, Department of Social Work

Melanie Sage, University at Buffalo, School of Social Work

Sara L. Schwartz, University of Southern California, Suzanne Dworak-Peck School of Social Work

Jenny Simpson, The Open University, School of Health, Wellbeing and Social Care

Jonathan B. Singer, Loyola University Chicago, School of Social Work

Nancy J. Smyth, University at Buffalo, School of Social Work

Amanda M.L. Taylor, University of Central Lancashire, School of Social Work, Care and Community

Jimmy A. Young, California State University San Marcos Department of Social Work

Karen Zgoda, University of Massachusetts Boston Department of Public Policy and Public Affairs

FOREWORD

In 2017, a new publication, *Standards for Technology in Social Work Practice*, was issued to address the intersections of professional social work practice and technology. The National Association of Social Workers (NASW), along with the Council on Social Work Education (CSWE), Association of Social Work Boards (ASWB), and the Clinical Social Work Association (CSWA), cosigned the *Standards*, developed by a committee of primarily social work practitioners. The CSWE clarified that the *Standards* are neither part of the *2015 Educational Policy and Accreditation Standards* competencies nor part of the accreditation process (CSWE, personal communication, June 30, 2017). The authors of the *Standards* also offered brief interpretations of each of the *Standards* and sub-standards.

Hearing a call for more thorough guidance, the editors of this document reached out to social work educators and supervisors with specialized knowledge of teaching and supervising with technology and asked them to help us think about Standard 4, *Social Work Education and Supervision*. In the early Fall of 2017, 23 people responded to the editors' request to contribute their best practice and research wisdom. We used technology to crowdsource (obtain input from a number of people online), which allowed us to co-create, co-edit, and gather rapid feedback on this document over the course of a month. The following pages include the original standards published by NASW, followed by interpretations developed by our full group of 26 social work academics and supervisors. It offers considerations for decision-making related to the benefits and risks of technology use in teaching and supervision, developed by those who have direct experience in these arenas.

We extend our appreciation to the contributors, and to all social work educators and supervisors who strive to see all the potentials and benefits of technology, innovate while upholding our professional values and ethics, and understand and educate about risks of technology while working with and on behalf of people who are the most vulnerable.

Thank you,

Laurel Iverson Hitchcock, University of Alabama
at Birmingham (lihitch@uab.edu)
Melanie Sage, University at Buffalo (msage@buffalo.edu)
Nancy J. Smyth, University at Buffalo (sw-dean@buffalo.edu)
Editors

INTRODUCTION

The latest *NASW Technology Standards* (2017a) offer updated guidance for thinking about the use of technology in social work practice, with brief interpretations. Standard 4.0 specifically addresses social work education and the role of educators and supervisors in maintaining professional standards related to technology-mediated practice and educational settings.

Discussions with educators revealed a need for broader consideration, which is why the interpretations below were written in collaboration with 26 social work educators and supervisors, whose names are listed at the beginning of this document. The purpose of this document is to shift the interpretations from a mostly risk-averse and micro-practice focus to a perspective that also acknowledges the potential strengths of technology in micro to macro levels of practice and social work education, supervision, and continuing education.

This document is not meant to replace the *NASW Technology Standards* interpretations; rather it offers expanded and alternative interpretations. For instance, although the *NASW Technology Standards* emphasizes educators who are utilizing or currently specifically teaching about technology, the following interpretations widen this scope to address the need for *ALL* social work educators to have some basic understanding and competence in the use of technology and its impact on our field.

Further, we acknowledge that all educators are using technology in some way and have important roles in helping students prepare for technology-mediated practice at all levels. The word "competence" is used but not defined in the *NASW Technology* standards. The CSWE considers competence to be "the ability to integrate and apply social work knowledge, values, and skills to practice situations in a purposeful, intentional, and professional manner to promote human and community well-being" (CSWE, 2015, p. 6). Further, CSWE notes that professional and ethical behavior for a social worker includes using "technology ethically and appropriately to facilitate practice outcomes" (CSWE, 2015, p. 7). Along with being professional and ethical with technology, we see competency with technology for social work practice as context-dependent and evolving as technology evolves. Using technology in social work education requires ongoing participation in learning networks and continuing education, just as in any other practice area.

We also encourage educators to acknowledge their personal biases and competencies related to the intersections of technology and social work, and to consider how those are transmitted to students, colleagues, and other constituents. Social work educators are ideally positioned to model and support students, colleagues, and other constituents in becoming lifelong learners in these areas and others.

Finally, in order for social work educators to practice these ethical standards, educational settings need to ensure they offer the infrastructure and technical support to educators to teach effectively in the classroom and in field placements.

> **Standard 4.01: Use of Technology in Social Work Education**
>
> *Social workers who use technology to design and deliver education and training shall develop competence in the ethical use of the technology in a manner appropriate for the particular context.*

All social work educators should develop competence in the ethical and professional use of technology; the best practices for utilizing technology in social work education and in social work practice; and be prepared to teach basic digital literacy skills to students which are needed for ethical practice and to meet the competencies required by *CSWE 2015 Educational Policy and Accreditation Standards* (e.g., from Competency 1, Professional and Ethical Behavior, using technology ethically and appropriately to facilitate practice outcomes). In addition to understanding the use of technology, social work educators should help students understand the norms, values, and culture of specific applications, which together with the use of technology, informs digital literacy.

While not everyone will adopt the many different forms of technology (nor should they), social work educators should have a working knowledge of how to use technology ethically, and model those skills for their students. Social work educators should have competency in the learning management systems and other classroom technologies that they utilize. Social work educators in any setting should utilize the tools and techniques for which they have training and support, keep updated on effective pedagogical practices for using technology in education, and should bring concerns about their training and support to the appropriate administrators when it may have a significant impact on students.

Some best practices for staying informed include developing a professional learning network in the area of technology in practice, attending institutional training about technology tools and practices, participating in formal continuing education opportunities, and reviewing scholarly literature and current news related to technology in higher education and social work practice.

Some best practices for using technology in social work education include careful attention to social presence, clear expectations, scaffolding learning, facilitated conversations, the use of active learning, and use of activities that are well-linked to learning objectives.

Social work educators have an ethical responsibility to ensure that diversity and difference across types of learners are respected when implementing technological innovations in classroom settings. Social work educators should not replicate existing structural inequalities when creating digital class environments and assignments for their courses. The use of classroom technologies should consistently fit with desired learning outcomes, and support students in the use of transferable technology skills. Student technology competence or access should not be assumed, and students should have opportunities to demonstrate and receive feedback about basic technology competencies both during classroom and practicum training. A best practice is to work with institutional supports such as instructional designers, disability services, and centers for teaching and learning.

Social work educators should [ensure] that they and their students understand the liabilities and risks associated with storing sensitive information about students, peers, and/or clients on cell phones, external drives, or other storage that may be lost, stolen, and exposed to viruses.

They should take appropriate actions to ensure privacy, confidentiality, and security of student records and other sensitive information.

Finally, social work educators, both with their current employers, their professional organizations, and with larger national or regional conferences, should advocate for training on evidence-based teaching and teaching-based evidence related to technology in the classroom and in the field.

Social work administrators should support ethical technology usage in the classroom and encourage grants or other research support to help develop research studies that allow social work educators to gain a better understanding of best practices or effective technology tools to use in the social work classroom.

> **Standard 4.02: Training Social Workers About the Use of Technology in Practice**
>
> *Social workers who provide education to students and practitioners concerning the use of technology in social work practice shall provide them with knowledge about the ethical use of technology, including potential benefits and risks.*

All social work educators should understand the benefits and risks in the ethical and professional use of technology, and prepare students with this knowledge. Ethical principles of the *NASW Code of Ethics* should guide decisions about when technology may cause benefit or risk (NASW, 2017b). Social work educators should help students consider the ways that technology intersects with core values and ethics of the profession such as commitment to clients, self-determination, informed consent, competence, diversity, privacy, and access to records.

When training students in technology-mediated interventions, social work educators should help students understand how to evaluate the impact of the intervention on their own clients, how to identify promising practices, evidence-based practices, and best practices regarding the use of technology, including when technology-mediated interventions are and are not appropriate.

Alongside discussions of risks related to technology use, educators should acknowledge the ways in which technology-mediated practice may be the best tool in some situations. They should educate students about the ethical risks that may be present by using and NOT using technology (e.g., the exclusion of services to certain populations, failure to reach constituents by not having information easily accessible, record-keeping deficiencies).

Social work educators should offer training in effective and ethical ways to use technology to mobilize communities, disseminate information, and reach constituents in mezzo and macro interventions. Best practices include using technology to bring qualified guest experts into the classroom, incorporating technology-mediated practice into assignments and learning experiences, discussing emerging technologies and their potential benefits and risks, demonstrating the ways that technology can be helpful in understanding client or agency outcomes, and selecting texts and readings for courses that include information about technology in social work practice.

Standard 4.03: Continuing Education

Social work educators who use technology in their teaching and instruct students on the use of technology in social work practice shall examine and keep current with relevant emerging knowledge.

All social work educators should stay current with the best and evidenced-based practices on (A) teaching with technology and (B) the use of technology/role of technology in the topics on which they consult, supervise, and instruct students, colleagues, and other constituents.

Teaching with technology relates to instructional methods, pedagogy, and teaching/learning philosophy. Thus, all social work educators need to stay current with best practices, and when available, evidence-based approaches for using technology in educating students, colleagues, and other constituents such as field supervisors and practicing social workers. Best practices include protecting student privacy; ensuring teaching materials are accessible; and organizing and sequencing content clearly. When teaching skills, the skills should be modeled for students and students should have opportunities to practice skills in simulations. Standard 4.01 also addresses the importance of competence in technology for all educators.

Educators must have basic understanding of technology-mediated social work practice, address their personal biases related to technology-mediated practice, and stay up to date in the areas they teach that intersect with technology so they can appropriately evaluate the risks and benefits from a social work lens. Examples of topics that require specialized knowledge include federal or state laws that impact the intersection of social work and technology, such as Health Insurance Portability and Accountability Act (HIPAA) standards for health and behavioral health settings and the Family Educational Rights and Privacy Act (FERPA) for school social workers, as well as emerging theoretical explanations and empirical findings about how technology shapes social settings, interactions, and human development (U.S. Department of Education, 2015; U.S. Department of Health & Human Services, 2017). Educators should instruct students on the importance of lifelong learning necessary to adapt to a changing landscape in fast-moving technological advancement.

> **Standard 4.04: Social Media Policies**
>
> *When using online social media for educational purposes, social work educators shall provide students with social media policies to provide them with guidance about ethical considerations.*

A social media policy, when developed and applied for professional purposes by a social worker, reflects the behaviors that the social worker aspires to when using social media for work with clients, colleagues, and communities. This offers the opportunity to provide informed consent about how the social worker uses social media, reinforces professional behavior, and gives an opportunity to address and avoid potential boundary crossings. Educators who are using social media either personally or professionally and publicly, or as part of the social work curriculum, can use the opportunity to model the relevant and transferable skill of creating their classroom social media policy. Ideal social media policies in social work education should reinforce digital literacy, reflect grounding in the core values of the profession, and be modeled in a strengths-based perspective. Both benefits and challenges of the use of social and digital media should be reflected in the policy.

When using technologies in the classroom that include public exposure (such as blogs and social media), social worker educators should provide and model informed consent, including an explanation of the risks and benefits of establishing a professional digital presence, and provide alternative forms of participation if the student declines participation in publicly accessible discussions.

Best practices for social media policies include written policies that are shared in a systematic way (i.e., on course syllabi or via student handbooks); consideration of the impact on the most vulnerable; periodic reviews of the policy; and amending the policy when a new risk or benefit is identified. The strongest social media policies will provide general guidelines that are linked to social work values, ethics, and professional behavior. Policies that are too prescriptive will fail to address every possible situation and will lose relevance quickly as the technology and applications change.

Social work educators should first be intentional in their efforts to understand ethical and professional use of social media as it relates to students, clients, colleagues, and other constituents, and second, strive to shape healthy digital presences as they relate to the social work profession and practice. Best practices for social work educators includes modeling ethical and professional use of social media for others, providing both positive and negative examples of social media use in professional practice, and offering opportunities to practice social and digital technology in the classroom and in field placements when deemed appropriate by the agencies.

Finally, social work educators should encourage the administrative units at their institutions to develop social media policies and/or best practices that help guide students, faculty, staff, agency field supervisors, and other constituents on how to ethically and professionally use social and digital technologies in the social work profession. Best practices include consulting and engaging all constituents in the development of organizational social media policies and providing resources and supports in the development of social media policies, such as professional development training and materials on how to use social and digital media in professional ways.

> **Standard 4.05: Evaluation**
>
> *When evaluating students on their use of technology in social work practice, social work educators shall provide clear guidance on professional expectations and how online tests, discussions, or other assignments will be graded.*

Consistent with good educational practice (which is expected in all higher education settings, and is not unique to social work), all educators should provide clear guidance as to how ALL assignments and other learning activities will be assessed. Best practices include clear connections to learning outcomes (i.e., social work competencies), the use of rubrics that specify how the student work will be graded, and the inclusion of self- and peer assessments.

When the use of specific devices or applications is required to complete an assignment, educators should ensure both that students have access to the appropriate equipment or applications, and that they receive instruction, or have access to training, in the appropriate use of the devices or applications. When the use of technology or technology competency will be included as part of student assessment, educators should consider whether specific technology training is needed as a stand-alone graded component of the assignment. When competency in the use of a particular technology is part of an assignment (e.g., creating an infographic vs. a website), educators should consider tailoring grading criteria to each type of assignment, because different digital literacy skills sets are required depending on the type of technology used in the assignment. Additionally, when technology competency is part of an assignment, the grading criteria should make it clear how much weight is assigned to the technology competency, as well as to the substantive content presented through the technology.

Educators also should provide information on their policies and expectations for students and other constituents when the technology needed for completing an assignment or exam fails. See Standard 4.06 for more guidance.

> **Standard 4.06: Technological Disruptions**
>
> *Social work educators shall provide students with information about how to manage technological problems that may be caused by loss of power, viruses, hardware failures, lost or stolen devices, or other issues that may disrupt the educational process.*

All social work educators should prepare for technological disruptions in synchronous and asynchronous courses or workshops, and online and onground courses. Examples include during an assignment submission via a learning management system, emailing, when showing a movie in a class, or joining a live online class via video-conferencing software. Social work educators should be aware of and educated about institutional supports and processes related to technology on their campuses (e.g., Informational Technology [IT] Help Services, Disability Support Services, computers labs on campus, Wi-Fi access information, etc.), and alternative means of addressing the content in the case of technology failure. This information should be shared with all students, and other constituents such as teaching assistants and administrative staff.

Best practices for preparing for disruptions include development of a course-level disruption readiness plan (DRP) for when technological disruption of a course, test, or assignment occurs. This should include plans for both asynchronistic assignments and live sessions; [as well as] working with students, workshop participants, and/or colleagues, and be applied in a consistent and ethical manner. Social work educators who make accommodations for students with disabilities should consider specific disruption plans for those students in consultation with the university disability office. Other best practices for a DRP include providing multiple avenues to reference a technological disruption policy for the classroom, and alternate ways of obtaining course information should disruptions occur. Social work educators should also have their own personal DRP in place should their course data be lost or compromised in some way.

> **Standard 4.07: Distance Education**
>
> *When teaching social work practitioners or students in remote locations, social work educators shall ensure that they have sufficient understanding of the cultural, social, and legal contexts of the other locations where the practitioners or students are located.*

Social work educators should advocate for quality student and faculty support services to assist with technological disruptions. They should serve as advocates for their students within the Office of Disability Services, by educating support personnel about the technology-related skills students are expected to perform.

Distance learning refers to education that is provided to students who are not always physically present at the institution. Examples include online programs or courses and programs where instructors travel to deliver courses at off-campus locations. All social work educators should be mindful that students will have diverse past and future experiences in both geography and client populations, and should instruct students on how to assess their local social, cultural, and legal contexts and apply their learning to local issues, while also understanding how local social work issues translate to other geographical contexts. Social work educators should draw on the strengths of students who attend campuses from remote geographic locations who may bring increased diversity and ranges of experiences, and take opportunities to use diverse student experience to enhance classroom discussions and learning for everyone.

All social work educators should help all students evaluate their current contexts, bring these contexts into the classroom, and encourage students to use them in the explicit and implicit curricula to enhance the student body culture, and to understand similarities and differences between communities. When planning curriculum, social work educators should prepare students for the varied experiences they will encounter with state laws for issues such as licensing or interpreting public policy, rather than teaching policies based on the university's physical location.

Social work educators may also consider consulting with colleagues, locally trained social workers, and other constituents when planning their curriculum. Social work programs should [ensure] that their programmatic policies comply with laws related to educating students across state lines via distance formats and the use of field sites in other states.

> **Standard 4.08: Support**
>
> *Social work educators who use technology shall ensure that students have sufficient access to technological support to assist with technological questions or problems that may arise during the educational process.*

All social work educators should provide students with specific information about how to access technical support for each relevant aspect of a social work course. Best practices would be to provide support information at the beginning of the course and in the course syllabus. Educators also should inform students at the beginning of the course (or before entering a fully online program) about the types of technology and devices needed to access the course through the institution's learning management system (LMS) and to complete course assignments.

Educators should be knowledgeable about the types of devices and software students are likely to access and use during their courses, and should appreciate the differences in how content might be displayed differently given the variety of devices and software. Additionally, educators should provide information about available technology support at their institutions, such as computer labs, free or affordable software, and/or IT services.

If educators find that technical support is not meeting students' needs, they should inform their administrators of this problem immediately, and, if necessary, modify course expectations to accommodate the situation so that students are not penalized for the educational institutions' failure to provide adequate support. See Standard 4.06 for guidance on how to support students during technology disruptions.

As part of the implicit curriculum, all social work educational programs should work to meet this standard as well. Specifically, programs should be transparent with students about all the technology requirements needed to successfully complete a degree, and provide adequate information about technical support. Additionally, social work programs should advocate on behalf of students, faculty, and staff for access to quality technological support to assist with technological questions or problems that may arise during the educational process.

> **Standard 4.09: Maintenance of Academic Standards**
>
> *When social work educators use technology to facilitate assignments or tests, they shall take appropriate measures to promote academic standards related to honesty, integrity, freedom of expression, and respect for the dignity and worth of all people.*

All social work educators should take appropriate measures to promote academic standards related to honesty, integrity, freedom of expression, and respect for the dignity and worth of all people. This includes being aware of and knowledgeable about institutional academic honor codes and policies; the *NASW Code of Ethics*; academic and non-academic support services (i.e., writing centers, disability services, IT help services, and supported software); and FERPA (NASW, 2017b; U.S. Department of Education, 2015). For each course taught, all educators should provide students with information about how the academic standards are applied in that course, including information about technology-based products that support academic standards such as plagiarism tools or proctoring services.

Best practices for this standard include describing academic support services in all courses regardless of the method of delivery; modeling professional boundaries and respectful language as an instructor and providing exemplars for students; being knowledgeable about the types of technology-based products and services that support academic integrity, how they are used, and how students access these services (i.e., how third-party applications operate; cost to students, etc.); knowing how to assess for social cues across different types of settings; and being knowledgeable about best practices for ensuring academic integrity in online and offline environments. For an additional best practice, see Standard 4.04 on social media policies.

As part of the implicit curriculum, all social work educational programs should promote a culture of academic honesty, integrity, freedom of expression, and respect for dignity and worth of all people that is consistent and equal across all courses (i.e., asynchronous, synchronous, online, or seated). Social work educators and programs should advocate for the institutional support that provides academic and non-academic support services and equal access for students in all types of courses and programs.

> **Standard 4.10: Educator-Student Boundaries**
>
> *Social work educators who use technology shall take precautions to ensure maintenance of appropriate educator-student boundaries.*

All social work educators should be proactive in developing and maintaining appropriate boundaries with students, colleagues, supervisors, alumni, community-based agencies, and other constituents. The *NASW Code of Ethics* provides guidelines for how to maintain boundaries with colleagues and within the profession, which should similarly be applied to relationships with students in both digital and onground contexts (NASW, 2017b). Educators should work to educate each other about how educator-student boundaries, including ensuring privacy, need to be managed when using technology such as email, texting, learning management systems, and mobile devices. This means that educators should be knowledgeable about the devices, software, apps, and social media platforms that they use as tools of communication and sharing with students (i.e., privacy settings, how to maintain secure Wi-Fi connections, and how to set up password protections and authentication tools). Similarly, educators should follow their institution's policies on the use of institutional and personal devices to access communications with students, educational records, and course materials.

Best practices for educators around educator-student boundaries include maintaining a social presence that balances professionalism and humanizing interactions, asking students to use and monitor their school email accounts for course-related information, developing a social media policy for interacting on social media with students (see Standard 4.04 for more guidance), [and] sharing guidelines for if, when, and how you will text with students, ground rules for class discussions (online and onground) and consequences for not adhering to the ground rules, and examples of dual relationships between educators and students and how to avoid them. Educators should also be aware of any policies at their institutions related to the use of mobile devices and social technologies and sharing with students, and share these policies with students.

All social work educational programs should also be proactive in helping students, faculty, staff, and field agency supervisors to develop and maintain appropriate boundaries with each other and other constituents in all situations. This can include developing guidelines or policies for student and faculty handbooks that promote professional boundaries, and helping students, staff, and faculty assess and manage the benefits and risks of using portable devices, social media platforms, and other related technology as tools of communication and sharing.

Standard 4.11: Field Instruction

Social workers who provide field instruction to students shall address the use of technology in organizational settings.

Social work educators and field instructors should encourage discussions of agency norms and values related to technology use, and be prepared to help guide students around the use of the *NASW Technology Standards* in their field settings (NASW, 2017a). Educators should understand both risks and benefits of use of technology in field practicum, prepare students to understand agency use of technology and be transparent about their own use, and ensure that they know how to get questions answered about technology use in their field setting when questions arise, as there may not be formal processes within the agency or university for managing these types of issues. Educators should ensure that students have the opportunity to demonstrate and be assessed on their ability for competent technology use during their field instruction experience.

Field instructors should ensure that students understand agency policies and procedures to ensure client privacy, and compliance with all regulations, for all types of data, including digital data. Field instructors also should ensure that students are knowledgeable about agency policies and practices related to the use of social media and other digital technologies with clients, clients' families, agency staff, community resources, and the field educator.

Additionally, universities may have (or choose to invoke) policies about technology use that reach beyond the standard levels of practice in an agency where policies or practices are not yet established or do not provide enough guidance. Examples include policies to help maintain professional boundaries with social media, the use of specific software programs that are HIPAA or FERPA compliant, and/or protocols to be followed when technology disruptions occur (U.S. Department of Education, 2015; U.S. Department of Health & Human Services, 2017). See Standard 4.04 for more guidance on social media policies and Standard 4.06 for information on technology disruptions.

Given rapid changes in technology, students may know more than others in their agencies about the intersections of social work values and technology, as well as promising uses for technology with clients. Therefore, students should be prepared for the possibility that their field agency is not utilizing the current best practices, and be supported regarding where and how to address technology-related ethical concerns that may present themselves in the agency. Students may also be in the unique position to help agencies evaluate or update their technology practices, placing them in a leadership role. This role reversal may require that students receive extra support about how to navigate student-generated recommendations or critiques.

> **Standard 4.12: Social Work Supervision**
>
> *Social workers who use technology to provide supervision shall ensure that they are able to assess students' and supervisees' learning and professional competence.*

All social workers who provide supervision should ensure that they are able to assess students' and supervisees' learning and professional competence, and provide appropriate feedback, regardless of whether the supervision is provided in the same onground physical space, or if it is mediated by some form of technology. When a client outcome is being assessed, the use of appropriate assessment tools should be considered. For all of these reasons, social workers providing supervision should be knowledgeable in the best practices and most effective research-based methods to assess students' and supervisees' learning, competence, and client outcomes, and should use these methods when appropriate.

Remote supervision that occurs over the telephone or video-conferencing software takes unique expertise by the supervisor, who must engage in successful interpretation of both verbal and nonverbal communication, manage emotionally charged discussions, and address professional identity and ethical boundaries. Educators and supervisors who provide supervision mediated by technology should ensure they are trained to provide supervision via these modalities (see Standard 4.03 for more guidance), and that their supervisees receive appropriate training and support with the technology, as well. Best practices include using HIPAA compliant software, having a disruption readiness plan (see Standard 4.06 for more information), and considering cost of and access to software and/or devices for supervisees or agencies. Additionally, social workers who provide supervision and/or who receive supervision may need to advocate for appropriate resources with agency-based administrators.

All social workers who provide supervision shall ensure they are providing appropriate and necessary protection of private and confidential information, regardless of the modality of supervision. All social workers, particularly those in educator and supervisory roles, will need to stay aware of how each state board and/or territory regulates technology in the scope of supervision, and when changes to those regulations occur. All involved professionals (supervisors, students, and supervisees alike) who engage with technology platforms for supervision must be knowledgeable about current state and federal regulations and guidelines for risk management, privacy, and security (e.g., HIPAA), and regulations related to practicing across state lines. See Standard 4.01 for best practices to stay informed and current on technology.

REFERENCES

Council on Social Work Education. (2015). *2015 Educational Policy and Accreditation Standards for Baccalaureate and Master's Social Work Programs*. Alexandria, VA: Council on Social Work Education. Retrieved from https://www.cswe.org/Accreditation/Standards-and-Policies/2015-EPAS

National Association of Social Workers. (2017a). *NASW, ABSW, CSWE, & CSWA Standards for Technology in Social Work Practice*. Washington, DC: National Association of Social Workers. Retrieved from http://www.socialworkers.org/includes/newIncludes/homepage/PRA-BRO-33617.TechStandards_FINAL_POSTING.pdf

National Association of Social Workers. (2017b). *Code of*

Ethics of the National Association of Social Workers. National Association of Social Workers. Retrieved from https://www.socialworkers.org/About/Ethics/Code-of-Ethics/Code-of-Ethics-English.aspx

U.S. Department of Education. (2015, June 26). *Family Educational Rights and Privacy Act (FERPA)*. Retrieved from http://www2.ed.gov/policy/gen/guid/fpco/ferpa/index.html

Department of Health & Human Services. (2017, August 31). *Health Insurance Portability and Accountability Act of 1996*. Retrieved from https://aspe.hhs.gov/report/health-insurance-portability-and-accountability-act-1996

RESOURCES

Association of Social Work Boards. (2015). *Model Regulatory Standards for Technology and Social Work Practice: ASWB International Technology Task Force, 2013–2014.*

Belluomini, E. M. (2016). *Digitally Immigrant Social Work Faculty: Technology Self-Efficacy and Practice Outcomes*. Walden University. Retrieved from: http://scholarworks.waldenu.edu/cgi/viewcontent.cgi?article=4383&context=dissertations

Berzin, S. C., Singer, J., & Chan, C. (2015). Practice innovation through technology in the digital age: A grand challenge for social work. *Grand Challenges for Social Work Initiative Working Paper* (12). Retrieved from http://aaswsw.org/wp-content/uploads/2015/12/WP12-with-cover.pdf

Brady, S. R., McLeod, D. A., & Young, J. A. (2015). Developing Ethical Guidelines for Creating Social Media Technology Policy in Social Work Classrooms. *Advances in Social Work, 16*(1), 43–54.

Culpeper, Virginia: Association of Social Work Boards. Retrieved from https://www.aswb.org/wp-content/uploads/2015/03/

ASWB-Model-Regulatory-Standards-for-Technology-and-Social-Work-Practice.pdf

Curington, A. M., & Hitchcock, L. I. (2017). *Social Media Toolkit for Social Work Field Educators*. Retrieved from http://www.laureliversonhitchcock.org/2017/07/28/social-media-toolkit-for-social-work-field-educators-get-your-free-copy/

Hitchcock, L. (2016, February 12). My Guidelines for Using Digital & Social Tech in the Classroom and Beyond [blog post]. Retrieved from http://www.laureliversonhitchcock.org/2016/02/12/my-guidelines-for-using-digital-social-tech-in-the-classroom-and-beyond/

Hollis, C., Morriss, R., Martin, J., Amani, S., Cotton, R., Denis, M., & Lewis, S. (2015). Technological innovations in mental healthcare: Harnessing the digital revolution. *The British Journal of Psychiatry: The Journal of Mental Science, 206*(4), 263–265. Retrieved from doi:10.1192/bjp.bp.113.142612

Robinson, L., Cotten, S. R., Ono, H., Quan-Haase, A., Mesch, G., Chen, W., . . . Stern, M. J. (2015). Digital inequalities and why they matter. *Information, Communication & Society, 18*(5), 569–582. Retrieved from doi:10.1080/1369118X.2015.1012532

Singer, J., & Sage, M. (2015). Technology and social work practice: Micro, mezzo, and macro applications. In K. Corcoran & A. R. Roberts (Eds.), *Social Workers' Desk Reference* (3rd ed.). New York: Oxford University Press.

Smyth, N. J. (2013, November 18). Intervention with SMS: What's Next? [blog post]. Retrieved from https://njsmyth.wordpress.com/2013/11/17/intervention-with-sms-whats next/

University at Buffalo School of Social Work. (n.d.). Social Worker's Guide to Social Media [infographic & videos]. Retrieved from https://socialwork.buffalo.edu/resources/social-media-guide.html

APPENDIX 4

REFLECTION QUESTIONS FOR DIGITAL LITERACY IN SOCIAL WORK

These questions are licensed under a Creative Commons Attribution-NonCommercial-Share with Attribution, No Derivatives International License. Belshaw's *Eight Essential Elements of Digital Literacies* (see http://digitalliteraci.es/) appear in this document as materials under fair use. Contact Nancy J. Smyth (swdean@buffalo.edu) with questions.

Many websites have assessments that purport to assess one's digital literacy. However, on closer look, they are often very dependent on the context of the technologies discussed, which means they become obsolete quickly and are not relevant to all contexts (such as how features of an app may look different on a smartphone compared to a laptop). To help readers understand their own digital literacies more deeply, we are presenting some questions that serve as a starting point for reflection as you consider teaching with technology, as well as helping students enhance their digital literacies. We agree with Belshaw (2014) that digital literacies are contextual. For example, if you are in a setting working with protected health information, questions would vary from those listed below. For this reason, these questions could never be exhaustive. However, they can provide a good starting place for personal reflection and professional growth for social workers and educators who use technology competently and ethically. The best time to consider these questions is when you are considering adopting a new application, solving a tech-related challenge, or using a new device.

CULTURE

This literacy includes having knowledge and skills, applying personal and professional values, and being about to think critically and reflectively about the context and culture of digital and social technologies.

- What is the purpose of what I am seeking to do right now?
    - What device and applications (apps) make sense given that purpose?
        - For each app:
            - If it is a social networking app, what are the norms and best practices for interacting/sharing with this app?
            - Does the *NASW Code of Ethics* or *Technology Standards* offer guidance as to how I should use this tool?
            - What is my experience using this app, and how different is this from my purpose or role now?
            - Does my user profile for this app reflect the activities that go with my goal/role/purpose? If not, do I need to set up a different user account on the app?
            - How will other people who use this app view what I am doing (i.e., my activities on this app)?
        - For each device:
            - What device best fits my role, the cultural context, and my purpose?

REFLECTION QUESTIONS FOR DIGITAL LITERACY

- How should this device best be used to fit the cultural context?
- What security settings and backups make the best sense for accessing this device, given my role, and the cultural context?
  - How can I best organize my work (i.e., on specific devices, with specific apps) to meet my purpose, including managing my attention?
    - Which apps will I need for my work?
      - If my purpose needs concentration, what devices need to be turned off or placed into "Do Not Disturb" mode to support that purpose?
      - Considering my needs, which device makes the most sense to use for my work?
  - What technology standards, legal standards, organizational policies, and professional ethics come into play to shape how I implement my purpose (i.e., what I am seeking to do right now)? Given this context, are there privacy protections that need to be employed?
  - Who is my audience for what I am doing?
    - What is my audience's cultural context (i.e., norms, values, knowledge base, and perspective) and how should that be considered for accomplishing my purpose?
    - What do I know about the use of this app by people in my target audience?
    - Are there other apps that might be more appropriate for me to use with this audience?
- What role am I in as I am working on my purpose?
  - How will others (e.g., peers, students, supervisors, my organization, clients, or the public) understand what I create?
  - What social work ethical principles and standards come into play to guide me in my role?
  - If my role is an educator and my audience is my students,

are there devices or apps I could use that would both fulfill my purpose and help my students meet additional goals, such as strengthen their digital literacy, enable them to build professional learning networks, or help them develop skills they could utilize in practice?

COGNITIVE

This literacy includes having knowledge about the structure and processes of digital and social technologies.

- For each app:
    - What category of app is this? (e.g., learning management system, presentation software, video sharing)
        - How will I use this app?
        - What other apps in this category do I know?
        - How is the structure of this app similar to and different from others I use?
            - If it is very similar to other apps I have used, how confident am I that I can use it?
            - If the similar apps are very different, are there tutorials or help sections I can use as a resource?
            - If not, is it different enough that I would benefit by doing an Internet search for "how to" articles for students and practitioners?
    - Do I know where to get support for app problems?
    - Is the app from a reputable vendor who is likely to continue supporting the app?
- Menus:
    - What options are available at the top level of the app? How knowledgeable am I with the functions indicated?
    - How do the menu options change based on the context of what's being done?

REFLECTION QUESTIONS FOR DIGITAL LITERACY

- o Are there backup options (i.e., a way to save drafts)?
  - ≫ If so, when do I need to use them to save my work?
  - ≫ If not, how can I protect my work? Do I need to copy it and save it somewhere else?
- o What settings are available for this app?
  - ≫ Given my purpose and role (i.e., cultural context), how do I need to customize the settings?
- o If the app works on a range of devices, are there key functions available across all the devices? If not, which functions are not available?
- o How knowledgeable am I about the unique features of the operating systems for each of my devices (e.g., settings for privacy and notifications)?
- For each device:
  - o Do I know how to
    - ≫ Customize security settings?
    - ≫ Use key operational feature to turn it on and off? Silence it?
    - ≫ Back up key information?
    - ≫ Purchase new apps? Delete apps I do not want?
    - ≫ Personalize the device display?
    - ≫ Recharge it?
    - ≫ Protect it from viruses and hacking?
  - o How comfortable am I working in this particular operating system environment?
  - o Do I know where to get support for device problems?

CONSTRUCTIVE

This literacy includes having knowledge and skills to create digital content such as text, images and videos.

- Do I know how to carry out the following key functions in all

the apps and other software that I work with?
- Copy
- Paste
- Cut
- Edit
- Save
- Undo/Delete
- Construct a complete profile
- Upload content
- Download content
- Publish online

- Am I able to use apps and other software to create text, images, audio, video, and mixed-media content?
- Do I know how to copy, cut, and paste content between apps on my devices?
- Do I know how to share content between my devices?
- Am I knowledgeable about how copyright regulations are applied in digital environments?
    - Do I know how to cite content that I have found in a digital environment?
    - Do I know how to create and apply a Creative Commons license to my work?
    - Do I know how to find public domain images? Music? Video?

COMMUNICATIVE

This literacy includes having knowledge and skills, applying personal and professional values, and being about to think critically and reflectively about the content created and shared in digital formats.

- Who is my primary target audience for this communication?
    - What is the best way to craft this message to

communicate clearly to that audience (given the all cultural context information)?
- What is the best app platform to use given my target audience?
- What words, abbreviations, and symbols will be known and not known by my audience?
- Am I looking for this message to catch the attention of people other than my primary audience?
- Do I want the content to be shared by others? If so, have I included all the key content that will ensure it continues to communicate what I intend?
• Are there secondary audiences that will see this this content?
- If so, how will they interpret it?
- Are there changes I can make to the content to make it appropriate for all audiences and to minimize miscommunication?
• Am I able to translate key information into compelling messages and formats, such as visual, audio, and video?

CONFIDENT

This literacy includes being able to think critically and reflectively about one's ability to use digital and social technologies.

• How confident do I feel about my ability to
    - Learn a new app, software program, or device settings?
    - Find a solution to a problem that I have encountered in working in a digital environment?
    - Identify a new app to fulfill a new goal?
• What would help increase my confidence in navigating digital environments in general?
• What digital environments do I need to increase my experience with so that I feel more confident?

- How confident do I feel about my ability to work across a range of devices?
- How comfortable am I working in this particular operating system environment?

CREATIVE

This literacy includes having knowledge and skills, applying personal and professional values, and being about to think critically and reflectively about creating digital content that adds value.

- Remix skills:
    - Have I successfully combined text and images to create new images?
    - Have I successfully combined video and/or audio clips to create new multimedia content?
- Am I able to create new content (through remixing or my own designs) to capture the attention and interest of my intended audience?
- Does my new content add value to the message I want to share with my target audience(s)?

CRITICAL

This literacy includes being about to think critically and reflectively about the quality, authenticity, and trustworthiness of digital content, software, hardware, websites, and other virtual environments.

- What websites and apps do I currently use to get my information?
    - Who are the authors or organizations of these sites or apps?
    - What do others say about these authors or organizations

(i.e., my colleagues, social work professional organizations, or the general public)?
- Have I used multiple strategies to verify the credibility of a digital source?
- Am I knowledgeable about how to use websites to use for fact checking?
- Do I know how to triangulate information to verify accuracy?
- Do I know my own digital identity, and does it reflect my professional self accurately?
- Do I know how to manage spam, inappropriate responses, or "trolls" in the places where I control or create content?

CIVIC

This literacy includes the knowledge, attitudes, and behaviors that support participation in the larger society with digital and social technologies such as with political and social action, community-based organizations, government agencies, and social action.

- Am I knowledgeable about how to
    o Locate proposed state and national legislation/regulation online?
    o Enter commentary or comments through digital channels?
    o Locate policy and practice guidelines through online searches?
- Am I familiar with digital advocacy tools (i.e., apps and websites) to:
    o Create or sign petitions?
    o Crowdsourcing feedback?
    o Organize ongoing communities to plan advocacy collaborations?
    o Connect regularly with elected officials?

- - o Raise money for causes (through crowdfunding sites or donation buttons)?
- Have I developed robust, trusted digital social networks related to key advocacy goals?
- Do I know what steps to take in attempts to correct inaccurate information about me or my profession online?
- Am I able to successfully use my digital social networks to collaborate on advocacy efforts?

REFERENCES

Belshaw, D. (2014). *The essential elements of digital literacies.* Retrieved from http://digitalliteraci.es/

APPENDIX 5

SOCIAL WORK DISTANCE EDUCATION ASSESSMENT OF READINESS (SW-DEAR)

Developed by Carol Schneweis, Melanie Sage, Carenlee Barkdull, Randy Nedegaard, Laurel Iverson Hitchcock, and Nancy J. Smyth, 2017.

This checklist is free to use under a Creative Commons License 2017 with attribution and no derivatives: https://creativecommons.org/licenses/by-nc-nd/4.0/, and has been reformatted for inclusion in this book.

This checklist is designed for social work programs that are offering or considering distance social work programming. It is a self-assessment related to best practices and resources for distance education. In each area, rate your current capacity using the following scale:

0 = No capacity
1 = Emerging capacity
2 = Operable capacity
3 = Full capacity

There is no minimum score; users should address areas in which scores are low and make efforts toward continuous quality improvement. In total, 129 points are possible. You may find this helpful to score as a committee before a discussion of how to further develop capacity.

University Capacity

1. The university has infrastructure that allows distance students to conduct business (including registration actions, financial aid, library, tutoring, and access to disability services) from a distance.
2. The university has infrastructure that allows distance students to conduct business (including registration actions, financial aid, library, tutoring, and access to disability services) from a distance.
3. For undergraduate programs: The university offers distance courses outside social work that fulfill the undergraduate degree requirements.
4. The institution uses learning management software products or processes that meet the needs of distance students and instructors, including remote authentication processes for off-site testing, plagiarism detection tools, and synchronous meeting spaces.
5. The university has a distance education unit that supports review of institutional practices and policies related to distance education.
6. The institution has a process for curriculum review for online courses that is equivalent to the process for on ground courses, and yet considers the unique aspects of online curriculum. [Note: In larger institutions, this review may not occur at the university level, but instead, at the college or school level].
7. The institution offers training, workshops, and technical support to faculty, including adjunct members, for designing and delivering online courses.
8. The institution offers training and technical support to students

for accessing and participating in online degree programs
9. The institution provides financial and public relations to support the program's distance education goals.

Program (College/School/Department) Capacity

1. The program has engaged key stakeholders in a process for embarking on the distance learning path.
2. The program has defined its target audience, specific niche, and has completed an environmental scan related to the market, reach, and applicable laws.
3. The program has reviewed its vision, mission, and context in relation to distance learning goals.
4. The program has broad support among faculty for engaging in distance learning.
5. The program has a distance coordinator who provides student and faculty support.
6. The program has adequate support staff who are knowledgeable about department offerings and can respond to numerous inquiries.
7. The program has developed policies and procedures that are specific to online programming and appropriate and ethical use of technology in education.
8. The program supports a consistent framework for the delivery of distance education content.
9. The program advocates the use of best practices and/or evidence-based teaching models for the delivery of distance education content
10. The program uses a range of software and teaching methods that support student engagement and critical reflection.
11. The program has access to instructional design support for development and design of the overall program and individual courses.

12. The program offers flexibility in deployment of distance education that acknowledges the extra training and preparation required for teaching technology-mediated courses.
13. If distance adjunct instructors are used, the program has a process for supporting their orientation, skill development, and engagement with the on-campus faculty.
14. The program offers an online orientation and supports students in appropriate use of technology in the program.
15. The program has a structure for academic and professional advising via distance that supports relationship building and ensures comparable quality to on-campus advising.
16. The program has a procedure for field placement agreements with distance agencies.
17. The program provides an equivalent level of field supervision to distance and campus students.
18. The program has equivalent methods for gatekeeping distance students, and faculty members are knowledgeable about warning signs of student difficulty in online environments.
19. The program offers opportunities for distance students to participate in social work student clubs or organizations and other implicit curriculum activities.
20. The program uses a process for evaluation of online teaching and supports a process of continuous quality improvement to make improvements based on assessment.
21. The program uses a process for assessment of student competencies in the online environment and uses a continuous quality improvement process to make improvements based on assessment.
22. The program has a process for reviewing and updating its technology-enhanced curriculum and uses a continuous quality improvement process to make improvements based on assessment.
23. The program has a back-up plan for technology failures.

Faculty Capacity

1. Faculty members have formal training or coursework in best practices and/or evidence-based teaching in distance teaching, including maintaining and supporting social presence.
2. Faculty members have formal training in universal design/American With Disabilities Act compliance in distance teaching.
3. Faculty members are knowledgeable in technology-mediated student engagement and use appropriate tools to support engagement and learning.
4. Faculty members are enthusiastic in supporting distance education and teaching with technology.
5. Faculty members have access to a course evaluation process and access to coaching for course improvements.
6. Faculty members understand how to assess and address the regional and cultural contexts that students bring to the classroom.

Student Support Capacity

1. Students have access to technical support related to the tools they are required to use in class.
2. Students are knowledgeable about the expectations for distance students prior to program admission, including all costs of tuition; technology required; and time expectations for class, homework, and field. They can engage in self-assessment about their match for distance education.
3. Students are knowledgeable about program context, including where to get help, standards for student behavior, how to find materials, and how to contact their advisors.
4. Students have access to implicit curriculum equivalent to students who take courses on campus, including opportunities to communicate in a community outside the classroom, and

are educated about the social work values and ethics regarding use of technology in online social environments.
5. Students have opportunities to offer feedback on the strengths and weaknesses of distance programming.

APPENDIX 6

TECHNOLOGY TIPS FOR SOCIAL WORK PRACTITIONERS AND ACADEMICS

The content in this appendix is licensed under a Creative Commons Attribution-NonCommercial-Share with Attribution, No Derivatives International License (https://creativecommons.org/licenses/by-nc-nd/4.0/). Contact Laurel Hitchcock (lihitch@uab.edu) with questions.

This section includes many tips, ideas, and recommendations about how technology can be used for professional development by social work practitioners and educators. All these tips were contributed by social workers in academic settings or practice and accompany the content from Chapter 9, "Technology for Professional Development." We selected these tips because they complement the discussions in Chapter 9 about how social workers can use technology for life-long learning, work productivity, virtual collaboration, and dissemination of scholarship.

USING TECHNOLOGY FOR LIFELONG LEARNING: PROFESSIONAL LEARNING NETWORKS

As noted in Chapter 9, professional learning networks (PLN) exist when social workers use social media to collect information related to professional interests, shares this information with others, and collaborates with others on projects (Richardson & Mancebelli, 2011; Hitchcock, 2015).

A PLN is unique to each person, and learning how others structure their PLN can be helpful in setting up your own network. Kelly Joplin, an assistant professor and director of field education from the Carver School of Social Work at Campbellsville University, uses a productivity app called Evernote to support her PLN. She writes:

> I love Evernote! It keeps me organized. It has folders where I collect articles, videos, audio clips, pdfs, maps, and links to resources for each of my classes. I use many different types of media in my classes and this makes pulling those different pieces onto the classroom screen seamless. I do not have to toggle back and forth between apps or the Internet therefore eliminating the uncomfortable classroom lag time while bringing up media. (I find I lose students in the lag.)
>
> It also has a web clipper tool. This allows me to grab interesting articles while I am surfing for future class discussion or activities. I can email those links to students or post them to social media. It is laid out with tiles so each article or link is easy to find and pull up at a glance.
>
> It has a work chat feature where you can send colleagues articles. The app can be put on smartphones and syncs. It also has a feature where you can work on a document as a group. Evernote Basic for 60 Megabytes is free. You can upgrade for additional features. (K. Joplin, personal communication, September 11, 2017)

In contrast, Ann M. Callahan, an associate professor of social work at Eastern Kentucky University's Social Work Program, shares how she incorporates several apps into her PLN:

TECHNOLOGY TIPS FOR SOCIAL WORKERS

I organize Web resources for course development and student collaboration through Flipboard, YouTube, and Pinterest.

Flipboard can be used to organize articles and is accessible for students with disabilities. There you can create your own magazine(s) where articles that you virtually "flip" appear. You can flip articles from other Flipboard magazines into your own magazines. To flip articles into Flipboard magazines from the web, you can download a "Flip It" add-on tool if using Google Chrome. You can invite others with a Flipboard account to flip articles into your magazine(s). You can post comments about flipped articles. You can also follow Flipboard magazines created by others. My social work magazines are at https://flipboard.com/@dranncallahan.

YouTube can be used to create, upload, and close caption your videos (for accessibility). There you can also create playlists to organize videos uploaded by others on YouTube and videos from websites that host on YouTube. Some videos on your playlists may be deleted over time, so it requires vigilance to discard old links. My social work playlists are at https://www.youtube.com/user/dranncallahan/playlists.

Pinterest can be used to organize infographics and pictures. There you can create your own board(s) and then virtually "pin" images to the board. You can pin images found on boards created by others on Pinterest. You can also pin images found on the Web with a "Pin It" add-on tool for Google Chrome. These images need to be described in the title and/or as a comment to support accessibility (Chiles, 2016). My social work boards are at https://www.pinterest.com/dranncallahan/.

If you have a website, you can insert script provided by Flipboard, YouTube, and Pinterest to create a "widget." I have widgets that direct people to all the social work materials I have collected on my website at http://dranncallahan.info/. In one of my classes, I asked students to share items that enhanced their understanding of course content through Flipboard and Pinterest. We discussed what they found in class. It was fascinating to engage with students this way. I still see some of my previous students using these applications. (A. Callahan, personal communication, September 5, 2017)

USING TECHNOLOGY FOR PRODUCTIVITY: MANAGING THE ACADEMIC WORKLOAD

Today's academic work environments are fast-paced and rely on digital technologies to handle the flow of communication and information such as email, digital calendars, and to-do apps. In this blog post, we asked social work educators and practitioners to share their best tips for using technology as a tool for productivity.

Managing email can be a difficult and time-consuming task. Andy Berkhout, the data quality coordinator from the St. Patrick Center in St. Louis, MO, shares his guidelines for managing e-mail:

> Clients and colleagues will notice if you are paying more attention to checking email on your phone than you are to them. Instead, set a dedicated time at the beginning or end of the workday to catch up on electronic communication. When it is time to pay attention to the person in front of you, do just that; put your phone away and give your complete focus. Your text messages and email will still be there later, but the chance to connect with a client or provide meaningful input during a meeting might pass if you're not giving the present moment your full attention. (A. Berkhout, personal communication, September 6, 2017)

Shelly Richardson, an assistant professor and director of undergraduate social work at the College of St. Scholastica in Duluth, MN, uses her prior practice experience to cope with her e-mail:

> In my role as an associate professor and director of an undergraduate program, I only check emails twice a day and spend no more than 45 minutes doing so. This forces me to prioritize activities and responses quickly. I only "touch" things once. If I need to take care of something or respond, I do it immediately on receiving the request. I also have files with names of my frequent contacts (such as co-workers, dean, chair); emails that are initiated by those individuals are easier to find. I also use folder titles for activities I am responsible for (advising, to be graded, coordinating, and committees). These folders allow me to clean up my inbox; as I read through emails, I flag emails that are in progress or I need to follow up on and review the flags once a week (usually Monday or Friday). These flagged items stay in my inbox and I work to keep this number around 15. I also have a rule, if I have to respond more than twice, I make a phone call immediately or schedule a face-to-face to follow up. This is usually indication that communication has broken down somewhere and needs to be resolved. (S. Richardson, personal communication, September 20, 2017)

Karen Zgoda, an instructor of social work at Bridgewater State in Boston, MA, combines scheduling and apps to manage her e-mail:

> Email volume can be crippling. I check email at breakfast, lunch, and once at night. I avoid responding to non-crisis emails outside these times and on the weekend. If an assignment is due, I check more often, but from my smartphone so I am limited to shorter replies. For productivity sanity, I also

use the "Do Not Disturb Mode" feature on my cell phone and SelfControl, a free app that locks down my computer for a period of time so I don't have access to email, the web and other distracting programs while I work. (K. Zgoda, personal communication, September 24, 2017)

Leah Hamilton, an assistant professor of social work at Appalachian State in Boone, NC, recommends using add-ons and other tools from one's e-mail software to control the flow of e-mail:

> For managing student email, I love Google Gmail's Canned Response and automated appointment scheduling. Canned Responses can be found in the Settings section, under Labs. When I get common student emails, I select from a list of auto responses, which I have created over time. Some of the most common responses I use are things like, "Thank you for letting me know that you will be out today. I hope you feel better soon!"; "Great question. I will look into this and get back to you as soon as possible"; and "Thanks for your question. Please see the course syllabus section X for more information on this topic." I also use Canned Responses to compose common emails such as "Welcome to the Department of Social Work! I am your new advisor. At your convenience, please make an appointment with me at the link provided below. Also, feel free to email or call me with any questions. I look forward to working with you!" Saving these few keystrokes really adds up and helps me to more frequently achieve the ever-elusive Inbox Zero (Mann, 2007)! Finally, my email signature also includes a hyperlink to "Make an appointment with me." This link currently directs students to make an appointment on my Google Calendar, but I have also used Schedule Once with great results. Eliminating the back and forth emails to schedule meetings and office appointments

saves a surprising amount of time. (L. Hamilton, personal communication, September 5, 2017)

Several other social work educators recommend using scheduling apps to eliminate back and forth emails with students to set up meetings. Kate Constable, the undergraduate academic advisor for the School of Social Work at Portland State University, uses an app called YouCanBook.Me:

> I just started using YouCanBook.Me for calendaring, and it has changed my life! Anyone can create a free account and use the service to connect with their calendars. I have also had great feedback from students about how easy it is to use, and how much they appreciate being able to see my availability, and make or reschedule appointments online. (K. Constable, personal communication, September 8, 2017)

Julia Kleinschmit, a clinical associate professor of social work at the University of Iowa in Sioux City, IA, uses a calendar management tool called SignUp Genius, which allows students to schedule meeting with her or sign-up for events:

> I love, love, love SignUp Genius. It is the easiest calendar management tool I have used to schedule time with students for advising, project reviews for class projects, and so on. It is free, provides reminders to students and me, and is easy to use with any device. (J. Kleinschmit, personal communication, September 6, 2017)

Liz Fisher, a professor of social work at Shippenburg University's Department of Social Work in Pennsylvania recommends Doodle for scheduling meetings not only with students but also with colleagues (L. Fisher, personal communication, September 5, 2017).

Keeping an online to-do list is another common practice by social work educators. Christine McKenna Lok, an academic coach at Dean College in Franklin, MA), uses an online list system called Workflowy:

> It allows headings and subheadings for the various components of the larger task and you can tag each item with as many labels as you want such as due dates, specific courses, specific committees, etc. (C. M. Lok, personal communication, September 11, 2017)

Similarly, Tina Jiwatram-Negrón, a postdoctoral research fellow at the University of Michigan, School of Social Work, uses Todoist for her workflow management:

> I use Todoist for workflow management, and it's wonderful. I started using Todoist about 3 years ago and it has helped me improve my productivity and stay sane! It has been designed in line with David Allen's method of Getting Things Done (GTD) (http://gettingthingsdone.com/)—and works great for individuals and groups (Allen & Fallows, 2015). The GTD method encourages folks to think broadly/see the big picture (identifying their values, goals, etc.) and all the way down to the daily stuff that takes up valuable brain space. Todoist essentially allows you to capture these details in one place, organizing projects and tasks, big or small, personal and professional. I use Todoist in conjunction with my Google Calendar, and that's all! (T. Jiwatram-Negrón, personal communication, September 9, 2017)

USING TECHNOLOGY FOR COLLABORATION: VIRTUAL COMMUNITIES OF PRACTICE

Virtual communities of practice (VCoP) are professional online communities that exist to improve work and education around disciplines and professions (Hara, Shachaf, & Stoerger, 2009; Adedoyin, 2016). We asked our colleagues (social work educators) to share their best tips for collaborating with other professionals using digital tools.

Christine McKenna Lok of Dean College in Franklin, MA, participates in a VCoP called Academic Writing Club:

> They set you up with a group of a dozen faculty in the social sciences (or health sciences, or whatever) and you have a private community to set goals for each 12-week cycle, check off which dates you've accomplished your goals, and write messages to each other about the process of writing rather than the content. They also have chat sessions available at various times with the entire enrollment for that session so you can log in at, say, 8 AM Central and say hello to other folks who have committed to a half-hour of writing and then wish them well at the end of the time. It's not free, but it's a worthwhile investment. (C. M. Lok, personal communication, September 11, 2017)

Similarly, Elizabeth Austic, research associate in social work and psychology at the University of Michigan, uses Google Drive for collaborative writing projects:

> My best tip is to use Google Docs and Google Drive for collaborative projects. Google Docs is free, and allows you to collaborate and make edits simultaneously on the same document. You can share Google spreadsheets, documents, calendars, and other types of files easily. You

> choose whether you want to share these files with the public, or only with certain people, and whether you want to give them permission to edit, or just to comment, or only reading access. The interface is a lot like Microsoft Office, so it is easy for people to learn to use. There are additional collaborative tools that allow you to review, make notes, comment, track changes, and revise a shared document, which you may then download to your desktop. (E. Austic, personal communication, October 3, 2017)

Roshini Pillay, lecturer in social work at the University of the Witwatersrand in Johannesburg, South Africa, notes that VCoPs can support student-centered learning within a classroom and across the curriculum:

> I believe that technology if used in a careful way to support student-centered learning is beneficial. Technology use should be linked to instructional design, pedagogical approaches and teacher practices. The effectiveness of technology enhanced learning (TEL) lies in how technology supports the learning outcomes and student learning. Key features of TEL that require course design consideration include the goals of instruction, pedagogy, teacher effectiveness, content, the students and the fidelity of technology implementation (Bates, 2015). Notably, one of the greatest advantages of using technology is to support students' efforts to achieve learning instead of acting as a tool to deliver content. Tools may include the use of discussion forums, blogs and Twitter links to establish a community of practice where students, social workers, members within the multidisciplinary team and others can share ideas, solve problems and develop the profession and themselves. In so doing communities of practice may emerge whereby groups of people who share a concern or a passion for

something they do and learn how to do it better as they interact regularly (Wenger, 2006). The community of practice members engages in collective and collaborative activities whereby members help each other share resources, experiences, stories, tools and ways of addressing recurring problems and work together. In this way, the members learn from each other and engage in some of the following activities:

- problem solving
- requests for information
- sharing experience
- reusing assets
- coordination and synergy
- discussing developments
- documentation projects
- visits
- mapping knowledge and identifying gaps (Wenger, 2006).

Some of the skills that can be developed and enhanced by TEL are reflection, critical thinking, rapport, empathy and becoming a better public good professional (Walker & McLean, 2010). (R. Pillay, personal communication, September 7, 2017)

Nadine McNeal, the director of social work and assistant professor of social work at Freed-Hardeman University, also promotes VCoPs with her students by using Google Docs and Google Drive:

> I love the Google Apps for the classroom. These resources make the courses and students much more manageable. I love Google Calendar to electronically catch all meetings (student, colleague, administration, or community). Without the color coded datebook, I am lost. Without the reminders, I would miss several meetings. It is especially

handy since it goes from my phone to my laptop, to my desktop. If it is scheduled on one, it is shared with all. That is a great plus of these items. I also love Google Docs and Google Drive. Sharing documents to review, alter, or add is wonderful. It is one of the best ways for the students to share their videos for me to review for the practice courses. I no longer have to run from room to room and try to schedule all sessions at certain times or in set rooms. Instead, the students complete the videos and I review them online from the comfort of my office. (N. McNeal, personal communication, October 18, 2017)

USING TECHNOLOGY FOR SCHOLARSHIP: CREATING AND SHARING YOUR WORK

Social and digital technologies offer many tools and opportunities to create and disseminate scholarship in social work. For example, social work educators can use blogs, podcasts, videos, and infographics to create and share content for professional purposes.

Jimmy A. Young, an assistant professor of social work at California State University San Marcos, shares how he uses social media to disseminate his research:

> Social media technologies offer exciting opportunities to disseminate scholarship with a broader audience and share your research with others. A few examples include using Twitter to share a quick highlight or quote with a direct link to the article, a blog post with a longer quote or summary and direct link to the article, or some sort of video message on YouTube or Snapchat that also shares a summary and direct link. Today's social media users enjoy rich content and video is an engaging way to share articles with others. I have also been successful in using professional academic

social networks such as ResearchGate or Academia.edu to host articles, post summaries and links, as well as to connect with others working in a similar area. The great thing about these websites is you can get some analytics that can be useful for demonstrating your scholarly impact. For example, I have open access articles on ResearchGate that have garnered thousands of views and many of these articles have found their way into other scholar's work as citations. Google Scholar is another great way to manage your academic profile online and keep track of your scholarship and citations. Remember that some publishers do not want their articles shared on these websites for copyright reasons, but more and more are beginning to allow academics to post pre-print copies and even full online print versions. ResearchGate has been very useful because they are establishing relationships with some publishers to ensure that your work is freely available to share with others. Also, remember that many publishers provide a number of free copies for authors to distribute, and these copies can be great to share on social networks and increase your citations, online presence, and maybe even make you famous. Perhaps just moderately famous. (J. A. Young, personal communication, November 3, 2017)

Jonathan B. Singer, an associate professor of social work at Loyola University and the founder of *The Social Work Podcast*, describes how he used social media to measure scholarly impact:

> How do you measure scholarly impact? Academic scholarship has long relied on a formula that counts citations. The more times you are cited the more impact your work is having. Citation count and impact is great in theory, but the current model for establishing impact is controlled by a for-profit corporation (Thompson/Reuters) that excludes

most social work journals. So, if you publish an important piece of scholarship in a journal without an impact factor score, many researchers in academia won't take it seriously. "That's ok," you say, "I'm interested in reaching a wider audience than just researchers." Most scholarship, however, is hidden from the general public behind a paywall. The issue of what qualifies as scholarship, and how institutions evaluate scholarly output and measure impact, takes on renewed importance with in the era of social media. The use of social media in scholarship has been called social scholarship (Greenhow & Gleason, 2014). Disseminating scholarship through blogs, podcasts, and other forms of social media makes content accessible to the general public and is therefore consistent with the social work values of social justice and service. But there is enormous pressure for social work scholars to publish in journals with high-impact factors, and to not publish content in mediums that do not have impact factors, including many social work journals, blogs, podcasts, and other forms of social media.

What else can we do? In recent years, there have been alternative ways of measuring impact. H-Factor is a citation count formula that is not behind a proprietary paywall and can be easily accessed through Google Scholar. Altmetric has become one of the most widely used services to measure the reach of peer-reviewed scholarship on social media. Altmetric looks at the number of times your scholarship has been tweeted, and included in a Mendeley database. Although you have to pay to access the deep analysis, basic information about the reach of your articles on these social media sites is free. Academic social network sites, such as ResearchGate and Academia.edu, encourage scholars to post their articles (pre-print or otherwise) so that other scholars can find them. Academia.edu cites an open access research article from 2016 that showed 69% increase in citations over

5 years for scholars who posted their work on Academia.edu (Niyazov et al., 2016).

Here's how all of this plays out in real life. Over the course of a year, Kim O'Brien, Mary LeCloux, and I wrote an article about psychotherapies for suicidal youth. In August 2016 *Child & Adolescent Social Work Journal* published the article online (Singer, O'Brien, & LeCloux, 2017). Since *Child & Adolescent Social Work Journal* is not listed in the Impact Factor journal list, I decided to run my own experiment on social media to see if posting about the article on a regular basis would increase reach as measured by Altmetric. I set up a daily tweet through the app *If This Then That* that said "Online access to Theory & Techniques for ABFT, DBT & I-CBT for #suicidal adolescents http://rdcu.be/ntfQ #SPSM #Socialwork #psychology." So, what happened as a result of this daily tweet? The article quickly became the most tweeted article from the journal and in the Top 5% of all research articles tracked by Altmetric. At least one person per day (other than me) shared the article with their followers.

When the publisher notified me that the article was being published in the physical journal I went to the journal website. I saw that the article had been shared 429 times and downloaded 262 times. There were 8 other articles in the issue. The second most widely downloaded article had 166 downloads and 0 shares.

The reach of this article is due to social media. Again, the article reached a wide audience BEFORE the article was published in the physical journal because of social media. My experiment was a success. The article was published in the April issue of the journal. I continued to share the article on Twitter, and the Altmetric score continues to go up.

I will continue to track the article to monitor the shares to download ratio and the citation count (which was at zero in March and currently at one). So, what about the paywall? Springer Publishing now offers an option where people cannot print or download the article but can read the article online free with this link http://rdcu.be/ntfQ.

I strongly encourage all academics to look to social media as a place to share scholarship. If you publish in peer-reviewed journal articles, ask them to provide an option similar [to] Springer Publishing. (J. B. Singer, personal communication, November 3, 2017)

REFERENCES

Adedoyin, A. C. A. (2016). Deploying virtual communities of practice as a digital tool in social work: A rapid review and critique of the literature. *Social Work Education, 35*(3), 357-370.

Allen, D., & Fallows, J. (2015). *Getting Things Done: The Art of Stress-Free Productivity* (Revised ed.). New York: Penguin Books.

Bates, T. (2015). *Teaching in a digital age.* Retrieved from http://dergipark.gov.tr/glokalde/issue/7240/95340

Bornmann, L. (2015). Alternative metrics in scientometrics: a meta-analysis of research into three altmetrics. *Scientometrics, 103*(3), 1123–1144. doi:10.1007/s11192-015-1565-y

Chiles, D. (2016, March 18). *Accessibility on Social Media.* Retrieved from https://technews.olemiss.edu/accessibility-social-media/

Greenhow, C., & Gleason, B. (2014). Social scholarship: Reconsidering scholarly practices in the age of social media. *British Journal of Educational Technology, 45*(3), 392-402.

Hara, N., Shachaf, P., & Stoerger, S. (2009). Online communities of practice typology revisited. *Journal of Information Science, 35*(6), 740-757.

Hitchcock, L. I. (2015, July 2). *Personal Learning Networks for Social Workers*. Retrieved from http://www.laureliversonhitchcock.org/2015/07/01/personal-learning-networks-for-social-workers/

Mann, M. (2007, March 3). Inbox Zero. Retrieved from http://www.43folders.com/izero

McLean, M., & Walker, M. (2010). Making lives go better: University education and professional capabilities'. *South African Journal of Higher Education, 24*(5), 847-869.

Niyazov, Y., Vogel, C., Price, R., Lund, B., Judd, D., Akil, A., . . . Shron, M. (2016). Open access meets discoverability: Citations to articles posted to Academia.edu. *PLOS ONE, 11*(2), e0148257. doi:10.1371/journal.pone.0148257

Richardson, W., & Mancabelli, R. (2011). *Personal learning networks: Using the power of connections to transform education.* Bloomington, IN: Solution Tree Press.

Singer, J. B., O'Brien, K. H. M., & LeCloux, M. (2017). Three psychotherapies for suicidal adolescents: Overview of conceptual frameworks and intervention techniques. *Child and Adolescent Social Work Journal, 34*(2), 95–106. doi:10.1007/s1056

Wenger, E. (2006). *Communities of practice: A brief introduction.* Retrieved from https://www.ohr.wisc.edu/cop/articles/communities_practice_intro_wenger.pdf

GLOSSARY

We often assume a shared understanding of what it means to have an online class or to use technology; however, there is a complex language associated with our rapidly changing technology-infused environments. Terms such as seated classrooms, online courses, asynchronous versus synchronous content, hybrid courses, MOOCs, and social media are routinely part of the daily conversations in administrators' offices, faculty offices, and curriculum committee meetings, as social work educators grapple to understand the available technology options and keep up with this new dictionary of terms and concepts.

This glossary provides a comprehensive and simplified guide to technology terms and jargon used in this book. General technology terms are separated from the brand-name products and organizations. For uniformity, we established some conventions for this glossary:

- Only those terms and definitions we consider the most useful to social work students, educators, and practitioners are included.
- Some terms appear as nouns and verbs (or a skill), such as blog or blogger and blogging, and we combined these terms into one definition.
- When explaining a brand-name product or tool, we provide the address to the company's Web page, also known as a URL, where you can find more information.

631

- If terms have common abbreviations or acronyms, such as apps for applications, we include the full term first and then the abbreviation or acronym along with the definition.

- When reading this glossary, you may need to look up a few terms to arrive at the definition for a phrase. For example, online videoconferencing software is broken down into three separate terms—online, videoconferencing, and software. By understanding that online means the computer is on and connected to the Internet, and that software is a computer program designed to perform a group of coordinated functions for the benefit of the user, then all you have to do is look up videoconferencing to fully understand the phrase.

Finally, new technologies are growing exponentially, and innovation will continue to change the way we educate future social workers. For example, Moore's law suggests that computers and the systems that use them double their capabilities every 18–24 months (Emerging Future, 2012). It is not uncommon for digital tools to fall out of use or for a specific type of software to become obsolete. Between starting this book in 2015 and going to press, at least six brand-name Web-based products initially mentioned in text were no longer available. Additionally, new applications will be released, or a company may start charging monthly fees for a service. Because of these challenges, we encourage you to check out the following resources:

- Edshelf: https://edshelf.com/education-technology-dictionary (a socially curated discovery engine of websites, mobile apps, desktop programs, and electronic products for teaching and learning)

- "Social Media Definitions: The Ultimate Glossary of Terms You Should Know" by Carly Stec: https://blog.hubspot.com/marketing/social-media-terms

- Technology Dictionary by Techopedia: https://www.techopedia.com/dictionary
- Webopedia: Online Tech Dictionary for Students, Educators and IT Professionals: http://www.webopedia.com
- Tech Terms Computer Dictionary: https://techterms.com

GENERAL TECHNOLOGY TERMS

adaptive release/adaptive release tools. In a learning management system, digital tools allowing course content to be released to learners based on rules such as date, time, assessment scores or attempts, and the review status. This gives the instructor control over what content is made available to which students (individuals or groups) and under which conditions.

add-on/add-on tools. (1) A hardware unit that can be added to a computer to increase its capabilities. (2) A type of software or a program utility that enhances a primary software program.

advanced searching. An option for a website, database, or Web browser that can combine search terms by setting specific parameters such as date or location to obtain narrower and more relevant search results.

algorithms. A detailed series of instructions for carrying out an operation or solving a problem, especially in software programs. These are commonly used with search engines to identify relevant content.

altmetrics/alternative metrics. Measurements of impact for research articles and other types of research output beyond a citation count; based on the reach of output on the World Wide Web. Complementary to citation-based metrics, these measures include peer reviews on research dissemination websites, citations on Wikipedia and in public policy documents, discussions on research blogs, mainstream media coverage, bookmarks on reference managers such as Mendeley, and mentions on social networks such as Twitter.

alt-text. A text description that can be added to an image using hypertext markup language (HTML), which is code used to display information on a Web page. Alt-text is a helpful tool for making Web pages accessible to individuals with vision difficulties or when a hyperlink is broken.

analytics/analytic tools. (1) Digital tools in a platform or program that assists in the gathering and analysis of patterns in data. (2) The process of discovering, analyzing, and sharing patterns in data, as well as the information resulting from the systematic analysis of data. Some software and social media have analytic tools such as helping users know who is following them or how often a student logs onto a learning management system.

annotate/annotating/annotation/annotation tools. (1) For educational purposes, a process of providing critical or explanatory comments about the content in a digital file. (2) A feature in software programs that allows a user to make a critical or explanatory comment in the digital file.

application/app. A software program or group of programs designed for users to perform a tasks or different functions. Also called end-user programs, examples in education include programs for word processing, social networking, and content management.

asynchronous/asynchronously. A term to describe learning that does not occur in the same time or place. Instructors and learners are online at different times and cannot communicate without time delay. Examples of these self-paced learning events include recorded video lectures and text-based discussion forums.

audio/audio files. Recordings of audio signals, usually made digitally. There are different audio file formats, such as .mp3, .wav, or .wma, for digital recordings that help to reduce the size of the file.

GLOSSARY

authentication. A process in a software application that ensures and confirms a user's identity.

automate/automating/automation. (1) For educational purposes, a process of using technology to convert a task from a human-initiated process to a computer-initiated process. (2) A feature in software programs that allows a user to set up a process that runs without continuous input from the user.

avatar. A personalized graphical illustration that represents a user within a digital environment or alter ego that represents that user.

back-loading. In a blended or hybrid class, the sharing of online content with students after the introduction of a topic in a class meeting; the reviewing of online content that reinforces what was learned in the class meeting.

backup/backing up. The process of making copies of data or data files to use in the event the original data or data files are lost or destroyed.

beta. In software development, it is the second phase of software testing in which a sampling of the intended audience tries the product.

big data. Simply, this refers to the digital byproducts of human interaction. Typically, this is a large volume of structured and unstructured data that is so big it is difficult to process using traditional database and software techniques.

blog/blogging/blogger. (1) A regularly updated website or Web page, typically one run by an individual or small group, that is written in an informal or conversational style. (2) The process of writing a blog. (3) A person who regularly writes material for a blog.

bookmark/bookmarking. (1) A hyperlink that is stored in a browser or other software program for quick access later. (2) The process of curating hyperlinks for later access.

Boolean search/searching. A type of search allowing users to combine keywords with operators such as *and*, *not*, and *or* to produce more relevant results.

bulletin board. A text-based online community with virtual space in which users with similar interests discuss topics. These conversations or discussions are available in the form of posted messages.

calendaring software. A computer program that allows users to create and manage an electronic calendar.

caption/captioning/captioner. (1) Text or subtitles that accompany videos or video streaming and capture the content of every sound and word in the video. (2) The process of translating sounds into a text-based format, either in real time or asynchronously. (3) A person who captions.

capture/capturing. (1) A digital content that is created from information currently displayed on a screen or monitor. In education, instructors use this to create content to be accessed by students asynchronously. (2) The act of saving content currently displayed on a screen or monitor.

Carnegie unit. A unit of academic credit in higher education based on how much time students spend in direct contact with an educator.

CD/CD player. (1) Also known as a compact disc, it is a flat disc that can store digital data. (2) A device that can read data from a CD.

chat/chatting. A method of communication in which people type text messages to each other, thereby holding a conversation over a network such as the Internet.

chat box/chat tools. A digital menu or other types of digital tools that allow a user to create and customize text for chatting.

chunk/chunking. (1) In education, a discrete unit of content that is part of larger learning unit. (2) The process of dividing information into small pieces and grouping them together so they can be stored and processed easily for learning.

clicker. A device or application that allows students to anonymously answer multiple-choice questions (also known as polling) during a live class session. Responses are aggregated in real time and shared with the class.

cloud/cloud based. A set of remote servers where data is stored and can be accessed from anywhere through the Internet.

cloud computing. Refers to the computer hardware and software that power the cloud. This includes servers (a computer with specialized software on it), data storage, applications, and more.

code/code source. An agreed-on set of unambiguous rules, which act as instructions for software programs on how to function.

cognitive overload. A situation in which an instructor gives too much information or too many tasks to learners simultaneously, resulting in the learner being unable to process this information.

collaborate/collaborating/collaboration. With technology, the process of two or more people or organizations working together to realize or achieve something successfully, using digital tools or within virtual environments.

comments/commenting. Text, audio, video, or images expressing an opinion or reaction in computer programs and applications, often found on blogs, news aggregators, and social media platforms.

computer. A programmable machine. The characteristics of a computer are that it responds to a specific set of instructions in a well-defined manner and can execute a prerecorded list of instructions.

content management systems. A computer program that allows for the display of learning content only.

contextual menus. A pop-up menu that appears with the right-click of a mouse on a certain area of the screen, providing information about other tools or information within the program.

copy and paste/cut and paste. A process in which digital text or other data is moved from one part of a document and inserted elsewhere. The copy feature leaves the data in the original location in document, whereas cutting removes the data from the original location.

course shell. A blank template within a learning management system that hosts a single online course.

crowdsource/crowdsourcing. The practice of obtaining information or input for a task or project by enlisting the services of many people, either paid or unpaid, typically via online communities or virtually.

dashboard. An electronic interface used to acquire and consolidate data across a computer platform or an organization.

delete/deleting. With technology, the process of removing digital text or other content from a file, Web page, or other digital product.

dialogue box. A digital area within a program screen in which the user is prompted to provide information or select commands.

digital/digitally/digital environment. A context, or a "place," that is enabled by technology and digital devices, often transmitted over the Internet, or other digital means.

digital access. An individual or community's level of access to digital and social technology.

digital device. A physical unit of equipment that contains a computer or microcontroller, such as smartphones and tablets.

digital equity. The belief that all individuals and communities have the information technology capacity needed for full participation in our society, democracy, and economy.

digital file. A collection of data or software stored in the computer. Everything permanently saved in a computer system is a digital file, identified by file type and name.

digital immigrant. A person born or brought up before the widespread use of digital and social technologies. It is assumed that such individuals do not have a strong grasp of digital technology because it was not a regular part of their lives growing up.

digital inclusion. The activities needed to ensure that all individuals and communities, including the most disadvantaged, have access to and use of information and communication technologies.

digital justice. (1) A term used to describe social justice in digital environments. Major principles include equal access to media and technology, common ownership of digital tools and knowledge, and consumer control of digital data. (2) The use of technology within the justice system of a government to reduce manual processes.

digital literacy. The knowledge and skills to find, evaluate, use, share, and create digital content using technology.

digital native. An individual born during or after the common use of digital technologies, such as the Internet. It is assumed that such individuals have a strong grasp of digital technology because it was a regular part of their lives growing up.

digital networks. An online community of users who communicate via the use of digital technologies such as mobile phones, the Internet, and e-mail.

digital self-efficacy. Users' confidence in their ability to understand, use, and participate with different digital and social technologies.

discussion board/discussion forum. (1) In an online class, a tool that allows text-based communication to occur asynchronously between different users. (2) An online discussion group. Using forums for discussion allows participants with common interests to exchange open messages.

discussion thread. A series of comments in an online discussion forum connected by a common theme.

domain name. A specific name used by Web browsers to identify specific Web pages or sites located on the Internet.

do not disturb mode. An option on a device or within a software program that when selected stops notifications, alerts, and calls from making any noise, vibrating, or lighting up a screen.

download/downloading/download button. (1) The process of retrieving data over the Internet or a file that is retrieved from the Internet onto a computer or device. (2) A tool within an application that allows a user to retrieve content from one location to a computer or device.

DVD/DVD player. A device that plays digital versatile disc, which is an optical disc used to store audio, video, or computer data.

e-advocacy. The use of digital and social technologies for activism, campaigning, fundraising, lobbying, and civic organizing.

e-book. A digital publication that consists of text and/or images. These publications are often proprietary and require special software or devices to read.

edit/editing. The process of correcting, condensing, or otherwise modifying text or content in digital files of all types including word, video, and audio files.

eLearning. Education or training that occurs via the Internet, a digital network, or a stand-alone computer. E-learning refers to using electronic applications and processes to learn, and includes Web-based learning, computer-based learning, virtual classrooms, and digital collaboration.

electronic database. A searchable electronic collection or repository of digitized content.

electronic mailing lists. A digital list of electronic mailing addresses used to deliver electronic messages.

electronic records. In education or social work, this is information about a person captured through electronic means and digitally

GLOSSARY

stored; it may or may not have a paper record to back it up. Examples include electronic medical records or student educational records.

e-mail/e-mailing. Short for electronic mail, it is the transmission of messages over digital communication networks.

e-mail merge. A process that enables automating the process of sending bulk e-mail to a list of individuals.

emporium model. An online learning model that eliminates all regular class meetings, replacing classes with a learning resource center featuring online materials and on-demand personalized assistance.

e-reader. A portable digital device that displays downloaded digital text primarily for reading, such as a digital book.

face-to-face. A method of course delivery that occurs in real time with participants in the same location or able to view each other's faces with videoconferencing software.

favoriting. An action taken by a user or member of an online community to express appreciation for another user's message or content, and bookmark it for future reference.

flipping/flipped classroom. Describes a reversal of traditional teaching where students gain first exposure to new material outside of class, usually via reading or lecture videos, and then class time is used to do the harder work of assimilating that knowledge through strategies such as problem solving, discussion, or debate.

follow/following/follower. (1) An action taken by a user, typically within social media sites, to subscribe to another user's feed or contents. (2) Someone who follows another user.

friend/friending/friend request. (1) An option on a social networking site to become digitally connected to another user on the site. Most commonly used with Facebook. (2) The act of asking someone to digitally connect with you via a social networking site.

front-loading. In a blended or hybrid class, the sharing of online content with students before a live class meeting.

game-based learning. A learning context designed to balance content with gameplay.

gaming/gamification. Applying elements of games, such as levels, awards, and badges, or competition with peers, to learning content, or placing that content into a gamelike framework for the purposes of learning.

geographic information system (GIS). A computer data system capable of capturing, storing, analyzing, and displaying geographically referenced information.

global positioning system (GPS). A system of satellites, computers, and receivers that can determine the latitude and longitude of a receiver on Earth by calculating the time difference for signals from different satellites to reach the receiver.

hacks/hacking/hacker. (1) Commonly, unauthorized access to or control over computer network security systems for some illicit purpose. (2) The process of completing a hack. (3) Someone who hacks.

hardware. For technology, these are the physical components that make up a digital system, such as the monitor, hard drive, and memory chips.

hashtag. A word, abbreviation, phrase, or term preceded by the symbol #. The hashtag connects the post with the broader online conversation about that topic; the hashtag serves as a label linking related content.

host/hosting. (1) A service for the storage of digital data and other resources to make a website accessible on the Internet. (2) The process of being a host.

GLOSSARY

hybrid course/hybrid program. (1) A course where at least half of the content is delivered via learning management system over the Internet. (2) A degree program where are all the courses are hybrid.

hyflex model. A course design model that presents the components of hybrid learning (which combines face-to-face with online learning) in a flexible course structure that gives students the option of attending sessions in the classroom, participating online, or doing both.

hyperlink/hyperlinking. (1) An element in an electronic document that links to another place in the same document or to an entirely different document. By using a mouse to left-click on the words, a user is directed to the content. Hyperlinks are the most essential ingredient of all hypertext systems, including the World Wide Web.

inbox zero. A rigorous approach to e-mail management aimed at keeping the inbox empty, or almost empty, at all times (http://whatis.techtarget.com/definition/inbox-zero).

infographics. Visual representations of information such as numbers, text, and images to share large amounts of information quickly.

information and communication technologies (ICT). Refers to technologies that provide access to information through telecommunications. Used by some as synonymous with IT, and by others as more expansive than IT, because it also includes communication technologies.

information technology (IT). (1) The study of computer science and technology. (2) The technology involving the design, development, installation, and implementation of information systems and applications.

insert/inserting. With technology, the process of adding digital text or other content to a file, Web page, or other digital product.

instructional design and technology. The systematic planning, implementation, and evaluation of course materials using technological processes and resources.

Internet/Internet based. A global network that connects millions of computers and includes the hardware and infrastructure.

keyboard. An input device with keys to represent letters, numbers, and other symbols that allows a user to enter text into a computer.

label/labeling. With technology, this is the act of describing someone or something with digital text.

learning content management system. A computer program that stores and delivers content with the ability to track course completion by specific learners.

learning management system (LMS). A computer program that stores and delivers course content while also tracking learners and tasks within courses.

level up/leveling up. The process of progressing to the next level of character play in role-play video games.

lightboards. A glass chalkboard filled with light that can be used to record video lectures (http://lightboard.info/home.html).

like. An action within an application or program by a user as a quick way to show approval.

link/linking. See *hyperlink*.

load. Refers to the time period (before or after) for which course materials are made available in online courses.

log on/logging on. A security action required for users to gain access to computer, social media platform, or other restricted online environment.

lurking. The act of reading discussions on message boards, newsgroups, and social networks but rarely or never participating in the discussion.

GLOSSARY

mash-up/mashing. The process of creating a digital project that integrates data, images, and other content from several sources to create a single project, document, or visual representation.

massive open online course (MOOC). A model for delivering learning content online to any person who wants to take a course, with no limit on attendance.

media. In education, refers to audio, video, animations, and graphics in an e-learning course.

media literacy. The ability to access, analyze, evaluate, and create media or messages across a variety of contexts, including print and digital. Based on an understanding of the role of media in society.

megabytes. A measurement of the storage capacity of a device.

meme. An image with text used to describe a thought, idea, joke, or concept that is widely shared online.

mention. In Twitter, a term used to describe an instance in which a user includes someone else's username in their tweet to attribute a piece of content or start a discussion.

menu. In a website or software program, a list of items grouped by topic that helps a user navigate content or perform tasks.

microphone. A device that translates sound into electrical signals that can be recorded, amplified, or transmitted to another location.

mix/mixing. The process of combining digital media to create a new product.

mobile device. A portable, handheld, electronic device such as a tablet or a smartphone that can run applications and connect to the Internet with wireless network access.

moderate/moderating. The process of reviewing other users' posts or comments and then assessing the post for quality, appropriateness, and contribution to the original content or discussion forum.

mouse. A handheld input device used to control the cursor on a computer screen when moved along a flat surface.

MP3. A common audio format for consumer audio streaming and storage, and the standard for the transfer and playback of music on most digital audio players.

MP4. A multimedia file format for audiovisual data; a file extension that can be thought of as metadata that helps an operating system identify the type of data a file holds and how to process the file.

multimedia. The combination of multiple forms of media, such as combining text, audio, and images, into a digital presentation for the purposes of communication or expression.

net neutrality. A digital justice principle that all data on the Internet should be treated the same and not segregated based on user, content, website, platform, application, type of equipment, or method of communication. This means governments and Internet service providers are unable to block or slow the streaming/downloading of content or charge additional fees for specific content. Also known as *network neutrality* or *Internet neutrality*.

network/networking. (1) A system of interconnected computers that can communicate with each other. (2) All the people that a user is virtually connected with via e-mail, social networking sites, and other digital platforms.

new media literacy. The ability to critically consume and produce messages in a variety of digital media channels. Inherent to these literacies is the use of Web 2.0 tools for social engagement, interaction, and collaboration.

notification/notification settings. Options available to users of software and applications to manage when and how they receive electronic messages such as text, voicemail messages, and e-mails.

GLOSSARY

offline. Refers to the state in which a computer or device is temporarily or permanently unable to communicate with another computer or device. Sometimes also refers to users who are not currently using their computer or device to connect with others online.

onground/on-the-ground. A descriptor for a traditional classroom that meets in a specific location at a set time and where the instructor and students are present in person.

online. Refers to the state in which a computer is connected to another computer or network. Sometimes also refers to users who are currently using their computer or device to connect with others online.

online class/online program. (1) A course in which all content and learning activities occur over the Internet via a learning management system. (2) A degree program in higher education that can be completed by an individual mostly via a learning management system.

online groups. A place for small group communication and for people to share their common interests and express their opinion on a social media site such as Facebook. Groups allow people to come together around a common cause, issue, or activity to organize, express objectives, discuss issues, post photos, and share related content.

online presence. An intentional or unintentional digital existence on the Internet by engaging with websites, blogs, social media, or other digital services. Also known as a Web or Internet presence.

online programs. Entire degree programs that can be accessed through online classes that require no regular in-person contact.

online program management (OPM)/online program manager or provider. A company, usually for-profit, that provides services and tools to educational institutions for the purpose of converting a degree program from onground to online delivery, typically for a significant cut of student tuition.

open/open source/open sourced. A program in which the source code is available to the public for use and/or modification from its original design free of charge.

operating/operating system. (1) The software that allows a user to start and shut down a computer and work with all the other software programs, manage files, and connect to the Internet. (2) The ability to use an operating system.

participatory culture. An approach to civic and community engagement that values the creating and sharing of members' work within a group, has low barriers to participation, and where members have some degree of social connection to each other.

PDF. Short for *portable document format*, a type of digital file that captures text, formatting, and graphics and that works across different types of operating systems.

pin/pinning. Commonly used with Pinterest, this is digital content that is found on the Internet and is saved by a user, usually representing an idea or something of interest to the user. Pinning is the action of saving digital content in Pinterest.

platform. A term used to define the type of operating system on which a computer or device is based.

play/playing. Involves the ability to successfully operate a device or hardware for the purposes of running software, viewing a video, or listening to a podcast, among other actions.

podcast/podcasting/podcaster. (1) An audio file that is available on the Internet as a series and is streamed or downloaded for listening. (2) The act of creating a podcast. (3) Someone who creates podcast.

post/posting. Refers to the ability to use software and/or Web 2.0 platforms to write and share ideas, thoughts, opinions, and other forms of feedback about written or visual content, such as a blog post about social work practice, a question on a discussion board, or an electronic news article from the local newspaper.

presenting/presentation. In the context of technology, this is the process of using digital presentation software to continuously display text, images, or types of digital content for educating or sharing information. A digital presentation typically consists of a collection of digital slides arranged to share with an audience.

privacy setting. Options available to users of software and applications to protect sensitive and private communications, data, and preferences.

professional learning network. Within an online environment, the practice of connecting to people who share interests and can learn from each other for professional reasons.

profile. A collection of settings and information associated with a user (i.e., individual or organization) that contains personal data that helps a program or an application identify the user.

publish/publishing. Includes all the activities necessary to share digital content with the public, including written text, photos, videos, or audio files.

real time. (1) In education, when students attend class at a specific time and specific location, at the same time as their classmates and instructor. (2) Being with other people at the same time and in the same location.

record/recording/recorders/recording device. (1) The process of capturing sound or movement for conversion to digital data that can be played back later as a podcast or video. (2) A device with a camera and/or microphone that allows users to record digital audio or video files.

reference management software/reference managers. A computer program that allows users to record bibliographic citation information from books, articles, and other types of scholarly artifacts, and then generate bibliographies and reference lists. Also known as citation managers.

remix/remixing. (1) An artifact (e.g., a video, song, or lesson) created by cutting and splicing various digital works together to create something new. (2) The process of making a remix.

retweet/retweeting. A tweet, or post, on Twitter that has been reposted by a user who is not the author. The act of reposting a tweet.

reverse image search. A search technique that starts with an image and returns results related to the origin of an image as well as derivations and manipulations of the image.

right-click/right-clicking. The action of using the right button on a mouse to control an action on a computer. Right-clicking is often used to open contextual menus, obtain help, or display background information related to a digital item.

RSS feed/RSS feed reader. (1) An abbreviation of Really Simple Syndication, RSS is feed format used to publish frequently updated content such as blogs and videos in a standardized format. Content publishers can syndicate a feed, which allows users to subscribe to the content and read it when they please from a location other than the website. (2) An RSS reader allows users to aggregate digital content from multiple websites into one place for viewing or playing.

run/running. The ability to operate software and hardware to complete a task.

save/saving. (1) A command in a software application that stores the data of a current document or image to a digital file for later retrieval. (2) The process of storing the data of a document or image to digital file.

scaffolding. Refers to a variety of instructional techniques used to move students progressively from simple toward more complex tasks. Teachers provide successive levels of temporary support that help students reach higher levels of comprehension and skill acquisition that they would not be able to achieve without assistance; higher levels of understanding; and ultimately, greater independence in the learning process.

scheduling/scheduling software. (1) In the context of technology, this is the process of using digital tools and applications to create and maintain an electronic calendar or schedule. (2) A computer program that automates the process of creating and maintaining a calendar or schedule.

screen capture/screen-capturing/screen-capture software. (1) A digital image that is created from information currently displayed on a screen or monitor. (2) The act of saving content currently displayed on a screen or monitor to an image. (3) A computer program that allows users to save content currently displayed on a screen or monitor as an image.

screencast/screencasting/screencast software. (1) A video that is created from information currently displayed on a screen or monitor. (2) The act of saving content currently displayed on a screen or monitor to video. (3) A computer program that allows users to save content currently displayed on a screen or monitor as a video.

search/searching. Requires the use of search engines and keywords by the user to locate digital content from the World Wide Web, online databases, and other types of websites.

search engine. A searchable database or index containing thousands or millions of websites, Web pages, or Web documents. It allows the user to search for digital content by entering keywords or phrases and then executes the search in its database to find matches to the query.

search engine optimization (SEO). The process of driving traffic to a website through the process of improving website search engine rankings by developing website content for expertise and to match common searches.

seated classroom. The traditional classroom setting that meets at a predesignated time where students gather in their seats in-person on campus with an instructor.

seat times. Equivalences of time for in-class and out-of-class time in online courses.

security settings. Options available to users of software and applications to protect one's identity in online environments.

selfies. A photograph that one has taken of oneself, typically one taken with a smartphone or webcam and shared via social media.

server. A device, computer, or program that is dedicated to maintaining a network; a utility that basically waits in a never-ending loop to send information to a user.

sexting. The sending of sexually explicit digital images, videos, text messages, or e-mails, usually by cell phone.

share/sharing/sharing services. The process of making a digital file or document available to other users via a computer network, as for viewing, downloading, or making changes to it.

signaling. A design principle for multimedia presentations that uses cues to highlight the important content that needs to be learned. Examples include bold or underline text, adding images, or incorporating audio clicks.

slide/side deck. A single page of a digital presentation. A group of slides is known as a slide deck.

smartphone. A mobile phone with advanced connectivity and computing capabilities such as e-mail, Internet connection, and data storage.

social. As related to technology, this is interactive and collaborative behavior between individuals or users via computers or digital devices using software or applications. Sometimes referred to as social computing.

GLOSSARY

social bookmark/social bookmarking. (1) A hyperlink that is stored in a browser or other software program for quick access later and shared with other users. (2) The process of curating hyperlinks for later access, and to be shared with other users.

social media. Web-based applications that enable users to create and share content or to participate in social networking.

social network/social networking. (1) A digital platform that allows users to create a profile, add friends, communicate with other members, and add their own media. (2) The act of socializing in an online community.

software. A computer program designed to perform a group of coordinated functions, tasks, or activities for the benefit of the user.

software update. A piece of software that can correct problems within a software program. These are usually free to download and are also known as a software patch.

spam/spamming/spammer. (1) The electronic equivalent of junk mail or sending an e-mail message to a great number of recipients without regard for their need to know. (2) The act of e-mailing spam. (3) A person who sends spam.

speakers. A device that converts audio signals to create audible sound such as music or dialogue. Speakers are typically included on computers, phones, and tablets.

spreadsheet. A program that provides a worksheet with rows and columns to be used for calculations and the preparation of reports.

streaming/streaming services. When data from an audio or video file is continuously delivered to a user via the Internet, to allow for listening or viewing.

student roadmap. A lesson outline or guide that allows students to track their progress through online learning modules.

subscribe/subscribing. (1) An option that allows a user to gain access to content for a fee or to be notified when content is available from a vendor or provider of content. (2) The act of paying for content or adding one's e-mail address to a vendor or provider's e-mailing list.

synchronous chat. A method of communication in which people type text messages to each other, thereby holding a conversation over a network such as the Internet but in real time.

synchronously. An online course delivered in real time, in which class members meet over a distance at a designated time within the learning management system by using video or audio connections.

tablet. A type of notebook computer that has an LCD screen on which the user can write using finger and swipe actions or by using a special purpose apparatus called a stylus.

tag/tagging. A social media functionality that allows users to create a link back to the profile of the person shown in the picture or targeted by the update.

technology-enhanced learning/technology-facilitated learning. The use of technology to enhance student learning. Often a synonym for eLearning, the focus is on learning with technology, not just via technology.

telehealth. A variety of digital technologies used to deliver medical care and education for enhancing care and educational delivery.

text/text message/texting/text messaging. (1) A short electronic message that occurs between two or more users of mobile devices over a network. Also known as short message service (SMS), a text is usually under 100 characters. Multimedia message service (MMS) allows for users to send audio, video, and images. (2) The act of creating and sending a short electronic message to another mobile device user.

time on task. The total learning time spent by a student in a college course regardless of delivery method. This includes instructional time, studying, and completing course assignments.

This is viewed as an alternative to the Carnegie, the traditional model for academic credit.

to-do list software. A computer program that allows users to create and manage an electronic list of tasks to complete.

track changes. A feature of most word-processing software programs that allows a user to record alterations made to a document, including additions or deletions of text, and restore a document to its original state.

troll/trolling. (1) A member of an online community who posts offensive, divisive, and controversial comments, which are meant to bait other members into reacting. (2) The act of posting offensive, divisive, and controversial comments to get a reaction from other members in an online community.

tweet/tweeting. (1) A post made on the microblogging platform Twitter. A tweet is limited to 280 characters or fewer. (2) The act of creating and publishing a post on Twitter.

undo/undoing. (1) A feature in a word-processing program or other type of publishing software that allows a user to restore the last editing activity, such as bringing back original text that was deleted or changed. (2) The act of restoring original text in a program or application.

uniform resource locator (URL). Also known as a universal resource locator, URL address, or Web address, this is the location identifying where files can be found on the Internet and the protocol used to access it.

universal design/universal design for learning. Designing online courses or content with the goal of making them usable to all learners, regardless of their age, technical savvy, or ability.

upload/uploading. This is the transfer of data from a local computer to a remote location such as the cloud, another computer, or a server.

user/username. (1) In the context of technology, an individual who uses a computer or digital or mobile device. (2) A username is created by a user and consists of alphanumeric characters and symbols that identify a user and allow access to a program or computing system.

video/video file. A recording of moving visual images, usually made digitally. There are different video file formats for digital recordings that help to reduce the size of the file. See also *MP4* and *MP3*.

video blogs. A Web log, or blog, that uses video to present information.

videocast/vidcast/videocasting. A method for the distribution of video clips over the Internet using the same supporting technology (RSS feeds) as that used for podcasting.

video clip. A segment of video or media files containing video, audio, graphics, or any other content.

videoconferencing/videoconferencing software. (1) The use of video technology (hardware and software) to create a virtual meeting between two or more people in different physical locations. Participants can see and hear each other through this technology. (2) A software program of application that facilitates initiating and conducting live conferences between two or more participants at different sites by using computer networks to transmit information in the form of audio, video, or text.

video sharing. When one user shares a video or video clip with another user or many others over the Internet.

video stream/video streaming. A type of media streaming in which the data from a video file is continuously delivered via the Internet to a remote user.

viral. Digital content such as an image, a video, or an advertisement that is circulated rapidly on the Internet.

GLOSSARY

virtual/virtually/virtual environment. In education, a computer-generated setting where courses or course materials are shared.

virus. A malicious software program loaded onto a user's computer or device without the user's knowledge that performs malicious actions.

wearable technology. Smart electronic devices (electronic device with microcontrollers) that can be worn on the body as implants or accessories that track a user's movement or other biological functions.

Web/Web based. Any program that is accessed over a network connection using hypertext transfer protocol (HTTP), rather than existing within a device's memory.

Web browser. A software program that allows a user to locate, access, and display Web pages.

webcam. A video camera that is attached to a computer or laptop that can transmit live images via the Internet and can also be used for recording.

Web page. A digital document created with hypertext markup language, making it accessible with a Web browser. In addition to text and graphics, Web pages may also contain downloadable data files, audio and video files, and hyperlinks to other pages or sites.

website. A single address on the World Wide Web, typically consisting of multiple pages organized around a topic or by an information provider.

Web 2.0. A term often applied to a perceived ongoing transition of the World Wide Web from a collection of websites to a full-fledged computing platform serving Web applications to end users. It refers to a supposed second-generation of Internet-based services, such as social networking sites, wikis, communication tools, and folksonomies, that emphasize online collaboration and sharing among users.

widget. Refers to an element within an application or a tiny application that displays information or interacts with a user. Examples include a digital button, a scroll bar, or a search box.

WiFi/WiFi access. Refers to wireless connectivity of devices and computers to the Internet.

wiki. A collaborative website that allows anyone who has access to it to add and edit content. Wikipedia, an online encyclopedia, is an example of a wiki.

word processing. The electronic process of creating, formatting, editing, proofreading, and printing documents.

World Wide Web. WWW for short; defined as a collection of computers and users on the Internet that is connected via protocols such as the hypertext transfer protocol.

Specific Brand Name Products and Organizations

Academia.edu. A Web-based service and platform for academics and researchers to network and share scholarship. https://www.academia.edu/about

Academic Writing Club. A Web-based writing club for students and professors that provides support and coaching in academic writing. http://academicwritingclub.com/

Adobe Connect. A videoconferencing software by Adobe. https://www.adobe.com/products/adobeconnect.html

agreeAdate. A Web-based scheduling service. Users can send invitations to schedules or events. http://www.agreeadate.com/

ALCEA Software. A software company that specializes in field intern placement software. https://www.alceasoftware.com/alcea/index.html

Altmetric. A Web-based tool for generating alternative metrics. https://www.altmetric.com/

GLOSSARY

American FactFinder. A Web-based search tool for the U.S. Census Bureau's website that allows for guided and advanced search of census data. https://factfinder.census.gov/faces/nav/jsf/pages/index.xhtml

Apple GarageBand. Apple's software application that allows users to create music or podcasts. https://www.apple.com/mac/garageband/

Apple iCloud Calendar. Apple's cloud calendaring software. https://www.icloud.com/#calendar

Apple iMovie. A video-editing software made by Apple that can be used on Mac products. https://www.apple.com/imovie/

Apple Keynote. A brand of presentation software developed by Apple. https://www.apple.com/keynote/

Apple Mac Mail. A brand of electronic mail software developed by Apple. https://support.apple.com/mail

Apple MacOS. Apple's operating system. https://www.apple.com/macos/high-sierra/

Apple Pages. Apple's brand of word-processing software. https://www.apple.com/pages/

ArcGIS. A brand of geographic information system (GIS). http://www.esri.com/arcgis/about-arcgis

Audacity. A free multitrack audio editor and recorder for multiple operating systems commonly used for podcasting. http://www.audacity.com/

BigBlueButton. An open-source Web conferencing system. https://bigbluebutton.org/

Bing. Microsoft's search engine. https://www.bing.com/

Blackboard. A virtual learning environment and course management system developed by Blackboard Inc. http://www.blackboard.com/index.html

Blackboard Collaborate. A Web-based conferencing tool, or virtual classroom. https://www.blackboard.com/online-collaborative-learning/blackboard-collaborate.html

Blogger. A free blogging platform owned by Google that allows individuals and companies to host and publish a blog typically on a subdomain. https://www.blogger.com/

BlogTalkRadio. A Web-based talk radio and podcast hosting platform. http://www.blogtalkradio.com/

Camtasia. A software application used for creating video tutorials and presentations directly via screencast or a direct recording plug-in to Microsoft PowerPoint. https://www.techsmith.com/video-editor.html

Canva. An online graphic designing software. https://www.canva.com/

Canvas. A learning management system developed by Instructure. https://www.canvaslms.com/?lead_source_description=instructure.com_

Cengage. An educational content, technology, and services company. https://www.cengage.com/

Change.org. A website where users can create petitions and collect digital signatures. https://www.change.org/

Cielo24. An online platform that creates searchable metadata, including indexes, transcripts, and captions. https://cielo24.com/

Creative Commons license. One of several public copyright licenses that enable the free distribution of an otherwise copyrighted work. https://creativecommons.org/

Del.icio.us. A social bookmarking Web-based service for storing, sharing, and discovering bookmarks. https://del.icio.us/

Digg. A brand of news aggregator with a curated front page that selects stories specifically for the Internet audience, such as science, trending political issues, and viral Internet issues. https://digg.com/

GLOSSARY

Diigo. A social bookmarking website that allows signed-up users to bookmark and tag Web pages. https://www.diigo.com/

DocuSign. A company that provides electronic signature technology and digital transaction management services for facilitating electronic exchanges of contracts and signed documents. https://www.docusign.com/

Doodle. An online scheduling tool that can be used to find a date and time to meet with multiple people. https://doodle.com/

DropBox. An online cloud-based technology where data is stored and shared. https://www.dropbox.com/

Dwellr. An application from the U.S. Census Bureau that provides access to demographic, socioeconomic, and housing statistics from the American Community Survey. https://www.census.gov/data/mobile-apps/dwellr.html

Educause. Provides, among other information, quality standards for teaching online. https://www.educause.edu/

Educreations. An interactive whiteboard and screencasting tool that allows users to annotate, animate, and narrate nearly any type of content. https://www.educreations.com/

EndNote. A brand of citation manager. http://endnote.com/

Evernote: A note-taking software program. https://www.evernote.com

Facebook. A social media platform and social networking service. https://www.facebook.com/

Factcheck.org. A fact-checking website that rates the accuracy of claims by elected officials and others on its Truth-O-Meter. https://www.factcheck.org/

Feedly. An RSS feed reader. https://feedly.com/i/welcome

Firestorm Viewer. An open source viewer for accessing virtual worlds. http://www.firestormviewer.org/downloads/

Fitbit. Wearable devices that track exercise, heart rate, and other health biometrics. https://www.fitbit.com/home

Flickr/Flickr: The Commons. A photo-sharing platform and social network where users upload and share photos. https://www.flickr.com/

Flipboard. A website that aggregates content from social media, news feeds, photo-sharing sites, and other websites; presents it in magazine format; and allows users to "flip" through the articles, images, and videos being shared. https://www.flipboard.com/

Flipgrid. A Web-based platform and app that allows users to record short videos from inclusion in a group discussion forum. https://flipgrid.com/

Free Music Archive. An interactive library of high-quality, legal audio downloads directed by WFMU, a free-form radio station. http://freemusicarchive.org/

Freesound. A collaborative database of Creative Commons licensed sounds and music. https://freesound.org/

Glogster. A cloud-based platform for creating presentations and interactive learning. http://edu.glogster.com/

Google/Googling. A popular Web-based search engine, or the process of using the search engine to look up information. https://www.google.com/

Google Apps/GSuite. A brand of cloud computing, productivity, and collaboration tools, software, and products developed by Google. https://gsuite.google.com/together/

Google Calendar. A brand of calendaring software that was developed by Google. http://www.calendar.google.com/

Google Chrome. A free Web browser produced by Google that fully integrates with its online search system and its other applications. https://www.google.com/chrome/

Google Docs. A group of Web-based office applications that includes tools for word processing, presentations, spreadsheet analysis, and so forth. https://www.google.com/docs/about/

Google Drive. A file storage and synchronization service developed by Google that allows users to store files on their servers, synchronize files across devices, and share files. https://www.google.com/drive/

Google Forms. A platform created by Google where users can create online surveys and quizzes and send them to other people. https://www.google.com/forms/about/

Google Gmail's Canned Response. A feature on Google's Gmail allowing users to create and save multiple e-mail templates in their inbox. https://google.oit.ncsu.edu/core/gmail/canned-response/

Google Maps. A Web mapping service developed by Google. https://www.google.com/maps

Google Play. Google's digital distribution service. https://play.google.com/store?hl=en

Google Reverse Image Search Engine. An application that lets users search by images instead of keywords. https://reverse.photos/

Google Scholar. A Web search engine that indexes the full text or metadata of scholarly literature across an array of publishing formats and disciplines. https://scholar.google.com/

Google Sites. A structured wiki and Web page creation tool offered by Google as part of the G Suite productivity suite. https://sites.google.com/

Google Slides. A platform created by Google where users can create and edit presentations. https://www.google.com/slides/about/

Google Spreadsheets. A platform created by Google where users can create and edit spreadsheets and databases. https://www.google.com/sheets/about/

GotoMeeting. An online meeting, desktop-sharing, and videoconferencing software that enables the user to meet with other computer users, customers, clients, or colleagues via the Internet in real time. https://www.gotomeeting.com/

Grid-Enabled Measures (GEM) Database. A Web-based compendium of behavioral and social science measures organized by theoretical constructs. https://www.gem-beta.org/Public/Home.aspx

GroupMe. An text-messaging application. https://groupme.com/

Hootsuite. A social media integration and management platform. https://hootsuite.com/

iClickers. A brand of clicker. https://www.iclicker.com/

iCloud Calendar. A brand of calendaring software that was developed by Apple. https://www.icloud.com/calendar

If This Then That (IFTTT). A Web-based service to create chains of simple conditional statements, called applets. https://ifttt.com/

Instagram. A photo-sharing application that lets users take photos, apply filters to their images, and share the photos instantly on a feed and other social networks. https://www.instagram.com/

Instapaper. A Web-based bookmarking service. https://www.instapaper.com/

Internet Archive. A nonprofit digital library offering free universal access to books, movies, and music. https://archive.org/

Intern Placement Tracking (IPT). A Web-based practicum monitoring system designed to keep track of students placed in internship programs with various agencies. https://www.alcea-software.com/alcea/index.html

iTunes. A media player, a media library, an Internet radio broadcaster, and a mobile device management application developed by Apple Inc. https://www.apple.com/itunes/

Jamendo. A Web-based music streaming platform. https://www.jamendo.com/?language=en

GLOSSARY

Jing. A screencasting software that allows users to record their computer or phone screen. https://www.techsmith.com/jing-tool.htm

Kaltura. An open-source video platform that enhances websites with customized video, photo, and audio functionalities. https://corp.kaltura.com/

LinkedIn. A professionally-oriented social media platform. https://www.linkedin.com/

Listly. A tool to create, curate, and collect digital lists. https://list.ly/

LISTSERV. An electronic mailing list application that distributes messages to subscribers of specific lists. Members of a LISTSERV usually join based on a common shared interest.

Livechat. A Web-based live chat software. https://www.livechatinc.com/

LiveText. A cloud-based software for assessment, accreditation, and e-portfolios to educational organizations. https://www.watermarkinsights.com/

LockDown Browser. A customized browser that increases the security of test delivery in Blackboard. When activated, students are unable to print, copy, go to another URL, or access other applications. https://www.respondus.com/

Loomio. A decision-making software designed to assist groups with the collaborative decision-making process. https://www.loomio.org/

Mendeley. A brand of citation manager. https://www.mendeley.com/

Microsoft Excel. A spreadsheet software developed by Microsoft for Windows, macOS, Android, and iOS. https://www.office.microsoft.com/excel/

Microsoft Movie Maker. A video editor by Microsoft. https://www.windows-movie-maker.org/

Microsoft Office. An application suite by Microsoft for Windows that includes Excel, PowerPoint, and Word. https://www.office.com/

Microsoft Outlook. Microsoft's e-mail service. https://products.office.com/en-us/outlook/email-and-calendar-software-microsoft-outlook?tab=tabs-1

Microsoft PowerPoint. A software package from Microsoft designed to create electronic presentations consisting of a series of separate pages or slides. https://products.office.com/en-us/powerpoint

Microsoft Windows. Microsoft's operating system. https://www.microsoft.com/en-us/windows/

Microsoft Word. Microsoft's word-processing software. https://products.office.com/en-us/word

MindMeister. An online mind mapping application that allows its users to visualize, share, and present their thoughts via the cloud. https://www.mindmeister.com/

Minecraft. A video game. https://minecraft.net/en-us/

Moodle. A brand of learning management system. https://moodle.org/

MySpace. A social networking platform. https://myspace.com/

Netiquette. A combination of the words *network* and *etiquette*, defined as a set of rules for acceptable online behavior. http://www.albion.com/netiquette/

Noodle Partners. An online program manager (OPM) that partners with schools to help with student and program management. https://www.noodle-partners.com/

NVIVO. A qualitative analysis software. http://www.qsrinternational.com/nvivo/what-is-nvivo

The Old Reader. A Web-based news aggregator that delivers website, blog, and other Internet content to a Web-based inbox. https://theoldreader.com/

Padlet. An app that enables users to create an online bulletin board to display information on any topic. https://padlet.com/

GLOSSARY

Pearson. A company that provides educational materials and services. https://www.pearson.com/us/

Pexel Videos. A website that provides free stock video downloads. https://videos.pexels.com/

PhotoGrid. A photo-editing application. http://www.cmcm.com/en-us/photo-grid/

Piktochart. A Web-based application that allows users to create infographics. https://piktochart.com/

Pinterest. A photo-sharing social network that provides users with a platform for uploading, saving, and categorizing "pins" through collections called "boards." https://www.pinterest.com/

PlayPosit. An online learning environment to create and share interactive video lessons. https://www.playposit.com/

Pocket. An app that enables users to manage a reading list of articles saved from the Internet to read later. https://getpocket.com/

Poll Everywhere. An audience response technology based on Web and cellular networks that allows students or others to provide feedback regardless of the device they are holding. https://www.polleverywhere.com/

Popplet. An online tool designed for capturing, organizing, and mapping ideas. https://popplet.com/

Prezi. A Web-based presentation platform. https://prezi.com/

ProctorU. An online proctoring service. https://www.proctoru.com/

Project Gutenberg. A free e-book library. https://www.gutenberg.org/

Public Domain Pictures Website. An online database of free stock photographs. https://www.publicdomainpictures.net/

PubMed. A search engine accessing primarily the MEDLINE database of references and abstracts on life sciences and biomedical topics. https://www.ncbi.nlm.nih.gov/pubmed/

Qualtrics. A company that provides products and services to collect and analyze data online. https://www.qualtrics.com/

Remind. Web-based software that allows text-based messages to be sent between faculty members and students, typically used as assignment reminders. https://www.remind.com/

ResearchGate. An academic social networking site designed to facilitate access to academic research and collaboration between researchers. https://www.researchgate.net/

SafeAssign. A Blackboard feature that compares submitted assignments against a set of academic papers to identify areas of overlap between the submitted assignment and existing works. https://help.blackboard.com/Learn/Instructor/Assignments/SafeAssign

Salesforce. A cloud computing provider that consists of multiple cloud services including Sales Cloud, Service Cloud, and Marketing Cloud. https://www.salesforce.com/

Schedule Once. An appointment scheduler with personal calendars that supports users in a wide range of scheduling scenarios. https://www.scheduleonce.com/

Screencast-O-Matic. A screen-recording software. https://screencast-o-matic.com/

Scrivener. A word-processing software. https://www.literatureandlatte.com/scrivener/overview

Second Life. An online virtual world. http://secondlife.com/

SelfControl. An application that allows the user to block access to websites or other applications. http://selfcontrolapp.com/

SignupGenius. An online software tool for volunteer management and event planning. http://www.signupgenius.com/

Skype. A video, voice, and instant messaging software application to communicate with people over the Internet. https://www.skype.com/

GLOSSARY

Slack. A cloud-based set of collaboration tools and services for teams. https://slack.com/

SlideShare. A Web 2.0–based slide hosting service. https://www.slideshare.net/

Snagit. A screencapture software. https://www.techsmith.com/screen-capture.html

Snapchat. A social app that allows users to send and receive time-sensitive photos and videos known as "snaps," which are hidden from the recipients once the time limit expires (images and videos remain on the Snapchat server). https://www.snapchat.com/

Snopes. A fact-checking website. https://www.snopes.com/

Social Pilot. A social media scheduling tool. https://www.socialpilot.co/

Social Work Podcast. A podcast that focuses on topics related to social work and social work practice. https://socialworkpodcast.blogspot.com/

Sonia. A student placement management application. https://www.sonia.com.au/

SoundCloud. An online music streaming platform. https://soundcloud.com/

Statistical Package for the Social Sciences (SPSS) software. A software package, distributed by IBM, used for statistical analysis. https://www.ibm.com/analytics/spss-statistics-software

SurveyMonkey. A website that allows users to create and distribute online surveys. https://www.surveymonkey.com/

Taskstream. A cloud-based software for assessment, accreditation, and e-portfolios to educational organizations. https://www.watermarkinsights.com/

Tegrity. A software system that allows instructors to record audio, video, and computer screen activity. https://www.mheducation.com/highered/platforms/tegrity.html

Tes Teach. Tes Teach is a Web-based software for creating digital lessons and offers free accounts. https://www.tes.com/lessons

3PlayMedia. A company that provides video captioning and transcription, audio description, translation, and subtitling services. https://www.3playmedia.com/

Tinychat. An online chat website that allows users to communicate via instant messaging, voice chat, and video chat. https://www.tinychat.com/#category=all

TK20. A cloud-based software for assessment, accreditation, and e-portfolios used by educational organizations. https://www.watermarkinsights.com/

Todoist. A task management application. https://en.todoist.com/

Trello. A Web-based project management application. https://trello.com/

Tumblr. A microblogging platform and social networking website allowing users to post multimedia and other content to a short-form blog. https://www.tumblr.com/

Turnitin. A Web-based plagiarism-detection service. http://turnitin.com/.

TweetDeck. A Twitter tool that provides users with a way to manage their Twitter presence through custom columns. The platform integrates with the Twitter API to allow users to send and receive tweets. https://tweetdeck.twitter.com/

Twine. A Web-based open-source tool for telling interactive, nonlinear stories. https://twinery.org/

Twitter. A real-time social network that allows users to share 140-character updates with their following. Users can favorite and retweet the posts of other users and engage in conversations

GLOSSARY

using @ mentions, replies, and hashtags for categorizing their content. https://www.twitter.com/

2U. An online program manager (OPM) educational technology company that partners with colleges and universities to offer online degree programs. https://2u.com/

Unsplash. A website where users can download copyright-free photography under a nonexclusive copyright license. https://unsplash.com/

U.S. Library of Congress. A website for the research library that officially serves the United States Congress. https://www.loc.gov/

Venngage. A free Web-based tool that aids creation of infographics. https://venngage.com/

VideoAnt. A Web-based platform on which students and teachers view and annotate videos. https://ant.umn.edu/

Videvo. A Web-based service that provides free stock video footage and motion graphics for use in any project. https://www.videvo.net/

Vimeo. A video-sharing platform. https://vimeo.com/

VoiceThread. A Web-based platform that enables teachers and students to upload images, video, or documents; record audio, video, or text comments; and then invite others to record comments. https://voicethread.com/

Wakelet. A content curation platform that lets users save and organize articles, videos, tweets, podcasts, and other content online to use later. https://wakelet.com/

WeVideo. An online video-editing application. https://www.wevideo.com/

Wikimedia Commons. A media file repository making available public domain and freely licensed educational media content. https://commons.wikimedia.org/wiki/Main_Page

Wikipedia. An open content, online encyclopedia. https://www.wikipedia.org/

WordPress. A Web publishing tool used for basic website creation worldwide. https://wordpress.com/

Words With Friends. A multiplayer word game that resembles Scrabble. https://www.zynga.com/games/words-with-friends-2

WorldCat. A large network of library content and services. https://www.worldcat.org/

World of Warcraft. A massively multiplayer online role-playing game. https://worldofwarcraft.com/en-us/

Wunderlist. A cloud-based task management application. https://www.wunderlist.com/

YouCanBookMe. An online scheduling software for teams and individuals that integrates with Google or iCloud Calendar. https://youcanbook.me/

YouTube. A free video-sharing website that allows uploading and viewing of video content. https://www.youtube.com/

Zoom. A brand of videoconferencing software. https://zoom.us/

Zotero. A free and open-source reference management software to manage bibliographic data and related research materials. https://www.zotero.org/

INDEX

Boxes, figures, and tables are indicated by b, f, and t following the page numbers.

A

AASWSW (American Academy of Social Work and Social Welfare), 359
Academia.edu, 362, 625, 626
Academic integrity. *See also* Ethical considerations for technology in education; Plagiarism
    e-learning tools for, 113*t*
    NASW on, 317*b*, 337, 589–590
    open-sourced content for assignments, 338–339, 338*b*
Academic workload, 370–372, 616–620
Academic Writing Club, 621
Access and accessibility issues. *See also* Technological disruptions
    accommodations in online programs, 218–219, 219*b*, 238
    class design and, 98
    digital inclusion and, 34–35, 36, 310, 328–329
    electronic devices, availability of, 111, 150
    ethical considerations for technology in education, 325–330, 326–328*b*
    identity and, 49–50*b*
    Internet access as human right, 310, 353, 360
    NASW on, 588–589
    people with disabilities and, 115, 181
    socioeconomic status and, 97–98
    student evaluation and, 585
    video kits for, 266*b*
Accreditation standards, 4–5, 240–241, 269, 287–288. *See also* Educational Policy and Accreditation Standards of CSWE
Active learning model
    defined, 95
    distance education and, 95–99
    instructional design and, 78, 80*f*
    scaffolding and, 99

social learning and, 88–89
technology in classrooms and, 108–109, 111
Active listening, 167
ADA (Americans with Disabilities Act, 1990), 218, 325, 327
Adaptive release tools, 171–172
Add-on tools, 129, 288–289, 370–371
Adedoyin, A. C. A., 374
Adjunct faculty, 225–228
Administrators
    nontraditional scheduling challenges for, 239
    online programs and, 223, 230
    social media policies and, 584
    support for technology in classrooms, 580
Admission to online programs
    assessing students for, 238
    competitiveness of, 235–236
    encroachment issues and, 247–248
    multiple dates for, 229, 231, 237
    nontraditional time clocks and, 239
    state regulations and, 248–250
    transfer credits and, 220
Adobe Connect, 136, 235
Adoption of new technology, 40–42, 41*f*, 349–351, 351*f*
Adult learning (andragogy), 76–81, 77–79*b*, 80*f*, 298. *See also*
    Pedagogical approaches to technology
Advanced searches, 130
Advocacy. *See* Human rights advocacy; Social justice
Agency tutorials assignment, 468–470
Agreeadate, 266*b*
ALCEA software, 288–289
Algorithms, 310, 342
Allen, I. E., 3
Altmetric (tool), 626–627
Altmetrics/alternative metrics, 362, 626–627
Alt-text, 327
American Academy of Social Work and Social Welfare (AASWSW), 359
American FactFinder tools, 489–492
Americans with Disabilities Act (ADA, 1990), 218, 325, 327
Analytic tools, 133–135
Anderson, T., 89
Annotating on digital content. *See* Commenting on digital content
Anthony, Becky, 227, 248
Apple GarageBand, 137, 415
Apple iCloud Calendar, 371
Apple iMovie, 137, 415, 529

INDEX

Apple iTunes, 452, 454, 547
Apple Keynote, 135
Apple MacOS, 529
Apple Pages, 131
Application of knowledge, tools for, 132–133
Applications (apps). *See also* Learning management systems; *specific apps*
    for calendar scheduling, 266*b*, 371–372
    case study on, 54–55*b*
    cognitive literacy and, 50–51
    ethical use in education, 322
    LMS compatibility with, 112, 113*t*
    notifications from, 379–380, 381–382*b*
    for photo-editing, 56
    professional use of, 47, 322
    rate of usage in BSW education programs, 109–110
    for self-care, 380
    for text messaging, 265, 266*b*
    for to-do lists, 371
    for videoconferencing, 301
ArcGIS, 543
Archer, W., 89
Article review assignment, 478–480
Artificial intelligence, 310
Assessment data, reporting of, 287–288, 361
Assignment compendium, 393–549
    ethical and legal considerations for assignments, 398
    field education, 429–442
    HBSE, 443–455
    navigation of, 393–398
    practice skills development, 456–530
    research, 530–549
    types of learning activities in, 142, 142–144*f*
Association of Baccalaureate Social Work Program Directors, 373–374
Association of Social Work Boards (ASWB), 4, 314
Asynchronous vs. synchronous online content
    effectiveness of, 178–179
    flipped classrooms and, 99
    learning activity examples, 176–177*t*
    online courses defined, 13
    social presence and, 92, 93*b*
    time requirements and, 172–174, 240–241
Attention. *See also* Distractions
    mindfulness and, 48, 82, 87*b*, 382
    motivation and, 84
Attribution. *See* Citations for digital work

Audacity, 137, 507
Audience response tools, 113*t*, 530–532
Audioconferencing software, 113*t*
Audio presentation assignments
    podcasts, 463–465, 497–499, 510–513
    radio show, 504–507
    recording and editing, 440–442
Authentication strategies, 337
Automation, 265–266, 288, 292, 618
Autonomy, 82
Avatars, 260, 268, 323, 402–409

B

Babson Survey Research Group, 159, 160*t*
Bachelor social work (BSW) degrees, 220–221
Back-loaded content, 164
Back-up plans, 328, 330, 357, 599, 601, 610
Backward mapping, 79, 178
Badging, 133
Barkdull, Carenlee, 607
Barth, A. M., 244
BASW (British Association of Social Workers), 314
Beal, B., 110
Behavior change project, 431–435
Belluomini, Ellen, 561
Belshaw, Doug
    on elements of digital literacy, 19, 38–40, 44, 45*f*, 48, 51–55, 58, 597
    SAMR Model and, 118–119
Best practices for technology use. *See also Standards for Technology in Social Work Practice*
    accessibility issues and, 326
    adult learners and, 76, 80
    classroom delivery methods, effect of, 12
    continuing education and, 579
    deleting online comments, 200
    for educational assessment, 150, 339, 607–612
    ethical considerations and, 312
    field education and, 303
    pedagogy and, 10–11
    public posting of personal information, 321, 323
    student engagement and, 188*b*
    training instructors in, 239, 277
Beta, 350

Biases
  against online programs, 264, 294
  personal, 556, 578, 582
BigBlueButton, 236
Big data, 310, 359–360
Bing, 129
Biometrics, 337
Blackboard, 46
Blackboard Collaborate, 236
Blended courses. *See* Hybrid courses
Blogger, 131, 136, 376
Blogging, 131, 320, 321, 375–377
BlogTalkRadio, 507
Bloom's Digital Taxonomy
  cognitive process dimension, 123, 124*f*
  digital knowledge dimension, 121, 122*f*
  digital tools in, 127–138
  learning outcomes from, 145–146, 147*f*
  overview of, 120–125
  for social work education, 125–126, 126–127*f*
  suggested uses for, 138–139
  technology-enhanced learning activities using, 142, 142–144*f*
Book groups, assignment on, 419–421
Bookmarking, 129, 367
Boolean searches, 130
Borton, T., 354
Boyer, E. L., *Scholarship Reconsidered*, 374
Bradley, Sarah
  on active learning, 97*b*
  on feedback and evaluation, 94*b*
  on field education, 271
  on foundational theories, 85*b*, 88*b*
  on instructional designers, 77–79*b*
  on scaffolding, 92*b*
  on self-regulation tools, 83*b*
  on social presence, 93*b*
  on student evaluations, 100*b*
  on technology use in training, 282
Brady, S. R., 335, 354
British Association of Social Workers (BASW), 314
Brokering skills, 416–419
Bulletin board systems, 33, 92–93
Buquoi, B., 109
Burns, K., 191

C

Calendar and schedule management
    for asynchronous or blended classes, 240–241
    e-mail communication and, 370–371
    nonstandard time clocks for online courses, 239
    software and digital tools for, 266b, 371, 619–620
California, field placement regulations for, 249–250
Campus visits, 244–247, 272. *See also* Orientation
Camtasia, 451
Canadian Association of Social Workers (CASW), 314
Canva, 135
Canvas, 112, 228
Captions, 326b, 327, 327–328b
Capture of digital content. *See* Content capturing e-learning tools
Carnegie units, 240
Carney, Michelle, 233, 242–243
Case examples, 319b
Case presentation assignment, 480–482
Castaneda, Silvana, 297
CASW (Canadian Association of Social Workers), 314
Cengage, 232–233
Census Bureau data, 489–492, 547–549, 563
Center for Humane Technology, 380
Change.org, 61
Chat boxes, 224, 301, 357
Chatting. *See* Text messaging
Cheating. *See* Academic integrity; Plagiarism
Chunking, 86
Churches, A., 123, 125, 128
Churches Digital Taxonomy, 128
Cielo24, 326
Citations for digital work, 52–53, 336–339, 338b
Civic element of digital literacy, 60–61
Classrooms
    online, 157–208. *See also* Online courses
    seated. *See* Seated classrooms
    technology in, 107–155. *See also* Technology in classrooms
Clickers (audience response tools), 113t, 530–532
Client information, 318–320, 319b
Clinical Social Work Association (CSWA), 4, 74, 313, 314
Cloud-based services, 110, 113t, 136, 301
Cloud computing, 263, 349, 361
CMSs (content management systems), 114
Code of ethics. *See* NASW Code of Ethics
Code source, 59

Cognitive element of digital literacy, 50–51, 600–601
Cognitive literacy, 50–51
Cognitive overload, 86–87, 88*b*
Cognitive presence, 89–90
Cognitive processes, 123–125, 124*f*
COI (Community of Inquiry) model, 89–90, 169
Collaboration. *See also* Interprofessional collaboration
    for digital tool use, 136
    for dissemination of research, 374–375
    e-learning tools for, 113*t*
    for field instructor training, 304
    learning environments and, 168
    PLNs and, 365
    technology tips for, 621–624
    virtual communities of practice for, 372–374, 621–624
    YouTube for, 128
Collaborative learning, 80*f*, 84, 88–94, 94*b*
Commenting on digital content. *See also* Discussion boards and forums
    to communicate understanding of content, 131–132
    feedback received from, 373
    quality of, 135
    text-based comments systems in LMSs, 46, 51, 83*b*, 85*b*
Commercial partners for online programs, 229–232, 251, 310
Communication. *See also* High-touch pedagogy model; *specific types of media and devices*
    automated, 189, 265, 266*b*, 370–371
    lurking vs., 53
    mailing lists, subscriptions to, 129–130
    nonverbal skills, assessing, 272
    professionalism in, 36, 553
    student-instructor, 184, 189, 190*b*, 265, 266*b*
    technological change and, 33
Communicative element of digital literacy, 53–54, 54–55*b*, 602–603
Communities of practice (CoP), 302–303, 372–374, 621–624
Community assessment assignments, 508–510, 541–543
Community connections, 95, 299–300
Community learning. *See* Professional learning networks
Community of Inquiry (COI) model, 89–90, 169
Competence
    access and accessibility issues, 585
    assessing acquisition of, 7, 241, 268
    defined, 577
    domains of, 268
    evaluations based on, 240–241
    feedback, giving and receiving, 199

field education and, 268
of instructors, 579
technological, 577–578. *See also* Digital literacy
Competency-based education, 4, 78, 121, 361
Competency outcome assessments, 241
Confident element of digital literacy, 55–56, 57*b*, 603–604
Confidentiality. *See* Privacy and confidentiality
Connected learning, 80*f*, 88–89, 94–95
Connected Learning Research Network, 95
Constructive element of digital literacy, 52–53, 601–602
Consultation. *See* Supervision and consultation
Consumer protections, 250
Content capturing e-learning tools, 113*t*, 137, 291–292
Content knowledge, 40
Content management systems (CMSs), 114, 367
Content repositories, 113*t*
Contextual menus, 52
Continuing education. *See also* Communities of practice
    best practices and, 579
    CSWE on, 581–582
    digital literacy and, 44, 578, 579
    ethics of, 280
    field coordinators and, 281–282
    NASW on, 316*b*, 581–582
    via websites, 114
Continuum of technology integration, 12–14, 16, 157
CoP (communities of practice), 302–303, 372–374, 621–624
Copy and paste, 51, 52, 185, 515, 537, 602
Copyright laws, 52–53
Council on Social Work Education (CSWE)
    accreditation standards of. *See* Educational Policy and Accreditation Standards of CSWE
    annual program meetings, 247, 303
    on assessment data reporting, 287
    competence defined by, 577
    on competency-based education in social work, 121
    on competency-based evaluations, 240
    on competency outcome assessments, 241
    on distance field supervision, 298
    on ethical use of technology, 4, 314, 577–578
    on field education, technology and, 268
    on implicit curriculum, 242
    on online education availability, 3
    on online MSW programs, 253
    on online program requirements, 214

on professional practice competencies, 32
on technology-based learning tasks, 17, 551–569. *See also* Technology-based learning tasks
on work-based field placements, 273
Counselman-Carpenter, Beth, 326–328*b*
Course shell, 181, 494
Craig-Oldsen, Heather, 275*b*
Creating, digital tools for, 136–137
Creative Commons license, 338–339, 376–377
Creative element of digital literacy, 57–58, 604
Credentials for digital content, 58–60, 59–60*b*
Credit hours, 240–241. *See also* Seat time and time on tasks
Critical element of digital literacy, 58–60, 59–60*b*, 604–605
Critical thinking
    assessing, 271
    COI model and, 90
    technology-based learning tasks for, 558–561, 563
    trustworthiness of digital information and, 58–60, 59–60*b*
Cross-campus curriculum, 220
Crowdsourcing, 575
CSWA (Clinical Social Work Association), 4, 74, 313, 314
CSWE. *See* Council on Social Work Education; Educational Policy and Accreditation Standards (EPAS) of CSWE
Cultural element of digital literacy, 44–49, 45*b*, 49–50*b*, 598–600
Culture
    of agencies for field placement, 283
    assignments on, 402–409, 478–480, 502–504
    competence in, 33
    digital literacy and, 328–329
    of online courses, 183–186, 184–187*b*
    of online program cohorts, 243
    participatory, 95
    social cues and, 81
    of social media platforms, 283–284
    sociocultural learning theory, 91
    socioeconomic status as factor for, 97–98
    technology-based learning tasks for, 555–556
Curating tools, 367
Curriculum and course design. *See* Design of online courses and curriculum; Instructional designers
Cut and paste, 51, 52, 185, 515, 537, 602

D

Dashboards, 289, 290

Data
  assessment data, reporting, 287–288
  collection of, 320–321, 324, 431–435
  management systems for, 287–289
  ownership of, 321
  social media, management of, 378
  storage of, 13, 148–149, 288–290, 580
Databases for field education programs, 284–291, 285*b*
Davidson, C., 37
Deleting online content, 200
Del.icio.us, 129, 131
Delivery of online courses
  class culture and, 183–186, 184–187*b*
  instructor and student engagement, 187–197, 188*b*, 190*b*, 192–194*b*, 195*f*, 198*b*
  providing feedback and, 198–200, 199*b*
Department of Education, 240
Design of online courses and curriculum. *See also* Instructional designers
  accessibility issues and, 98, 326*b*, 327
  for adult learning, 76–77
  consistency in, 182*b*
  course mapping and aligning, 178–179
  ethical considerations for, 313, 360
  for field education, 273
  hardware and software skills and, 180*b*
  HIPAA compliance in, 319*b*
  for online courses and programs, 168–182, 180*b*, 182*b*, 233–234
  pedagogy and, 169–172
  planning learning activities, 172–175, 176–177*t*
  social presence in, 92
  state law variability and, 587
  suggestions for, 180–182
  time requirements for, 223
Devices. *See* Electronic devices
Diagnostic and Statistical Manual of Mental Disorders, 5th Edition (DSM5) assignment, 457–460
Dialogue box, 51, 129
Digg, 130
Digital access, 311
Digital boundaries, 379–380, 381–382*b*
Digital devices. *See* Electronic devices
Digital equity, 36, 310, 353, 360
Digital file, 132
Digital forms, 284, 289
Digital immigrants, 35–36

INDEX

Digital inclusion, 34–35, 36, 310, 328–329
Digital justice. *See* Social justice
Digital literacy, 20, 31–71
    access and accessibility issues, 585
    civic element of, 60–61, 605–606
    class participation rates and, 98
    cognitive element of, 50–51, 600–601
    communicative element of, 53–54, 54–55b, 602–603
    confident element of, 55–56, 57b, 603–604
    constructive element of, 52–53, 601–602
    course design considerations and, 178–179
    creative element of, 57–58, 604
    critical element of, 58–60, 59–60b, 604–605
    cultural element of, 44–49, 45b, 49–50b, 598–600
    culture and, 328–329
    defined, 37–39, 38–39b
    digital technology and, 40–42, 41f
    ethical considerations for, 321, 325, 333
    of field coordinators, 261–262, 273–274, 276–277
    of field personnel, 277–281
    of instructors, 109–111, 168, 579
    necessity of, 32–35
    overlap and interplay of elements, 61–63, 62f
    privacy considerations and, 590
    reflection questions for, 597–606
    research on, 63–64
    SAMR Model and, 118
    social work education, application to, 42–44, 43b
    student competency, 11–12, 35–36, 263, 279, 592–593
    teaching, 578–579
    transferability of skills learned, 110, 173
Digital natives, 35–36
Digital networks, 53, 410
Digital rights, 556–557
Digital self-care, 379–384, 381–383b
Digital self-efficacy, 55
Digital storytelling, assignment on, 414–416
Digital thinking skills, 123
Digital tracking systems, 285–291, 287b
Dignity, academic standards and, 589–590
Diigo, 129
Disabled students. *See* People with disabilities
Discussion boards and forums
    culture of, 46
    deleting comments from, 200

feedback on, 173, 198–200
field education, assessment of readiness for, 272
instructors' use of, 85*b*, 189
netiquette for, 167
posting comments on digital content, 135
requirements for number of posts, 83*b*, 196
social presence and, 92
time requirements and, 172–173
variations in, 51
video, 272
virtual communities of practice, 373
Discussion threads, 171, 196
Disruption readiness plans (DRPs), 586
Distance education. *See also* Online courses; Online programs and degrees
    institutional assessment of readiness, 210–211, 607–612
    NASW on, 586
    technological considerations for, 586–587
Distractions, 48, 84, 87, 87*b*, 361–362. *See also* Time management skills
Diversity and difference in practice, 555–556
Documentary films, 426–428
DocuSign, 289
Domain names, 59, 60
Do not disturb mode, 599, 618
Doodle, 266*b*
Dorminey, Carrie, 297
Drake, P., 321
Drisko, J., 335
DropBox, 362, 555
DRPs (disruption readiness plans), 586
DSM5 assignment, 457–460
Dual processing, 86
Dual relationships, 7, 330–331. *See also* Instructor-student boundaries
Dwellr, 547, 548

E

E-advocacy. *See* Human rights advocacy; Social justice
E-books, 139
Economic justice, 556–558
Editing digital content, 132
Educational Policy and Accreditation Standards (EPAS) of CSWE
    on assessment data collection, 287
    to assess quality of assignments, 145
    on competency outcome assessments, 241
    on ethical use of technology, 578
    on field education, 269

INDEX

  NASW standards and, 575
  social work competencies from, 145–146, 147f, 394–395
  technology-based learning tasks using, 17, 551–569. *See also* Technology-based learning tasks
  on technology in education, 4–5
Educational records, 320–324
Educational websites, assignment on, 412–414
Educause, 9
Educreations, 488
E-learning tools, 112, 113t, 178. *See also* Learning management systems
Electronic communication (e-mail)
  digital tracking systems for, 288
  LISTSERVs for online communities, 373–374
  in LMS, 56
  norms of, 46
  notifications from, 379–380
  privacy issues and, 324
  professional behavior in, 36, 553
  rate of usage, 109–110, 349
  time management skills and, 370–371, 616–619
Electronic devices. *See also* Smartphones
  access to, 111, 150
  common types of, 132
  costs of, 150, 161
  personal, institutional policies on, 590
  rate of usage in BSW education programs, 109
  skills needed for online courses, 180b
  tool knowledge and, 40, 127–128
  variations in, 588–589
  for web facilitated courses, 161
Electronic Frontier Foundation, 556
Electronic media project, 438–440
Electronic records, 349
Electronic resumes, 435–437
E-mail. *See* Electronic communication
E-mail merge, 288
Emotional support, 265, 266b. *See also* High-touch pedagogy model
Employers, 7, 215, 248
Employment-based field education placements, 272–273
Emporium model, 165
EndNote, 129
Environmental justice, 556–558
E-portfolios, 113t, 322
E-readers, 396, 420, 421
Ethical considerations for technology in education, 23–24, 309–346

685

academic integrity and, 312, 336–339, 338*b*
   access and accessibility issues, 325–330, 326–328*b*
   assignment compendium and, 398
   boundary issues and, 330–336
   categories of, 311–312
   in citations and remixing practices, 52–53
   CSWE on, 4, 577–578
   FERPA issues and, 320–324, 323–324*b*
   HIPAA concerns and, 318–320, 319*b*
   overview, 311–312
   practice skills, teaching, 312–314
   privacy and confidentiality, 318–324
   social media use and, 331–333, 354
   standards for, 4–5, 314–318, 316–317*b*
Ethics. *See also NASW Code of Ethics*
   assignments on, 492–494, 525–527
   field education and technology use, 283
   social work practice and technology use, 359–360, 581
   technology-based learning tasks for, 551–554
Evaluation of assignments. *See also* Feedback
   best practices and, 339
   culture of communication and, 185*b*
   grading and rubrics for, 147–148
   NASW on, 316*b*, 584–585
   student self-efficacy and, 82
   technology-based assignments, 145–148, 147*f*
Evaluation of digital content, tools for, 135–136
Evernote (app), 614
Evidence-based practice, 582
Evidence-based teaching, 9, 580
Excel, 110, 285, 397, 491
Experiential service-learning assignment, 527–530
Explicit curriculum, 241–242

F

Facebook. *See also* Social media
   case study on, 43*b*
   culture of, 46
   profile photos for, 51
   social presence through, 170, 237, 300*b*
Face-to-face, 12, 23, 33, 93*b*, 99, 160, 227, 236, 369
Faculty. *See* Instructors
Family Educational Rights and Privacy Act (FERPA, 2015), 320–324, 582, 592
Favoriting, 129, 367

INDEX

Feedback
    on assignments. *See* Evaluation of assignments
    asynchronous, 199
    comments on digital content, 135
    on discussions, 173
    to enhance motivation, 84
    flipped classrooms and, 99
    online courses and, 170, 198–200, 199*b*
    from peers, 94*b*, 95, 199–200
    on scholarship, 375–377
Feedly, 130
FERPA (Family Educational Rights and Privacy Act, 2015), 320–324, 582, 592
Field coordinators
    approval of field sites, 296
    digital literacy of, 261–262
    digital tracking system use and, 288
    distance vs. campus programs and, 270, 270–271*b*
    duties of, 276–277
    emotional support provided by, 266*b*
    field placement sites and, 263–264
    GIS software use of, 263*b*
    ideal traits of, 274–275*b*
    meetings with supervisors and students, 296–302, 300*b*
    student ratios for, 281
Field education online programs, 23–24, 259–307
    assignments for, 429–442
    campus field education programs vs., 270–273, 270–271*b*
    community building, 302–303
    directors and coordinators for, 276–277
    emotional support through, 266*b*
    face-to-face meetings, necessity of, 296–302, 300*b*
    field placement assignments, 438–442
    GIS software for, 263*b*
    instructors and supervisors for, 278–279
    journaling for reflection on, 429–431
    liaisons for, 278
    NASW on, 317*b*
    out-of-state field placements, 293–295, 294*b*
    preparing students for, 291–293, 293*b*
    regulatory bodies on, 267–269
    social work faculty members for, 279–280
    specialized software and databases for, 284–291, 285*b*, 287*b*
    staff for, 277–278
    stakeholders for, 280–281

state regulations on, 249–250
students of, 279
technology skills of coordinators and instructors, 273–284, 274–275b, 591–592
telehealth settings for, 232
Field journal website, 429–431
Field liaisons, 275, 278, 281, 288, 296
Field placement agreements, 264, 269, 295
Field seminars, 297–298
Field staff, 277–278
Fill-in-the-blanks assignment, 424–426
Firestorm Viewer, 403, 405
Fisher, Liz, 120b
Fiske, H., 191
Fitbit, 380
Fitch, D., 110
Flexible-mode courses, 165–166
Flickr, 131
Flipboard, 615–616
Flipgrid, 97
Flipped classrooms, 98–99, 162–163
Florida, online MSW programs in, 252
Flynn, Marilyn, 231–232, 247
Following and friending. *See* Social media
For-profit businesses, 229, 231, 232, 251, 310
For-profit career colleges, 250
For-profit data exchange, 321
Foundational learning theories, 79–80, 80f, 83–85b, 88b
Free Music Archive, 338b
Freesound, 338b
Front-loaded content, 164

G

Game-based learning, 133, 143, 144
Gaming/gamification, 133, 502–504, 564
GarageBand, 137, 415
Garrison, D. R., 89
Gatekeeping, 7, 244, 270
Gates, T., 165
GEM (Grid-Enabled Measures) Database, 533, 534, 535
General Data Protection Regulation (GDPR, EU), 324
General education courses, 220
Gentle-Genitty, Carolyn Sherlet, 184–185b
Geographical challenges, 232, 247, 262. *See also* Rural students

Geographic information system (GIS) software, 262, 263*b*, 284, 360
    assignment, 541–543
Gleason, B., 374
Glogster, 451
Gmail Canned Response, 618
Goals. *See also* Learning objectives
    active learning model and, 95
    to enhance motivation, 84
    technology distractions vs., 48
Goldkind, L., 349
Google, 128–129
Google Apps, 623
Google Calendar, 371, 620, 623
Google Chrome, 615
Google Docs, 131, 136
Google Drive, 621, 623, 624
Google Forms, 284, 285*b*
Google Gmail Canned Response, 618
Google Maps, 134
Google Reverse Image Search, 60
Google Scholar, 130, 566, 625, 626
Google Sites, 413
Google Slides, 126
Google Spreadsheets, 134, 179, 397, 558, 621
GotoMeeting, 136, 236
Grade point average (GPA), 238
Grading. *See* Evaluation of assignments; Feedback
Greenhow, C., 374
Grid-Enabled Measures (GEM) Database, 533, 534, 535
Group-based learning, 93–94, 96, 194, 196–197, 198*b*
GroupMe, 265

H
Hacking, 124, 601
Hague, C., 37
Hardware. *See* Electronic devices
Hashtags, 49–50*b*, 60, 131, 426–428
Hayward, Elizabeth, 297
HBSE (human behavior in the social environment) assignments, 443–455
Health Insurance Portability and Accountability Act (HIPAA, 1996),
    318–320, 319*b*, 582, 592
Hearing impairment, 326*b*, 327–328*b*
Heiser, J., 85
Help-seeking abilities, 82

High-touch pedagogy model, 235, 265, 302
Hitchcock, Laurel Iverson, 376–377, 607
Honesty, 589–590. *See also* Academic integrity
Honor codes, 337
Hootsuite, 381
Hosting platforms, 55, 131, 185, 262
Human behavior in the social environment (HBSE) assignments, 443–455
Human rights advocacy. *See also* Social justice
    assignments on, 416–419, 422–424, 460–462, 475–477
    Internet access and, 310, 353, 360
    technology-based learning tasks for, 556–558
Hybrid courses, 13, 160*t*, 162–164, 241
Hybrid learning, 77*b*
Hyflex model, 165, 301
Hyperlinks, 134

I

ICAI (International Center on Academic Integrity), 336
iClickers, 113, 531
iCloud Calendar, 371
Identity in online postings, 49–50*b*
If This Then That (IFTTT), 627
iMovie, 137, 415, 529
Inbox Zero, 618
Independent contractors, 250
Infographics, 134–135, 377, 416–419, 456–457
Informatics, 431–435
Information and communication technologies (ICTs). *See also specific types of techologies*
    adoption/diffusion curve, 40–42, 41*f*
    competency in use of. *See* Digital literacy
    importance for social work profession, 34
Information for Practice, 559
Information technology (IT), 166, 205, 288, 329, 372
Informed consent, 583
Innovators, 349–351, 351*f*
Inserting content, 51, 118, 615
Instagram, 37, 50, 51, 56, 111, 135, 284, 322, 334, 483, 522, 536, 564
Instapaper, 129, 559
Institutional considerations
    in assessment of readiness for online programs, 608–610
    in online courses, 158, 159
    in online program support, 212–216, 228–229, 240–241, 249–253
    policies on technology use, 592
Institutional Review Boards (IRBs), 320

Instructional designers (IDs)
    on collaborative learning, 94*b*
    consultations for course design, 166, 181
    defined, 76–77
    foundational theory incorporation and, 83–84*b*, 88*b*
    on synchronous components of online classes, 93*b*
    working with, 77–79*b*

Instructors. *See also* Best practices for technology use
    boundaries. *See* Instructor-student boundaries
    burnout of, 239
    campus-based vs. online, 225–226
    concerns about technology use, 7–9
    continuing education for. *See* Continuing education
    curriculum and course development. *See* Design of online courses and curriculum
    digital literacy of, 109–111, 168, 579
    discussion board communications, 85*b*, 189
    disruption readiness plan for, 586
    ethical considerations for, 309–346. *See also* Ethical considerations for technology in education
    field instruction and, 260, 278–279, 294–295, 591–592
    grading and evaluation of. *See* Evaluation of assignments
    knowledge areas for technology use, 358–362, 363*b*
    learning management systems and, 114–115
    modeling behavior, 52–53, 167–168, 170, 174–175, 184, 191, 338–339
    of online programs, 221–228, 221–223*b*, 224–225*t*, 230, 611
    out-of-state employees, 250
    professional development of, 347–391. *See also* Professional development
    publishing research, technology for, 348–349, 374–379, 624–628
    rates of technology adoption and use, 348–351, 351*f*
    self-care and, 379–384, 381–383*b*
    social media policies for, 584
    social presence in online classes, 92, 169
    student communication with, 85*b*, 184, 189, 190*b*, 265, 266*b*. *See also* Feedback
    teaching personas of, 169–170, 189
    technology-based assignments, readiness for, 149–150, 151*b*
    willingness to attend online training, 281–282

Instructor-student boundaries
    electronic communication and, 189
    ethical considerations for, 330–336
    NASW on, 317*b*
    social media use and, 283, 331–333, 591
    technology use and, 590–591

Integrative learning theories, 79–80, 80*f*, 92–94*b*, 97*b*, 170
Intensives, 244–247
Interdisciplinary ethics assignment, 492–494
International Center on Academic Integrity (ICAI), 336
International students, 297
Internet. *See also* Social media
    access as human right, 310, 353, 360
    advanced searches, 130
    digital inclusion and, 34
    evolution of, 33
    patient information and HIPAA compliance, 320
    rate of usage in BSW education programs, 109–110
    research of self, 552
    search engines, 128–129
    smartphones for, 42
Internet Archive, 338
Intern Placement Tracking (IPT) software, 288–289
Internships. *See* Field education online programs
Interprofessional collaboration, 10, 34, 566–567
Interventions, 564–567, 581
IRBs (Institutional Review Boards), 320
Isolation, 300
iTunes, 452, 454, 547

J
Jamendo, 338*b*
Jing, 183, 459
Jones, J., 349
Journaling for reflection, 163, 429–431

K
Kaltura, 112, 113, 326
Kanter, Beth, *The Happy Healthy Nonprofit*, 381–382*b*
Kaplan, C. D., 226
Karpman, H. E., 335
Keynote, 135
Keywords, 128–129
Knowledge
    content, 40
    digital dimension of, 121, 122*f*
    for professional development, 358–362, 363*b*
    of technology, 31–71. *See also* Digital literacy
    of tools, 40, 127–128
Krause, Denise, 21, 157

INDEX

L

Labeling digital content, 131
Labor laws, 250
Lave, Jean, 372
Learning
    active. *See* Active learning model
    adult learning (andragogy), 74, 76–81, 77–79*b*, 80*f*, 298. *See also*
        Pedagogical approaches to technology
    collaborative, 80*f*, 84, 88–94, 94*b*
    community. *See* Professional learning networks
    connected, 80*f*, 88–89, 94–95
    e-learning tools, 112, 113*t*, 178. *See also* Learning management systems
    foundational learning theories, 79–80, 80*f*, 83–85*b*, 88*b*
    group-based, 93–94, 96, 194, 196–197, 198*b*
    hybrid, 77*b*
    integrative learning theories, 79–80, 80*f*, 92–94*b*, 97*b*, 170
    multimedia learning theories, 80*f*, 85–87, 170
    network-based, 364
    passive, 89, 95, 108, 110
    problem-based, 91, 93
    progressive components for, 171–172
    scaffolding. *See* Scaffolding
    social, 80*f*, 84, 88–94, 94*b*
    sociocultural learning theory, 91
    universal design for learning, 115, 218–219, 219*b*
Learning Content Management Systems (LCMSs), 114
Learning House Instructor Readiness Questionnaire, 149
Learning management systems (LMSs)
    collaboration tools in, 96
    consistency in, 182
    course design and, 178
    defined, 114
    digital self-efficacy, 55–56
    distractions in, 87
    overview of, 112–115
    privacy in, 320, 322
    progressive learning components in, 171–172
    rate of usage, 109–110, 348–349
    for storage of data, 13
    text-based comments systems in, 46, 51, 83*b*, 85*b*
    types of e-learning tools in, 113*t*
    uploading digital assignments to, 149
Learning objectives
    Bloom's Digital Taxonomy for, 121, 145–146, 147*f*
    course design based on, 178

skill transferability and, 84
Learning outcomes
  assessment data for, 361
  course design based on, 78, 125, 145
  digital literacy as requirement, 34
  game-based learning for, 133
  in seated vs. online classrooms, 8, 158
  self-regulated learning and, 82
Leveling up, 502
Lewis, Laura, 23, 259
Library databases assignment, 535–538
Library of Congress, U.S., 338*b*
Licensing, 52–53, 248–249, 304–305
Licensing boards, 314
Lightboards, 113
Likes, 362, 379, 528
Lindsay, C., 321
LinkedIn, 51, 136, 435–437
Linking to digital content, 134
Listly, 129
LISTSERVs, 33, 373–374
Literature review assignment, 535–538
Livechat, 38
Live support specialists, 224, 224–225*t*
LiveText, 286
LMSs. *See* Learning management systems
Loading content, 164
Lock Down Browser, 113
Lonn, S., 85
Loomio, 565
Lurking, 53

M

MacOS, 529
MacroSW (online community), 373
Mailing lists, 129–130
Mapping courses, 178–179
Marketing assignment, 456–457
Marketing of online programs, 216, 230
Marquat, Matthea, 326–328*b*
Mashing/Mash-ups, 134
Massive open online courses (MOOCs), 164–165
Master's of social work (MSW) programs. *See also* Field education online programs; Online programs and degrees
  commercial partners for online programs, 229–232

online, examples of, 212, 216–217
state and local regulations for, 248–250
topical focus and, 217
tuition costs for, 232
Mayer, R. E., 85
McLeod, D. A., 354
Media literacy. *See* Digital literacy
Medical records, 359–360
Meditation, 87*b*
Melanie Sage, Social Work Geek (blog), 376
Memes, 56
Mendeley, 626
Mentions, 362
Mentors, 283, 293*b*, 376
Menus, 50, 51, 600
Meta-tags, 131
Microsoft Excel, 110, 285, 397, 491
Microsoft Movie Maker, 529
Microsoft Office, 622
Microsoft Outlook, 285, 371, 429
Microsoft PowerPoint, 424–426, 451
Microsoft Word, 131
Mindfulness, 48, 82, 87*b*, 382
Mind mapping tools, 134
MindMeister, 134, 566
Minecraft, 504
Mixing digital content, 137
Mobile devices. *See* Electronic devices; Smartphones
Mock interviews, 246
Mock testimony assignment, 470–473
Moderating comments on digital content, 135–136, 200
MOOCs (massive open online courses), 164–165
Moodle, 112
Moore's law, 127
Motivation. *See also* Self-regulation
adult learners and, 80*f*, 81–82, 84, 85*b*
online courses and, 171, 174
MP3s, 131, 498
MP4s, 498
MSW programs. *See* Master's of social work programs
Multimedia learning theories
adult learners and, 80*f*, 85–87
online courses and, 170
MySpace, 334

N

NASW. *See* National Association of Social Workers
NASW Code of Ethics
    CSWE competencies and, 551
    on digital literacy of social workers, 42
    digital literacy to advance, 34
    on dual relationships, 330–331
    on ethical responsibility to broader society, 61
    on ethical use of technology, 314
    on instructor-student boundaries, 590
    technology standards and, 580–581, 589
    on technology use in education, 5–6
National Association of Black Social Workers, 243
National Association of Social Workers (NASW), 4, 114, 337. *See also NASW Code of Ethics; Standards for Technology in Social Work Practice*
National Center for Education Statistics, 3
National Council for State Authorization Reciprocity Agreements (NC-SARA), 249–250, 269
Nedegaard, Randy, 607
Netiquette, 167, 398, 553
Net neutrality, 310
Network-based learning, 364
Networking. *See also* Professional learning networks; Social media
    assignment on, 435–437
    connected learning and, 95
    digital skills for, 129, 136
    informal, 226–227
    virtual communities of practice, 372–374, 621–624
New media literacy, 37, 63
News media statistics assignment, 538–541
New York, online MSW programs in, 251–252
Nonverbal communication, 272
Noodle, 18
No Significant Difference Phenomenon, 8
Note-taking programs, 367
Notifications, 56, 129–130, 189, 379–380
NVIVO, 378

O

Objectives. *See* Goals; Learning objectives
Office hours, 184, 191
Offline, 60–61, 200, 290, 590
OLC (Online Learning Consortium), 159, 166, 228
The Old Reader, 130
Onground classrooms. *See* Seated classrooms

INDEX

Online courses, 21–22, 157–208
    class culture for, 183–186, 184–187*b*
    course mapping and aligning, 178–179, 180*b*
    defined, 13, 159, 160*t*, 164–165
    designing, 168–182. *See also* Design of online courses and curriculum
    design suggestions, 180–182
    feedback on, 198–200, 199*b*
    instructor and student engagement with, 187–197, 188*b*, 190*b*, 192–194*b*, 195*f*, 198*b*
    pedagogy, 169–172
    planning learning activities, 172–175, 176–177*t*
    resources for, 166
    seated classrooms compared to, 75, 159, 167, 172–174, 176–177*t*, 181
    skill requirements for, 182*b*
    social presence and, 88–90, 92, 93*b*
    teaching, 167–168
    types of, 159–166, 160*t*
Online groups and communities. *See* Discussion boards and forums; Professional learning networks; Social media
Online Learning Consortium (OLC), 159, 166, 228
Online presences, 323–324*b*, 334
Online program management (OPM), 228, 295
Online programs and degrees, 23, 209–257
    accessibility issues for, 218–219, 219*b*
    admission to. *See* Admission to online programs
    availability of, 3
    campus visits for, 244–247
    capacity for, 212–214
    centralized organic model of, 233–239, 236*b*
    competency outcome assessment for, 241
    concerns about, 7–9
    costs of, 214, 229, 231, 232–233, 236, 251–253, 310–311
    criticism of, 74–75
    decentralized vs. centralized approach to, 228–233
    defined, 13
    employers on, 7
    encroachment issues, 247–250
    ethical considerations for, 309–346. *See also* Ethical considerations for technology in education
    for field education, 259–307. *See also* Field education online programs
    funding models for, 251–253
    human relationships, lack of, 7
    implicit curriculum in, 241–243
    instructor training for, 227–228

motivation for creating, 211–212
NASW on, 316*b*
nontraditional time clocks for, 239
seat time, 240–241
students for, 215–218
teaching, 221–228, 221–223*b*, 224–225*t*
tuition considerations, 214
undergraduate social work degrees and, 220–221
Online support group assignment, 516–520
Open-sourced content, 338–339, 338*b*
Operating system, 132
OPM (online program management), 228, 295
Orientation
assignments for, 404
for field education, 269, 272, 291–292, 293*b*, 301
in-person vs. online, 296
for online classes and programs, 174, 237, 244–247, 296
Out-of-class time, 159, 173–174

P

Padlet, 453
Parker, Jamie, 263*b*
Parks, Cheryl, 230–231
Participatory culture, 95
Passive learning, 89, 95, 108, 110
Passwords, 590
PDF files, 131, 132, 219, 327, 545–546
Pearson (educational company), 233, 281
Pedagogical approaches to technology, 20, 73–105
adult online learning, 76–81, 77–79*b*, 80*f*
best practices for technology in education, 10–11
converting seated class to online class, 169–172
definition of pedagogy, 76
self-regulation, motivation, and multimedia theories, 81–87, 83–85*b*, 87–88*b*
student engagement and, 88–99, 92–94*b*, 97*b*
theory and, 74–75
Peer feedback, 94*b*, 95, 199–200
People with disabilities
accessibility of digital content for, 115, 181
disruption plans for, 586
ethical considerations for technology in education, 325–330, 326–328*b*
online program considerations for, 218–219, 219*b*, 238
universal design for learning and, 115, 181, 218–219, 219*b*

INDEX

Perron, B. E., 34
Personal biases, 556, 578, 582
Personal digital and social technology policies, 552–553
Personal learning networks. *See* Professional learning networks
Persuasive speeches, 463–465
Pew Internet Research Center, 33
Pew Research Center, 561
Pexel Videos, 338*b*
PhotoGrid, 56
Piktochart, 135
Pinterest, 443–445, 615–616
Pintrich, P. R., 84
Placement management systems, 285–291, 287*b*
Plagiarism, 93*b*, 113*t*, 312, 336–339, 338*b*
Platform, 132
Playing. *See* Gaming/gamification
PlayPosit, 458, 459
PLNs. *See* Professional learning networks
Pocket, 129
Podcast assignments, 463–465, 497–499, 510–513
Podcasts, 137, 266*b*
Policy change assignment, 470–473
Policy critique assignment, 465–467
Policy practice, technology-based learning tasks for, 559–561
Poll Everywhere, 113, 464, 465
Popplet, 134
Portland State University (PSU)
    active learning, 97*b*
    campus visit requirements, 246–247
    field education of, 271
    instructional designers (IDs), 77–78*b*
    MSW online program development, 238–239
    scaffolding, 92*b*
    self-regulation tools, 83–84*b*
    social presence and, 93*b*
    student evaluations on, 100*b*
Posting comments. *See* Commenting on digital content; Discussion boards and forums
PowerPoint, 424–426, 451
Practice-informed research, 558–559
Practice outcomes, 554, 568–569
Practice skills development
    assignments for, 456–530
    case presentation models for, 197
    pedagogy for, 169

through online programs, 97b, 239, 245–246, 271–272, 313–314
videoconferencing for, 313
Prezi, 126, 449, 450, 491
Privacy and confidentiality
  as concern for technology use, 7, 318–324
  FERPA concerns and, 320–324
  field instruction and, 592
  HIPAA concerns and, 318–320, 319b
  instructor-student boundaries and, 590
  online presences and, 323–324b
  settings for, 51
  storing sensitive data and, 580
Problem-based learning, 91, 93
ProctorU, 113
Professional behavior
  app use and, 47, 322
  CSWE on, 32
  distractions from technology and, 48
  in electronic communications, 36, 553
  of instructors, modeling, 52–53, 167–168, 170, 174–175, 184, 191, 338–339
  netiquette and, 167, 398, 553
  in online environments, 167, 168, 184, 323–324b, 332, 334, 338–339
  social media use and, 43b, 348
  technology-based learning tasks for, 551–554
Professional community networks, 299–300
Professional development, 24–25, 347–391
  academic workload, management of, 370–372
  comfort level for technology use, 322, 352–356, 353b, 356–358b
  for field instructors, 304
  knowledge areas for technology use, 358–362, 363b
  in LMSs, 115
  online programs, instructor training for, 227–228
  personal devices, digital boundaries for, 381–382b
  professional learning networks for, 364–368, 366–369b
  rates of technology adoption and use, 348–351, 351f
  scholarship creation and sharing, technology for, 374–379
  self-care and, 379–384, 381–383b, 382–383b
  social media assignments, 482–484, 499–502, 520–522
  in universal design for learning, 219
  virtual communities of practice for, 372–374
Professional learning networks (PLNs)
  benefits and importance of, 363b
  best practices for staying informed, 579
  book groups, 419–421

case study on, 368–369*b*
on digital literacy, 65
for lifelong learning, 339, 364–368
setting up, 366–369*b*
social media policies and, 334
tips for, 613–616
virtual communities of practice and, 373
Profile photos, 51, 92
Progressive learning components, 171–172
Project Gutenberg, 338*b*
Pseudonyms, 323
Public domain, 338–339, 338*b*
Public Domain Pictures, 338*b*
Publishing
    digital content, 137
    research, technology for, 348–349, 374–379, 624–628
PubMed, 129, 566
Puentedura, Ruben, 115, 116, 118, 397

Q

Quality Matters, 166, 228
Qualtrics, 284
Quinn, A., 110, 244

R

Radio show assignment, 504–507
Ranking Digital Rights, 556
Real time, 13, 38, 88, 162, 176, 366
Recordings
    podcast assignments, 463–465, 497–499, 510–513
    podcasts, 137, 266*b*
    radio show assignment, 504–507
    recording and editing, 440–442
Records
    educational, 320–324
    electronic, 349
    medical, 359–360
Recruitment of students, 216, 229–230
Reference management software, 367
Reflection
    journaling for, 163, 429–431
    questions for, 597–606
    reflection-in-action model, 355–356, 356–358*b*, 380
    technology-based learning tasks for, 552–553
    technology use, assessing comfort level for, 352–355, 353*b*

Rehabilitation Act (1973), 559
Relationships in digital spaces, 53–54
Remembering, digital tools for, 128–130, 367
Remind, 265, 266, 285
Remixing digital content, 52–53, 137
Remote supervision, 593–594
Research
    assignments on, 431–435, 530–549
    blogs for publication of, 375–377
    case-based health education, 378–379
    creating and sharing, technology for, 374–379
    on digital literacy, 63–64
    ethics in, 551
    on online program effectiveness, 8
    social media for data collection, 377–378
    social media for dissemination of, 348–349, 624–628
    on technology and field education, 304–305
ResearchGate, 362, 625, 626
Research-informed practice, 558–559
Residencies, 244–247
Resumes, electronic, 435–437
Retweeting, 501
Reverse image search, 60
Rheingold, Howard, 11, 19, 48, 53, 59
Rightclicking, 40
Rogers, Everett, 349–351, 351*f*
Role-play assignments, 495–497, 513–515
Role-playing, 91, 313
RSS feed readers, 129–130
Rubrics for technology-based assignments, 147–148
Rumors, social media and, 238
Running software, 132
Rural students, 232, 237, 291, 300

S

SafeAssign, 337
Sage, Melanie, 376, 607
Salesforce (software), 232, 284
SAMR (substitution, augmentation, modification, redefinition) Model for Technology Integration
    application for social work educators, 118–120, 119–120*b*
    application to assignments, 397–398. *See also* Assignment compendium
    converting seated class to online class, 168
    overview, 116–118, 117*f*, 397–398
    questions for assignment transitions, 141*b*

suggested uses for, 138–139
Saving. *See* Storage of data
Scaffolding
    active learning and, 99
    collaborative learning and, 91, 92*b*
    course design considerations and, 179
    progressive learning components and, 171
    SAMR model and, 120
    student engagement and, 187
Schedule management. *See* Calendar and schedule management
Schedule Once, 618
Schneweis, Carol, 23, 235–236, 259, 607
Scholarships, 231
Schon, D. A., 352–354, 353*b*
Schools. *See* Institutional considerations
Schwartz, S. L., 226
Screen-capture software, 113, 405, 537
Screencast assignment, 535–538
Screencast-O-Matic, 459
Scrivener, 45
Seaman, J., 3
Seaman, J. E., 3
Search engine optimization (SEO), 230
Search engines, 128–129, 130
Searching for online content, 128–129
Seated classrooms
    active learning in, 96
    collaborative learning in, 88–89, 93
    converting to online classrooms, 169–172
    credit hour requirements for, 240–241
    defined, 12–13, 160–161, 160*t*
    digital literacy and, 179
    hybrid courses and, 13, 160*t*, 162–163
    online environments compared to, 75, 159, 167, 172–174, 176–177*t*, 181
    social presence and, 88–90, 92
    technology use in, 110–111
Seat time and time on tasks, 159, 173–174, 240–241
Second Life (SL) assignments, 402–409, 513–515
Security settings, 483, 599, 601
Self-awareness, 354–356, 356–358*b*, 556
Self-care, 379–384, 381–383*b*
Self-disclosure, 332
Self-efficacy, 82, 84, 174, 182
Selfies, 194

Self-regulation
   adult learners and, 80*f*, 81–82, 83–84*b*
   online courses and, 171, 174, 182
   rubrics for technology-based assignments, 148
   technology-based learning tasks for, 552–553, 556
SEO (search engine optimization), 230
Servers, 132, 136, 287, 328, 504
Service-learning project assignments, 475–477, 527–530
Sexting, 566
Shah, Nivisha, 263*b*
Sharing digital content, 132–133
Sherbino, J., 378
Siemens, George, 364
Signaling, 87
Signatures, authenticated, 289
Signup Genius, 619
Singer, Jonathan, 119*b*, 373
Skill requirements for online courses, 182*b*
Skype, 136, 236, 301, 555
Slack, 565
SL (Second Life) assignments, 402–409, 513–515
SlideShare, 133
Sloan Consortium. *See* Online Learning Consortium
Smartphones, 40–42, 381–382*b*, 547–549. *See also* Text messaging
Smyth, Nancy J., 363*b*, 376, 379, 382–383*b*, 607
Snapchat, 50, 522, 624
Snopes, 59
Social action movements, 60–61. *See also* Hashtags
Social bookmarking, 129, 367
Social cues, 81
Social justice. *See also* Human rights advocacy
   assignments on, 416–419, 422–424, 487–489
   Internet access and, 310, 353, 360
   technology-based learning tasks for, 556–558
   technology worldview and, 353–354
Social learning, 80*f*, 84, 88–94, 94*b*
Social media. *See also* Professional learning networks; Social media assignments; Social media policies
   as advocacy tool, 557
   for case-based health education, 378–379
   case study on, 43*b*
   for connected learning, 95
   cultural competence and, 33
   cultural context for, 46–47, 283–284
   as data source, 378

INDEX

    for dissemination of research, 348–349, 374–375, 624–628
    ethical considerations for use of, 331–333, 354
    instructor-student boundaries and, 283, 331–333, 591
    netiquette for, 398, 553
    networking through, 129
    for participant outreach and recruitment, 377–378
    personal boundaries for, 380–381
    privacy considerations for, 321–322
    for professional use, 43*b*, 348
    profile photos and, 51, 92
    rate of usage among instructors, 348
    rumor control and, 238
    social presence through, 170, 237, 300*b*
    technology-based learning tasks for, 552–553, 565
    as virtual communities of practice, 302–303
Social media assignments
    creating digital networks, 410–411
    electronic resumes, 435–437
    lifelong learning, 443–445
    live tweeting documentary films, 426–428
    professional development, 499–502
    professional profiles, 482–484
    professional use, 520–522
    social media agency policies, 484–487
    Twitter chats, 473–475
Social media policies
    assignment on, 484–487
    for classrooms, 335
    drafts, creating, 565
    for individual students, 335–336
    NASW on, 316*b*, 583–584, 591
    for social work degree programs, 334–336
Social Media Policy Database, 565
Social networking, 129, 135, 136, 283, 302, 349
Social Pilot, 381
Social presence. *See also* Seated classrooms
    collaborative learning and, 88–90, 92–93, 93*b*
    distance field supervision and, 298–300
    Facebook groups for, 170, 237, 300*b*
    in online classrooms and programs, 169, 246
Social scholarship, 374
Social Work and Technology (online community), 373
Social Work Distance Education Assessment of Readiness (SW-DEAR), 210–211, 607–612
    faculty capacity, 611

institutional capacity, 608–609
program capacity, 609–610
student capacity, 611–612
Social Work Distance Education Conference, 247, 303
Social Work Distance Education Field Consortium, 303
Social Worker's Guide to Social Media (University of Buffalo), 333
Social work faculty. *See* Instructors
Social Work Podcast, 440, 510, 511, 512, 625
Social work practice, 5–6, 359–360. *See also* Practice skills development
Society for Social Work Research, 247
Sociocultural learning theory, 91
Socioeconomic status, 97–98
Software. *See also specific types*
    for assignments, 397
    for audioconferencing, 113*t*
    for calendar and schedule management, 266*b*, 371, 619–620
    course design considerations and, 179
    for field education offices, 284–291, 285*b*
    to prevent cheating, 337
    rate of usage in BSW education programs, 109–110
    skills needed for online courses, 180*b*
    skills needed for use, 132
    skill transferability and, 110
    technological disruptions and, 325
    training in use of, 297
    for videoconferencing, 110, 113*t*, 235, 236*b*
Software updates, 186, 325
SOLR (Student Online Learning Readiness), 150
Sonia (software), 289
SoundCloud, 464–465
Spamming, 54
Speech assignment, 463–465
Standards for Technology in Social Work Practice (NASW)
    on access and accessibility issues, 325
    cultural element of digital literacy and, 46
    on dual relationships, 333
    ethical considerations, 314–315
    learning objectives, connecting to, 145
    overview, 4, 575, 577–578
    requirements of, 42, 269
    "Social Work Education and Supervision" (Section 4), 4–5, 314–315, 316–317*b*, 337, 578–596
State and local laws
    on field internships, 249–250, 269
    licensing boards, technology standards for, 314

on online programs and degrees, 233, 248–252
 on social media tools, 46
 on supervision, 297
Statistical Package for the Social Sciences (SPSS), 110, 179, 397
Storage of data, 13, 148–149, 288, 580
Streaming services, 113*t*
Structural inequalities, 579
Student engagement
 active learning and, 96–98. *See also* Active learning model
 best practices for, 188*b*
 case presentation guidelines, 198*b*
 case study on, 192–194*b*
 coaching, 192*b*
 collaborative learning and, 90–94
 flipped classrooms and, 98–99
 guidelines for responding to students, 190*b*
 integrative theory for, 92–94*b*, 97*b*
 in online courses, 7, 187–197, 195*f*
 pedagogical approaches to technology and, 88–99
 practical tips for, 190*b*
 reinforcement of learning beyond classrooms, 95–96
Student loans, 310–311
Student Online Learning Readiness (SOLR), 150
Student response system assignment, 530–532
Student roadmap, 181
Students
 adult learners, 74, 76–81, 77–79*b*, 80*f*. *See also* Pedagogical approaches to technology
 assessment for programmatic fit, 238, 611–612
 benefits of technology in education for, 2
 connecting with other distance students, 299–300
 digital literacy and competence of, 11–12, 35–36, 263, 592–593
 with disabilities. *See* People with disabilities
 engagement of. *See* Student engagement
 evaluation of. *See* Evaluation of assignments
 of field education online programs, 264–265, 270–272, 279, 291–292
 instructor boundaries and. *See* Instructor-student boundaries
 instructors, communicating with, 184, 189, 190*b*, 265, 266*b*. *See also* Feedback
 of online courses. *See* Online courses
 of online programs, 215–218. *See also* Online programs and degrees
 peer feedback for, 94*b*, 95, 199–200
 peer support and, 242–243
 perceptions of online courses, 174
 privacy of educational records, 320–324

professionalism. *See* Professional behavior
recruitment of, 216, 229–230
seated classrooms vs. online learning, assessing, 75
self-regulation, motivation, and multimedia theories of, 81–87, 83–85*b*, 87–88*b*
student-affiliated organizations, 243
technology-based assignments, readiness for, 150
Student-student interaction, 94*b*, 194–197, 195*f*, 199–200
Subscriptions to mailing lists, 129–130
Supervision and consultation
    NASW on, 317*b*, 593
    remote, 593–594
    technology-based learning tasks for, 554
    technology use in, 593–594
Support for technology. *See* Technological support
Support group assignment, 516–520
SurveyMonkey, 284
Surveys
    assignment on, 544–546
    audience response tools for, 113*t*, 530–532
    digital tools for, 134, 284, 349
SW-DEAR. *See* Social Work Distance Education Assessment of Readiness
Synchronous distributed courses, 162, 235, 236*b*, 240–241. *See also* Asynchronous vs. synchronous online content
Systems theory, 566

T

Tablets, 6, 109, 132, 137. *See also* Electronic devices
Tagging, 129, 131
Taskstream (software), 289–290
Taxonomies, 128. *See also* Bloom's Digital Taxonomy
Teachers. *See* Instructors
Teaching and Learning in Social Work (blog), 376–377
Teaching associates, 224, 224–225*t*
Teaching-based evidence, 580
Teaching online courses. *See* Delivery of online courses
Teaching personas, 169–170, 189. *See also* Social presence
Technological change
    adoption of new technology and, 40–42, 41*f*, 349–351, 351*f*
    communication and, 33
    digital literacy and, 64–65
    field agencies and, 592–593
    tool knowledge and, 40, 127–128
Technological disruptions
    institutional policies and, 592

INDEX

NASW on, 316*b*, 325, 585–586
planning for, 330
readiness plans for, 586
reflection questions for, 354–356, 356–358*b*

Technological support
  access to, 588–589
  for digital tracking systems, 288, 290
  disruption readiness plans and, 586
  ethical considerations for technology in education, 325
  for instructors of online programs, 224, 224–225*t*
  NASW on, 317*b*, 588–589
  for online programs, 238

Technology-based learning tasks, 17, 551–569
  for diversity and difference in practice, 555–556
  for ethical and professional behavior, 551–554
  for human assessment, 563–565
  for human engagement, 561–562
  for human rights advocacy, 556–558
  for interventions, 565–567
  for policy practice, 559–561
  for practice evaluation, 268–269
  for research and practice, 558–559

Technology-enhanced learning activities. *See* Assignment compendium

Technology in classrooms, 20–21, 107–155
  assignments for. *See* Assignment compendium
  assignment transitions, questions for, 141*b*
  Bloom's Digital Taxonomy and, 120–138, 122*f*, 124*f*, 126–127*f*
  case study on, 139–141*b*
  converting assignments for, 138–142, 142–144*f*
  evaluating assignments on, 145–146, 147*f*
  grading of assignments on, 147–149
  learning management systems and, 112–115, 113*t*
  learning tasks. *See* Technology-based learning tasks
  overview of, 109–111
  readiness, assessment questions for, 151*b*
  SAMR Model for Technology Integration and, 116–119, 117*f*, 119–120*b*
  structural inequalities and, 579

Technology in education, 1–29. *See also* Online courses; Online programs and degrees
  accessibility issues and. *See* Access and accessibility issues
  assignments using, 396–397. *See also* Assignment compendium
  benefits of, 2, 9–11
  common questions on, 15
  competency-based education and, 4–7

concerns for, 7–9
continuum of technology integration and, 12–14, 16, 157
ethical considerations for, 309–346. *See also* Ethical considerations for technology in education
for field education, 259–307. *See also* Field education online programs
knowledge areas for instructors, 360–361
NASW on. *See Standards for Technology in Social Work Practice*
student competency and, 11–12
trends in, 3–4
Technology standards of NASW. *See Standards for Technology in Social Work Practice*
Technology tips, 613–629
    academic workload, 616–620
    creating and sharing work, 624–628
    professional learning networks, 613–616
    virtual communities of practice (VCoPs), 621–624
Tegrity, 236
Telehealth settings, 232, 268, 294*b*, 305, 359
Tes Teach, 468–470
Text-based comments systems in LMSs, 46, 51, 83*b*, 85*b*
Text messaging
    apps for, 265, 266*b*
    instructor-student boundaries and, 591
    managing, 616
    norms of, 46
    rate of usage, 349
Theoretical constructs and measures assignment, 533–535
Thinking skills, 123, 124*f*. *See also* Critical thinking
3PlayMedia, 326
Time clocks, online programs and, 239
Time management skills
    e-mail and, 370–371, 616–619
    learning new technology and, 179, 362
    motivation and self-regulation, 82
    personal boundaries for technology use, 380–381
    for PLNs, 367*b*, 369*b*
    seat time and time on tasks, calculating, 159, 173–174, 240–241
    technology for, 370–372
Time on tasks. *See* Seat time and time on tasks
Time requirements
    asynchronous vs. synchronous content and, 172–174
    discussion boards and forums and, 172–173
    field education, 272
    online courses and programs, 223–224
Tinychat, 518

INDEX

Tips. *See* Technology tips
TK20, 113, 286
Todoist, 555, 620
To-do lists, 371, 620
Tool knowledge, 40, 127–128
Track changes, 132, 199, 622
Training. *See* Continuing education; Professional development
Transferability of digital skills, 110, 173
Transfer credits, 220
Trauma assessment assignment, 457–460
Trello, 371
Trolling, 605
Trustworthiness. *See also* Academic integrity
    of digital content, 58–60, 59–60*b*
    digital relationships and, 53–54
Tuition
    for-profit businesses sharing, 229, 231, 232, 251, 310
    high cost of online programs, 310–311
    model expectations for, 214
    program funding models and, 251
    scholarships and, 231
Tumblr, 131, 136
Turnitin, 113, 337
Tweetdeck, 45
Twine, 525, 526–527
Twitter
    assignments on, 410–411, 426–428, 473–475, 499–502
    as blogging platform, 131
    case study on, 54–55*b*
    culture of, 46
    for dissemination of research, 348–349
    professional vs. personal use of, 47, 136
    use in education, 120*b*
    virtual communities of practice, 373
2U (online program manager), 230–231, 295

U

Undergraduate social work degrees, 220–221
Understanding, tools for, 130–132
Undo, 51, 52, 602
Uniform resource locator (URL), 59, 151, 327, 405
Universal design for learning (UDL), 115, 218–219, 219*b*
Unsplash, 338
Uploading digital content, 132–133, 149
User authentication, 320, 337

V

Values
- of agencies for field placement, 283
- concerns about technology use, 8
- NASW on, 581
- social justice and, 353
- technology-based learning tasks for, 552–553, 556
- technology use, assessing comfort level for, 352–354

VCoPs (virtual communities of practice), 302–303, 372–374, 621–624
Venngage, 135
Vernon, Bob, 237–238
VideoANT, 92b
Video-based discussion tools, 272
Video blogging, 124, 137, 524
Videocasting, 137
Videoconferencing
- for field liaison visits, 296
- for field supervision, 296–297, 302
- for high-touch pedagogy model, 265, 266b
- for live modeling of practice skills, 313
- for social work practice, 359
- software for, 110, 113t, 235, 236b
- for synchronous courses, 162, 235, 236b

Video demonstrations
- included with published work, 377
- of practice skills development, 271

Video files, 117, 131, 199, 498
Video kits, 266b
Video presentation assignments
- case presentation, 480–482
- experiential service learning, 527–530
- practice skills, 523–524
- social justice, 487–489
- walking tours, 508–510

Video sharing, 47, 117, 118, 141, 148, 171, 472, 510, 528. *See also specific applications and websites*
Video streaming, 114, 234, 420, 421
Videvo, 338b
Vimeo, 560
Viral content, 65, 66, 377
Virtual communities of practice (VCoPs), 302–303, 372–374, 621–624
Virtual Connections (blog), 376
Virtual worlds, assignments on, 513–515
Viruses, 316, 504, 580, 585, 601
Vision impairment, 218

VoiceThread, 112, 132, 272, 326, 458
Vygotsky, Lev, 91

W
Wakelet, 134
Walking video tour assignment, 508–510
Walters, A., 165
Wearable technologies, 360
Web browsers, 1, 113, 122, 129, 151, 396
Webcams, 313, 337, 481
Web facilitated courses, 160*t*, 161–162
Web pages, 40, 131, 134, 151, 160, 191, 423, 444
Website creation, assignments on, 412–414, 429–431
Web 2.0, 33, 133, 135, 137, 143, 144, 376
Wenger, Etienne, 372
WeVideo, 488
White papers, 377
Widgets, 615–616
Wi-Fi, 266, 586, 590
Wikimedia Commons, 338*b*
Wikipedia, 37, 38, 129, 424
Wiki tools, 125–126, 422–424
Wiley, J. L., 226
Wolf, L., 349
WordPress, 131, 136, 376
Word processing, 132, 136, 151, 180*b*, 327, 396. *See also specific applications*
Words With Friends, 504
Work productivity. *See* Distractions; Time management skills
WorldCat, 130
World of Warcraft assignment, 502–504
Wunderlist, 371, 555, 566

Y
YouCanBookMe, 619
Young, J., 63–64, 354
YouTube, 507
    e-advocacy assignment using, 460–462
    professional vs. personal use of, 47
    for students who are deaf, 327*b*
    uses for, 615
    video-editing tools of, 128

Z
Zone of proximal development, 91
Zoom (software), 235, 236, 301, 555
Zotero, 129